■ Eating Disorders

Assessment and Treatment

David G. Schlundt
Vanderbilt University

William G. Johnson
University of Mississippi School of Medicine

Allyn and Bacon
Boston   London   Sydney   Toronto

Copyright © 1990 by Allyn and Bacon
A Division of Simon & Schuster, Inc.
160 Gould Street
Needham Heights, Massachusetts 02194

All rights reserved. No part of the material protected by this copyright notice may be reproduced or utilized in any form or by any means, electronic or mechanical, including photocopying, recording, or by any information storage and retrieval system, without written permission from the copyright owner.

Series Editor: John-Paul Lenney
Series Editorial Assistant: Susan Brody
Cover Administrator: Linda Dickinson
Manufacturing Buyer: Tamara McCracken
Production Coordinator: Superscript Associates
Editorial-Production Service: Kailyard Associates
Cover Designer: Linda Dickinson/Suzanne Harbison

Library of Congress Cataloging-in-Publication Data

Schlundt, David G.
    Eating disorders : assessment and treatment / by David G. Schlundt, William G. Johnson.
      p.   cm.
    Includes bibliographical references.
    ISBN 0-205-12086-5
    1. Eating disorders.   I. Johnson, William G., 1939–
II. Title.
  RC552.E18S37   1989
616.85'26--dc20

Printed in the United States of America

10 9 8 7 6 5 4 3 2 1 93 92 91 90 89

Contents

Preface xi

1 Introduction to Eating Disorders 1
Eating Disorders: The Clinical Picture 1
   Anorexia Nervosa: The Clinical Syndrome 1
   Bulimia Nervosa: The Clinical Syndrome 3
Terminological and Diagnostic Confusion 5
   Bulimarexia 5
   Dietary Chaos Syndrome 6
   Dysorexia 6
   Bulimia 7
   Bulimia Nervosa 8
   Confusion and Overlap 8
Current Diagnostic Categories 10
   Anorexia Nervosa DSM-III-R 11
   Bulimia Nervosa DSM-III-R 13
Eating Disorders: Common Misconceptions 15
   Eating Disorders in Males 16
   Atypical Eating Disorders 17
   Pica DSM-III-R 17
   Rumination Disorder of Infancy DSM-III-R 17
   Anorexia and Bulimia Nervosa in DSM-III-R 18
Incidence of the Diagnosis of Anorexia Nervosa 18
Incidence of the Diagnosis of Bulimia 19
Spectrum of Eating Disorders 21
The Anorectic-Bulimic Conflict 23
A Three-Dimensional Eating Disorder Continuum 25
Summary 31

2 The Biobehavioral Control of Eating Behavior 33
Hunger and Satiety 34
Neuroanatomy and Neurotransmitters 35

Energy Balance and Resting Metabolic Rate 37
Exercise, Resting Metabolic Rate, and Caloric Intake 38
Weight Regulation 39
    Counter-Regulation in Obesity and Anorexia Nervosa 40
Mechanisms of Weight Regulations: Set-Point Theory 41
    Body Weight: Naturally Occurring Variations 42
Composition of the Diet and Weight Regulation 43
Food Cravings, Overeating, and Binge Eating 44
    The Role of Insulin 45
    Diet Composition and Insulin 46
    The Role of Carbohydrate Restriction in Food Craving 47
Biobehavioral Responses to Extreme Weight Loss Efforts 48
    Starvation Response 48
    Hypokalemia 50
    Reproductive Hormones 50
The Role of Dieting in the Development of Eating Disorders 51
Summary 54

3 Dieting, Fear of Weight Gain, and Body Image 55

Restrictive Dieting and Fasting 55
Fear of Weight Gain 58
    Fear of Interpersonal Consequences of Being Fat 60
    Being Fat Is Equated with Failure 61
    Compulsive Weighing and Checking 61
    The Social Comparison Process 62
    The Fear of Being Seen 62
    Avoidance of Situational Cues 63
Body Image 63
    Conceptual Issues in Body-Image Assessment 65
    A Cognitive Science Approach to Body Image 66
    Schemata 68
Food Phobia 73
Summary 75

4 Bingeing and Tasting 77

Disturbed Eating Behavior 77
    Binge Eating 78
Frequency of Eating Disturbances in the Population 82
Frequency of Binge Eating in Bulimia 85
Food Obsession 86
Tasting 87
Variations and Case Descriptions 89
Summary 91

5 Vomiting and Other Compensatory Strategies 93
Self-Induced Vomiting 93
 Frequency of Vomiting in the Population 96
 Vomiting in Eating Disorder Patient Samples 98
Laxatives 99
 Frequency of Laxative Abuse in the Population 100
 Laxative Abuse in Bulimic Patient Samples 101
Diuretics 103
 Frequency of Diuretic Abuse in the Population 103
 Diuretic Abuse in Bulimic Patient Samples 104
Fasting and Dieting 104
Excessive Exercise 106
 Frequency of Excessive Exercise in the Population 107
 Excessive Exercise in Bulimic Patient Samples 108
Case Descriptions 108
Summary 110

6 Biogenetic Theories of Anorexia and Bulimia Nervosa 113
The Clinical Course of Anorexia Nervosa 114
Physiological Theories of Anorexia Nervosa 114
 Hypothalamic Theories 115
 Auto-Addictive Model of Anorexia Nervosa 118
 Family Resemblance 119
 The Genetics of Anorexia Nervosa 120
Physiological Theories of Bulimia Nervosa 121
 The Clinical Course of Bulimia Nervosa 122
 Bulimia Nervosa as a Seizure Disorder 123
 The Physiological Consequences of Dieting 124
 Substance Abuse Models of Bulimia Nervosa 125
 Bulimia and Major Affective Disorders 127
Summary 133

7 Psychosocial Theories of Eating Disorders 135
Functional Analysis 136
Naturalistic Functional Analysis 136
Behavioral Medicine and the Biopsychosocial Approach 139
 Clinical Implications of a Biopsychosocial Functional Analysis 140
The Psychosocial Determinants of Anorexia and Bulimia 141
 Environmental Antecedents 141
 Behavioral Antecedents 156
 Cognitive Antecedents 159
 Emotional Antecedents 163

       Physiological Antecedents 168
    Consequences of Anorexic and Bulimic Behavior 169
       Environmental Consequences 170
       Behavioral Consequences of Eating Disorders 172
       Cognitive Consequences of Eating Disorders 173
       Emotional Consequences of Eating Disorders 175
       Physiological Consequences of Eating Disorders 176
    Summary 177

8 Assessment in Eating Disorders 181
    Measures Specific to Eating Disorders 182
    General Psychological Tests 188
       SCL-90 188
       Minnesota Multiphasic Personality Inventory 190
       Beck Depression Inventory (BDI) 191
       Fear of Negative Evaluations 192
       Social Avoidance and Distress (SAD) 193
    Other Assessments of Eating Behavior 194
       The Dieter's Inventory of Eating Temptations (DIET) 194
       Food Survey 195
       Three-Factor Eating Questionnaire 199
       Restraint Scale 200
    Semistructured Interviews and Interview Forms 201
    Physical Measures 203
       Body Composition 205
       Resting Metabolic Rate 207
       Physical Fitness 213
    Assessment of Body Image 214
    Methods for Assessing Body Image 214
       Projective Methods 215
       Questionnaire Approaches 215
       Psychophysical Approaches to Body Image 216
       Methods That Contrast Different Body-Image Schema 222
       Body Image Testing System 224
    Behavioral Assessment of Eating 228
       Estimating Food Intake 228
       Functional Analysis of Eating Behavior 232
       Test Meals 233
    Clinical Recommendations 235
    Summary 236

9 Medical and Pharmacological Therapies for Eating Disorders 239
    Biological Therapy for Anorexia Nervosa 239

Nutritional Support **239**
Medication for Anorexia Nervosa **245**
Biological Therapy for Bulimia Nervosa **247**
Nutritional Support **247**
Laxative Reduction Therapy **248**
Medication for Bulimia Nervosa **251**
Summary **256**

10 Psychoanalytic and Family Therapy Approaches 259
Understanding Psychotherapies **259**
The Problem of Evaluating Treatment Outcome **260**
Psychoanalytic Therapy for Eating Disorders **262**
Basic Theory **262**
Conceptualization of Eating Disorders **264**
Methods of Treatment **265**
Family Therapy for Eating Disorders **266**
Basic Theory **266**
Conceptualization of Eating Disorders **267**
Methods of Treatment **270**
Summary **273**

11 Cognitive Interventions 275
Purpose and Objective **275**
Rationale **275**
Cognitive Therapy for Eating Disorders **276**
An Information-Processing Model of Cognition **278**
Perceptual Processing **279**
Interpretation **281**
Decision Making **283**
Response Execution **284**
Feedback **285**
Procedures **286**
Teaching the System **286**
Assessment of Schemata and Cognitions **286**
Countering **287**
Imagery **293**
Role Playing **294**
Homework **294**
Summary **294**

12 Behavioral Treatment of Bingeing and Purging 297
Exposure with Response Prevention (ERP) **297**
Purpose and Objective **297**
Rationale **297**

    Procedures   300
   Temptation Exposure with Response Prevention (TERP)   305
    Purpose and Objective   305
    Rationale   305
    Procedures   307
   Clinical Recommendations   317
   Summary   319

13 Nutrition Education and Management   321
   Purpose and Objective   321
   Rationale   321
   Procedures   322
    Carbohydrates, Fats, and Proteins   322
    Clinical Intervention   327
    Fluid Balance, Minerals, and Electrolytes   331
    Vitamins   332
    Nutrient Density   334
    Dietary Goals   335
    The Basic Food Groups   335
   Clinical Recommendations   335
   Summary   338

14 Energy Balance Training   339
   Purpose and Objectives   339
   Rationale   339
   Procedures   341
    Increasing Resistance to Temptation   341
    Reducing the Likelihood of Binge Eating   343
    Modifying Food Choices   345
    Learning to Eat in Positive Social Situations   346
    Negative Emotions   349
    Exercise   355
   Summary   358

15 Personal Social Problem Solving   361
   Purpose and Objective   361
   Rationale   361
    The Situational Specificity of Behavior   362
    The Importance of Learning in the Development of Psychological Problems   362
    An Emphasis on Competence   363
    The Problem-Solving Approach   363
   Procedures   365
    Problem Definition and Description   365

Setting Intervention Goals **366**
Brainstorming Potential Intervention Strategies **368**
Strategy Evaluation and Selection **369**
Implementation and Follow-Up **370**
Summary **373**

16 Body-Image Treatment **375**
Understanding Body-Image Disturbance **375**
Body-Image Distortion **376**
Body-Image Dissatisfaction **377**
Cognitive Distortions **378**
Problem Situations **379**
Impact of Therapy on Body-Image Disturbance **380**
Assessment of Body-Image Disturbance **381**
Intervention **381**
Summary **387**

17 Group and Inpatient Treatment **389**
Group Therapy for Eating Disorders **389**
Basic Theory **389**
Conceptualization of Eating Disorders **391**
Methods of Treatment **391**
General Considerations in Forming Therapy Groups **395**
Inpatient Treatment Programs **399**
Basic Theory **399**
Conceptualization of Eating Disorders **401**
Methods of Treatment **402**
Clinical Recommendations **410**
Summary **411**

18 Therapeutic Programming: Integrating Assessment and Treatment **413**
The Outcome of the Assessment Process **414**
Therapeutic Programming **417**
Therapeutic Techniques **417**
Case Descriptions **419**
Nancy, a Case of Bulimia Nervosa **419**
Leigh's Treatment Plan **421**
Andi's Treatment Program **423**
Summary **425**

References **427**

Appendix A **457**

Appendix B 469

Name Index 497

Subject Index 507

Preface

Anorexia and bulimia nervosa are eating disorders that are encountered by physicians, nurses, dietitians, psychologists, and other therapists. There are many myths about eating disorders and there is much that we truly do not understand. In the last fifteen years, research in this area has exploded. Anorexia and bulimia nervosa have been approached from a variety of perspectives. Some have viewed these problems as arising from biological processes originating in the hypothalamus. Others have viewed the current cultural context with its emphasis on slimness as the culprit, while still others blame eating disorders on the family and the kinds of early childhood experiences the family provides.

Our task in preparing this book was to gather this information, make sense of it, then to translate it into a form that will be useful to the many different professionals who study and treat individuals with anorexia and bulimia nervosa. Our goal was to produce an up-to-date, comprehensive, yet useful volume that will be accessible to students just beginning to study eating disorders while of sufficient depth that experts in the field will find new material not previously encountered.

Chapter 1 begins with a discussion of issues surrounding the definition and diagnosis of anorexia and bulimia. We cover the evolution of terminology both in the scientific literature and in the official diagnostic criteria of the American Psychiatric Association's DSM-III and its recent revision. We review data on the incidence of anorexia nervosa, bulimia, and their co-occurrence. At the end of Chapter 1, we propose a model that describes the relationship between anorexia and bulimia, and the relationship of these eating disorders to the common behaviors of dieting and overeating. Anorexia and bulimia are not separate disorders. Instead, they represent different possible outcomes of the same underlying process, which revolves around the pursuit of thinness, the fear of gaining weight, and the struggle between dieting and biological and behavioral pressure to eat. Viewing anorexia and bulimia as outcomes of biological, psychological, and cultural processes leads us to consider these various components in detail.

Understanding how eating behavior gets out of control requires that we understand the normal mechanisms that regulate food intake and energy balance. In Chapter 2, we examine the psychology and biology of normal eating behavior with an emphasis on its biological underpinnings. This chapter provides basic concepts and findings that will be of use throughout the book.

Chapters 3, 4, and 5 describe the core behaviors observed in eating disorders. In Chapter 3, we cover dieting, the fear of weight gain, and body-image problems. In our discussion of body-image problems, we attempt to extend current conceptualizations of this phenomenon by drawing upon cognitive science theories of information processing and knowledge representation. Chapter 4 deals with binge eating while Chapter 5 covers purging. We have attempted in these chapters first to describe these behaviors in detail, drawing upon the published literature and various case histories. We then examine the prevalence of these behaviors in the general population and learn that these behaviors are indeed common. We finally examine the prevalence of the core behaviors in samples of patients with eating disorders.

Chapters 6 and 7 deal with the issue of what causes some people to cross the line from the apparently widespread practices of dieting and overeating to develop into the more extreme manifestations of these behaviors observed in anorexia and bulimia nervosa. Chapter 6 presents biological theories of anorexia and bulimia. Chapter 7 attempts to integrate the biological and psychological data to develop a behavioral model of eating disorders. This model is based on a functional analysis of antecedents, behaviors, and consequences where these are broadly conceived to include environmental, emotional, cognitive, and physiological events. This behavioral model not only helps organize a wide range of available data, but also has definite implications for the assessment and treatment of eating disorders.

Chapter 8 covers approaches to the assessment of eating disorders. In this chapter, we have assembled a variety of specific and general measures that are useful in the clinical diagnosis of eating disorders or their scientific study. This chapter covers eating disorder questionnaires, general questionnaires, interview schedules, body-image assessment, and behavioral assessment. We provide tables that quickly summarize each assessment instrument to allow for comparison shopping.

The remainder of the book, Chapters 9 through 18, is devoted to the treatment of eating disorders. Chapter 9 covers biological approaches to treatment and includes useful sections on nutritional management of anorexia nervosa and laxative withdrawal in bulimia nervosa. Chapter 10 covers two important schools of psychotherapy that have been used in the treatment of eating disorders: psychoanalysis and family systems therapy. Chapter 11 provides detailed coverage of the theory and methods of cognitive therapy for eating disorders. While readers familiar with cognitive therapy will recognize most of the techniques and procedures described, we have updated the theoretical underpinnings of cognitive therapy by describing it from an information-processing approach.

Chapter 12 begins our presentation of behavioral techniques for the treatment of eating disorders. It presents a detailed outline for exposure with response prevention, a behavioral treatment intended to eliminate vomiting in bulimia. Chapter 12 also contains the first detailed presentation on a related behavioral technique, temptation exposure with response prevention, designed to treat binge eating. Chapter 13 covers nutrition education and management, a necessary therapeutic intervention for both anorexics and bulimics. It emphasizes the basic information about human nutrition that must be understood by the therapist and taught to the patient. Chapter 14 describes a set of behavioral methods for teaching patients appropriate self-management skills for controlling their energy balance. Many of the techniques presented in Chapter 14 will be familiar to those who have experience in weight loss therapy with obese individuals. In many respects, the obese and those with an eating disorder will all benefit from adopting a sensible life-style with proper nutrition and regular exercise. Chapter 15 covers what we call personal social problem solving, a behavioral approach to treating eating-disordered patients by helping them reduce or eliminate the emotional antecedents that tend to disrupt their eating behavior. Chapter 16 presents a cognitive/behavioral approach to the treatment of body-image problems. This approach combines behavioral exposure treatments with cognitive therapy.

In Chapter 17, we present alternative modalities for the treatment of eating disorders. Specifically we discuss the use of group therapy and the role of hospitalization.

In presenting treatment approaches to eating disorders, we have separated the various tactics used by therapists into distinct chapters and treated them as though they were independent techniques. In many respects, Chapters 11 through 16 could be combined into a single chapter titled cognitive/behavioral treatment of eating disorders. In each chapter, we attempt to note when other techniques can be used appropriately in combination with the treatment we are describing. However, in order to encourage clinicians to combine these separate techniques into a treatment plan that is responsive to the patient's needs, we have written Chapter 18. Chapter 18 addresses the issue of therapeutic programming. In this chapter, we discuss the role of assessment in treatment planning and the selection of treatment strategies based on assessment data. While one could easily devote an entire volume to the issue of integrating assessment and treatment, we hope that this chapter will provide the clinician with some guidance when it comes to selecting ways to treat individuals with an eating disorder.

We hope that the reader will find this volume both informative and thought-provoking. The conceptual, empirical, and clinical approaches to anorexia and bulimia are evolving quickly. If our analysis and presentation make a contribution to furthering understanding of eating disorders, we shall be extremely gratified.

Acknowledgments

William G. Johnson is indebted to Kimberly Cranston Bergeron for her careful reading and editorial review of the chapters and to Tricia Warner for her secretarial assistance. David G. Schlundt would like to thank Harriet Simpkins and Douglas Arnold for their help in proofreading the manuscript. My graduate students Tracy Sbrocco, Barbara Stetson, Betsy Sementilli, and Crystal Bell have all in one way or another contributed information or ideas that have found their way into the book. My wife, Zada Law, has been very patient with the mountain of reprints and late nights spent writing. I would especially like to thank Cindy Johnson for sacrificing her antique dining room table during my numerous trips to Mississippi while writing this book.

In addition, we would both like to express our appreciation to Dr. Stewart Agras, Stanford University, Dr. Arnold Andersen, Johns Hopkins University, and Professor Donald Williamson, Louisiana State University at Baton Rouge, for their assistance in reviewing the manuscript. Their comments greatly contributed to the book's development.

We would also like to acknowledge the staff at Allyn and Bacon for their efforts, including Susan Brody for her assistance in seeing the text through to production. Finally, we would like to thank our series editor, John-Paul Lenney, for his patience in working with us through the entire process of writing and publishing the book.

1

Introduction to Eating Disorders

EATING DISORDERS: THE CLINICAL PICTURE

Anorexia Nervosa: The Clinical Syndrome

Dramatic and often life-threatening weight loss is the primary clinical feature of anorexia nervosa that brings it to the attention of health care professionals. While severe weight loss can result from metabolic disease, the weight loss in an anorexic patient appears voluntary and often pleasing to the patient. Semistarvation, severe weight loss, and techniques of purging have health consequences that range from uncomfortable to fatal.

Fear of obesity and the pursuit of thinness represent the driving force in both anorexia and bulimia nervosa. In anorexia nervosa, this fear is expressed through a number of secondary symptoms including the desire to maintain a suboptimal body weight, body-image disturbance, and food avoidance. These forces interact and influence the individual's food intake and exercise to culminate in substantial weight loss. The fear of obesity, expressed either as an intense fear of getting fat or as an obsession with being thin, is well developed and is the most prominent cognitive feature of anorexia nervosa. The body image disturbance in many anorexics manifests itself as a perceptual distortion in which the body is perceived to be fat in spite of its emaciated appearance or as an extreme dissatisfaction with the size or shape of the body or certain body parts. Other anorexics may be able to perceive accurately their emaciated state but prefer an inappropriately thin shape. Still others have been able to achieve and maintain a reduced body weight and are pleased with their size in spite of its emaciated state. Many of these patients deny or fail to recognize that they are in fact emaciated, often arguing that they still have several pounds to lose.

Food avoidance and aversions are another secondary symptom of anorexia. Many anorexic patients will only eat so-called diet foods, such as salads, fruits, and cottage cheese. The fear of eating "forbidden" foods may become so great that the anorexic patient will deliberately throw up afterwards if forced by circumstances to consume some of these foods.

The ability to maintain oneself on a semistarvation diet provides the basis for differentiating two types of anorexics, namely, restrictor and bulimic types. Restricting anorexics are very capable of adhering to a strict caloric limitation that subsequently leads to dramatic weight loss. In a sense, restrictor anorexics are the perfect dieters because they are successful in achieving stringent control over their food intake. In contrast, bulimic anorexics are not always able to maintain severe dietary restraint. These patients alternate between a semistarvation diet that they cannot maintain and uncontrolled eating episodes or binges that are often followed by self-induced vomiting. It has been estimated that approximately 50 percent of women with anorexia nervosa display the bulimic symptoms of binge eating and purging (Casper, Eckert, Halmi, Goldberg, & Davis, 1980; Chapter 5). In addition to self-induced vomiting, bulimic subtype patients may also purge with laxatives, exercise, or diuretics.

Anorexia Nervosa—Restrictor Type: A Case Description

At the time of treatment, Leigh was a twenty-two-year-old white female who taught school in a large metropolitan area. She was tall at 5' 11" and weighed 116 pounds with 12 percent body fat. The onset of Leigh's eating disorder occurred when she was fourteen and weighed 140 pounds. With the help of her mother, Leigh initiated a series of diets and effectively reduced her weight to 112 pounds. The diets were low in calories but consisted of a balanced intake across the four food groups. Unfortunately, at this time Leigh inadvertently associated a low body weight with love and felt rejected by her peers and family at the higher weight. Somehow, the fear of a higher weight was also associated with her physical maturation (twelve to fourteen years) since her precocious development (height, weight, and breasts) was in marked contrast to other girls her age. Her mother and father were within normal weight limits, but her mother frequently dieted and informed Leigh that any weight over 140 pounds was very unhealthy.

In spite of her obviously low body weight, Leigh's perceptions of her body were distorted. She experienced herself as much heavier than her actual weight and described her ideal weight as much less than 112 pounds. Leigh engaged in severe caloric restriction, consuming approximately

500–800 calories each day. She ate no breakfast, had a salad and crackers for lunch, and the same supper with frequent diet cokes. She did not binge or purge but exercised at least five times per week for one hour in some combination of jogging and cycling. While Leigh was socially skilled, she stated that she preferred the lower body weight because it kept her from becoming the center of attention. She also stated that a higher body weight would be difficult as it would place more pressure on her to interact with others and to form closer social relationships, particularly with men.

Anorexia Nervosa—Bulimic Type: A Case Description
Andi was a twenty-year-old white female college student who was 5'3" and weighed 102 pounds, with 16 percent body fat at the time of diagnosis. In an effort to control her weight, Andi alternated between severe caloric restriction and uncontrolled bingeing and purging. She was able to fast or severely diet for about four days eating only 500 calories or fewer each day. The third and fourth days of dieting were difficult, and she would eventually eat a very small meal such as a salad with no dressing. It was not unusual for this meal to initiate a binge of cookies, cakes, and pies. Typically, the uncontrolled eating took place in the evening when she was alone in her college dormitory room after having a late night snack with her boyfriend. The episodes of bingeing as well as some of the low calorie meals were followed by self-induced vomiting.

Two years previously, Andi had achieved a low body weight of eighty-seven pounds. At that time, she was able to restrict her caloric intake more effectively and vomited less frequently. She also used exercise as a form of purging. For example, Andi swam at least thirty minutes and jogged several miles six or seven days a week. She would increase her exercise after eating as a way to rid herself of the calories. She also worked as an aerobics instructor and led six to ten one-hour classes each week.

Bulimia Nervosa: The Clinical Syndrome

Young women with bulimia nervosa share many of the symptoms of anorexia nervosa. Specifically, the fear of obesity and attempts to lose weight are core clinical features of bulimia nervosa. Many bulimic women also display a body-image disturbance that takes the form of dissatisfaction with current body weight and shape and, in some cases, misperception of actual body size. While they practice caloric restriction, in contrast to anorexics, bulimics are not as effective in dieting and thus usually weigh within the normal range. In contrast to anorexia, which involves extreme weight loss, the normal body weight exacerbates perceptual disturbances and body dissatisfaction. In addition, since bulimic individuals are not forced into treatment by life-threatening weight losses, most avoid treatment for many years. As their condition worsens, some seek help by initiating contact with health care professionals.

Severe restriction of caloric intake often precipitates binge eating. The classification of food intake as a binge is subjective and differs from person to person. Many experts define a binge as the intake of a large quantity of food in a short period of time. For some young women, however, eating a single doughnut, brownie, or other forbidden food constitutes a binge. For others, the consumption of thousands of calories—dozens of doughnuts, packages of cookies, or several pies—would constitute an eating binge. For still others, a binge would be the consumption of a normal-sized meal. In general, a binge is the ingestion of any food substance or quantity that violates the individual's idea of dieting and thereby increases anxiety regarding weight gain.

Eating binges and the subsequent weight-related anxiety arouse the desire to purge the calories consumed to avoid weight gain. Purging can occur by either self-induced vomiting, laxative abuse, fasting, or intense exercise. These binge/purge episodes occur infrequently in some patients but in others may happen ten to fifteen times a day.

For many bulimic individuals, the act of eating is associated with the feeling of being out of control. As we noted, this loss of control is a common experience for bulimic anorexics as well. The fear of losing control is warranted, as both groups of individuals are in a chronic state of semistarvation. In this semistarved state, there are strong biological pressures to eat. Eating a small morsel of food in these circumstances can easily elicit a larger food intake than intended.

For bulimia nervosa, eating food in an unrestrained fashion gives rise to sensations of fullness and bloatedness that result in intense fears of gaining weight. In the overwhelming majority of cases, anxiety over weight gain is eliminated by purging via self-induced vomiting. Typically, vomiting occurs within one-half hour or less after the binge. Initially, most bulimic individuals stimulate vomiting via the gag reflex. With vomiting occurring on a regular basis, the response may become easier requiring little more than a diaphragm contraction with no retching or tears evident.

Other bulimics abuse laxatives by taking several times the recommended dosage on a daily basis thinking that the induced diarrhea will flush out the excess food. A substantial proportion of bulimics also combine laxative abuse with self-induced vomiting. Laxatives are often taken according to some regimen the bulimic believes will be effective in purging. This results in widely varying patterns of laxative use, including before eating, after eating, or before going to bed, to name a few.

Bulimia Nervosa: A Case Description
Nanci was a nineteen-year-old white female, 5′1″ at one hundred pounds with 20 percent body fat. She had completed one-and-a-half years of college

but dropped out and was unemployed because of her eating disorder. Nanci's strong fear of obesity resulted in a pattern of semistarvation involving meal skipping and fasting for one or two days followed by self-induced vomiting after a regular meal or a binge of junk foods, such as chips and cookies. She evidenced no body-image distortion, but was aware of and dissatisfied with her shape.

The health and medical complications of her disorder included periods of dizziness, generalized weakness, fluid retention, irregular heartbeats, and irregular menstrual cycles. It was not unusual for her to go seven months without a period.

The onset of Nanci's disorder occurred when she was fifteen years old at which time she began self-induced vomiting once a day with a gradual progression to two or three times a day. Prior to that time, she had a long history of participation (preschool, elementary school, and junior high) in gymnastics, dancing, and modeling. Many instructors warned her to keep her weight down or she would never be a successful dancer or gymnast.

TERMINOLOGICAL AND DIAGNOSTIC CONFUSION

While there is fair agreement on the standards for evaluating obesity and some degree of consistency regarding the specifics of anorexia nervosa, the terms used to describe and distinguish bulimia and anorexia nervosa have been quite problematic. A plethora of terms has arisen over the past fifteen years to describe eating disorders including bulimia, bulimia nervosa, bulimarexia, the dietary chaos syndrome, and dysorexia. The lack of consistency in terms is also evident in the criteria for various diagnostic categories. Stein and Laakso (1988) traced references to binge eating over the past 300 years. They concluded that while conceptualizations and specific descriptions of the disorder have varied considerably, there is a core problem whose fundamental features have remained constant over time. We will first take a look at relevant terms, their origins, and their descriptions prior to discussing diagnosis.

Bulimarexia

The term *bulimarexia* was introduced by Boskind-Lodahl (1976) to describe normal weight women who engaged in a pattern of binge eating followed by purging. This term was introduced prior to the inclusion of bulimia in the *Diagnostic and Statistical Manual* (DSM) of the American Psychiatric Association. In choosing the term bulimarexia, Boskind-White and White

(1983) attempted to identify bingeing and purging as a distinct eating problem in normal weight women. They also attempted to distance the term from medical and psychoanalytic theories of causation.

In bulimarexia, the binge/purge pattern is conceptualized as a learned form of behavior. It is acquired through the individual's interaction with other people within a sociocultural context that places great value on thinness as a prerequisite to feminine beauty. Early psychoanalytic formulations attributed bulimia to a fear of oral impregnation and a deep-seated rejection of femininity (Waller, Kaufman, & Deutsch, 1940). In contrast, Boskind-White and White (1983) argued that the etiology of bulimia involved the acceptance of a stereotypic cultural definition of the ideal female that culminated in an obsession with thinness and weight loss.

The work of Boskind-White and White on bulimarexia was important for several reasons. They provided some of the first detailed clinical descriptions of bingeing and purging in normal weight women and also called attention to the sociocultural origins of the disorder (Boskind-White & White, 1986). Their work on bulimarexia also resulted in some of the earliest published work on the cognitive behavioral treatment of the disorder (Boskind-Lodahl & White, 1978).

The term bulimarexia, however, has not been adopted in general use. The criteria for diagnosing someone as bulimarexic has always been somewhat vague, and the category has considerable overlap with many other terms.

Dietary Chaos Syndrome

Palmer (1979) introduced the term *dietary chaos syndrome* to describe gorging and vomiting consistently observed in a subset of patients with anorexia nervosa. In addition, there were patients who did not meet the weight-loss criteria for anorexia, but who were clearly quite distressed by the behavioral pattern of compulsive overeating followed by self-induced vomiting. Vomiting and laxative abuse were seen as important features of the dietary chaos syndrome because they broke the natural link between overeating and weight gain allowing the compulsive overeating to progress out of control. The term, however, has not been well accepted and is currently not used.

Dysorexia

Recognizing the inherent similarity of anorexia and bulimia, Guiora (1967) introduced the term *dysorexia* as a potential diagnostic label. Guiora's formulation of dysorexia was based on his experience in the psychoanalysis of six patients with varying forms of eating disorders. While Guiora's formulation is subjective and presented without supporting data, his behavioral observations are interesting and worth examining.

Guiora argued that anorexia and bulimia are two poles of a single disorder, dysorexia. The anorexic behaviors, food restriction and severe weight loss, and the bulimic behaviors, bingeing and in some instances purging, are seen as symptomatic of a single eating disorder. The dysorexic individual is seen as alternating between the two sets of symptoms. The common elements, according to Guiora, consist of excessive concern with body weight along with psychodynamic conflicts that result from an oral fixation and the subsequent failure to develop a mature sexuality. While the merit of Guiora's psychodynamic formulation is debatable, his observation that both anorexia and bulimia nervosa represent different behavioral manifestations of an underlying obsession with a thin body weight has had an impact on current thinking.

Bulimia

The term *bulimia* was introduced as a diagnostic category in 1980 (APA, 1980) in the third version of the American Psychiatric Association's *Diagnostic and Statistiscal Manual* (DSM-III). The DSM-III diagnostic criteria are as follows*:

1. Recurrent episodes of binge eating (rapid consumption of a large amount of food in a discrete period of time, usually less than two hours);
2. At least three of the following:
   - Consumption of high-caloric, easily ingested food during a binge;
   - Inconspicuous eating during a binge;
   - Termination of such eating episodes by abdominal pain, sleep, social interruption, or self-induced vomiting;
   - Repeated attempts to lose weight by severely restrictive diets, self-induced vomiting, or use of cathartics or diuretics;
   - Frequent weight fluctuations greater than ten pounds due to alternating binges and fasts;
3. Awareness that the eating pattern is abnormal and fear of not being able to stop voluntarily;
4. Depressed mood and self-deprecating thoughts following eating binges;
5. The bulimic episodes are not due to Anorexia Nervosa or any known physical disorder.

In many ways, the DSM-III category was very important in that it introduced standardized diagnostic criteria that were widely adopted. While there are a number of shortcomings that will soon become apparent, the

---

*Diagnostic Criteria for Bulimia: DSM-III reprinted with permission from the *Diagnostic and Statistical Manual of Mental Disorders. Third Edition. Revised.* Copyright 1987 American Psychiatric Association.

DSM-III has been so widely employed that one must understand the criteria in order to evaluate much of the current literature on bulimia.

Bulimia Nervosa

The term *bulimia nervosa* was introduced by Russell (1979). This category has three primary features: (1) the patients suffer from powerful and intractable urges to overeat; (2) they seek to avoid the perceived fattening effects of food by inducing vomiting or abusing purgatives or both; and (3) they have a morbid fear of becoming fat. Originally, Russell used the term bulimia nervosa to refer to a subgroup of patients with anorexia nervosa. When Russell's data is examined, however, it is clear that 20 percent of his original patients had no history of anorexia nervosa. Russell's identification of bulimia as an ominous variant of anorexia nervosa had more to do with similarity of psychopathology than with weight history. In fact, Thompson (1988) compared bulimic patients with differing current weights and weight histories on eating disorder symptoms and psychopathology and found few differences between underweight bulimics, normal weight bulimics with a history of being underweight, and normal weight bulimics with no previous history of being underweight. The major differences among the groups were that the underweight bulimics were more satisfied with their current weight than the two normal weight groups. The current thinking (Fairburn & Garner, 1986) is that bulimia nervosa refers to a pattern of behaviors that occur in individuals with a variety of current body weights and weight histories.

Russell (1983) revised the criteria for bulimia nervosa to include a previous overt or cryptic episode of anorexia nervosa. Thus, the individual who begins as obese and then develops behavior patterns that meet the criteria for bulimia nervosa could not be diagnosed because of the absence of a previous episode of anorexia.

Recent usage of the term is not restricted to patients with any particular body weight or weight history.

Confusion and Overlap

Unlike the DSM-III category, bulimia nervosa explicitly recognizes that some form of purging as a weight control strategy is a defining feature. The requirement that purging be present to render a diagnosis of bulimia nervosa has the advantage of leading to a more homogeneous grouping of patients than DSM-III bulimia. The presence of purging, either self-induced vomiting or laxative abuse, leads to a different constellation of behaviors than binge eating alone. Individuals who frequently binge but who do not purge usually become obese, further complicating the clinical picture. The differences between obese binge eaters and those who binge and purge have important implications for treatment. Wilmuth, Leitenberg, Rosen, and Cado (1988) compared twenty women who binged and purged, twenty women who only binged but did not purge, and twenty women without eating disorders and found greater eating disturbance, body-image distortion, and psychopathology among the purging bulimics than the nonpurgers or the controls. Those who binged but did not purge had more psychological problems than the control group, but they were not nearly as severe as those found among the purgers. These data suggest that the presence or absence of vomiting or laxative abuse is an important distinction in the diagnosis of an eating disorder.

Another problem with bulimia nervosa is the use of body weight as a diagnostic criteria. For example, Fairburn and Cooper (1982) surveyed 499 women who met the first three diagnostic criteria for bulimia nervosa (bingeing, purging, and fear of fat). The majority of these women (83 percent) were within 15 percent of normal body weight for their height. A prior episode of anorexia (less than 85 percent ideal body weight) was reported by 43 percent of the women surveyed. In addition, 45 percent of the sample reported a history of obesity (more than 15 percent above ideal body weight). The problem of weight history, however, is more a criticism of the early usage of the term bulimia nervosa since recent usage is based on bingeing, purging, and fear of obesity regardless of weight history.

It is clear that the behavioral syndrome of bingeing and purging occurs in women with a variety of weight histories. Using body weight or weight history to make diagnostic distinctions can lead to essentially artificial separations. Many women who binge and purge show considerable variability in their adult body-weight histories. The important clinical feature is not body weight or weight history but is instead the use of purging as a weight control strategy, the loss of control over eating behavior, and the obsession with becoming thin or staying thin.

When examined in detail, the criteria for the diagnosis of the dietary chaos syndrome, bulimia nervosa, bulimarexia, and DSM-III bulimia are quite similar. The definitions all refer to a disturbance in eating behavior described as binge eating. Some of the definitions emphasize body weight, weight changes, or endocrine disturbances (e.g., amenorrhea). A somewhat unique feature of the category of dietary chaos syndrome is the inclusion of an obsessive preoccupation with food. However, this feature appears to be sufficiently similar to binge eating and preoccupation with weight as not to create a functional difference. The dietary chaos syndrome has not been used as a category in the research literature, which may be due in part to the appearance of the DSM-III category of bulimia in the year following its publication and the lack of specificity of its diagnostic criteria. It is subject to the same criticism as DSM-III bulimia (purging need not be present). In addition, dietary chaos syndrome does not specifically require that binge eating be present. Like the DSM-III, use of the dietary chaos syndrome results in heterogeneous groupings of patients.

There is a definite need for an empirically reliable and valid system for classifying eating disorders. Such a system will improve communication among clinicians and researchers, facilitate basic research, and lead to the development and testing of clinical interventions. There are several ways to approach classification and different ways of interpreting the meaning or significance of diagnostic categories.

An eating disorder is an abnormal pattern of behavior with respect to food intake and energy balance. Unfortunately, the current language that we use to talk about eating disorders is permeated with medical connotations. We talk about our clients as patients. We attempt to diagnose anorexia and bulimia. We talk about complications of the disorder and its prognosis. In this book, we will find it impossible to escape the use of the current language to talk about eating disorders. However, we would like to make it clear that we are not assuming that bulimia or anorexia nervosa represent manifestations of an underlying mental illness. Instead, the use of these terms refers to constellations of behavior that are consistent across many individuals. As such, a diagnosis is merely an attempt to classify people according to patterns of behavior that are commonly observed.

The reader should note, however, that our view on this matter is not universally held. Pope and Hudson (1988) have argued that bulimia is in fact a disease and that it is caused by biological abnormalities in neurotransmitters involved in the regulation of affect. Beumont (1988), on the other hand, argued that while bulimia is clearly a constellation of symptoms, it may not be useful to view it as a disease entity or even a medical syndrome. Instead, bulimia is considered a response to the current cultural demands for thinness and dieting, making it a behavioral and cultural, not medical, phenomenon.

CURRENT DIAGNOSTIC CATEGORIES

In 1987, the American Psychiatric Association published a revised version of the DSM-III, the DSM-III-R (APA, 1987). Since we believe that standardization of terminology is important, we will present these latest diagnostic criteria and note some of the shortcomings of this current system. However, we will adopt the position of Guiora and argue in a later section that anorexia and bulimia (even in DSM-III-R) along with binge eating in the obese are subordinate categories of an overriding diagnostic category called "eating disorders." While the behavioral manifestations and consequences differ, anorexia and bulimia nervosa arise from similar causal processes.

Anorexia Nervosa DSM-III-R

Although anorexia nervosa has long been identified as a psychopathological condition, it was not recognized by the American Psychiatric Association as a psychopathological condition until it was listed in the 1980 version of the DSM-III.

The term *anorexia nervosa* has been in use for many years to describe a type of patient who usually presents with severe emaciation in the absence of any metabolic disease. The criteria for the diagnosis of anorexia in DSM-III-R are*:

1. Refusal to maintain body weight over a minimal normal weight for age and height (e.g., weight loss leading to maintenance of body weight 15 percent below that expected; or failure to make expected weight gain during period of growth, leading to body weight 15 percent below that expected);
2. Intense fear of gaining weight or becoming fat, even though underweight;
3. Disturbance in the way in which body weight, size, or shape is experienced (e.g., the person claims to "feel fat" even when emaciated, believes that one area of the body is "too fat" even when obviously underweight);
4. In females, the absence of at least three consecutive menstrual cycles when otherwise expected to occur (primary or secondary amenorrhea). (A woman is considered to have amenorrhea if her periods occur only following hormone, for example, estrogen, administration.)

There are a number of problems with the DSM-III-R category of anorexia nervosa, one of the major ones being the use of body weight as a criteria to establish diagnosis. The revised version has fewer problems than the previous version, which *required* a minimum loss to 25 percent below expected body weight. The revised version suggests but does not require 15 percent below ideal body weight for a diagnosis. Halmi (1985a) argued that there are no data showing that patients can be separated into distinctly different groups on the basis of their degree of weight loss. The degree of emaciation that anyone will display depends upon initial body weight. For example, obese individuals who lose a great deal of weight using the same behaviors as an anorexic will be automatically excluded from this category unless they drop 15 percent or more below the expected weight for their height and age. Others who lose considerable amounts of weight and who share the psychological and behavioral characteristics of

---
*DSM-III-R Criteria for Anorexia Nervosa reprinted with permission from the *Diagnostic and Statistical Manual of Mental Disorders. Third Edition. Revised.* Copyright 1987 American Psychiatric Association.

anorexia nervosa will be excluded from this diagnosis until they fall well below normal body weight. Despite these arguments, patients who present severely emaciated will require different treatment than persons closer to normal weight who engage in similar dieting behaviors.

Additionally, the DSM-III-R criteria do not specify behavioral criteria related to methods of weight loss. However, two distinct subgroups of patients with anorexia nervosa have been identified, namely, those who maintain a low body weight through strict food restriction and those who binge and purge. For example, Casper, et al. (1980) divided 105 anorexic patients into two groups, bulimics (47 percent) and restrictors (53 percent). Restrictors were patients who lost weight predominantly through dieting and food restriction. The bulimic patients employed vomiting and laxative abuse as weight loss strategies. While the weight history of the two groups did not differ, the bulimic patients were significantly older and were much more likely to resort to self-induced vomiting as a weight control measure. Measures of psychological adjustment showed that bulimic patients were more disturbed and distressed by their problems than the restrictors.

Similarly, Garfinkel, Moldofsky, and Garner (1979) reported on a series of 135 patients treated for anorexia nervosa. Based on extensive clinical interviews, the patients were classified as restrictors or bulimics. Bulimic patients had more severe depression, mood lability, used more alcohol and drugs, and were more sexually active than the restrictor group. These studies demonstrate the importance of distinguishing patients with anorexia nervosa based on the behaviors used to produce the weight loss.

Another difficulty with the DSM-III-R category is that it does not provide specific criteria for determining the presence of fear of weight gain and body-image disturbance. While the literature supports the inclusion of these two features as a core element of an eating disorder (Halmi, 1985a), no method for ascertaining if a particular patient meets these two criteria is provided.

A final problem with the DSM-III-R category of anorexia nervosa is the requirement that the individual experience amenorrhea. There is much evidence that disruption of reproductive hormones and cessation of the menses occurs as a consequence of chronic self-induced starvation (Henley & Vaitukaitis, 1985). Many other endocrine changes also occur as a result of starvation due to anorexia nervosa. It is not clear why one particular consequence of starvation was singled out to become a diagnostic criteria. Henley and Vaitukaitis (1985), in describing the physiological impact of starvation or malnutrition on reproductive hormones, state that the regular occurrence of menses requires maintenance of some minimum body fat percentage. The primary feature of anorexia nervosa is behavior designed to minimize nutrient intake and/or maximize energy expenditure in order to maintain voluntarily an excessively low body weight. Amenorrhea is therefore a consequence of weight loss and should probably not be considered a core symptom required for a diagnosis.

Bulimia Nervosa DSM-III-R

The data on the heterogeneity of patient groups treated for anorexia eventually led to the development of bulimia as an alternative diagnostic group. The previous version of the DSM-III had the problem of splitting individuals who binge and purge into two groups solely on the basis of body weight. Those who had lost more than 25 percent of their body weight were classified as anorexic while those whose weight remained above the cutoff were classified as bulimic.

The DSM-III-R criteria for bulimia nervosa are as follows*:

1. Recurrent episodes of binge eating (rapid consumption of a large amount of food in a discrete period of time);
2. Feeling of lack of control over eating behavior during the eating binges;
3. Regular self-induced vomiting, use of laxatives or diuretics, strict dieting or fasting, or vigorous exercise in order to prevent weight gain;
4. Minimum average of two binge eating episodes a week for at least three months;
5. Persistent overconcern with body shape and weight.

There are a number of changes in the revised version of the bulimic eating disorder including its name. As before, a diagnosis of bulimia nervosa requires that the individual engage in binge eating. The revised bulimia nervosa category requires in addition a minimum average of two binges per week for at least three months. This requirement insures that only those with a chronic and persistent binge-eating problem will receive a diagnosis.

A big difference between the old DSM-III category of bulimia and the revised category of bulimia nervosa is the specific requirement that some form of purging be present in order to render a diagnosis. Four major categories of purging are mentioned: (1) self-induced vomiting, (2) laxative or diuretic abuse, (3) strict dieting or fasting, and (4) vigorous exercise. The criteria no longer require depression, self-deprecating thoughts, or awareness that the pattern is abnormal. Instead of these less essential features, the revised bulimia nervosa criteria include overconcern with body weight or shape.

There are still several problems with the DSM-III-R category of bulimia nervosa. We have treated a number of patients who show overconcern with their weight, vomit after every meal, and who feel unable to control this behavior pattern. However, they do not lose control and engage in rapid consumption of large amounts of food. Unless these in-

---
*DSM-III-R Criteria for Bulimia Nervosa reprinted with permission from the *Diagnostic and Statistical Manual of Mental Disorders. Third Edition. Revised.* Copyright 1987 American Psychiatric Association.

dividuals are significantly below expected body weight, they can only be given a diagnosis of eating disorder not otherwise specified.

Examples of disorders of eating that do not meet the criteria for a specific eating disorder are*:

1. Person of average weight who does not have binge-eating episodes, but frequently engages in self-induced vomiting for fear of gaining weight;
2. All of the features of anorexia nervosa in a female except absence of menses; and
3. All of the features of bulimia nervosa except the frequency of binge-eating episodes.

The requirement that binge eating be present raises an additional question of definition. What is an eating binge? Does binge eating differ from overeating? Can binge eating be objectively defined, or is it a cognitive and emotional reaction to one's eating behavior? There are many situations in our culture in which overeating is considered appropriate. Holidays, such as Christmas and Thanksgiving, and other social events are frequently occasions at which people eat too much food. Schlundt, Johnson, and Jarrell (1985) compared a group of twenty-three overweight patients to eight bulimic patients using a microanalysis of self-monitored eating behavior. The same kinds of events that precipitated the binge/purge cycle in bulimics were found to precipitate overeating in the obese group. These events included being alone at home in the evening, negative moods, and positive social occasions. This study suggests that not only is it difficult to draw an arbitrary line between overeating and binge eating on the basis of the amount of food consumed but that it may not be possible to distinguish the two on the basis of their behavioral dynamics.

Basing a diagnosis of bulimia nervosa on the regular occurrence of binge eating is problematic unless an arbitrary distinction is drawn between the common occurrence of overeating and an eating binge. It does not make sense to draw an arbitrary boundary on a behavior that is so prevalent. Nor does there seem to be evidence that the physiological, psychological, or environmental causes of overeating and binge eating are qualitatively different (see Chapters 2, 4, 6, and 7).

Some investigators have suggested that the term bulimia be used just to refer to binge eating behavior (Halmi, 1985a). However, this not only confuses binge eating with overeating, it also creates an unfortunate overlap with DSM-III-R terminology.

Food intake exists on a continuum from fasting to gorging. It is sensible to have words to distinguish behaviors on the extremes of this continuum. However, it is difficult to draw an arbitrary boundary between

---

*DSM-III-R Eating Disorder not Otherwise Specified reprinted with permission from the *Diagnostic and Statistical Manual of Mental Disorders. Third Edition. Revised.* Copyright 1987 American Psychiatric Association.

dieting and restrictive dieting and between overeating and binge eating.

Bulimia nervosa is a behavior pattern that extends over time. By seeing the patterned nature of this behavior, many of these problems can be at least partially resolved. The bulimic behavior pattern begins with the consumption of an amount of food that the individual deems excessive given the circumstances. The evaluation of the amount of food allowed in various situations relies on a set of self-imposed standards designed to induce weight loss or avoid weight gain. Violation of these standards elicits a fear of gaining weight that results in the initiation of a compensatory behavior designed to remove or ameliorate the effects of excessive eating. Purging results in a reduction in fear of weight gain and a return to a state of vigilance in which the individual must be careful not to eat too much for fear of gaining weight.

Basing a diagnosis of bulimia nervosa on a pattern of behavior in which overeating arouses fear of weight gain that results in use of some purging strategy avoids some of the problems inherent in the DSM-III-R category. This approach also has the advantage that highly trained athletes are not accused of having an eating disorder. For an eating disorder to be present, vigorous exercise must occur as a way of compensating for a specific instance of perceived violation of dietary restraint rules.

A problem occurs with thinking about bulimia as an interrelated pattern of overeating, fear of weight gain, and purging in chronic bulimics. Once this pattern of behavior is well established, the individual learns that self-induced vomiting is a very effective method of weight control. As a result, there is little attempt to restrain food intake and very little fear of gaining weight because the individual plans in advance to throw up after the binge. In these individuals, when the opportunity to purge is prevented, dietary restraint and fear of weight gain will reappear.

While the DSM-III-R requirement that purging be present in order to render a diagnosis of bulimia nervosa results in more homogeneous patient groups than with the previous criteria, an important group of eating-disordered individuals is left without a name to describe their pattern of behavior. This group consists of people who regularly engage in binge eating, are concerned about excess body weight, and fear additional weight gain but do not rely on purging (Wilmuth et al., 1988). They also have attempted to gain control over their eating behavior in the past but have met with little or no success. Until a future revision of the American Psychiatric Association's diagnostic manual comes up with a category for these individuals, we propose the term *compulsive overeater*.

EATING DISORDERS: COMMON MISCONCEPTIONS

The majority of eating disorders occur in middle- and upper-middle-class white females. However, anorexia and bulimia do occur in other social strata, racial and ethnic groups, and in men (Nevo, 1985; Robinson & Andersen, 1985; Oyebode, Boodhoo, and Schapira, 1988; Rosen et al., 1988; Silber, 1986). The fear of obesity, desire for a thin body shape, and sociocultural pressures equating attractiveness with a thin figure are increasingly apparent in these other groups and will undoubtedly result in increased incidence of eating disorders in these populations.

Eating Disorders in Males

Although most eating disorders occur in females, cases of males with anorexia or bulimia, while rare, nonetheless do occur. In a review of the literature, Beumont, Beardwood, and Russell (1972) concluded that of the many cases of anorexia attributed to males, only twenty-five or 10 percent, would appropriately be diagnosed as displaying anorexia nervosa. In the other cases, the evidence was not available or was too sketchy to support a definite diagnosis. Interestingly, of the twenty-five cases that did fit the diagnosis, the condition was strikingly similar to that of anorexia in women. The onset of the disorder occurred in late childhood or early adolescence. Slightly more than half had thought themselves to be obese, and an equal number desired to be thin and showed a definite fear of weight gain. Additionally, most were preoccupied with their eating and weight and approximately half purged via self-induced vomiting and/or exercise.

A surprising difference between men and women with anorexia nervosa is the SES distribution. Most research finds that 90–95 percent of anorexics are female and that these women are predominantly from the upper and middle classes (Bemis, 1978). The available data with males is somewhat different. Crisp and Toms (1972) found that approximately half of their male anorexics come from working- and lower-class backgrounds.

Male anorexics may also display a significant homosexual conflict, and it is postulated that this conflict is similar to the threat of maturity and fears of intimacy found in many young women with anorexia nervosa (Crisp in Darby et al., 1983).

Oyebode et al. (1988) compared thirteen male anorexic patients to a set of carefully matched female anorexics. They found that the clinical features of the disorder were essentially the same for men and women, but their data suggested that the outcome was worse for men.

Garner, Olmstead, and Garfinkle (1983) speculated about why women are more likely to develop eating disorders and fears of maturity than men. In contrast to males who display increased growth of facial hair and deepening voice, females display much more pronounced body changes at the onset of puberty. The enlargement of the breasts and changes in the shape of the hips can often be mistaken for getting fat in someone who has already developed body-weight concerns.

Atypical Eating Disorders

Most individuals with anorexia or bulimia display the common core symptoms discussed. It is not unusual, however, to see cases that do not fit the exact clinical syndrome. Those patients with core anorexic symptoms who maintain a body weight slightly below or just within normal limits should still be considered to be eating disordered. These preanorexic cases should be treated aggressively and not dismissed. They are at high risk for a lower body weight, a more complicated clinical picture, and a longer course of therapy. The presence of core anorexic symptoms is all that is necessary to identify and treat these cases, not a lower body weight and physical complications such as amenorrhea.

Atypical cases, by their very nature, offer a wide spectrum of confusing presentations. Many older women, for example, will display significant weight loss and the resulting medical complications. These women are often pleased with their lower body weight but do not display the deliberate food aversion, intense fear of obesity, or body-image disturbance of the typical anorexic. Their restricted food intake is more likely to be the result of stress from marital and family discord or other personal adjustment problems. Contributing to the lower body weight is excessive caffeine intake (coffee, tea, diet cola), cigarette smoking, and alcohol or drug abuse. Because they are pleased with their lower body weight and the addictive nature of their caffeine and nicotine intake, these patients display an extreme resistance to therapeutic efforts to increase food intake and restore body weight.

Pica DSM-III-R

Consumption of nonnutritive substances often occurs in children and is widespread in different cultures. There are two criteria for the diagnosis of pica: (1) repeated eating of a nonnutritive substance for at least one month and (2) the person does not meet the criteria for either autistic disorder, schizophrenia, or Kleine-Levin syndrome (APA, 1987). While pica in children can present serious health risks (e.g., lead poisoning from old paint), it is very different from anorexia and bulimia nervosa in that regulation of body weight is not an issue.

Rumination Disorder of Infancy DSM-III-R

There are two criteria for diagnosis of rumination disorder: (1) repeated regurgitation, without nausea or associated gastrointestinal illness, for at least one month following a period of normal functioning and (2) weight loss or failure to make expected weight gain. Unlike bulimia nervosa, the

the vomiting is experienced as automatic and uncontrollable rather than self-induced.

Related to ruminative disorders in children is psychogenic vomiting in adults (Johnson, Corrigan, Crusco, & Jarrell, 1987). While this condition is rare, it is often confused with bulimia. Clinicians who treat many eating disorder patients will undoubtedly see a few of these patients over the course of several years. Psychogenic vomiting consists of an involuntary regurgitation of food into the oral cavity. Whether the regurgitation is entirely involuntary or to some extent deliberate is somewhat controversial. In many cases, the rumination syndrome combines with psychogenic vomiting. Here food is rechewed and may be reswallowed.

Several features of psychogenic vomiting/rumination syndrome that distinguish it from anorexia and bulimia nervosa include the following: (1) a general absence of core symptoms such as fear of obesity, binge eating, or body-image disturbance and (2) an indication that the vomiting is involuntary rather than self-induced. Available information suggests that psychogenic vomiting is related to possible gastrointestinal tract dysfunction, poor eating habits, and stress during the process of eating (Johnson, Corrigan, & Mayo, 1987).

Anorexia and Bulimia Nervosa in DSM-III-R

One of the major criticisms of the DSM-III classification of eating disorders has been the distinction between bulimia and anorexia with bulimia. Nearly 50 percent of the patients who qualify for a diagnosis of anorexia nervosa engage in a behavior pattern similar to bulimia. The DSM-III-R has responded to this problem by creating sets of diagnostic criteria that allow for an individual to qualify as having bulimia nervosa if a pattern of bingeing and purging is present and a concurrent diagnosis of anorexia nervosa if this behavior pattern results in maintenance of a low body weight.

It is too early to tell how researchers and clinicians will deal with the concurrent diagnosis of anorexia and bulimia nervosa. While the overlap may lead to some confusion in practice, it may also have the beneficial effect of leading to the development of a typology and/or conceptualization of eating disorders that can easily encompass these overlapping cases.

INCIDENCE OF THE DIAGNOSIS OF ANOREXIA NERVOSA

In some respects, it is easier to study the incidence of anorexia nervosa than bulimia since it is more difficult to hide a dramatic weight loss than secretive bingeing and purging. However, over the years, it has been difficult to evaluate the incidence of anorexia nervosa. Lucas, Beard, Kranz, and Kurland (1983), in a review of the early literature on the epidemiology of anorexia nervosa, point out that many different methodological factors influence prevalence estimates. Prevalence estimates have ranged from 0.37 per 100,000 to 460 cases per 100,000. One of the major factors influencing the prevalence estimate is the population from which the samples are drawn. Younger populations with higher concentrations of women from upper-income families tend to yield the highest estimates.

Eight studies reporting prevalence rates for anorexia nervosa (see Appendix A) show that the particular population surveyed has a large effect on the estimated prevalence rate. The highest rate, 9 percent, was reported by Szmukler, Eisler, Gillies, and Hayward (1985) in a survey of one hundred students attending an exclusive school for ballet dancers. Rodin, Daneman, Johnson, Kenshole, and Garfinkel (1985) found a 6 percent rate of anorexia nervosa in a sample of forty-six adolescent females with diabetes mellitus. The lowest rates are given by studies that examined the prevalence of anorexia in community psychiatric registries. Hoek and Brook (1985) reported a rate of 0.04 percent and Szmukler et al. (1986) reported a rate of 0.004 percent.

Three studies of students lead to a combined prevalence rate of 2.5 percent, while a study by Pope, Hudson, and Yurgelun-Todd (1984) in which urban shoppers were surveyed leads to an estimated lifetime prevalence of 0.7 percent. We must conclude that the prevalence of anorexia nervosa in the general population is well below 1 percent. However, when specialized populations are sampled, the prevalence rate can become much higher.

INCIDENCE OF THE DIAGNOSIS OF BULIMIA

Twenty-two studies of the prevalence of bulimia in various populations (see Appendix A) employed a variety of criteria for diagnosing bulimia. However, the DSM-III criteria or some slight modification is the most common.

Estimates of the prevalence of bulimia vary widely between studies. Low estimates were given by Hart and Ollendick (1985) of 1.0 percent in a population of working women, Fairburn and Cooper (1983) of 1.9 percent in a population of women drawn from a family planning clinic, and Rand and Kuldau (1986) of 0.4 percent in a population of community volunteers. These studies used older, more heterogeneous populations and obtained generally lower rates of bulimia. However, Pope et al. (1984) surveyed shoppers at a mall and obtained an estimated prevalence of bulimia of 10.3 percent. High estimates were given by Hamilton et al.

(1985) of 15.2 percent in ballet dancers, Pertschuk, Collins, Kreisberg, and Fager (1986) of 21.6 percent in college students, Pope et al. (1984b) of 18.6 and 12.5 percent in two college populations, Nevo (1985) of 11.0 percent in a college population, Halmi, Falk, and Schwartz (1981) of 13.0 percent in a college population, and Williams, Schaefer, Shisslak, Gronwaldt, and Comerci (1986) of 12.5 percent in a junior high and high school population. While several of the results may be high for methodological reasons (e.g., Pertschuk, 1986; Nevo, 1985), or due to the use of special high-risk populations (Hamilton, 1985), the high rates cannot easily be explained away in all cases.

When the rates of bulimia are averaged across the twenty-two studies, a mean rate of 7.6 percent is obtained. This rate will be a high estimate for older, more heterogeneous populations, and may be low for younger, more homogeneous high-risk populations. Taken at face value, the literature would suggest that somewhere between 6–8 percent of young female populations, especially on college campuses, will qualify for a DSM-III diagnosis of bulimia. These estimates correspond quite well with a recent study by Gross and Rosen (1988). Gross and Rosen surveyed 1,373 male and female high school students from geographically, racially, and ethnically diverse backgrounds. They distinguished between binge eating with and without purging (roughly corresponding to the difference between DSM-III and DSM-III-R). To be diagnosed bulimic, binge eating had to occur at least once per month. The rate of bulimia with purging was 2.2 percent among girls and 0.1 percent for boys and without purging 7.4 percent for girls and 1.1 percent for boys.

Schotte and Stunkard (1987) surveyed 1,965 college students using a questionnaire that assessed not only the presence but also the frequency of bingeing and purging. Binge eating was very common, being reported as occuring at least once a month by 45 percent of the women and 38 percent of the men. While vomiting was much less common, occuring once a month or more in 3 percent of the women and 1 percent of the men, it was almost always reported in conjunction with binge eating. When both the DSM-III and the DSM-III-R criteria were applied to this sample, the prevalence estimates were identical for women (0.9 percent). For men, the prevalence rate for DSM-III diagnosis was zero since none of the men reported self-deprecating thoughts. However, when this item was not considered, the DSM-III and DSM-III-R criteria both resulted in a prevalence estimate of 0.3 percent. Interviews were conducted with a sample of students who met the diagnostic criteria in order to estimate the rate of false positives resulting from diagnosis by questionnaire. Twenty-two percent of the women who met the criteria based on questionnaire responses could not be diagnosed (using either DSM-III or DSM-III-R) based on the interviews. The prevalence rates, adjusted for false positives, dropped to 1.3 percent for women and 0.1 percent for men. While DSM-III and

DSM-III-R resulted in similar overall prevalence estimates, there was very little overlap between those individuals identified using the two sets of criteria.

The Schotte and Stunkard (1987) rates stand in marked contrast to many of the other studies. The major difference results from Schotte and Stunkard obtaining frequency estimates on all of the diagnostic criteria and requiring a rating of "often" or "usually" for a symptom to be considered present for the purposes of diagnosis. While some of the core behaviors of bulimia are quite common, the pattern of behavior (bingeing and purging) itself is not quite so common, and the frequent occurrence of this pattern may be rare.

The sensitivity of the prevalency estimates from survey studies to the exact diagnostic criteria used is nicely illustrated in a study by Whitehouse and Button (1988). Data collected on 578 college students in 1981 was analyzed for the prevalence of anorexia nervosa and bulimia using a variety of diagnostic criteria. The rates for anorexia varied between 0.2 percent and 0.4 percent; the rates for bulimia varied from 0.9 percent, using Russell's (1983) criteria for bulimia nervosa, to 2.5 percent, when Palmer's (1979) criteria for dietary chaos syndrome were applied.

It is of interest to examine the extent to which the diagnosis of anorexia overlaps with that of bulimia. A review of seven studies that reported rates of bulimic versus restrictor anorexics in patient samples (see Appendix A) concludes that 55 percent of the anorexic patients were classified as restrictors and 45 percent were classified as bulimic.

SPECTRUM OF EATING DISORDERS

Two findings argue that a more comprehensive model of eating disorders is needed: (1) the substantial overlap between anorexia and bulimia nervosa and (2) the core behaviors (binge eating, methods to compensate for overeating, and the desire to lose weight or avoid weight gain) exist on a continuum within the population. Following logic similar to Guiora (1967), Andersen (1983) suggested that anorexia and bulimia nervosa represent a spectrum of eating disorders. The concept of a spectrum of disorders has been used with both schizophrenia and depression. Andersen compared the similarities and differences between anorexia and bulimia nervosa and concluded that similarities between the two disorders are striking. His comparison found similarities in the epidemiology, natural history, psychopathology, and social impact of the two disorders.

Support for the notion of an eating disorder spectrum is provided by Mikalide and Andersen (1985) who studied over 240 patients. Among the 165 females, the investigators found that 75 percent could be diagnosed with an eating disorder as follows: 33 percent anorexic restrictor, 10 percent anorexic bulimic type, 26 percent normal weight bulimic with prior history of anorexia, and 31 percent normal weight bulimic without prior anorexia. The remaining fifty patients were diagnosed with some form of psychopathology (e.g., schizophrenia) in which eating was disturbed as a secondary consequence of the primary psychiatric disorder. Twenty-six of the patients with a diagnosis of bulimia nervosa had a prior episode of anorexia nervosa that would have qualified for a DSM-III diagnosis at the time while the remaining bulimic patients never had an episode of anorexia nervosa.

In eating disorders, there is a tendency for patients to alternate between anorexia nervosa and bulimia nervosa diagnostic criteria, and between bulimia nervosa and obesity. The alternation between the diagnoses is illustrated by Fairburn and Cooper (1982) who surveyed 499 women meeting the criteria for bulimia nervosa. After excluding all individuals who were more than 15 percent underweight they found the weight histories of these individuals to be quite variable with substantial numbers having histories of either anorexia nervosa, obesity, or both. Andersen (1983) argued that the reason that the incidence of bulimia is usually reported to be higher than anorexia nervosa is because no specific weight criteria are involved in diagnosing bulimia but both involve a similar struggle with attempts to lose weight.

While a diagnosis of anorexia nervosa is in part based on a weight loss of 15 percent or more of body weight, a substantial number of patients with anorexia nervosa display a behavior pattern similar to bulimia nervosa. Oppenheimer, Howells, Palmer, and Chaloner (1985) reported on the diagnosis of a series of seventy-eight eating disorder patients. Bulimia was the primary diagnosis in 42 percent while anorexia was the diagnosis for 58 percent. Of those patients diagnosed as anorexic, 21 percent engaged in gorging and vomiting. Also, Halmi and Falk (1982) reported on fifty consecutive cases of anorexia nervosa with 47 percent also engaging in bingeing and purging characteristic of bulimia nervosa. Bhanji and Mattingly (1981), in a report on twenty cases of anorexia, described bulimic behavior in 50 percent of the patients. In a large series of 141 patients, Garfinkel, et al. (1979) found that 48 percent of the patients diagnosed as having anorexia nervosa reported engaging in bulimic behavior. While it is difficult to draw strong conclusions about the incidence of bulimic behavior in anorexia from consecutive hospital admissions because of potential biases in referrals, these data do suggest that there is not a clear distinction between anorexia and bulimia nervosa.

Andersen (1983) argued that the spectrum of eating disorders has two basic components; a fear of gaining weight and a fear of losing control over eating. Both anorexia and bulimia nervosa are motivated by a desire to be thin and a fear of becoming fat. The basic difference is whether the individual is coping with the fear of losing control by strict food restriction (anorexic restrictor) or whether the individual has given in and lost control over eating, in which case purging is adopted as a compensatory strategy. Andersen (1983) suggested that premorbid personality characteristics may in part determine whether the spectrum of disorders expresses itself as anorexia or bulimia. He speculates that the anorexic restrictor is more perfectionistic and compulsive (the perfect dieter) while the bulimic is more outgoing and impulsive. However, he explicitly recognizes that the eating disorders and their expression are determined by a multiplicity of variables.

THE ANORECTIC-BULIMIC CONFLICT

Further information on the spectrum concept is provided by Holmgren et al. (1983) who studied a series of seventy-nine eating disorder patients who were diagnosed using the DSM-III criteria for anorexia nervosa and bulimia. At intake, sixteen patients were diagnosed as anorexic, forty-three were diagnosed as bulimic, seven qualified for both diagnoses, and thirteen displayed many of the characteristics but did not meet all the criteria for a diagnosis. The thirteen patients did not meet the weight loss criteria for anorexia and were considered to be in preclinical or residual states of anorexia.

Detailed patient histories were taken to reconstruct the course of the eating disorder over time. For those patients who received a diagnosis of anorexia, 38 percent had a previous episode of bulimia. For those who were considered anorexic-like, 77 percent had engaged in bulimic behavior in the past. When histories of the patients were taken into consideration, Holmgren et al. were more impressed with the similarities than the differences. Since the mean duration of eating disorder was 5.8 years, there was considerable opportunity for patients to have experienced different phases or manifestations of their eating disorder.

Holmgren et al. suggested that the various groups of eating-disordered patients displayed the outcome of a core anorectic-bulimic conflict. This conflict centers on the control of food intake. It is essentially an approach-avoidance conflict. On the anorexic side, the desire to become thinner and the fear of getting fatter motivates the individual to limit food intake and reduce body weight through dieting. On the bulimic side, there is a strong biological push towards eating food and a tendency to lose control over food intake once eating has started. Patients resolve this conflict in different ways at different times. During some periods, extreme dietary restriction is practiced resulting in loss of weight and qualification for a diagnosis of anorexia nervosa. At other times, loss of control occurs and results in the bingeing and purging pattern of bulimia. At any given time, a particular patient may be in the anorexic phase, the bulimic phase, or a transitional period.

The anorectic-bulimic conflict is thought to be motivated by an underlying fear of becoming fat. The fear of gaining weight is considered to be unrelated to actual body weight. This fear motivates behavior that is designed to reduce body weight. The basic conflict is between efforts to lose weight by food restriction or purging and the preoccupation with food and the compulsion to binge eat. According to Holmgren et al., this conflict between overeating and losing weight tends to become the focal point of the lives of individuals who suffer from an eating disorder. It is the dynamics of this conflict, motivated by the fear of gaining weight, that are the central features of all eating disorders.

Because of the fear of weight gain, individuals with an eating disorder develop an approach-avoidance conflict to food. At any time, one of the two tendencies may win out over the other. When the approach to food is dominant, binge eating occurs. After binge eating, the fear of weight gain strengthens the avoidance response which motivates behaviors like vomiting, laxative abuse, fasting, and excessive exercise. After a period of food restriction, the strength of the food preoccupation increases and pushes the individual toward eating and the possibility of losing control and bingeing. The alternation between approach and avoidance accounts for the behavioral manifestations of eating disorders and for changes in body weight over time. The patient who rapidly alternates between approach (binge eating) and avoidance (purging) will be engaging in bulimic behavior. The patient who engages in avoidance for long periods of time will first be diagnosed as preclinical anorexic and then, when sufficient weight loss has occurred, will be considered anorexic. At any time, the approach side of the conflict can win and the anorexic or preclinical anorexic will lapse into an episode of bulimia nervosa.

Body weight, rather than being a feature entering into the diagnosis, is merely a complication or consequence of the particular phase of the eating disorder. Body weight is determined by energy balance, which is a function of food intake and energy expenditure (see Chapter 2). The relative energy balance is dependent upon which behavioral characteristics are dominant, dieting or binge eating. Likewise, endocrine disturbances such as amenorrhea are also consequences of food restriction and purging, rather than being clinical features. As such, body weight and endocrine problems should not enter into the diagnosis of eating disorder. Instead, the diagnosis, according to Holmgren et al., should be based on the presence of a morbid fear of weight gain and the approach-avoidance conflict between food intake and caloric restriction or elimination.

The anorectic-bulimic conflict model has some advantages over the approach embodied in the DSM-III-R. First, it accounts for the diversity in patients with eating disorders by a single underlying conceptualization. It avoids making arbitrary distinctions between individuals who differ only in body weight. The clinician is prepared for changes in body weight and lapses between anorexic and bulimic behavior patterns. The clinician need not be concerned about changing the diagnosis when these lapses occur. Instead, the clinician can be concerned with the underlying problem of weight phobia and the resulting approach-avoidance conflict with its various behavioral manifestations.

The anorectic-bulimic conflict also has the advantage of including the group of patients Holmgren et al. referred to as preclinical anorexics. This group consists of individuals who are in the initial phase of developing an eating disorder, in a recovery phase, or in an intermediate phase between anorexia and bulimia. These patients will be characterized by behaviors designed to restrict food intake and ultimately control body weight, and these behaviors will be motivated by a strong desire to become thinner and to avoid weight gain.

Focusing on the weight phobia and the alternation between dieting and overeating as the core features of eating disorders allows us to see more clearly that diagnosed cases of eating disorders are merely the tip of an iceberg. As we shall see in detail in Chapter 3, weight concerns and dieting are widespread among young women. The possibility that fear of weight gain and alternation between overeating and dieting represent a spectrum of eating disorders may have important implications for prevention.

A THREE-DIMENSIONAL EATING DISORDER CONTINUUM

As we have seen from the review of diagnostic conceptualizations and their epidemiology, there are several major issues that must be addressed by any diagnostic scheme:

1. To what extent should body weight, and changes in body weight enter into the diagnosis and classification of eating disorder patients?
2. How do we reconcile the fact that two very different behavior patterns, bingeing versus dieting, are associated with eating disorders? The association involves observation of both patterns in patients who are otherwise quite similar (restrictor versus bulimic anorexics), and alternation between the two behavior patterns within the same subject over time.
3. To what extent should diagnostic distinctions be made on the

basis of the metabolic and endocrine consequences of calorie deprivation and emaciation or the metabolic consequences of overfeeding or purging?
4. Is a common psychological problem present in all of the different manifestations of eating disorders?
5. To what extent are the categories and classes of eating disorders describing qualitatively different psychiatric illnesses or are we instead classifying people according to patterns of abnormal cognition and behavior?
6. Do eating disorders represent discretely different states, or do they exist on a continuum with normal eating behavior? If so, how do we decide when the problem is serious enough to require medical or psychological intervention?

One approach to addressing these questions of description and diagnosis is to use the three-dimensional model depicted in Figure 1.1.

Body weight is one dimension in the description and diagnosis of eating disorders. It varies on a continuum from extreme emaciation to massive obesity. Individuals move back and forth on this continuum over time. Body weight and changes in body weight are determined by a multitude of variables. For example, set-point theory (Keesey, 1986; Chapter 2) proposes that body weight is a homeostatically regulated

FIGURE 1.1 A Three-Dimensional Model of Eating Disorders

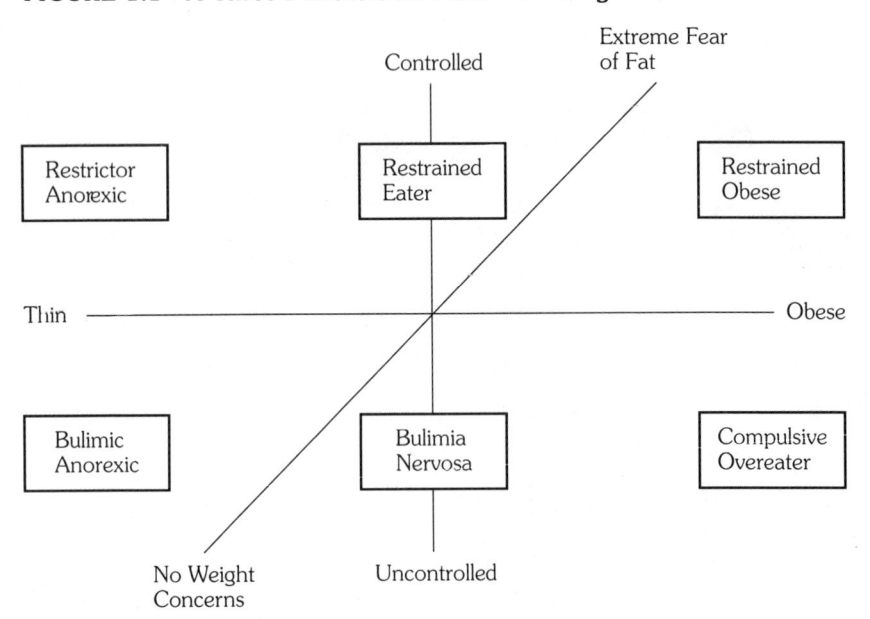

physiological system. Obesity, according to this view, is a matter of a physiologically high body-weight set point. The body defends a certain weight by altering its efficiency of energy utilization. While set point may be affected by certain behavioral variables such as smoking, dietary fat, and habitual levels of exercise, there is considerable evidence to suggest a large genetic component (Stunkard et al., 1986), especially for body fat percentage (Bouchard, Perusse, Leblanc, Tremblay, and Theriault, 1988). In addition to hereditary constraints, weight can be influenced deliberately through increased energy expenditure, decreased food intake, or both. Some aspects of weight, such as the amount of subcutaneous fat, show very little genetic contribution and are instead influenced by cultural and behavioral variables (Bouchard et al., 1988).

Because so many variables, both behavioral and genetic, determine body shape and composition, it does not make much sense to make diagnostic distinctions purely on the basis of body weight. In particular, drawing an arbitrary line at 85 percent of premorbid body weight will divide a continuum into two arbitrary groups. In addition, there are many ways to calculate relative body weight, leading to some unreliability in the use of relative weight as a diagnostic criteria (Pyle, Mitchell, & Eckert, 1986). Weight and changes in body weight should be included in the clinical description of any eating-disordered patient. However, the clinical meaning of the individual's body weight only makes sense if considered in the context of behavioral attempts to modify weight and the individual's biological and genetic makeup, which is difficult if not impossible to determine.

The second dimension in the model is behavioral control. This dimension represents the approach-avoidance conflict discussed earlier as the anorectic-bulimic conflict. This dimension represents the primary behavioral manifestation of eating disorders. At one extreme, we observe prolonged fasting while at the other extreme we observe a high frequency of bingeing. This dimension primarily reflects control over food intake. However, different levels of control over eating behavior may be accompanied by clusters of behaviors. For example, the individual who chronically restricts food intake may also engage in excessive exercise. Those whose eating is out of control may indulge in vomiting and laxative abuse as a way to try to minimize the impact of the loss of control on energy balance and body weight. Individuals can change their location on the behavioral control dimension quite rapidly. That is, the day might begin with the intention to fast all day only to be broken by a loss of control and binge eating in the evening. Clinically, an eating-disordered patient needs to be described in terms of the frequency and timing of the alternations between dieting and bingeing.

The third dimension of the model represents the intensity of the individual's obsession with body weight. The fear of being fat is assumed to be the central feature of all eating disorders. This fear is manifest in a number of ways including fear of gaining weight, fear of the consequences of being overweight, obsession with losing weight, unrealistic ideal weight, body-image disturbances, and specific food phobias (see Chapter 3). The fear of fat is the primary motivational force that drives the approach-avoidance conflict between dieting and bingeing. It is the fear (or the consequences) of eating high-calorie "forbidden" foods that motivates the individual to attempt to diet and maintain restrictive control over eating behavior. Biological, emotional, and social pressures drive the dieting individual toward overeating (see Chapter 7). When overeating does occur, the fear of gaining weight is aroused and motivates the individual to engage in compensatory behaviors, such as exercise or vomiting. When this fear is weak, the individual can be characterized as "weight conscious" or perhaps as a "restrained eater" (Herman & Polivy, 1975). When the fear is moderate, the individual will show more frequent or more intense alternations between controlled and uncontrolled eating behavior. As the concern with body weight becomes extreme, behaviors and consequences develop that meet the criteria for anorexia or bulimia nervosa.

The traditional diagnostic categories for describing eating disorders are depicted in Figure 1.1. The two dimensions, body weight and behavioral control, can be used to divide the continuum of eating disturbances into various regions. At the low body-weight, high control end of the model fall individuals who would be considered as having anorexia nervosa, restrictor type. Behaviorally, these individuals are characterized by constant dieting, periods of fasting, and sometimes excessive exercise. At the low end of the weight continuum, there are individuals who have lost control over eating behavior. This group is typically considered to have anorexia nervosa, bulimic type. Most individuals who are at the low end of the weight continuum will experience metabolic consequences of semistarvation such as amenorrhea, hypothermia, laguno, changes in thyroid function, and lowered levels of growth hormone (Root, 1984). When body weight drops too low, significant risk of mortality occurs due to starvation (predominantly in restrictors) or severe electrolyte disturbance (in patients who purge). Hsu (1980) reviewed sixteen outcome studies of anorexia nervosa and reported an average mortality rate across the studies of 6 percent.

At the middle of the weight continuum are individuals who maintain a stable weight within the normal range or whose weight varies within the normal range. At the high end of the control continuum is a group that is best described as restrained eaters (Herman & Mack, 1975; Herman & Polivy, 1975; Ruderman, 1986). Restrained eaters may vary from those who simply watch their calories to keep from putting on a few pounds to formerly obese individuals who practice a more extreme form of restriction in order to hold their body weight below their biological set point.

Restrained eaters may experience some metabolic consequences of their attempts to diet such as reduced resting metabolic rate (Garrow, 1986). As long as weight remains near normal, there is little chance of observing the severe and life-threatening complications that are observed in anorexia nervosa. Yet as Ruderman (1986) argues, restrained eaters do engage in occasional bouts of overeating, especially in situations involving strong negative emotions (Ganley, 1988). This finding suggests that the idea of an approach-avoidance conflict between dieting and overeating is relevant to this group of the population. If restrained eating does in fact exist on a continuum with the more severe forms of the same behaviors observed in anorexic and bulimic patients, a sizeable portion of the population may be at some risk for developing an eating disorder. Polivy and Herman (1985) reviewed data on restrained eating in obesity and bulimia and argued that a number of studies show that dieting usually precedes binge eating. Kirkley, Burge, and Ammerman (1988) showed that binge eating and dietary restraint were related to bulimic tendencies. Johnson, Corrigan, Crusco, and Schlundt (1986) showed that bulimic patients had higher levels of dietary restraint than obese dieters, who were more restrained than a normal weight comparison group.

At the middle of the weight range but at the low end of the control continuum are individuals that would be diagnosed as bulimic according to DSM-III-R. The absence of control takes a wide variety of behavioral manifestations. If loss of control is not severe, then the individual may be able to maintain normal weight by alternating between bingeing and dieting. However, when loss of control over food intake becomes severe, either in terms of frequency of occurrence or caloric content of eating binges, it becomes unlikely that the individual will maintain a normal weight without resorting to some form of purging in order to minimize the consequences. In many binge eaters, once purging starts, the frequency and size of the eating binges gets further out of control since weight gain is no longer a definite consequence of overeating. There may be a threshold point after which a positive feedback loop gets established and the behavior becomes qualitatively different from normal dieting and overeating.

While the bulimic at normal weight does not suffer the starvation syndrome that occurs at levels of emaciated body weight, there can be negative metabolic consequences of bulimia. In particular, individuals who purge through self-induced vomiting, laxatives, or diuretics often experience electrolyte disturbances that can vary in severity from discomfort to sudden death due to cardiac arrest (Mitchell, 1986; Neuman & Halverson, 1983). However, it is clear that many of the metabolic consequences observed in normal weight individuals who engage in bulimic behavior are a function of the methods of purging used.

At the obese end of the weight continuum, at least two basic groups of individuals can be singled out on the basis of variations in their control over food intake. First are the obese individuals at the controlled end of the continuum who are obese in spite of the fact that they exercise restraint over their food intake. These individuals probably have a strong genetic component to their obesity and are probably below their set point in spite of the fact that they are above ideal body weight. These individuals, like others who practice dietary restraint, may have occasional episodes of overeating but probably do not meet the criteria for a diagnosis of DSM-III bulimia let alone DSM-III-R bulimia nervosa. At the other end of the control continuum are individuals who might be best described as obese bingers or compulsive overeaters. Mitchell et al. (1981) reported on a series of forty bulimic patients in which 8 percent were obese at the time they presented for treatment. Telch, Agras, and Rossiter (1988) reported in a sample of eighty-one obese patients that the prevalence of binge eating increased as adiposity increased. In this study, 40 percent of the patients with a body-mass index greater than 34 engaged in binge eating as defined by the DSM-III criteria. George et al. (1989) presented data from the analysis of food and activity records of 431 subjects showing that there are two populations of individuals at any given weight that can be distinguished on the basis of their energy intake, small eaters and large eaters.

Individuals who binge but either do not engage in any form of purging or who use an ineffective method, such as diuretics, are at risk of becoming obese, especially if the frequency of binges is high or the size of binges is large. It is also possible for an individual to engage in bingeing and purging and to still maintain an obese body weight. It is unlikely that compulsive overeaters or obese bingers will experience the endocrine abnormalities that are common among patients who lose extreme amounts of weight. However, the emotional and social consequences of being obese become more prominent for these individuals. In addition, many years of food abuse may result in the health complications of obesity such as adult onset diabetes, hypertension, or hyperlipidemia.

It is possible to conceptualize eating disorders as a phenomenon driven by an underlying fear of obesity that is manifest in an individual's perception of body weight and feelings about food and its ingestion. This fear is the motivational engine that drives the behavioral manifestations of eating disorders. The primary behavioral dimension of eating disorders consists of a control continuum. At one end of this continuum, we observe fasting and food restriction. At the other end, we observe frequent episodes of gorging on large quantities of food. Toward the middle, we observe dieting and occasional overeating. An individual can change status on this dimension quite quickly, such as when a diet is broken by a single bout of overeating. However, this dimension can be used to describe the individual's predominant mode of behavior over a longer period of time. Some individuals, when they experience a disinhibition of eating, will resort to purging in order to minimize the impact on energy balance, while others will only feel guilty and depressed.

As a consequence of short- and long-term alternations in control over eating, individuals will vary in body weight. The variations in body weight represent a true continuum from extreme emaciation to massive obesity. Most of the metabolic disturbances that are associated with eating disorders, such as amenorrhea and hypokalemia, are consequences either of severe weight loss or of the behaviors that are used to attempt to induce weight loss.

This conceptualization leaves us with a dilemma. If eating disorders are motivated by a common source of anxiety and obsession concerning body weight, and if body weight and behavior exist on a continuum, then does it make sense to use discrete diagnostic categories like the DSM-III-R categories of anorexia and bulimia nervosa? The answer to this question is "it depends." If the goal of diagnosis is to identify discretely different categories of mental disorders, then the underlying continua of weight obsession, body weight, and food intake regulation suggest that any diagnostic system will contain arbitrary distinctions. However, if the process of diagnosis is to form relatively homogeneous clusters of individuals that will have utility for suggesting treatment approaches, then these groupings may be meaningful. Diagnostic groupings, rather than being seen as representing different mental illnesses, represent instead different regions in a three-dimensional space that can be used to match treatments with problems.

SUMMARY

The two major categories of eating disorders, anorexia nervosa and bulimia, have been troubling people for many years, with some historical accounts tracing them back into the seventeenth century. Only in the last twenty five years, however, has the scientific and medical community begun to focus on understanding and treating persons with eating disorders.

There has been and continues to be confusion and controversy surrounding the definition and diagnosis of eating disorders. The data suggest that even though the psychiatric diagnostic criteria recognize two distinct disorders, anorexia nervosa and bulimia nervosa, the similarities between the two categories are often greater than their differences.

We argued that anorexia and bulimia nervosa are not distinctly different disorders. A three-dimensional model of eating disorders was presented as a way of seeing the inherent continuity between anorexia, bulimia, and, in some cases, obesity. Weight is seen as a consequence of genetic predisposition along with dietary behavior. The core of all eating disorders is an obsessive concern with weight, which manifests itself as an intense desire to lose weight or a morbid fear of gaining weight. A pattern of dieting develops as a way to cope with these fears. Almost as a physiological consequence of dieting, overeating or binge eating develops when the individual is not able to constantly restrict food intake. The person with an eating disorder thus alternates between dieting and bingeing. The rapidity of this alternation along with the use of compensatory behaviors, such as self-induced vomiting, determines the eventual weight consequences of these behavior patterns.

When viewed from a strictly medical and psychiatric perspective, the prevalence of anorexia nervosa is less than 1 percent and the prevalence of bulimia nervosa is probably between 1 and 2 percent in the population of women under forty years old. When viewed from the perspective of the three-dimensional model, we see that the psychiatric diagnosis misses another group, namely those who binge but do not purge. We have labeled this group compulsive overeaters. However, the three-dimensional model also implies that there are a large number of normal weight individuals who exercise dietary restraint and engage in occasional bouts of overeating, but probably do not meet the psychiatric criteria for an eating disorder. When eating disorders are seen as existing on a continuum with dietary restraint, it is easy to see that the 3 percent or so of the women who develop a diagnosable eating disorder merely represent the tip of an iceberg. Further evidence to confirm this conclusion will be presented in Chapters 3, 4, and 5.

2

The Biobehavioral Control of Eating Behavior

EATING IS THE PERIODIC intake of food and nutrients necessary for survival. Research with animals and humans has revealed that biobehavioral mechanisms integrate internal and external stimuli to control food intake. These biobehavioral mechanisms involve the interaction of physiology, behavior, and the external environment through the neuroendocrine system. Examples of external stimuli that affect eating behavior include the sight, smell, and taste of food and aspects of the social environment such as seeing others eat, the time of day, and the food practices of one's culture. Similarly, internal stimuli include hormones such as insulin, the brain neurotransmitters, and endogenous opioids.

These internal and external stimuli rarely act in isolation; instead they function together through the neuroendocrine system. For example, the role of insulin in metabolism is fairly well known. The presence of food in the gastrointestinal tract leads to increased levels of insulin, which aids the transport of glucose into cells. Insulin is also secreted in a "preparatory" or cephalic phase prior to eating. It is secreted at certain times of the day associated with eating and increases upon seeing or thinking about food (Johnson & Wildman, 1980). Insulin secreted when there is no food entering the gastrointestinal tract decreases available blood glucose and is responsible for food cravings and perhaps bingeing.

In this chapter, we will first consider some of the basic neurophysiological and endocrine mechanisms that influence and control eating behavior. We will then apply these concepts to the understanding of weight regulation through consideration of set-point theory. Consideration of the neuroendocrine and behavioral effects of carbohydrates concludes the discussion.

HUNGER AND SATIETY

Current research suggests that there is a relatively constant neural signal to eat and that appetite regulation is a function of the number, strength, and nature of the inhibitors to this signal (Hoebel, 1985). The eating drive may be inhibited by competing physiological, psychological, or social needs such as sleep, sexual activity, thirst, work, the desire to socialize, or the intention to diet.

Hunger ratings increase with food deprivation and as customary mealtime approaches. In contrast, ratings of satiety gradually increase during the course of a meal and decrease postprandially. The relationship between hunger ratings and the amount of food consumed varies widely with only weak to moderate relationships observed (Hill & Blundell, 1982/83). Furthermore, individuals with eating disorders display unique relationships between hunger and food intake. Bulimic patients will continue to eat even after they feel stuffed and bloated. This continuation of eating in the presence of a full stomach is in part motivated by psychological stimuli that induce negative affect and by the intention and opportunity to purge. Also, anorexics often experience intense levels of hunger, which they effectively deny, and consequently they eat very little.

The role of hunger in the regulation of food intake then is not entirely clear (Keesey & Poweley, 1986). Hunger is thought to initiate eating, yet not all eating occurs in response to hunger, and the experience of hunger is not the same for every person. For some, the subjective experience of hunger may be directly related to food and nutrient deprivation. For others, however, the physiological cues that are labelled as hunger may be related to fatigue or negative emotions.

For example, Schlundt, Johnson, and Jarrell (1985) looked at hunger as an antecedent to bulimic behavior and to overeating in a sample of obese subjects. They found that extreme ratings of hunger were predictive of overeating, bingeing, and purging. Moderate levels of hunger were associated with much lower probabilities of overeating. Surprisingly, eating episodes that occurred when the individual was not at all hungry tended to be binges. Also, when the caloric content of the meals was examined for these obese subjects, there was no relationship between hunger ratings and the amount of food consumed.

Extreme levels of hunger tend to influence the style of eating behavior. When someone begins to eat when very hungry, their speed of eating is increased and the total amount of food consumed is greater. Meal skipping has been observed to cause this kind of change in behavior. There is probably a physiological basis for this. Extreme dieting often results in a change of eating style that tends to promote binge eating (Kirkley, Burge, & Ammerman, 1988).

The internal mechanisms and stimuli responsible for hunger and satiety include the following: (1) the taste, smell, and texture of food that originate primarily in the oral-nasal cavity; (2) internal body temperature; (3) stimuli in the gastrointestinal tract such as sensations of fullness and gastric hormone secretions; (4) energy depletion and metabolic needs primarily in the form of blood glucose levels or glycogen stores; and (5) neurotransmitters, insulin, and endogenous opiates. The available data suggest that the initiation of eating is controlled primarily by physiological energy demands, characteristics of food, neurotransmitters in the brain, and aspects of the social environment. In contrast, the termination of a meal appears to originate primarily from signals in the gastrointestinal tract and peripheral nervous system as well as through cognitive mechanisms, such as the exercise of dietary restraint.

More specifically, neurochemicals regulate the transmission of sensory information in the brain and several have been strongly implicated in eating, including the catecholamines, endogenous opiates, and brain-gut peptides. These neurochemicals act primarily through the hypothalamus, including the lateral and ventromedial nuclei structures. The most prominent neurotransmitters influencing eating include epinephrine, norepinephrine, dopamine, serotonin, and the endogenous opiates. Recent evidence also suggests that small changes in insulin concentrations in cerebral spinal fluid may be involved in the regulation of satiety, appetite, and energy metabolism (Rothwell & Stock, 1988).

In summary, human eating behavior is very complex and includes an integration of the external environment, cognition, and physiological systems. Examples of external stimuli include the sight and smell of food, its taste and texture, the time of day, emotional distress, and seeing others eat. Many of these stimuli are so powerful that they initiate eating regardless of the level of food deprivation or satiety. Likewise, humans are able to override strong physiological signals of hunger cognitively in order to lose weight voluntarily. When these physiological signals are strong, the environmental stimuli may be potentiated, resulting in the rapid consumption of a large amount of food, or binge eating.

NEUROANATOMY AND NEUROTRANSMITTERS

A number of studies have attempted to identify the neurological basis of eating behavior. In the 1950s and 1960s, most studies concentrated on the hypothalamus. This research indicated that the lateral hypothalamus (LH) was involved in the initiation of eating, and lesions in this area caused animals to cease eating. The ventromedial hypothalamus (VMH) was considered the satiety center, and lesions in this area were found to increase eating and produce obesity.

Continuing research of the neuroanatomy of eating has indicated, however, that it is not the particular LH or VMH area per se but the various nerve tracts associated with these areas that are responsible for the disruptions in eating behavior. LH lesions produce many other effects on behavior. For example, rats with LH lesions are relatively unresponsive to both internal and external stimuli. LH-lesioned rats display a generalized neglect of sensations including touch, taste, and smell. These animals refuse both food and drink and may starve themselves to death. The bulk of the data indicate that the LH lesions responsible for these behavior changes have also disrupted the nigrostriatal bundle, which passes through the LH area (Hernandez & Hobel, 1980).

According to Keesey (1986), LH lesions lower the set point for body weight. To support this hypothesis, Keesey notes that LH-lesioned animals maintain lower stable body weights with a near constant percent body fat. This lowered set point will be defended against a variety of challenges including caloric increases and decreases.

In contrast to the sensory neglect resulting from LH lesions, lesions in the VMH area accentuate response to a wide variety of stimuli. VMH-lesioned animals are hyperphagic and also evidence disrupted hormonal and metabolic functions, such as hyperinsulinemia. It is difficult to differentiate whether these hormonal and metabolic changes are consequences or direct causes of the eating disturbance. As with lesions in the LH area, current research on the VMH area focuses on surrounding areas, such as the paraventricular nucleus.

VMH lesions augment responses to a wide variety of internal and external stimuli. VMH-lesioned animals are hyper-responsive, irritable, and finicky eaters. VMH lesions may prevent signals of satiety from being activated, thereby causing the usual mechanisms that inhibit eating to fail.

Research on neurotransmitters has focused primarily on norepinephrine (NE), dopamine, serotonin, and the endogenous opioids. Norepinephrine appears to have paradoxical effects on eating behavior as a function of its site of action in the hypothalamus. When NE is injected in the paraventricular area, eating increases, yet both NE and dopamine decrease eating when injected in the medial hypothalamus. As summarized by Hernandez and Hobel (1980), research integrating neuroanatomical sites and neurotransmitters indicates that feeding is primarily located in the lateral hypothalamus, which contains dopamine receptor fibers of the nigrostriatal tract and beta-adrenergic synapses that induce satiety. The medial and paraventricular hypothalamus contain alpha-adrenergic synapses and serotonin pathways and synapses. The associated neuroanatomical structures and neurotransmitters reveal an intricate pattern in which receptors in the ventromedial and lateral hypothalamus are responsive to nutritional, olfactory, visual, gustatory, and sensory inputs. The VMH and paraventricular areas are primarily responsive to serotonin and NE while the lateral hypothalamus and nigrostriatal tract are responsive to dopamine and endorphins.

The endorphins (endogenous opiates) are involved in eating both directly and through their interactions with other neurotransmitters and glucose. Beta-endorphin levels increase with food deprivation. Injections of beta-endorphin and dynorphin in the hypothalamus increase eating. Stress-induced eating is also associated with increased dopamine and beta-endorphin with glucose-insulin levels possibly mediating these effects. These data suggest that beta-endorphins may serve as a chemical signal to initiate eating behavior.

There are also data to suggest that the regulatory function of opiates on eating is related to their reinforcement properties. Eating is obviously a very rewarding and pleasurable activity. Opiates may therefore function as a drive-reward mechanism by increasing in response to food intake. Low levels of opiates initiate a drive for specific stimuli, including food and food cues, which will result in stimulation of opiate production. The behaviors, such as food seeking and eating, that remove the deficit of endogenous opiates will be reinforced.

The role of endogenous opiates in eating has been further explicated by using compounds antagonistic to the opiates. Specifically, naloxone and naltrexone have been shown in animal and human studies to block the initiation of eating induced by endogenous opiates. Naloxone and naltrexone decrease food intake acutely. However, studies involving twenty-four-hour infusions have shown no effect on overall caloric intake while a reduction in carbohydrate consumption has been noted (Morley, Levine, Gosnell, & Billington, 1984).

The current evidence points to a role for the endogenous opiates in regulation of normal and disordered eating behavior. The exact role of these substances has yet to be worked out in detail. For example, how can increased levels of endogenous opiates function both as a signal to turn on eating behavior and as a drive-reduction mechanism to reward eating? More research is needed to clarify the various actions of these substances and their interactions with hormones and other neurotransmitters.

ENERGY BALANCE AND RESTING METABOLIC RATE

It is a simple matter of physics that if body weight is to remain constant, energy intake and energy expenditure must balance. When intake chronically exceeds expenditure, weight gain occurs. When expenditure exceeds intake, body weight decreases. In the energy balance equation, expenditure and intake are separate but nonetheless interacting sources of influence on body weight. Body weight is regulated through changes in energy intake, variations in energy expenditure or both.

Resting metabolic rate (RMR) is the rate of energy consumption when the body is completely at rest and is the result of the energy requirements needed to maintain vital functions, such as circulation and respiration. RMR accounts for the largest proportion of energy expenditure with activity representing the next largest proportion. The caloric requirements of RMR average about 1 kcal per kg of body weight per hour (1 kcal/kg/hr). RMR accounts for between 70–80 percent of energy expenditure depending on individual differences and overall activity level. The amount of fat-free body mass (lean body weight) is the single largest determinant of RMR. The RMR for men is generally higher than for women while the RMR for obese individuals is greater than the RMR for lean. These differences are due to greater lean body mass in men than women and in obese persons than lean. RMR is also affected by temperature, activity, exercise, sleep-wake cycle, intermeal interval, and emotional arousal. RMR is high in the growth period and decreases in late adolescence and early adulthood. Gradual reductions begin to occur after age ten with more dramatic reductions occurring between eighteen and twenty years of age and again between forty-five and fifty.

The second major component to energy expenditure is activity, which is calculated in multiples of the RMR or MET. One MET is equivalent to the RMR, whereas, two METs would be two times the RMR. Activities such as a slow walk or light housework are 2 METs. Other examples of activities and their MET values include the following: golf = 3 METs; casual cycling = 4–5 METs; and jogging = 7–8 METs. Life-style and activity variations can account for a large degree of variability in energy expenditure. These differences in activity are often very subtle, yet they can play a highly significant role in body-weight regulation.

EXERCISE, RESTING METABOLIC RATE, AND CALORIC INTAKE

The effect of exercise on RMR and eating is an interesting question. Research suggests that over the long course, exercise does not dramatically influence caloric intake. The influence of exercise on food intake may be related to body fat stores such that intake decreases in the overweight while food consumption is enhanced in the underweight. The fear of many overweight individuals that exercise will lead to an increase in appetite is essentially unfounded. For the obese, exercise may have appetite suppressing rather than enhancing effects (W.G. Johnson, 1989).

Exercise effects on energy expenditure occur both as a result of the work of exercising and the effect of exercise on RMR between periods of exercise. For example, Tremblay et al. (1986) investigated the effects of exercise on RMR in lean and overweight individuals. In an initial study, these investigators measured RMR in groups of physically trained and untrained individuals and found an 11 percent higher RMR in trained subjects. To study further the effects of exercise training on RMR, eight moderately obese individuals exercised five hours a week for eleven weeks by aerobic dancing. The results of this study showed a significant reduction in body weight and body fat over the period and a significant increase in RMR.

McGowen, Epstein, Kupfer, and Bulik (1986) have also examined the short-term impact of exercise on food intake. Seven male joggers who jogged 2.5 to 4 miles/day, five times a week were studied when they were not exercising at their normal level, when they were exercising regularly, and when they doubled their level of exercise. Caloric intake was determined by self-monitoring. Energy expenditure from exercise averaged zero in the no exercise condition, over 500 kcal/day in the regular exercise condition, and 869 kcal/day in the double exercise condition. These values represent daily energy expenditures in the no exercise condition of 18 percent below normal and in the double exercise condition of 13 percent over their customary levels of energy expenditure.

Caloric intake remained relatively stable over different conditions ranging from 2,529 kcal/day in the no exercise condition to 2,695 kcal/day in the double exercise condition. Similarly mean body weight varied little over the periods ranging from 73.8, 73.4, and 73.3 kilograms. It appears then that caloric intake and weight remained relatively stable over these weekly variations in energy expenditure. Since these men were well-trained physically, their metabolic processes apparently adjusted to periods of prolonged exertion. However, untrained persons with higher body fat compositions may respond differently to a doubling in the typical level of physical activity.

WEIGHT REGULATION

In general, the biobehavioral mechanisms regulating food intake act to create a homeostatic metabolic condition through the integration of the internal and external environments with behavior. Given a relatively constant pattern of food intake (nutrients) and energy output (activity), weight is quite closely regulated. However, with advancing age and resulting decreases in activity and RMR, there is a gradual, yet evident, decrease in lean body mass with a corresponding increase in body fat. These changes often occur with little variation in total body weight.

The stability of body weight in spite of drastic changes in caloric intake is illustrated by several studies. Keys, Brozek, Henschel, Mickelsen, and Taylor (1950) placed a group of volunteer subjects of various body weights on a semistarvation diet approximately 1,000 kcal/day below their customary intake. After approximately eight months, their body weights dropped an average of 25 percent. Following a refeeding phase lasting three months, the subjects gradually regained approximately their original body weights. Similarly, Simms and Horton (1968) increased the caloric intake of human volunteers for six months thereby increasing their body weights by 15–25 percent. With a resumption of customary caloric intake, these subjects returned to their original weights.

Counter-Regulation in Obesity and Anorexia Nervosa

While homeostatic weight regulation is the rule, there are exceptions that are most notable in the weight extremes of marked obesity and anorexia nervosa. Here, the biobehavioral mechanisms responsible for regulating eating, activity, and weight appear to be reset at higher or lower levels. They appear to display a counter-regulation with the mechanisms in obesity and anorexia appearing to be organized to increase and decrease weight, respectively. Accordingly, for individuals who are considerably overweight or underweight, regulation appears to favor a body weight that is heavier or lower respectively. Under these circumstances, when very heavy and very light individuals tend to become heavier or lighter, the term counter-regulation is used to indicate the failure of homeostatic processes to adjust weight to moderate levels.

Intuitively, one would expect that given an ample supply of body fat stores, appetite and further food intake would be regulated in order to return body weight to moderate levels. Similarly, given a deficit in available body energy as in the case of anorexia, one would expect sufficient impetus from biobehavioral mechanisms to initiate more substantial eating in order to return weight to more appropriate levels. Unfortunately, counter-regulation appears to be the rule in these weight deviations. For individuals who are obese, increases in weight appear likely to be due to associated high insulin levels and their stimulation of appetite and to a decrease in physical activity and the resulting lower energy expenditure. Correlated with the decreased activity would be the increased association with and proximity to food (Rodin, 1981).

Contrastingly, for those individuals who are below an ideal body weight as in the case of anorexia nervosa, biobehavioral mechanisms responsible for weight regulation appear to be organized for further weight loss rather than weight restoration, although the information here is mostly anecdotal and clinical. It appears that a hypometabolic state accompanies the decrease in weight with semistarvation. All essential body functions are slowed and body temperature is reduced in an effort to adjust for the decreased caloric intake. Further reductions in food intake may be the result of the failure of adequate nutritional intake to stimulate appetite, and again insulin may play a prime role. Also, as we shall discuss in Chapter 6, endogenous opiates appear to reinforce further weight loss. Based on a review of animal and human data, Epling and Pierce (1988) provide a framework that has the potential for integrating the counterregulation of eating seen in obesity and anorexia. They argue that both animals and humans display increased food consumption as weight increases and activity decreases. Contrastingly, in the face of food restriction there are increases in activity correlated with decreases in body weight. The authors suggest that strenuous exercise decreases the value of food as a reinforcer, thereby leading to decreased food intake. This reduction in food intake further serves to increase the motivational value of exercise. The biobehavioral mechanisms responsible for these changes appear to involve the neuroendocrine system and endogenous opiates.

MECHANISMS OF WEIGHT REGULATION: SET-POINT THEORY

As we noted, with the exception of extremely high and low body weights, compensatory mechanisms function to regulate weight within relatively narrow limits. In fact, most researchers agree that weight stability in adults is the rule rather than the exception. Food intake, energy expenditure, and metabolic rate interact in complex ways to maintain a stable weight with changes in one accompanied by compensatory changes in another. For example, decreased food intake in healthy adults is followed by a decrease in resting metabolic rate, a decrease in the specific dynamic action (SDA) of food following ingestion, and both an increase in activity specifically designed to secure food and a decrease in extraneous activity to conserve energy. Much of this research on weight regulation is organized around what is now referred to as set-point theory (Nisbett, 1972). According to this theory, physiological and metabolic processes function so as to compensate for deviations from an established set-point weight. Changes in food intake, energy expenditure, or internal metabolic rate result in compensatory responses that act to maintain a stable body weight.

While noting that weight stability is the rule, changes in weight, both increases and decreases, obviously occur. How are we to understand these weight changes in light of set-point theory? Keesey and Powley (1986) note that set-point weights are not fixed but only approximate weights that are established over a period of time—perhaps on the order of at least six months. They argue that neither weight stability nor change is necessarily an argument for or against set-point theory. Changes in set point can occur in response to long-term changes in diet and exercise. Keesey (1986) describes how high fat diets elevate and exercise lowers set point.

The action of compensatory mechanisms in the defense of a body weight has been documented in both animal and human studies. These studies indicate that when individuals are force fed, they gain less weight than would be expected on the basis of the food (caloric) intake alone (Simms and Horton, 1968). The same is true for decreased caloric intake and weight loss, which is all too familiar to dieters, many of whom decrease their caloric intake yet lose considerably less than expected on the basis of their decreased caloric intake alone. In both cases, metabolic rate and other energy expenditure adaptations have compensated for the changes in food intake.

Changes in RMR may result from changes in lean body mass that occur during weight gain and weight loss. The specific dynamic action (SDA), also known as the thermic effect of food intake, is an additional compensatory mechanism that is used to adjust total energy requirements. The SDA of food refers to the production of heat (energy) immediately following ingestion. As such, SDA represents the initial step in the metabolism of a meal and represents the energy required to digest and absorb nutrients. SDA increases approximately twenty minutes postprandially and remains elevated for several hours. The SDA varies widely, ranging from 10 to 35 percent of the energy ingested and depends on many variables including the macronutrient composition of the meal. Food restriction decreases SDA, which can also be decreased in obese and highly trained individuals. Reductions in SDA promote energy storage. Caloric restriction decreases SDA and caloric increase produces a rise in SDA. Recent animal research suggests that a large portion of dietary induced thermogenesis is due to sympathetic activation of brown adipose tissue. The stimulation of brown adipose tissue by noradrenaline is also the mechanism involved in other forms of nonshivering thermogenesis that occur in adapting to a cold environment. It appears that the SDA of food is centrally mediated by sympathetic outflow from the VMH to brown adipose tissue (Rothwell & Stock, 1988).

Body Weight: Naturally Occurring Variations

There are many naturally occurring variations in weight that are not reflected in attempts at dieting or the result of an eating disorder. Increases in physical activity such as result from a job change, sports participation, or the like, can result in changes in body weight, body composition, and resting metabolic rate. While long-term increases in activity may result in increased food consumption, often the increased food consumption is not sufficient to maintain the initial body weight. These changes will reverse if the increased energy expenditure is lowered.

Body weight can also fluctuate as a result of food availability. During famine and periods of low food supply, there is a decrease in weight as people rely more on endogenous body fat stores and lean tissue to meet their energy needs. Contrastingly, with increased food availability, weight increases as body fat stores and lean body mass are replenished.

COMPOSITION OF THE DIET AND WEIGHT REGULATION

At any given level of caloric restriction, a low-fat/high-carbohydrate diet may lead to greater total weight loss, more favorable changes in body composition, and less reduction in RMR than a high-fat/low-carbohydrate regimen. Flatt (1987) has suggested that body composition remains constant over time because substrate oxidation on the average corresponds to the ratio of fat:carbohydrate in the diet. (McNeill, Bruce, Ralph, & James, 1989). Carbohydrate oxidation is determined by carbohydrate intake whereas fat oxidation is unrelated to fat intake. When fat intake is relatively high and total calories are adequate, the excess fat is readily deposited in adipose tissue leading to the development of a high percentage of body fat.

In addition, fat and carbohydrate differ in their specific dynamic action. Greater heat is produced (as lost energy) by the consumption of carbohydrate than by the consumption of fat. It has been estimated that only 75 percent of the available energy in carbohydrate becomes available as energy for work or storage as fat compared to 94–97 percent of the available energy in dietary fat (Danforth, 1985; Schutz & Bessard, 1984).

Recent studies have suggested that when patients are placed on a low-fat diet, weight loss occurs in spite of the fact that the subjects are not attempting to restrict total caloric intake (Lisner, et al., 1987; Brown et al., 1984). The elimination of large amounts of dietary fat is not compensated for by increased carbohydrate consumption, thus leading to a negative energy balance. In addition, the high carbohydrate intake on a low-fat, *ad lib* carbohydrate diet may have a protein-sparing effect leading to less loss of lean body mass during weight reduction and consequently a smaller change in resting metabolic rate.

Clinically, patients may find it easier to approach weight loss as a long-term life-style change program when they are only trying to limit fat intake and are allowed to eat as much carbohydrate as they wish than when they are attempting to restrict total caloric intake by dieting. Many of the compliance problems that occur during attempts at weight loss derive from feelings of deprivation that are from attempts at strict dietary restraint; some compliance problems may be physiologically induced by deficits in carbohydrate intake. Patients on a low-fat *ad lib* carbohydrate diet will have to use less dietary restraint and may feel less deprived since they can eat as often as they wish as long as the food they eat is very low in fat and high in carbohydrates. In addition, consumption of adequate amounts of carbohydrate will lead to a physiological state of satiety.

Clinically, we have noted recently that hospitalized anorexic patients will fail to gain weight on a high-carbohydrate/low-fat regimen. A recent patient failed to show weight gain even when total caloric intake was increased to 3,000 kcal/day. However, when the composition of the patient's diet was changed and substantial fat was added, weight restoration occurred quickly.

In conclusion, variations in body weight are regulated by compensatory mechanisms. Regardless of weight, the same mechanisms apply. The weight of an obese man is as regulated as that of an anorexic teenager. In the latter case, weight gain can be resisted by compensatory increases in metabolic rate and SDA, changes in physical activity, and continued avoidance of dietary fat. Similarly, weight loss is resisted in the overweight by the reduction of metabolic rate and continued consumption of high-fat foods.

The idea that body weight is regulated by homeostatic mechanisms around a set point needs to be qualified by several considerations. First, during early phases of development, body metabolism is directed toward growth and weight gain. With aging, a gradual decline in resting metabolic rate and activity results in a gradual increase in body-weight set point. Within these broad time frames, set point may be responsive to dietary intake and physical activity. In addition, conditions such as obesity and anorexia may reflect temporary or permanent alterations in body set point due to poorly understood counter-regulatory processes.

FOOD CRAVINGS, OVEREATING, AND BINGE EATING

It is common to distinguish between hunger for food in general and cravings that are linked to specific foods or nutrients. Current research suggests that cravings for food in general are instigated by energy depletion and arousal, whereas cravings for specific foods are related to dietary deficiencies as well as individual tastes acquired through learning. Several lines of human and animal research indicate that the biobehavioral mechanisms responsible for food cravings are mere extensions of those underlying hunger and satiety. These mechanisms involve interactions between external/environmental influences, behavior, and thoughts, on the one hand, and internal neurotransmitters and hormones, on the other.

As we indicated in Chapter 1, there is a fine line between what is considered overeating and what is considered binge eating. To a great extent, both are subjective experiences that involve eating a large amount of food, eating in a ritualized fashion, violating one's diet, or feeling guilty after eating. All of these may give rise to fears of weight gain in eating-disordered patients. These examples of overeating typically involve the intake of food in an excessive amount, the intake of certain forbidden foods or both. As we shall describe in Chapter 3, epidemiological surveys indicate that overeating in the general population occurs in approximately 40–50 percent of women at one time or another. As many as 15 percent to 20 percent of the female population report overeating several times a month or more. It is likely that the same psychological and physiological mechanisms that are responsible for overeating also are responsible for binge eating.

The Role of Insulin

Research on the role of insulin as an instigator of eating has been particularly prominent in the last several years. A major function of insulin is to facilitate the transport of glucose into cells. Several distinct phases of insulin secretion have been differentiated with the most prominent being the postprandial and the cephalic. In the postprandial phase, insulin is secreted in response to food intake to utilize glucose and deposit fat. During the cephalic state, however, insulin appears to trigger increases in appetite and food cravings. This phase occurs *prior to eating* and prepares the internal environment for the ingestion of nutrients. Insulin has been shown to increase as a result of nearing the time of day associated with eating, smelling food, seeing food, preparing to eat, and even thinking about food. Secretions of insulin prior to the consumption of food act to decrease blood glucose and give rise to an experience of hunger. Since insulin secretion occurs in response to a variety of internal and cognitive stimuli, it can serve as a powerful impetus to eat.

The obese and those on a diet appear to show higher levels of insulin secretion during the cephalic phase. The increases in insulin secretion along with other predigestive responses during the cephalic phase probably serve to stimulate eating (Johnson & Wildman, 1980; Klanjer, Herman, Polivy, & Chhabra, 1981).

Diet Composition and Insulin

A common observation among dieters is that eating breakfast makes practicing dietary restraint difficult for the remainder of the day. It is not unusual, for example to hear dieters say, "If I eat something now, I will have blown my diet." One line of research suggests that it may not be the individual act of eating, but more likely, what is eaten and its effect on insulin that is responsible for the difficulty in continuing dietary restraint.

To study this phenomenon, Spitzer and Rodin (1987) examined how the intake of various sugars eaten in the morning influenced a later meal. Following an overnight fast, normal weight male and female subjects drank either glucose, fructose (fruit sugar), or water. Solutions were isocaloric and equivalent in terms of pleasantness. Approximately two hours after the sugar and water preloads, the subjects were exposed to buffet trays of various meats, cheeses, breads, fruits, sweets, and drinks as well as necessary condiments. The results showed important differences in the amount of food eaten some two hours later as a function of the type of morning preload. Those subjects who drank the glucose ate significantly more than those who drank water or fructose.

The basis of the increased food intake following the glucose preload relative to water and fructose is in the glucose/insulin relationship. Specifically, the simpler chemical structure of glucose results in speedy absorption from the gut. Blood glucose and insulin levels rise quickly and are soon followed by a rapid reduction as a result of glucose uptake. This subsequent dramatic fall in the level of blood glucose appears responsible for increased hunger, and the subsequent larger food intake for those in this glucose preload condition.

The influence of fructose on insulin is not as dramatic. Following fructose ingestion, there is less of a rise in glucose and insulin levels, and more importantly, a much more gradual decline in these levels. As Spitzer and Rodin note, approximately two to three hours following the ingestion of the preload, plasma glucose levels produced by the ingestion of fructose are actually higher than those produced by glucose. This influence has the effect of minimizing the reports of hunger and food-seeking behavior. Thus, it appears that eating simple sugars, which quickly enter the digestive process, leads to high levels of insulin that soon reduce glucose levels giving rise to a desire to eat. This reactive hypoglycemia may be responsible for patients' reports of sugar or carbohydrate cravings and may function as a trigger for binge eating. These data support the merit of a balanced breakfast that is metabolized at a slower rate without the rapid drop in blood glucose levels associated with eating simple sugars. In Chapter 6, we will review data indicating how insulin and glucose levels potentiate the binge/purge cycle in bulimia nervosa.

The Role of Carbohydrate Restriction in Food Craving

Dietary intake of carbohydrate has been implicated in food cravings. Research by J.J. Wurtman (1984) and colleagues revealed that low carbohydrate meals result in neurotransmitter changes that influence dietary intake at later meals. Specifically, this research focuses on the intake of carbohydrate, its effect on tryptophan (a precursor to brain serotonin) and consequently, brain serotonin.

The available data indicate that a high protein meal will create a ratio of tryptophan relative to other large neutral amino acids such that the competition across the blood brain barrier does not favor tryptophan. After a high protein meal, tryptophan is not readily in the brain and serotonin levels fall. Serotonin deficits create a specific appetite for carbohydrate. The effect of higher carbohydrate meals is to raise brain serotonin levels and create satiety in the appetite for carbohydrate.

As a neurotransmitter, brain serotonin is associated with decreased alertness and increased drowsiness. Because of serotonin's dependence on carbohydrate intake, dietary intake may have fairly direct effects on mood. To study this relationship, Lieberman, Wurtman, and Chew (1986) investigated the impact of carbohydrate consumption on the mood of two groups of subjects, namely, carbohydrate snackers and noncarbohydrate snackers. The investigators measured mood before and two hours after a standard, high-carbohydrate meal. The results showed that noncarbohydrate snackers reported feeling sleepy, tired, and less alert while carbohydrate snackers displayed little or no changes in mood. These investigators suggest that different snack patterns may be maintained due to their mood-altering consequences and that a preference for carbohydrate by carbohydrate snackers may be related to serotonin-mediated changes in mood that are perceived as positive. The noncarbohydrate snackers may avoid carbohydrate snacks due to the induction of these same moods, which are perceived as annoying or adverse (i.e., drowsiness).

This research on the influence of carbohydrate on serotonin levels is important not only for its contribution to the understanding of food cravings but also for a variety of other observations in those who diet or have an eating disturbance. Many popular diets are low in carbohydrates due to the myth that carbohydrates are dangerously fat-producing. Coupled with the knowledge that eating disorders often develop as a consequence of dieting, it is not unusual for those with eating disorders to diet by restricting their carbohydrate intake. Typically, these individuals have periods of low caloric intake lasting from one day to a week, which are then interrupted by an episode of binge eating prior to the onset of the next bout of dieting. It appears that the biological consequences of low-carbohydrate intake are profound, predisposing these individuals to overeat or binge as a result of both energy depletion (blood glucose and glycogen stores) and low brain serotonin levels. Moreover, research by J.J. Wurtman (1984, 1986) also suggests that a preference for carbohydrate snacks may be related to their soothing and mood-altering effects. As we shall discuss in detail in Chapter 7, the presence of negative moods as a result of an inability to cope successfully with problem situations is a strong predictor of binge episodes (Schlundt, Johnson, & Jarrell, 1985, 1986). There seems to be a strong preference for carbohydrate snacks (with or without a high level of dietary fat) as preferred binge foods.

It appears then that serotonin functions as a controlled-feedback system in the brain. That is, the intake of carbohydrate increases brain serotonin which then inhibits further carbohydrate intake. There is also evidence linking decreased brain serotonin with depression (Silverstone & Goodall, 1986), and as we shall see in Chapter 6, there is a strong association of bulimic nervosa and depression. Antidepressive medications, some of which increase brain serotonin levels, have been used successfully to treat bulimia. Additionally, one drug widely used in weight reduction, fenfluramine, directly increases the brain levels of serotonin and suppresses food intake (Silverstone & Goodall, 1986).

BIOBEHAVIORAL RESPONSES TO EXTREME WEIGHT LOSS EFFORTS

Starvation Response

When the human body is subjected to prolonged, extreme caloric restriction, a number of compensatory responses occur (Dwyer, 1985). These responses are designed to conserve energy and promote survival. The starvation response is relevant to bulimia because bingeing and purging are often intermixed with periods of dieting. The various aspects of the starvation response are organized to conserve physiological resources and initiate eating. Among the responses to starvation or semistarvation are the following:

1. *Reduction in resting metabolic rate.* Resting metabolic rate can be decreased by as much as 15 to 30 percent as a result of prolonged semistarvation (Keesey, 1986). In an evolutionary perspective, the function of this reduction in RMR was to conserve energy and to minimize weight loss during periods of famine. The result is that once the individual begins to refeed, weight gain can be rapid since the reduced metabolic rate persists for some time. Two processes may be involved: (1) an actual reduction of the body's metabolic requirements due to adjustments at the cellular level and

(2) a reduction in RMR due to loss of lean body tissue. Women with both anorexia and bulimia nervosa have lower RMR and caloric requirements and often have high body-fat percentages due to the wasting of body tissue that occurs due to chronic dieting.

These changes in RMR may influence eating disorders in several ways. First, changes in metabolic rate during extreme dieting slow the rate of weight loss thereby creating frustration and anxiety for these dieters. Weight gained once bingeing begins intensifies fears of being fat, and will elicit purging or other behaviors designed to mitigate the effects of food consumption. Rapid weight gain is usually due to storage of body fat since lean tissue is restored much more slowly. Repeated episodes of weight loss followed by weight regain may chronically lower RMR by causing an increase in body fat and a long-term reduction in lean tissue.

2. *Reduced thermic effect of food.* In addition to the reduction in RMR, starvation results in a reduction in the SDA or thermic effect of a meal. That is, part of the energy contained in a meal is released as excess heat during digestion. In the starved state, the amount of excess heat produced by a standardized test meal is reduced (Keesey & Powley, 1986).

3. *Hypothermia.* If caloric restriction occurs for a prolonged period of time, hypothermia may be observed (Nishita, Knopes, Ellinwood, & Rockwell, 1986). The hypothermia is initially limited to the extremities in order to preserve body temperature. While it is not clear that hypothermia itself has a direct effect on eating behavior, it certainly contributes to an unpleasant outcome of extreme dieting.

4. *Irritability.* The studies by Keys et al. (1950) and Fitcher et al. (1986) have documented that prolonged reduction of caloric intake can result in irritability and other emotional disturbances. Depression, insomnia, and inability to concentrate are other potential psychological impacts of starvation (Dwyer, 1985). Since negative affective states are a potent trigger of binge eating, this irritability tends to contribute to the unstable nature of emotions during extreme caloric restriction.

5. *Heightened cue sensitivity.* Caloric restriction and semistarvation have been shown to result in heightened sensitivity to eating cues in the environment (Nisbett, 1972). Since bulimic behavior is very responsive to environmental cues, a heightening of this sensitivity would tend to make long-term food restriction more difficult to endure. Other authors claim that prolonged starvation results in an obsession with food and an inability to think of anything else (Dwyer, 1985).

Hypokalemia

Three of the major strategies of purging—vomiting, laxatives, and diuretics—can result in depletion of potassium stores. While it is not clear that this has any direct effect on eating behavior, low serum potassium (hypokalemia) does create negative subjective feelings. For example, hypokalemia can cause weakness, blurred vision, muscle spasms, heart palpitations, and disorientation. These subjective experiences contribute to a general feeling of malaise after purging. The individual may learn that eating relieves some of these negative symptoms (possibly by restoring potassium balance), which may contribute to the repetition of eating binges. In addition, negative physical feelings may contribute to the negative emotional states that are strong elicitors of binge eating.

Reproductive Hormones

There is considerable literature on the effects of anorexia on reproductive hormones (Henley & Vaitukaitis, 1985; Warren, 1985). Amenorrhea is so common in anorexia nervosa that it is considered by some to be a diagnostic feature (Halmi, 1983b; APA, 1987). Warren (1985) reports that amenorrhea may also occur in bulimia, but that its occurrence is much more variable than in anorexia. Menstrual dysfunction may not be just limited to individuals with diagnosable eating disorders. Rippon, Nash, Myburgh, and Noakes (1988) showed that anorexic-like eating attitudes were more predictive of menstrual difficulties than body mass or level of physical activity in eighty-eight lean runners, dancers, and models. These data suggest that nutritional deficiencies that are too subtle to lead to a full-blown case of anorexia may be serious enough to disrupt menstrual function.

The changes in menstrual function are a result of reduction in the secretion of luteinizing hormone and follicle-stimulating hormone. Warren reports that the level and diurnal variation in these hormones revert to a prepubertal pattern. These changes are also observed in starvation due to other causes besides anorexia nervosa. The consequences of severe food restriction for reproductive function, however, do not appear to create conditions that stimulate bulimic behavior.

The role of monthly variation in reproductive hormone levels and its effect on eating behavior is often reported clinically. Many women claim that one of the symptoms of the premenstrual syndrome (PMS) is increased appetite and carbohydrate craving. Very little scientific data exists to document this phenomenon. PMS may play a role in the stimulation of bulimic behavior in women who have not lost a sufficient amount of weight to induce amenorrhea.

THE ROLE OF DIETING IN THE DEVELOPMENT OF EATING DISORDERS

As we discuss in Chapter 3, dieting is very widespread, particularly in females who show an exponential increase from the early preadolescent years where 10 to 15 percent of young girls diet to the age of eighteen years where 60 to 70 percent are dieting. Moreover, the extent of dieting often goes beyond caloric restriction to include semistarvation, carbohydrate avoidance, and the abuse of laxatives, diuretics, and appetite suppressants, as well as purging via exercise and self-induced vomiting. Given the widespread practice of dieting, the obvious question concerns the role that dieting plays in the initiation of eating disorders.

Dieting is strongly implicated as a precursor to eating disorders. Several investigators, namely Nylander (1971) and Rodin, Silberstein, and Streigel-Moore (1985), have suggested a continuity between dieting and eating disorders. Specifically, this position suggests that dieting and eating disorders are quantitatively and not qualitatively different. Other investigators propose a discontinuity between dieting and eating disorders relying on data indicating that the vast majority of dieters do not develop an eating disorder. As summarized by Polivy and Herman (1987), the available data indicate individuals with eating disorders share many characteristics with those who diet and are preoccupied with food and weight. As they note, however, there appears to be a fundamental difference in that individuals with eating disorders display some form of psychological vulnerability, such as a sense of personal ineffectiveness or interpersonal distress. An obvious question then, is whether individuals who have eating disorders develop the psychopathology prior to the onset of their eating disorder or following it.

Individuals who are not dieting appear to regulate their food intake primarily by physiological cues emanating from energy depletion and the gastrointestinal tract. In contrast, patients who are preoccupied with food and weight have established cognitive controls that signal when, where, and how much to eat. As the research on dietary restraint indicates, many of these individuals overregulate their eating and are susceptible to disinhibition as a result of a wide variety of cues, including the presence of food, seeing others eat, alcohol, and stress. Additionally, strong dietary restraint may give rise to a variety of internal responses creating biological imperatives that are difficult to withstand. We can examine how a semistarvation diet can influence eating, thoughts about food, and psychopathology. The many parallels between the experimental study of starvation and clinical examples of eating disorders will be striking.

The foregoing strongly implicates dieting in the development of eating disorders. Prior to discussing the role of excessive and inappropriate dieting, we shall review how humans have coped with severe decreases in food supplies that have occurred under famine conditions. Famines can be traced to the earliest recordings in human history. The Bible contains repeated references to starvation and famine. More recently, reports of famine and starvation have been associated with drought and other severe weather conditions, overpopulation, world wars (particularly WWI and WWII), marooned sailors and travelers, and animal and human experiments. Over the course of human evolution (possibly mammalian evolution), the ability to withstand periods of decreased food availability for months at a time has emerged. In this adaptation process, humans are able to store excess calories as fat in times of plenty and to use these stores during these periods of lower food availability.

Although there are many reports of human starvation occurring under natural conditions, Keys et al. (1950) studied the biological and psychological changes that are induced by starvation and subsequent refeeding in a controlled experiment. Thirty-two normal, healthy men who were conscientious objectors to military service served as subjects. Throughout the study, the subjects lived in a controlled environment under close supervision and ate prepared meals from a dietary kitchen. In the first three months, the men ate a *normal amount of food* after which they were placed on a semistarvation diet (average = approximately 1,600 kcal/day). During this period of reduced food intake their weight fell an average of 25 percent. A final three-month period was devoted to a *refeeding phase* where caloric intake ranged from 3,200 to 4,500 kcal with extremely high levels up to 10,000 kcal noted.

These subjects, who were normal weight, physically healthy, and psychologically normal in every respect, displayed disturbed patterns of eating, negative emotional states, and disturbed cognitions during semistarvation that appear directly related to their reduced caloric intake. They reported increased tiredness and appetite, muscle soreness, irritability, apathy, social isolation, hunger, and depression. They also displayed decreased ambition, self-discipline, concentration, and sexual interest. Physically, they complained of cold hands and feet, dizziness, fainting spells, visual impairment, and reduced strength. Body temperature and heart and respiration rates decreased. RMR also dropped approximately 40 percent below normal levels. Weight losses averaged approximately 25 percent, and corresponding decreases in fat of almost 70 percent and muscle of 40 percent were also noted.

These men became preoccupied with food, constantly talking about eating, cooking, and recipes. In fact, reading cookbooks became a favorite pastime and many daydreamed about food and eating. As a group, they became very finicky and picky eaters—toying with their food and consuming everything served. The subjects also attempted to prolong each meal, some taking up to two hours to eat. Surprisingly, the men also began collecting and hoarding food utensils and almost half developed an interest in cooking that they intended to pursue following the experiment.

Binge eating was also evident as several subjects were not able to adhere to the diet and reported eating cookies, popcorn, ice cream sundaes, and candy. During these episodes, the men ate enormous amounts of food even after having just completed a meal. They reported feeling out of control and unable to stop eating, consuming between 8,000 and 10,000 kcal at a time.

As indicated, all subjects were psychologically well-adjusted prior to the study but many reported emotional maladjustment including increased irritability and anger during the six months of deprivation. There was an increase in depression and two of the subjects developed clinically abnormal behavior that bordered on psychosis.

During the three months of refeeding, the preoccupation with food and eating persisted for some time. It was very difficult for the men to return to their normal manner of eating. As the refeeding phase continued, most of the men were able to return to normal patterns, but overconsumption and binge eating persisted for many. During this refeeding stage, their weights increased to original levels but their body fat was up 140 percent with complaints of feeling fat and flabby.

This study by Keys et al. highlights the physiological, behavioral, emotional, and cognitive changes that accompany starvation. Surprisingly, in spite of severe reductions in caloric intake over a six-month period, the men lost only 25 percent of their body weight, possibly due to further reductions in RMR. Moreover, during the refeeding phase, weight gain was largely fat.

The changes in eating habits and preoccupation with food during starvation were striking as were the strong tendencies to break the diet with binge eating and the difficult adjustments encountered during the refeeding period. All in all, the study points to the potential dangers of diets involving drastic and even moderate caloric reductions for prolonged periods. Many of the physical, behavioral, and psychological changes observed in these normal, healthy male volunteers are very similar to those occurring in people who set out to lose weight by dieting.

Fitcher, Pirke, and Holsber (1986) studied the neuroendocrine and psychological disturbances induced by starvation. Five females between the ages of twenty-one and twenty-five who were normal weight and medically and psychologically healthy were studied over four successive three-week periods alternating between normal caloric intake and fasting. During the fasting period, disturbances in the hypothalamic-pituitary-adrenal axis consisted primarily of hypercortisolism and deviations in thyroid function. All of these functions returned to normal during refeeding. Disturbances in psychological functioning consisted primarily of increased irritability, distress, anxiety, and depression. The authors conclude that the alterations observed were the direct result of fasting and semistarvation. They further state that their results do not support a common neuroendocrine basis for eating disorders and affective disorders. Instead, the emotional and neuroendocrine disturbances associated with eating disorders may be a result of the dieting and purging rather than the cause.

SUMMARY

Biological mechanisms control eating and weight regulation. The hypothalamus, together with the neurotransmitters and endogenous opiates, plays a central role in eating as it integrates biological and environmental information on energy deprivation, nutritional status, and hormonal variations. Weight stability is the rule rather than the exception, and it is maintained by a delicate balance of energy and nutrient intake, energy expenditure, and internal metabolic adjustments in RMR and SDA. The weights of volunteers who have been either force-fed or starved return to previous levels upon the resumption of their customary diet and activity routines. Deviations from optimal energy and nutrient intake common in dieting can have drastic consequences for health and are implicated in the development of eating disorders. Studies show striking similarities in the psychological and physiological changes accompanying stringent dieting and eating disorders.

3

Dieting, Fear of Weight Gain, and Body Image

IN ORDER TO DEAL EFFECTIVELY with eating disorders, it is important to understand how they are manifested behaviorally. The spectrum of eating disorders described in Chapter 1 will apply to many patients who are diagnosed as anorexic, bulimic, or both.

Four constellations of behaviors will be discussed: dieting, fear of weight gain, body-image disturbance, and food phobias. Unfortunately, these behaviors are not unique to individuals with a diagnosis of anorexia nervosa or bulimia nervosa. Consequently, we will also consider the distribution of these behaviors in the general population so that the behavioral manifestations of eating disorders can be appreciated within their cultural context.

RESTRICTIVE DIETING AND FASTING

Dieting is the attempt to lose weight by restricting caloric intake. There is no lack of information available on how to diet. There are hundreds of diet books. Most women's magazines feature monthly articles on dieting; some magazines are even devoted exclusively to the topic. Nicholas and Dwyer (1986) reviewed the features of nine published diet books. The diets varied in terms of the kinds of claims made, the use of behavior modification techniques, the type of approach to weight loss (low-carbohydrate/

high-fat versus high-carbohydrate/low-fat), and the nutritional adequacy of the diet. From a nutritional standpoint, almost all of the popular diets can be criticized as having several areas of gross inadequacy.

Grunewald (1985) conducted a survey of college students in order to better describe dieting behavior. The most popular approaches were exercise (60 percent), moderate calorie restriction (55 percent), fasting/starvation (35 percent), and diet pills (34 percent). Questions about where subjects obtained information about weight loss showed that information in the media about dieting is readily available and frequently used. Most dieters report avoiding the more drastic methods of weight loss (e.g., vomiting) with the exception of fasting. Respondents classified as chronic dieters gained an average of 3.5 pounds during the school year and those classified as periodic dieters showed an average weight gain of 7.8 pounds. In spite of all the efforts to diet, these women were by and large not successful in controlling their weight.

When reviewing the literature on the incidence of restrictive dieting and fasting as weight control strategies, we must keep in mind that the way in which the questions are worded in surveys will have a large effect on the resulting estimate of incidence. Unfortunately, the focus of most surveys in the literature on eating disorders is on binge eating. Very few surveys that report on the incidence of dieting offer a definition of dieting or fasting or give the wording of the questions used to assess the frequency of this behavior. Subtle differences in the way questions are worded can lead to very different incidence estimates.

Johnson, Lewis, Love, Stuckey, and Lewis (1983) surveyed 1,268 adolescent females representing 98 percent of the total female population from an urban high school. The term diet was defined as "... changing your eating behavior for the purpose of losing weight" (p. 16). Given this definition of dieting, it would appear that the ages of twelve to fifteen are the ages at which the majority of high school girls start to practice food restriction for the purpose of losing weight. While dieting did occur in ten- and eleven-year-old girls, it was relatively rare. By the age of fifteen, 62 percent of the girls had dieted and by the age of eighteen, 69 percent had attempted to lose weight through dieting. When asked if they were currently on a diet, 37 percent reported that they were. Although no definition of chronic dieting is presented, Johnson et al. reported that 14 percent of the girls were classified as chronic dieters.

Nevo (1985) reported the results of a survey of 689 college women at the University of California at Berkeley. When asked how often they tried to lose weight, 52 percent reported dieting on a weekly or monthly basis. When the definition of dieting was changed from trying to lose weight to crash dieting, only 15 percent of the women reported crash dieting on a weekly or monthly basis. When asked about fasting to lose weight, 16 percent reported fasting on a weekly or monthly basis. It is not possible to know from the data presented the extent to which the "fasters" and the "crash dieters" represented different or overlapping groups of individuals.

Rosen and Gross (1987) provide further evidence for the high prevalence of dieting among adolescent girls. Three separate schools were surveyed in semirural, suburban, and metropolitan areas. Students were selected by randomly selecting classes and having the entire class complete a questionnaire. A 90 percent participation rate was obtained for a total sample of 1,455 students. There were equal numbers of males and females with proportional representation from grades 9 to 12. Over 90 percent of the students were middle to upper class with a racial mix of 78 percent white, 16 percent black, 4 percent hispanic, and 3 percent Asian.

The results of the study indicated that girls were more likely to report reducing weight than boys (63 percent versus 16 percent) whereas boys were more likely to report gaining weight (28 percent versus 9 percent). The students were also asked to list all the major methods they used to control their weight. For both boys and girls, exercise, decreasing calories, cutting out snacks and junk foods, and skipping meals were the most frequently mentioned methods.

Fasting was found to be a common weight control method with almost twice as many girls as boys using it for two to fourteen days. A similar pattern is evident for vomiting, laxatives, and appetite suppressants. However, the percentages for these more drastic behaviors were relatively low with 5 percent of the girls reporting vomiting and laxative abuse on at least a weekly basis and only 2 percent of the boys. Ten percent of the girls reported using diet pills on a weekly basis as compared to 4 percent of the boys.

Within each sex, whites and Hispanics were much more likely to be attempting to lose weight than Asians and blacks, while black girls were more likely to be attempting to gain weight. Regarding social class, girls with higher socioeconomic status were more likely to be attempting to lose weight, whereas those in middle and lower classes were more likely to be gaining.

Regarding weight status and efforts to control weight, an interesting pattern emerged. Of the eighty-one overweight girls, nearly all were attempting to lose weight. In addition, approximately two-thirds of the average weight girls and even 18 percent of those who were underweight were trying to lose weight. Granted that there are some difficulties in ascertaining the validity of these self-reports, these data are a striking indication that dieting is extremely widespread among adolescent girls.

At least ten population surveys include reports on the frequencies of various forms of dieting or caloric restriction (see Appendix A for detailed documentation). The reports include behaviors such as dieting, fasting, meal skipping, crash dieting, and avoidance of carbohydrates. Most studies reported the presence or absence of these behaviors, although several contained estimates of the frequency of fasting.

Table 3.1 summarizes the prevalence of dieting behaviors in young female populations as estimated from the ten studies reviewed. The rate of dieting in the female population seems to be quite high, with an overall estimate of 40 percent. Harsh dieting and fasting are not quite as common, yet still occur at a rate of around 20 percent. These behaviors seem to become quite common in young women by the age of fifteen and continue into college and adulthood.

We cannot tell accurately from these data, however, how many young women use dieting or fasting as a purging strategy, or how many of these women meet the criteria for anorexia nervosa or bulimia nervosa. The majority who diet are either normal weight or overweight. There is a subtle difference between being on a diet because you think you are a few pounds overweight and fasting in order to compensate for a loss of control over your eating behavior. We should perhaps conclude that dieting behavior is so common that while it is employed by eating-disordered individuals, it is not unique to them. Dieting and fasting may lead to the development of an eating disorder, and will almost always be present in eating-disordered individuals during some phase of their history. However, a diagnosis of eating disorders cannot hinge on the presence of dieting since it is such a common behavior among young women.

FEAR OF WEIGHT GAIN

We live in a culture in which appearances are important and in which "thin is in." The pursuit of thinness is a billion-dollar-a-year industry in America. Obesity is not only a health concern (Burton, Foster, Hirsch, & Van Itallie, 1985) but also constitutes a significant social stigma (see Bray, 1986). When shown pictures representing various disabilities, both children and adults indicate that obesity is the type of disability they would least prefer

TABLE 3.1 Summary of the Incidence of Dieting and Fasting in Young Female Populations

Dieting	40%
Harsh Dieting	14%
Fasting	
Ever	20%
Monthly	21%
Weekly	5%

(Richardson, Hastorf, Goodman, & Dornbusch, 1961; Goodman, Richardson, Dornbusch, & Hastorf, 1963; Maddox, Back, & Liederman, 1968). Obesity creates obstacles to marriage and dating, especially in women (Elder, 1969; Walster, Aronson, Abrahams, & Ratlmann, 1966). Obesity may also create obstacles to employment and promotion (Matusewich, 1983; Rothblum, Miller, & Garbutt, 1988).

With obesity having so many negative physiological and social consequences, it is no wonder that many people fear becoming fat. Boskin-White (1985) points out that the cultural emphasis on thinness has created special difficulties for women. For example, she points out a discrepancy between the ideal female figure as currently seen by men and women. Most men find the image of Twiggy, the emaciated model of the early 1960s, to hold very little sexual attraction. Women, on the other hand, appear to have subscribed to the adage that "You can't be too thin or too rich." The fashion magazines, television, movies, and other institutions of our culture are all giving young women the message that to be loved, accepted, and successful, you must be thin. The ideal female figure as portrayed in the magazines and media has pencil-thin legs, a flat stomach, very small hips, and almost no breasts. The reality of the situation is that very few women have any reasonable chance of looking this way. Fallon and Rozin (1985) showed that females tend to have a thinner idea of what the ideal female figure should look like than men do. Franzoi and Herzog (1987), in a study of 193 female and 150 male college students, showed that women's physical attractiveness was judged along the dimension of body thinness while men were judged more in terms of upper body strength.

As we documented in the previous section, the pursuit of thinness has become the national pastime. The women's magazines are full of diet and exercise tips intended to help their readers get thin and stay thin. Weight loss clinics and programs have sprung up in nearly every city and town in the country. Books on dieting and weight loss routinely make the best-seller list. Health spas catering to young men and women who desire to be thin are in business everywhere. At the societal level, we are spending a tremendous amount of time, energy, and money trying to lose weight.

The cultural ideal of the emaciated fashion model has been internalized by millions of young women. The end result is that many women have adopted a set of goals and standards for their appearance that is literally unattainable. These women are chronically unhappy, think they are too fat, are afraid they are unattractive, and fear rejection because of their perception of being overweight. Being fat (or at least feeling that way) is bad enough, but gaining weight and getting fatter is even worse.

The fear of obesity, like the other core behaviors, is not unique to eating-disordered men and women. However, this fear definitely appears to be a core feature of both anorexia and bulimia. Empirical literature dealing with the fear of fat is sparse, which is somewhat surprising since it has long been considered an essential component in the diagnosis of anorexia nervosa.

First and foremost, is a fear of gaining weight. Like all other fears, there is a strong emotional component. The fear is not omnipresent, but comes and goes varying in intensity from time to time and situation to situation. At mild levels of intensity, it is a concern over gaining weight and a wish to get thin and stay thin. At more intense levels, it becomes an intense feeling of panic. It is a feeling that the individual wishes to avoid. Once it is aroused, it creates a motivation to do something to reduce it. The more intense the fear of gaining weight and getting fat, the stronger the motivation to do something to remove or reduce it.

Fear of Interpersonal Consequences of Being Fat

The fear of gaining weight carries with it a fear of the consequences of being fat. The stronger the fear, the more likely the individual is to think about and anticipate the terrible consequences that would accompany obesity. The fears are interpersonal. With friends and family, the weight-phobic fears being rejected or ridiculed for being too fat. There may be some basis in experience for this fear since many young women have been criticized or teased about their weight. One of our patients, Sandy, grew up with a very obese aunt. She recalled her mother and father teasing her saying that if she did not stop eating so much she would end up looking like her aunt. When Sandy's fear of getting fat was aroused, she feared ridicule from her parents and her husband, who was constantly bragging about how thin and beautiful she was.

In the area of heterosexual relationships and intimacy, the fear of becoming fat can be devastating. The anorexic or bulimic woman fears that those close to her, especially her husband or boyfriend, will reject her if she gains weight. For the woman who is not involved in an intimate relationship, the fear is that no one will ever want her because she is fat and ugly. Unfortunately, when aroused, this fear may motivate the bulimic to avoid social engagements since she is afraid that "if he sees me looking this fat, he surely will hate me." One of our patients routinely avoided dates and other social contacts using the excuse that she would start to go out when she lost weight and looked better. This patient was chronically unable to lose enough weight to get over her fears of social rejection and consequently lead a fairly isolated and unhappy existence.

The fear of being fat extends into anticipated consequences in the workplace as well. The anorexic or bulimic is often convinced that the evaluation of her performance and her potential for raises and advancement is based partly on her appearance. She fears that getting fat will hold her back in her career. Trudy was working as a secretary, but had interests in going back to school and getting advanced training so she could move into a management position. She had the intellectual ability to succeed, and she was aware of this. However, she hesitated to make any changes because she felt fat and was afraid that she was getting fatter. (In fact, Trudy was about 10 percent below ideal body weight.) She told herself that she would not quit work and go back to school until she was thin. She was sure that no one would want to hire a fat woman even if she had an advanced degree.

Being Fat Is Equated with Failure

When patients with eating disorders talk about their weight and their feelings about their weight, they often talk about success and failure. Losing weight is seen as being successful, gaining weight is seen as a failure. By equating body weight with personal success and failure, the individual places her self-esteem on the line every time she steps on the scale. Sharon, an attractive and slender young woman from a prominent southern family, was devastated whenever her weight rose. While she was accustomed to success in academics and in her career, she reported feeling like a complete failure whenever she thought she was gaining weight. The fact that Sharon often weighed herself several times a day simply insured that her life and her self-esteem were on a constant roller coaster ride.

Compulsive Weighing and Checking

Because of the fear of getting fat is a central theme in the lives of people with eating disorders, many strategies are developed that allow the individuals to monitor and check whether the dreaded event is happening. Each person has certain key items of clothing that are used to determine whether or not weight gain is occurring. Other cues are appearance of the stomach, general feelings of bloatedness, fullness and roundness of the face, and a feeling of fatigue and sluggishness that is often equated with fatness. Often the fear of gaining weight can be held partially in check as long as all of the cues are telling the person that her weight is fine. However, if the individual's jeans are too tight or stomach seems to stick out, an intense fear is elicited that then motivates behavior designed to lose weight.

Repeated daily weigh-ins are such a commonly encountered behavior in clinical situations that it deserves separate comment. Many patients report weighing themselves three or four times a day for months at a time. Weighing oneself once a day, at the same time and place each day, is a generally effective way to detect quickly actual changes in body weight. However, body weight is inherently variable both from day to day and from one time to the next within the day. The fear of gaining weight is constantly reinforced by multiple daily weighing since, on the average, about half of the time body weight will appear to be going up. When the fear of weight gain results in behavior designed to lose weight (such as purging), multiple daily weigh-ins deliver an intermittent partial reinforcement to this kind of behavior since much of the time a reduction in body weight will be observed at a later weigh-in. This schedule of intermittent partial reinforcement leads to high, sustained frequency of the behavior (Bandura, 1969).

The Social Comparison Process

The fear of getting fat has a powerful impact not only on the eating-disordered individual's self perception, but can also affect the way the individual sees other people. Many patients report an intensely distressing process of social comparison that seems to be related to the fear of obesity. For example, whenever Mary Ann walked into a room with other women, she immediately compared her weight to the weight of others in the room. When she found someone she believed to be thinner than herself, she reported becoming anxious and depressed. Other patients who lived in a group situation with other women such as a sorority, have reported a very competitive atmosphere in which each woman worked to become thinner than the others. When the anorexic or bulimic woman perceives someone else as thinner than herself, two things can happen: (1) she begins to feel anxious and afraid that she is getting fat and (2) she resents the other woman and has difficulty developing mutually satisfying same-sex friendships. Some patients compensate for this by becoming good friends with women who are quite overweight. Others have few satisfying friendships since they resent thin women and see fat women as failures.

The Fear of Being Seen

When the fear of being fat is fully aroused, the individual is afraid of being seen by other people. While convinced that she is fat, the anorexic woman does not want others to see her this way and thus to find out what a failure she is. This may result in the development of a number of behaviors designed to hide the body. These behaviors can include wearing loose fitting, large clothes that are seen as hiding the fat areas. The choice of where to sit in a room is often dictated by a desire to remain hidden from view. Hiding behind desks, sweaters, and purses are other ways of hiding a fat stomach from the world.

Avoidance of Situational Cues

For many eating-disordered individuals, certain situations serve as cues that evoke the fear of weight gain. For example, even if the fear were not present prior to the situation, putting on a bathing suit and going to a swimming pool will often elicit a strong fear of being fat. What we have not mentioned thus far is that eating, especially eating forbidden foods, is a strong elicitor of the fear of weight gain. Thus, many social situations that involve eating, such as dates and banquets, are guaranteed to elicit the fear of weight gain. Many learn that an easy way to avoid becoming upset about weight is simply to avoid the types of situations that routinely elicit these fears. The unfortunate consequence is an impoverishment of the individual's social life.

BODY IMAGE

As we have seen from our discussion of the diagnostic criteria for anorexia nervosa and bulimia, the idea that a disturbance of body image is a central feature of both disorders is included as a criteria for diagnosis by several sets of standards, including DSM-III-R. Our discussion at this point will review several studies that have used different methods to demonstrate that a problem with self-perception is a core feature of eating disorders. We will then present a cognitive-behavioral model of body perception and satisfaction and discuss how cognitions related to the body can influence behavior. We will cover assessment of body image in Chapter 8 and treatment of body-image problems in Chapter 16.

Most investigators studying body image have approached the problem using the definition of body image given by Garner, Garfinkel, and Moldofsky (1978) as ". . . the mental image that a person has of the physical appearance of his body" (p. 250). Garner et al. reviewed the literature on obesity and anorexia and concluded that both groups had a tendency to overestimate their body size as compared to normal controls but that there were some discrepant studies.

Freeman, Thomas, Solyom, and Koopman (1985) investigated body-image distortion in seventeen restrictor anorexics, twenty-three bulimics with a history of anorexia, twenty-four bulimics with no history of anorexia, eighteen phobic controls, and thirty-three normal individuals. While all groups tended to overestimate their body size on a distorted video image, the previous anorexic bulimics showed the greatest body-image distortion. In addition, bulimics in both groups gave ideal body size estimates that were much more discrepant with their perceived body size than the other groups of subjects. Anorexic patients did not display large distortions and were fairly accurate in seeing themselves as thin.

Huon and Brown (1985) used a complex set of procedures involving viewing oneself in a distorting mirror and adjusting the degree of horizontal distortion in a video image of oneself. The study involved ten bulimic, ten anorexic, and ten noneating-disordered control subjects. When asked to adjust the television image to reflect how fat their bodies felt, the anorexic and bulimic patients made the images significantly fatter than the controls. Huon and Brown concluded that the basic issue in body-image disturbance is a reaction to the fear of being too fat.

Thompson, Berland, Linton, and Weinsier (1986) used an adjustable light-beam method to assess distorted perception of specific body parts in seven different groups of eating- and noneating-disordered subjects. Normal weight bulimics showed a significant distortion in their perception of their thighs and stomachs while the other groups showed less disturbance of body image.

Hsu (1983), after reviewing the data on body-image disturbance in anorexia, concluded that there was very little evidence for its existence as a core feature. The literature on bulimia, while still young, seems to indicate that some disturbance in the perception of and feelings about body size, especially breasts, stomach, hips, and thighs, may occur in bulimia. It seems fairly clear that normal weight bulimic individuals desire to be thinner than they currently are and that anorexic and anorexic/bulimic individuals are pleased with their low body weight.

Thompson (1986) argues, however, that this desire to be thinner is true about most normal weight women as well. Cash, Winstead, and Janda (1986) analyzed a random sample of 2,000 of the 30,000 responses that were received to a body-image questionnaire published in *Psychology Today*. Overall, 55 percent of the women responding reported being dissatisfied with their weight. Over 55 percent of the women who actually fell into the normal weight range described themselves as overweight while 40 percent of the women who were actually underweight considered themselves normal weight.

When working with patients clinically, body image often becomes a very salient issue. We have been confronted many times with a slim, attractive patient who refused to see herself as anything but fat and repulsive. When asked to describe in detail what these patients do not like about their bodies, the responses indicated that there are usually one or two parts of their bodies that are perceived as too fat. We have also noted that the degree of dissatisfaction does not necessarily remain constant. Body dissatisfaction seems to covary with the fear of gaining weight that was described in detail in the previous section. At this point, it is not possible to conclude that body-image distortion is an independent core feature of anorexia nervosa or bulimia. Instead, findings related to body dissatisfaction and misperception are most likely to be a manifestation of the underlying fear of being fat. Body perception and satisfaction seem to depend on current body weight and perhaps weight history.

A major problem with the body-image construct is that a clear conceptual framework for the assessment and study of body image that includes both perceptual and emotional variables has not been formulated. Most techniques used for assessment of body image are based on a purely visual conceptualization of body image. Because this dominant conceptualization ignores emotional, proprioceptive, and other perceptual aspects of body image, there are great difficulties in interpreting research results and their clinical significance. There is a need to formulate a conceptual framework for the body-image construct that integrates the entire range of cognitive and affective components into a coherent theory.

In developing a better conceptualization of body image, it is important to first make some distinctions. Four different concepts are critical: (1) perceived body image, (2) ideal body image, (3) actual body size, and (4) body satisfaction. When there is a discrepancy between perceived body image and actual body size, this phenomenon will be referred to as perceptual distortion. Perceptual distortion per se does not necessarily lead to body dissatisfaction. Instead, body dissatisfaction results when there is a discrepancy between perceived and ideal body image. Perceptual distortion is a perceptual/cognitive problem whereas body dissatisfaction is a cognitive/affective problem.

Conceptual Issues in Body Image Assessment

The construct of body image has meant many different things to different people. At the simplest level, body image refers to a mental image each person has of what his or her body looks like. This mental image is a spatial-perceptual phenomenon. It is in essence the picture of ourselves that we carry in our heads. Very few psychologists today would accept such a simple definition of body image.

Body image has a cognitive as well as a perceptual component. That is, we all have certain thoughts and ideas about our bodies. These ideas are stored in long-term memory and are accessed whenever we have to think or talk about our bodies. The cognitive element of body image consists not only of ideas pertaining to body size, shape, and texture but also involves ideas of the implications of body shape for life and relationships with other people.

At a slightly more complex level, body image refers to how we feel about our bodies and body shape. These feelings may be positive or negative. Whenever we have to talk, think, or picture our bodies, these feelings exert a subtle influence on the entire process.

At an even more complex level, body image is a blending of perceptual, cognitive, and affective elements. Whenever our bodies come to mind, the way we manipulate and deal with the information involves an interaction of the three elements.

It is very important to make a clear distinction between the underlying construct (or set of constructs) and the methods and techniques used to measure body image. To a certain degree, the underlying perceptual images, ideas, and feelings about our bodies are relatively stable. However, the task or situation in which these stable elements are called into play can exert a tremendous influence on how perception, cognition, and affect combine. Some tasks are very perceptual and as a consequence may downplay the impact of cognitions and emotions. Other tasks tap more directly into the emotional component of body image, and thus performance is more of a reflection of feelings about the body and less of a measure of a perceptual image.

The concept of a schema has developed in cognitive psychology to refer to interconnected sets of ideas, beliefs, and feelings that are used to process and interpret information. The meaning of any particular stimulus or event is determined through an application of cognitive schemata to incoming sensory data. Barrios, Ruff, and York (1989) suggest that body image is in fact a result of the individual's application of a body schema to the body-image assessment task. The body-image schema is itself imbedded in a broader self-schema, a set of ideas and feelings that are used to evaluate oneself in relation to the world. Because of this imbeddedness, the body-image schema can come to have a substantial influence on a variety of seemingly disparate behaviors. For example, a negative body schema can result in both social isolation and withdrawal (because the individual comes to anticipate rejection for being fat and ugly) and bulimia (because the individual is highly motivated to lose weight to overcome that fatness and ugliness).

Recently, the concept of schema (particularly self-schema) has been applied to the study of depression (Beck, 1976). One of the more interesting results has been the growing conclusion that we may possess a multitude of schemata that we use to interpret the world. In manic depressives, for example, the self and the world are interpreted and responded to very differently depending upon the current mode of affect (elation or depression). At a less dramatic level, we all have experienced optimistic and pessimistic moments during which we interpreted the same event very differently. A variety of events determine which schema will be accessed for information processing and behavior at any given time.

A Cognitive Science Approach to Body Image

Cognitive scientists have provided theories of knowledge representations, imagery, and memory processes that are grounded in empirical research.

Cognitive theorists are much more explicit in identifying properties and criteria for images, memory processes, and schemata than the investigators of the body-image construct. Understanding cognitive mechanisms may benefit researchers in the area of body image by providing an empirically grounded conceptual framework, the lack of which has hindered previous investigations.

According to Anderson (1985), sensory memories are repositories in which sensory information is stored for a few seconds. To last beyond that, the information must be processed and transformed into more permanent cognitive representations. Some of these permanent representations preserve the sensory information as perceptual images and are called *perception-based knowledge representations*. Other representations are formed by abstracting conceptual information from the perceptual details and are called *meaning-based knowledge representations*. Understanding these two modalities of knowledge representations may help explain how body images are formed and modified.

Anderson stated that "people have a natural tendency to think of images as 'pictures in the head'" (p. 89), but that there are important distinctions between images and mental pictures. Anderson proposed that images are not precise like pictures. Instead, images are segmented into meaningful pieces and can be distorted.

Anderson identified six general properties of images from scientific studies of spatial imagery. (1) Images are capable of representing continuously varying information. This property implies that an image of an object can be identified as the original object even when presented in a novel fashion. (2) Images are capable of having operations performed on them that are analogues of spatial operations. For example, mental rotations are one such analogue. (3) Images are not exclusively tied to the visual modality but seem to be part of a general system for representing spatial and continuously varying information. This general system of knowledge is based on perceptions from a number of sensory modalities that have been acquired over time and across a variety of situations. (4) Quantities and qualities, such as size, are harder to discriminate in images as the quantities or qualities of the images become more similar to one another. (5) Images are more malleable and less crisp than pictures. According to Anderson, some operations are easier to perform on a picture than on an image because a picture is precise. (6) Images of complex objects are segmented into meaningful pieces.

Meaning-based knowledge representations do not preserve the exact structure of an experience or an event. Sensory and perceptual details become less important, and only the meaning of the experience is remembered.

One concept of how meaning is represented in memory is through the use of propositional units (Anderson, 1985, p. 114). According to

Anderson, a proposition is the smallest unit of knowledge. This unit must provide just enough information that a judgement of true or false can be made based on that information. Words, experiences, and events are made up of numerous propositional units that are linked together by association into a propositional network. Propositions can have hierarchical organizations in which one proposition is a unit within a larger propositional unit. This hierarchical organization is known as bottom-up processing in which the smallest units of knowledge are incorporated into larger units of knowledge.

Abelson and Black (1986) took exception to the propositional theory for representing knowledge structures because it is a bottom-up processing approach. Abelson and Black contended that people use their knowledge in a top-down processing approach in the real world. People tend to begin processing information at a very broad level and refine their knowledge about a situation into more specific information relevant to that situation. However, the theories of both Anderson (1985) and Abelson and Black (1986) are not necessarily incompatible. Studies using the bottom-up approach have provided much of the information that we know about perception, categorization, and information storage. Likewise, studies using the top-down approach have much to offer in our understanding of schemata and behavioral scripts.

Schemata

Anderson commented that "propositions are fine for representing small units of meaning, but they fail when it comes to representing the large sets of organized information that we know about particular concepts" (p. 124). For this we use schemata. Schemata are complex units of knowledge that represent general concepts. Schemata are designed to facilitate making inferences about objects and events and dealing with the exceptions to a concept in a specific situation. Abelson and Black contended that schematized knowledge is organized in chunks or packages such that, given some situational information, an individual can make many possible inferences as to what might happen next. Schemata determine not only how much will be remembered but which parts of the information will be recalled as more relevant.

Most schemata involved in the body-image construct are concerned with inferences about the concept of self. Markus (1977) defined self-schemata as "cognitive generalizations about the self, derived from past experience, that organize and guide the processing of self-related information contained in the individual's social experiences" (p. 64). According to Markus, self-schemata include cognitive representations derived from specific situations as well as general representations derived from repeated categorizations and evaluations of self-information.

Markus contended that self-schemata influence both the perception of incoming information and the behaviors that are emitted based on that information. These schemata function as selective mechanisms that determine what information will be attended to, how it is structured, what is most important about the information, and what subsequently happens to the information. As experiences accumulate, self-schemata become increasingly resistant to inconsistent or contradictory information. When inconsistent information is encountered, processing occurs so that the inconsistency is resolved within the self-schemata. A change in the self-schemata may occur or a new schema may develop if the inconsistent information is frequently encountered, especially salient, or cannot be resolved in the general self-schemata.

Markus posited that self-schemata are constructed from past experiences and that no two individuals have the same experiences; therefore, individual differences in self-schemata would be apparent. Markus contended that if people have developed specific self-schemata, they should be able to: (1) process information about the self in that given domain with relative ease, (2) retrieve instances of behavioral evidence from the domain, (3) predict their own future behavior in that domain, and (4) resist counter-schematic information in that domain. Markus called people who develop a self-schema in a specific domain *schematic*. Individuals who have not developed a self-schema in a specific domain would not exhibit consistency in their responses, would not process information efficiently, and would not be able to predict future behavior in that domain. People who have no schema in a specific domain are called *aschematic*.

Markus found that people were self-schematic on dimensions that were important to them. That is, people make rapid judgements of acceptance or rejection on dimensions that did or did not pertain to their self-schemata. Markus, Hamil, and Sentis (1987) examined the effect of self-schemata on the processing of weight-relevant information. Two groups of females were identified. The schematics were forty-two female students who had elaborate body size and weight schemata whereas the aschematics were twenty-two females for whom body weight played little or no role in their self-definition. The schemata group processed information concerning body shape, body fat, and food more quickly than the aschematic group.

Other research by Markus and associates demonstrated that when people are asked to predict their own behavior, they make predictions that are consistent with their self-schemata, usually making these self-schematic judgements rapidly (Markus, 1977; Markus, Crane, Bernstein, & Siladi, 1982). People who are self-schematic on a given attribute also notice this attribute in other people (Fong & Markus, 1982; Markus &

Smith, 1981). This implies that people who are schematic on one attribute respond in more detail based on that schemata than with an aschematic dimension. For example, someone with a well-developed body schema could generate many words to describe hips.

Body images, at the lowest level, are perception-based knowledge representations. A multitude of perceptions are integrated to form a composite image. That image would then conform to the six general properties of images described earlier.

At the second level, body image is a meaning-based knowledge representation in the form of a propositional network. Facts are associated with perceptions of body segments in a hierarchical organization. Additional associations are formed for the total body appearance in the highest level of the hierarchy. This chunk of information about the general appearance of the body becomes part of the larger knowledge structure known as a self-schema.

Meanings and feelings are attached or associated with many propositions and also to schemata as part of a complex propositional network. The literature review on body image suggests that we know very little about how these concepts become associated with the images. However, consider body image as a propositional network, with each perception being the smallest proposition or node. The nodes are connected by their associations with one another. Body parts become the larger propositional units and those units combine to form total body image, which is the largest proposition in the hierarchical organization. Both perception-based and meaning-based knowledge representations are integrated in this memory network. Figure 3.1 presents a graphic representation of the hierarchical organization of body-related information in long-term memory.

Like physical characteristics, quantities and qualities ascribed to different body parts are linked in the propositional network. Cognitive researchers demonstrated that the more frequently a fact is encountered, the more rapidly it is accessed in the network. Consider the qualities of fat and ugly as facts that have been consistently paired with the proposition hips. This association would then be accessed more quickly than the association of attractive. In this situation fat and ugly are schematic attributes that are accepted and attractive is quickly rejected as an attribute of hips. The different perceptions involved in body image may thus be affected by quality/quantity associations that have come to be paired with them. These types of associations are an integral part of the overall self-schemata.

The propositional network illustrates how facts may be stored and accessed as important attributes in self-schema relevant information. Given a situation in which hips are recalled as an unattractive attribute, this self-schema may affect behavior. For example, when attending an exercise class for the first time, would this individual be more likely to wear

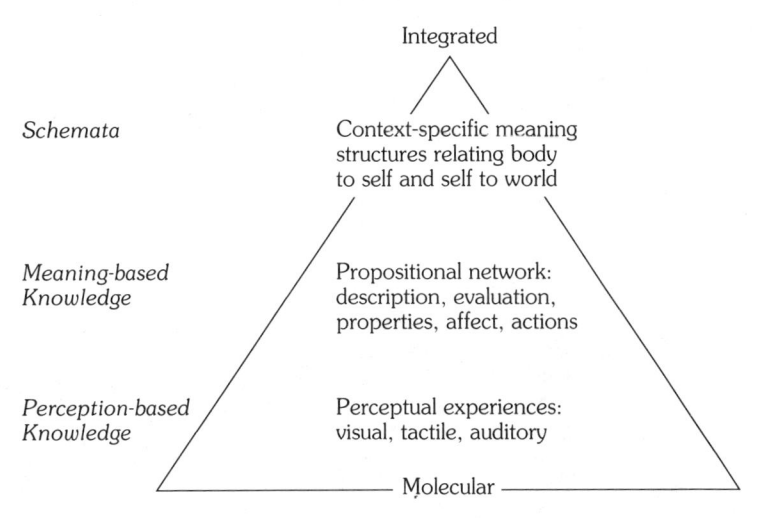

FIGURE 3.1 A Three-Tiered Model of Body Condition

Schemata — Integrated / Context-specific meaning structures relating body to self and self to world

Meaning-based Knowledge — Propositional network: description, evaluation, properties, affect, actions

Perception-based Knowledge — Perceptual experiences: visual, tactile, auditory

Molecular

tights or a warm-up suit? If this individual is looking for information in the biased, self-enhancing direction, then perhaps the warm-up suit would call less attention to the hip area. Given the same situation, perhaps this individual would wear tights under a warm-up suit which could be discarded after noticing how fat and ugly hips are in other people, provided that attribute is important enough to notice in other individuals.

People may have multiple body schemata at their disposal that are situation specific. Individuals who have sophisticated knowledge structures pertaining to the body may differentiate between schemata that become more content specific than the general self-schema, such as the "attractive me," the "sexy me," the "fat me," or the "athletic me." Conceptual, perceptual, or affective information may differentially activate these schemata, subsequently influencing perceptions in that specific situation, which in turn, influences the behaviors that result from these perceptions. These types of schemata contain body-relevant information that may influence body image as measured by various assessment techniques.

These schemata are linked to other self-schemata. Their use is highly dependent upon emotional and situational factors. For example, any given individual may have body schemata for herself as a fat person, as an athletic person, as a well-dressed person, and as a sexual person. When it comes to choosing food, the fat-person schema may be evoked. The result may be stringent dieting and eventually anorexia or bulimia. However, when the situation involves seducing her lover, the sexual-person body schema is evoked, calling forth an entirely different set of images, thoughts, feelings, and behaviors.

An outline of this conceptual model of body image is presented in Figure 3.2 The model has several main components. First, the environment is depicted as being both the source of input in the form of stimulations and the target of output in the form of behavior. Not only do we derive stimulation from the environment, but one aspect of this stimulation is information about the consequences and outcomes of our actions.

The central portion of the figure is a representation of the individual as an information processor. In the present context it is unimportant to be specific about the operations that occur during information processing or their exact order. Let it suffice to say that perception, interpretation, decision making, and response programming are the major processes that intervene between stimulus input and behavior. Two internal components are depicted as interacting with the information processing system. Long-

FIGURE 3.2 A Conceptual Model of Body Image

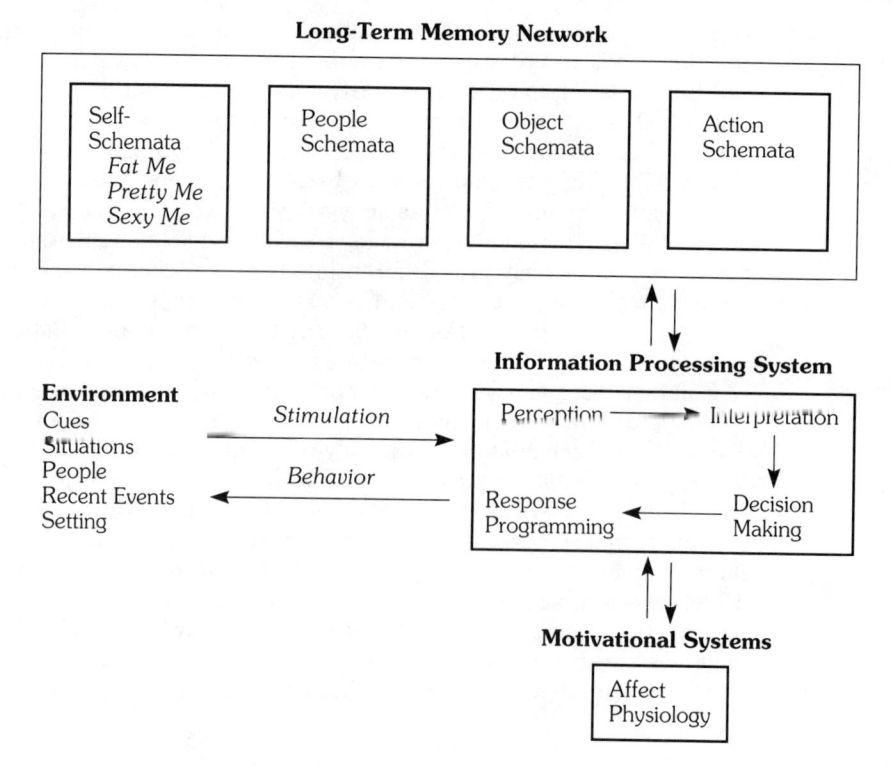

Long-Term Memory Network

Self-Schemata *Fat Me* *Pretty Me* *Sexy Me*	People Schemata	Object Schemata	Action Schemata

Information Processing System

Environment
Cues
Situations
People
Recent Events
Setting

Stimulation →

Behavior ←

Perception → Interpretation
↓
Response Programming ← Decision Making

Motivational Systems

Affect
Physiology

term memory is depicted on the top of the figure. Memory is assumed to be organized as a hierarchical semantic network. Nodes in this network represent schemata or sets of schemata. The network aspect of memory organization is highlighted through the many interconnections among various schemata. Three different body-schemata are included in the figure as illustrations. The specific schemata are shown as bundles of information consisting of ideas, meanings, and relationships, perceptual information used to form images, affective and evaluative information, and behavioral information on how to act.

The information processing component is linked not only to the semantic network of schemata but also to the individual's motivational system. While the motivational system is itself quite complex, the main point is that the current emotional tone along with the body's physiological state feed into information processing. Affect and physical status also interact with memory and serve as contextual variables affecting retrieval of various schemata. For example, if a person is feeling depressed and tired, then retrieval of memory schemata that have negative affect connections is more likely.

FOOD PHOBIA

The fear of getting fat and staying fat manifests itself in another way that has not been adequately studied. Many patients appear to have developed strong and irrational fears of certain specific food items. These fears are often so strong and irrational that we refer to them as food phobias.

A food phobia is a fear that eating a certain food will make one fat. The sight of or even idea of eating the food can arouse anxiety, and steps are taken to avoid it. Williamson, Prather, Goreczy, Davis, and McKenzie (in press) used psychophysiological measures to evaluate the reaction of bulimic subjects to ingesting a high-calorie meal. Heart rate and galvanic skin response (GSR) showed a significant increase in bulimic subjects in response to the meal. Arousal levels in normal weight controls decreased after eating while obese subjects showed a gradual increase in arousal. In a subsequent study, bulimics' fears of foods were assessed using a food survey (Ruggiero, Williamson, Davis, Schlundt, & Carey, 1988). Half of the bulimic subjects were given forbidden foods and the other half were given a standard meal. In this study and a subsequent study, no difference was found in psychophysiological response to forbidden foods. However, the studies were not able to disentangle the physiological effects of food ingestion from the arousal supposedly due to fear of gaining weight.

When psychological rather than physiological reactions are assessed, bulimic subjects, as compared to noneating-disordered individuals, show specific food phobias. Ruggiero et al. compared bulimic purgers with binge eaters and obese and normal-weight subjects on the food survey. The food survey is a sample of forty-five common foods representing different calorie levels from the four food groups plus beverages (see Chapter 8). Subjects rate how they would feel about themselves after eating each food. The results showed that bulimic purgers displayed the greatest degree of food phobia.

While the specific foods that are feared will vary somewhat from one person to the next, there are some common elements of feared foods. In general, foods that are considered junk foods are usually on the list of foods to be avoided. Junk foods are typically high in calories relative to the other nutrients they contain. In addition, there is a curious tendency for anorexic and bulimic individuals to single out breads as a class of foods to be avoided as fattening. While many eating-disordered persons are quite knowledgeable about the caloric content of foods, they sometimes behave inconsistently. For example, some patients we have seen are quite fearful of high-calorie breads and meats but do not seem to recognize the high fat and calorie content of milk and cheeses.

Like body dissatisfaction, food avoidance based on the perceived fattening properties of certain food is not unique to eating-disordered individuals. Many people who are health conscious avoid eating certain foods because of their high caloric content. However, a food phobia differs from normal weight consciousness in the reactions that occur to eating the particular food. Most weight-conscious individuals are able to eat pizza occasionally without precipitating crash dieting or vomiting.

Melinda, a thirty-year-old nurse who had reduced from 250 to about 130 pounds, was a patient who presented a clear example of food phobias. Her phobias were notable because they were so widespread. There was a period in her weight loss when she was afraid to eat anything except turnip greens and watermelon. She considered almost anything else too fattening. The very idea of eating a piece of fried chicken was enough to make Melinda cry and seek ways to escape the situation. Melinda was easily able to develop a hierarchy of feared food during her therapy by sorting a set of note cards with food items on them from least feared to most feared. Her therapy consisted of gradual exposure to foods increasingly high on the list. Unfortunately, the intensity of Melinda's fear prevented her from getting past hard-boiled eggs and cottage cheese, both relatively low on the list.

The concept of a food phobia may or may not be an accurate description of the behavior of restricting anorexics. In one respect, it is not accurate to talk about the reaction of anorexic patients (with or without concurrent bulimia) to high-calorie foods as a food phobia. In other phobias, the feared object is avoided at all costs. With food, there is an approach-avoidance conflict. That is, the individual fears eating the food and the consequences believed to follow in terms of weight gain. However, because the forbidden foods are usually quite palatable, the individual is attracted to them. The true phobia in this case is the fear of gaining weight, which can be avoided by not eating the fattening foods.

SUMMARY

To summarize, the fear of getting fat expresses itself as a fear of the consequences of eating certain forbidden foods. These fears can take on an intensity that is reminiscent of phobic anxiety. The anxiety, expressed in affect and behavior, may not necessarily show up as grossly undifferentiated autonomic nervous system arousal. What is clear is that many eating disordered individuals live daily with an approach-avoidance conflict that is fueled on the one side by their intense fear of getting fat and on the other side by physiological need and desire for food. The food phobia idea can certainly account for the fact that many patients alternate between two modes of eating, dieting and bingeing. Because of their fears of certain foods, some eating-disordered patients are unable to consume a well-balanced nutritious diet without arousing an intense fear of getting fat and triggering bingeing and purging. Restrictive anorexics, on the other hand, become very astute at avoiding their forbidden foods.

The fear that one is fat and getting fatter is a core feature of both anorexia nervosa and bulimia nervosa. The fear, like any other fear, is manifest as affect, cognition, and behavior. Affectively, the fear results in feelings of anxiety, panic, and eventually depression. Cognitively, being thin is equated with being beautiful, competent, and successful while being fat is equated with being ugly, incapable, and a failure. Behaviorally, the fear is manifest in almost every area of life. Socially, it can result in reluctance to take risks. And generally, it results in avoiding situations that are likely to elicit or exacerbate the fear. Many cues, including food, are effective elicitors of the fear of gaining weight. Many of the cues, such as frequent weighing, function to constantly reinforce and maintain the fear of getting fat.

Most workers in the area of eating disorders have approached body image from one of several rather simplistic conceptual frameworks. It is time to apply modern cognitive science to the study of body image and to recognize the complex nature of the construct. The following conclusions about body image can be drawn:

1. Body image is more complex than a picture in our heads.
2. Cognitive science theories of perception and

knowledge-based information representation may further our understanding of body image.
3. The concept of a cognitive schema is a way of organizing our understanding of the representation of body-relevant information in memory.
4. Individuals differ in the content and degree of elaboration of body-relevant schemata.
5. In addition to self-schemata relevant to body size and shape, individuals have schemata that represent idealized shapes of men and women.
6. Body-relevant schemata contain information on perception, knowledge, affect, and implied behaviors.
7. Body schemata are used as the basis of performance on the various body-image assessment tasks.
8. Multiple body-related schemata may exist, each of which pertains to knowledge, cognition, affect, and behavior in different environmental situations.
9. Future research on body image should go beyond simply comparing the performance of different groups of eating-disordered individuals on assessment measures. Greater progress will be obtained by studying the structure, elaborateness, and content of body-relevant schemata in eating-disordered and normal populations.

4

Bingeing and Tasting

THE BEHAVIORS ASSOCIATED with bulimia nervosa can be separated into core behaviors, behaviors that are used to define bulimia and ancillary behaviors often present in bulimia but not central to its definition. The core behaviors are derived from Russell's (1979) definition of bulimia nervosa and the DSM-III-R criteria. They include an obsessive desire to overeat, purging behaviors designed to minimize the effects of food, and fear of being fat. Since we reviewed the literature on fear of fat in Chapter 3, we will describe bingeing and behaviors closely related to bingeing in this chapter while purging will be discussed in Chapter 5. The frequencies of these behaviors in bulimic and noneating-disordered populations will be described. We will also describe several cases and indicate some of the variations that can be expected in these behaviors.

DISTURBED EATING BEHAVIOR

There is no doubt that bulimia nervosa involves a severe disturbance in eating behavior. We will approach this disturbance by looking at three different aspects of disturbed eating behavior. The primary disturbance involves binge eating. Related to binge eating is a preoccupation with food, which in some cases becomes an obsession. We will discuss the preoccupation with eating but in less detail since there is less research on this aspect of the bulimic pattern. Finally, we will cover tasting, chewing food and spitting it out, a behavior about which very little is currently known.

Binge Eating

All of the definitions and diagnostic descriptions of bulimia include binge eating as one of the primary or defining characteristics. Several major problems are involved in developing an adequate definition of an eating binge. First, eating behavior exists on a continuum from extreme restraint to gluttony. There is no *a priori* basis for drawing a line somewhere on this continuum. Second, the size of a meal is a multidimensional phenomenon. That is, should meal size be a function of the caloric content of the food, the number of servings of food, the types and varieties of foods eaten, or the nutrient density of the food? Which is more important, carbohydrate or fat concentration in a meal? Even if we were to settle on caloric content as the way to express the size of a meal, we must still deal with the question of what is an appropriate number of calories. The appropriateness of any meal depends not only on its caloric content but on the type of meal (breakfast, lunch, supper, or snack), the social context in which the meal occurs, and on other situational factors.

Whether a particular meal should be considered an eating binge is mainly a matter of perception on the part of the individual consuming the food. Instead of trying to develop a definition of an eating binge that focuses on the amount and kinds of foods eaten, the definition can be based on the subjective response the individual has to eating particular kinds and amounts of food. An eating binge from this perspective is a matter of the person feeling that he or she has consumed more food than is appropriate. That is, binge eating occurs when the individual perceives having violated internalized rules of dietary restraint. The problem with this approach is that some individuals will report that they have binged after consuming only minute amounts of certain forbidden foods. These meals are certainly not comparable to binges in which the patient gorges until unable to take another bite of food.

The DSM-III-R definition of an eating binge is the ". . . rapid consumption of a large amount of food in a discrete period of time" (American Psychiatric Association, 1987, p. 68). Others have included the proviso that the individual experiences the overeating as uncontrolled (Crowther, Lingswiler, & Stephens, 1984). The DSM-III includes several other statements that describe or qualify binge eating in bulimia, for example, binge foods are high caloric, easily ingested, and eating during a binge is often inconspicuous. It is interesting that most of the literature on eating disorders employs the term "binge eating" while very few authors offer a definition of the term. Some authors also use the term bulimia to mean binge eating and bulimic to refer to a person who binge eats.

Several studies have provided data that allow us to describe eating binges behaviorally. The subjects of some of these studies have used subjective criteria to identify meals or snacks that were considered to be eating binges. These binges were then analyzed in some detail in order to characterize the behaviors involved. Interviews, eating diaries, and direct observation of behavior were all used to gain descriptive information on binge eating in bulimia. Some of these descriptive studies will be reviewed in order to gain a greater insight into what patients with bulimia mean when they say they have been binge eating.

Rosen, Leitenberg, Fisher, and Khazam (1986) asked twenty bulimic patients to self-monitor their food intake for a seven-day period. Eating episodes the subjects identified as binges were analyzed for the type and amount of foods consumed. The average eating binge involved 1,459 calories as compared to 321 calories for nonbinge-eating episodes. Binges consisted of significantly fewer fruits and vegetables and significantly more snacks and desserts. Although 27 percent of the binge-eating episodes contained more than 2,000 calories, one-third contained 600 calories or fewer.

Mitchell and Laine (1985) observed six bulimic patients binge eating on a hospital research ward and analyzed the caloric content of their eating binges. The mean number of calories per binge was 4,394 ranging from 1,436 to 8,585. Cumulative calorie intakes during the twenty-four-hour period of hospitalization ranged from 1,436 to 25,755. When asked how the binges in the hospital compared to those at home, several patients reported that they typically consumed less food at home. It is likely that the very large quantities of food made available during the study had the effect of increasing the size of eating binges.

Abraham and Beumont (1982) asked thirty-two bulimic patients to describe their behavior in detail during clinical interviews. All of the patients reported that they preferred to engage in binge eating while alone, although a few engaged in occasional binges with someone else. Binges occurred predominantly at home but not always. Some patients reported that they engaged in discrete bouts of binge eating and that they frequently had multiple binges during a single day while others described eating binges as lasting for days or weeks at a time. Seventy-five percent of the patients admitted to planning their binges, and most patients admitted to buying food for the express purpose of bingeing on it. According to patient reports, all eating binges did not involve the rapid ingestion of food.

Abraham and Beumont identified an additional pattern of eating behavior common among their bulimic patients that they referred to as picking. This behavior involved repeatedly going to the cupboard or icebox and eating one or two bites of food at a time over a long period of time. Picking was described by some patients as a strategy to avoid detection by family members. For other patients, picking was a result of their inability to resist the urge to eat whenever food was present.

Typically, binge eating involved the consumption of forbidden foods (i.e., foods that were considered fattening). Sometimes, specific foods were chosen not so much for their palatability but rather because they were easy to throw up at the end of the binge. An analysis of reported binge foods typically showed foods high in both fats and carbohydrates.

In describing binge eating, Abraham and Beumont draw the following conclusions:

1. Bulimia was seen by all patients as a phenomenon quite distinct from simple overeating.
2. In all patients the amount of food eaten during most of their binges was excessive when judged against nutritional requirements or social expectations.
3. All patients attempted to resist the urge to overeat.
4. Bulimia was invariably associated with forms of behavior directed at weight loss.
5. All patients were secretive about the behavior, at least initially.
6. There was an association with dysphoric mood states, which were often relieved after the binge. (p. 633)

The quality of binge eating, however, may be a function of whether and how the individual purges. Lacey and Gibson (1985) compared the binge-eating behavior of twenty patients who regularly vomited to that of ten who abused laxatives. Average daily intake of the group that vomited averaged 6,024 calories, ranging from 2,524 to 14,322, while the mean for the laxative group was 2,220, ranging from 1,870 to 2,526. Variations in daily values were large for the group that vomited, ranging from 1,200 to 29,700. While both groups described themselves as bulimics, the nature of the binge-eating behavior varied substantially as a function of the method of purging.

Crowther, Lingswiler, and Stephens (1984) compared eating episodes of twenty-nine college undergraduate subjects who engaged in binge eating to twenty-seven who did not. Subjects recorded each meal or snack along with information about the corresponding situation and their mood and rated each episode according to whether or not it was an eating binge. Subjects who engaged in binge eating ate more frequently during the evening than those who did not binge. Binges were more likely to occur in inappropriate places such as the living room, bedroom, or car. The average number of binges per week was 3.2. The caloric content of binges ranged from 30 to 2,024, and the mean size of an eating binge was 605.5 calories. While it is difficult to argue that the sample in this study actually represented individuals with eating disorders, these data do show that there is great variability in what is subjectively experienced as an eating binge.

Mitchell, Pyle, and Eckert (1981) had forty patients diagnosed as bulimic using the DSM-III criteria keep an eating diary for one week. The subjects kept track of the frequency, duration, and content of binge-eating episodes. The mean duration was 1.18 hours ranging from fifteen minutes to eight hours. The average patient reported 11.6 binge-eating episodes per week ranging from one to forty-six. On the average, these patients devoted over thirteen hours per week to binge eating with one patient reporting having spent over 40 hours per week eating. The average caloric intake for a binge-eating episode was 3,415 ranging from 1,200 to 11,500 calories. A few patients in the study were consuming over 50,000 calories per day during eating binges while several other patients showed near normal caloric intakes. The typical binge-eating episode occurred during the afternoon or evening and consisted of high-calorie foods, such as ice cream, candy, or doughnuts.

Russell (1979), in describing a series of thirty patients with bulimia nervosa, gave a detailed description of binge-eating behavior. Russell was impressed with the degree to which food and eating were constantly on the minds of his patients with bulimia nervosa. The preoccupation with food was so extreme in some patients that it resulted in impairment of concentration and interfered with the ability to function effectively in interpersonal and vocational situations. These patients reported that certain foods could not be eaten in small amounts. Whenever even a bite of a forbidden food was ingested, the patients would lose control and eat the food until stuffed or until all of the food was gone. Binge eating, then, took on an all-or-none pattern in which foods high in carbohydrates or fats were either avoided or consumed voraciously.

Leon, Carroll, Chernyk, and Finn (1985) compared self-reported bingeing habits of male and female college students who responded positively to the question, "Have you ever experienced occasions over the past few years when you have engaged in gorging or eating excessive quantities of food, i.e., consuming 4,000 calories or more in a period of one to two hours or less?" Sixty-one percent of the females preferred to binge on pastries and other soft and easily consumed foods high in carbohydrates and fat as compared to 11 percent of the males. Forty-seven percent of the males preferred to binge on high-protein foods like hamburgers as compared to none of the females. The females in this study reported more regularity in their eating habits (three-meals per day) while the males reported a much higher incidence of between-meal snacking. While there is not a lot of data on sex differences in binge eating, this study suggests that sex differences should be examined in more detail.

Binge eating is a label that is applied to certain eating episodes in which the individual perceives having violated implicit rules of appropriate eating. These rules of dietary restraint place limits on the amount of certain foods that can appropriately be eaten and absolutely forbid eating other kinds of foods. Once the individual has broken the dietary restraint rules, a loss of control often occurs and eating continues until the individual is forced to stop because of running out of food or because of abdominal pain or discomfort. However, the important feature is that a binge is experienced as a violation of self-imposed rules of dieting.

The loss of control is an important aspect of binge eating. Once an individual perceives him or herself to be out of control, the rules of dietary restraint may be abandoned altogether and the individual may start planning ahead and bingeing intentionally. The feeling of being out of control is one of the features that distinguishes binge eating from everyday overeating. Most people who practice dietary restraint will eat more food from time to time than their implicit dietary rules will allow. The defining characteristic of an eating binge is not so much that the individual has eaten too much but that the ability to stop eating is perceived as out of control.

We can also see that binge eating is not independent of the methods that the individual uses to try to avoid gaining weight. Once the individual starts to use self-induced vomiting as a weight control strategy, it is as if a brake is released and binge eating gets out of control. The reports in the literature of patients who consume 5,000 calories per binge or 40,000 to 50,000 calories per day indicate that they are all vomiting after their eating binges. Removing the possibility of gaining weight by throwing up eliminates the incentive to stop eating before the food is all gone. Loss of control over food intake is actually not all-or-none but can be a matter of degree. Eating continues until a stop condition is met, until some threshold is crossed. Stopping conditions can include running out of food, becoming uncomfortably full, being interrupted or the threat of being interrupted, arousing a sufficient fear of gaining weight, or biological satiety signals.

FREQUENCY OF EATING DISTURBANCES IN THE POPULATION

In this next section, we will look at the results of a number of epidemiological surveys that examined the frequency of binge eating in a variety of populations. We have argued that binge eating is difficult to distinguish from normal overeating. It is important to keep in mind that the rates of binge eating are much higher than the rates of diagnosable cases of bulimia. However, it is quite useful and informative to examine the rate of binge eating in a variety of populations.

Sixteen population surveys were reviewed (see Appendix A) in order to estimate the incidence and frequency of binge eating. (Note that when data was presented separately for males and females, only the female data was summarized.) The populations ranged from junior high school, to high school, to college, to community samples from the United States, England,

and Ireland. Sample sizes ranged from 72 to 1,355. Binge eating was not measured uniformly. Some studies provided subjects with a definition of an eating binge, while others just asked subjects how often they engaged in binge eating. Most studies only asked if subjects ever engaged in binge eating. However, a few of the studies asked subjects to report how often they binged.

When asked if they ever binged, the average response rate across nine different studies was 44 percent. In four of the nine samples, over 50 percent of the respondents reported engaging in binge eating. Taken at face value, these data seem to suggest an epidemic of bulimia. However, given the vague nature of the term eating binge, these studies are more likely to suggest that overeating is a very common behavior and that many individuals are willing to call overeating an eating binge. In fact, it is not surprising that over half of the adult population will admit to overeating from time to time.

When studies examine the frequency of binge eating, a different picture emerges. Herzog, Pepose, Norman, and Rigotti (1985) surveyed 212 medical students and examined the relative frequency of bulimia in this population. The data for 121 females are discussed. While 19 percent reported binge eating once a month, and 13 percent reported binge eating two to three times a month, only 4.2 percent reported binge eating at least daily. This represents five female medical students out of a sample of 121. An additional eight medical students (6.7 percent of the sample) binged on a weekly basis. While it is of concern that thirteen female medical students out of a sample of 121 (10.7 percent) binged more than once a week, this is far less than half of the sample.

Johnson, Lewis, Love, Stuckey, and Lewis (1983) surveyed 1,268 female students (98 percent of the total population) in an ethnically diverse urban high school. Table 4.1 presents the responses to several questions concerning binge-eating behavior. Note that like other surveys that asked if subjects had ever engaged in binge eating, over 50 percent of the subjects said that they had binged. However, when frequency of bingeing is examined, only 4 percent binged daily and 17 percent binged weekly. It is of great concern that 21 percent of high school females are binge eating once a week or more, but the incidence of serious binge eating is certainly far below 50 percent.

Fairburn and Cooper (1983) reported the results of a survey of 369 women attending a family-planning clinic in Sussex, England. A binge was defined as an episode of uncontrollable excessive eating. When asked if they had ever binged, 26.4 percent responded positively. When asked if an eating binge had occurred during the previous two months, 20.9 percent said they had binged recently. However, when the frequency of binge eating was examined, only 7.3 percent binged weekly and only 0.5 percent binged daily. This study also demonstrates that while overeating on

TABLE 4.1 Results of a Survey on Binge Eating

Question	Percentage of Responses	
	Yes	No
1. Do you get uncontrollable urges to eat then eat until you feel physically ill?	19%	81%
2. Are there times when you are afraid you cannot stop eating voluntarily?	24	76
3. Have you ever had an episode of eating an enormous amount of food in a short space of time (an eating binge)?	57	43
4. Do you feel miserable and annoyed with yourself after an eating binge?	42	24[a]
5. Do you consider yourself a binge eater?	15	85

[a]Not all subjects consider themselves binge eaters.
Source: C.L. Johnson et al., "A Descriptive Survey of Dieting and Bulimic Behavior in a Female High School Population," *Report of the 4th Ross Conference on Medical Research,* 1983. Table compiled by author.

occasion is quite common, binge eating on a regular basis (once a week or more) is less common. The study also suggests that when the criteria for a binge is spelled out more explicitly and includes the criteria that the eating be experienced as out of control, only one-quarter rather than one-half of the female population will admit to binge eating.

It would appear, on the basis of the studies reviewed, that a large segment of the female population perceive themselves as having at least occasional problems with binge eating. When asked if they have ever binged, over 50 percent of young women surveyed will say that they have. However, when the frequency of binge eating is examined, a somewhat different picture emerges. When binge eating at a rate of greater than once a week is examined, the prevalence is closer to 10 percent of the young female population. This figure may be even higher in younger age groups as evidenced by the C.L. Johnson et al. (1983) study. Binge eating, while perhaps not an epidemic, is a relatively common pattern of behavior in young female populations. However, the population surveys do not provide information on the amount of food consumed. We should not conclude that 10 to 20 percent of the female population suffers from bulimia on the basis of these data. As we discussed previously, binge eating in bulimia differs from overeating in several ways. None of these surveys allow us to determine the extent to which individuals who overeat on a regular basis suffer from the obsession with food, fear of weight gain, or body dissatisfaction characteristic of bulimia.

FREQUENCY OF BINGE EATING IN BULIMIA

We have already described binge eating in eating-disordered populations in considerable detail. A large number of studies have reported data on the frequency of binge eating in groups of patients with eating disorders (see Appendix A). Because a diagnosis of bulimia is based on the presence of binge eating, those studies that did not report binge-eating frequencies (C.L. Johnson et al., 1983; Lacey, Coker, & Birtchnell, 1986; Russell, 1979) end up with estimates of 100 percent of the bulimic patients engaging in binge eating. The study by Beumont, George, and Smart (1976) included anorexic restrictors and therefore reported only a 43 percent incidence of binge eating. The remainder of the studies reviewed, however, provide valuable information on the frequency of binge eating in eating-disordered groups.

A large proportion of bulimic patients binge eat on a daily basis. Across eight studies that reported the percent of patients binge eating on at least a daily basis, 57 percent of the patients were found to be bingeing daily. While the exact percentage depends on a number of factors, such as the inclusion of anorexia patients, whether the sample is inpatient or outpatient, and the method used to estimate the frequency of bingeing, there is considerable consistency in these data. Thus, binge eating in bulimia is so severe in over half of the cases that it is occurring on a daily basis.

These studies, however, tend to be biased in that they mostly consist of patients who have sought treatment for an eating disorder. We cannot conclude that the rate of daily bingeing would be this high in an untreated population of bulimics. The study by Fairburn and Cooper (1982) of a sample of 499 subjects who met the criteria for bulimia nervosa suggests that in fact patients who seek treatment may be more severe. This study involved an analysis of questionnaires completed by women who responded to a magazine article on bulimia nervosa. In this sample, binge eating was a daily affair for only 27 percent of the women responding. Weekly bingeing was reported by an additional 33 percent of the respondents. The study by Johnson and Love (1985) utilized a similar methodology of obtaining questionnaires from women responding to a magazine article. A total of 544 women meeting the DSM-III criteria for bulimia completed questionnaires. Of this sample, 49 percent reported binge eating on at least a daily basis with an additional 42 percent bingeing weekly.

While over 50 percent of the bulimics studied tended to binge on a daily basis, the remainder were bingeing at least weekly. Three studies reported rates of binge eating of less than once a week in their patients. Johnson and Berndt (1983) reported that 8 percent of their patients binged less than once a week but more than once a month. Mitchell et al. (1985) in a large series of 275 patients reported that only 2 percent of the patients binged less than once a week. The study by Johnson and Love (1985) reported that 10 percent of the respondents binged less than once a week, with 2 percent bingeing less than once a month.

Binge eating is a core behavior in bulimia. An individual who does not binge eat, cannot be given a diagnosis of bulimia or bulimia nervosa. Most of the diagnostic definitions do not specify any particular frequency of bulimia. The DSM-III-R is an exception. The data reviewed here suggest that binge eating in bulimia typically occurs once a week or more, and that over half of the cases will involve daily eating binges. When population surveys are examined, eating binges of once a week or more are fairly common, occurring in approximately 10 percent of the young female population.

FOOD OBSESSION

There is more to the disturbance in eating behavior than not being able to stop eating until all the food is gone. If a failure to stop were the only problem, then it would be a simple matter of avoiding forbidden foods and strictly limiting quantities. However, most patients with bulimia cannot stop thinking about food. Bulimia involves a preoccupation with food and eating. Food is a constant struggle for the bulimic individual. Thoughts of food and eating are nearly constant, often making it difficult to concentrate on work or other daily activities. The binge itself often becomes a ritual in which food is bought, prepared, consumed, then purged. A period of remorse and physical discomfort may follow the binge. However, the urge to overeat soon returns, forcing many patients to plan their next eating binge.

While many authors have mentioned a preoccupation with food as a characteristic of bulimia (e.g., Crisp, 1981; Palmer, 1979; Russell, 1979), relatively little empirical data exists documenting this particular feature of the eating disorder. Russell, in his descriptive paper on bulimia nervosa, presented three case histories. He described these patients as "plagued by the urge to keep on eating," "much preoccupied with food and derived great pleasure from eating," and "overeating as an involuntary almost unconscious habit" (p. 43). Russell described preoccupation with food as a common feature, but gave no estimate of its frequency of occurrence.

Lacey (1982) described normal weight bulimic patients as ". . . fascinated and haunted by food, particularly carbohydrate" (p. 63). Pyle, Mitchell, and Eckert (1981), in a descriptive study of thirty-four bulimic patients, indicated that many of their patients were so preoccupied with food that they took jobs as waitresses or food handlers, and that many of their patients enjoyed cooking for others. Casper, Eckert, Halmi, Goldberg, and Davis (1980) compared anorexics with and without bulimic behavior patterns and found a positive correlation ($r = .26$) between a questionnaire measuring preoccupation with food and the presence of binge eating.

Some of the best data on food preoccupation comes from a large questionnaire survey of 499 women meeting the criteria for bulimia nervosa by Fairburn and Cooper (1982). When asked if they had an "intense preoccupation with food and eating such that their concentration and everyday activities were impaired" (p. 1154), 81.9 percent responded affirmatively.

In part, our knowledge of the cognitive side of binge eating, the incessant craving for and preoccupation with food, is limited because we lack reliable and valid means of measuring it. In addition, as we saw in Chapter 2, craving food may be the outcome of certain physiological processes. It is clear that part of the disorder involves a constant battle with cravings and intrusive thoughts about food and eating. We need more systematic research into the nature of the food preoccupation in bulimia. In the absence of such research, however, we can postulate that one of the core features of bulimia is a preoccupation with food that is manifest by the following:

1. Intrusive thoughts about food and eating that disrupt concentration and ability to perform work
2. Cravings for specific foods, especially high-fat and carbohydrate foods, such as ice cream, cookies, and doughnuts
3. Time and activities structured around eating
4. Planned eating binges
5. Hyper-responsiveness to external food cues
6. High level of interest in preparing or handling food
7. Uncontrollable urges to eat unrelated to physical hunger

TASTING

Binge eating is not the only aberration in eating behavior that occurs in eating disorders. There is another behavior, which may occur quite frequently, that has not been studied systematically. This behavior, which we call tasting, involves chewing food then spitting it out without swallowing. The purpose of this behavior is to obtain much of the pleasure of eating and to enjoy the taste of food without running the risk of gaining weight.

Mitchell, Hatsukami, Eckert, and Pyle (1985) reported on the characteristics of 275 patients diagnosed as bulimic according to the DSM-III criteria. While the frequency of tasting was not reported, 64.5 percent of the patients reported engaging in tasting at one time or another. Fairburn and Cooper (1984) in a clinical description of thirty-five bulimic patients reported that 37 percent had engaged in tasting and spitting and that 20 percent were currently doing so.

Melinda, a patient who admitted to tasting behavior, was a thirty-year-old married woman with two young children. Melinda had been obese most of her adult life, but started to lose weight when she began to use vomiting and laxatives. Melinda had a long history of binge eating, dating back to early adolescence. She had always sneaked food against her parent's wishes and preferred to binge on foods like hamburgers, pizza, chips, and milk shakes. When Melinda began treatment, she was alternating extreme food restriction (300–400 calories per day) with days of bingeing and purging. After several months in treatment, Melinda admitted that she had been tasting food. She would buy her favorite foods, such as hamburgers or M & M's, and chew on them while driving in her car. Once she had chewed and gotten a good taste of the food, she would spit it out into a soft drink cup or bag. She would continue to taste the food until all of it was gone. She would then stop her car and throw away the chewed remains so as to avoid detection. She reported having one or two tasting episodes per day. While we could see no immediate harm in this behavior, we eventually targeted it for treatment since it did seem to reinforce her constant obsession with food and eating.

At this point, we cannot really assess the importance of tasting in bulimia. The few patient series that have included an assessment of this behavior lead to the suggestion that it is fairly common. The extent to which this behavior is a central feature of bulimia is not clear. Nor do we understand the importance of treating this behavior. It may be that tasting will spontaneously subside when binge eating is effectively treated. However, it is possible that many patients who are treated for an eating disorder may continue to chew food and spit it out long after they have gained control over binge eating.

It is possible to argue that there is nothing wrong with tasting in that it is a harmless behavior. While it probably results in the ingestion of some calories that become dissolved in saliva, it probably does not lead to high caloric intakes. Spitting food out before swallowing does not have the negative metabolic consequences that accompany self-induced vomiting and laxative abuse. A nationally prominent weight loss company has recently introduced a flavor spray product that allows people to get the taste of their favorite foods (e.g., chocolate) without ingesting any of the calories.

However, tasting may have its drawbacks. Most people find the sight of chewed food somewhat disgusting. Tasting certainly creates a mess. From a psychological point of view, tasting is a way of maintaining an inappropriate pattern of behavior. As long as the individual continues to taste foods high in calories while low in nutritional quality, the craving for these foods is maintained. It is a very small step from chewing and spitting to chewing and swallowing. The problem with tasting is that it will predispose people to relapse by maintaining a form of eating behavior that is very close to binge eating. In addition, to the extent that tasting stimulates insulin production, it may stimulate physiologically based food craving.

VARIATIONS AND CASE DESCRIPTIONS

In order to provide a greater understanding of binge eating in bulimia, several cases will be presented to illustrate some of the variability encountered in this behavior. These will focus on the behavioral patterns that we have observed in binge eating and will not be complete case descriptions.

Case 1. Sandy was a twenty-eight-year-old mother of two children who worked part-time selling real estate. Sandy would binge eat 3 or 4 times per week. Her favorite binges involved baking cookies for her children, then eating six to eight cookies after the children had eaten and while they were napping. She would also binge on snack foods, such as chips or brownies, that she had bought for the children. Late afternoon, while her husband was at work, was her preferred time for bingeing. Because her husband sometimes worked in the evenings, she would also binge later in the day when he was not there. These binges sometimes involved eating leftovers from the evening meal, especially casseroles and starchy foods like pasta. Sandy's binges were not very large and usually involved fewer than 1,500 calories. However, she was quite disturbed by her inability to exercise control over her food intake and was distressed by frequent thoughts of food and eating.

Case 2. Sally was a thirty-eight-year-old housewife and mother of two who had been bulimic for nearly twenty years. She engaged in binge eating about three times per day on the average. Because her husband was employed as a manual laborer, the family did not have much excess income. Sally had developed a pattern of binge eating that allowed her to stuff herself but which did not cost a great deal of money. She would buy loaves of day-old bread and large jars of generic brand jelly. Her binges would involve eating half a loaf of bread with jelly on it. She would also binge on leftovers, fried pies, day-old doughnuts, and cooked rice. She was very careful to hide her binges from her husband and children, and had been able to avoid detection for twenty years. Sally preferred to consume large quantities of food, eating until it was all gone or until she felt stuffed. She had considerable difficulty keeping her mind off food during the day.

Case 3. Ellaine was a twenty-five-year-old single woman with a college degree in accounting. Ellaine was completely obsessed with food and spent as much of her time as possible bingeing and purging. Because her financial resources were limited while in school and during periods of subsequent unemployment, she had developed a number of strategies for bingeing when she was out of money. She had a boyfriend who worked for a major motel chain and had learned from him how to charge meals to his employee account. She would also walk into a restaurant, sit down at a recently vacated table, and finish any food that was left on the plates. She also reported that the garbage dumpsters at certain restaurants were good places to find edible leftovers. For example, steak houses were good places to find uneaten or half-eaten baked potatoes, and fast-food restaurants were good sources of hamburgers. When Ellaine had money, she would drive from one fast-food restaurant to the next. She would order a large meal (three sandwiches, two large fries, milk shake, apple pie, large coke), consume it in the car in the parking lot, vomit, then drive to the next fast-food restaurant. Ellaine's frequency of binge eating was often as high as twenty binges per day. When food was readily available, she could consume very large quantities, such as two dozen doughnuts or an entire large box of cereal with a half-gallon of milk.

Case 4. Amanda Sue was a twenty-two-year-old single female from a small southern town. Her parents owned a grocery store, and she worked in the store from time to time. She was living at home but had a good paying job. Amanda Sue binged from ten to twenty times a day and consumed enormous amounts of food during her typical binge. Breakfast would consist of a dozen eggs scrambled, a pound of sausage, a dozen jelly rolls, and a gallon of milk. She would throw up as soon as she had eaten it. She would leave work on her break and buy food at a nearby convenience store in order to binge. In the evenings, she would drive from one fast-food restaurant to the next bingeing and vomiting in the parking lot at each one. Amanda Sue would steal small items from stores in order to account to her parents for the money she had spent on eating. She would also steal food from her parents' store, take it into her car, and binge. Amanda Sue's obsession with food was so great that she often found it difficult to concentrate at work, especially as breaktime or lunchtime grew near. Her life quite literally revolved around bingeing and around the efforts she had to make to pay for it and to cover it up.

Case 5. Melinda had a pattern of alternating between very strict dieting and bulimia. (See description of Melinda in earlier section, "Tasting.") When she was dieting, her husband and children were aware of her low food intake. Since Melinda had been obese much of her life, her husband and children were not alarmed whenever she was on another diet. Melinda developed a pattern of not eating meals with her family. She would use the excuse that she was dieting and couldn't eat what she had prepared for the family. During periods of food restriction, Melinda would either not eat or just eat some vegetables or fruit. During periods of bulimia, Melinda would wait until the family had eaten, then binge while she was cleaning up the kitchen. She would then go into the bathroom, telling her family that she was taking her evening bath. While the water was running into the tub, Melinda would make herself throw up. The noise of the running water helped her avoid detection.

SUMMARY

A severe disturbance in eating behavior is one of the core features of bulimia. This disturbance is manifest through several different behaviors. The most observable and salient feature is binge eating. As we have seen, binge eating involves the following:

1. A subjective judgement that an inappropriate amount or kind of food has been eaten
2. A perceived loss of control over the ability to stop eating after a normal amount of food has been eaten
3. The use of an extreme stopping rule, such as running out of food, abdominal pain, or the possibility of detection
4. Out-of-control eating patterns when purging occurs, since the fear of weight gain no longer functions as a stopping rule

Binge eating is driven by the second prominent behavioral feature, an all-consuming preoccupation with food. The drive to eat conflicts with the individual's desire to avoid gaining weight. This tension may set the stage for frequent binge-eating episodes. Binge eating is hard to avoid when the individual cannot get the idea of food or eating out of his or her mind, when thoughts of food and eating interrupt daily activities and interfere with concentration. It is this preoccupation with food and the near constant desire to be eating that distinguishes an eating disorder from ordinary overeating. The normal person who overeats, usually does so in specific situations, such as holidays, parties, or times of negative emotion or fatigue. In between these episodes of overeating, the normal person is not constantly obsessed with food and is not spending the greater part of each day struggling with the conflict between wanting to eat and being afraid of gaining weight.

Finally, we reported on a variation of binge eating which we called tasting. Tasting typically involves the same kinds of food consumed in eating binges. The only difference is that the food is only chewed, not swallowed. Tasting is clearly an abnormal way to relate to food and is driven by the same obsession with eating that drives binges.

5

Vomiting and Other Compensatory Strategies

ALTHOUGH PURGING IS NOT NECESSARY for a diagnosis of bulimia using the DSM-III criteria (the criteria used in most of the studies reviewed here), it is frequently present and can be considered to be one of the core behaviors of bulimia nervosa. Purging refers to behavioral strategies that are designed to minimize the impact of eating binges. Each of these behaviors shares the common feature that it is used as a way to compensate for having eaten too much food. Purging strategies include self-induced vomiting, laxative abuse, diuretics, excessive exercise, and fasting. Each of these strategies differs somewhat in its effectiveness as a way to restore energy balance and in people's ability to use them consistently. In the following sections, we will describe each of the methods of purging in detail referring to the available literature and to case examples. We will examine the frequency of various methods of purging in the general population and among eating-disordered populations.

SELF-INDUCED VOMITING

Self-induced vomiting is the form of purging most frequently associated with bulimia. When an individual has consumed too much food during an eating binge, she learns that it is possible to restore energy balance and regain control over eating by simply throwing up. Most patients begin vomiting by stimulating the gag reflex, either with a finger or through mechanical stimulation using a toothbrush or a spoon. Many patients develop voluntary control over vomiting such that they merely bend over and flex their diaphragm in order to induce vomiting at will. Fairburn and Cooper (1982), in a survey of 499 women meeting the criteria for bulimia nervosa (binge eating and vomiting), related that 67 percent of the women reported that stimulation of the gag reflex with their fingers was necessary in order to vomit while 15.3 percent were able to regurgitate spontaneously.

Patients who engage in self-induced vomiting vary in the extent to which they empty their stomachs. Some patients will vomit only once or twice in order to relieve the pressure of being full. This leaves some food in the stomach and allows the individual to maintain either a normal or sometimes an obese body weight. Others will continue to vomit until all food has been purged from their stomachs. Some will consume large quantities of water and throw it up in order to ensure that all food has been purged. Others begin a binge with a specific food which serves as a marker. When this food is observed in the vomitus, the patient knows that purging is nearly complete.

Many patients eat certain foods during their binges in order to facilitate vomiting. Soft, creamy foods, such as ice cream, are easier to throw up than dry, crunchy foods, like crackers. Many end a binge with a large quantity of fluid, such as a liter of cola, in order to make throwing up easier. Some patients report that one of the reasons they eat until they are painfully stuffed is that extreme fullness makes vomiting easier. Most of the time, bulimics who vomit plan to do so before beginning the eating binge. That is, vomiting is typically a premeditated action.

Vomiting is usually concealed by the bulimic individual. Typically, the bulimic throws up into a toilet. Often, water is turned on and the toilet is flushed during retching in order to avoid detection. Sometimes, when it is not practical to find a bathroom, the bulimic individual will vomit into some kind of container, such as a plastic bag, then dispose of the container to hide the evidence. Martin and Wollitzer (1988) obtained questionnaires from 277 women attending a family practice outpatient clinic. Fourteen percent of the women reported a history of self-induced vomiting while 3 percent reported vomiting at least once a week. Of those who admitted to purging, 57 percent had never told anyone while only 2 percent of the vomiters had ever shared this information with a physician.

The use of self-induced vomiting as a purging strategy has a profound effect on eating behavior. Vomiting is such an effective way to compensate for bingeing that there is no longer any incentive to limit the amount or kind of foods eaten. Self-induced vomiting, at least at first, allows the binge eater to "have her cake and eat it too." Binge eating can quickly get out of control when the fattening consequences of eating too much food can be removed by simply throwing up.

Self-induced vomiting is a very effective way to eliminate calories, and functions quite nicely as a weight control strategy. Lacey and Gibson (1985) studied twenty bulimic women who used vomiting as a weight control strategy an average of 3.2 times per day over a fourteen-day period. Average daily caloric intake was 6,025 calories. Given that no significant change in body weight occurred during the two-week test period, it was estimated that vomiting eliminated an average of 3,770 calories a day. The average binge/purge episode resulted in vomiting away approximately 1,200 calories of food. There were significant individual differences in the number of times per day vomiting occurred (one to eight) and the average number of calories purged per episode (274 to 1,640). However, the use of self-induced vomiting as a weight control strategy can have very negative long-term health consequences.

Vomiting does not always occur in conjunction with eating binges. Some patients will throw up regular meals, even meals of only moderate caloric content. This sometimes occurs because the social presence of others prevents the individual from losing control and bingeing. Other times, vomiting regular meals occurs as part of the individual's overall strategy for losing weight. Many patients are able to maintain very low body weights by throwing up after every food intake, regardless of whether it was an eating binge or not.

There is little published data describing self-induced vomiting in any detail. Russell (1979) described variations in vomiting in a number of cases of bulimia nervosa. One of the problems is that vomiting is difficult to measure. There are several issues to be considered in the measurement of self-induced vomiting. First, unless the subject is confined to a hospital or other controlled institutional setting, the measurement of vomiting must rely on self-reported data. Mitchell and Laine (1985) studied binge eating and vomiting in subjects confined to a hospital research ward. Of interest to this discussion, vomitus was collected and weighed after each binge-eating episode. An analysis of the collected vomitus allowed a better understanding of the degree to which purging resulted in a removal of calories eaten. When studying or treating bulimia on an outpatient basis, the utility and practicality of collecting vomitus as a method of behavioral assessment seems somewhat limited.

Although vomiting is initially seen by most bulimics as a way to eat all the food they want and never gain weight, it is not a panacea. There are a number of metabolic consequences of self-induced vomiting that make it a dangerous and destructive behavior. Damage to the teeth is one of the primary long-term consequences of vomiting (Dwyer, 1985). The acidic contents of the stomach are brought up into the mouth during vomiting, bathing the teeth with acid. Some of the acid and residual vomitus sticks to the tongue which tends to rub against the inside of the teeth causing erosion of the enamel. In addition, dehydration reduces the production of saliva, which contributes to the continuation of an acidic environment in the mouth. The stomach acid may also do damage to the esophagus and throat. Repeated vomiting leads to inflammation and occasionally infection in the parotid salivary glands.

Electrolyte depletion is the other major negative consequence of self-induced vomiting. Of particular concern is the depletion of body potassium leading to dangerous hypokalemia. Severe potassium depletion interferes with cardiac electrical conduction leading to arrhythmias and in some cases sudden death. Short of its fatal consequences, hypokalemia produces headache, weakness, shakiness, cramps, and inability to concentrate.

Frequency of Vomiting in the Population

A number of population studies have examined the incidence and frequency of various purging behaviors in different groups. Sixteen studies in which populations were surveyed for the occurrence of self-induced vomiting (see Appendix A) were identified. These studies covered a range of subject groups, including junior high and high school students, college students, working women, and patients in a family practice clinic. The age of subjects surveyed in these studies tends to be young, with the average age being under twenty-five for all studies but two.

The estimated prevalence of self-induced vomiting is partly a function of how the question about the behavior is asked. Seven of the surveys asked subjects to report if they had *ever* engaged in self-induced vomiting as a weight control strategy. On the average, 6.7 percent of the respondents reported having used self-induced vomiting as a weight control strategy at some time in their lives. The range was between 1.7 percent in a survey of older community volunteers (Rand & Kuldau, 1986) and 8 percent in a survey of junior high and high school students (Williams, Schaefer, Shisslak, Gronwaldt, & Comerci, 1986).

Leon, Carroll, Chernyk, and Finn (1985) surveyed 231 college students, 141 females and 72 males, using a seventy-six-item eating-patterns questionnaire. Of the female students, 13 or 9.2 percent admitted to using self-induced vomiting. Four of the 13 indicated that the vomiting occurred after binge eating and the other 9 indicated that the vomiting occurred after eating small amounts of food. Two of the male students (2.7 percent) admitted to using self-induced vomiting.

Fairburn and Cooper (1983) reported the results of a survey of 384 consecutive female patients under the age of forty at a family-planning clinic in Sussex, England. A total of 369 of the patients (96.1 percent) returned the questionnaires. This survey obtained a more representative sample of the female population than the surveys of students. Since the sample was from a family-planning clinic, there was no bias toward including individuals with more illnesses, which would favor the inclusions of chronic eating-disordered patients. While 26 percent of the sample reported binge eating, only 6.5 percent reported that they had ever used self-induced vomiting as a weight control strategy, and only 2.9 percent admitted to having vomited during the previous two months. Only two patients (0.5 percent) admitted to vomiting on a daily basis with another two admitting to using vomiting at least once a week. Recently, Martin and Wollitzer (1988) have obtained prevalence estimates of 14 percent who have ever vomited and 3.3 percent who have vomited at least once a week using a similar outpatient medical sample. Of those who admitted to purging, half were currently engaging in the practice.

Katzman, Wolchik, and Braver (1984) reported the results of a survey of eating behaviors in 485 college women and 327 men. Of the 147 females who reported engaging in binge eating, 105 were contacted for more detailed questioning. Of these, 21 admitted to using purging strategies in the last month. Given the nature of the questions asked and the way the data was reported, it is difficult to come up with an exact estimate of the number of women using self-induced vomiting. Our best estimate from these data is that 20 percent of the binge eaters or 4.3 percent of the entire sample admitted to the use of self-induced vomiting.

Williams et al. (1986) selected fifty students in each of the grades seven through twelve in Tucson, Arizona, for a survey of eating habits. Of the 300 students selected, only seventy-two, or 24 percent, completed the questionnaire and clinical interview. While the sex of the subjects completing the study was not reported, a total of 8 percent of the subjects admitted to using self-induced vomiting.

Rand and Kuldau (1986) examined disordered eating behaviors in 232 normal weight adults. Subjects were recruited from a variety of community sources including churches, industries, and hospitals. While 42 percent of these subjects admitted to binge eating during the previous two months, only 1.7 percent admitted to the use of self-induced vomiting. Kuldau and Rand (1986) surveyed 174 morbidly obese adults and reported that 6 percent admitted to using self-induced vomiting as a weight control strategy.

Eleven other studies obtained estimates of the frequency of self-induced vomiting in a variety of populations. Six studies identified individuals who reported self-induced vomiting on a daily basis. The mean percentage of subjects vomiting daily across the six studies was 0.8 percent. The percentages were fairly consistent from study to study with the low estimate being 0.5 percent by Fairburn and Cooper (1983) and the high estimate being 1.6 percent by Johnson, Lewis, Love, Stuckley, and Lewis (1983). Nine studies identified subjects who vomited at least weekly. The mean percentage across these studies was 1.7 percent. There was more variation in the rates with a low estimate of 5.0 percent given by Hart and Ollendick (1985). Vomiting at least once a month was reported by five studies with a mean percentage of 5.9 percent. Three of the five studies, however, were surveys of high school students, which may account in part for the high percentages. The mean percentage of high school students in these three studies vomiting on a monthly basis was 7.9 percent compared to 5.0 percent for the survey of medical students by Herzog et al. (1985) and only 0.8 percent in the study of college students by Halmi et al. (1981). The frequencies were combined across the studies in order to derive best estimates of the incidence of self-induced vomiting. The results are presented in Table 5.1.

The best estimate of the prevalence of self-induced vomiting as a weight control strategy that can be derived from the available literature is about 6 percent of females under thirty. When more extreme uses of vomiting (on at least a weekly basis) are examined the prevalence estimate drops to about 2 percent of the population. Less than 1 percent of the population can be expected to have a serious problem with bulimia in which self-induced vomiting occurs at least daily. These data suggest that the use of throwing up as a weight control strategy is used by a significant portion of the young female population. However, only a relatively small number of individuals will be hooked on vomiting as a weight control strategy and use it on a weekly or daily basis.

Vomiting in Eating Disorder Patient Samples

The rates of vomiting as a method of purging in groups of bulimic patients were reviewed. Comparison of the studies is somewhat difficult since a variety of diagnostic criteria were used. Also, some studies mixed anorexics and bulimics together, and the criteria and methods used to assess the frequency of the core behaviors varies considerably.

Table 5.2 summarizes the data for self-induced vomiting in bulimia. It is evident from this table that over half of the patients diagnosed as bulimic are vomiting daily and over 80 percent are vomiting weekly. Only

TABLE 5.1 Estimated Prevalence of Self-Induced Vomiting in Young Females

Frequency	Percentage	Cumulative Percentages
Daily	0.8	0.8
Weekly	1.7	2.2
Monthly	5.9	6.3
Ever[a]	6.6	

[a]This question was usually worded, "Have you ever used vomiting as a way to lose weight?" The estimates for *ever* include data from studies not included in the frequency estimates.

TABLE 5.2 Rates of Self-Induced Vomiting in
Bulimic Patient Samples

Frequency	Percentage	Cumulative Percentages
Twice daily or more	37.5	37.5
Daily	56.6	62.7
Weekly	26.2	82.1
Monthly	9.0	84.7
Less than monthly	5.0	86.1
Present[a]	76.4	

[a]This question was usually worded, "Do you currently use vomiting as a way to lose weight?" Estimates of the presence of vomiting include more studies than the frequency estimates and include studies that may have mixed anorexics and bulimics in the sample.

a small percentage of patients with bulimia who vomit do so less than once a week. Since the DSM-III criteria did not require self-induced vomiting for a diagnosis of bulimia, it is not surprising that about 15 to 20 percent of the patients diagnosed as bulimic did not engage in self-induced vomiting.

Three of the studies reported the average number of vomiting episodes per week. The mean of the three studies was nine episodes of self-induced vomiting per week. These data add support to the contention that daily vomiting is common in bulimia.

LAXATIVES

Purging by taking an overdose of laxatives is another common method used by bulimics to try to avoid gaining weight after binge-eating episodes. The amount of laxatives taken usually exceeds the recommended dosage by three to ten times. In general, overdosing on laxatives induces diarrhea. The effects of laxatives are twofold. First, they eliminate a relatively small percentage of the calories consumed by speeding the movement of material through the gastrointestinal tract. Second, the diarrhea associated with laxatives tends to slightly dehydrate the individual, thus diminishing feelings of fatness and bloatedness and helping the individual feel thin.

Laxatives are usually taken during or just after an eating binge. However, some patients will binge all day and take a large dose of laxatives at night before going to bed. This usually results in diarrhea in the morning. Often, laxatives will be used when vomiting is not possible because of social circumstances. Other patients find vomiting difficult or distasteful and rely on laxatives as their sole method of purging.

Lacey and Gibson (1985) reported data on ten bulimic patients who abused laxatives but did not vomit. Each patient used an average of five different brands of laxatives and took an average of six times the recommended dosage. Average daily caloric intake for laxative abusers was 2,220 calories a day, which was very close to the required caloric intake for weight maintenance. Eight of the ten patients increased their dosage of laxatives as their food intake increased. When these patients were compared to bulimics who purged using self-induced vomiting, it was found that the sizes of the eating binges were much smaller for those patients who only used laxatives. Vomiters were able to eat two or three times more food than laxative abusers without gaining weight.

Bo-Linn, Santa Ana, Morawski, and Fordtran (1983) evaluated the effect of laxative ingestion on calorie absorption in two bulimic patients and five normal volunteers. Caloric intake was compared to the caloric value of rectal effluent and stool on two test days after a complete gut washout. On one of the two days during which identical meals were eaten, the subjects took a large dose of laxatives. The effect of laxatives (up to fifty Correctol tablets a day) on calorie absorption was minimal, decreasing absorption by only 12 percent. The authors conclude that laxatives are ineffective as a method of purging in order to eliminate ingested calories.

In addition to not being a very effective way to eliminate absorption, laxatives can have a variety of negative metabolic consequences. As with vomiting, laxative abuse tends to deplete the body's potassium stores, potentially leading to life-threatening hypokalemia. Frequent overuse of chemical stimulant types of laxatives can lead to an eventual loss of peristolic muscle action in the intestines. The long-term result is that the individual becomes dependent on laxatives in order to have normal bowel movements. Laxative abuse can also lead to intestinal inflammation, urinary and kidney problems, gastrointestinal bleeding, pancreatic dysfunction, and metabolic acidosis (Dwyer, 1985; Mitchell & Boutacoff, 1986; Mitchell, Pomeroy, & Huber, 1988; Willard & Winstead, in press). Withdrawal from laxatives after chronic use has been associated with constipation and reflex peripheral edema (Mitchell, et al., 1988). The alternation of dehydration followed by edema may provide a powerful reinforcement mechanism since many bulimic individuals will perceive the gain and loss of fluid as feeling fatter and thinner.

Frequency of Laxative Abuse in the Population

Nine studies of the prevalence of laxative abuse in young female populations were reviewed (see Appendix A). Three of the studies only allowed a determination of the percentage of the population that had ever abused laxatives. Rand and Kuldau (1986) in their survey of 232 community volunteers reported that 3.8 percent admitted to using laxatives. Williams et al. (1986), in a survey of junior high and high school students, reported that only 1.0 percent had abused laxatives as compared to a 4.9 percent estimate given by Fairburn and Cooper (1983) in their survey of consecutive patients in a family-planning clinic.

The remainder of the studies provided estimates of the frequency of laxative abuse in a variety of populations. Killen et al. (1986) surveyed 1,728 tenth grade students in California from diverse ethnic and racial backgrounds. For the girls, the percentage admitting to the use of laxatives was 6.8 percent. Of that group, only 0.2 percent admitted to daily use, 0.5 percent to weekly use, and 6.1 to using laxatives once a month or less. The rates for the boys were fairly similar with 5.7 percent admitting to the use of laxatives for weight control purposes. For the boys, 1.1 percent reported daily use, 0.6 percent reported weekly use, and 4.1 percent reported using laxatives once a month or less.

Pyle, Halvorson, Neuman, and Mitchell (1986) reported the results of two similar surveys of college populations, one conducted in 1980 and the other, in 1983. In 1980, ten subjects (or 1.7 percent of the females) admitted to the use of laxatives, with four reporting weekly use (0.7 percent) and two (0.3 percent) reporting daily use. In the 1983 sample, only six women reported current use of laxatives (0.8 percent), with one reporting weekly use and none reporting daily use.

Crowther, Post, and Zanor (1985) surveyed 363 girls in the ninth through twelfth grades in Ohio. Of the 363 girls surveyed, 17 or 4.6 percent admitted to laxative use. When the rates of use were examined, 3.3 percent of the girls used laxatives monthly, 0.8 percent used them more than once a month but less than once a week, 0.6 percent used them weekly, and none reported daily use.

Johnson et al. (1983) surveyed 1,268 adolescent females between the ages of thirteen and nineteen. This survey represented 98 percent of the female population of an ethnically and socioeconomically diverse urban high school. Laxative use was reported by 7.7 percent of the population, with 4.6 percent reporting monthly use, 1.7 percent weekly use, and 1.0 percent daily use.

Table 5.3 summarizes the review of laxative abuse in young female populations. The best estimates available is that daily laxative abuse occurs in 0.4 percent of the population. Less than one percent of the population uses laxatives on a weekly basis. The overall rate of ever using laxatives as a compensatory strategy appears to be around 4 percent of the young female population.

Laxative Abuse in Bulimic Patient Samples

Table 5.4 summarizes the available data on the rate of laxative abuse among bulimic patient groups. Daily laxative abuse is not nearly as common as daily

TABLE 5.3 Estimated Prevalence of Laxative Abuse in Young Females

Frequency	Percentage	Cumulative Percentages
Daily	0.4	0.4
Weekly	0.5	0.9
Monthly	4.0	4.9
Ever[a]	4.1	

[a]This question was usually worded, "Have you ever used laxatives as a way to lose weight?" The estimates for *ever* include data from studies not included in the frequency estimates.

TABLE 5.4 Rates of Laxative Abuse in Bulimic Patient Samples

Frequency	Percentage	Cumulative Percentage
Daily	15.8	15.8
Weekly	28.7	44.5
Monthly	38.0	82.5
Less than monthly	2.0	84.5
Present[a]	4.1	

[a]This question was usually worded, "Do you currently use laxatives as a way to lose weight?" Estimates of the presence of laxative abuse include more studies than the frequency estimates and include studies that may have mixed anorexics and bulimics in the sample.

vomiting in bulimia. Our best estimate is that about 16 percent of bulimic patients will report using laxatives on a daily basis. However, when weekly laxative abuse is examined, nearly 50 percent of the bulimic patients in four studies reporting frequencies were using laxatives on at least a weekly basis. According to these studies, a substantial number of bulimic patients are using laxatives on a monthly basis. However, this estimate is higher than the estimate of presence of laxative abuse derived from twelve studies. When this larger group of studies is examined, it appears that about 50 percent of bulimic patients will admit to abusing laxatives. Because a larger number of studies is involved, we think it safer to conclude that about half of bulimic patients will have a history of at least occasional laxative abuse. This is an alarming figure since laxative abuse does not effectively eliminate caloric content of a binge and has a wide range of serious side effects. While we cannot directly estimate the number of patients who vomit and abuse laxatives, these data suggest that a substantial number use both behaviors. If 85 percent of bulimic patients vomit and 50 percent use laxatives, then substantial overlap between the two behaviors must exist.

DIURETICS

Diuretics, or water pills, cause the body to excrete sodium by inhibiting the renal tubular reabsorption of electrolytes. The loss of body sodium is compensated for by a loss of body water. The effect of diuretics is to lessen feelings of bloatedness and to induce mild dehydration. Subjectively, this is experienced as feeling thinner. Diuretics are commonly abused in bulimia.

Diuretics have absolutely no effect on energy metabolism. Anyone abusing diuretics needs to know that the only effect is to cause loss of electrolytes and body water. While the main effect is to cause sodium excretion, diuretics also cause loss of potassium. When diuretics are combined with laxatives or self-induced vomiting, hypokalemia is very likely. The symptoms of hypokalemia include dry mouth, weakness, lethargy, drowsiness, restlessness, muscle pain, fatigue, hypotension, oliguria, tachycardia, muscle cramps, and gastrointestinal disturbance.

Mitchell, Pomeroy, Seppala, and Huber (1988) described several medical consequences of diuretic abuse. Diuretic abuse can lead to a condition called Pseudo-Bartter's syndrome, a kidney disorder characterized by hypokalemia, alkalosis, aldosteronism, nephropathy, and hyperplasia of the juxtaglomerular apparatus. In addition, diuretic abuse can lead to idiopathic edema, which is also called cyclical or periodic edema. These patients complain of puffiness and bloating in the upper part of the body during the morning and in the lower extremities by evening. Diuretic abuse, like laxative abuse, sets off a cyclical pattern in which bloating and dehydration alternate and are perceived as gaining and losing weight.

The use of diuretics is not limited to eating-disordered individuals. Many women use diuretics, which are available over the counter, to relieve water retention and bloatedness associated with their menstrual periods. The use of diuretics as a purging strategy involves taking the drugs to compensate for overeating and to relieve some of the subjective distress associated with feeling full, bloated, and too fat.

Frequency of Diuretic Abuse in the Population

Only five studies reported the prevalence of diuretic abuse in the young female population. Two studies (Pyle, Halvorson, et al., 1986; Pyle et al.,

1983) did not present frequency information and just reported the presence of diuretic use in females who met the diagnostic criteria for bulimia. This method may give an underestimate of the rate of diuretic use since those who used diuretics but who did not meet the other criteria for bulimia would have been excluded.

The frequency data is summarized in Table 5.5. The overall rate of diuretic abuse appears to be lower than that of vomiting or laxatives. Our best estimate is that about 2 percent of the population will be using diuretics, and that only 1 percent will be abusing them on a weekly basis. Because diuretics are used to ameliorate the symptoms of premenstrual syndrome, monthly use of diuretics cannot necessarily be considered a form of purging for weight control purposes.

Diuretic Abuse in Bulimic Patient Samples

Four studies provided data on the prevalence of diuretic abuse in bulimic patient samples. Considered together, these studies lead to an estimate that about 40 percent of bulimic patients will at one time or another abuse diuretics. Since the estimate by Beumont et al. (1976) stands out as much higher than the rest, the actual rate is probably between 20 percent and 30 percent. The one study that reported rates (Mitchell, Hatsukami, Eckert, & Pyle, 1985) showed that 10 percent of bulimic patients use diuretics daily while an additional 14 percent use them weekly, and 10 percent use them less than once a week.

FASTING AND DIETING

Bulimia, for many people, involves an alternation between periods of uncontrolled binge eating and periods of fasting or severe dieting. The length

TABLE 5.5 Estimated Prevalence of Diuretic Abuse in Young Females

Frequency	Percentage	Cumulative Percentages
Daily	0.4	0.4
Weekly	0.5	0.9
Monthly	2.0	2.9
Ever[a]	2.2	

[a]This question was usually worded, "Have you ever used diuretics as a way to lose weight?" The estimates for *ever* include data from studies not included in the frequency estimates.

of these periods is quite variable. For some, dietary restriction begins each morning and ends each evening. For others, dieting may last for weeks or months. As we saw in Chapter 1, the alternation between control and loss of control, between bingeing and dieting, is at the very core of eating disorders.

When a bulimic woman enters a controlled period, she attempts to avoid eating foods that she believes will make her fat. She may try fad diets, restrict herself to just fruits and vegetables, eat only salads, or use other behaviors that are typical of dieting in order to minimize caloric intake. Many bulimic individuals are quite knowledgeable concerning nutrition and can often recall the caloric content of many foods from memory. With the wide availability of new diets and weight loss plans in the magazines, there is no lack of new methods for restricting food intake. Many individuals have very specific and almost ritualized patterns of dieting that are followed during periods of abstinence. Dieting behaviors include avoidance of foods high in carbohydrates or fats. The behaviors also include meal skipping and even fasting for days at a time.

For some individuals, dieting and food restriction are an accepted way of life in their social context. College women who live in a sorority, for example, find that nearly everyone around them professes to be constantly on a diet. Behaviors designed to limit caloric intake in this social context will not be unusual and may, in fact, be socially reinforced. A woman in this context will probably feel compelled to hide her bingeing and to proudly display her dieting. Others will live in contexts where food restriction is less socially appropriate and will have to hide their dieting. This forces some bulimics to avoid social situations in which food is involved. When living at home, the bulimic who is attempting to restrict food intake may have to face pressure from family members to eat, since family members will often not approve of restrictive dieting. In either case, the bulimic individual will find that she has to hide some aspects of her eating (or lack thereof) from friends and family. Most of the descriptions of dieting and fasting among bulimic patients in the literature are in case studies or first-hand accounts (e.g., Boone-O'Neill, 1982). Rates of dieting and fasting in the population were reviewed in Chapter 4.

The use of over-the-counter appetite suppressants is closely related to dieting and fasting. Phenylpropanolamine HCL is the active ingredient in these drugs, which may also include caffeine and vitamins. These pills tend to reduce appetite by stimulating the sympathetic nervous system. Mitchell, Hatsukami, Eckert, and Pyle (1985) reported that 52 percent of 275 bulimic patients studied had used diet pills, with 25 percent having gone through a period of daily use. Mitchell, Pomeroy, and Huber (1988) reported that in a series of 100 bulimic patients, 26 had used diet pills in the month prior to treatment. Several patients reported patterns of abusive diet pill usage including two patients who admitted to taking ten or more diet pills at a time. The dangers of phenylpropanolamine HCL are not well documented. When used in medically supervised weight-loss clinical trials, they have been shown to be safe and to facilitate short-term weight loss (Altschuler, Conte, Sebok, Marlin, & Winick, 1982). However, there have been anecdotal reports of serious side effects and toxicity, including hypertension, seizures, renal failure, anxiety, agitation, stroke, and neurological impairment (Mitchell, Pomeroy, & Huber, 1988).

EXCESSIVE EXERCISE

Energy balance is a matter of matching caloric intake with caloric expenditure. Vomiting helps maintain energy balance by eliminating food prior to digestion and thus limiting caloric intake. Laxatives also prevent absorption of calories but to a much lesser degree than vomiting. Fasting and strict dieting, of course, manipulate energy balance by lowering or preventing nutrient intake. Exercise, however, is different in that it can be used to manipulate energy balance by increasing energy expenditure.

Like binge eating, it is difficult to draw a line between appropriate amounts of activity and exercise and excessive exercise (Leon, 1984). However, some have suggested that when running reaches the point of marathon training, the purpose may be closely related to body-image problems associated with anorexia (Yates, Lechey, & Shisslak, 1983).

Most health professionals are recommending regular exercise as a way to improve physical health and improve psychological well-being. Current recommendations are that people should be exercising three to five times per week and should be engaging in twenty to sixty minutes of vigorous activity at each session. A complete fitness program should also include exercises for building strength and flexibility.

Exercise can be used as a form of purging. That is, when an eating binge has occurred, the individual can engage in a prolonged period of exercise in order to burn off the excess calories consumed. Typically, these bouts of exercise exceed the recommended twenty to sixty minutes in duration. Running is often a preferred method of purging through exercise. Most eating-disordered individuals realize that very long distances must be covered in order to burn off enough calories to compensate for an eating binge. Many patients will engage in multiple forms of physical activity such as running, followed by swimming, followed by cycling.

Richert and Hummers (1986) examined the relationship between disordered eating behavior and exercise in 328 college students classified as normal and 29 students classified as being at high risk for an eating disorder. Scores on the Eating Attitudes Test (Garner & Garfinkel, 1979) were correlated with the number of hours a week spent jogging and the number of hours a week spent exercising alone. Subscale scores on the dieting factor were correlated with total number of sports activities, number of hours spent jogging, and preference for exercising alone. Subjects at risk for eating disorders were more likely to jog (71 percent versus 45 percent) and spent more hours a week jogging (2.43 versus 1.25) than the normal comparison group. Unfortunately, this study did not provide information on whether exercise was used to compensate for overeating.

Nudelman, Rosen, and Leitenberg (1988) attempted to test the hypothesis that high-intensity exercise in men is similar to bulimia in women. Three groups of subjects were compared: twenty males who ran six to seven times per week with sessions lasting at least forty minutes, twenty men who were sedentary to moderately active, and twenty normal weight women who had bulimia for at least three years. The groups were compared on body satisfaction, body-image distortion, eating attitudes, and psychopathology. No differences were found between the two groups of men, but the bulimic women showed the expected pattern of weight concerns, disordered eating behavior, and poor emotional adjustment. Brooks-Gunn, Burrow, and Warren (1988) compared eating attitudes, body weight, and food intake in three groups of female athletes. Dancers ($n = 64$) and figure skaters ($n = 64$) were lighter and more concerned about weight control than swimmers ($n = 72$), with dancers showing the most evidence of dieting and weight concerns. The swimmers did not differ from a comparison group of nonathletes ($n = 424$). Pasman and Thompson (1988) compared male and female runners, weightlifters, and sedentary controls on measures of body image, eating disturbance, and psychopathology. Weightlifters showed less body-image distortion than runners, who did not differ from the controls. Both weightlifters and runners showed more evidence of eating disturbances than the controls, with the female athletes showing more disturbance than the males.

These three studies suggest that there is no simple relationship between eating disorders and exercise. Some populations of athletes appear to have greater weight concern, body-image disturbance, and disturbances in eating behavior than others. The data suggest that the role of exercise must be evaluated on an individual basis. There are some sports, like dancing and figure skating, that place a great deal of emphasis on body size. Participants in these sports will appear more eating disordered, but it is not clear if this is because eating-disordered individuals are attracted to the sport or if weight concerns and dieting are considered necessary to be a top athlete. In any sport, there may be certain individuals whose motivation to be active is related to an underlying fear of obesity and who use exercise as a purging technique.

Frequency of Excessive Exercise in the Population

While exercise as a method of purging is very interesting, little data on its prevalence in female populations exists. Fairburn and Cooper

(1983) in a survey of 369 female patients in a family-planning clinic, reported that 7.3 percent used exercise as a method of controlling body weight.

Halmi, Falk, and Schwartz (1981) surveyed 355 college students and observed that 4.5 percent reported using exercise as a weight control strategy. Garner, Rocket, Olmstead, Johnson, and Coscina (1985) argued that the prevalence of exercise as a weight control strategy in women is actually much higher. They cite the results of a survey of 33,000 women done by *Glamour* magazine, which showed that 95 percent of the respondents said they exercised in order to control their weight. The actual use of exercise as a purging strategy is certainly much lower. However, our understanding of exercise as a purging technique is currently limited by a relative absence of data.

Excessive Exercise in Bulimic Patient Samples

Excessive exercise as a purging strategy was reported by four studies of bulimic patients. The study by Fairburn and Cooper (1984) yielded a low estimate of 29 percent. Fairburn and Cooper's (1982) report of 499 individuals meeting the criteria of bulimia nervosa who responded to a magazine article showed that 61 percent admitted to using exercise as a weight control strategy. Pyle et al. (1981) and Mitchell, Hatsukami, Eckert, and Pyle (1985) gave the highest estimates of 76 percent and 91 percent respectively. Mitchell et al. also reported rates of exercise as a weight control strategy. In their sample of 275 bulimic patients, 57 percent reported exercising on a daily basis in order to control their weight with an additional 28 percent reporting weekly exercise. From these data, we would estimate that approximately 64 percent of bulimic patients will engage in excessive exercise as a way to control weight.

CASE DESCRIPTIONS

In order to provide a better sense of the range and variability in purging strategies that can be observed in bulimic patients, several case descriptions are included.

Case 1. Bonnie was a twenty-three-year-old female who was married with two small children. She had a long history of weight problems. Several years before presenting for treatment, she had successfully lost eighty pounds using Weight Watchers. Within the six months before entering treatment, she had relapsed and had regained seventy-five pounds. Bonnie engaged in binge eating two or three times per day. She would binge mainly on junk foods, such as candy bars, snack cakes, potato chips, and cookies. She would justify having these foods in the house because her children liked to have them for snacks and with lunch. Bonnie had tried vomiting, but found that it was too painful and unpleasant. She had been using diuretics, which she had talked a physician into prescribing for premenstrual bloating, off and on for about five years. She learned that she was able to manipulate her weight by three or four pounds by taking diuretics, and would take them the night before her clinic appointments when she had to weigh in.

Case 2. Mindy was a twenty-two-year-old single woman who was employed as a dental assistant. Mindy would alternate between periods of bingeing and vomiting, and strict dieting. These periods would typically last one or two months. Toward the end of a period of strict dieting, Mindy would start to overeat occasionally. Since she knew that if she started vomiting, she would lose control and fall back into her pattern of bingeing and vomiting one or two times per day, she would counteract some of the effects of overeating by using diuretics. The diuretics would help her feel less bloated, keep her clothing from feeling tight, and would help her avoid panicking over possible weight gain. Once Mindy started vomiting again on a regular basis, she would stop using diuretics.

Case 3. Mary was a twenty-nine-year-old female who worked as a secretary for a small business. She was engaged to be married, but was quite ambivalent about the relationship since her fiancee was pathologically jealous. Mary, who was 5′6″ tall and weighed 105 pounds, never ate breakfast. Three days a week she would skip lunch in order to try to lose more weight. On the other days, she would go to lunch with her co-workers and usually limit her intake to a salad. On the weekends during the summer, she would spend the entire day by the pool working on her tan and drinking diet sodas. She explained that her reason for doing so was to help her keep from eating so that she would lose weight. Mary, however, was unable to diet for more than two or three days at a time. Her pattern was to stop at the store on the way home, buy food, then binge and purge. The next day she would get up, determined that she would eat nothing all day.

Case 4. Trudy was a twenty-three-year-old single female who worked as a secretary at a bank. She had been bulimic for about five years. During this time, she had gained control over her bingeing and vomiting on six different occasions. She would follow a sensible eating pattern for one or two months. Gradually, she would become increasingly strict about dieting, and attempt to lose weight. When she dropped below 800–1,000 calories a day, she would start to have difficulty again with overeating. Her dieting periods would end when she would throw up after eating a large meal, precipitating a loss of control and another bout of bingeing and purging lasting one to six months.

Case 5. Marilyn was a twenty-nine-year-old female, married with one child. She taught school and was the basketball coach for the girls' high school basketball team. Marilyn had been very athletic as a child and young adult and had been an excellent basketball player herself in college. Marilyn binged and vomited four or five times per week. She also compensated for other food intake by engaging in very long bouts of exercise. She would run seven or eight miles, then ride her bicycle for an hour. On other days she would play racquetball, work out with weights, or attend an aerobics class. All of this exercise was in addition to the activity associated with coaching the basketball team. When initially evaluated, Marilyn was administered a fitness test. On a five-minute step test, her heart rate did not exceed 110 beats per minute. She had rapid heart rate recovery, and had a resting heart rate of 55 beats per minute.

Case 6. Betsy was a twenty-one-year-old female who had been married for about eight months when she presented for treatment. She had been bingeing and vomiting for four years and wanted to try to stop before her husband found out. As a part of her treatment program, Betsy was encouraged to begin to exercise on a regular basis as a way to help manage her energy balance and avoid unwanted weight gain while she was working on gaining control over the bingeing and vomiting. About two months into treatment, Betsy was no longer throwing up, but had started to use exercise as a way to compensate for excessive food intake. Betsy mainly relied on running. She worked part-time and was able to get home around two o'clock in the afternoon. To compensate for bingeing the night before, Betsy would run between six and ten miles.

Case 7. Marny was a twenty-year-old college student who first started vomiting at the age of seventeen. When the vomiting first started, she was very active in school, being one of the varsity cheerleaders. She had also been in gymnastics and other sports since she was a child. Marny reported that she had never really had a problem with binge eating. When she started purging, the vomiting occurred after regular meals. Her family had become concerned with her weight loss during her senior year of high school and began to force her to eat a well-balanced supper with the family. Eating these meals aroused fear of weight gain, and Marny would compensate by throwing up. Over the three-year period before seeking treatment, Marny would vomit only when she was living at home with her parents or at stressful times while away at college. Marny was also an excessive exerciser engaging in daily exercise lasting anywhere from one to four hours and usually involving multiple activities.

SUMMARY

We have reviewed four strategies that are used by bulimics to purge, to compensate for the effects of excessive food intake due to bingeing. Purging methods actually function on two levels, physical and psychological. At the physical level, purging acts to restore energy balance by preventing absorption of calories or by burning extra calories. At the psychological level, purging reduces anxieties about gaining weight and creates the feelings of being thin. Some of the feelings of thinness are a by-product of the dehydration and electrolyte imbalances created by the various methods of purging. The problem with dehydration is that body water is rapidly replenished, and the feelings of fatness and bloatedness quickly return, possibly setting the stage for another eating binge. In fact, repeated use of laxatives and diuretics create a cycle in which stopping use of the drugs leads to edema, which is perceived as feeling fat and which can only be relieved by further abuse of the drugs.

Voluntary regurgitation of the stomach's contents can be a very effective way to eliminate calories and prevent their absorption. It is immediately effective, which quickly helps reduce anxiety. The feeling of fullness is eliminated, and the individual has the immediate perception of being thinner. Laxatives are a relatively ineffective way of preventing the absorption of calories. However, an overdose of laxatives, which usually cause diarrhea, can lead to temporary dehydration and the psychological perception of thinness. In addition, the individual may believe that she is preventing the digestion of her food by overdosing on laxatives, which may psychologically relieve much of her anxiety. Diuretics have no effect on energy metabolism. They cause loss of body water and eliminate feelings of bloatedness that the bulimic interprets as being fat. However, eventually the body water will be restored and the individual will feel fat again. Fasting and restrictive dieting are often used as ways to cope with eating binges. Physiologically, food restriction is a very effective way to restore energy balance. Food restriction, especially after a period of gross overeating, will cause rapid weight loss due to a loss of body water. This occurs as the body excretes the excess sodium consumed during the eating binges and as a natural response to a rapid reduction in carbohydrate intake. The problem with fasting and dieting is that most individuals cannot maintain very low calorie intakes in the face of the biological and cognitive pressure to eat that starvation produces. While exercise is important to health, excessive exercise can be used as a method of purging. Increased activity does burn off the excess calories consumed during an eating binge. However, the amount of exercise needed to burn off the calories of a moderate-sized eating binge is enormous. The use of exercise as the only compensating strategy will necessitate spending several hours each day working out. Exercise, however, does have some beneficial psychological effects as well. It tends to increase muscle tone and decrease body fat percentage, helping the individual feel that she looks better. A long bout of exercise, especially in hot weather, will cause dehydration, which may be experienced psychologically as feeling thin. Thus, the perceived effect of exercise on feelings of fatness may be greater than its actual effect on energy balance.

Table 5.6 presents a summary of the estimated rates of various purging behaviors in bulimic patient samples. Vomiting is by far the most frequently used purging strategy, being used by over 80 percent of bulimic patients. Exercise is probably the next most common behavior, being employed by an estimated 64 percent. Laxatives are abused by about half of the bulimic individuals while 25 percent abuse diuretics.

While we have been able to estimate roughly the prevalence of purging behaviors in groups of bulimic patients from the available literature, we have not been able to estimate the prevalence of combinations of purging behaviors. For example, what percentage of the patients with bulimia vomit *and* use laxatives? What percent of the laxative abusers also use diuretics? Who are the exercisers? Does the group that exercises overlap with the group that uses other purging strategies? Are there many individuals who are diagnosed as bulimic (DSM-III) who do not use any purging strategy at all? While there is much we do not know about the core behaviors of bulimia, we do know that we are justified in considering the various forms of purging as central to the behavioral manifestations of bulimia.

TABLE 5.6 Rates of Purging Behaviors in Bulimic Patient Samples

Vomiting	81%
Laxatives	52%
Diuretics	25%
Exercise	64%

6

Biogenetic Theories of Anorexia and Bulimia Nervosa

AS WE POINTED OUT in Chapter 1, there is a great deal of overlap in the symptoms of anorexia and bulimia nervosa. The clinical profiles of both disorders can include a drive for thinness, body-image disturbance, aberrant eating habits, and purging. The most discriminating feature is the lower body weight typically found in anorexia. Against the background of these clinical similarities, current conceptualizations of these twin eating disorders are also similar as they attempt to explain the origin, development, and maintaining variables. In both cases, theories of etiology run the gamut of physiological, psychological, and sociocultural perspectives. In spite of these similarities, there are several unique conceptualizations of anorexia and bulimia nervosa.

Before we discuss the etiology of eating disorders, a note of caution is in order. Anorexia and bulimia nervosa have been viewed from physiological, psychological, and sociocultural perspectives and their various combinations. The variables or factors influencing the development of an eating disorder may not contribute to maintaining it. Similarly, variables maintaining a particular disorder may have had little or no role in its origin or development. As we shall soon see, several theories have proposed biological variables as playing various initiating and maintaining roles. As an additional caution, most of the available research indicates that no one, two, or even three variables are necessary or sufficient for development of anorexia or bulimia nervosa. Rather, both disorders appear to represent final common pathways that are entered from any number of multiple, interacting biological, psychological, and sociocultural sources.

THE CLINICAL COURSE OF ANOREXIA NERVOSA

Prior to our discussion of etiology, it will prove helpful to describe briefly the clinical course of anorexia nervosa in order to sequence our discussion of etiology. This description will aid the differentiation of initiating and maintaining variables.

While there are exceptions, most clinical investigators agree that anorexia nervosa begins with some form of psychological distress that increases vulnerability. Against this background of increased susceptibility, efforts are made to control eating behavior in order to lose weight. Dieting efforts are mostly successful for younger women with the classical restricting anorexic being able to pursue relentlessly a lower body weight through strict adherence to a semistarvation diet. As we noted in Chapter 2, semistarvation diets and the resulting weight loss are associated with important and ofttimes dramatic physiological and psychological changes, such as those evident in the volunteers of Keys, Brozek, Henschel, Mickelsen, and Taylor (1950) and Fitcher, Pirke, and Holsber (1986). For females these changes include disruptions of hormone and neuroendocrine mechanisms in a variety of physiological subsystems including the hypothalamic-pituitary-adrenal (HPA) axes. These axes refer to feedback loops in which stimulating, releasing, and circulating hormones are reciprocally related. For example, production of luteinizing hormone is in part related to luteinizing releasing hormone (LHRN). However, increased levels of luteinizing hormone result in lower LHRN levels.

Psychological changes associated with the lower body weight include irritability; depression; preoccupation with body shape, weight, and food; resistance and denial; and social isolation and withdrawal. Furthermore, it is not unusual for family members and close friends to attempt to assist or otherwise aid these individuals to gain weight. These efforts are often perceived by the young dieter as intrusive and designed to make her fat. There is some degree of uncertainty over the nature of the initial psychological vulnerability and whether the social deficits emerging in the latter stages of anorexia nervosa are present at the onset.

PHYSIOLOGICAL THEORIES OF ANOREXIA NERVOSA

Not surprisingly, the focus of physiological theories of anorexia nervosa has centered on the role of the hypothalamus and its relationship to the pituitary, thyroid, adrenal, and reproductive glands. More recently, an auto-addictive model of anorexia has been proposed that is based on the role of neuropeptides in eating behavior. Also, there is renewed interest in the possibility of a genetic predisposition in the development of anorexia nervosa. While investigations of the physiological influences on anorexia nervosa are being pursued aggressively, these studies are severely hampered by the degree of starvation and inanition of these young women. As we noted in Chapter 2, severe dietary restriction produces major alterations in metabolism and neuroendocrine function, and makes the differentiation of antecedent from consequent variables very difficult.

Hypothalamic Theories

The Role of the Ventral-Medial Hypothalamus

Leibowitz (1983) proposed that anorexia nervosa symptoms may be related to deviations in the hypothalamic control of eating including the associated catecholamines and neuropeptides. While recognizing that many anorexia nervosa symptoms develop as a consequence of starvation, Leibowitz points out that these same symptoms may also be produced by hypothalamic dysfunction. To support her argument, Leibowitz focused on the alternation of fasting and bingeing typical of many anorexics and considered this behavior in light of animal research. Specifically, Leibowitz notes that a decrease in medial hypothalamic norepinephrine activation produces a sequence of behavior similar to that seen in anorexia. These changes include a reduction in carbohydrate intake, loss of body weight, decreased rate of eating, increased fluid intake, decreased insulin responsiveness, increased activity, and a tendency to rebound with overeating. Research supporting her contention that decreased norepinephrine activity in the medial hypothalamus underlies anorexia is presented. Leibowitz is well aware of the heuristic nature of her proposal and the notion that at the human level, anorexia nervosa is a complex disorder influenced by a variety of variables.

The Role of the Lateral Hypothalamus

Keesey and Corbett (1984) discussed animal research on the hypothalamic control of eating and its relevance to the etiology of anorexia nervosa. Whereas Leibowitz focused on the medial and paraventricular hypothalamic areas, Keesey and Corbett reviewed research on the lateral hypothalamic (LH) syndrome. In this LH preparation, lesions in the medial zone of the LH produce aphagia and lower body weights. Moreover, long after recovery and the opportunity for refeeding, these lesioned animals still display aphagia and weight loss. Interestingly, the animals maintain a near constant percentage body weight below normal that is proportional to the extent of this LH lesion. Furthermore, this body weight is defended against a variety of challenges much like anorexic women fervently cling to a particular body weight.

The results of these LH experiments are interpreted by Keesey and his colleagues as lowering the set point for body weight. Specifically, Keesey notes how a particular body weight is defended against force-feeding, food restriction, and palatable diets among others. The experiments on force-feeding dramatically illustrate this defense of a lower body weight. LH lesioned animals that are force-fed until their weight approximates that of nonlesioned animals will again become aphagic and lose weight to their previous, postlesion level at the end of the force-feeding regimen. Also, LH-lesioned animals whose food is restricted lose weight, yet regain weight to their postlesion level following ad lib feeding. Also, a wide variety of diets varying in palatability and caloric density have little or no effect on the maintenance of body weight loss in LH-lesioned animals. The lower body weight of LH-lesioned animals results initially from an increase in heat production involving the beta-adrenergic system. Much like Leibowitz, Keesey recognizes that research on LH-lesioned animals has not been directly compared to studies of human anorexia. But, as he notes, neither have studies been done that suggest such comparisons are not possible.

The Role of Hypothalamic Changes in Anorexia

Wakeling (1985) reviews hypothalamic changes in anorexia with particular emphasis on the adrenal, gonadal, and thyroid axes. He notes that the physiological changes seen in anorexia nervosa and other eating disorders are not specific. They also occur in starvation and these changes in physiological function revert to normal following refeeding or weight gain.

According to Wakeling, changes in the hypothalamic axes (HPA, HPO, and HPT) and the neuroendocrine system play a role in maintaining anorexia. Yet the fact that some changes are present prior to the development of anorexia nervosa and others may persist after weight restoration leaves open the possibility of a role for disturbed physiology at onset. For example, there is evidence that a small proportion, perhaps on the order of 10 percent, of anorexics have a primary amenorrhea prior to significant weight loss rather than secondary to the eating disorder.

Developmentally, menses typically begins when a body fat-to-lean ratio of approximately 17 percent is reached. Although there is considerable variability, a certain proportion of body fat or nutritional intake is necessary for the onset as well as the regular maintenance of menses. Additionally, amenorrhea is common in athletes, such as runners, swimmers, and gymnasts who are active in endurance events or who otherwise require low body fat for high levels of performance.

A stress-induced primary amenorrhea with associated HPO changes can occur subsequent to difficulties in coping with family, peer, and personal problem situations (Weiner, 1983). It may well be that this stress-induced amenorrhea preceding the onset of anorexia has a basis in deficient problem-solving and coping competencies. Studies reporting primary amenorrhea in anorexia, however, suffer methodological problems including inaccurate reports of menarche, the presence of aberrant dietary practices, and the possibility of purging prior to the development of the low body weight. Also, approximately half of the anorexics with amenorrhea resume menstruation during the process of weight restoration due to improved nutrition and the accumulation of body fat stores.

Other changes in the HPO axis include a decrease in the reproductive hormones, luteinizing hormone (LH), and follicle-stimulating hormone (FSH) as well as a blunted response of luteinizing hormone to its releasing hormone (LHRH). These and other changes in the HPO axis resemble a return to the prepubertal state and most occur as a result of poor nutrition and low body weight. Further, a variety of challenges to the HPO axis indicates no fundamental hypothalamic dysfunction and most hormone levels return to normal with weight restoration or improved nutrition (Garfinkel & Garner, 1982).

Changes in the HPT axis include low free triiodothyronine (T3) and low to normal thyroxine (T4) levels. Similarly, disruptions of the HPA axes include low cortisol. These changes are a result of the low body weight and poor nutrition and can only be viewed as adaptive and secondary to caloric restriction and weight loss in anorexia nervosa (Doer, Fichter, Pirke, & Lund, 1980; Gold et al., 1986). Thus, the malnourished state seen in anorexia nervosa is largely responsible for the physiological changes observed in hypothalamic axes, and these changes are thought to play an as yet unidentified role in the maintenance of lower body weight.

One possible indicator of abnormal neuroendocrine or hypothalamic function is growth rate, and there is some evidence to suggest that anorexics mature early. For example, Crisp (1970) found that anorexic patients had an earlier onset of menses as well as higher growth rates in childhood. Similarly, Nielsen (1985) studied approximately eighty anorexics and was able to obtain data on height and weight at least two years prior to the onset of the eating disorder. In comparison to a reference population, females displayed a slight trend toward overweight prior to the onset of anorexia with a weight-by-height ratio being significantly higher than expected. Also, male anorexics were taller and heavier for their age with some indication of premorbid obesity. Whether this precocious physical development is related to unique neuroendocrine mechanisms controlling feeding is open to question. Regardless, these data suggest early maturation and perhaps a heavier weight in comparison to peers contribute to the development of anorexia nervosa.

Anorexia and experimental starvation produce similar neuroendocrine profiles, yet hyperactivity and body-image disturbance are unique to anorexia. As Casper (1984) indicates, starvation is typically characterized by hypoactivity as a function of attempts to conserve energy. Moreover, individuals who are malnourished or starving are well aware of their emaciated state, and thus do not appear to entertain a body-image disturbance in terms of their current condition or their ideal. Casper suggests that the extreme caloric restriction, nutrient deprivation, and the resulting lower body weight all combine to induce central nervous system changes that in turn yield hyperactivity and the body-image disturbance. Moreover, within the sociocultural context with its emphasis on thinness, these symptoms serve to drive and reinforce further attempts at weight loss. The continued drive for thinness can be appreciated at a physiological level in terms of both the auto-addictive model and the proposal by Casper of subtle and perhaps unidentified central nervous system changes.

Auto-Addictive Model of Anorexia Nervosa

As discussed in Chapter 2, endogenous opioids, primarily beta-endorphin, influence eating behavior. Investigators in this area (Morley, Levine, Gosnell, & Billington, 1984a) note considerable variation among species regarding the control opioids exercise on eating. However, the data suggest that this system is operative in human feeding, and changes in the opioid system may represent the ill-defined hypothalamic and neuroendocrine alterations alluded to by Wakeling and Casper.

Using this data base, Marrazzi and Luby (1986) propose that endogenous opioids are the driving force in anorexia nervosa. Specifically, they suggest that psychological explanations appear sufficient to account for the development of dieting and exercise behaviors that instigate a lower body weight. However, the relentless pursuit of dieting in the face of overwhelming physiological, familial, and social negative consequences ultimately points to an auto-addictive process mediated by endogenous opioids. They suggest that the opioid system is the physiologic substrate for this auto-addictive process and that it is responsible for the maintenance of anorexic behavior.

Clinical observations of the phenomenological experiences of anorexics illustrate their drive for a lower body weight, resistance to eating, and the failure to explain rationally these consequences in otherwise bright young women. It is a common observation that eating disordered patients have not given much thought to the overall consequences of a lower body weight. They are uniformly caught up in the process of weight loss and fantasize that a low weight is the answer to their problems. It is rare for these patients to appreciate fully the many adverse consequences of a low body weight. Additional indirect evidence for an addictive process in anorexia is suggested by the fact that a wide variety of psychological interventions and drug treatments have not led to any change in recovery rates. Also, there is an increased resistance to treatment as a function of chronicity and duration of the disorder. It is precisely this chronicity in the face of negative social and personal consequences and the resistance to treatment where psychological explanations do not suffice. So, while the initial drive for a lower body weight may have a psychological origin, the continuing relentless pursuit of low body weight may be grounded in pathophysiology.

Marrazzi and Luby propose that increased endogenous opioids during starvation serve to increase food intake as well as down-regulate physiological and metabolic processes in an adaptation for starvation. The increased levels of endogenous opioids reinforce anorexic behavior perhaps by contributing to an analgesic euphoria. This reinforcement mechanism may underlie anorexics' resistance to treatment and the denial of their weight and eating difficulties.

The essence of Marrazzi and Luby's position is a feedback mechanism in which increased opioids during starvation served to reinforce the continuation of severe, restrictive dietary practices and the drive for a lower body weight. As the lower body weight persists, metabolic, behavioral, and psychological processes become organized to defend it. Thus, anorexics appear to become psychologically and physically dependent on the mood and energy levels mediated by endogenous opioids. As repeatedly mentioned by other investigators, there is no real loss of appetite in anorexia, merely an effective suppression that is perhaps aided by the analgesic properties of the endogenous opioids. Also many anorexics may succumb to the cravings for food due to the appetite stimulating properties of opioids that may underlie the occasional bingeing observed in anorexia nervosa.

Marrazzi and Luby also noted that physical exercise stimulates endorphin levels, and so, exercise may add an additional, complementary component to the opioid addiction process. The auto-addictive model of anorexia nervosa has considerable intuitive appeal. However, the data supporting this model is not currently available.

Family Resemblance

Several studies have explored the occurrence of eating disorders and other psychiatric diagnoses in the relatives of patients with eating disorders. The data on family resemblance are then compared with the occurrence of similar diagnoses in control groups. For example, Gershon et al. (1984) studied eating disorders in the relatives of patients with anorexia nervosa. They found that anorexia nervosa and bulimia nervosa were present in 1 percent of the relatives of medically ill controls. In contrast, eating disorder diagnoses were present in approximately 6 percent of the relatives of anorexic patients.

Strober, Morrell, Burroughs, Salkin, and Jacobs (1985) studied first- and second-degree relatives of sixty patients with anorexia and compared them to the relatives of ninety-five patients with psychotic diagnoses. The prevalence of eating disorders was 27 percent in relatives of patients with anorexia and 6 percent in relatives of psychotic patients. Specific significant differences were obtained between the anorexic and control patients for the percentage of anorexia in sisters (11.45 percent versus 1.8 percent), mothers and sisters combined (10 percent versus 1.4 percent), and aunts (9.5 percent versus 2.4 percent). The pattern of family resemblance in these data is striking and restricted to females. Questions remain about what and how characteristics are transmitted as well as the gender-specific nature of the transmission.

The Genetics of Anorexia Nervosa

Given the positive findings from family resemblance studies, it appears that anorexia is more frequent in families in which other individuals suffer from an eating disorder. It is not unusual then to suspect that genetic endowment, early learning, life experiences, and family atmosphere are involved in the development of eating disorders. In recent years, there has been a noticeable increase in investigation on the genetic basis of a variety of behaviors ranging from social shyness to the extreme psychopathology seen in schizophrenia. Regarding eating disorders, the influence of the environment is robust and omnipresent with its emphasis on thinness as a cultural ideal. However, because they may be less obvious, genetic influences and their potential impact on the hypothalamus and neuroendocrine system should not be denied.

In an extensive review of studies on the heritability of anorexia, Scott (1986) concluded that the evidence supports a significant genetic contribution. He notes that a major methodological shortcoming of this research is the determination of zygosity in identical twins studies. To correct for the weakness, he classified studies into three classes: (1) cases with loose criteria for zygosity, (2) substantiated cases, and (3) cases utilizing more explicit biological or chromosomal markers for zygosity. In the thirty-seven studies using loose criteria for monozygosity (MZ), 40 percent of the cases were concordant for anorexia. Of sixteen pairs utilizing stricter criteria, seven of sixteen or 44 percent were concordant for anorexia. A similar 50 percent level of concordance was found in six reports utilizing chromosomal markers of zygosity. The concordance levels are similar in spite of the criteria for determining zygosity.

A major problem with studies on the heritability of anorexia nervosa has been the small sample size and the almost exclusive reliance on MZ twins. In an attempt to address these issues, Holland, Hall, Murray,

Russell, and Crisp (1984) studied thirty-four pairs of twins and one set of triplets where the proband was diagnosed with anorexia. This particular study was a collaborative project between two hospitals in England, and the investigators utilized standard criteria to diagnose anorexia nervosa and to determine zygosity. Holland et al. determined concordance for anorexia if both twins had an episode that met the criteria for anorexia nervosa for at least three months' duration. Also, these diagnoses were categorized as severe or mild. Diagnostic criteria utilized in this study included a fear of overweight and a pursuit of thinness, weight loss induced by caloric restriction, purging via self-induced vomiting, laxative abuse, and amenorrhea. Information used to evaluate the patients was obtained in semistructured interviews with the twin and the parents, and this information was evaluated over the diagnostic criteria.

Of the thirty female twin pairs, sixteen were monozygotic (MZ) with nine (55 percent) being concordant for anorexia. Of the fourteen dizygotic (DZ) female twins, one (7 percent) was concordant and thirteen, discordant. These data yielded highly significant relationships between zygosity and anorexia with concordance rates for probands of .66 for MZ and .25 for DZ pairs. None of the three male/female DZ pairs, nor the male MZ triplets were concordant for anorexia nervosa.

Holland et al. concluded that the data rather convincingly point to a genetic predisposition for anorexia that becomes manifest under conditions of dieting or emotional stress. The nature of this predisposition or genetic vulnerability may be in the form of a personality type, psychiatric illness, a body-image disturbance, or perhaps even a hypothalamic dysfunction.

While these data are impressive in terms of the concordance rates observed and the differences between MZ and DZ twins, they also suffer from methodological difficulties that preclude strong, unequivocal conclusions, that is, the presence of a shared environment and the possibility that the family may have treated the MZ twins more similarly than the DZ twins. More convincing data would emerge from studies that explored MZ and DZ twins raised in the same versus different environments with a proband for anorexia.

PHYSIOLOGICAL THEORIES OF BULIMIA NERVOSA

The physiological theories of bulimia nervosa have taken three major directions, namely, a view of bulimia nervosa as a seizure disorder, a focus on the role of neurotransmitters in perpetuating the binge/purge cycle, and consideration of bulimia nervosa as a variant of a major affective disorder. Before reviewing these theories, the clinical course of the disorder will be described.

The Clinical Course of Bulimia Nervosa

Like anorexia nervosa, bulimia nervosa has a clinical course that can be quite varied. Although some discrepancies in the data exist, women with bulimia nervosa appear to be older than those with anorexia nervosa, and it is not unusual for those with bulimia to have had a prior history of anorexia.

In contrast to the restricting anorexic, data on the onset and frequency of bulimia obtained in surveys may be more precise due to the directly observable and discrete nature of bulimic behavior (bingeing and purging). Severe dieting is difficult to distinguish from normal adolescent behavior, and it may not attract attention until weight loss becomes noticeable. In contrast, the onset of bulimia is more definitive given the nature of binge eating and purging via self-induced vomiting, laxative use, and excessive exercise. Most women when granted anonymity can clearly date the onset of bingeing and purging in contrast to when they began dieting.

On the basis of anecdotal clinical reports and survey data, it appears that bulimia nervosa begins with dieting, perhaps against a background of vulnerability not unlike that ascribed to anorexia. Because dieting does not achieve its intended results in terms of the expected weight loss, food restriction becomes more severe and approaches semistarvation levels. This reduction in caloric intake results in further energy and nutrient depletion which, as we noted in Chapter 2, increases the probability of overeating and eventually bingeing. Eating and even bingeing are reinforcing but quickly lose their appeal as the individual becomes aware of sensations of bloatedness, which give rise to fear of weight gain. Sometime thereafter, purging, primarily in the form of self-induced vomiting, develops to reduce the fear of weight gain. According to the available data (Fairburn & Cooper, 1982), a pattern of erratic eating in which there is an alternation between severe caloric restriction and binge eating may persist for six to nine months prior to the onset of purging.

Purging may be crucial for the continuation of bulimia, as it enables increased binge eating. That is, young women will binge less frequently and consume less food if there is no opportunity to purge. The association between bingeing and purging then becomes quite strong, and this relationship is the focus of psychosocial theories of bulimia nervosa (see Chapter 7).

As we noted in our discussion of anorexia, some theories concentrate on the initiation and development of bulimia nervosa while others are organized around the maintenance of the eating disorder. Additionally, with an increased duration, the binge/purge cycle becomes associated with a variety of antecedents and consequence stimuli—external environmental and internal cognitive and physiological. The binge/purge cycle is precipitated by antecedents, such as being alone at home, the presence of negative moods, and energy-nutrient depletion among others. The psychological and physiological consequences of the disorder are positive and maintaining. While negative consequences are also evident, they appear to decrease binge/purge cycles only temporarily and may actually increase binge/purge episodes due to their arousing ability. These negative consequences include a disruption in family life, vocational/occupational instability, poor academic performance, low self-esteem, and depression.

Bulimia Nervosa as a Seizure Disorder

The phenomenological experience during the binge/purge cycle is often described as a confused depersonalized state with many bulimics reporting an incomplete awareness of what they are doing. On the basis of such clinical reports, Green and Rau (1974) proposed that patients with bulimia have abnormal electroencephalogram (EEG) patterns that resemble those of epileptic seizures. Furthermore, they hypothesized that these abnormal EEGs reflect either a localized hypothalamic dysfunction of the satiety center or a generalized dysfunction that may increase the state of arousal, and thereby cloud consciousness. In a preliminary study, Green and Rau found that phenytoin (dilantin) restored eating to normal in nine of ten patients.

Subsequent studies investigating the relationship of EEG, bulimia, and response to phenytoin, however, have not been as positive as Green and Rau's initial report. For example, the study of abnormal EEGs and bulimia nervosa have found that many patients do not display abnormal EEG patterns, and, of those who do, the EEG patterns are not similar or uniform (Lacey, 1982). Also, in a controlled evaluation of phenytoin, Wermuth, Davis, Hollister, and Stunkard (1977) compared the drug with a placebo in a six-week double-blind, randomized crossover design. The results of this trial were largely equivocal in terms of the effectiveness of phenytoin on binge eating. Patients in the drug-to-placebo condition showed an initial decrease in binge eating compared to estimates of their binge eating prior to treatment. Yet, when these patients were switched from the active drug (phenytoin) to the placebo, there was no increase in the frequency of binge eating. Patients in the placebo-to-drug condition displayed a significant decrease in bingeing when switched to phenytoin.

The failure to observe an increase in bingeing when switched from drug-to-placebo limits any definitive conclusions about the relationship between the drug action and the reduction in bingeing. Additionally, the investigators found no relationship between the response to phenytoin and EEG status. That is, patients with and without EEG abnormalities displayed the same degree of improvement in their bingeing. To summarize, the results of this controlled evaluation merely showed that patients on an active medication decreased bingeing, and that no relationship existed between improvement in bingeing and EEG status. Thus, any phenytoin effect was not related to abnormal EEG pattern.

It appears likely that the positive results obtained in this study may be due to the ability of the patients to discriminate the physiological side-effects of the medication. That is, the patients could tell when they were on active medication as opposed to the placebo. This knowledge may have accentuated their "placebo" response.

The Physiological Consequences of Dieting

The onset of eating disorders, and bingeing in particular, is related to dieting. In epidemiological surveys of eating-disordered women, dieting looms as one of the most significant antecedents in the development of their eating problems. In this section, we shall consider the influence of dieting on selected physiological parameters with respect to their potential role in the development of bulimia nervosa.

The research by Keys et al. (1950) and Fitcher et al. (1986) documented the cognitive, behavioral, and physiological effects of semistarvation. The physiological adaptations as a result of restrictive dieting are accentuated by purging and together with the cognitive disinhibition created by bingeing create a cascading sequence of events that strongly reinforce repeated binge/purge episodes (Johnson & Jarrell, 1988; Polivy & Herman, 1985).

One of the major consequences of dieting is a reduction in RMR (Hill, Sparling, Shields, & Heller, 1987). Most diets provide from 800 to 1,200 kcal and often represent drastic reductions from predieting intake levels. However, Hill et al. (1988) recently failed to find any reduction in resting metabolic rate beyond that accounted for by reductions in lean body mass. They studied a group of forty obese women who decreased their caloric intakes from 2,009 kcal/day at baseline to a mean of 1,178 kcal/day during the twelve-week weight loss program. The diet used in this study, however, was composed of 55 percent carbohydrate, 20 percent fat, and 25 percent protein, which is different from the high-protein/low-carbohydrate diets used in studies showing significant RMR reductions (Hill et al., 1987). RMR reductions do occur but the degree of the reduction and how it is affected by the fat-lean body mass ratio and dietary composition is unknown. What is obvious is the failure of repeated dieting to yield the desired weight loss, the tendency to increase the fat-lean body mass ratio with repeated dieting, and the weight cycling of repeated dieting. The results of an animal study on weight cycling provide an interesting analogue to the dieting effects of bulimics. Lab animals exposed to a series of weight gains by high-fat feeding and weight losses by food restriction over repeated cycles display a more efficient energy utilization. It took twice as long to lose the same amount of weight the second time as it did the first. Also, the weight gain occurred three times faster in the second cycle as compared to the first. These weight-cycled animals had high percentages of body fat and a greater number of fat cells than comparable controls while maintaining similar weights on significantly fewer calories (Brownell, Greenward, Stellar, & Shrager, 1986).

Regardless, an overall effect of caloric reduction observed in bulimia is the induction of a state of chronic hunger that is poorly tolerated and increases the probability of eating unplanned meals or forbidden foods. Once dietary restrictions have been broken, counter-regulation can occur resulting in an eating binge (Polivy & Herman, 1985).

Another major influence of dieting and severe caloric restriction is the accentuation of hormone responses to the sight, thought, or smell of food (W.G. Johnson & Wildman, 1980; Klanjer, Herman, Polivy, & Chhabra, 1981). These hormonal responses (e.g., insulin) appear to exert strong pressures to eat.

Yet another physiological consequence of dieting is the restricted carbohydrate composition of most diets. Compared to proteins and fats, carbohydrates constitute a greater proportion of nutritional intake. Unfortunately, most popular diets advocate reductions in carbohydrates because they yield faster weight loss. Unbeknownst to most dieters, the weight loss is predominantly a result of diuresis secondary to the restriction of carbohydrate intake. Many individuals believe that carbohydrates are fat producing, and so they often specifically target carbohydrate reductions. The research of Wurtman and colleagues (Wurtman & Wurtman, 1982) indicates that carbohydrate restriction leads to subsequent carbohydrate intake and even craving. Thus, when dieters consume meals low in carbohydrates relative to proteins, they reduce their brain levels of tryptophan, an amino acid precursor to serotonin. Lowered serotonin levels instigate a preference for the consumption of carbohydrates in later meals. The end result of dieting with decreased consumption of carbohydrates is the stimulation of subsequent carbohydrate intake. When weight loss plateaus in several weeks after diuresis and possibly decreased RMR, violations of the diet by partaking of the forbidden carbohydrates typically results in termination of the diet. It should be noted that most of these carbohydrate foods typically contain high levels of dietary fat as well (e.g., potato chips, doughnuts).

Substance Abuse Models of Bulimia Nervosa

Support for the substance abuse model of bulimia derives from the role of endogenous opiates on eating, similarities in the clinical experience of patients with bulimia nervosa and substance abuse disorders, and the efficacy of opioid antagonists to decrease eating. Hardy and Waller (1988) review the many parallels between bulimia nervosa and substance abuse disorders. They note the many similarities in the diagnostic criteria of the disorders, the cravings for food and the abused substance, the euphoric experiences associated with eating and substance abuse, and the developmental progression of bulimia and substance abuse disorders. Lastly, they note how both bulimic and substance abuse disorders may be mediated by endogenous opioids.

It is clear that endogenous opioids are involved in the regulation of food intake. Elevated levels of endorphins are found in obese animals, and endorphin injections in the hypothalamus instigate eating. It appears that endogenous opiates are activated by both starvation and the incentive-reward value of highly palatable food (Dum, Gramsch, & Herz, 1983).

In a human study, Waller et al. (1986) compared thirty-four bulimic women with thirty-four controls on a measure of anorexic attitudes (Eating Attitudes Test) and beta-endorphin levels. The bulimic women scored more pathological on the EAT and had significantly lower beta-endorphin levels. Within the bulimia group, there was a significant inverse relationship between beta-endorphin levels and severity of the eating disorder as measured by the EAT, suggesting that the greater the severity of bulimia, the lower the beta-endorphin level. These authors suggest that these low levels of endorphins may provide the stimulation for food cravings.

Fullerton, Swift, Getto, and Carlson (1986) also pursued the role of endorphins in bulimia. They suggested that binge eating is a function of the release of endogenous opiates, which occurs as a result of eating under stressful conditions. Increased opiate levels enhance their sensitivity in the brain and augment the reward value of food. The authors observed increased levels of endorphins in bulimics when compared to normals in multiple samplings. More recently, these researchers studied endorphin levels in vomiting and nonvomiting bulimics and observed increased levels in the vomiting group. This difference could be related to either the increased caloric intake or vomiting in this subsample of bulimics (Fullerton, Swift, Getto, Carlson, & Gutzmann, 1988).

The data regarding opioid antagonists have been positive, although weak. Several studies (Jonas & Gold, 1986, 1987; Mitchell, Laine, Morely, & Levine, 1986) suggest that naltrexone can reduce bingeing and purging. For example, Jonas and Gold (1987) observed 75 percent to 100 percent reductions in bingeing and purging for nine of thirteen bulimics in an open trial. In the Mitchell et al. study, naltrexone was compared to cholecystokinin (CCK), a gut hormone strongly associated with satiety in animal studies. Naltrexone, but not CCK, reduced binge eating. Together, these studies indicate that opioid antagonists decreased food intake and bingeing and, by implication, indirectly support the role of endorphins in the development and maintenance of bulimia.

Bulimia and Major Affective Disorders

The most controversial issue in the literature on eating disorders is the hypothesis that bulimia nervosa is a variation of major affective disorders in general and depression in particular. Evidence from four areas of research are offered to support this proposition (Hudson, Pope, & Jonas, 1984b).

Clinical Symptomatology
According to Hudson et al. there is considerable overlap in the symptoms of bulimia nervosa and affective disorder. To study the association between bulimia and depression, Hudson et al. administered a semistructured interview to seventy-four patients with bulimia nervosa. From this group, 89 percent had a concomitant diagnosis of affective disorder with many being major depression and dysthymic disorders. Additionally, 34 percent satisfied the diagnosis for substance abuse disorder, 50 percent anxiety disorders, 34 percent had disorders of impulse control, and 15 percent were diagnosed with a personality disorder, primarily borderline type.

Given the association between bulimia and depression, the overlap in symptom sets is also remarkable and particularly evident for depression. Depression is a symptom that is pervasive and commonly observed in most diagnostic categories including psychotic, neurotic, and personality disorders. Thus, individuals with these diagnoses could also receive the concomitant diagnosis of depression much like that proposed by Hudson et al. for bulimia.

While not denying the extent of depression in bulimia nervosa, the nature and degree of the symptom set is decidedly different from that seen in the depressive diagnosis. For example, Cooper and Fairburn (1986) investigated the symptoms of depression in thirty-five patients with bulimia nervosa and forty-four with depression. The evaluation consisted of various tests and a semistructured interview. The results revealed similarities between the two groups but also important differences regarding the nature of depressive symptoms. Those with bulimia were significantly lower than the pure depressives on sadness and suicidal thoughts and plans. Patients with bulimia nervosa were also more likely to be anxious, and the depressive symptoms they displayed were more specific to their eating problems.

Also, the experience of guilt in bulimia nervosa was related to eating forbidden foods and feeling out of control while eating (Cooper & Fairburn, 1986). A discriminant analysis yielded a bimodal distribution in which obsessional ideas and ruminations were present in 80 percent of the patients with bulimia nervosa and in only 2.5 percent of the depressives. A second analysis based on ten variables correctly classified over 90 percent of the cases in their respective diagnostic group. Five percent of the depressed patients were misclassified in the bulimia group, and 14 percent of the patients with bulimia nervosa were incorrectly classified as depressive. These data run counter to the notion that the experience of depression in bulimia is similar to that in major affective disorders. Also, they suggest that the depression observed in bulimia nervosa is focused specifically on eating and its problems rather than being more generalized.

The diverse nature of depressive symptoms in bulimia nervosa are also evident in a study by Swift, Kalin, Wambolt, Kaslow, and Ritholz (1984) who followed thirty-one patients with bulimia for two to four years following their inpatient treatment. The patients were administered standard measures of depression as well as a semistructured interview. Twenty-six of the thirty patients continued to meet the criteria for bulimia (DSM-III), yet the intensity of the bulimic symptoms was reduced markedly over the period. There was an 84 percent reduction in episodes of bingeing and an approximately 75 percent reduction in self-induced vomiting. Interestingly, depression was quite low with 95 percent of the patients indicating no or only mild levels of depression. Moreover, measures of bulimic behavior at follow-up were significantly correlated with depression, being .56 for bingeing and .35 for vomiting. Also, the greater the degree of clinical improvement over time, the lower the depression score. These data are consistent with those of Cooper and Fairburn in suggesting that the depression experienced by bulimics is secondary rather than primary to the eating disorder.

Given the proposal of a common etiology for bulimia and depression as suggested by Hudson et al., the expectation would be that young females presenting for treatment with depression would also evidence an increased number of eating disorders. However, as Strober and Katz (1987) note, the data suggests otherwise. The incidence rates for anorexia nervosa and bulimia nervosa are similar to that observed in the general population and not enhanced as the common etiology hypothesis would predict. Moreover, the natural course and history of these disorders are quite diverse and not consistent with a common, underlying etiology. Strober and Katz suggest the patterns of recovery, relapse, and duration of illness among patients with eating and affective disorders are quite different. Full recovery from episodes of depression at six months is evident in approximately two-thirds of the patients with nearly 80 percent having recovered within two years of seeking treatment. In contrast, eating disorders are more resistant to treatment with slightly more than one-third of the patients recovered at six months. Additionally, the incidence of eating disorders and depression differs with rates of 1 percent and 3 percent for anorexia and bulimia nervosa, respectively, which contrasts with the 10 percent rate for depression.

Physiological Tests

Further evidence relating bulimia nervosa to affective disorders is provided in studies using physiological tests of the HPA axis that are presumably linked to depression. The prime tests used in the diagnosis of depression are dexamethasone suppression test (DST) and the thyrotropin response (TSH) to thyrotropin releasing hormone stimulation test (TRH). The DST involves administering one mg of dexamethasone in the evening with cortisol levels taken the following day. Studies indicate that approximately 50 percent of patients with depression fail to suppress cortisol in response to the dexamethasone. Hudson et al. (1984) found that 47 percent of patients with bulimia nervosa failed to show suppression on the DST in contrast to 9 percent in a normal control group. The specificity of DST for depression is a problem since many patients with other diagnoses also are positive on this test.

The TSH test involves measuring TSH in response to TRH administration. Patients with a diagnosis of major affective disorder displayed a blunted TSH response. Hudson et al. reviewed data indicating that the majority of bulimics also show a blunted TSH response to a TRH challenge.

In reviewing the literature in response to DST and TRH tests, Strober and Katz (1987) noted that for anorexia at least, the DST normalizes with improved nutrition in the presence of sustaining core anorexic symptoms, such as striving for thinness and body-image disturbance. The fact that DST test results vary with nutritional status is obvious in data demonstrating a failure to suppress cortisol in noneating-disordered controls who fast (Fichter, Pirke, & Holsber, 1986).

The variability in the DST performance with nutritional status was also evident in a study by Abou-Saleh, Oleesky, and Crisp (1985). In studying fifty patients with anorexia nervosa, compared with a group of controls, these investigators found a strong and highly significant relationship between cortisol and body weight yet no significant relationship between cortisol and measures of depression. Thus, there was a strong relationship between DST nonsuppression and lower body weight indicative of the state of negative energy balance, but no association between DST nonsuppression and depression.

The data on DST abnormalities and symptom remission in eating disorders are contrasted by Strober and Katz with that of recovery from depression. Thus, DST results in eating-disordered patients normalize with improved nutrition while eating problems and body-image disturbances remain. For depression, however, suppression of cortisol is more likely to be congruent with recovery from depression.

Norris, O'Malley, and Palmer (1985) studied the TSH response of both bulimics and anorexics compared to noneating-disordered controls. TSH was measured before and after an injection of 500 mg of TRH. Bulimics did not differ from the healthy controls in their TSH response. Prior to weight gain, the anorexics had a later peak TSH, but no significant differences emerged between them and controls after weight restoration. More recently, Hudson et al. failed to observe nonsuppressed cortisol in the DST in bulimics.

In summary, studies investigating the relationship between bulimia and depression have relied on physiological measures of the HPA and HPT axes. Initial studies with DST and TSH tests indicated a similarity between the responses of bulimic, anorexic, and depressed patients. More recent experiments have demonstrated the sensitivity of these tests to nutritional status, weight, and presumably purging, with many failing to show abnormal values in bulimics.

Family Resemblance Studies

Family resemblance studies represent a third research area relevant to the relationship between bulimia nervosa and depression. To date, most studies on family resemblance have investigated the association between the diagnoses of bulimia nervosa and affective disorders in families. These studies stand in contrast to the more explicitly genetic studies previously discussed for anorexia nervosa.

In a large scale family investigation, Hudson, Pope, Jonas, and Yurgelun-Todd (1983) evaluated 350 first-degree relatives of 75 patients who were diagnosed with bulimia nervosa. The extent of major affective disorders in the relatives of bulimia nervosa patients was compared to the extent of major affective disorders in patients with other diagnoses, such as bipolar and borderline personality disorders. The first-degree relatives in the study were classified as either at risk for major affective disorder or having a definite diagnosis. The results indicated that 28 percent of the relatives of patients with bulimia nervosa were at risk and 53 percent had a definite diagnosis of major affective disorder which did not differ from the relatives of the bipolar patients. Furthermore, the extent of major affective disorders in relatives of schizophrenics was 3 percent and the relatives of those with borderline personality disorders showed a similar low level. These data indicate a significant degree of family resemblance in bulimia nervosa and major affective disorders, yet, these studies remain only suggestive of biological influences.

In a well-controlled study of family resemblance, Strober, Morrell, Burroughs, Salkin, and Jacobs (1985) studied over 600 first-degree relatives of patients with anorexia, depression, bipolar affective disorder, and schizophrenia. Diagnosis of affective disorder and eating disorder were made blindly from interviews with relatives. The results indicated that the rates of eating disorders in relatives of patients with affective disorders and schizophrenia were low, ranging from 0.6 to 1.3 percent, which does not differ from the expectancies in the general population. In contrast, the presence of affective disorders was large in relatives of patients who also had an affective disorder. In summarizing these data, Strober and Katz (1987) note that ". . . the evidence accumulated thus far seems to indicate that anorexia nervosa and primary affective disorders are not genetically related; rather they are transmitted independently in families, although the two disorders do coexist within a subgroup of patients" (p. 176).

Wilson and Lindholm (1987) also studied family resemblance in patients with bulimia nervosa. As these authors note, a critical question is whether depression is antecedent and causally related to bulimia nervosa, simply a correlate and thus coexisting, or perhaps a consequence of the eating disorder. Wilson and Lindholm studied over fifty patients with bulimia nervosa on standard psychological and eating questionnaires as well as semistructured interviews. Patients were categorized based on their depression scores as normal, mild, moderate, or severe; and these data were related to the family history of affective disorder. A highly significant correlation ($r = .63$) between patient's level of depression and the probability of having a first-degree relative with depression was observed. However, as Wilson and Lindholm note, the bulimia nervosa patients exhibited a much broader range of psychopathology than mere depression. They concluded that the extent to which bulimia nervosa patients have a depressed first-degree relative is strongly correlated with their own level of depression and not the eating disorder.

Response to Antidepressant Therapy
Therapeutic response to antidepressant medication is another area of research that is cited as supporting the relationship between bulimia nervosa and major affective disorders. Several double-blind, placebo-controlled clinical trials of antidepressants have been conducted. One of the first of these studies was conducted by Pope, Hudson, Jonas, and Yurgelun-Todd (1983) who randomly assigned twenty-two patients with bulimia nervosa to imipramine or placebo for six weeks. The results of this study indicated that at six weeks, subjects on imipramine had decreased their binges approximately 7.5 times per week whereas those on placebo showed little or no change. The improvement demonstrated by those in the imipramine group represented an average reduction of approximately 70 percent over their pretreatment level. Additionally, the imipramine group decreased on other measures of bulimic behavior, including preoccupation with food and intensity of binges as well as their depressive symptoms. Moreover, at follow-up ranging from one to eight months, the treatment gains made by the imipramine group continued, with approximately 90 percent considered markedly improved. The authors remark that this pattern of response to antidepressant medication is similar to that observed in the drug treatment of depression.

The Pope et al. study supporting the efficiency of antidepressant medication generated a host of subsequent investigations using a variety of antidepressant medications with increasing levels of sophistication, including attempts to correlate changes in depression and blood levels of medication with clinical improvement.

In an extension of the Pope et al. study, Agras and colleagues (Agras, Dorian, Kirkley, Arnow, & Bachman, 1987) randomly assigned twenty-two patients with bulimia nervosa to either imipramine or placebo for a sixteen-week period. In contrast to the retrospective recall of binge/purge episodes typical of many studies, these investigators had patients monitor bingeing, purging, and laxative abuse at weekly intervals three separate times during the study. Similar to previous reports, the results were positive, showing a 72 percent reduction in bingeing in the imipramine group compared with a 35 percent reduction in placebo. In spite of this drug effect, however, this research generated questions regarding the mechanism of action of the medication since there was no association between initial levels of depression and improvement in eating behavior.

Hughes and colleagues (Hughes, Wells, Cunningham, & Ilstrup, 1986) attempted a more definitive study that explored not only the efficacy of antidepressant medication, but also the mechanism of action by correlating blood levels with clinical improvement. Twenty-two patients with bulimia nervosa (twenty-one females, one male) were randomly assigned to desipramine or placebo for six weeks. On the basis of frequency ratings of binges per week, this study reported a 91 percent decrease in binge frequency for the desipramine patients and a 19 percent increase for those taking the placebo. Global clinical status improvements were evident in those on desipramine with worsening observed for those on the placebo. Moreover, patients initially taking the placebo who crossed over to desipramine at the completion of the study also attained a decrease in binge frequency of over 80 percent and improvements in global clinical status. Interestingly, only six of twenty patients available for blood testing had desipramine levels within the therapeutic range. The values of ten patients were subtherapeutic while four patients with supratherapeutic values had their dosages lowered due to intolerable side effects with no corresponding changes in bulimic symptoms.

These data are the best reported regarding a reduction in bulimic symptoms of patients on antidepressant medication. Yet there appeared to be little relationship between dosage levels, serum levels of medication, and clinical improvement, with some patients achieving therapeutic improvement on low serum levels.

Other studies have used different antidepressants, namely monoamine oxidase inhibitors (MAOI) and mianserin with mixed results. For example, Sabine and colleagues (Sabine, Yonace, Farrington, Barratt, & Wakeling, 1983) found no difference between placebo and medication on 60 mg of mianserin, which has been criticized as a low level.

The question remains as to the mechanism of drug action on bulimic symptoms. As Pope and Hudson (1986) state, there is an imperfect correlation between the antidepressant effects of the medications and their antibulimic effect. These authors note, however, that the dosage and plasma levels of antidepressant medication necessary to effect a change in eating disorders are similar to those for treating major depression. Also, the time course of recovery appears to be the same. In surveying these result, Agras and McCann (1987) suggest that the antidepressants work by altering negative moods that are antecedent to the binge/purge cycle. Other reviews, most recently by P.B. Mitchell (1988), suggest that their action may be due to their antianxiety effects rather than the treatment of an underlying depression. Regardless of the effect of antidepressant pharmacological agents on bulimic symptoms, these data neither support nor disconfirm the argument that bulimia nervosa is a variant of major affective disorder.

SUMMARY

In this chapter, we have reviewed the major physiological theories of anorexia and bulimia nervosa. While explicitly focused on either anorexia or bulimia, the respective theories display a similarity that mimics the core symptoms of the twin disorders. The physiological theories of anorexia are organized around the role of the hypothalamus in eating, the family resemblance and genetic basis of anorexia, and most recently, the autoaddictive model. Theories of bulimia include the substance abuse model, the variation of affective disorder, and the physiological consequences of dieting.

There is no questioning the role of the hypothalamus and neuroendocrine system involvement in eating, be it normal or disordered. Animal research on the ventromedial and lateral hypothalamic areas and the neurotransmitters present interesting analogues and promising heuristics. With the exceptions of the relationship between dietary tryptophan and serotonin, the human research is only tangentially related to these basic investigations. Thus, while the similarities between the autoaddictive and substance abuse models of anorexia and bulimia are obvious, in terms of the two-dimensional model of eating disorders, these seemingly distinct conceptualizations actually deal with the same phenomenon. Yet both suffer from an estrangement from basic research and are in need of reconciliation one with the other. It is unlikely, for example, that the neuroendocrine system in general and the endogenous opiates in particular contain two separate feedback systems corresponding to DSM-III-R categories. This criticism does not undermine the role of endogenous opioids reinforcing further reductions in body weight or precipitating binge eating, but rather speaks to the failure to appreciate the similarities of the two disorders and the need for a unified physiological conceptualization.

The family resemblance and genetic studies indicate these disorders run in families and that females and identical twins are more likely to be affected. Because environmental influences are not controlled in these studies, these effects are also likely to result from modeling, family atmosphere, and other experiential influences. The viability of the environmental influences are all the more likely when we recognize that what is being transmitted may be a fear of obesity and the initiation of inappropriate dieting.

The controversy regarding bulimia and affective disorder may have run its course. While not denying the utility of antidepressant medication, the bulk of available data indicate no unique role of major affective disorders in the etiology of bulimia. Moreover, why has the literature focused on depression and bulimia to the virtual exclusion of anorexia? Depression in anorexia is not very prominent when these young women are at low body weights. Depression becomes more obvious with weight gain as does the prospect of bulimia.

Instead of focusing primarily on diagnostic categories, the focus of theories of eating disorders must be on helping us understand the core phenomenon of fear of weight gain and the regulation and disregulation of food intake as was discussed in Chapter 1. We need to understand how these physiological systems contribute and adapt to changes in body weight, keeping in mind that eating-disordered patients often cycle between a diagnosis of anorexia nervosa and bulimia, or bulimia and obesity.

7

Psychosocial Theories of Eating Disorders

IN THIS CHAPTER, we will consider a broad array of psychosocial variables that play an important role in the development and maintenance of disordered eating behavior and how these variables interact with the biological causes discussed in Chapter 6. Our objective is both to integrate much of the known data and develop a model that will have heuristic value for assessment and treatment of eating disorders. In constructing this model, we have drawn from several theoretical perspectives in modern psychology, including social learning theory (Mischel, 1973; Bandura, 1969), interactional personality theory (Magnusson & Endler, 1977), applied behavior analysis (Baer, Wolf, & Risely, 1968), interpersonal skills training (Schlundt & McFall, 1985), information processing (Carver & Scheier, 1988), and the biopsychosocial model of behavioral medicine (G.E. Schwartz, 1982). The conceptual model presented in this chapter is also an outgrowth of our own research (Schlundt, Johnson, & Jarrell, 1985, 1986; Johnson, Schlundt, & Jarrell, 1986).

Much of the current work in the area of eating disorders suffers from a lack of a theoretical direction. As clinicians, we are forced to assess and intervene with problems we do not fully understand. While many workers have a specific theoretical orientation, such as psychodynamic or cognitive/social learning, most researchers and clinicians have not fully articulated how their orientation can be used to account for the full range of cognitions and behaviors seen in eating disorders. Researchers are too often content to conduct surveys in which questionnaires are given to simply find out which variables are correlated or to determine which measures discriminate eating-disordered individuals from normal controls. Our understanding of eating disorders will progress more rapidly as studies are guided by an explicit theory. The model presented in this chapter is a first step toward organizing the psychosocial data on eating disorders into a theory.

FUNCTIONAL ANALYSIS

The term *functional analysis* best describes our theoretical approach to understanding the psychology of eating disorders. Behavior is the primary focus of a functional analysis. We will focus on the core behaviors of binge eating, purging, restrictive dieting, and fear of weight gain. The goal of functional analysis is to identify the antecedents and consequences that influence and control behavior. We will use the functional analysis approach to address the following questions:

1. What environmental, emotional, cognitive, and behavioral events elicit bingeing, purging, dieting, and fear of obesity?
2. What are the consequences (environmental, affective, cognitive, and behavioral) of these behaviors?
3. How do these antecedents and consequences interact to make anorexia and bulimia resistant to behavior change efforts?

NATURALISTIC FUNCTIONAL ANALYSIS

Since much of our discussion of data in this chapter will refer to studies by Schlundt, Johnson, and Jarrell (1985, 1986), a brief description of these studies will be presented in order to avoid redundancy and to provide a concrete illustration of a functional analysis of bulimia (Schlundt, 1985). The methods of both studies were similar with subjects keeping a diary of eating behaviors and the situational context during the course of a behavior therapy program. Schlundt et al. (1985) used a multiple-choice format for coding environmental antecedents. For example, the place at which the eating episode occurred was coded as home or away. A sample of eight bulimic patients contributed 1,707 eating episodes, and twenty-three obese patients contributed 1,976 eating episodes. In the Schlundt et al. (1986) study, eight bulimic patients kept diaries in which descriptions of the environment were written in and coded by the experimenters. One important difference between the two studies is that subjects judged for themselves whether each episode was a binge in the 1985 study. Unfortunately, whether or not each meal was a binge could not be reliably determined from the free response diary (Schlundt et al., 1986). The data analysis strategy differed between the two studies. In the 1985 study, a nonsequential data analysis strategy was employed whereas the 1986 study used a sequential analysis approach.

The results of the two studies were remarkably similar. Table 7.1 summarizes the results for the following variables: social context, physical context, hunger, activity prior to eating, time of day, meal content, and mood. Schlundt et al. (1985) account for 33 percent of the uncertainty in vomiting, and 25 percent of the uncertainty in overeating and bingeing. When sequential analysis was used (Schlundt et al., 1986), 69 percent of the uncertainty in vomiting was accounted for using combinations of predictor variables.

Because the concepts used in a naturalistic functional analysis are based on correlational relationships, they are not identical to the corresponding concepts derived from an experimental analysis of behavior. Thus a positive reinforcer in an experiment is an event that increases the probability of a behavior. In a correlational analysis, a positive reinforcer is a desirable event that is observed to occur more frequently subsequent

TABLE 7.1 Naturalistic Functional Analysis of Bulimia

Variable	Study	Results
Social Context	1985	1. No association with bingeing or vomiting in bulimia 2. Social situations associated with overeating in obese subjects 3. Social situations associated with high calorie intake in the obese
	1986	1. Vomiting more likely when alone 2. Vomiting even more likely when coming from social situation to being alone 3. Vomiting very likley when alone and last episode was vomited
Physical Context	1985	1. Bingeing and vomiting more likely at home 2. Higher calorie meals in obese when away from home
	1986	1. Vomiting more likely when eating at home 2. Vomiting even more likley if ate away from home 3. Vomiting very likely when at home and last episode was vomited
Time of Day	1985	1. Bingeing and vomiting more likely in the evening and night 2. Overeating and high caloric intake occur more often in the evening and at night

(continued)

TABLE 7.1 (continued)

Variable	Study	Results
	1986	1. The later in the day, the higher the probability of vomiting 2. The second meal in a given time period more likely to be vomited in morning and afternoon 3. At evening and night, vomiting more likely if the previous meal was in the previous time period. 4. Skipping the morning or evening meal associated with more vomiting 5. If vomiting occurs early in the day, more likely later in the day
Activity	1985	1. Binge eating more likely to occur after exercise. 2. Overeating in the obese associated with socializing and relaxation/television 3. Activity not related to vomiting
	1986	1. Activities coded as recreation, especially if they followed work or recreation, were associated with vomiting 2. Recreation after socializing associated with a reduced probability of vomiting
Mood	1985	1. Negative moods strongly associated with bingeing, vomiting, and overeating 2. Positive moods associated with lower probabilty of bingeing and vomiting 3. For the obese, neutral moods associated with reduced probability of overeating
	1986	1. Positive and neutral moods associated with lowered probability of vomiting 2. Negative moods associated with high probability of vomiting 3. Affect changes in negative direction (positive to neutral, neutral to negative) associated with much higher rates of vomiting 4. Affect changes in positive direction predicted low rates of vomiting 5. Negative moods and mood changes predicted initiation of sequences of vomiting episodes
Meal Content	1986	1. Junk food predictive of vomiting 2. The greater the variety of foods at a meal, the higher the probability of vomiting
Hunger	1985	1. Bingeing, vomiting, and overeating most likely to occur when either very hungry or not at all hungry 2. No relationship between hunger and calorie size of meal for the obese

to the occurrence of a behavior than in the absence of the behavior. Although not identical, the two uses of the term positive reinforcers are similar enough to make naturalistic functional analysis useful. Causal attribution cannot be made with certainty from correlational data. However, the empirical documentation of associations between antecedents and behavior and behaviors and consequences can provide information that is useful for theory building and behavioral assessment.

BEHAVIORAL MEDICINE AND THE BIOPSYCHOSOCIAL APPROACH

The area of behavioral medicine is emerging as an approach to understanding the interface between medical problems and behavior (Weiss & Schwartz, 1982). According to G.E. Schwartz (1982), behavioral medicine has developed as a multidisciplinary field concerning itself with the relationships among lifestyle, biology, environment, and disease. The etiological and clinical complexity of medical problems has forced many biomedical and behavioral scientists to adopt general systems theory as a metatheoretical framework (Miller, 1978; von Bertalanffy, 1968). General systems theory is a way of conceptualizing causal mechanisms that is particularly applicable to living organisms. The behavior of a system is seen as resulting from the interactions of multiple components. From interacting components emerges a whole, the system, which is greater than the sum of its parts. That is, the system's behavior cannot be predicted from the properties of single components in isolation.

From a systems perspective, behavior results from the interaction between the organism, its past behavior, and its environment. Systems thinking in behavioral medicine has led to the development of the *biopsychosocial model,* which states that understanding a disease requires studying the pathophysiology as it interacts with psychological, behavioral, and interpersonal processes (G.E. Schwartz, 1982). Thus, the consideration of any disorder, such as cancer or bulimia, must take into account how biological, psychological, and environmental variables interact to produce specific symptoms and complications.

A rigorous use of the functional analysis perspective leads directly into systems thinking. The consequences of one behavior become the antecedent to the next behavior. Behavior is determined by a reciprocal interaction between the person and the environment over time in which behavior alters and influences the environment and the environment shapes and guides behavior. Being derived from radical behaviorism, the functional analysis approach to date has overemphasized environmental and underemphasized biological, cognitive, and emotional influences on behavior.

The psychosocial causes of bulimia will be approached using the biopsychosocial model of behavioral medicine in conjunction with the functional analysis model of learning theory. The range of antecedents and consequences include environmental, biological, cognitive, and emotional events while behavior will be considered in terms of affect, cognition, and action.

Clinical Implications of a Biopsychosocial Functional Analysis

The primary objective in formulating a model of disordered eating behavior is to have a framework to use to generate strategies for assessment and treatment. Towards this end, a functional analysis using biopsychosocial variables has several strengths and weaknesses.

In terms of assessment, the functional analysis approach forces attention both to detail and to collection of a broad range of data. Assessment is focused on describing the interaction between the patient and the environment over time. Focusing on antecedents, behaviors, and consequences requires collecting detailed, specific information. Including environmental, cognitive, biological, and emotional variables encourages a comprehensive assessment.

The ability to handle individual differences easily is another strength of the functional analysis approach to assessment (Cone, 1986). For complex biopsychosocial systems, the same pattern of behavior (e.g., bingeing and purging) can arise in many different ways. Bulimic behavior, for example, is obviously rewarded in every case, but the exact rewards and their relative importance may differ from one person to the next.

A systems perspective also provides advantages in the treatment of eating disorders. According to systems theory, change in one component can cause changes in all other components of the system. Thus, biological interventions should have psychological impacts, and behavioral interventions will have biological impacts. It is naive to think that eating disorders have a single cause, and that there is therefore only one way to effect a cure. Instead, complex interactions of biological, environmental, and psychological variables cause anorexia and bulimia, and interventions that affect any one of these variables may lead to clinically beneficial outcomes.

In terms of drawbacks, taking a multi-component systems approach causes us to sacrifice any sense of certainty that we derive from adhering to simple theories of anorexia and bulimia. For example, the theory that bulimia is a manifestation of an underlying major depressive disorder implies antidepressant medication as a treatment. From a biopsychosocial perspective, antidepressant medication may be needed for some individuals and not for others. One begins with an initial position of uncertainty and then collects assessment data to reduce this uncertainty, tailoring the treatment to the individual's problems.

THE PSYCHOSOCIAL DETERMINANTS OF ANOREXIA AND BULIMIA

In this section, we present a comprehensive model of anorexia and bulimia nervosa with major emphasis on understanding bingeing and purging. As we argued in Chapter 1, the behaviors in anorexia and bulimia exist on a continuum with dieting and overeating behaviors in the general population. We will therefore include occasional studies of eating behavior in normal populations. In keeping with the biopsychosocial perspective, we will point out where biological variables come into play. Since biological variables were discussed in detail in Chapters 2 and 6, our comments on these variables will be brief.

Table 7.2 presents an overview of the functional analysis model. The model identifies the three major classes of variables that must be considered: antecedents, behaviors, and consequences. Antecedents and consequences have been classified as environmental, behavioral, cognitive, emotional, and physiological. The behavior section of the model represents the core behaviors of eating disorders discussed in Chapters 3, 4, and 5: binge eating, fear of fat, purging, and restrictive dieting.

Environmental Antecedents

Environmental antecedents can be divided into two general categories: situational cues and environmental systems. Situational cues refer to the immediate context in which behavior occurs. Environmental systems refer to more general aspects of how the individual interacts with the environment that accrue over time yet have a significant impact on behavior.

Situational Cues

A fair amount of information is available on how cues in the immediate environmental situation effect bingeing and purging in bulimia. There is less information on the effects of the immediate situation on the fear of fat and restrictive dieting.

PHYSICAL SETTING The physical setting refers to the place or location of the individual in the physical environment. Examples of physical settings are home, work, a cafeteria, the library, the bedroom, in your mother's kitchen, and so forth. Physical setting not only includes the place at which behavior occurs but also includes a variety of features of the setting that can serve as stimuli and reinforcers. With respect to eating, food and food-related cues are important elements of the physical setting that can have a dramatic influence on behavior. For example, the kitchen contains many

TABLE 7.2 A Functional Analysis of Bulimia

Antecedents	Behaviors	Consequences
Environment	Binge Eating	Environmental
Situational Cues	Amount of Food	Family
Physical Setting	Kinds of Food	Friendships
Time of Day	Stopping Rules	Vocational
Social Context	Fear of Fat	Financial
Behavior Setting	Cognitions	Sexual/Intimate
Environmental Systems	Emotions	Health Care Systems
Family	Behaviors	Behavioral
Friendships	Purging	Competing Activities
Vocation	Vomiting	Chaining
Financial Resources	Laxatives	Dieting Behavior
Sexual/Intimate	Diuretics	Cognitive
Health Care Systems	Dieting	Self-evaluation
Cultural Systems	Exercise	Rules of Dieting
Behavioral	Restrictive Dieting	Outcome Expectancies
Ongoing Activity		Body Image
Previous Eating		Emotional
Restrictive Dieting		Guilt
Cognitive		Depression
Knowledge of Food		Anxiety
Rules of Dieting		Food Phobias
Outcome Expectancies		Body Dissatisfaction
Body Image		Fear of Fat
Emotional		Physiological
Transient Mood Changes		Insulin/Glucose
Psychopathology		Starvation Response
Fear of Fat		Hunger
Body Image		Hypokalemia
Food Phobias		Reproductive Hormones
Physiological		Catecholamines
Insulin/Glucose		Endogenous Opiates
Starvation Response		
Hunger		
Hypokalemia		
Reproductive Hormones		
Neurotransmitters		
Endogenous Opiates		

food and eating cues. Plates, forks, knives, and the table are all cues associated with eating and with thoughts about eating. The sight and smell of food, such as freshly baked bread, can function as a cue within the physical setting.

Schachter (1971) extensively studied the role of environmental cues in the regulation of eating behavior. The elicitation of eating behavior by an environmental cue is referred to as external cue sensitivity. Schachter's objective was to identify personality or behavioral differences between normal weight and obese individuals that would account for obesity. Schachter and his colleagues showed that many cues could influence both whether food was consumed and the amount of food eaten. These cues included the passage of time, the taste and sight of food, and the number of food cues present (Schachter & Rodin, 1974). Based on Schachter's early work, it was believed that obese individuals were more sensitive to external cues than the nonobese. In fact, Schachter and Rodin went so far as to postulate externality as a personality trait that distinguished obese and normal weight persons. The argument was that normal weight individuals used internal physiological cues to regulate their eating behavior while obese individuals were at the mercy of the food and eating cues in their environment because of their high level of externality.

Rodin (1981), in a review and critique of the literature on externality in obesity, concluded that the data do not support externality as a trait that specifically distinguishes obese from normal weight individuals. Instead, people at all weights can be induced to eat by external cues depending upon the circumstances of the study (Nisbett & Temoshok, 1976; Price & Grinker, 1973; Rodin, Slochower, & Fleming, 1977).

In bulimia, a number of cues and situations associated with the physical setting have been shown to elicit binge eating and vomiting. Schlundt et al. (1985, 1986) showed that bingeing and vomiting occurred more frequently at home than away from home. A sequential analysis of the data showed that when the previous eating episode was eaten away from home, vomiting became very likely if the next episode was eaten at home. Abraham and Beumont (1982) reported that going home was an antecedent to binge eating for 72 percent of their thirty-two bulimic subjects. Other places, such as eating in the car or going to the movies, may function as cues that not only elicit eating but that lead to the consumption of specific foods. Even if these food and eating cues do not directly elicit eating behavior, they may stimulate thoughts about eating that translate later into a binge.

The relationship between situational cues and the fear of fat is not well documented. We can speculate that certain places and cues do function to elicit or intensify the fear of fat. For example, going to the beach where everyone is wearing a bathing suit may be a physical setting that elicits a strong fear of fat. Likewise, being in the mere presence of forbidden foods may arouse a fear of gaining weight. It is reasonable to assume that the fear of obesity can be influenced by the physical setting. It is also likely that the specific eliciting stimuli will differ from one person to the next and one setting to the next.

TIME OF DAY   Much of our eating behavior occurs on a regular schedule. We get up at the same time each day, eat breakfast at a certain time, take breaks from work at certain times, and have our other meals at fairly regular times. It is not surprising, therefore, that people rely on temporal cues to regulate their food intake. The time of day was investigated by Schachter as one external eating cue. He found that some people were stimulated to eat when they were led to believe that it was dinner time, in spite of the fact that it was much earlier in the day (Schachter & Gross, 1968).

Stunkard (1959) identified a pattern of eating behavior, which he called the *night eating syndrome,* that occurred in some obese patients. It was characterized by skipping meals early in the day followed by binge eating in the evening. Some patients developed insomnia and would stay up late eating. These patients often awakened at night and ate before going back to bed. Stunkard reported that the night eating syndrome was present in about 60 percent of the obese patients referred to a university clinic for obesity treatment. In a less selected sample, only about 12 percent of the obese individuals showed the night eating syndrome.

In bulimia, time of day serves as a cue that elicits bingeing and vomiting. Sachlundt et al. (1985, 1986) showed that bingeing and vomiting were more likely to occur in the evening and at night. The later in the day, the higher the probability an eating episode will be purged. When two or more eating episodes occur during the same time period, the subsequent episodes are more likely to be purged. In addition, when a meal is eaten in the evening or at night, vomiting is more likely if the meal during the previous time period was omitted. However, once vomiting starts during the day, it tends to persist at the later meals during the day. Pyle, Mitchell, and Eckert (1981) reported that 32 percent of their bulimic patients reported bingeing when they were unable to go to sleep at night and Mitchell, Hatsukami, Eckert, and Pyle (1985) in an analysis of 275 bulimic patients reported that only 21 percent ate two or more normal meals a day while 18 percent ate only one meal a day, and 60 percent did not eat regular meals. The later the time of day, the harder the individual has to struggle to keep from eating. This may in part be due to the buildup of a physiological drive to eat. It may also be due to the fact that the physical setting changes to home in the evening and the degree of structure on time is typically lessened while the density of food cues is increased. Once dieting has been broken by a violation of the rules of restraint, repeated episodes of bingeing and vomiting may subsequently occur.

The fear of obesity may also vary as a function of time of day. This will be especially true if the individual is weighing in many times a day. As the day progresses and food and fluids are consumed, body weight will have a tendency to increase. This increase in weight, which may be a simple matter of diurnal variation, may be a strong cue for eliciting the fear of weight gain.

SOCIAL CONTEXT There are very few social events or rituals in our society that do not involve food in some way. Weddings, church socials, parties, sporting events, celebrations, dates, birthdays, and so forth all involve social interaction and food. Each social event may involve specific kinds of food, some of which will be forbidden foods for anorexic and bulimic patients. For example, the menu for a family meal at Thanksgiving is usually prescribed by tradition.

Schlundt and Zimering (1988) used the DIET questionnaire, a situation-specific measure of weight control competence, to form a behavioral taxonomy of obese and normal weight individuals. For the obese men and women, a cluster emerged that involved well-controlled eating when alone or at everyday meals and overeating in positive social situations. A similar cluster emerged in the normal weight subjects. Schlundt et al. (1985, 1986) showed that being alone was specifically associated with vomiting in bulimia. The probability of vomiting was highest when the individual's previous eating episode occurred in a social context while the current episode was alone. This, along with our clinical experience, suggests that many bulimic patients are reluctant to lose control and binge and vomit when out in a social situation. However, the eating that does occur in a social situation will often stimulate the fear of gaining weight. This fear can become strong enough to elicit bingeing and vomiting once the individual is alone again after leaving the social event.

Abraham and Beumont (1982) reported that eating alone led to bingeing in 78 percent of their sample of bulimic patients. However, in the same sample, 25 percent said that dates were an antecedent to binges, 22 percent reported that eating out stimulated binges, and 22 percent reported that parties were an occasion for binge eating. Others have also reported that bulimic patients preferentially binge when alone (C.L. Johnson & Berndt, 1983; Larson & Johnson, 1985).

Social context may exert a powerful control over the core behaviors of bulimia in several ways. First, like other people, many bulimics eat more high-calorie foods when socializing. These foods elicit a fear of fat that stimulates a desire to vomit. Vomiting will either occur right away or may be delayed until after the individual is alone and has a chance to binge again. In this situation, the bingeing may also be stimulated by the individual's preoccupation with food as a result of the social eating episode. Many times, the availability of high-calorie forbidden foods at a social occasion serves as a great temptation to binge eat. Because the individual fears that others will learn of the bulimia, binge eating is not allowed in front of others. Instead, an obsession with food and thoughts of bingeing develops and can only be satisfied later when the individual is alone.

BEHAVIOR SETTING Barker (1968) has developed a concept that he refers to as the behavior setting that helps account for the way environments organize and constrain behavior. Behavior settings, while primarily associated with specific places, are characterized by normative rules that prescribe patterns of behavior. For example, a grocery store is a behavior setting in which people engage in certain behaviors, such as pushing a cart, selecting food, trying food samples, and reading magazines in the cash register line. Barker's argument was that when you actually study how people behave in the natural environment, the behavior setting rather than individual differences is the best available information for predicting behavior.

This concept of behavior settings can be applied to bulimia. For each bulimic patient, certain behavior settings will be associated with a high frequency of binge eating. These settings occur at regular time intervals, happen at a particular place, may involve certain people, and usually are associated with normative patterns of behavior. Many behavior settings regularly involve food and food cues. For example, cooking supper in the kitchen or socializing at McDonalds are examples of specific behavior settings that involve stereotyped patterns of action.

Part of performing a functional analysis of bulimia is becoming familiar with the behavior settings in which bulimic behavior is most likely to be observed for each individual patient. There are individual differences in the range and type of situations that are associated with bulimia. However, organizing the information on physical setting, time of day, and social context around the concept of a behavior setting is a very useful way to proceed in a functional analysis of bulimic behavior.

The restrictor anorexic is somewhat different than the bulimic. The problem with the anorexic patient who is restricting food intake is not that certain situations are associated with uncontrolled food intake, but that food intake is restricted or curtailed to only a very few situations. The functional analysis of the restricting anorexic patient involves identification of those few situations in which any eating behavior is allowed to occur. It may also be important to apply the functional analysis approach to understanding how physical and social context elicit other behaviors, such as fear of weight gain and excessive exercise in the restrictor anorexic patient.

Environmental Systems and Eating-Disordered Behavior
The environmental context can exert a powerful influence on the occurrence or nonoccurrence of the core behaviors of anorexia and bulimia. Other aspects of the individual's environment, referred to as environmental systems, play an important role in the development and maintenance of eating behavior. Unfortunately, psychology has neglected developing constructs and methods for the systematic study of how natural environments influence and constrain behavior (Schlundt & McFall, 1987). Therefore, we will only be able to identify the kinds of environmental systems that

are important to consider in bulimia and offer very little detail on how and why these influences occur.

FAMILY SYSTEMS There has been a great deal of interest in how family systems relate to bulimic behavior. This line of interest dates back to the early work of Bruch (1973) who approached eating disorders from a psychoanalytic perspective. She argued that early childhood experiences in the family are the origin of these personality problems.

The family systems school of thought has approached bulimia as a set of behaviors that are maintained by maladaptive family interaction patterns (Root, Fallon, & Freidrich, 1986). According to this perspective, bulimic families are characterized by enmeshment, rigidity, and inability to deal with the expression and resolution of strong feelings.

Kog and Vandereycken (1985) reviewed the literature on the characteristics of the families of anorexic and bulimic patients. Social class of the families has been shown to be associated with eating disorders. Eating disorders in general tend to occur in upper-class and upper-middle-class families. Documented trends support the idea that the social class bias is breaking down somewhat over time and that it is less true for bulimia than anorexia (Pope, Champoux, & Hudson, 1987).

Several studies have shown that anorexia and bulimia are likely to be found in other members of an eating-disordered patient's family (Gershon et al., 1984). In addition, the rate of obesity has been shown to be higher in families of bulimic patients than families of restricting anorexics (Garfinkel, Moldofsky, & Garner, 1979). The evidence for psychiatric disturbances in the families of eating-disordered patients is mixed. Some studies have found no differences (Weiss & Ebert, 1983) while other studies have shown that the incidence of affective disorders is much higher in families of anorexics and bulimics than the general population (Hudson, Pope, Jonas, & Yurgelun-Todd, 1983). Hudson et al. also reported a higher incidence of alcohol abuse in families of eating-disordered patients. While eating and other psychiatric disorders tend to run in families, it is not possible to determine the extent to which this represents genetic inheritance versus transmission of these problems through social learning.

Recently, Strober and Humphrey (1987) reviewed the literature on family contributions to the etiology of anorexia and bulimia. The descriptive data suggest that maladaptive communication patterns and high levels of psychological distress exist within the families of eating-disordered patients. Humphrey (1983), in an analysis of family interaction patterns of anorexics and bulimics, suggested that the issues of autonomy and control were readily observable in the interpersonal behavior of family members. However, the extent to which these patterns are causes of weight concerns, dieting, or binge eating as opposed to consequences remains unknown.

Family variables may influence whether the fear of weight gain is translated into restrictive anorexia or bulimia. The data suggest that families of patients who develop bulimia are characterized as more disorganized, hostile, nonsupportive, and chaotic than families of restricting anorexics (Strober & Humphrey, 1987; Kog & Vandereycken, 1989). It may be that more hostile and disorganized family environments do not allow children to develop the self-efficacy and self-control necessary to maintain restrictive dieting to the point of becoming anorexic, a suggestion at least partially supported by Toner, Garfinkel, and Garner (1987) who presented data showing that bulimic anorexics displayed an impulsive style of cognition compared to restricting anorexics. Stern et al. (1989) used the Family Environment Scale to compare family functioning in twenty restricting anorexics, thirteen bulimic anorexics, twenty-four normal weight bulimics, and fifty-seven age-matched controls. Families of eating-disordered patients differed from the controls on cohesion, expressiveness, conflict, achievement orientation, and active-recreational orientation, with families of the eating-disordered patients showing more pathology.

For older patients, relationships with one's spouse and children may be more important than relationships with parents. Van Buren and Williamson (1988) compared twelve couples in which one of the persons was bulimic to fourteen couples in marital therapy and fifteen normal control couples on a variety of measures of marital satisfaction and conflict resolution style. Essentially, the marriages of bulimic women did not differ significantly from those of patients seeking marital therapy. They were highly dissatisfied, had a number of dysfunctional cognitive beliefs about their relationships, and were deficient in the ability to utilize conflict resolution skills. Because of the correlational nature of these data, it is not possible to tell whether the bulimia interfered with the development of a satisfactory marital relationship or if a poor marital relationship was a primary source of stress exacerbating the bulimia.

From a functional analysis perspective, there are several ways in which family systems can function as antecedents to bingeing, purging, and the fear of obesity:

1. The patient has acquired her fear of obesity from family interactions. For example, a mother who is herself afraid of getting fat and who diets constantly may teach this fear to her daughter. Comments and criticisms from parents, siblings, and other family members may help establish or reinforce a fear of obesity.

2. The family is the context in which an individual acquires appropriate or inappropriate eating habits. Someone who is raised in a family where overeating is common or where snacks are frequently substituted for meals may develop similar eating habits. It may be that dieting is

learned within the family and that some of the behaviors that the anorexic uses to restrict food intake were initially learned from the mother or an older sister. Purging techniques may also be learned within the family. In a survey of 499 bulimics, 27 percent reported learning to purge from family members (Fairburn & Cooper, 1982).

3. Bulimic behavior may be elicited and maintained by family interaction patterns. For example, a father's attempt to control his daughter's behavior may be met with refusal to eat as a coping response. The individual may be using the anorexia or bulimia as a way to fight back against her parents' efforts at control. The subsequent attempts of family members to get an anorexic daughter to eat may serve to further elicit food refusal and restrictive dieting.

4. Family interaction patterns may create situations that elicit bulimic behavior. For example, if the entire family is very busy, a situation may be created in which eating in restaurants is a common occurrence that exposes the eating-disordered individual to many forbidden foods. Likewise, the kinds and amounts of food that are stored in the house create a physical environment that may make restrictive dieting difficult and lead to bingeing.

5. Family interaction patterns, such as enmeshment or disengagement, create stress that serves as an antecedent to bulimic behavior. Conflict with parents or siblings may create stress and negative emotions that are responded to with eating. The role of stress and emotions as an antecedent to bulimic behavior will be covered in a later section.

While each of these mechanisms whereby family systems can influence the development and maintenance of the behavioral manifestations of eating disorders is plausible, much more research is needed before we can be confident that we understand the family system as an antecedent in eating disorders.

FRIENDSHIPS While the family environment is very important in the development of eating and weight-related attitudes and behaviors, peer interactions may be of equal or greater importance. During adolescence, when eating disorders are most likely to develop, much time is spent away from the family interacting with friends. Peer interactions may function as antecedents to eating disorders in several ways:

1. Peers can influence attitudes towards body weight and size by talking with each other and sharing their views.

2. Negative feelings can be created about one's body or body weight when peers ridicule or tease.

3. Methods of dieting and weight control are learned from one's peers. Grunewald (1985) in a survey of college students found that 27 percent of the subjects surveyed said that they obtained information about how to diet from friends and family.

4. Dieting becomes a behavior that is expected and rewarded by the peer group. Johnson, Lewis, Love, Stuckey, and Lewis (1983) showed that 69 percent of adolescent girls had engaged in dieting by the age of eighteen, suggesting that dieting is indeed a normative behavior within the peer culture.

5. Interactions with friends may involve exposure to foods that will elicit fear of weight gain and lead to bingeing and purging after the social interaction is over. Many adolescents spend much of their time socializing in parking lots, near grocery stores and fast food restaurants. Many adolescents obtain much of their nutrition from eating junk foods. The peer culture creates an environment in which there is strong demand to be thin but also many opportunities to eat forbidden foods.

Smith, Pruitt, Mann, and Thelen (1986) did a survey of knowledge and attitudes about eating disorders in high school and college students. Ratings were collected concerning the extent to which someone with an eating disorder was acceptable as a friend, a best friend, or a dating partner. Males were less willing to accept a woman with any form of eating disorder as a friend than were females. Males were most rejecting of average weight females who vomited as a friend, and most rejecting of both anorexic and obese females as a dating partner. An average weight female who binged but did not purge was least rejected by the males as either a friend or a dating partner. Females, on the other hand, were much more accepting of eating disorders than males. They showed the highest rejection ratings for an anorexic as a friend, and for a vomiter and anorexic as a best friend. Like males, females were least rejecting of an average weight binge eater.

The data from Smith et al. show that there are strong attitudes among young people about eating disorders. It is clear that being too fat can lead to rejection. However, it is interesting to note that losing too much weight and becoming anorexic can lead to rejection as well. There is pressure within the peer culture to be thin and to hide one's eating disorder from friends. It is good to lose weight, but losing too much weight is considered pathological and may lead to peer rejection. It is alright to admit to bingeing, but vomiting is considered to be more pathological and is more likely to lead to peer rejection.

There have been some suggestions that peer interactions are disturbed in patients with an eating disorder. In a study of anorexic bulimics, 33 percent reported that their social relationships could be characterized as isolated, 14 percent, as rare and unsatisfactory, and 30 percent, as intermittent and unsatisfactory (Garfinkel et al., 1979). The sample, however, was hospitalized for treatment of anorexia nervosa and may not be representative of normal weight individuals with bulimia. Lacey, Coker, and Birtchnell (1986) also reported that 28 percent of their bulimic sample had problems with peer relationships. Unsatisfactory relationships with friends or lack of friendships can become a source of stress that leads to binge/purge episodes. Social isolation also creates situations in which bingeing is more likely to occur.

VOCATION Most of us spend more time at our jobs than anywhere else. It is not surprising that job satisfaction is an integral part of psychological adjustment. We have noted in many of our bulimic and anorexic patients that conflict and dissatisfaction at work is very often a source of negative affect that disrupts their eating patterns, precipitating episodes of bingeing and purging.

Certain jobs can prove very problematic for a person with an eating disorder. We have had several bulimic patients who work at restaurants and are around food all day. Several of these patients have used their employment as an opportunity to have easy access to binge foods. Others find the constant exposure to food and food cues creates an obsession with food that leads to bingeing after work.

Some vocations place stringent demands on people to maintain a specific weight or appearance. Professional modeling and dancing, for example, are professions that require, for the most part, very thin people. Actors and actresses in the public eye, professional athletes, and people in the health professions, such as dieticians, are often under considerable pressure to maintain a thin, healthy appearance. These jobs create tremendous pressure to diet and can drive the individual to begin purging when efforts at food restriction fail to work.

FINANCIAL RESOURCES We all know how important our financial resources are to the quality of our day-to-day lives. The ability to solve problems and accomplish many important goals is enhanced by having adequate personal finances. It is surprising, however, that very little research has directly examined the role that personal financial resources play in behavior or in emotional adjustment.

Eating disorders tend to occur predominantly in the middle and upper social classes (Fairburn, Cooper, & Cooper, 1986). However, the social class distribution of bulimia tells us very little about how financial variables can serve as antecedents to binge eating and vomiting. In addition, eating disorders most often occur during adolescence and young adulthood when individuals' control over financial resources may be quite limited.

Money has its most direct effect on bulimia through its influence on the availability of food for binge eating. Without money, it is not possible to buy food. Without food, it is not possible to binge. While lack of money does not always prevent bingeing, it does force individuals to resort to drastic strategies, such as eating garbage and stealing. Garner, Olmstead, and Garfinkel (1985) reported 27 percent of their sample of anorexic bulimics engaged in stealing. Norton, Crisp, and Bhat (1985) compared anorexics who admitted to stealing with those who did not and concluded that stealing money and food was related more to financial pressures than to psychopathology.

The extent to which financial resources are available will also affect the kind and quality of food consumed. When there is little money, bulimics will often binge on very cheap food, such as a loaf of day-old bread. When money is more plentiful, preferred foods, such as ice cream, fried chicken, or pizza, will be purchased.

Financial resources also affect bulimic behavior indirectly by influencing the individual's emotional state. Poor financial resources may create stress in several ways. First, there is the worry about not being able to pay bills and meet financial obligations. This worry can be exacerbated by the fact that binge eating consumes a large portion of the individual's available cash. Second, when little money is available, many problems such as transportation are much more difficult to solve. Third, financial pressures can create stress and interpersonal conflict within the family that in turn acts as a precipitant of bulimic behavior.

Financial pressures then contribute to bulimia through several direct and indirect routes. When assessing a patient with bulimia, it is important to determine the patient's financial status and feelings about finances.

INTIMACY AND SEXUALITY The establishment of an intimate sexual relationship is one of the major developmental tasks facing an individual during the transition from adolescence into adulthood. The task is a difficult one that often generates intense emotion. It is therefore not surprising that events in the area of sexuality and intimacy can have an impact on eating-disordered behavior.

There have been several suggestions that eating disorders are related to early sexual experiences. Some of the early psychoanalytic thinkers suggested that bulimia was a symbolic expression of an underlying sexual conflict or arrestment of sexual development (Bruch, 1973). While some of the formulations are elaborate and interesting, very little data exists supporting a psychoanalytic interpretation of anorexia and bulimia. In fact, Bruch (1985) admits that she abandoned a psychoanalytic approach in favor of a less theoretical, more pragmatic approach.

Others have suggested that physical and sexual abuse in childhood are precipitants of eating disorders. Oppenheimer, Howells, Palmer, and Chaloner (1985) had seventy-eight consecutive cases of eating-disordered patients fill out a sexual history questionnaire. Sexual experiences that occurred between the ages of thirteen and sixteen with a partner who was at least five years older were singled out for study. About two-thirds of the sample reported such sexual experiences with most finding these experiences distressing.

There have also been several reports comparing subtypes of eating-disordered patients on their sexual behavior patterns. Garfinkel et al. (1979) compared bulimic anorexics to restrictors and found greater sexual promiscuity among the bulimics. Beumont et al. (1976) also reported greater sexual activity in bulimic than restrictor anorexics. However, it is not clear whether there is an association between sexual promiscuity and bulimia or whether bulimic groups show normal sexual activity while the restrictors are unusually inactive (Norton, Crisp, & Bhat, 1985).

At this point, we can only speculate as to whether sexual abuse or promiscuity plays a role in the etiology of bulimia. Of greater interest is the role that current relationships of an intimate sexual nature play in bulimia. A number of surveys of bulimic patients have reported that changes in relationships with boyfriends or husbands have played an important role as an antecedent to bulimic behavior (Lacey et al., 1986; Pyle et al., 1981). Dieting, bingeing, and fear of weight gain may be influenced by a variety of events:

1. When a relationship moves from friendship to a sexual relationship, intense emotion and stress may result. This is especially true for a first sexual experience in adolescence. Exposing one's body and being touched may exacerbate feelings of being too fat. Sexual experiences may trigger either bingeing and purging or restrictive dieting.

2. Conflict in a relationship can serve as an antecedent of bulimic behavior (Johnson et al., 1986; Pyle et al., 1981).

3. When a relationship ends through breaking up, divorce, or death, the experience of loss may precipitate anorexic or bulimic behavior (Johnson, Stuckey, Lewis, & Schwartz, 1983; Lacey et al., 1986).

4. Fear, anxiety, or ambivalent feelings about a lover can play an important role as an antecedent of bulimic behavior. In this kind of situation, the bulimic behavior functions as a way of escaping and avoiding having to deal with these feelings. After a date during which unwanted sexual advances occurred, binge eating enables the individual to avoid feeling guilty or upset about her behavior.

Establishing and maintaining an intimate sexual relationship requires a number of interpersonal skills. When severe bulimia develops in early adolescence, the eating disorder can interfere with the development and acquisition of these skills. These women are often naive and immature in the way they deal with men in dating situations. This leads to frustrating interactions, and to a relatively high level of fear and anxiety about sex and intimacy. One of the goals of treatment must be to help these patients achieve the interpersonal and emotional maturity necessary to develop and maintain satisfying intimate relationships.

HEALTH CARE SYSTEMS   Most individuals in this country receive regular health care. There is really no systematic research on how bulimia interfaces with the health care system. Anorexic patients are probably more likely to come into contact with the health care system than normal weight bulimics. However, their entry is usually not voluntary and is most often at the insistence of concerned parents.

Most of the patients we have seen have hidden their bulimic behavior from their primary physician. Those who have disclosed their behavior to their physicians have often been very disappointed. The reaction from most physicians has been less than helpful. We have received many reports from patients who said that the reaction of their physician was to tell them that bulimia is dangerous and disgusting and that they should stop. Other physicians have said that there was nothing they could do to help and left it at that.

Nurses and primary care physicians are in a position to detect early cases of bulimia and to make appropriate referrals. These professionals should understand that bulimia is a pattern of behavior that the individual cannot control, and that simply admonishing the individual to stop will have little or no effect. Some of the patients had such a negative experience with the health care system that they literally waited years before trying again to seek help in overcoming their problem.

Eating disorders has now become a big business. Most cities now have eating disorder units in private hospitals. There is no way to know currently what quality of care these businesses are offering, what kind of success rates they have, or what impact their methods of treatment are having on patients. Interactions with the health care system, especially when an attempt at treatment has failed, certainly will have an effect on the individual's emotional state and behavior. Any assessment of a bulimic patient must include an inquiry into past experiences with the health care system, feelings about these experiences, and the effect this has had on behavior.

CULTURAL SYSTEMS   A great deal has been written on the extent to which eating disorders are influenced by cultural factors. The culture fosters a desire to be thin and a fear of getting fat. Many observers have described our current culture as being obsessed with thinness (Garner, Garfinkel, Schwartz, & Thompson, 1980; Orbach, 1978, 1985; Wooley, Wooley, & Dryenforth, 1979).

From a social psychological perspective, there is little doubt that cultural variables such as magazines, television, and movies have a profound influence on peoples' attitudes and beliefs. It has been estimated that 56 percent of women between twenty-four and fifty-four regularly diet. Of those who diet, 76 percent admit it is for cosmetic rather than health reasons. Each culture has an idea or ideas of what the ideal female body should look like. Several have argued that the ideal body image for women is currently represented by Twiggy (Orbach, 1985).

Garner et al. (1980) examined the evolution of the ideal female body image over the past twenty years by examining changes in *Playboy* centerfolds and contestants and winners of Miss America Pageants from 1959 to 1978. For both groups, mean weights of the feminine ideals were substantially less than the population weights of women during the same time period. When age and height were controlled, there was a significant decline in weight of the cultural exemplars over time. After 1970, the weights of Miss America winners were significantly less than the weights of the other contestants, further adding to the argument that there has been a change in cultural standards.

Garner et al. (1980) also examined the emphasis on dieting and weight loss in popular magazines during this time period. They found a significant increase in the number of diet-related articles in women's magazines over the twenty year period.

In addition to the desire to be thin, it is possible to document a cultural bias against being fat (Wooley et al., 1979). Fat people are viewed as weak, lazy, and ultimately as personally responsible for their reprehensible physical condition. The prejudice against fat appears to be stronger for women than men.

Mori, Chaiken, and Pliner (1987) showed that women altered their eating behavior when they believed their femininity was being judged by an attractive male partner. In addition, Chaiken and Pliner (1987) showed that when students believed a small meal was eaten by a woman, she was rated as more feminine and attractive. Perceptions of males, however, were uninfluenced by meal size. These studies suggest that cultural stereotypes concerning sex roles contain strong assumptions about how men and women are expected to eat.

The difficulty in dealing with cultural factors and eating disorders is not so much one of establishing cultural trends and biases, rather it is a problem of describing how these cultural variables come to influence individual behavior. Schwartz, Thompson, and Johnson (1981) have argued that individual behavior must be viewed as an attempt to adapt to the given cultural context. Young women want to be accepted and liked by others and come to see being thin (looking like the culturally ideal woman) as a way to achieve acceptance. The individual who is bombarded with information telling her that she is too fat and that she needs to follow the latest diet eventually incorporates these values into her personal value system. While many variables influence the importance that any given individual attaches to a single outcome, such as being thin, the greater the cultural emphasis on thinness, the greater the likelihood that this will become a central value.

On a functional analysis level, cultural information can serve as an immediate antecedent of bulimic behavior. For example, a women reads the latest magazine article on weight loss strategies and takes the self-assessment quiz that is part of that article. She may learn from this that according to the author's standards she is too fat or doesn't eat right. This kind of information can function as a cue that elicits the fear of obesity, which then leads to restrictive dieting and eventually binge eating. Even watching models on TV commercials can invoke a social comparison process that results in the arousal of the fear of obesity. Since we are bombarded on a daily basis by messages telling us that we are too fat and that thin is beautiful, there is ample opportunity for these kinds of events to function as antecedents to bulimic behavior.

Behavioral Antecedents

The main point of the functional analysis approach is the recognition that anorexic and bulimic behavior exists and occurs in a context. Understanding and modifying this behavior involves, in part, developing an understanding of the specific context for any given individual. Part of the context of any act is the activity or behavior that occurred in the recent past. In the next several sections, we will examine how the behavioral context plays a role in bingeing, purging, and the fear of weight gain.

Ongoing Activity
Eating behavior often occurs either just after or concurrent with other activities. These activities can have a dramatic influence on the amount and kind of food that is eaten, and on the extent to which the fear of weight gain is elicited. Schlundt et al. (1985) examined the relationship between ongoing activity and binge eating in bulimic and overweight subjects. For the bulimic subjects, binge eating was more likely to occur after exercise. For the obese subjects, overeating was associated with socializing, relaxation, and watching television. Schlundt et al. (1986) extended these results by conducting a sequential analysis of the relationship between activity and self-induced vomiting in bulimic subjects. Activities coded as recreation

were predictive of vomiting, especially if they followed work or other recreational activities. These two studies provide very little detailed information about the role of ongoing activity in bulimia. In fact, very little detailed data is available. Ongoing activity may function as an antecedent to bulimic behavior on several levels:

1. The occurrence of unstructured activity during leisure time allows the individual a chance to think about food and to engage in binge eating. This is partly a function of a low demand on the individual's concentration and attention during unstructured leisure activities. It may also be a function of the absence of competing activities. This allows the person the free time to binge eat.

2. Different activities generate cues that can affect the fear of fat or the desire to binge. For example, some activities, like exercise, may involve wearing a leotard in front of other people, which could act to stimulate the fear of fat. Other activities, like socializing, can put the person in a situation where the desire for food can be stimulated by watching another person eat.

3. Certain activities can develop into habit patterns. For example, if a person gets used to exercising every day then coming home and bingeing, the exercise-binge association becomes a habit that is difficult to change. Thus, binge eating can become one behavior in a habitual chain of behaviors that the individual engages in without really giving it much thought.

Previous Eating
Prior food intake is one aspect of the behavioral context of a bulimic episode that must be taken into consideration. Johnson et al. (1986) showed quite clearly that bulimic behavior tends to occur in chains. The unconditional probability of vomiting in the patient sample was 0.36. When it was known that the previous eating episode had resulted in vomiting, the conditional probability of vomiting the next episode increased to 0.54. Schlundt, Sbrocco, and Bell (in press) performed a sequential analysis of overeating in a population of obese subjects enrolled in a weight loss program. The results indicated that overeating tended to occur in chains. Additional ability to predict overeating occurred when the particular meal was taken into consideration. For example, if overeating occurred at breakfast, there was over a 50 percent probability that overeating would occur at the next meal compared to an approximately 13 percent unconditional probability of overeating. This effect carried over from the evening to the next day. If the last meal of the evening was overeaten, then there was a 60 percent probability that overeating would occur at breakfast.

R. Davis, Freeman, and Solyom (1985) had twenty-one bulimic and twenty-one control subjects keep self-monitoring diaries of their eating behavior, mood, and hunger on an hourly basis over several days. In a sequential analysis of this data, Davis et al. reported that the consumption of food during the hour prior to eating predicted that the meal or snack would be a bulimic episode. Empirical observations are essentially in agreement with clinical reports that bulimic episodes tend to occur in bouts. There may be several reasons for this:

1. A bulimic episode represents violation of abstinence rules. We have already argued that bulimia involves an alternation between highly restricted dieting and a complete loss of control over food intake (Chapter 1). The violation of abstinence rules has been observed to result in the abstinence violation effect (Marlat & Gordon, 1980). The abstinence violation effect involves an increased frequency or intensity of a forbidden behavior after a single occurrence of the behavior. Other researchers have referred to essentially the same phenomenon as counter-regulation (Ruderman & Wilson, 1979).

2. Once a single binge-eating episode has occurred, the fear of gaining weight may be stimulated. The increase in fear of weight gain leads to an impulse toward restrictive dieting that leads to further violations of abstinence rules making self-control difficult.

3. A loss of control over eating results in feelings of guilt and depression. These negative emotions become the context for later eating episodes, making self-control more difficult. As we shall discuss shortly, negative emotions are a powerful precipitant of bulimic behavior.

Restrictive Dieting
We have discussed thus far how previous episodes of overeating can lead to bouts of bulimic behavior. It is important to note that undereating and meal skipping can also have a similar effect. Many bouts of bulimic behavior occur as a reaction to extreme dietary restriction. Schlundt et al. (1986) reported that meal skipping was associated with increased probabilities of self-induced vomiting. Schlundt et al. (1985) showed that extreme hunger was a significant predictor of binge eating but that moderate levels of hunger were not.

Davis, Freeman, and Solyom (1985) compared the eating patterns of bulimic and normal subjects showing that the bulimics ate fewer regular meals. Perceived hunger was not related to bulimic episodes in this data set. Johnson, Stuckey, Lewis, and Schwartz (1983) reported that 34 percent of 316 bulimic patients attributed the onset of bulimic behavior to restrictive dieting. Mitchell, Hatsukami, Eckert, and Pyle (1985) in a study of 275 bulimic women reported that meal skipping was very common. Only 22 percent reported eating two or more normal meals per day, 19 percent reported eating one normal meal per day, 39 percent reported eating a normal meal several times a week, while 21 percent said they never ate normal meals. Lacy et al. (1986) reported that 96 percent of their patient sample described carbohydrate craving as an important antecedent to bulimic episodes. In a study of thirty-two bulimic patients, Abraham and Beumont (1982) reported that 84 percent of the patients described eating any kind of food as precipitating episodes of binge eating. Most of the patients reported attempting to follow strict rules of dieting between binge-eating episodes.

As described in an earlier chapter, we believe that the alternation between restriction and binge eating is one of the core features of bulimia. The longer the individual restricts caloric intake, the greater the pressure to eat. When rules of dieting are extremely strict, as is often the case in eating disorders, the consumption of almost any food represents a violation of rules and leads to an abstinence violation effect (or counter-regulatory response). The end result is that the consumption of almost any food can result in a loss of control over food intake, the initiation of a chain of binge/vomit episodes, and a large increase in the fear of gaining weight.

Cognitive Antecedents

The effects of environmental and behavioral events are often mediated by cognitive variables. The abstinence violation effect or counter-regulation response is a prime example of a cognitively mediated behavior pattern. The meaning of any particular event to the individual depends on how the individual processes environmental information. People use stereotypes, interpretations, misconceptions, and biases to process environmental and behavioral information. In the next few sections, we will talk about some of the cognitive processes that may interact with environmental information to precipitate bulimic episodes or intensify the fear of weight gain.

Knowledge of Food

We have found that many bulimic patients, because of the years of dieting, are quite knowledgeable about the caloric content of food. This knowledge is used to categorize some foods as acceptable diet foods and others as unacceptable forbidden foods. Only acceptable foods are eaten during successful periods of dieting while during a binge the individual will usually consume forbidden foods. While many authors have discussed the role of carbohydrates in bulimia, most of the forbidden foods are also very high in dietary fat. It is not clear whether fat content and palatability or physiologically induced carbohydrate cravings are the basis for the strong attraction to eating forbidden foods.

While many patients are quite knowledgeable about food and nutrition, others show grossly distorted ideas about certain foods and their caloric content. We have observed that many of our patients greatly overestimate calories, particularly for breads and other starchy foods. Many with an eating disorder will religiously avoid breads as forbidden foods, but will allow themselves to eat cheese which is actually a more calorically dense food because of its high fat content.

Whether accurate or not, most patients have a cognitive map of the food world telling them which foods are diet foods and which are fattening. The consumption of a forbidden food, as we have seen, can precipitate binge eating. In the assessment of an eating-disordered patient, it is important to obtain information on how the individual categorizes foods as diet foods and forbidden foods.

Rules of Dieting
Along with an implicit set of rules differentiating between diet foods and fattening foods, most bulimics have a set of rules that prescribe proper dieting behavior. For example, a weight loss rule might be to never eat anything right before bedtime because foods eaten late at night turn to fat. There are great individual differences in the degree to which the rules of dieting are explicit and rigid. In general, patients can articulate a set of rules that describe what behavior is or is not allowed during dieting.

To understand the behavior of bulimic patients, it is necessary to become acquainted with each patient's list of forbidden foods and the rules of dieting that patient attempts to follow. The degree to which the list of forbidden foods is extensive and the rules of dieting are very strict increases the chances of violating these rules and thus precipitating a bout of bingeing and vomiting. However, this is not always the case since some patients will have very stringent dietary rules and will develop the restrictor type of anorexia as a result.

Outcome Expectancies
Outcome expectancies refer to the consequences that an individual believes will occur as a result of various actions. People in general behave in a way that they believe will result in positive and desireable outcomes. What often happens is that outcome expectancies are distorted or erroneous, and the individual behaves in a way that appears illogical to the external observer.

Of interest in bulimia are the outcome expectancies an individual has for various eating and exercise behaviors. For example, if an individual believes that the diarrhea caused by ingesting a large quantity of laxatives will rid the body of unwanted calories, then the behavior of taking laxatives may be used as a way to cope with an eating binge. Also, behavior that may in fact be an effective way of coping will not be used if the outcome expectancies for that behavior are negative. For example, the individual may believe that eating three meals a day will result in rapid weight gain when in fact spreading food out over three meals a day might contribute greatly to the ability to regulate food intake.

Closely related to outcome expectancies are a host of irrational beliefs that affect the behavior of bulimic individuals (Fairburn, 1985). The following list is a sample of erroneous outcome expectancies and irrational beliefs that are observed in anorexic and bulimic patients. The beliefs have a profound effect on the individuals' behaviors and must be addressed before permanent behavior change can occur.

- High-calorie foods are immediately stored as fat.
- Breads and other starchy foods are very fattening.
- Any change in weight is a result of getting fat.
- Laxatives get rid of extra calories. The more laxatives I take, the more calories I get rid of.
- Fasting is the best way to lose weight.
- Missing a single day of exercise will result in getting fat.
- Being unable to control my appetite means that I am weak and a failure.
- Once I start to overeat, it does not matter how much I eat since all hope is lost.
- If I go to bed with a full stomach all of that food will turn to fat.
- If I look fat, people will notice and will reject me.
- Eating just a little bit of this food will make me feel better.
- Vomiting is O.K. as long as no one else finds out about it.
- I will gain weight if I eat more than 1,000 calories a day.
- Eating breakfast will only make me hungrier and want to eat more all day.
- Diuretics help me lose weight.
- If I get fat, I will be an unhappy, unattractive failure.
- Indulging myself is bad because it is a sign of weakness.
- Anything less than perfection is a failure.
- The way I see myself in the mirror is the way others see me.

Israel, Stolmaker, and Andrian (1985) studied the relationship between cognitive expectations about eating and obesity. The authors developed a scale to measure the occurrence of both positive and negative thoughts that were presumed to be related to success in weight reduction efforts. In the first study, seventy-two female and sixty-nine male college students were administered the scale. The relative occurrence of positive thoughts was correlated with lower body weights while the occurrence of negative thoughts was associated with greater degrees of obesity. In a second study, the occurrence of negative thoughts was associated with a failure to lose weight in a behavioral weight loss program. These studies suggest that cognitions play an important role in the regulation of eating behavior in a noneating-disordered population.

Schulman, Kinder, Powers, Prange, and Gleghorn (1986) reported the development of a twenty-five-item scale to measure cognitive distortion in bulimia. The scale easily discriminated between bulimic and a matched sample of normal subjects. Two factors emerged in a factor analysis. One factor consisted of items related to the onset of bulimic eating (e.g., "If I am lonely, I must eat"). The other factor related to beliefs about body and physical appearance (e.g., "My value as a person is related to my weight"). Scores on this scale were also correlated with depression scores.

Bulimia is characterized by a number of distorted and mistaken beliefs and expectations about food, the effect of food on weight, and the role that food plays in one's life. There is much that we do not understand about cognition in bulimia, and this is an area in which further investigation is necessary. When assessing a patient with bulimia, it is important to learn as much as possible about that person's specific beliefs and expectations and how these cognitions affect eating behavior.

Body Image
Much has been written about body image and its role in eating disorders (Barrios, Ruff, & York, 1988; Garner, 1981; Wilmuth, Leitenberg, Rosen, Fondacaro, & Gross, 1985). While body image is also discussed in detail in Chapters 3, 8, and 16, here we will consider how distorted body perceptions and body dissatisfaction can stimulate dieting and weight loss behaviors.

Body image has a cognitive component that consists of perceptions and beliefs about one's body (see Chapter 3). Perceptions include how one sees and interprets the shape of certain body parts and the features of one's body that are prominent when looking in a mirror or at a photograph. The relevant beliefs include ideas of what each body part should look like, ideas of what is attractive in general, and ideas about the consequences of being too large or small in different body parts. Body image also consists of an affective component in which people have different emotional reactions to each body part. Body image may also have a behavioral component in which body parts of a certain size or shape imply certain actions, such as dieting when the stomach is not perfectly flat. These feelings and beliefs are linked in cognitive structures known as schemata. Situational events activate body-related schemata. Once activated, the schema guides further processing of information and affects the individual's choice of behavior. For example, observing one's reflection in a window while walking down the street and thinking that your hips look large can result in invoking a negative body schema that will result in negative affect, fear of weight gain, and the initiation of efforts designed to lose weight.

While the literature on body image is becoming rather extensive (Barrios, Ruff, & York, 1988), most of the research has involved attempts to demonstrate that eating disorders are characterized by perceptual distortion. These efforts have led to mixed results. Instead of making crude between-group comparisons, research needs to examine how cognition and affect with respect to body size and shape are related to disordered eating behavior.

Emotional Antecedents

Transient Mood Changes

There is very little doubt that negative emotions are a strong antecedent of bulimic behavior. Schlundt, Johnson, and Jarrell (1985) showed that negative moods were strongly predictive of bingeing and vomiting. Positive moods, however, were associated with a reduced probability of bingeing and vomiting. Schlundt et al. (1986) also reported a strong association between negative moods and self-induced vomiting. A sequential analysis of the data showed that even better prediction could be obtained when affect changes from one eating episode to the next were examined. When mood changed from positive to neutral or negative or from neutral to negative, a very high rate of self-induced vomiting was observed.

Since bulimic episodes tend to occur in bouts or chains, it is important to look for antecedents that initiate bulimic episodes. In terms of a sequential analysis, this involves looking for a variable that predicts a high probability of vomiting when vomiting did not occur at the previous eating episode. Schlundt, Johnson, and Jarrell (1986) showed that negative moods and mood changes were strong predictors of the initiation of bulimic bouts.

Johnson-Sabine, Wood, and Wakeling (1984) had fifty bulimic patients keep self-monitoring diaries for an eight-week period. The data clearly showed that depression, anxiety, and hostility were predictive of bingeing and purging. Subjects whose bulimia was more severe showed greater levels of affective disturbance during the eight weeks of monitoring. Davis, Freeman, and Solyom (1985) compared self-monitoring records of twenty-one bulimic to twenty-one normal subjects. Overall, the bulimics experienced more negative affect than the normal control group. In addition, a sequential analysis showed that a decrease in mood was a significant predictor of the occurrence of a bulimic episode.

Abraham and Beumont (1982) asked thirty-two bulimic patients to report the kinds of events that precipitated binge eating and vomiting. Tension was mentioned by 91 percent, loneliness and boredom by 59 percent, and arguments with parents, boyfriends, or husbands by less than 20 percent. Mitchell et al. (1985) looked at precipitants of binge eating in 275 patients. The most frequently mentioned precipitant was feeling tens or anxious, which was endorsed by 83 percent of the patients. Two-thirds of the patients also mentioned feeling unhappy as a reason for binge eating. Pyle, Mitchell, and Eckert (1981) in a report on thirty-four cases of bulimia identified feeling unhappy, anxious, frustrated, bored, and hating oneself as feelings that patients reported as causing the onset of binge eating. Johnson et al. (1983), in a report of 316 cases of bulimia, stated that over 40 percent of the sample attributed the onset of bulimia to an inability to handle negative emotions, such as depression, anger, and anxiety. Greenberg (1986) showed that measures of stress and depression were predictive of the severity of binge eating in both an eating-disordered and a college student population. Wolfe and Crowther (1983) showed that the amount of stress in the previous year was significantly associated with the frequency of binge eating in a college student sample.

Cooper, Morrison, Bigman, Abramowitz, Levin, and Krener (1988) examined time sequences of mood in the binge/purge cycle in bulimic patients with and without a concurrent major affective disorder. They found that moods were lowest after the binge and improved after purging. After bingeing, patient affect was described as guilt, disgust, anger, panic, and helplessness. After purging, the patients reported higher levels of security and relief. It is surprising, given the literature on the role of affect in the binge/purge cycle, that these authors failed to assess mood prior to bingeing, thus rendering the results of this study somewhat inconclusive. No differences in mood were found when the patients with and without the concurrent diagnosis of major affective disorder were compared.

Negative moods clearly precipitate bingeing and vomiting but their role in fear of obesity and onset of dieting is less clear-cut. Striegel-Moore, McAvay, and Rodin (1986) conducted a study examining the relationship between psychological and behavioral variables and feeling fat. While a number of variables were predictive of feeling fat, included in these variables was a measure of the extent to which the individual feels bad about having failed. To summarize, there is clear evidence that bulimic behavior is elicited by transitory mood states. These changes in mood can be brought about by changes and events in almost any area of life. The role of negative mood is particularly important in initiating the first bulimic episode in a chain of episodes. In assessing a patient with bulimia, it is important to learn about the frequency and duration of negative mood states, the kinds of events that precipitate transitory mood changes, and the way these changes impact on bulimic behavior.

Cattanach and Rodin (1988) discussed the role of environmental stress in eating disorders. These authors proposed that stress be viewed as a process whereby an individual interprets and copes with challenging events in the environment and suggested that the important variables are appraisal of the stressor, perception of control, coping responses, and social support. We agree with these authors that the effects of stress on bulimia must be examined at the level of how persons perceive, process, and respond to challenging environmental situations. However, the functional analysis approach employed in this chapter is a more specific approach than simply enumerating a set of apparently relevant variables.

Psychopathology

We have seen that transient changes in mood state produce bingeing, purging, and possibly increased fear of obesity in bulimia. In this section, we will show that long-term fluctuations in mood that can be characterized as affective or anxiety disorders may also play a role in the onset and maintenance of bulimic behavior.

A number of clinical reports have shown a high prevalence of depressive symptoms in both anorexic and bulimic patients. Rates of depression in anorexic patients have been typically reported in the 25 percent to 50 percent range. G. Russell (1979) in a report on thirty patients with bulimia nervosa, classified twenty-six out of the thirty to be at least moderately depressed. Williamson, Kelley, Ruggiero, and Blouin (1985) compared fifteen bulimic subjects to matched control groups of obese and normal weight individuals finding that bulimic subjects appeared more depressed on the MMPI depression subscale, the depression subscale of the SCL-90, and the Beck depression inventory.

Fairburn and Cooper (1982) described 629 women who met the diagnostic criteria for bulimia nervosa. Scores on the General Health Questionnaire showed significant elevations on both the depression and the anxiety subscales.

Casper, Eckert, Halmi, Goldberg, and Davis (1980) compared anorexic patients who purged with those who lost weight through food restriction alone. Higher levels of depression, guilt, interpersonal sensitivity, and anxiety were observed in the bulimic subgroup along with more antisocial behavior, stealing, and drug and alcohol abuse than in the restrictor subgroup. In a similar comparison by Yellowlees (1985), high rates of anxiety and depression were reported for both the bulimic and the restrictor subgroups. The bulimic subgroup was bothered more by guilt than the anorexic subgroup. Piran, Kennedy, Garfinkel, and Owens (1985) compared thirty-three bulimics to fourteen anorexic restrictors on a variety of measures of psychological functioning. There were high rates of both depressive and anxiety-based disorders in both groups with no significant difference between the two.

Weiss and Ebert (1983) compared a group of fifteen bulimic patients to a matched control group of fifteen normal weight noneating-disordered patients. The bulimic group showed higher rates of substance abuse, stealing, and impulse control problems. The bulimia patients showed higher levels of distress on questionnaire measures of psychopathology, with larger differences found for anxiety and depression. Ordman and Kirschenbaum

(1986) compared twenty-five bulimic patients to a matched control sample and found large differences on measures of psychopathology, such as anxiety, depression, obsessive compulsion, and psychoticism.

Hatsukami, Eckert, Mitchell, and Pyle (1984) reported on rates of depression and substance abuse in a sample of 108 female bulimics using the DSM-III diagnostic criteria. When all types of depressive disorders are considered, 38 percent of the patients were currently diagnosed as depressed while 53 percent had either a current or past diagnosis of depression. While only 2 percent of the patients qualified for a current diagnosis of substance abuse, 22 percent had a history of severe substance abuse.

Swift, Andrews, and Barklage (1986) reviewed the data on the relationship between eating disorders and primary affective disorder and concluded that there is ample data showing that persons with an eating disorder display high levels of anxiety and depression. As we saw in Chapter 6, one of the biological theories of bulimia holds that it is an expression of an underlying affective disorder. The authors conclude that there is no question but that there is some relationship between eating disorders and depression. However, the nature of this relationship is still open to debate.

From the viewpoint of a functional analysis of bulimia, we have seen that transient changes in mood are a strong antecedent to bulimic behavior. When mood changes are less transient, such as in an episode of severe depression, the susceptibility of the individual to the inducement of bulimic behavior is heightened. Chronic depression may lower the threshold for stimulating bulimic behavior by making long-term adherence to food restriction more difficult. It may also worsen the severity of weight gain phobia. In addition, one of the outcomes of bulimic behavior is the inducement of guilt and depression. The bulimia interacts with the depression to form a positive feedback system in which depression leads to more bulimic behavior and more bulimic behavior intensifies the depression.

It is notable that most of the studies of psychopathology have shown that bulimic and anorexic patients are distressed on almost every dimension measured. While some of the family history evidence argues that there is a specific role of depression in bulimia, an argument can be made that people with an eating disorder are generally upset and unhappy. All of this negative affect interacts and combines to further encourage bulimic behavior.

More recent attention of clinicians has been focused on personality disorders in anorexia and bulimia nervosa, especially borderline personality disorder (Piran, Lerner, Garfinkel, Kennedy, & Brouillette, 1988). Because of the heterogeneity of borderline personality disorder in terms of its clinical presentation, it appears to be the nonpsychotic diagnostic equivalent of schizophrenia. For example, borderline personality disorder includes the following range of characteristics: impulsivity, dependency, antisocial, schizoid, and histrionic to name a few of the most prominent.

Enright and Sansone (in press) estimate that somewhere between 10 percent and 40 percent of the bulimia nervosa patients can also be diagnosed as borderline personality disorder. They argue that these borderline patients should be identified since their treatment is more complex and arduous. They propose ten *indices of suspicion* that are intended to sensitize clinicians to the presence of borderline personality disorder and, when present, encourage them to conduct a thorough assessment to determine if borderline personality disorder can be diagnosed. The indices of suspicion include:

1. Chronic bulimia nervosa for ten or more years.
2. Multiple treatment failure in inpatient and outpatient settings with drugs and psychotherapy.
3. Multiple diagnoses, including mood disorder, substance abuse, and other personality disorders.
4. Chronic impulsivity and self-destructive behavior, including suicide attempts, shoplifting, substance abuse, and sexual promiscuity.
5. Symptom substitution wherein reduction in one symptom set (e.g., drug abuse) is associated with an increase in another (e.g., binge eating).
6. Chronic dysphoria characterized by mood shifts, anxiety, and depression.
7. Spectrum weight disorders progressing through obesity and anorexia.
8. Transient quasi-psychotic episodes including brief, episodic depersonalization, impulsivity, and rage reactions.
9. Use of multiple weight control methods.
10. Unresponsiveness to drug therapy.

Cooper, Morrison, Bigman, Abramowitz, Blunden, Nassi, and Krener (1988) compared thirty-one bulimic patients to ten patients with bulimia and a concurrent diagnosis of borderline personality disorder. The borderline group had more severe bulimic symptoms and suffered greater levels of psychological and emotional distress. When the borderline subgroup of bulimic patients was compared to thirty-two patients with borderline personality disorder who did not have a concurrent diagnosis of bulimia, few differences between these two groups were found.

Pope and Hudson (1989) reviewed seven studies examining the prevalence of borderline personality disorder among patients with an eating disorder. The studies showed considerable variability, with results ranging from 0 percent to 42 percent. They argue that the lack of specific diagnostic criteria for borderline personality disorder, the similarity of the symptoms of borderline personality disorder and depression, and the lack of a validated method for making the borderline diagnosis may have led some of the researchers to overestimate the prevalence of borderline personality disorder in bulimic patient samples. Borderline patients are viewed very negatively by mental health professionals because they are believed to be difficult if not nearly impossible to treat. Pope and Hudson caution that until we are sure the term borderline refers to a homogeneous subgroup of patients and we are able to make reliable and valid diagnosis of borderline personality disorders, it is wise to be careful not to overapply this label to patients.

Physiological Antecedents

We are often as aware of our physiological state as we are of environmental stimuli. When we are aware of our physiology, biological events can function as cues that influence our behavior. For example, hunger is a physiological cue we are all aware of that can stimulate us to eat. Fatigue is another cue that tells us to rest (or perhaps to get something to eat).

Because we are animals who evolved from cognitively less complex organisms, there are many physiological systems affecting our behavior that operate below the level of awareness. Some of these, like respiration, are absolutely necessary to survival. Other biological processes, like thirst for example, can operate either above or below the level of awareness. The neural and hormonal processes involved in regulation of eating, dieting, and bingeing were described in Chapters 2 and 6.

Most of the research on neural control of feeding has been done with rats and other nonhuman species. While in many cases much has been learned about neural mechanisms that control behavior, it is not clear how well this literature generalizes to the human being, especially someone with an eating disorder (Blundell & Hill, 1986). In animals, it has been established that there are separate brain sites that control meal initiation and meal termination. Both meal initiation and meal termination are problems in eating disorders. Some bulimics binge 10 to 20 times a day. Most eating binges involve failure to stop eating when an appropriate amount of food has been consumed. However, we cannot tell from animal studies whether binge eating in humans is a failure of brain biochemistry or instead a problem that is best conceptualized as resulting from faulty learning, cognitive events, or an interaction among psychological and physiological systems.

For example, Schlundt et al. (1985, 1986) looked at hunger as an antecedent to bulimic behavior and to overeating in a sample of obese subjects. They found that extreme ratings of hunger were predictive of overeating, bingeing, and purging as would be expected from our knowledge of the neurophysiology of eating. Moderate levels of hunger, however, were associated with reduced probabilities of losing control over food intake while eating episodes that occurred when the individual was not at all hungry tended to be binges. When calorie size of the meal for obese subjects was examined (Schlundt, Johnson, & Jarrell, 1985), there was no relationship between hunger ratings and the amount of food consumed.

The task at hand is not to decide whether physiological or environmental influences are more important, but to specify each of these influences and then to study how they interact to produce fear of obesity, dieting, bingeing, and purging. In terms of physiological variables, two mechanisms of action are likely. First, physiological state can serve as a cue that affects behavior through cognitive processes. Second, physiological systems affect behavior without the individual's awareness through the creation of motivational drives.

We have looked at the antecedent side of the model and documented how environmental, behavioral, cognitive, emotional, and physiological events can act to stimulate disordered eating behavior. In the remaining sections of the chapter, we will focus on some of the consequences of these behaviors, and how they act as rewards and punishments.

CONSEQUENCES OF ANOREXIC AND BULIMIC BEHAVIOR

One of the basic ideas of behavioral analysis is that each and every behavior has a function. That is, for every behavior that is observed in someone's repertoire, there is a consequence that rewards or reinforces that behavior. Anorexic and bulimic behavior is no exception. In order to gain a better understanding of eating-disordered behavior, we need to examine how it is rewarded and maintained by a variety of consequences.

In the following sections, we will cover the environmental, behavioral, cognitive, emotional, and physiological consequences of bulimia. As there is much less empirical literature on consequences than there is on antecedents, some of our discussions will be speculative and will be based mainly on our clinical experience in the assessment and treatment of anorexia and bulimia.

We will examine four types of consequences in each of the areas: (1) positive consequences that reward a behavior, (2) negative consequences that punish a behavior, (3) consequences that reward a behavior through escape or avoidance of something unpleasant, and (4) the removal of positive consequences that acts as a punishment to a behavior. As we shall see, it is easily possible for any given behavior to be both rewarded and punished at the same time. Short-term consequences often exert a powerful influence over behavior. Long-term consequences, while sometimes devastating, do not exert as powerful a controlling effect. In looking at the consequences of dieting and bingeing, we will attempt to identify both short-term and long-term consequences.

Environmental Consequences

Disordered eating behavior has an impact on the individual's environment and on other people in that environment. Table 7.3 lists some of the environmental consequences of anorexia and bulimia. There are very few positive social consequences for bingeing and purging. There may be a few individuals who binge in social situations who derive some positive reward from social bingeing. There are, however, positive social consequences in many people's environments for dieting and for fear of fat. Parents, friends, boyfriend, husband, and coaches may all either overtly or subtly encourage dieting and obsession with being thin. When the individual makes statements about her weight or engages in obvious dieting behavior, the reaction of others may prove most rewarding.

Many of the social consequences in eating disorders are either negative or escape/avoidance consequences. For some patients, the social consequences of anorexic and bulimic behavior are very important in maintaining the disorder. Some use their bulimia as a way to avoid threatening social interactions. Thus, staying home and bingeing is rewarded by escaping the ordeal of going on a date.

There are many negative environmental consequences of bulimia. Many of these accrue over a long period of time and therefore do not have a controlling effect on behavior. However, after five to ten years of bulimia, many of these consequences can be quite devastating. All of the deception that is necessary in order to keep the bulimia a secret interferes with the development and maintenance of close interpersonal relationships with friends and families. When friends, families, or co-workers find out about the bulimia, the results can be disastrous. Even family members with good intentions can create a tremendous amount of conflict and bad feelings after severe weight loss or once bingeing and purging has been discovered.

Bulimia can interfere with social and sexual development in several ways. First, the amount of time spent eating and purging takes away from time that most adolescents spend with friends in situations in which significant social learning occurs. This partial isolation can retard social development. If the individual is using bulimia as a way to avoid anxiety-provoking social interactions, then the chances and opportunities to establish and develop intimate relationships are lessened.

Food obsession and bingeing can also interfere with work performance. Some suffer in their work from the depression that accompanies an eating disorder, while others use their bulimia as an excuse to avoid taking risks and improving their vocational situation.

TABLE 7.3 Environmental Consequences of Anorexia and Bulimia

Positive Consequences	Negative Consequences	Escape and Avoidance	Removal of Positive Consequences
1. Socializing while bingeing 2. Increased attention from family and friends who know 3. Friends and family may approve of attempts to diet and lose weight 4. Fear of fat is valued by members of peer group 5. Boyfriends/spouse may respond positively to weight loss and obsession with weight 6. When weight loss does occur, the reactions and comments of others are quite rewarding	1. Friends and family may be disgusted 2. People at work might find out and discriminate against you 3. Costs a lot of money and prevents from buying many needed goods and services 4. Must constantly lie to friends and family and run the risk of being caught lying 5. May interfere with or prevent the development of an intimate sexual relationship 6. Creates family conflict 7. Treatment of the medical/dental complications is expensive 8. May result in poor job performance, loss of job, or failure to advance	1. Avoid facing social anxiety 2. Escape from sexual commitments 3. Excuse for inactivity in area of vocational improvement 4. Escape taking risks in interpersonal relationships	1. Destroys savings and other aspects of financial security 2. May result in break up or divorce in intimate relationships 3. Destroys social support systems 4. Prevents individual from getting proper health care

Bulimia can be very expensive financially. These expenses take money that could be used either for necessities or desired luxuries. Many bulimic women have very little to show for years of work because so much of their money has been flushed down the toilet. Another significant source of expense is medical treatment for the long-term physical complications of bulimia.

Eventually bulimia can take its toll on a person's social environment. Good relationships go bad, friends are alienated, and overall the individual is left without much social support. The financial costs destroy savings, ruin credit ratings, and create other problems, such as having to drive an automobile in poor repair. Finally, fear of telling health care professionals and facing up to the problem of bulimia may lead to avoidance of health care contact and end up preventing the individual from receiving comprehensive health care.

Behavioral Consequences of Eating Disorders

Behavioral consequences occur when one activity leads to the performance of another activity. Some activities are preferred and have a reward value in and of themselves. Other activities are aversive and are either punishing or become activities to be avoided. Table 7.4 summarizes the behavioral consequences of disordered eating behavior.

Eating in and of itself is a preferred activity. One of the positive consequences is that the bulimic woman gets to eat everything she wants. A direct pleasure arises from the act of eating, especially forbidden foods. In addition, the activities associated with buying and preparing food may be experienced as enjoyable.

One of the negative consequences of bulimia is that one binge leads

TABLE 7.4 Behavioral Consequences of Anorexia and Bulimia

Positive Consequences	Negative Consequences	Escape and Avoidance	Removal of Positive Consequences
1. Eating is a preferred activity 2. Get to consume lots of good food 3. Food preparation behavior is enjoyable	1. The behaviors involved in purging are unpleasant 2. Dieting is difficult 3. One binge leads to another 4. Very bad eating habits develop 5. Leads to meal skipping and erratic eating	1. Escape or avoid unpleasant tasks 2. Purging save from dieting	1. Takes up time that could be spent in more enjoyable activities

to another. Once the individual loses control and starts bingeing, a long chain of binges may occur before control is regained. All of the negative consequences of bulimia are compounded when this kind of chain-reaction bingeing occurs.

The act of purging is experienced by most individuals as unpleasant. A few will describe purging in terms of gaining relief, but most find that the actual act of throwing up or having diarrhea is downright unpleasant. Most cope with it by not thinking about it.

Dieting is itself unpleasant. Many of the dieting strategies, such as fasting or meal skipping, result in the development of bad eating habits, which take considerable time to correct. One of the consequences of bulimia is the development of an erratic pattern of eating, which cannot be maintained and which sets the person up for alternation between periods of control and loss of control.

An important consequence of every behavior is that it takes a certain amount of time to perform. Given that each person has only twenty-four hours in a day to engage in all of the activities that lead to achieving their important goals in life, the devotion of significant amounts of time to a single activity has numerous implications for the individual's quality of life. Bulimia can affect this quality of life in a profound way. In the first place, bulimia can be used to avoid tasks that are perceived as unpleasant. Often, avoiding these tasks, such as paying bills, will have long-term negative consequences. Not only does bulimia serve as an aid to avoidance and procrastination, it also takes away time from activities that are potentially pleasant and fulfilling.

Cognitive Consequences of Eating Disorders

The cognitive consequences of a behavior are the effects that the behavior has on a person's ideas and thoughts. Typically, the most important cognitive consequences are the effects that behaviors have on our thoughts and images of ourselves, our self-schema. These cognitive consequences can have a profound effect on subsequent behavior. Table 7.5 summarizes the cognitive consequences of disordered eating behaviors.

On the positive side, dieting and food restriction can have the cognitive consequences of confirming the individual's image of oneself as a good person who is in control. It helps develop the expectation that others will like one and approve of one's dieting. Both purging and dieting have the positive consequence of allowing the bulimic woman to see herself as a thin person. Purging and dieting also allow her to believe that she is controlling her weight, which is valued as a good and important thing to do.

Bulimia is also rewarded by some consequences that avoid negative cognitions. The bulimic woman is able to escape having to think and worry

TABLE 7.5 Cognitive Consequences of Anorexia and Bulimia

Positive Consequences	Negative Consequences	Escape and Avoidance	Removal of Positive Consequences
1. Act the way you think other people expect you to act	1. Leads to negative self-evaluation	1. Avoid thinking about troubles while bingeing	1. Takes away your sense of being in control of yourself
2. Purging and dieting allow you to see yourself as a thin person	2. May distort body-image perception	2. Avoid having to think of yourself as a fat person by purging	
3. You think you are controlling your weight	3. Develop negative outcome expectancies with regard to self-control		
	4. Abstinence violation effect		
	5. Rules of dieting become more stringent		

about other problems when she is engaged in the act of bingeing. Also, purging and dieting allow her to avoid unpleasant thoughts about getting fat.

On the negative side, there are some very devastating cognitive impacts of bulimia. When dietary restriction rules are broken, the abstinence violation effect often occurs and an uncontrolled eating binge often results. As a consequence of the loss of control, the individual begins to see herself as weak, ineffective, and out of control. Negative thoughts about the self and negative expectations about the future contribute to a very negative self-image. These negative thoughts about the self then become the antecedents to future episodes of bulimic behavior creating a vicious cycle of negative cognitions and behaviors. The more the individual experiences a loss of control and develops negative expectations about her ability to maintain control over her eating, the more stringent her demands for dieting become. This also creates a situation in which it becomes progressively easier to violate a dietary abstinence rule and to experience a loss of control via the abstinence violation effect.

Bulimic behavior may also have a negative impact on how the individual perceives her body and parts of her body. The idea that parts of the body are fat and the cognitive image of what the body parts look like may change as bulimic behavior gets out of control. Again, these cognitive changes will act to intensify the fear of weight gain and the strictness of the dietary rules that the individual imposes on herself.

Emotional Consequences of Eating Disorders

Emotional consequences refer to feelings that occur as a result of behaviors. While it is often difficult to separate cognition and emotion, identifying something as an emotional consequence is often more a matter of emphasis. For example, the idea that one's hips are too fat is difficult to separate from the feeling of panic that goes along with the idea. Table 7.6 summarizes the emotional consequences of disordered eating behaviors.

There are very few positive emotional consequences of bulimic behavior. There is an emotional satisfaction that comes from eating food. Some individuals describe the feelings they have while eating in terms that are reminiscent of sexual feelings.

Dieting and weight loss are rewarded by feelings of pride, happiness, and satisfaction. Being in control of oneself is a positive emotional experience.

Other positive emotional consequences of bulimia have to do with escape and avoidance. One of the most powerful reinforcing aspects of bulimia is the fact that purging removes the fear of weight gain, provides a sense of relief, and takes away a considerable amount of anxiety. Dieting and exercise are also rewarded by taking away or reducing the fear of weight gain. In addition, bingeing itself is strongly rewarded because it, at least temporarily, removes or reduces negative affect.

TABLE 7.6 Emotional Consequences of Anorexia and Bulimia

Positive Consequences	Negative Consequences	Escape and Avoidance	Removal of Positive Consequences
1. Eating food is very satisfying 2. Dieting results in a sense of satisfaction over being in control 3. Losing weight makes you feel happy	1. Bingeing and vomiting result in guilt 2. Being out of control is depressing 3. Fear of getting fat 4. Hatred of body 5. Chronic depression can occur 6. Fear of the long-term effects of purging 7. Self-hatred 8. Shame	1. Purging gets rid of the fear of weight gain 2. Dieting prevents the fear of weight gain 3. Purging gives a sense of relief 4. Bingeing takes away the bad feelings	1. Bingeing and purging takes away my feeling of being in control 2. Bingeing takes away any good feelings I had about myself 3. Bingeing takes away any good feelings I had about my body

Many of the emotional consequences of bulimia are quite negative. Bingeing and vomiting result in feeling guilty and ashamed. The person feels out of control. An episode of bulimia can result in feeling anxious, guilty, and depressed. A chain of bulimic episodes can result in a more chronic state of depression. The bulimic hates herself, her behavior, and her body. She feels helpless to do anything to regain control. This self-hatred and helplessness is depressing. The depression, guilt, and anxiety create a state of negative affect that carries over to later eating episodes and provokes violations of dietary restriction. The affective outcomes in bulimia, like the cognitive ones, result in a vicious cycle of negative emotions that lead to bingeing and purging, which further intensifies the negative emotions.

Physiological Consequences of Eating Disorders

At this point, our understanding of the physiological consequences of bulimia is incomplete in many areas. Some of the consequences we suggest are speculative and are based more on theory than research. However, we think that it is important to be attuned to the antecedents and consequences of bulimia on the biological level. Table 7.7 summarizes some of the physiological mechanisms that may be serving as positive and negative reinforcers for disordered eating behavior.

There are some positive biological consequences that reward bulimic behavior. For example, eating a meal high in carbohydrate and low in protein may have the effect of reducing anxiety through the action of serotonin in the central nervous system (Wurtman, 1986, Chap. 2, 6). Dieting, exercising, and purging are reinforced by weight loss. In addition, there is some indication that regular bingeing and purging may result in an opioid high (Morley, Levine, & Willenbring, 1986, Chap. 6).

Purging is also rewarded by removing a number of negative physiological states, such as bloatedness, and excess calories consumed. Bingeing may be rewarded by removing some negative conditions, such as hypoglycemia, hypokalemia, and opioid withdrawal. When someone is using laxatives as a purging strategy, continual laxative use is necessary in order to prevent constipation occurring as a withdrawal response.

A number of negative consequences of bulimic behavior occur at the biological level. Some of these are immediate, such as hypoglycemia and hypokalemia, and others are long-term, such as mechanical damage to the gastrointestinal tract and to the teeth. Purging, either by vomiting or laxatives, is an unpleasant and painful act. Dieting may also be punished by allowing an endogenous opioid withdrawal syndrome to occur.

TABLE 7.7 Physiological Consequences of Anorexia and Bulimia

Positive Consequences	Negative Consequences	Escape and Avoidance	Removal of Positive Consequences
1. Eating reduces arousal 2. Dieting results in weight loss 3. Exercise burns calories 4. Bingeing and purging may result in endogenous opioid high 5. Regular purging results in weight loss	1. Purging causes hypoglycemia 2. Purging causes hypokalemia 3. Purging is painful 4. Purging causes damage to gastrointestinal tract and teeth 5. Purging may cause cardiac abnormalities 6. Weight loss results in starvation response consisting of reduced metabolic rate, hypothermia, amenorrhea, irritability, and other symptoms 7. Dieting may result in endogenous opioid withdrawal	1. Purging reduces bloatedness 2. Eating alleviates hypoglycemia 3. Eating alleviates hypokalemia 4. Bingeing and vomiting avoid endogenous opioid withdrawal 5. Purging rids excess calories 6. Continual use of laxatives prevents constipation	None

SUMMARY

Our intent in the discussion of the consequences of bulimia was to argue that anorexia and bulimia are complex disorders. The various behaviors involved—bingeing, purging, fear of weight gain, restrictive dieting—are all rewarded and punished on the environmental, behavioral, cognitive, emotional, and physiological level. These multiple concurrent schedules of reinforcement are what make eating disorders so difficult to treat. Unlike some authors (e.g., Williamson, Prather, Goreczy, Davis, & McKenzie, in press), we do not advocate a simple model of bulimia. We do not think, for example, that it is accurate to say that bulimic behavior is rewarded solely by anxiety reduction that occurs after vomiting (W.G. Johnson & Brief, 1983). Nor is it accurate to state that bingeing is caused by poor eating habits. The most sophisticated approach to bulimia is to realize that each of the behaviors is rewarded by multiple positive consequences, multiple negative consequences, and multiple escape and avoidance consequences.

In this chapter, we presented a model of disordered eating behavior to guide our thinking and action in the realm of assessment and treatment. Our model incorporates the following principles:

1. General systems theory.
2. Anorexia and bulimia must be approached at a behavioral level.
3. To understand behavior, we employ the tools of functional analysis, the study of how behavior is molded by antecedents and consequences.
4. The entire range of biopsychosocial variables must be considered. Many events, biological, cognitive, environmental, social, and emotional, can function as antecedents and consequences.
5. The loss of certainty is more than compensated for by the gain in specificity and comprehensiveness that comes from taking this approach to the assessment and treatment of anorexia and bulimia.

The functional analysis model, taken as a whole, shows that in order to understand the bulimic behavior of any given patient, you must understand the specific antecedents and consequences that operate in that individual's life. The functional analysis needs to be performed at different levels of analysis, including environmental, behavioral, cognitive, affective, and physiological levels. Our description of the antecedents and consequences of disordered eating behavior was, in fact, somewhat simplified. We did not try to describe all of the interactions that occur among events at the different levels of analysis. Environmental events interact with cognitions, behaviors, emotions, and physiology. Likewise, the impact of a physiological variable (opioid withdrawal) will depend on the environmental situation and the individual's cognitive and emotional state at the time.

The functional analysis model of eating disorders is important. Our recommendations for assessment and treatment of anorexia and bulimia follow directly from this model. Conducting an individualized functional analysis is far more important than rendering a single diagnostic judgment. The cost of conceptualizing eating disorders in this way is that we must abandon simple explanations that try to account for anorexia and bulimia on the basis of one variable or one mechanism. The benefit of seeing anorexia and bulimia in their full complexity is that the functional analysis model gives us multiple points of intervention. No one treatment strategy is considered the only way to treat an eating disorder. There are many points of intervention—environmental, behavioral, cognitive, affective, and pharmacological. Each of these will have a different impact, but all of them have the potential of synergistically changing the behaviors of interest. When one intervention does not work, the functional analysis model can be used to generate ideas for other interventions. Our hope is that through appropriate use of assessment data, we can match treatments with patients and obtain the best outcome at the lowest cost in time, money, and tears. An outline of the functional analysis model structured as an assessment form that the clinician can use to guide the collection and analysis of assessment data is presented in Appendix B (B.1).

8

Assessment in Eating Disorders

THIS CHAPTER WILL FOCUS on methods of assessment in the diagnosis and treatment of eating disorders. We will cover a variety of measures and measurement approaches. We have not attempted to be exhaustive in our coverage. We have included the most commonly used measures along with some of our own that are not so commonly used but which may have some merit.

Many of the measures we will discuss were designed for use exclusively with eating-disordered populations. Other measures were designed with the general population in mind or to be applied to obesity. Measures that are designed for specific populations can be much more focused and yield precise information. This precision can often be had without requiring a great deal of time and effort on the part of either the clinician or the patient. On the other hand, it is often useful to have some way of separating people with an eating disorder from those without an eating disorder. This kind of measure, while general in its target population, is usually fairly specific. It is sometimes of interest to compare someone with an eating disorder to members of other populations on much more general measures, such as depression. These kinds of measures that are applicable to the general population must by their very nature be less specific in the kind of information gathered.

The enterprise of psychological and behavioral assessment is a complex one, which offers many alternative methods and approaches to the clinician. In order to utilize assessment procedures, the clinician must have clearly articulated and well-defined questions to ask. Only after the questions have been defined can the clinician select the assessment approach that is most likely to give satisfying and useful answers. In the remainder of this chapter, we will present a basic battery of assessment methods that clinicians and researchers can use to find the best way to answer specific questions about anorexia and bulimia nervosa.

MEASURES SPECIFIC TO EATING DISORDERS

Not surprisingly, a number of assessment instruments, mainly questionnaires, have been developed in the last few years that are specifically for the study and treatment of eating disorders. In this section, we will profile and review some of the more widely used measures of this type.

Probably the most extensively used rating scale in the study of eating disorders is the **Eating Attitudes Test (EAT)**. The scale was developed by Garner and Garfinkel (1979) and has appeared in a forty-item and a twenty-six-item version. The test was originally intended as a way to diagnose anorexia nervosa in epidemiological studies. However, it has not proven particularly useful for this purpose mainly because it is a measure of a psychological construct, anorexic attitude, rather than a measure of actual behavior. The characteristics of the EAT are summarized in Table 8.1.

The **Anorectic Attitudes Questionnaire** was developed by Goldberg, Halmi, Eckert, Casper, Davis, and Roper (1980) to measure changes in attitudes of anorexic patients over time and as a function of treatment. Table 8.2 summarizes the Anorectic Attitudes Questionnaire.

Garner, Olmstead, and Polivy (1983) developed the **Eating Disorder Inventory (EDI)** as a questionnaire measure designed to assess psychological characteristics relevant to both anorexia nervosa and bulimia. The scale was well developed and has known reliability and validity (Garner et al., 1983). Table 8.3 presents a summary of the EDI.

Williams, Schaefer, Shisslak, Gronwaldt, and Comerci (1986) reported a study comparing the EAT, the EDI, and a structured clinical interview on the accuracy of each method in detecting people who potentially have an eating disorder. Subjects were seventy-two adolescent females who were diagnosed using the structured interview with fifty-four considered normal, nine as dieters, eight as suspected bulimics, and one as bulimic. Overall, the different groups showed more differences on the EAT than the EDI. A discriminant analysis using the total EAT score along with three items from the EAT and four items from the EDI was able to correctly classify 86 percent of the subjects. The greatest number of errors were made by classifying dieters as normals. Five of the eight suspected bulimics were correctly classified. Raciti and Norcross (1987) also compared the EAT and the EDI and found both to give similar results in the classification of weight-preoccupied college students.

TABLE 8.1 An Evaluation of the Eating Attitudes Test

Element	Comments
Name	Eating Attitudes Test (EAT)
Citation	Garner and Garfinkel (1979)
Type of measure	Psychological measure of anorexic-like attitudes and beliefs
Potential uses	Population surveys, evaluating the effect of treatment
Populations	Normal populations, anorexia nervosa
Format	26-item or 40-item self-report questionnaire in which the frequencies of attitudes and beliefs are rated using 6-point scales
Scoring	A single score is computed. A cutoff is sometimes used to identify eating-disordered or eating disorder-prone individuals.
Evaluation	Scores on the EAT are correlated with general measures of psychopathology. The scale is not very useful for diagnosing eating disorders. It may be good for identifying individuals at risk for an eating disorder and for tracking the impact of treatment.
Availability	26-item version is published by Halmi (1985b); 40-item version is available from D.M. Garner, Toronto General Hospital, Toronto, Canada.

TABLE 8.2 An Evaluation of the Anorectic Attitudes Questionnaire

Element	Comments
Name	Anorectic Attitudes Questionnaire
Citation	Goldberg, et al. (1980)
Type of measure	Self-report questionnaire measuring attitudes common in anorexia nervosa
Potential uses	Evaluating the impact of treatment of anorexia
Populations	Females diagnosed with anorexia nervosa
Format	63-item rating scale
Scoring	Five subscales: (1) negative attitudes toward hospital staff, (2) fear of fat, (3) denial of illness, (4) negative attitudes towards parents, and (5) experiences hunger.
Evaluation	May be useful in treatment outcome studies; has not been extensively used
Availability	Published in Halmi (1985b)

TABLE 8.3 An Evaluation of the Eating Disorder Inventory

Element	Comments
Name	Eating Disorder Inventory (EDI)
Citation	Garner, Olmstead, and Polivy (1983)
Type of measure	Psychological assessment of constructs presumed to be characteristic of patients with eating disorders
Potential uses	Epidemiological studies, testing research hypotheses by comparing groups, treatment outcome studies
Populations	Eating disorders, comparison groups, normals
Format	64-item rating scale
Scoring	Eight subscales: (1) drive for thinness, (2) bulimia, (3) body dissatisfaction, (4) ineffectiveness, (5) perfectionism, (6) interpersonal distrust, (7) interoceptive awareness, (8) maturity fears
Evaluation	Well-constructed and validated scale; one of the most widely used measures in research
Availability	Garner, Olmstead, and Polivy (1983); Halmi (1985b)

Hawkins and Clement (1980) developed a short self-report measure, the **Binge Scale,** designed to quantify some of the behavioral characteristics of bulimia. Although short, the scale has adequate reliability. It is, however, strongly correlated with the restraint scale (Herman & Polivy, 1975), a measure of tendency to diet. Table 8.4 presents a summary of the Binge Scale.

Halmi, Falk, and Schwartz (1981) developed the **Binge Eating Questionnaire** to quantify behavioral characteristics associated with bulimia for an epidemiological study. The questionnaire consists of twelve demographic items and eleven items asking about bingeing and purging behaviors. Its primary purpose is to provide a method for establishing a diagnosis of bulimia, since its questions assess most of the behaviors required for a DSM-III diagnosis. The Binge Eating Questionnaire is summarized in Table 8.5.

Schulman, Kindwer, Powers, Prange, and Gleghorn (1986) developed the **Bulimia Cognitive Distortions Scale** to measure cognitive beliefs and irrational thoughts associated with bulimia. The scale easily discriminates eating-disordered from normal subjects. It is not known whether it can discriminate bulimic from anorexic subjects. The Bulimia Cognitive Distortions Scale is summarized in Table 8.6.

Slade and Dewey (1986) developed a scale for screening individuals at risk for developing anorexia and bulimia nervosa. The scale, named the **SCANS,** is a forty-item, self-report inventory that measures psychological

TABLE 8.4 An Evaluation of the Binge Scale

Element	Comments
Name	Binge Scale
Citation	Hawkins and Clement (1980)
Type of measure	Behavioral assessment of binge eating
Potential uses	Screening for eating disorders, epidemiological studies, treatment planning, treatment outcome
Populations	Normal and eating disorders
Format	Nine-item, multiple choice self-report questionnaire
Scoring	Single total score derived from a weighted sum of the nine items
Evaluation	Good choice in research when a short scale is needed; provides descriptive data on behavior that may be useful clinically; may be too short for some purposes especially in epidemiological studies
Availability	Hawkins and Clement (1980); Halmi (1985b)

TABLE 8.5 An Evaluation of the Binge Eating Questionnaire

Element	Comments
Name	Binge Eating Questionnaire
Citation	Halmi, Falk, and Schwartz (1981)
Type of measure	Behavioral assessment of bulimic behavior
Potential uses	Diagnosis and screening for bulimia in populations
Populations	Normals
Format	12 demographic, and 11 multiple-choice items describing bulimic behaviors
Scoring	Not scored; each item is used separately
Evaluation	May be useful as a quick screening device
Availability	Halmi (1985b)

constructs presumed to be associated with eating disorders. Table 8.7 summarizes the SCANS.

Smith and Thelen (1984) developed the **BULIT** questionnaire as a way to diagnose bulimia and to distinguish bulimic from anorexic patients. The questionnaire consists of thirty-two multiple choice items that describe thoughts, feelings, or behaviors associated with bulimia. The BULIT is summarized in Table 8.8.

TABLE 8.6 An Evaluation of the Bulimia Cognitive Distortions Scale

Element	Comments
Name	Bulimia Cognitive Distortions Scale
Citation	Schulman et al. (1986)
Type of measure	Psychological assessment of irrational thoughts associated with bulimia nervosa
Potential uses	Testing research hypotheses, planning cognitive behavior therapy, treatment outcome studies
Populations	Bulimia nervosa
Format	25-item rated on a five-point agreement scale
Scoring	Total score plus two factor analytically derived subscales: (1) automatic eating, (2) cognitive distortions about appearance
Evaluation	Not that useful for diagnosis; may have some use clinically and for research
Availability	Write: Bill Kinder, Dept. of Psychology, University of South Florida, Tampa, FL 33620

TABLE 8.7 An Evaluation of the SCANS

Element	Comments
Name	SCANS
Citation	Slade and Dewey (1986)
Type of measure	Psychological assessment of constructs believed to measure characteristics of people who are at high risk for developing an eating disorder
Potential uses	Testing research hypotheses in prospective studies
Populations	Normals, high risk individuals
Format	40 items in which the subject compares self to a person with certain described characteristics
Scoring	Five factor analytically derived subscales: (1) general dissatisfaction, (2) social and personal anxiety, (3) perfectionism, (4) adolescent problems, (5) weight control
Evaluation	The usefulness of the SCANS in predicting who will develop an eating disorder is currently unknown.
Availability	Slade and Dewey (1986)

TABLE 8.8 An Evaluation of the BULIT

Element	Comments
Name	BULIT
Citation	Smith and Thelen (1984)
Type of measure	Questionnaire measure for diagnosis of bulimia
Potential uses	Epidemiological studies, research, diagnosis
Populations	Normal and eating-disordered
Format	32-item multiple-choice questionnaire. Items are descriptions of feelings and behaviors associated with bulimia.
Scoring	A total score is calculated and can be compared to a cutoff for diagnostic purposes.
Evaluation	Adequate reliability and validity; may be useful for the measurement of degree of disordered eating behavior in nonclinical populations
Availability	Smith and Thelen (1984)

The **Bulimic Investigatory Test Edinburgh (BITE)** is a brief self-report instrument designed to measure the occurrence and severity of either DSM-III bulimia or bulimia nervosa (Henderson & Freeman, 1987). While relatively new, the authors report reliability and validity data. The questionnaire was designed to resolve some of the ambiguities of previous questionnaires that merely asked subjects if they ever binged. The BITE is summarized in Table 8.9.

TABLE 8.9 An Evaluation of the BITE

Element	Comments
Name	Bulimic Investigatory Test Edinburgh (BITE)
Citation	Henderson and Freeman (1987)
Type of measure	Questionnaire measure for diagnosis of DSM-III bulimia and/or bulimia nervosa
Potential uses	Epidemiological studies, research, diagnosis
Populations	Normal and eating-disordered
Format	Modeled after the Eating Attitudes Test. Items are descriptions of feelings and behaviors associated with bulimia.
Scoring	A total score is calculated and can be compared to a cutoff for diagnostic purposes.
Evaluation	Adequate reliability and validity reported
Availability	Henderson and Freeman (1987)

GENERAL PSYCHOLOGICAL TESTS

An enormous variety of psychological tests are available today. As with the tests specific to eating disorders, other psychological and behavioral assessments differ widely in their purpose, format, and specificity. We will not be able to present all of the possible tests that might be useful to answer the many questions that arise concerning a patient with eating disorders. Instead, we will focus on basic information that may prove useful to clinicians who do not have a strong background in psychological or behavioral assessment.

We suggest that each clinician choose one or two objective tests that give a multidimensional profile of psychopathology to use with all patients to screen for severity of psychological distress. There are several advantages to using one or more of these tests routinely:

1. The content areas covered by these tests are often quite broad.
2. Some patients feel more comfortable admitting to certain feelings or behaviors on a test than discussing them in an intake interview.
3. The results of testing will alert the clinician to areas that need to be explored in greater detail in an interview.
4. The use of a standard battery of tests on all patients allows the clinician to build a database that can be used to compare patients.
5. Patients who are more severely disturbed (e.g., major depression, psychosis) can be quickly identified using standardized objective tests.
6. The severity of the disturbances seen in eating-disordered patients can be put into the context of the disturbances experienced by other patients seeking psychological or psychiatric help by referring to the test's normative data.
7. Some psychological states, such as depression and anxiety, are common elements of eating disorders.

SCL-90

The Symptom Checklist 90 (SCL-90) asks patients to rate the severity of each of ninety psychological or somatic symptoms on a five-point distress scale (Derogatis, Lipman, & Covi, 1973). The items were selected to reflect the kinds of distressing symptoms often experienced by psychiatric patients. The scale, however, has been extensively used in general medical settings to measure degree and type of psychological distress.

The scale is easy to administer, takes only about twenty to thirty minutes to complete, and is relatively simple to score. It provides the clinician with a quick overview of areas of distress, and can then serve as a basis for more detailed assessment or interviewing. It provides screening for a broad range of psychological problems. The existence of norms allows the clinician to evaluate the relative severity of each set of symptoms and greatly contributes to the interpretability of test results. The SCL-90 is summarized in Table 8.10.

Ordman and Kirschenbaum (1986) compared twenty-five bulimic subjects to thirty-six normal controls on a variety of psychological measures including the SCL-90. The eating-disordered patients expressed significantly more psychopathology on all nine of the SCL-90 subscales than the normal control group. Williamson, Kelley, Ruggiero, and Blouin (1985) compared fifteen bulimic women to fifteen obese and fifteen normal weight women on a variety of psychological measures. The bulimic subjects scored significantly higher on all of the SCL-90 scales than the normal weight and obese group with the exception of the hostility scale. Weiss and Ebert

TABLE 8.10 An Evaluation of the SCL-90

Element	*Comments*
Name	Symptom Checklist 90 (SCL-90)
Citation	Derogatis et al. (1973)
Type of measure	Psychological assessment of symptoms of psychopathology
Potential uses	Clinical screening instrument, testing research hypotheses, treatment outcome studies
Populations	Eating-disordered patients
Format	90-item self-report questionnaire. Each symptom is rated on a 5-point distress scale.
Scoring	General Symptom index, nine subscales: (1) somatization, (2) obsessive-compulsive, (3) interpersonal sensitivity, (4) depression, (5) anxiety, (6) hostility, (7) phobic anxiety, (8) paranoid ideation, (9) psychoticism. A normative profile can be drawn.
Evaluation	Very good way to screen for areas of psychological distress; does not result in much specific information to use in treatment planning; good source of data for comparing the severity of different cases
Availability	Clinical Psychometric Research, 1228 Wine Spring Lane, Townson, MD 21204

(1983) compared fifteen bulimics to fifteen normal controls on a number of measures including the SCL-90 and reported that the bulimic group scored significantly higher than the normals on all of the nine scales. Johnson, Schlundt, Kelley, and Ruggiero (1984) examined SCL-90 data on eight bulimic patients undergoing outpatient treatment. When the response patterns were compared to the normal female norms, the bulimics were found to be deviant on all scales. When the norms for female outpatient psychiatric patients were used, the profiles were very near the mean. The SCL-90 data seems to suggest that, overall, patients seeking treatment for bulimia show considerable psychological distress in almost all areas. However, when compared to other women seeking psychiatric help, no particular area of distress stands out.

Minnesota Multiphasic Personality Inventory

The MMPI is one of the most extensively used and studied personality tests. It was developed in the late 1930s as an objective way to make psychiatric diagnoses. The test is used less for making diagnoses and more for measuring areas of psychopathology or psychological disturbance. As such, the MMPI is widely used as a screening test that is given to all patients in psychiatric and mental health settings.

In treating eating disorders, the primary use of the MMPI is as an initial screening instrument that can alert the clinician to areas of potential distress and psychopathology. Since the MMPI is long, and takes a considerable amount of the patient's time to complete, it may not always be the most efficient way to screen for psychopathology. The validity scales are able to detect when individuals are trying to make themselves look better or worse than they really are. The characteristics of the MMPI are summarized in Table 8.11.

Williamson, Kelley, Davis, Ruggiero, & Blouin (1985) in a study comparing fifteen bulimic to fifteen obese and normal controls administered the MMPI to all subjects. The bulimic group scored higher (showed more psychopathology) than both the normal and obese group on the depression, hypochondriasis, and hysteria scales. The bulimics also scored higher on the psychopathic deviate scale than the normal group but did not differ from the obese group. Both the bulimic and obese groups had higher scores on the psychasthenia and schizophrenia scales. When the MMPI profiles were plotted using the norms, thirteen of the fifteen bulimic subjects showed significant elevations (more than two standard deviations above the mean) on at least one of the MMPI scales. The most frequent deviations were observed on the depression, hysteria, psychopathic-deviate, and schizophrenia scales.

TABLE 8.11 An Evaluation of the MMPI

Element	Comments
Name	Minnesota Multiphasic Personality Inventory (MMPI)
Citation	Dahlstrom et al. (1972)
Type of measure	Personality test that measures the extent to which an individual's responses resemble those of different psychiatric diagnostic groups
Potential uses	An instrument for screening eating-disordered patients for psychopathology. Most useful at intake or treatment initiation.
Populations	Eating-disordered patients
Format	566 item true/false questionnaire
Scoring	Ten subscales that reflect 10 areas of psychopathology: (1) hypochondriasis, (2) depression, (3) hysteria, (4) psychopathic-deviate, (5) masculinity-femininity, (6) paranoia, (7) psychasthenia, (8) schizophrenia, (9) hypomania, (10) social introversion. Three validity scales are also computed. The scores are compared to norms and the deviations from the norm are plotted on a profile.
Evaluation	Very widely used test. However, takes a long time to administer, and age of test norms creates some difficulties in interpretation. Much literature is available on how to interpret the MMPI.
Availability	NCS Interpretive Scoring Systems, P.O. Box 1416, Minneapolis, MN 55440

Beck Depression Inventory (BDI)

As we have seen in reviewing eating disorders, depression is a common feature. In assessing a patient with an eating disorder, it is very important to determine whether the patient is depressed and if so, how severe the depression is. While both the SCL-90 and MMPI contain depression subscales, the Beck Depression Inventory (BDI) was developed by Beck and Beck (1972) to scale severity of depression more precisely than screening instruments such as the SCL-90. The BDI is summarized in Table 8.12.

The BDI can provide useful information to the clinician throughout the process of treating someone with an eating disorder. At intake and screening, it is important to know the severity of depression experienced by a patient. The severity of depression has clear implications for the treatment approach to be selected. For example, a bulimic patient with

TABLE 8.12 An Evaluation of the Beck Depression Inventory

Element	Comments
Name	Beck Depression Inventory (BDI)
Citation	Beck and Beck (1972)
Type of measure	Psychological assessment of the severity of depression
Potential uses	Screening instrument, treatment planning, monitoring the effects of treatment, testing research hypotheses
Populations	Adults
Format	21-item multiple-choice questionnaire. The choices for each item represent different behavioral manifestations of depression
Scoring	A total score is computed as a sum of the item scores. The scores are interpreted as follows: 0–9 normal, 10–15 mild depression, 16–19 mild to moderate depression, 20–29 moderate to severe, and 30–63 severe depression.
Evaluation	Very good instrument for measuring severity of depression and for identifying behavioral manifestations of depression for a particular patient; useful throughout the process of treating someone with an eating disorder.
Availability	Beck and Beck (1972)

moderate to severe depression may greatly benefit from a trial on antidepressant medication. During treatment, the BDI can be administered repeatedly to keep track of any changes in severity of depression that might be occurring. A standardized questionnaire like the BDI is a better way to keep track of changes in affect over time than simply asking patients if they feel better.

Fear of Negative Evaluations

The SCL-90 and MMPI measure a broad range of psychological constructs. While both the SCL-90 and MMPI have a subscale measure of interpersonal sensitivity, neither is a very specific measure of interpersonal function. The Fear of Negative Evaluations (FNE) scale, developed by Watson and Friend (1969), is a more specific measure of social functioning that may have more direct utility for clinical work than the MMPI or SCL-90 subscales. The FNE measures the degree of evaluative anxiety an individual has concerning social situations, interactions, and relationships. The items are very specific and could be used directly as material for cognitive behavior therapy sessions. While norms for eating-disordered populations have not been published, we have found clinically that many eating-disordered patients score high on this scale, indicating extreme concern over what people think about them. The FNE is summarized in Table 8.13.

Social Avoidance and Distress (SAD)

The social avoidance and distress scale (SAD) is a companion measure to the FNE. While the FNE measures fear of interpersonal evaluation, the SAD assesses social anxiety and social avoidance behavior. While many eating-disordered patients will show a high fear of negative evaluation, only some experience high levels of social anxiety and actively avoid social interactions. These two scales, the FNE and the SAD, used together will give a fairly specific assessment of how the patient thinks, feels, and behaves with respect to social interactions. Like the FNE, the items on the SAD are very specific and could be used directly in cognitive behavior therapy. Table 8.14 summarizes the SAD.

TABLE 8.13 An Evaluation of the FNE

Element	*Comments*
Name	Fear of Negative Evaluation (FNE)
Citation	Watson and Friend (1969)
Type of measure	Questionnaire to assess the extent to which an individual anticipates that social interactions will have negative outcomes and fears negative evaluations from others
Potential uses	Research, treatment planning, treatment evaluation
Populations	Adults
Format	30-item true/false questionnaire. The items describe thoughts and feelings associated with social interactions.
Scoring	A total score is calculated reflecting degree of evaluative fear.
Evaluation	Adequate reliability and validity; may be useful for planning social problem-solving therapy and for obtaining information for cognitive behavior therapy
Availability	Watson and Friend (1969)

TABLE 8.14 An Evaluation of the SAD

Element	Comments
Name	Social Avoidance and Distress (SAD)
Citation	Watson and Friend (1969)
Type of measure	Questionnaire to assess the extent to which an individual actively avoids social situations and experiences anxiety when unable to avoid social interactions
Potential uses	Research, treatment planning, treatment evaluation
Populations	Adults
Format	28-item true/false questionnaire. The items describe feelings and behaviors associated with social interactions.
Scoring	A total score is calculated reflecting degree of avoidance and distress.
Evaluation	Adequate reliability and validity; may be useful for planning social problem-solving therapy and obtaining information for cognitive behavior therapy
Availability	Watson and Friend (1969)

OTHER ASSESSMENTS OF EATING BEHAVIOR

Since all eating disorders involve some kind of disturbance in eating behavior and in thoughts and feelings associated with food and eating, it may sometimes be useful to use assessment methods that focus on eating behavior but not specifically disordered eating behavior. Several of these measures will be presented in this section.

The Dieter's Inventory of Eating Temptations (DIET)

The Dieter's Inventory of Eating Temptations (DIET) was developed by Schlundt and Zimering (1988) as a structured behavioral assessment of weight control competence. The inventory was originally designed for use with obese individuals who are trying to lose weight, but may have some use with individuals with an eating disorder. A complete copy of the DIET questionnaire appears in Appendix B.

In order to identify different eating styles, Schlundt and Zimering performed a cluster analysis of subjects based on their responses to the DIET questionnaire. A separate analysis was conducted on overweight men and women since there may be sex differences in eating patterns. The results suggest that there are, in fact, very different patterns of behavior that may underlie a weight problem. For the overweight women, six different behavior patterns were identified, which were interpreted as follows:

1. *Impulse control.* These women have great difficulty resisting temptation and knowing when to stop overeating. They did not show much of a tendency to eat in response to negative emotions and were conscientious about exercising.

2. *Poor food choice.* This group of women were able to handle most of the situations pretty well. Their main problem area concerned preference for high-fat foods and for fattening food preparation techniques.

3. *Social eaters.* This group made very good food choices when they were alone. They could resist temptation and did not show any great difficulty with emotional eating. Their problem occurs when they have to eat in a positive social situation. These women have a very hard time controlling their food intake when they must eat at social affairs.

4. *Socially restrained.* This group showed great restraint in public but had problems resisting temptation when alone. They are good dieters in that they choose low-fat foods and food preparation techniques, but have problems resisting the temptation to snack when they are by themselves.

5. *Emotional eaters.* This group did fairly well in most situations with the exception of eating in response to negative emotions. This group of women use food as a way to comfort themselves when they feel bad.

6. *Uncontrolled.* This group of women had problems across the board. They reported that almost all of the situations were difficult for them to handle.

Similar clusters were identified for men. Men tended to have more problems with social eating and food choice and fewer problems with emotional eating than women.

With respect to eating disorders, the DIET questionnaire may be quite useful in helping the clinician identify the kinds of situations that may potentially precipitate binge eating. Table 8.15 summarizes the DIET questionnaire.

Food Survey

The Food Survey was developed as a device for measuring the construct of food phobia. That is, some individuals develop fears of eating specific

TABLE 8.15 An Evaluation of the DIET Questionnaire

Element	Comments
Name	Dieter's Inventory of Eating Temptations (DIET)
Citation	Schlundt and Zimering (1988)
Type of measure	Behavioral assessment of weight control competence
Potential uses	Treatment planning
Populations	Any group attempting to restrict food intake or exercise for weight control purposes
Format	30-item situational inventory. Each item presents a situational description along with a competent response. The subject rates the percentage of time he or she would behave as described in similar situations.
Scoring	A total score and six subscales are computed. The subscales are: resisting temptation, positive social, food choice, exercise, overeating, and negative emotions. Two profile plots are available, the average rating and normative based T-scores.
Evaluation	May be useful for identifying the kinds of situations most likely to trigger loss of control (binge eating) in bulimic patients; very useful in behavioral weight loss programs.
Availability	Appendix B

foods or specific types of food. These fears, while quite pronounced in patients with eating disorders, may also be present in other populations as well.

The scale consists of a sample of forty-five food items. The items are from five food groups (milk, meat, grains, fruits/vegetables, and beverages). From each food group, three items were selected at each of three calorie levels (low, medium, high). The format of the test requires the subject to rate "how would you feel about yourself after eating this food."

The Food Survey results in eight scores: one for each of the five food groups and a score for low, medium, and high calorie foods. The scores represent the extent to which the individual fears and avoids each food group or various caloric levels of food. The raw scores are then converted to T-scores so that the extent to which the individual shows an unusual phobic reaction to each food group or calorie level can be measured. The Food Survey, a form for scoring the Food Survey and plotting profiles, and instructions for scoring and interpreting the Food Survey are contained in Appendix B. Table 8.16 summarizes the internal consistency and test-retest reliability of the Food Survey. These data indicate the scales of the Food Survey have moderate to good reliability. Some of the subscales, milk and beverage for example, consist of very diverse sets of items and would not be expected to show great internal consistency for most subjects. However, responses to the caloric levels and to other food groups showed good internal consistency.

To establish convergent validity of the Food Survey, the Food Survey along with several other measures of the tendency to diet and the concern with one's weight were administered to fifty-one undergraduate females. The measures included the Body Cathexis Scale, the Three-Factor Eating Questionnaire, and the BULIT. Several of the Food Survey scales, particularly meat, grain, and medium calorie foods, are strongly correlated with the BULIT, a self-report measure of bulimic behavior (Smith & Thelen, 1984). In addition, these scales also show good correlation with the Body Cathexis Scale, a general measure of body dissatisfaction. It is also interesting that subjects with a strong tendency towards dieting (scored high on the restraint subscale of the Three-Factor Eating Questionnaire of Stunkard & Messick, 1985) were likely to be sensitive to the calorie content of fruits, vegetables, and beverages. Table 8.17 summarizes this validity data for the Food Survey.

Ruggiero et al. (1988) compared bulimic subjects who purged, to women who only binged and to a normal eating control group. The low-calorie foods, fruits/vegetables, and beverage scales did not discriminate between the groups. The purgers differed from those who only binged by showing more phobic responses to grains and high-calorie foods. The eating-disordered subjects differed from the normal controls on the milk, meat, grain, high calorie, and medium calorie food scales. In a separate experiment, Ruggiero et al. compared purgers to obese and noneating-disordered subjects. Again, the fruits/vegetables, beverages, and low-calorie food scales did not differentiate between the groups. The obese group showed more food avoidance than the normal control group on the high-calorie food scale. The purgers showed more phobic reactions than the obese on the grain

TABLE 8.16 Reliability of the Food Survey

Scale	Internal Consistency	Test-Retest Reliability
Meat	0.85	0.90
Milk	0.60	0.63
Fruits/Vegetables	0.82	0.85
Grains	0.85	0.73
Beverage	0.52	0.67
Low Calorie	0.79	0.83
Medium Calorie	0.80	0.82
High Calorie	0.85	0.78

TABLE 8.17 Validity of the Food Survey

	Milk	Meat	Fruits/ Vegetables	Grain	Beverage	High Calorie	Medium Calorie	Low Calorie	Body Cathexis Scale	BULIT	Restraint Subscale	Disinhibition Scale
Milk	1.0	.36*	.41*	.53#	.29	.13	.72#	.49#	.26	.32	.30	.39*
Meat		1.0	.00	.62#	.20	.44*	.56#	−.04	.43#	.49#	.35*	.42*
Fruits/Vegetables			1.0	−.02	.36*	−.18	.54#	.85#	−.03	−.08	−.06	−.05
Grain				1.0	.25	.50#	.71#	−.06	.34*	.50#	.45#	.52#
Beverage					1.0	.16	.50#	.46#	−.17	.07	.02	−.03
High Calorie						1.0	.34*	−.06	.23	.28	.06	.32
Medium Calorie							1.0	.45#	.23	.42*	.28	.43#
Low Calorie								1.0	−.08	−.15	−.14	−.17
Body Cathexis Scale									1.0	.46#	.41*	.35*
BULIT										1.0	.27	.84#
Restraint Subscale											1.0	.24
Disinhibition Scale												1.0

*$p < 0.01$
#$p < 0.05$

and medium-calorie food scales, and differed from the normal control group on the milk, meat, grain, high-calorie, and medium-calorie scales.

The Food Survey is primarily intended as an individual assessment tool for treatment planning. Before initiating treatment (especially the exposure treatments described in Chapter 12), it is very useful to get an idea of the kinds of foods the person can and cannot eat comfortably. The Food Survey will identify food groups that the person fears eating, along with providing information on how comfortable that person is with medium- and low-calorie foods. The individual items can be used to form a hierarchy of foods ranging from least anxiety provoking to most anxiety provoking that can then be used to introduce foods gradually into the patient's diet. Table 8.18 summarizes the Food Survey.

Three-Factor Eating Questionnaire

Stunkard and Messick (1985) have developed a self-report questionnaire that measures three aspects of human eating behavior: dietary restraint, disinhibition, and hunger.

TABLE 8.18 An Evaluation of the Food Survey

Element	Comments
Name	Food Survey
Citation	Ruggiero, Williamson, Davis, Carey, & Schlundt (1988)
Type of measure	Psychological measure of food phobia
Potential uses	Treatment planning, testing research hypotheses, evaluating the impact of treatment
Populations	Normal weight, obese, and eating-disordered
Format	45-item self-report measure. Each item is a common food. The subjects rate how they would feel about themselves after eating each food on a 1–5 scale.
Scoring	Subscale scores are formed measuring fear and avoidance of: meat, milk, fruits/vegetables, grains, beverages, low calorie foods, medium calorie foods, and high calorie foods.
Evaluation	Correlates with measures of eating disorder and distinguishes normals from eating disordered. In addition, it is related to the severity of the eating disorder. May be very useful in treatment planning to help identify specific food fears.
Availability	Appendix B

As seen in Table 8.17, the restraint subscale of the Three-Factor Eating Questionnaire was correlated with several of the Food Survey measures of food avoidance. In addition, it was correlated with body dissatisfaction as measured by the Body Cathexis Scale. However, restraint was not correlated with scores on the BULIT. The disinhibition scale showed a stronger pattern of correlations with food avoidance and was highly correlated with the BULIT. The hunger scale was not correlated with any of the measures of food avoidance but was associated with body dissatisfaction, bulimic eating behavior, and the disinhibition scale. The Three-Factor Eating Questionnaire is summarized in Table 8.19.

Ganley (1988) conducted a factor analysis of the Three Factor Eating Questionnaire using a large sample ($n = 442$) of adult women. Instead of three factors, Ganley replicated Stunkard and Messick's (1985) restraint and hunger factors. Their disinhibition factor, however, split into two distinct factors in Ganley's analysis, weight lability and emotional eating. Contrary to previous findings, Ganley found no correlation between dietary restraint and emotional eating or weight lability.

Restraint Scale

Dietary restraint refers to the voluntary restriction of food intake for purposes of weight control. While originally developed to account for

TABLE 8.19 An Evaluation of the Three-Factor Eating Questionnaire

Element	Comments
Name	Three-Factor Eating Questionnaire
Citation	Stunkard and Messick (1985)
Type of measure	Measures psychological constructs of cognitive restraint, disinhibition, and hunger
Potential uses	Testing research hypotheses, treatment planning, monitoring the effects of treatment
Populations	Normal, obese, and eating-disordered
Format	51-item self-report questionnaire consisting of both true/false and multiple-choice ratings.
Scoring	Three subscales based on factor analysis: cognitive restraint, disinhibition, and hunger. Norms are published.
Evaluation	Better measure of the restraint concept than the original restraint scale and should be used instead. Data indicates good reliability and validity.
Availability	Stunkard and Messick (1985)

differences between obese and normal weight individuals (Herman & Mack, 1975), restraint has been shown to be relevant to individuals with eating disorders (Johnson, Corrigan, Crusco, & Schlundt, 1986). The Restraint Scale is a short questionnaire that assesses the extent to which an individual practices dietary restriction for purposes of weight control. The Restraint Scale is closely related to the restraint subscale of the Stunkard and Messick (1985) Three Factor Eating Questionnaire. In fact, many of the items are identical. Table 8.20 summarizes the Restraint Scale.

SEMISTRUCTURED INTERVIEWS AND INTERVIEW FORMS

Thus far, we have covered a variety of questionnaires that we believe will prove useful in the assessment and treatment of eating disorders. Questionnaires tend to be very specific, measuring only a few well-focused constructs and behaviors. In addition, questionnaires are almost always quantified in one way or another giving the clinician a number or profile of numbers as the end product. Questionnaires can be extremely useful. They are highly reliable, can be constructed to minimize faking, and provide an excellent way to compare one person to another on quantitative dimensions. However, the clinician who is conducting an assessment of a patient with an eating disorder needs a great deal of information that is not provided by psychometric questionnaires. In the treatment of eating disorders,

TABLE 8.20 An Evaluation of the Restraint Scale

Element	*Comments*
Name	Restraint Scale
Citation	Herman and Mack (1975)
Type of measure	Measures the tendency to restrict food intake for purposes of weight control
Potential uses	Testing research hypotheses, treatment planning, monitoring the effects of treatment
Populations	Normal, obese, and eating-disordered
Format	Self-report true/false questionnaire
Scoring	Total score measuring degree of dietary restraint
Evaluation	Shorter than the three-factor eating questionnaire; can be used to obtain a quick quantitative index of dietary restraint.
Availability	Herman and Mack (1975)

it is often useful and expedient to use a structured form or interview schedule in order to gather a large body of behavioral and psychological information in a short period of time. A number of useful interviews and interview forms have been published.

The **Diagnostic Survey for Eating Disorders** was developed by C. Johnson (1985) as a questionnaire designed to elicit a broad range of information from patients with eating disorders. The survey can be used either as a self-report inventory or as a semistructured interview. Johnson suggests that the form be completed by the patient as a questionnaire prior to the first interview. The first interview then involves going over the form with the patient and obtaining additional detail on various areas and assessing the patient's affective response to certain topics. The Diagnostic Survey for Eating Disorders is described in Table 8.21.

The **Bulimia Interview Form** was developed by Walsh and Gladis (Halmi, 1985b). It is a structured interview designed to obtain specific and detailed information about bulimic patients. It was developed to facilitate coding and quantification of the interview results so that it can be used to form a computerized patient data base. A summary of the bulimia interview form is presented in Table 8.22.

TABLE 8.21 An Evaluation of the Diagnostic Survey for Eating Disorders

Element	*Comments*
Name	Diagnostic Survey for Eating Disorders
Citation	C. Johnson (1985)
Type of measure	Interview form or structured interview
Potential uses	Diagnosis, treatment planning, research
Populations	Anorexia and bulimia nervosa
Format	Form provides a way to code and quantify answers to questions on demographic background, weight history and body image, dieting behavior, binge-eating behavior, purging, exercise, other related behaviors, sexual history, menstrual history, medical and psychiatric history, life adjustment, and family history.
Scoring	No scores are derived; used to gather descriptive information; may be entered into computer data base
Evaluation	Excellent screening instrument for diagnosis and treatment planning; works well if completed before the initial interview and then used as a basis for the first clinical interview with the patient.
Availability	C. Johnson (1985)

TABLE 8.22 An Evaluation of the Bulimia Interview Form

Element	Comments
Name	Bulimia Interview Form
Citation	Walsh and Gladis (in Halmi, 1985b)
Type of measure	Structured interview with coding instructions
Potential uses	Bulimia research, diagnosis, treatment planning
Populations	Bulimia Nervosa
Format	Printed interview schedule with places to code and record responses
Scoring	Interviewer uses his/her judgment to score the responses
Evaluation	Good interview that focuses mainly on the eating disorder. Very good if a detailed computerized data base is being instructed. Interview format allows for more flexibility in how the information is obtained. More detail can be obtained about important areas.
Availability	Halmi (1985b)

The eating disorders group at the University of Minnesota (Mitchell, Hatsukami, Eckert, and Pyle) have developed an interview form for patients with eating disorders that can be self-administered by patients (Halmi, 1985b). The **Minnesota Eating Disorders Questionnaire** is summarized in Table 8.23.

Powers (Powers & Fernandez, 1984) has developed an interview form for the diagnosis and assessment of patients with eating disorders. The form is designed to be completed by patients as a questionnaire. The **South Florida Eating Disorders Questionnaire** is summarized in Table 8.24.

The **Health Habit Survey** (see Appendix B) is a questionnaire designed to obtain specific, broad-based information about a prospective patient's eating behavior, exercise, and health history. We routinely use the Health Habit Survey as a baseline assessment instrument to obtain a systematic self-report of a patient's eating and exercise patterns. The Health Habit Survey is summarized in Table 8.25.

PHYSICAL MEASURES

The routine assessment of eating-disordered patients typically involves the collection not only of psychological and behavioral data but also of medical and physiological information. Patients with an eating disorder who are seeking treatment should always have a thorough physical exam by a

TABLE 8.23 An Evaluation of the Minnesota Eating Disorders Questionnaire

Element	Comments
Name	Minnesota Eating Disorders Questionnaire
Citation	Mitchell, Hatsukami, Eckert, and Pyle (in Halmi, 1985b)
Type of measure	Detailed interview that is completed by the subject as an interview form
Potential uses	Treatment planning, diagnosis, research
Populations	Anorexia and bulimia nervosa
Format	Self-report questionnaire that can be keypunched into a computer data base. Covers demographic information, weight history, dieting behavior, binge-eating behavior, purging behavior, exercise, substance abuse, suicide, self-mutilation, menstrual history, marriage and pregnancy, medical and psychiatric history, and life adjustment.
Scoring	No scores are obtained.
Evaluation	Very complete interview; can be self-administered as a questionnaire; quantifies many of the feelings and behaviors
Availability	Halmi (1985b)

TABLE 8.24 An Evaluation of the South Florida Eating Disorders Questionnaire

Element	Comments
Name	South Florida Eating Disorders Questionnaire
Citation	Powers and Fernandez (1984)
Type of measure	Interview completed by the patient as a questionnaire
Potential uses	Diagnosis, treatment planning, research
Populations	Anorexia and bulimia nervosa
Format	An interview form; covers weight history, binge eating, purging, medical history, social history, weight profile, and autobiography
Scoring	No scores are derived; can be coded and entered into a computer data base.
Evaluation	Very thorough interview form; can be used to gather a large amount of information with little professional time involved
Availability	Powers and Fernandez (1984)

TABLE 8.25 An Evaluation of the Health Habit Survey

Element	Comments
Name	Health Habit Survey
Citation	W.G. Johnson, unpublished
Type of measure	Interview questionnaire used to obtain description of eating, exercise, and other health behaviors
Potential uses	Clinical assessment, treatment planning
Populations	Normal, obese, and eating-disordered
Format	Questionnaire with a variety of open-ended, multiple-choice, and fill-in-the blank items.
Scoring	Not scored
Evaluation	Clinically useful screening instrument for pretreatment assessment with eating-disordered and obese patients
Availability	Appendix B

physician. This requires that anyone who works with eating-disordered patients develop a working relationship with a physician. The physician should investigate the possibility that any of the physical symptoms experienced by the eating-disordered patient are due to some physical disease or abnormality rather than merely consequences of the disordered eating behavior. Powers (1984) discusses the physical symptoms encountered frequently in eating-disordered patients, the types of laboratory or clinical tests used, and their connection with disordered eating behavior. A number of physical tests may be useful in the assessment of an eating-disordered patient. These tests are summarized in the next few sections.

Body Composition

We have found that it is useful to estimate body fat percentage in eating-disordered patients. This information is often more useful than body weight in determining the extent of weight loss or emaciation since body frame size and muscle mass contribute to considerable variability in relative weight measures. There are several methods available for studying body composition: sum of skinfolds, underwater weighing, electrical resistance techniques, and radioactive potassium studies. However, the use of radioactive potassium (K_{40}) requires sophisticated radiologic equipment and, hence, is not cost effective for most nonresearch purposes.

The electrical resistance technique involves obtaining an estimate of body composition through an analysis of the body's resistance to a low voltage current. The device is relatively inexpensive and is currently used by many fitness centers and health promotion facilities. There are some problems with the accuracy of this technique, particularly in populations that were not part of the calibration studies, such as children, the elderly, and blacks.

Numerous protocols are available for estimating body-fat percentage from skinfolds measurements. We prefer the sum of seven skinfolds because (1) multiple measurements increase the reliability of the procedure and decrease the chances of making errors and (2) the sum of seven skinfolds involves measurements below the waist, which makes it a better method for evaluating women than other protocols that take only above the waist measurements. The seven skinfolds sites are:

1. *Chest.* Diagonal fold on the lateral border at the pectoralis major muscle, halfway between the nipple and the shoulder crease
2. *Axilla.* Diagonal fold at the middle of the side on a line bisecting the armpit and hip at a level equal to the xiphoid process
3. *Triceps.* Vertical fold over the belly of the triceps halfway between the acromion and olecranon processes
4. *Subscapular.* Diagonal fold just under the bottom angle of the scapula halfway between the spine and the side of the body
5. *Abdomen.* Vertical fold one inch to the right of the umbilicus
6. *Suprailiac.* Diagonal fold just above the iliac crest slightly anterior to the middle of the side
7. *Thigh.* Vertical fold at the middle and front thigh halfway between the greater trochanter and the patella

The skinfolds thickness is read with a special skinfolds caliper. A skinfolds caliper is designed to exert a constant resistance (pinch) at any degree of opening of the caliper. The readings are taken by pinching the layer of fat above the muscle between the thumb and forefinger. The tips of the calipers are placed just next to the finger and thumb, and the reading is taken while still pinching the skin. Readings are made to the nearest millimeter. Usually two readings are taken at each site and then averaged to increase the reliability of the procedure. The results are then added together to get the sum of seven skinfolds. Table 8.26 gives conversion of skinfolds sums into body fat percentages for men and Table 8.27 gives the conversions for women. Note that the body fat percentage depends upon the subject's age.

Skinfolds have the advantage of being very easy to perform, they require very little training and are relatively inexpensive. However, skinfolds measurements are not very reliable. This is particularly true for overweight subjects and is partly due to the difficulty in measuring the thickness of the large fat pads in an obese individual. Weits, Van Den Beer, and Wedel (1986) discuss an ultrasound method for estimating skinfolds thickness that is more reliable than calipers. However, when used for clinical purposes, body fat percentages estimated from skinfolds in normal weight individuals are easy to obtain and reasonable to use.

The most accurate method for determining body fat percentage is underwater weighing. The method involves getting a weight in the air and another while the individual is submersed in a tank of water. The individual exhales as much air as possible while being weighed in the water. Since fat and lean tissue have different specific gravities, body fat percentage is a function of the difference between the air and water weights (recall that fat floats in water). After obtaining the weight, the residual air volume in the lungs is estimated and body fat percentage is calculated taking into consideration air and water temperatures.

Typically, the equipment for doing underwater weighing involves a sizable financial investment and considerable space. Unless a clinician is involved in research that requires frequent measures of body composition, it does not make sense to invest in this kind of equipment. However, many medical research centers and private health promotion facilities now have the proper equipment for underwater weighing. The amount of time and expense for the patient to be referred to one of these facilities for body fat determination is usually minimal.

There are many different ways to interpret the results of a body fat percentage assessment. Different groups of health professionals tend to provide different interpretations. Exercise physiologists, for example, tend to apply the standards for highly trained athletes to the general population. Recently, several of the women's magazines advocated that to be in good physical shape, women should be between 15 percent and 18 percent body fat. In the first place, such a low body fat percentage may cause some women to stop menstruating. In the second place, only a very small percentage of the population has a reasonable chance of being healthy at such a low body fat. We have developed a set of interpretive standards that we use to give feedback to our patients. These interpretations are more readily achievable and reflect good health rather than optimum athletic training. The standards are presented in Table 8.28.

Resting Metabolic Rate

Great individual differences exist in the number of calories it requires to maintain any given body weight. While the body's caloric requirements are in part a function of body weight (the more you weigh, the more calories it takes to maintain that weight) there are still large differences between individuals whose weight is exactly the same. Energy expenditure can be

TABLE 8.26 Body Fat Proportion for Sum of Seven Skinfolds—Male

Sum of Seven	\multicolumn{10}{c}{Age to Nearest Five Years}
	15	20	25	30	35	40	45	50	55	60
50	0.053	0.059	0.065	0.071	0.077	0.083	0.089	0.095	0.101	0.103
55	0.060	0.067	0.073	0.079	0.085	0.091	0.097	0.103	0.109	0.116
60	0.068	0.074	0.080	0.087	0.093	0.099	0.105	0.111	0.117	0.124
65	0.076	0.082	0.088	0.094	0.101	0.107	0.113	0.119	0.125	0.132
70	0.084	0.090	0.096	0.102	0.108	0.114	0.121	0.127	0.133	0.139
75	0.091	0.097	0.104	0.110	0.116	0.122	0.128	0.135	0.141	0.147
80	0.099	0.105	0.111	0.117	0.123	0.130	0.136	0.142	0.148	0.155
85	0.106	0.112	0.118	0.125	0.131	0.137	0.143	0.150	0.156	0.162
90	0.113	0.120	0.126	0.132	0.138	0.145	0.151	0.157	0.163	0.170
95	0.120	0.127	0.133	0.139	0.145	0.152	0.158	0.164	0.171	0.177
100	0.128	0.134	0.140	0.146	0.153	0.159	0.165	0.172	0.178	0.184
105	0.135	0.141	0.147	0.153	0.160	0.166	0.172	0.179	0.185	0.192
110	0.141	0.148	0.154	0.160	0.167	0.173	0.179	0.186	0.192	0.199
115	0.148	0.155	0.161	0.167	0.174	0.180	0.186	0.193	0.199	0.206
120	0.155	0.161	0.168	0.174	0.180	0.187	0.193	0.199	0.206	0.212
125	0.161	0.168	0.174	0.181	0.187	0.193	0.200	0.206	0.213	0.219
130	0.168	0.174	0.181	0.187	0.193	0.200	0.206	0.213	0.219	0.226
135	0.174	0.181	0.187	0.193	0.200	0.206	0.213	0.219	0.226	0.232
140	0.181	0.187	0.193	0.200	0.206	0.213	0.219	0.226	0.232	0.239
145	0.187	0.193	0.200	0.206	0.212	0.219	0.225	0.232	0.238	0.245
150	0.193	0.199	0.206	0.212	0.219	0.225	0.232	0.238	0.245	0.251
155	0.199	0.205	0.212	0.218	0.225	0.231	0.238	0.244	0.251	0.257
160	0.205	0.211	0.218	0.224	0.231	0.237	0.244	0.250	0.257	0.263
165	0.210	0.217	0.223	0.230	0.236	0.243	0.249	0.256	0.263	0.269
170	0.216	0.222	0.229	0.235	0.242	0.249	0.255	0.262	0.268	0.275
175	0.221	0.228	0.235	0.241	0.248	0.254	0.261	0.267	0.274	0.281
180	0.227	0.233	0.240	0.246	0.253	0.260	0.266	0.273	0.280	0.286
185	0.232	0.239	0.245	0.252	0.258	0.265	0.272	0.278	0.285	0.292

(continued)

TABLE 8.26 (continued)

| Sum of Seven | Age to Nearest Five Years ||||||||||
	15	20	25	30	35	40	45	50	55	60
190	0.237	0.244	0.250	0.257	0.264	0.270	0.277	0.284	0.290	0.297
195	0.242	0.249	0.256	0.262	0.269	0.275	0.282	0.289	0.295	0.302
200	0.247	0.254	0.261	0.267	0.274	0.280	0.287	0.294	0.300	0.307
205	0.252	0.259	0.265	0.272	0.279	0.285	0.292	0.299	0.305	0.312
210	0.257	0.264	0.270	0.277	0.283	0.290	0.297	0.304	0.310	0.317
215	0.262	0.268	0.275	0.281	0.288	0.295	0.301	0.308	0.315	0.322
220	0.266	0.273	0.279	0.286	0.293	0.299	0.306	0.313	0.320	0.326
225	0.270	0.277	0.284	0.290	0.297	0.304	0.310	0.317	0.324	0.331
230	0.275	0.281	0.288	0.295	0.301	0.308	0.315	0.322	0.328	0.335
235	0.279	0.285	0.292	0.299	0.306	0.312	0.319	0.326	0.333	0.339
240	0.283	0.289	0.296	0.303	0.310	0.316	0.323	0.330	0.337	0.344
245	0.287	0.293	0.300	0.307	0.314	0.320	0.327	0.334	0.341	0.347
250	0.290	0.297	0.304	0.311	0.317	0.324	0.331	0.338	0.345	0.351

TABLE 8.27 Body Fat Proportion for Sum of Seven Skinfolds—Female

Sum of Seven	\multicolumn{10}{c}{Age to Nearest Five Years}
	15	20	25	30	35	40	45	50	55	60
50	0.113	0.116	0.119	0.122	0.124	0.127	0.130	0.133	0.135	0.138
55	0.122	0.125	0.128	0.130	0.133	0.136	0.139	0.142	0.144	0.147
60	0.131	0.134	0.136	0.139	0.142	0.145	0.148	0.150	0.153	0.156
65	0.140	0.142	0.145	0.148	0.151	0.154	0.156	0.159	0.162	0.165
70	0.148	0.151	0.154	0.157	0.159	0.162	0.165	0.168	0.171	0.173
75	0.157	0.159	0.162	0.165	0.168	0.171	0.174	0.176	0.179	0.182
80	0.165	0.168	0.171	0.174	0.176	0.179	0.182	0.185	0.188	0.191
85	0.173	0.176	0.179	0.182	0.185	0.188	0.190	0.193	0.196	0.199
90	0.182	0.184	0.187	0.190	0.193	0.196	0.199	0.202	0.204	0.207
95	0.190	0.193	0.195	0.198	0.201	0.204	0.207	0.210	0.213	0.215
100	0.198	0.201	0.203	0.206	0.209	0.212	0.215	0.218	0.221	0.224
105	0.206	0.209	0.211	0.214	0.217	0.220	0.223	0.226	0.229	0.232
110	0.213	0.216	0.219	0.222	0.225	0.228	0.231	0.234	0.237	0.240
115	0.221	0.224	0.227	0.230	0.233	0.236	0.239	0.241	0.244	0.247
120	0.229	0.232	0.235	0.238	0.240	0.243	0.246	0.249	0.252	0.255
125	0.236	0.239	0.242	0.245	0.248	0.251	0.254	0.257	0.260	0.263
130	0.244	0.247	0.250	0.253	0.255	0.258	0.261	0.264	0.267	0.270
135	0.251	0.254	0.257	0.260	0.263	0.266	0.269	0.272	0.275	0.278
140	0.258	0.261	0.264	0.267	0.270	0.273	0.276	0.279	0.282	0.285
145	0.265	0.268	0.271	0.274	0.277	0.280	0.283	0.286	0.289	0.292
150	0.272	0.275	0.278	0.281	0.284	0.287	0.290	0.293	0.296	0.299
155	0.279	0.282	0.285	0.288	0.291	0.294	0.297	0.300	0.303	0.306
160	0.286	0.289	0.292	0.295	0.298	0.301	0.304	0.307	0.310	0.313
165	0.293	0.296	0.299	0.302	0.305	0.308	0.311	0.314	0.317	0.320
170	0.299	0.302	0.305	0.308	0.311	0.314	0.317	0.320	0.323	0.326
175	0.306	0.309	0.312	0.315	0.318	0.321	0.324	0.327	0.330	0.333
180	0.312	0.315	0.318	0.321	0.324	0.327	0.330	0.333	0.336	0.339
185	0.318	0.321	0.324	0.327	0.330	0.333	0.336	0.339	0.342	0.345

(continued)

TABLE 8.27 (continued)

| Sum of Seven | Age to Nearest Five Years ||||||||||
	15	20	25	30	35	40	45	50	55	60
190	0.324	0.327	0.330	0.333	0.336	0.339	0.343	0.346	0.349	0.352
195	0.330	0.333	0.336	0.339	0.342	0.345	0.349	0.352	0.355	0.358
200	0.336	0.339	0.342	0.345	0.348	0.351	0.354	0.357	0.361	0.364
205	0.342	0.345	0.348	0.351	0.354	0.357	0.360	0.363	0.366	0.369
210	0.348	0.351	0.354	0.357	0.360	0.363	0.366	0.369	0.372	0.375
215	0.353	0.356	0.359	0.362	0.365	0.368	0.371	0.375	0.378	0.381
220	0.358	0.362	0.365	0.368	0.371	0.374	0.377	0.380	0.383	0.386
225	0.364	0.367	0.370	0.373	0.376	0.379	0.382	0.385	0.388	0.391
230	0.369	0.372	0.375	0.378	0.381	0.384	0.387	0.390	0.394	0.397
235	0.374	0.377	0.380	0.383	0.386	0.389	0.392	0.396	0.399	0.402
240	0.379	0.382	0.385	0.388	0.391	0.394	0.397	0.400	0.404	0.407
245	0.384	0.387	0.390	0.393	0.396	0.399	0.402	0.405	0.408	0.412
250	0.388	0.391	0.394	0.397	0.401	0.404	0.407	0.410	0.413	0.416

TABLE 8.28 Interpretation of Body Fat Percentages for Men and Women

Interpretation	Men	Women
Very lean	below 15%	below 20%
Lean	15–20	20–25
Normal	21–25	26–30
Mild obesity	26–30	31–35
Moderate obesity	31–35	36–40
Very obese	above 35	above 40

partitioned into four components (Garrow, 1986): resting metabolic rate, the thermic effect of food, the thermic effect of exercise, and other thermogenesis.

Resting metabolic rate is typically measured under a standard set of conditions: the subject is at rest, in bed, in a comfortable room, between 8 a.m. and 9 a.m., after an overnight fast. The most common method for measuring resting metabolic rate is by indirect calorimetry. By measuring oxygen uptake and carbon dioxide production over a period of time, it is possible to infer the rate of energy metabolism. Metabolic rate is estimated in Kcal per hour or it is adjusted according to lean body mass and measured as Kcal/kg/hr. Resting metabolic rate is interpreted as the energy required to maintain blood flow, respiration, and other biological functions necessary for survival. Typical values will fall in the range of 45–90 kcal/hour. Total energy requirements for resting metabolic rate can be extrapolated to twenty-four hours by simply multiplying the rate in kcal/hour by twenty-four.

Resting metabolic rate expressed in this manner is a function of total body weight. People who are heavier will on the average have higher resting metabolic rates. However, there are large individual differences at any given body weight that place definite limits on how much food an individual can eat before weight gain begins to occur. From resting metabolic rate and knowledge of the individual's typical activity level, it is possible to estimate total daily caloric needs for weight maintenance. Typically, twenty-four-hour resting caloric requirement is multiplied by 1.5 for very sedentary to 1.8 for very active individuals to obtain estimated total daily caloric needs.

Clinically, there is great value to the measurement of resting metabolic rate. From resting metabolic rate, it is possible to determine an individual's approximate caloric needs. This no longer makes it necessary to use crude formulas to set dietary goals. When counseling a patient with anorexia nervosa, it will be very useful to be able to estimate rate of weight gain at different caloric intake levels by knowing daily caloric requirements as estimated from resting metabolic rate. Likewise, with bulimic patients who have not eaten normally for years, it is important to prescribe a level of caloric intake that will result in weight maintenance.

Unfortunately, indirect calorimetry requires the use of sophisticated gas analyzers. The cost of this type of equipment and the technical skill required to calibrate and maintain the equipment is beyond the reach of most clinicians. An increasing number of medical centers and health promotion programs, however, are now offering metabolic rate determinations for a fee.

Physical Fitness

Over recent years there has been an increasing emphasis on physical fitness both among practicing health professionals and in the popular media. For some eating-disordered patients, it may be sensible to assess their level of physical fitness.

Physical fitness is measured by estimating the body's ability to take in and utilize oxygen. All of the fitness tests are different ways to infer vO_2-max (maximum oxygen uptake). This is a measure of the body's capacity to utilize oxygen and indirectly an indication of the body's capacity for doing work.

The best method for measuring maximum oxygen uptake is to measure gaseous exchange during a maximal treadmill test (McArdle, Katch, & Katch, 1986). Essentially, the individual is exercised on a treadmill until maximum heart rate is reached (the point at which exhaustion occurs). While maximal tests allow the estimation of both maximum heart rate and oxygen uptake, they have several disadvantages including: (1) high dependency on subject motivation to reach maximum exertion, (2) sophisticated EEG monitoring required both to measure heart rate and to guard against potential arrhythmias, (3) the measurement of oxygen consumption requires expensive gas analyzers, (4) the procedure is aversive to most and dangerous for some individuals, and (5) direct medical supervision is required adding to the expense.

A wide range of submaximal fitness testing protocols have been developed for estimating maximum oxygen uptake. These alternative protocols are summarized in Table 8.29. This table clearly shows that it is possible for the clinician to conduct submaximal fitness testing easily in the office without the requirement of expensive equipment. The American College of Sports Medicine (1980) has published guidelines for fitness testing with and without medical supervision.

TABLE 8.29 Submaximal Fitness Testing Protocols

Test	Procedure	Reference
Harvard Step Test	Subject steps up and down on a step at a fixed pace for 5 minutes. Pulse is taken at 1-minute intervals during recovery. Fitness is inferred from maximum heart rate and speed of recovery.	Committee on Exercise and Physical Fitness (1967)
Queens College Step Test	Three minutes of continuous stepping with pulse measured for 15 seconds during recovery beginning 5 seconds after the end of exercise.	Katch & McArdle (1977)
Astrand Ergometer Test	Workload of a bicycle ergometer is systematically varied to keep the individual's heart rate at a predetermined submaximal level. For the subject's weight and the amount of work performed, vO_2-max can be estimated.	Astrand & Rodahl (1977)
Fixed time/ distance run	Subject runs as far as possible during a 12-minute time period. The distance covered is highly correlated with vO_2-max.	Cooper (1977)

ASSESSMENT OF BODY IMAGE

As we discussed in earlier chapters, problems with body image are considered by many to be one of the core features of anorexia and bulimia nervosa. The scientific and empirical study of body image as a psychological phenomenon is relatively recent. Bruch (1962) is often credited as having first suggested that body-image disturbance was a core feature of anorexia nervosa. The concept of body image, however, dates back to the early part of this century. In the last twenty years, there has been an explosion in empirical research on body image (for reviews see Garner & Garfinkel, 1981; Barrios, Ruff, & York, 1989). It might seem logical that after more than sixty years of existence and over twenty years of intensive study, the construct of body image would be well-defined and easily measured. On the contrary, new conceptual models and methods of assessment are appearing all the time.

METHODS FOR ASSESSING BODY IMAGE

In the following sections, we will describe a number of assessment methods that have been used to study body image. We will focus mainly on describing the techniques, procedures, and apparatus. For each method, we will describe a study in which it was applied.

There are several general approaches to assessing body image: (1) projective techniques, (2) questionnaire approaches, (3) psychophysical methods, and (4) methods that contrast different body-image schemata (e.g., actual versus ideal). Each of these methods has been implemented in several different ways. In addition, some assessment techniques involve a combination of the different approaches.

Projective Methods

Some of the earliest approaches to the assessment of body image were taken by individuals trained in psychoanalysis. Not surprisingly, early approaches to measurement involved the use of projective testing methods.

A projective technique involves presenting the subject with an ambiguous stimulus or task. Because the task itself is ambiguous, the individual's personality is presumed to play the dominant role in performance. A trained clinician observes the subject's response and by treating aspects of the response as symbolic is able to draw inferences about the individual's personality.

Actual methods involved in the projective evaluation of body image include the Rorschach inkblot test (Fisher & Cleveland, 1958), the Draw-a-Person test (Machover, 1957), word association (Secord & Jourard, 1953), and field independence (Witkin, 1965).

There is very little recent literature on the use of projective techniques to assess body image. In general, projective techniques have been extensively criticized for being unreliable and subjective. While there are probably a number of clinicians treating eating disorders who employ projective assessment techniques, there is no evidence that they are a good method for measuring any aspect of the body-image construct. Most therapists who use projective assessment techniques in eating disorders are more interested in general personality assessment than in using projective methods as an indirect way to assess body image.

Questionnaire Approaches

Several questionnaires have been developed to measure different aspects of the body-image construct. In addition to the questionnaires presented in this section, the Eating Disorders Inventory (EDI), which was presented earlier in the chapter, has a subscale related to body-image distortion, the body dissatisfaction subscale.

The **Body Shape Questionnaire (BSQ)** was developed by Cooper,

Taylor, Cooper, and Fairburn (1987) in order to have a psychometrically valid way to assess the dissatisfaction with one's body that is commonly observed in anorexia and bulimia. Each item presents a thought or concern associated with body dissatisfaction, and subjects are asked to rate how often they have felt this way in the last four weeks. The BSQ clearly discriminated between eating-disordered and noneating-disordered populations. It was correlated highly with the Eating Attitudes Test and the body dissatisfaction subscale of the Eating Disorders Inventory. Within the normal group, the BSQ was higher for those who were dieting than for those who were not. Finally, the BSQ was much higher in community samples for women who engaged in bulimic behaviors (bingeing or purging) than for women who ate normally. The BSQ is summarized in Table 8.30.

The **Body Cathexis Scale,** developed by Secord and Jourard (1953), is a 40-item self-report measure of general satisfaction with one's body. It is primarily useful as a research instrument in studies validating new measures of body-image or body satisfaction since it is a well-established questionnaire. The Body Cathexis Scale is presented in Table 8.31.

The **Body Image Automatic Thoughts Questionnaire (BIATQ)** measures specific cognitions, both positive and negative, associated with the patient's body. The subject rates the frequency of occurrence of each of fifty-two body-related thoughts. The BIATQ can be scored in order to derive positive thoughts and negative thoughts subscales. Table 8.32 summarizes the BIATQ.

The **Body Parts Rating Scale (BPRS)** (Berscheid et al., 1973) is a self-report measure that allows patients to rate their degree of satisfaction or dissatisfaction with each of twenty-four specific body parts or characteristics (e.g., face, hands, teeth, breasts, height). The items are grouped into body regions (e.g. face, lower torso) and summary scores are computed. The BPRS is summarized in Table 8.33.

The **BSQR** is a 140-item questionnaire in which subjects rate their agreement with each attitudinal item. It can be scored using seven-factor analytically derived scales that measure (1) appearance evaluation, (2) appearance orientation, (3) fitness evaluation, (4) fitness orientation, (5) health evaluation, (6) health orientation, and (7) illness orientation (Butters & Cash, 1987; Cash & Green, 1986; Noles, Cash, & Winstead, 1985). The BSQR is summarized in Table 8.34.

Psychophysical Approaches to Body Image

A number of methodologies have been developed and widely used to study body-image disturbance as an error in size estimation of one's own body. These methods are similar in that all require the subject to perform some task that involves reproducing the size of his or her body. The methods

TABLE 8.30 An Evaluation of the Body Shape Questionnaire

Element	Comments
Name	Body Shape Questionnaire (BSQ)
Citation	Cooper, Taylor, Cooper, and Fairburn (1987)
Type of measure	Psychological assessment of dissatisfaction with body shape
Potential uses	Epidemiological research, treatment planning, monitoring the effects of treatment
Populations	Adult females
Format	34-item self-report inventory. Each item represents a thought or feeling about one's body. The subject rates how often she has felt this way in the last month using a 6-point frequency scale.
Scoring	A single total score is derived by summing the frequency ratings.
Evaluation	Good way to get a quick measure of body dissatisfaction; norms allow clinical determination of severity; probably better for research than clinical practice
Availability	Cooper, Taylor, Cooper, and Fairburn (1987)

TABLE 8.31 An Evaluation of the Body Cathexis Scale

Element	Comments
Name	Body Cathexis Scale
Citation	Secord and Jourard (1953)
Type of measure	Psychological measure of overall body satisfaction
Potential uses	Clinical and epidemiological research, treatment planning, monitoring the effects of treatment
Populations	Adult males and females
Format	40-item self-report inventory. Each item is a part of the body or bodily activity. The subject rates how positive or negative he/she feels on a 5-point scale.
Scoring	A total body satisfaction (cathexis) score is computed by summing the ratings of the 40 items.
Evaluation	More useful as a research tool than as a clinical assessment
Availability	Secord and Jourard (1953)

TABLE 8.32 An Evaluation of the Body Image Automatic Thoughts Questionnaire

Element	Comments
Name	Body Image Automatic Thoughts Questionnaire (BIATQ)
Citation	Unpublished
Type of measure	Questionnaire for the assessment of positive and negative thoughts associated with the body
Potential uses	Testing research hypotheses, treatment planning, monitoring the effects of treatment
Populations	Normal, obese, and eating-disordered
Format	Rating scale
Scoring	Two subscales, positive and negative thoughts
Evaluation	Reliability and validity not yet established; may be clinically useful for patient assessment
Availability	Thomas Cash, Department of Psychology, Old Dominion University, Norfolk, VA 23529

vary in whether the entire body is reproduced as a whole or whether each part is done separately. The methods also vary in the extent to which the cues appear real or are completely abstract.

These methods seem to be well-suited for two purposes, the scientific study of the nature of body image and its disturbance in eating disorders and as an outcome measure in treatment research. While there has been considerable published research using these techniques (Garfinkel & Garner, 1982; Barrios et al., 1988; Slade, 1985) the vast majority of the studies have been concerned with either establishing that body-image disturbance is a characteristic of eating disorders or with presenting data on a new technique of psychophysical assessment.

Askevold (1975) developed an approach to the evaluation of body image called the **Image Marking Method.** This is one of the simplest approaches available. A large white sheet of paper is attached to a wall. The subject stands in front of the paper and uses a marking pen to indicate the width of specific body parts, such as chest, waist, and hips. The actual width of each part is measured, and the discrepancy between estimated and actual width is calculated. Several studies have shown that the image marking approach differentiates anorexic patients and normal controls (Pierloot & Houben, 1978; Wingate & Christie, 1978). The Image Marking Method is summarized in Table 8.35.

A very widely used set of psychophysical procedures can be collectively referred to as visual size estimation tasks. These methods were originally developed by Reitman and Cleveland (1969) and have been

TABLE 8.33 An Evaluation of the Body Parts Rating Scale

Element	Comments
Name	Body Parts Rating Scale (BPRS)
Citation	Berscheid, Walster, and Bohrnstedt (1973)
Type of measure	Questionnaire for the assessment of satisfaction and dissatisfaction associated with the body
Potential uses	Testing research hypotheses, treatment planning, monitoring the effects of treatment
Populations	Normal, obese, and eating-disordered
Format	Rating scale consisting of 24 body parts or characteristics. Satisfaction with each part is rated on a 6-point scale.
Scoring	Eight subscales: face, extremities, lower torso, mid torso, breast, height, and overall
Evaluation	Reliability and validity well-established; may be clinically useful for patient assessment
Availability	Thomas Cash, Department of Psychology, Old Dominion University, Norfolk, VA 23529

TABLE 8.34 An Evaluation of the Body-Self Relations Questionnaire (BSRQ)

Element	Comments
Name	Body-Self Relations Questionnaire (BSRQ)
Citation	Butters and Cash (1987), Cash and Green (1986)
Type of measure	Questionnaire for the assessment of attitudes towards appearance, physical fitness, and health
Potential uses	Testing research hypotheses, treatment planning, monitoring the effects of treatment
Populations	Normal, obese, and eating-disordered
Format	Rating scale consisting of 140 attitudinal items. Agreement with each item is rated on a 5-point scale.
Scoring	Seven subscales: appearance evaluation, appearance orientation, fitness evaluation, fitness orientation, health evaluation, health orientation, illness awareness
Evaluation	Reliability and validity well-established; may be clinically useful for patient assessment
Availability	Thomas Cash, Department of Psychology, Old Dominion University, Norfolk, VA 23529

TABLE 8.35 An Evaluation of the Image Marking Method of Body Image Assessment

Element	Comments
Name	Image Marking Method
Citation	Askevold (1975)
Type of measure	Psychological measure of body size misperception
Potential uses	Testing research hypotheses, treatment outcome studies
Populations	Normal and eating-disordered individuals
Format	A large white piece of paper is placed on the wall. Subjects mark the width of their bodies at various sites. The actual width of the body is measured.
Scoring	A discrepancy index is computed for each body site. An overall body-image distortion index can be computed by summing the individual discrepancy scores.
Evaluation	The easiest of the psychophysical methods to use since it does not require any specialized equipment; has been shown to differentiate normal from eating-disordered individuals.
Availability	Askevold (1975)

adapted by Slade and Russell (1973) and Ruff and Barrios (1986). All of the methods involve the subject adjusting either calipers, lights, or light beams to correspond to the width of different body parts. Objective measures of body size are obtained and are used to compute the **Body Distortion Index:**

$$\frac{\text{estimated size}}{\text{actual size}} \times 100$$

The BDI can be analyzed separately for each body site or combined across body sites to yield an overall score that reflects distortion of body size perception. Numbers higher than one-hundred reflect the tendency to overestimate one's body size while numbers less than one-hundred indicate a tendency to underestimate body size.

Slade (1985) has reviewed the literature on the use of body size estimation procedures and the image marking procedure. He found that the Body Distortion Index was remarkably stable across studies. BDI scores have also been reported for bulimic subjects as well (J.K. Thompson, Berland, Linton, & Weinsier, 1986). Table 8.36 presents norms for anorexic, bulimic, and normal weight subjects' BDI scores. Note that the normal and anorexic norms are based on considerably larger sample sizes than the bulimic

TABLE 8.36 Norms for the Body Distortion Index for Different Populations

Population	Mean	Standard Deviation
Normal	116	25
Anorexic	124	30
Bulimic	147	55

norms. However, J.K. Thompson (1987) has recently shown that some of the differences between eating-disordered and normal control subjects that have been reported in the literature may be an artifact of differences in their initial weight rather than differences in perceptual distortion per se. This is because small errors are proportionally larger in small people than the equivalent error in a larger person.

Both Slade (1985) and Garfinkel and Garner (1982) have criticized these techniques on the grounds that adequate reliability and validity data have not been reported. Recently, however, Barrios et al. (1988) have conducted an extensive study showing that the adjustable light beam technique is quite reliable. The size estimation approach to body-image assessment is summarized in Table 8.37.

A number of researchers have experimented with special mirrors, lenses, or video cameras that allow the image of an individual's body to be systematically distorted. Glucksman and Hirsch (1969) pioneered the use of a special photographic lens that distorts images only in the horizontal dimension. Basically, a photograph of the subject is projected onto a screen and can be made to appear from 20 percent thinner to 20 percent wider than its actual size. The subject's task is to adjust the distorting lens until the image appears to look just like her actual appearance. This anamorphic lens has been used extensively by the group in Toronto (Garfinkel and Garner, 1982). The test is scored by observing the percent of distortion in the image the subject chooses compared to the undistorted image. Recent advances in technology have replaced the distorting lens with an electronic system that distorts the image from a video camera (J.K. Collins, 1987; J.K. Collins et al., 1987; Touyz, Beumont, Collins, McCabe, & Jupp, 1984). Although studies using these techniques have had mixed results, the general finding is that normal subjects slightly underestimate body size while eating-disordered subjects tend to overestimate body size.

The data derived from these techniques do not suggest that they are superior to the size estimation or image marking procedures that are less expensive and involved. In addition, the distorted image technique distorts all parts of the body equally. Several studies have suggested that individuals with an eating disorder do not distort all parts of their bodies

TABLE 8.37 An Evaluation of Visual Size Estimation Methods for Assessing Body Image

Element	Comments
Name	Adjustable calipers, adjustable light beam
Citation	Slade and Russell (1973), Ruff and Barrios (1986)
Type of measure	Psychological measure of body size misperception
Potential uses	Testing research hypotheses, treatment planning, treatment outcome studies
Populations	Adult males and females
Format	Subject adjusts the width of calipers, lights, or light beams to correspond to the actual size of several body parts (face, chest, waist, hips, thighs)
Scoring	Estimated and actual size are compared using the body distortion index.
Evaluation	Fairly reliable technique; some difficulties in interpreting the results; with norms available, can be used for individual assessment. The method is most useful for research on body image.
Availability	Slade and Russell (1973), Ruff and Barrios (1986)

equally (Wilmuth, Leitenberg, Rosen, Fondacaro, & Gross, 1985). The distorted image approach is summarized in Table 8.38.

Methods That Contrast Different Body-Image Schema

Another set of methods for assessment of an individual's body image involves making a direct comparison between two or more of the individual's body schemata. Typically, the individual's actual perception of her body is compared to her idea of how she would like to look (ideal body image). Williamson, Kelley, Davis, Ruggiero, and Blouin (1985) have developed a set of stimuli that are useful for making this actual versus ideal body-image comparison. The stimuli are nine cards that contain drawings of a female figure that varies from very thin to quite obese. The subject is first instructed to choose the card that comes closest to her actual body size. The subject then is told to choose the card that is closest to the body size she would most prefer. The cards are numbered sequentially from smallest to largest and the body-image discrepancy score is simply the difference between the two card numbers. The entire procedure takes only two to five minutes to complete.

TABLE 8.38 An Evaluation of Distorted Image Techniques in the Assessment of Body Image

Element	Comments
Name	Anamorphic lens, distorted video image, distorted mirror
Citation	Garfinkel and Garner (1982), J.K. Collins (1987), Glucksman and Hirsch (1969)
Type of measure	Psychological measure of degree to which subjects misperceive their body size
Potential uses	Testing research hypotheses
Populations	Adult males and females
Format	An image of the subject is distorted in the horizontal dimension. The subject's task is to adjust the image until it looks just like he or she actually appears. The distortion is accomplished with mirrors, lenses, or electronic processing of video signals.
Scoring	The percentage deviation of the adjusted image from the unadjusted image is the score.
Evaluation	Too limited and expensive to be of much use for any purpose other than research on body image
Availability	See citations above.

Williamson et al. showed that the body-image discrepancy for bulimic subjects was significantly greater than for a matched group of normal controls. This was due to a significant tendency to see their actual bodies as larger and to choose thinner ideal bodies. When compared to a control group of obese subjects, the obese showed a greater body-image discrepancy. The ideal body size for the obese subjects did not differ from the one chosen by normal controls, but was significantly larger than the ideal selected by the bulimic group.

Freeman, Thomas, Solyom, and Koopman (1985) also approached the assessment of body image through a comparison of actual versus ideal images. Instead of using cards, they had subjects make adjustments of their own image on a video distortion camera. In this study, they found that body-image disturbance (either measured by overestimation or actual-ideal discrepancy) was greatest for normal weight bulimics with a history of anorexia nervosa.

Thompson, Dolce, Spana, and Register (1987) reported a study in which an adjustable light beam technique was used to obtain body size estimates under two instructional sets. In the first set, the subject was instructed to adjust the lights according to how she felt about each of the body parts. The second set of instructions asked the subject to make the adjustment according to how her body actually appeared. The subjects, thirty-four noneating-disordered college women, gave larger estimates of their thighs under the feeling instructions.

Basically, any of the psychophysical techniques could be adapted to generate comparisons of perceived versus ideal body images. The methods that involve contrasting different body schema (the way I look, the way I wish I looked, the way I feel) are quite promising. As soon as good norms are developed on some of these tasks, it may be useful to use these techniques clinically. It would be useful to know: (1) if a patient overestimates her actual body size, (2) if the patient has an unrealistically low ideal body size, (3) if the patient feels larger than she sees herself, and (4) the total size of the discrepancy between various body schema. Table 8.39 summarizes the contrasting body schema methods.

Body Image Testing System

Schlundt and Bell (1988) have been developing and testing a new computerized system for testing and research on body image, the Body Image

TABLE 8.39 An Evaluation of Contrasting Body Schema Techniques

Element	Comments
Name	Contrasting Body-Image Schema
Citation	Williamson, Kelley, Davis, Ruggiero, and Blouin (1985) Thompson, Dolce, Spana, and Register (1987)
Type of measure	Psychological measure of the discrepancy between different body schemata
Potential uses	Epidemiological research, testing research hypotheses, treatment planning, treatment outcome studies
Populations	Adult males and females
Format	An estimation of body size is obtained under two different sets of instructions (actual versus ideal)
Scoring	The discrepancy between actual and ideal body size estimates is computed as a body-image disturbance index
Evaluation	The card sorting task may be a very quick yet useful way of measuring body dissatisfaction. The measure does not distinguish between people who are overweight and people with an eating disorder.
Availability	Don Williamson, Department of Psychiatry, Louisiana State University

Testing System (BITS). The system consists of a computer program written in Borland's *Turbo Pascal* version 3.0. BITS is written for MS-DOS (IBM-PC and compatible) systems with either color or monochrome graphics. The program is written so that a variety of assessment tasks can be constructed by sequencing commands in a control file. The user is able to construct files containing instructions to the subject, instruct the system to collect ratings, and tell the system to write collected data to the disk.

The heart of the system is the profile of a body, which is generated on the screen. The body is constructed from overlapping ellipsoid shapes. Each ellipsoid has two parameters corresponding to the length of the horizontal and vertical axes on the screen. The subject interacts with the program through a menu. The subject continues to interact with the computer changing any part as many times as she wants until she is satisfied that the image on the screen corresponds to the instructions.

In a preliminary study, fifty-one female undergraduates completed the BITS task, filled out a battery of questionnaires, and had their height and weight measured. Three sets of instructions were used with the BITS. First, subjects made the screen match an image from a piece of paper, then they were told to make the screen look the way they saw themselves, and finally, they were instructed to make the screen look the way they wish they looked (ideal body). At the end of the session, subjects rated their satisfaction with each of the nine body parts.

The accuracy of the matching task was evaluated by comparing subjects' scores to the scores used to generate the figure. Subjects on the average were very accurate in reproducing all parts of the figure except the face, which was slightly overestimated.

Four sets of scores were derived from the testing session. Subjects were categorized into groups based on their quetelet's (weight divided by height^2) index so that ratings could be adjusted normatively on the basis of relative body weight. The mean score from each body part was computed for each weight group on the actual and ideal body-image tasks. Two sets of scores were formed by subtracting the weight group mean from the subject's score and then dividing by the within-group standard deviation. These actual and ideal normative deviation scores measure the extent to which the individual's self-perception differs from the average perception of other subjects who are the same relative body weight. Scores were computed separately for each body part. Total scores were also computed by summing across body parts.

A difference score was computed for each body part by subtracting the ideal score from the actual score. The difference scores and the satisfaction ratings were summed across body parts to form total scores. Table 8.40 presents the mean difference scores and satisfaction ratings for the sample of fifty-one undergraduate women. All of the difference scores were significantly greater than zero with the exception of the score for the

TABLE 8.40 Actual-Ideal Differences and Satisfaction Ratings on the BITS

Body Part	Mean Difference	Standard Deviation	Mean Satisfaction	Standard Deviation
Face	0.53[c]	0.97	9.65	1.03
Arms	0.35[c]	0.69	8.55	1.67
Neck	0.31[a]	0.91	7.98	2.00
Shoulders	0.43[c]	0.73	7.40	2.09
Chest	0.51[a]	1.59	6.67	2.27
Stomach	2.82[c]	2.34	4.92	2.56
Hips	1.68[c]	1.44	4.67	2.57
Thighs	1.98[c]	1.46	4.06	2.71
Breasts	−0.67	2.61	5.94	2.85
Total	7.62[c]	7.97	53.11	15.66

[a] $p < 0.05$; [c] $p < 0.001$

breasts. However, much greater dissatisfaction was associated with the stomach, hips, and thighs than the other body parts.

Total scores and scores related to the stomach, hips, and thighs were correlated with the Body Cathexis Scale, the BULIT, the Three-Factor Eating Questionnaire, and quetelet's index and are presented in Table 8.41.

The normative deviation scores for the actual body task measure the degree to which an individual sees herself as larger than others who are the same relative body weight. The actual deviation measures for hips and thighs were significantly correlated with the body cathexis, BULIT, restraint, and disinhibition scores. The normative deviation scores on the ideal body-image task measure the extent to which an individual wishes to be larger or smaller than others of her own relative weight. The stomach and thigh scores were associated with the disinhibition scale, a measure of the tendency to lose control over eating. The hips scores were correlated with the Body Cathexis Scale and the stomach scores were associated with the BULIT. The process of norming these measures by relative body weight was successful as indicated by the lack of any significant correlations with quetelet's index. When the individual's relative weight is allowed to enter in, the actual ideal discrepancy scores and the satisfaction ratings show a strong pattern of correlation with all of the measures except the hunger scale of the Three-Factor Eating Questionnaire.

Preliminary validation data on the BITS indicates that several interesting measures of body image can be derived from the computer interaction task. First, it is possible to derive a measure of perceptual distortion by identifying those individuals who see themselves as excessively large compared to others of similar relative weight. A measure of ideal body image could be derived in the same fashion. In addition, two measures of dissatisfaction could be derived, the actual-ideal discrepancy and satis-

TABLE 8.41 Preliminary Validation of the BITS

BITS	Body Cathexis	BULIT	Restraint	Disinhibition	Hunger	Quetelets
Stomach-A	0.123	0.141	0.102	0.127	-0.026	0.033
Hips-A	0.413[b]	0.054	0.250[a]	0.008	-0.029	0.187
Thigh-A	0.375[b]	0.254[a]	0.266[a]	0.250[a]	-0.087	-0.033
Total-A	0.178	0.132	0.151	0.084	-0.048	0.024
Stomach-I	-0.112	-0.264[a]	0.040	-0.307[a]	-0.179	-0.099
Hips-I	-0.275[a]	-0.085	0.141	-0.073	-0.061	0.037
Thigh-I	-0.164	-0.103	-0.049	-0.234[a]	-0.134	-0.005
Total-I	-0.019	-0.129	0.101	-0.171	-0.096	-0.068
Stomach-D	0.368[b]	0.387[b]	0.208	0.445[a]	0.157	0.526[c]
Hips-D	0.545[c]	0.283[a]	0.343[b]	0.230[a]	0.065	0.293[a]
Thigh-D	0.506[a]	0.438[c]	0.285[a]	0.420[b]	0.164	0.449[c]
Total-D	0.308[a]	0.386[b]	0.141	0.397[b]	0.076	0.604[c]
Stomach-S	-0.317[a]	-0.389[b]	-0.183	-0.440[b]	-0.135	-0.367[b]
Hips-S	-0.603[c]	-0.424[b]	-0.478[c]	-0.415[c]	-0.362[b]	-0.306[a]
Total-S	-0.317[b]	-0.290[b]	-0.130	-0.287[b]	-0.153	-0.200

A—deviates from the norm on actual size estimate; I—deviates from the norm on ideal size estimate; D—difference between actual and ideal; S—satisfaction rating (higher numbers more satisfied).
[a] $p<0.05$; [b] $p<0.01$; [c] $p<0.001$

faction ratings. The data suggest that these scores are a function of the individual's relative body weight with heavier individuals showing larger discrepancies and lower satisfaction ratings. However, the normative scoring process showed that measures of perceptual distortion and stringent ideal body image that were independent of body weight could be derived.

The BITS, because it is flexible and programmable, can be adapted for use in the experimental study of body image. The assessment can be self-administered and automatically scored. This makes it easier and more practical than the light beam or video distortion techniques. However, the major advantage of the BITS over the other techniques is that it simultaneously measures perceptual distortion, body dissatisfaction, and discrepancy between the actual and the ideal body schemata. The BITS is summarized in Table 8.42.

BEHAVIORAL ASSESSMENT OF EATING

Schlundt (in press) has criticized most of the assessment approaches used in studies of eating disorders as being too far removed from the behaviors of interest. For example, we saw that the EAT and the EDI, two of the most commonly used measures in the study of eating disorders, measure attitudes rather than behaviors. In this section, we will cover approaches that allow us to obtain more direct and specific information about eating, bingeing, and purging in eating-disordered patients.

Estimating Food Intake

The energy content and nutritional adequacy of a patient's diet is often information needed for evaluation and treatment. The assessment task is to gather data on the patient's food intake and to derive estimates of typical energy or nutrient intake (Block, 1982). In this approach, meal-by-meal and day-to-day variations in food intake are ignored. In the next section, we will cover an approach to understanding and studying variability in food intake.

We will describe three basic methods used to gather the data on food intake and two approaches to the estimation of energy or nutrient content. In order to estimate, for example, typical protein, carbohydrate, and fat intake for a patient it is necessary first to obtain data on the kinds and amounts of food eaten. Three methods have been used to obtain the raw data on food intake.

TABLE 8.42 An Evaluation of the BITS

Element	Comments
Name	Body Image Testing System (BITS)
Citation	Unpublished
Type of measure	Computer program for the assessment of body image; allows for the assessment of perceptual distortion, body dissatisfaction, and measurement of different body schemata
Potential uses	Research, treatment planning, treatment evaluation
Populations	Female adolescents and adults
Format	Computer-generated body image is presented on video display; subject interacts with the computer to make 9 different body parts appear fatter or thinner; can be programmed to obtain body image under different instruction sets; also obtains satisfaction ratings for the 9 body parts.
Scoring	Scores for each body part are obtained under each set of instructions. Difference scores can be calculated to compare different schemata. Regression equations are used to calculate perceptual distortion measures.
Evaluation	Preliminary validity data reported; may be useful for individual assessment and for research on weight and body-related cognition.
Availability	D. Schlundt, 323 A&S Psychology Bldg., Vanderbilt University, Nashville, TN 37240

Dietary recalls consist of interviews during which the patient is asked to remember all foods eaten and their amounts over a given time period, usually twenty-four or forty-eight hours. The interviewer typically probes for detailed information concerning the kind, amount, and method of preparation for each food reported. The interviewer also prompts the individual to determine if all foods eaten have been reported. The advantage of the dietary recall interview is that the interviewer can obtain detailed information from the patient about food and the amounts. There are several disadvantages. First, specific memory for foods eaten and their amounts does not extend too far into the past and is probably not valid beyond twenty-four to forty-eight hours into the past. Second, since the recall is conducted by an interview, demand characteristics of the situation may prevent patients from giving accurate and complete reports. For example, a bulimic patient may be embarrassed to admit to the actual number of doughnuts eaten during a binge. Finally, Schlundt (1988) has shown that one or two days of food information will rarely give a reliable estimate of typical nutrient consumption for an individual. In order to arrive at a reliable estimate, multiple twenty-four-hour recalls (at least four to seven) are needed.

Food diaries are the second method used to gather information about food intake for nutritional analysis. In a food diary, the patient is instructed to write down everything he or she eats over a given period of time (usually one to seven days). The patient is instructed on how to provide accurate descriptions of foods, amounts, and preparation methods in order to maximize the validity of the diary. Diaries get around the problem of memory by having patients record foods as, or soon after, they are eaten. Poor compliance can be a major problem with diaries, both in terms of recording all foods eaten and in terms of completing the record-keeping task. However, since diaries can be used to gather food intake data over multiple days, they are better suited to obtaining reliable estimates of an individual's typical food intake.

Food frequency questionnaires are the third method used to gather data on typical food intake. A food frequency questionnaire consists of a large list of food items. The patient indicates how often he or she typically eats each food item. In some questionnaires, the individual is also asked to indicate typical portion size. These questionnaires take very little time to complete and can yield very stable estimates of food intake. However, since these methods are geared toward estimating food intake in the general population, they may be less applicable to eating-disordered patients since many of the questionnaires will not be sensitive to the quantities of food eaten during binges (Krall & Dwyer, 1987). Schlundt and Pope (1988) have developed a food frequency questionnaire that can be administered and scored using a personal computer. This measure is summarized in Table 8.43.

Once the data on food intake has been obtained, it must be processed in order to obtain an estimate of the nutrient content of the food. We will cover two methods of processing food data. The first method is called computer nutrient analysis. Essentially, a large computer data base containing data on the nutrient composition of thousands of different foods is used to look up each food and to calculate total nutrient contents for meals or days (Adams, 1975; Hoover, 1983).

Programs exist for performing nutrient analysis on mainframe and microcomputers (ESHA research, 1987). These programs can calculate total values for over twenty specific nutrients and can summarize the percentage of the RDA for nutrients that have recommended values.

In a variation on nutrient analysis, patients are given a counter that contains information on a specific nutrient (usually kcal) for commonly eaten foods and are asked to calculate daily totals for that nutrient by hand. We have used this approach with subjects (Schlundt, Johnson, & Jarrell, 1985).

TABLE 8.43 An Evaluation of the Vanderbilt Food Frequency Questionnaire

Element	Comments
Name	Vanderbilt Food Frequency Questionnaire
Citation	Unpublished
Type of measure	Food frequency questionnaire for the estimation of typical nutrient intake
Potential uses	Research, treatment planning, treatment evaluation, population surveys
Populations	Adolescents and adults
Format	Administered as a paper-and-pencil questionnaire or as an interactive computer task; subject rates how often each food was eaten during the previous month
Scoring	Computer estimates typical intake of kcal, protein, carbohydrate, fat, alcohol, vitamin A, vitamin C, calcium, and iron. The program also lists the foods according to the amount of fat they contribute to the diet and indicates the proportional contribution each food makes to total fat intake.
Evaluation	May be more accurate in anorexic, obese, and normal subjects than bulimia because portion sizes vary substantially during eating binges
Availability	D. Schlundt, 323 A&S Psychology Bldg., Vanderbilt University, Nashville, TN 37240

The second approach to analyzing diet composition is to code foods using a food group system (Suitor & Crowley, 1984). Coding can be used to qualitatively evaluate an individual's dietary intake by examining the frequency of intake from each of the food groups. In addition, the typical nutrient value of a serving from each food group can be used to estimate energy content of the food (Schlundt, Hill, Sbrocco, Pope-Cordle, & Kasser, 1988). We have had subjects self-monitor food intake using a six food-group system (meat, milk, vegetable, fruit, grains, fats). Subjects were given a counter, which described the food group composition of many commonly eaten foods, and were taught to tally the total number of servings from each food group for each meal (Schlundt et al., 1988).

To summarize, typical nutrient intake information can be obtained using recalls, food frequency questionnaires, and diaries. This data can be summarized either by nutrient analysis or through classification of foods into food groups. Our recommendation for eating disorders is to use computerized nutrient analysis with seven-day food diaries in order to obtain an assessment of typical nutritional intake of anorexic or bulimic patients.

During treatment, however, we advise having patients monitor their food intake using diaries and calculating daily calorie intake or food group utilization on their own since this process also provides valuable immediate feedback to the patient.

Functional Analysis of Eating Behavior

There are many aspects of human eating behavior that are not easily captured by designation of average daily nutrient intakes or typical food group usage. Neither of these approaches provides a way of characterizing the range or degree of variability in food intake over time. When the data has been gathered using diaries or recalls from three or more days, it is possible to compute indices of variability as well as measures of central tendency. However, there are many temporal patterns in eating behavior that are still not captured by reporting standard deviations of daily macronutrient or micronutrients values.

Studying variability in eating behavior over time has been termed the microanalysis of food intake (Schlundt et al., 1985). The basis of this approach is that food intake is episodic, and that a variety of constructs and measures can be used to differentiate one eating episode from another. For example, eating episodes can be classified into meals (breakfast, lunch, supper, or snacks). Other constructs have been employed to differentiate eating episodes. For example, episodes characterized by the rapid consumption of a large quantity of food have been classified as eating binges (see Chapter 4). Meals can also be characterized using temporal parameters through description of meal duration, meal frequency, or intermeal interval. Questionnaires have typically been used to characterize qualities of food intake, such as binge eating, dietary restraint, and disinhibition, as we have seen in earlier sections of this chapter.

There is much room for further development of ways to describe eating behavior at the microanalysis level. As we have seen in Chapters 2, 6, and 7, most theories of food intake hold that eating behavior is influenced by a variety of biological and environmental variables.

Schlundt (1985, in press) suggested that the microanalysis of eating behavior can be structured to identify the specific antecedents and consequences that influence food intake. The study of how environmental antecedents and consequences influence behavior has been called functional analysis of behavior (see Chapter 7). In a naturalistic functional analysis of food intake, the unit of observation is the eating episode. As each eating episode occurs, measurements are taken to describe the behavior, the antecedents, and the consequences. Antecedents and consequences can be environmental, behavioral, physiological, or emotional events. The goals of functional analysis are to describe how qualities of eating behavior vary as a function of the environmental context and to derive detailed measures of eating behavior pattern.

Schlundt et al. (1985) used the naturalistic functional analysis to describe the environmental, behavioral, and affective antecedents of binge eating in eight bulimic subjects and overeating in twenty-three overweight subjects. Schlundt, Johnson, and Jarrell (1986) employed the methodology to describe the sequential structure of eating behavior in eight bulimic subjects. Schlundt, Sbrocco, and Bell (1988) described social and emotional antecedents to overeating and unplanned eating episodes in thirty-five subjects undergoing behavioral treatment for obesity. Diaries were entered into a microcomputer and were analyzed using the Self-Monitoring Analysis System (SMAS), a set of microcomputer programs for managing and analyzing data on the occurrence of behavior over time (Schlundt, 1985; Schlundt & Bell, 1987; Schlundt, in press).

Essentially, the method involves having subjects keep diaries over extended periods of time. In addition to recording food intake and/or coding calories or food groups, information about the situational context is recorded. We have employed diaries constructed using multiple-choice formats. Multiple choice eliminates coding problems and facilitates analysis of the diary information. Once the diary is collected, it is entered into a microcomputer using the Self-Monitoring Analysis System software. The clinician or researcher can then run analysis programs to describe the patient's eating behavior pattern in terms of means, probabilities, conditional means, and conditional probabilities. Schlundt et al. (1988) have described the reliability and validity of this approach to assessment when studying the eating behavior patterns of obese women. Table 8.44 summarizes the Self-Monitoring Analysis System.

Test Meals

Rosen and associates (Rosen, Leitenberg, Fondacaro, Gross, & Wilmuth, 1985; Rosen, 1988) presented an additional method of behavioral assessment for the evaluation of eating-disordered patients. The basic idea is that much can be learned about an individual with an eating disorder by actually observing the patient consume food. Consequently, standardized test meals have been used as a way to obtain information about eating behavior in a manner that can be used to gather data for clinical or research purposes.

The approach is to have the patient consume a standardized meal and to observe and measure the patient's response to the meal. Rosen et al. (1985) have used a full-course dinner, a spaghetti dinner, and candy

TABLE 8.44 An Evaluation of the Self-Monitoring Analysis System

Element	Comments
Name	Self-Monitoring Analysis System (SMAS)
Citation	Schlundt (in press)
Type of measure	Behavioral assessment of bingeing, purging, or nutrient intake; functional analysis of behavior.
Potential uses	Individual assessment of eating behavior patterns, research, treatment evaluation
Populations	Eating-disordered, obese
Format	All meals and snacks are recorded in a diary along with information on the situational antecedents and/or consequences.
Scoring	Diary data is entered into a computer data base and summary programs are used to extract probabilities, means, conditional probabilities, and conditional means.
Evaluation	Reliable and valid method for obtaining data on individual behavior under a variety of situational circumstances
Availability	D. Schlundt, 323 A&S Psychology Bldg., Vanderbilt University, Nashville, TN 37240

as standardized test meals. Patients are given a measured amount of each food and are instructed to eat as much as they feel comfortable eating. The dependent measures are the amounts of each type of food consumed and the subjects' ratings of fear, anxiety, and the urge to vomit. In addition, they asked subjects to think out loud into a tape recorder while eating in order to gather information on cognition and affect associated with the consumption of forbidden foods. The instructions for bulimic subjects include that they are not allowed to vomit for at least one-and-one-half hours after eating the test meal.

Rosen et al. showed that bulimic subjects ate less food and experienced more anxiety than normal weight, noneating-disordered subjects in response to the three test meals. Eating the forbidden foods elicited a strong urge to vomit in the bulimic subjects. Rosen (1988) suggests that this procedure may be useful for both diagnosis of the approach/avoidance behavior of eating-disordered patients with respect to forbidden foods and as a sensitive way to evaluate outcome in the treatment of bulimia. Williamson, Kelley, Davis, Ruggiero, and Veitia (1985) have also employed test meals in their research on the physiological arousal that occurs in bulimic, obese, and normal subjects. Table 8.45 summarizes the standardized test meal assessment technique.

TABLE 8.45 An Evaluation of Standardized Test Meals

Element	Comments
Name	Standardized Test Meals
Citation	Rosen (1988), Rosen et al. (1985)
Type of measure	Behavioral assessment
Potential uses	Diagnosis of food phobia, treatment outcome
Populations	Anorexia and bulimia nervosa
Format	Subjects eat a standardized meal with the instruction that they are not to vomit for at least 1½ hours after eating
Scoring	Amount of food consumed, ratings of anxiety, ratings of urge to vomit, description of thoughts that accompany consumption of forbidden foods
Evaluation	Provides information that cannot be obtained from questionnaire or diaries
Availability	Rosen (1988), Rosen et al. (1985)

CLINICAL RECOMMENDATIONS

In this chapter, we have presented a large number of assessment instruments and approaches that may be of some use in both research and treatment of eating disorders. We have described the format, uses, and scoring of each approach in detail and have indicated where copies of most instruments can be obtained.

The task for the clinician, however, is to choose which assessment instruments, out of the many available, to use with which patients. Our recommendation is that at least a minimal battery of measures be routinely employed so that information about a patient's eating disorder is not obtained only from clinical interviews. At least one of the short diagnostic questionnaires, such as the BULIT, should be employed along with a general measure of psychological distress such as the SCL-90. In addition, clinicians may want to obtain more specific information about body satisfaction using the BSQ, about cognition using the SCANS, or about interpersonal function using the FNE and SAD. We strongly recommend that eating-disordered patients be asked to keep a food diary, at least during the first few weeks of treatment. Even if the patient fails to keep the diary as assigned, valuable information has been obtained that will influence the clinician's evaluation of the patient and probably the plan for therapeutic intervention.

Whenever questionnaires are used, there is the danger of overloading the patient with probing questions early in the treatment process before an adequate therapeutic alliance has been forged. However, if the task of completing questionnaires is presented to the patient positively, with an adequate rationale, the majority of patients will comply and will not be driven away from therapy. It is probably wise to conduct at least one initial interview and begin the process of building rapport before asking the patient to spend an hour or so taking psychological measures. Patients will be more cooperative with future requests to complete assessment instruments if they are given at least minimal feedback on the results.

Most therapists recognize the importance of reliable and valid measurements when treatment is part of a research evaluation. However, some of these measures can also be quite useful when the treatment is being delivered purely as a clinical service. The utility of structured psychological and behavioral assessments occurs when the clinician scores the instruments, looks at the scores, and incorporates this information into conceptualization of the patient's problems and prioritization of treatment goals. Some measures, such as eating diaries, body composition assessment, image marking technique of body-image assessment, or the Vanderbilt Food Frequency Questionnaire, are useful for giving the patient direct feedback and can be actively incorporated into the therapeutic plan. The measures can be readministered later in order to give the patient specific feedback on the amount and kinds of changes made during therapy. The integration of assessment data into treatment planning and evaluation is discussed in more detail in Chapter 18.

Clinicians who routinely employ psychological assessment in their clinical practice may note the absence of one or more of their favorite assessment instruments. We deliberately omitted any discussion of general projective tests, such as the TAT or Rorschach, intellectual assessments, such as the WAIS, and neuropsychological tests. If these tests are part of a clinician's routine assessment protocol, there is no harm in administering them to eating-disordered patients. In fact, a clinician experienced with these measures may find them useful in treatment planning. However, we have not included them in our recommendations because they do not provide enough information specific to eating disorders.

SUMMARY

Every clinician engages in some form of assessment when treating a patient with an eating disorder. In this chapter, we have described a set of tools that can make the assessment task easier. First, there are a group of questionnaires that are specifically designed to assess the attitudes and behaviors characteristic of anorexia and bulimia nervosa. These include the EAT, Anorectic Attitudes Questionnaire, EDI, Binge Scale, Binge Eating Questionnaire, Bulimia Cognitive Distortions Scale, SCANS, BULIT, and BITE. While no clinician would administer all of these to patients, most clinicians will use several of these to assess attitudes, beliefs, and behaviors related to the diagnosis of an eating disorder.

While there are a vast number of general psychological tests that might be useful in the assessment of eating disorder patients, we described the MMPI, SCL-90, Beck Depression Inventory, Fear of Negative Evaluations, and Social Avoidance and Distress Scale. These measures are useful to screen for severe psychopathology, to determine the patient's level of emotional distress, and to describe specific areas of distress such as depression or social anxiety.

There are several useful questionnaires that have been developed to assess eating behavior, which are not specific to eating disorders. We discussed the DIET questionnaire, the Food Survey, the Three-Factor Eating Questionnaire, and the Restraint Scale. Two of these measures, the DIET and the Food Survey, appear in Appendix B with instructions for scoring and plotting profiles.

Questionnaires provide only a limited amount of quantitative information. Five detailed semistructured interviews or interview questionnaires that are available for use with eating disorder patients were also presented. (The Health Habit Survey is reproduced in Appendix B.) These interview protocols provide a broad ranging yet detailed description of the patient's health and psychiatric history, eating behavior, social adjustment, and lifestyle.

Several useful physical assessment approaches were described. Tests of body composition are used to estimate the patient's body fat percentage. Detailed instructions for using the sum of seven skinfolds along with tables for determining body fat percentage in men and women were included. We suggested that assessment of resting metabolic rate using indirect calorimetry can provide information that is useful in the treatment of eating-disordered patients. Assessment of physical fitness can also be important and several simple protocols were described.

The assessment of body image is a growing area of interest among scientists and clinicians working with eating-disordered patients. We described a variety of methods for assessing body image, including projective techniques, questionnaires, psychophysical methods, and approaches that contrast different body-image schemata. The Body Image Testing System (BITS), a computer program for assessment of body-image constructs, is described in some detail.

Behavioral assessment approaches to understanding a patient's eating behavior were presented. These included methods for estimating typical nutrient intake using recalls, diaries, and food frequency questionnaires.

We discussed the use of nutrient self-monitoring as another approach to studying typical nutritional intake. The microanalysis of eating is an assessment approach that examines the variability in food intake from one time to the next. The analysis of the antecedents and consequences of food intake using computer analysis of self-monitoring diaries was discussed as a potentially useful microanalysis approach. We also described the use of test meals as a behavioral assessment approach that can provide valuable information about the eating behavior of an anorexic or bulimic patient.

The question facing the clinician is not whether to conduct an assessment of a patient. Rather, the question is how to gather useful assessment data within a reasonable amount of time at an acceptable cost. This chapter described a variety of tools that can be used to evaluate the person with an eating disorder.

9

Medical and Pharmacological Therapies for Eating Disorders

IN THIS CHAPTER, current medical therapies for eating disorders will be reviewed. Given the possibility of a very low body weight in anorexia, aggressive medical intervention relies primarily upon nutritional support. Specifically for anorexia, nutritional support can take the form of a nasogastric tube or hyperalimentation. In contrast, nutritional support in bulimia nervosa consists primarily of education and behavior modification regarding proper eating habits and appropriate nutrition. For both eating disorders, a variety of medications have been utilized with none being clearly superior in treating either disorder. In general, neuroleptics are more likely to be prescribed for patients with anorexia, whereas antidepressants are more likely to be prescribed for those with bulimia.

BIOLOGICAL THERAPY FOR ANOREXIA NERVOSA

Nutritional Support

When body weight falls to 15 percent below ideal and body fat levels are below 10 percent, weight restoration becomes a treatment priority. Many patients can be effectively treated without hospitalization. However, when they fail to improve by showing appropriate meal patterns and significant weight gain after several weeks of therapy, the hospital environment becomes necessary for their physical well-being and effective treatment.

There are three approaches to weight restoration: (1) soft solid foods and oral liquid nutrition supplements, (2) liquid nasogastric tube feeding, and (3) hyperalimentation or total parenteral nutrition. These nutritional interventions vary in their ease of implementation, intrusiveness, and the likelihood of patient cooperation. All have the primary objective of restoring the individual to a safe and physically appropriate body weight.

By far the least intrusive and easiest path to weight restoration is regular meals with nutrition supplements. While many patients may resist or be unable to consume solids at regular meals, soft solids with liquid nutritional supplements represent a compromise that is readily implemented and well-tolerated. Soft solid foods are less likely to produce the uncomfortable fullness and bloatedness that often occurs as a result of delayed gastric emptying or the consumption of regular meals against a background of erratic eating habits. Also, the prospects of spontaneous gastroesophageal reflux is reduced along with the motivation to engage in self-induced vomiting.

The Relationship between Caloric Intake and Weight Gain

Wide variations in body weight increases are observed on similar caloric intakes. Some patients display dramatic increases in body weight on relatively few calories. This may be due to a low RMR resulting from a semistarvation diet and loss of lean body mass. With no opportunity for purging, other patients lag considerably behind in weight gain while taking in a level of calories that should theoretically promote weight gain. Unfortunately, there are no validated algorithms relating caloric intake to predicted weight gain. Clinicians must carefully titrate caloric intake against weight gain and recognize that rapid increases may foster patient resistance and potentially lead to relapse.

Caloric intakes begin in the 1,000–1,200 kcal/day range in four to six feedings per day and, depending on the patient's response, progress gradually up to 3,000 kcal per day in five-day increments of 500 kcal. A nutritional balance of carbohydrates (55 percent to 60 percent), proteins (15 percent), and fats (20 percent to 25 percent) is recommended with approximately 1.5 gm/kg of ideal body weight of high quality protein provided. Patients should be given a wide variety of food selections over the food groups, and encouraged to choose and eat each of the selections. Clinicians should be aware that very low-fat diets yield lower rates of weight gain.

The use of regular meals, soft solids, and nutritional supplements must be integrated within the total treatment program. Specific expectations and goals for eating and weight gain must be clearly communicated to the patient. The treatment program is ideally organized within a behavioral framework that allows increasing self-control and responsibility over both eating and behavior and weight gain (see Chapter 17).

When the patient's physical condition or continuing refusal to eat requires it, the nasogastric tube or total parenteral nutrition are appropriate medical interventions. The nasogastric tube consists of a plastic surgical tube that is inserted down the nose and swallowed into the stomach. Nutritional supplements are passed down the tube on a regular feeding schedule calculated to provide the patient with a sufficient quantity of macronutrients and micronutrients for a weight gain approximating one quarter pound or more per day. Coupled with encouragement of regular ad lib fluid intake, patients quickly adapt to the tube. For most patients the use of the nasogastric tube is aversive, and they are willing to relinquish it in favor of soft solids and eventually a schedule of regular meals. For a few patients, however, the presence of the nasogastric tube represents a relief from confronting the difficulties of eating. These individuals must be gradually weaned from the nasogastric tube. In either case, a solid therapeutic relationship and integrated treatment plan are extraordinarily important.

Total parenteral nutrition, also referred to as hyperalimentation, is a procedure in which hyperosmolar solutions of glucose, amino acids, fatty acids, and other essential nutrients are infused into the superior venae cavae through the subclavian vein. The nature of these solutions necessitates infusion in large veins where sufficient blood flow allows for rapid reductions in concentration. Hyperalimentation was initially developed to feed burn and other surgical patients who could not readily absorb food into the gastrointestinal tract. Total parenteral nutrition techniques should be reserved for emergency cases and for those patients who are most severely malnourished with body weights approaching 35 percent and below ideal.

Maloney and Farrell (1980) described the implementation of total parenteral nutrition with four patients who had lost at least 35 percent of their body weight and were resistant to a wide variety of other interventions including medication, individual and family psychotherapy, and behavior modification. Maloney and Farrell determined the amount and content of hyperalimentation fluid based on calories required for weight gain, protein level based on ideal body weight, and electrolyte balance. Infusion was continued until patients gained a significant amount of weight that yielded improved electrolytes, were eating regular meals, and displayed increased alertness and sociability. At admission, the percent of ideal body weight ranged from 55 percent to 64 percent in these patients who were from twelve to sixteen years old. One case, a fourteen-year-old girl, weighed a mere 16.6 kg with the authors indicating this to be one of the lowest body weights ever reported in the literature. Obviously, these patients required the kind of emergency medical intervention that only hyperalimentation or the nasogastric tube could provide.

With the hyperalimentation procedure, the patients gained an average of 8.5 kgs, and their average percent of ideal weight increased from 59 percent to 81 percent during the twenty-five days on total parenteral nutrition. Following weight restoration, the focus of therapy shifted to individual personality difficulties, conflicts, and family life. At follow-up sessions all were above 88 percent of ideal body weight.

Another report on total parenteral nutrition is provided by Pertschuk, Forster, Buzby, and Mullen (1981) who examined the records of patients admitted for anorexia nervosa at the Hospital of the University of Pennsylvania between January 1968 and 1979. Seventy-seven patients met the criteria for a diagnsosis of anorexia and eleven of these were placed on total parenteral nutrition. Those patients receiving hyperalimentation were compared with a matched control group receiving standard behavioral inpatient treatment. The patients averaged 31 kg and 57 percent of ideal body weight at admission. The total calories supplied by total parenteral nutrition were in excess of 150 percent of their calculated basal metabolic rate. Solid food was always available to the patients and total parenteral nutrition was discontinued when ad lib food intake was sufficient to promote weight gain. Patients in the behavioral treatment without hyperalimentation had privileges made contingent on a weight gain of approximately one half pound per day. In addition, some patients were also taking antidepressant medication.

The data indicated that total parenteral nutrition was very effective in generating weight gain with discharge weights averaging 38 kg or approximately 76 percent of ideal body weight. The total parenteral nutrition group had a significantly lower admission weight (57 percent of ideal versus 63 percent of ideal) and longer length of hospitalization (9 weeks versus 4.4 weeks) than the comparison group. The rate of weight gain during total parenteral nutrition of 2.5 kg/week was significantly higher than the 1.3 kg/week in the comparison group. These data on percent of ideal body weight, rate of weight gain, and length of treatment document the effective use of total parenteral nutrition in emergencies.

Both the nasogastric tube and total parenteral nutrition are associated with considerable risks including infection, pneumonia, and a variety of metabolic abnormalities. While patients may gain weight at a faster rate on total parenteral nutrition and the nasogastric tube, these procedures are indicated only for cases in which body weight has fallen 35 percent to 40 percent below ideal, or where there has been a rapid weight loss of 25 percent to 30 percent in a period of several months. Total parenteral nutrition and nasogastric tube feedings should not be used as punishment or out of desperation on the part of the therapist due to noncompliance with other forms of treatment. Their indications are clear: body weight 35 percent or lower than ideal or a medical emergency.

The Nature and Rate of Weight Gain

Several studies have attempted to document the nature and rate of weight gain in anorexic patients during weight restoration. For example, G.F.M. Russell and Mezey (1962) conducted detailed metabolic studies on four anorexics who were not maintained on tube or total parenteral nutrition feedings but were simply encouraged to eat. Homogenous liquid diets were provided with increasing levels of caloric intake raised over five- to ten-day periods until a maximum level between 3,500 and 5,500 calories per day were reached. The typical diet consisted of 266g carbohydrates, 97g proteins, and 109g fats. The results revealed that the surplus calories required to gain 1 kg of weight varied from 7,800 to 8,200 kcal with an average of 7,900 kcal/kg. Patients gained from 5.6 to 11.8 kg in the five- to six-week period with a weight gain of .2 to .3 kg/day. Interestingly, most of the weight gained was in the form of fat, which is consistent with the observations of Keys et al. (1950).

In a similar study, Pertschuk et al. (1981) studied weight gain and nutrition in four anorexic patients who were 52 percent of ideal body weight and required total parenteral nutrition for an average of sixty-three days. There was no significant correlation between either daily, nonprotein caloric excess and weight change or between weekly caloric excess and weekly weight change for any individual patient or for the entire group. However, over a longer time interval of two weeks, correlations were observed between weight gain and caloric excess. Not surprisingly, there was a significant correlation (.82) between the cumulative caloric excess and cumulative weight gain for the entire group over the duration of the study. The low individual correlations resulted from frequent weight plateaus in which there was no or little weight change for up to five days and variability in the caloric cost of weight gain. Like previous studies, including that of Keys, Brozek, Henschel, Mickelsen, & Taylor (1950), the estimates of the caloric cost of weight gain are often as high as 6,000 kcal/kg and in some cases even higher with considerable interindividual variability. These investigators suggested a number of variables that may influence the differences in individual rates of weight gain and caloric intake, including fluid accumulation and shifts, differences in the composition of newly synthesized tissue, and alterations in specific dynamic action and basal metabolic rate.

Maintaining and Enhancing Weight Gain

As previously indicated, there is a variable relationship between caloric intake and the weight restoration process for most anorexics (Pertschuk et al., 1981). An interesting problem facing clinicians is the level of caloric intake required to maintain weight at 85 percent to 90 percent of ideal body weight. Studies have shown that up to 50 percent of anorexics experience difficulty in maintaining their improved weight status following termination of a weight restoration program (Hsu, Crisp, & Harding, 1979). Thus, after weight restoration, the required caloric intake necessary to maintain the anorexic patient within a healthy percent of ideal body weight is uncertain.

To study this problem, Kaye and colleagues (Kaye, Gwirtsman, George, Ebert, & Petersen, 1986) observed thirteen anorexics soon after weight restoration, and nine additional patients after their weight had been recovered for at least six months. All subjects were studied over a three to five day period during which they stayed on an isolated inpatient unit. Food intake was documented and motor activity was continuously recorded for twenty-hour periods over the three to five days using electromechanical devices.

The recently weight-restored anorexics were studied two to four weeks after completing the treatment program and the long-term patients were studied from six to thirty-five months after obtaining and maintaining a stable, normal weight. The short-term group had significantly higher caloric intakes than the long-term recovered group. The short-term, weight-recovered group also had higher levels of activity compared to the long-term patients. For example, the caloric intake of the short-term weight-recovered group was just over 2,000 kcal per day while the long-term recovered group averaged approximately 1,350 kcal per day. Activity-wise, the recently recovered anorexics displayed a significantly higher level of activity, which was approximately 1.5 times that of the long-term recovered patients. Moreover, there was a high positive correlation between activity and daily caloric intake for the recently recovered anorexics (.58), whereas no such relationship was observed for the long-term patients. Thus, the increased caloric intake for the recently recovered group was directly proportional to their activity.

These data appear to indicate a need for high caloric intake following the weight restoration period and the importance of regular exercise. The higher need for calories in the short-term group could be related to their higher levels of activity or because metabolic processes were still organized around weight gain rather than weight maintenance. Regardless, following weight restoration and with normal cardiac function, regular aerobic exercise in the maintenance phase appears indicated for a number of reasons. First, regular aerobic exercise is important in appetite regulation (Epling & Pierce, 1988). Second, restricting anorexics in the process of weight restoration and maintenance are at risk for the development of binge eating and purging and can profit from learning healthy techniques of weight control (Johnson, Schlundt, & Jarrell, 1986). Finally, exercise may influence the ratio of lean to fat tissue synthesized during weight restoration.

Medication for Anorexia Nervosa

A variety of medications have been used to treat anorexia with none demonstrating a specific therapeutic action. The choice of medication, then, has generally been determined on an individual basis targeting associated symptoms, such as anxiety, depression, and cognitive distortions. The range of drugs used for anorexia have included neuroleptics, antianxiety agents, antidepressants, lithium, L-dopa, and cyproheptadine. With the exception of a few case reports, formal studies of medication have not found a drug of choice, and most drugs have not proved to be superior to placebos (Rockwell, Ellingwood, Dougherty, & Brodie, 1982).

Neuroleptics are the major tranquilizers, and they are typically used in the treatment of schizophrenia and psychosis. Phenothiazines such as chlorpromazine (Thorazine) are the most widely prescribed neuroleptic drugs for psychotic disorders, and they appear to affect behavior by interfering with neurotransmitters such as dopamine, norepinephrine, and serotonin. The use of neuroleptics, such as the phenothiazines, in anorexia is based primarily on clinical experience rather than research evidence. In fact, a side effect of the medication, namely inactivity and weight gain, is largely responsible for its use.

According to Garfinkel and Garner (1982), chlorpromazine has been the most widely used neuroleptic for anorexia. They recommend dosages ranging from 400 to 1,000 mg/day and note a recent trend toward lower dosages in the 50–150 mg range. Chlorpromazine is indicated to reduce the patient's anxiety over weight gain and for agitation, impaired judgment, and impulsivity. By reducing the patient's anxiety and tension, these drugs may promote weight restoration efforts and make the patients more amenable to changes in core symptoms of their eating disorder. Garfinkel and Garner also note a number of side effects of chlorpromazine including a reduction in the seizure threshold, lower body temperature, postural hypotension, and sedation.

Other neuroleptics have been used to treat anorexia, including pimozide and sulpiride in controlled trials with no definite outcome in favor of active medication versus placebo (Vandereycken & Pierloot, 1982; Vandereycken, 1984). Several systematic studies have documented the ineffectiveness of pimozide. Vandereycken and Pierloot (1982) studied various doses (4 mg and 6 mg) of pimozide or placebo within the context of a behavior therapy program and found initial differences favoring the drug that were not statistically significant or maintained. In a recent review, Vandereycken (1987b) expressed dismay over the continued use of neuroleptics in spite of the overwhelming evidence to the contrary. He notes that the antianxiety benefits associated with neuroleptics are better obtained with minor tranquilizers and that the side effect of weight gain is short-lived and better achieved with behavior therapy. Judd, Norman, and Burrows (1987), in reviewing the data on the pharmacological management of anorexia and bulimia nervosa, also concluded that neuroleptics have little proven value.

Antianxiety medications are also commonly prescribed for anorexia and the most frequently used are the benzodiazepines. These drugs decrease anxiety and are recommended only in specific cases and at low doses. Andersen (1987) recommends .5 mg lorazepam one hour prior to eating and notes that approximately 50 percent of his patients use the medication for about two and one half weeks. Antianxiety medications also have a number of side effects, including sedation, dependency, and ataxia. The indication for the use of antianxiety drugs is to reduce anxiety associated with eating and weight gain. Again, support for the use of these drugs is based on clinical experience as no controlled trials have been reported.

According to Hsu (1987), antidepressants are the most widely used drugs for anorexia yet these drugs and others, such as lithium, have not been shown effective with weight gain or core symptoms. A study by Biederman and colleagues is characteristic (Beiderman et al., 1985). They compared amitriptyline (3 mg/kg) to placebo in twenty-five anorexia patients in a five-week double-blind trial. Amitriptyline did not lead to a greater weight gain nor improved depression.

Cyproheptadine has been used with anorexia because of its effect on serotonin. Cyproheptadine is used primarily as an antihistamine with children, and experience with this medication suggested it caused weight gain, presumably due to its antagonistic effects on serotonin. Vigersky and Loriaux (1977) studied the influence of cyproheptadine on weight gain in outpatient anorexics who were randomly assigned to 4 mg cyproheptadine three times a day or placebo for eight weeks. Fewer than one third of the patients on cyproheptadine gained weight, and the level of weight gained was minimal, ranging from 2 percent to 20 percent. Interestingly, two of the patients taking the placebo gained 12 percent and 13 percent of their body weight over the eight-week trial.

A subsequent large-scale trial involving three hospitals explored the efficacy of cyproheptadine versus placebo combined with behavior therapy to induce weight gain (Goldberg, Halmi, Eckert, Casper, & Davis, 1979). Cyproheptadine was chosen not only because of its serotonin antagonist effect but also because it has few side effects compared to other psychiatric medications. All patients in the active treatment were begun on a liquid 12 mg dose that was increased 5 mg/day unless there was a weight gain of .5 kg in the preceding five-day period. Following thirty-five days of treatment, the average weight gain was 5.1 kg for the drug group and 4.3 for the placebo group, a nonsignificant difference. Also Halmi and colleagues (Halmi, Eckert, LaDu, & Cohen, 1986) reported a comparison of cyproheptadine, amitriptyline, and placebo with slight nonsignificant effects noted for the drugs.

BIOLOGICAL THERAPY FOR BULIMIA NERVOSA

Like anorexia nervosa, biological interventions in bulimia nervosa include nutritional support and medication. There are, however, several distinct differences in how the two conditions are treated. One such difference in nutritional support and medication is the increasing use of phenelzine in the treatment of bulimia. Phenelzine is a monoamine oxidase inhibitor and its use must be accompanied by a tyramine-restricted diet. In addition, therapy for bulimia often involves medical treatment of some of its complications, such as laxative addiction.

Nutritional Support

Since many bulimics are within a normal weight range, drastic nutritional support, such as the nasogastric tube and total parenteral nutrition, is rare. There are isolated cases, however, of electrolyte imbalance, dehydration, and metabolic alkalosis resulting from inadequate nutrition, purging, and the abuse of laxatives and diuretics that require emergency care. These patients are seen in hospital emergency rooms for dehydration and electrolyte imbalance. They have become weak, dizzy, and may have even fainted. Unfortunately, referrals for continuing psychological treatment are not made because the underlying eating disorder is not recognized. These patients not only require emergency rehydration, but also long-term treatment of the eating disorder. The nature of the nutritional intervention is brief, consisting of rehydration and electrolyte infusion. Thereafter, the patient can resume a regular diet and should enter treatment.

In the majority of cases, nutritional interventions with bulimia consist of providing information and counseling to insure adequate dietary intake of macro- and micro-nutrients. The nutritional information presented is similar to that reviewed in Chapter 13 and is often done by either a nutritional support team or a dietician with expertise and training in eating disorders.

Some of the most common difficulties presented by bulimics are food myths and the failure to eat what are called forbidden foods as discussed in Chapter 3. Treatment consists of exploring the irrational nature of the avoidance (see Chapter 11) and exposure with response prevention therapy (see Chapter 12). The basis of the inaccurate nutrition information is discussed and more appropriate information is supplied (see Chapter 13).

Many patients with bulimia nervosa are prescribed monoamine oxidase inhibitors with phenelzine (Nardil) being the most widely used. Due to the nature of their biotransformation, these medications require a diet that is tyramine-free or at least severely restricted. Tyramine is an amino acid that reacts negatively with monoamine oxidase inhibitors and can produce violent, nearly lethal reactions. Unfortunately, there is little in the way of quantitative information available on the tyramine content of various foods. However, most items high in tyramine are those that have served as a growth medium, such as cheeses, aged and smoked meats and fish, products containing yeast, high-protein fermented foods, bean pods, eggplant, and spoiled fruit. Beverages containing caffeine, such as coffee, tea, and soft drinks, should also be restricted. These foods and drinks should be avoided one day before and up to two weeks after taking these monoamine oxidase inhibitors. The reactions presumably vary with the amount of tyramine and can include a rapid elevation in blood pressure, severe headache, pounding heart rate, and flushed feeling.

Laxative Reduction Therapy

Laxative abuse is a problem frequently encountered in the treatment of eating disorders. Abuse of laxatives refers to their use solely to purge calories or lose weight. The purpose of laxative reduction therapy is to eliminate laxative abuse and in the process develop healthy, more appropriate strategies for weight control.

In many respects, the behavioral dynamics of laxative abuse parallel those of other forms of purging (see Chapters 5 and 7). Patients often recognize the irrationality and self-defeating nature of laxative abuse, yet they persist until they become physically and psychologically dependent. Because tolerance and dependency develop, it is unreasonable to expect that laxative abuse will be reduced or eliminated solely by exhortation or education alone. Rather, specific management and therapeutic techniques are necessary.

Laxative abuse in bulimic women develops, like other forms of purging, in an attempt to eliminate calories, thereby reducing the fear of weight gain. Many laxative-abusing women also vomit regularly, others have attempted to vomit but are physically unable, while still others cannot bring themselves to vomit. These latter women become exclusive laxative abusers.

Patterns of usage and types of laxatives are quite variable. No inherent rationale seems to exist for the selection of one brand of laxatives over another in terms of ability to eliminate calories or to create psychologically satisfying results. Rather, most decisions as to the types of laxatives or brands are based on taste, experience, superstition, cost, and the appeal of increasingly prominent advertisements.

It is not unusual for bulimic women to alternate types of laxatives. Timing of the laxatives is based on convenience or when the individual feels that a laxative will eliminate the greatest portion of the calories consumed during a binge. Thus, some women regularly take laxatives at certain times during the day, such as in the morning and evening, others use laxatives before and after eating meals or bingeing, while still others use laxatives whenever they feel fat or look fat.

The physiological and psychological effects of using laxatives are, unfortunately, continued use and greater dependency. The desired result is to eliminate calories by increasing the gastrointestinal transit time, thereby creating a malabsorption of food. However, research has shown that only a small amount (approximately 12 percent) of ingested nutrients are eliminated in the diarrhea, an amount considerably less than hoped for by the bulimic.

Laxatives have their effects by stimulating the colon and altering fluid retention. The short time required to produce diarrhea no doubt contributes to the psychological dependency. The resulting soft stools and diarrhea contribute to the belief that calories have been lost. Also, a secondary effect is to restrict the bulimic's mobility and social interactions due to the necessity of maintaining proximity to toilet facilities. The regular use of laxatives eventually results in a decreased function of the colon due to muscle atrophy and neural deterioration with chronic abuse holding the prospect of permanent damage. Consequently, gastrointestinal functions are severely compromised with regular laxative abuse, and the individual becomes physically dependent on laxatives in order to have bowel movements.

The major effect of laxatives that contributes to psychological dependence is dehydration. This diuretic effect appears largely responsible for the volume in bowel movements and contributes to the interference with calorie absorption. Due to loss of sodium in the diarrhea, renal function adjusts to conserve sodium at the expense of greater potassium loss. Subsequently, hypokalemia may develop and renal damage is a distinct possibility.

Like alterations in the gastrointestinal tract, the fluid and electrolyte complications of regular laxative use must be addressed in therapy. A reduction in the use of laxatives often causes constipation as a result of decreased gastrointestinal motility while peripheral edema is common due to sodium retention. Many patients are keenly aware of swelling in the abdomen, fingers, face, and ankles. They regularly monitor specific areas of their bodies by looking in the mirror, noting the tightness of their shoes, bracelets, and rings. The perception of bloating followed by taking laxatives and achieving relief is a powerful reinforcement mechanism that helps create psychological dependence on laxatives.

The goal of laxative reduction therapy is the elimination of their use. Since both physiological and psychological mechanisms regulate the continued use of laxatives, therapy must take both into account. The constipation and edema have the effect of maintaining the psychological abuse pattern through negative reinforcement. In treating laxative abuse, it is important to assess the association of eating, laxative abuse, and the nature and timing of bowel movements and related changes in fluid retention.

Therapy for laxative abuse involves an integrated program of education on the ineffectiveness of laxatives, the amelioration of the consequences of withdrawal, including constipation and fluid retention, and promotion of increased dietary fiber and regular exercise to improve regularity and establish more appropriate weight control behaviors.

Education on the effects of laxative abuse and nature of the physical and psychological dependency are extremely important as the first step in laxative reduction therapy. Many patients entertain myths as to the effectiveness of laxatives and are often quite surprised when informed of the minimal amount of caloric malabsorption. However, in spite of these educational efforts, the behavior of using laxatives is firmly entrenched as a result of the physiological and psychological dependence related to constipation and dehydration. Education must therefore address the specific nature of the dependency process. Additionally, laxative abusers should be warned not to confuse fluid retention with fat accumulation. In this regard, education about the side effects of withdrawal is particularly important. Equal emphasis, however, is placed on the short-term nature of these side effects and how increased dietary fiber and regular aerobic exercise can overcome the brief period of constipation and edema.

It is also important to assess the individual's thoughts about the use of laxatives, the pattern and frequency of use, and other aspects that may be maintaining the use, including the medical and interpersonal consequences of laxative abuse. Likewise, the individual's dietary patterns, including the current consumption of fruits and vegetables, high-fiber grains and breads, and fluid intake, should be assessed.

The next phase after education and assessment involves deciding whether abrupt or gradual cessation will be attempted. Unfortunately, there are no data available to guide such a decision. On the basis of our clinical experience and behavioral analysis, we prefer abrupt cessation. It is likely that gradual withdrawal will maintain both the physical and psychological dependance due to an intermittent or partial reinforcement schedule. In fact, we strongly suspect that most abusers have attempted to reduce laxative use gradually but soon revert to old patterns in response to constipation, edema, and arousal of the fear of weight gain.

When hospitalization is indicated, laxatives are terminated upon admission. In outpatient treatment, the individual begins an aerobic exercise program consisting of at least twenty or thirty minutes of vigorous activity each day while simultaneously increasing intake of fiber and fluids. Fiber can be increased by supplementing what the patient is already eating with more fruits, vegetables, whole-grain breads, and bran cereals. Table 9.1 presents a list of some high-fiber foods that can be added to the patient's diet. Once these dietary changes and exercise are in place for a week or so, the individual gradually learns more effective ways of weight regulation thereby diminishing the fear of obesity that psychologically underlies the laxative abuse. Subsequently, the individual terminates the use of laxatives while being prepared to cope with the constipation and fluid retention that develop. Glycerine suppositories are used if there is no bowel movement for three days. With continuing problems, a bran-fiber bulking agent, such as Metamucil is given. Because of the exercise and dietary changes, it is our experience that the levels of constipation and edema are much less than they were after previous attempts at cessation.

Medication for Bulimia Nervosa

Drug interventions for bulimia are related to specific conceptualizations of the disorder. For example, as we mentioned in Chapter 6, phenytoin was administered to bulimics based on the idea that bulimia is a seizure-like disorder. Similarly, the use of antidepressants, including the tricyclics and monoamine oxidase inhibitors, is based on conceptualizing bulimia

TABLE 9.1 Some Common Sources of Fiber in the Diet

Food	Serving Size	Grams of Fiber
Avocado	½ medium	2.2
Broccoli	½ cup	3.2
Baked beans	½ cup	11.0
Chili with beans	½ cup	8.5
Carrots (raw)	1 medium	2.3
Corn on the cob	1 ear	5.9
Green peas	½ cup	4.2
Baked potato	1 medium	3.0
Tomato (raw)	1 medium	2.0
Apple	1 medium	3.3
Apricots, dried	¼ cup	7.8
Banana	1 medium	3.5
Stewed prunes	½ cup	8.0
All-bran cereal	⅓ cup	9.0
Raisin Bran	¾ cup	4.0
Whole wheat bread	1 slice	2.1

as a variation of a major affective disorder. Likewise, the use of fenfluramine is linked to serotonin and carbohydrate cravings, and the opioid antagonists naloxone and naltrexone have been employed on the basis of their ability to block eating induced by endorphins.

As noted in Chapter 6, the research data on the relationship between bulimia nervosa and affective disorder indicate that depression develops secondary to the eating disorder and that there does not appear to be a common etiology for bulimia and affective disorders. Regardless, the data indicate that several medications are effective. The most commonly used drugs for bulimia nervosa are tricyclic antidepressants including imipramine, desipramine, amitriptyline, and mianserin.

Table 9.2 summarizes the results of drug studies of bulimia nervosa. In an initial study, Pope, Hudson, Jonas, and Yurgelun-Todd (1983)

TABLE 9.2 Controlled Studies Evaluating Antidepressants for Bulimia Nervosa

Study	Drug	Number of Patients	Treatment Duration	Outcome
Pope et al., 1983	Imipramine	9	6 weeks	70% reduction in binge eating
	Placebo	10		2% reduction in binge eating
Agras et al., 1987	Imipramine	10	16 weeks	72% reduction in binge eating
	Placebo	13		35% reduction in binge eating
Mitchell & Groat, 1984	Amitriptyline (150mg) and behavior therapy	16	10 weeks	79% reduction in vomiting
	Placebo and behavior therapy	16		53% reduction in vomiting
Hughes et al., 1986	Desipramine (200mg)	13 (10)	6 weeks	91% reduction in binge eating
	Placebo	12 (12)		19% increase in binge eating
Sabine et al., 1983	Mianserin (60mg)	19	8 weeks	Binge eating and self-induced vomiting unchanged in both groups
	Placebo	17		
Walsh et al., 1984	Phenelzine (60mg)	12	8 weeks	76% reduction in binge eating
	Placebo	13		No Change

randomly assigned twenty-two subjects to imipramine or placebo for a six-week period. As indicated in Table 9.2, the imipramine group displayed a 70 percent reduction in binge eating over baseline while the placebo group displayed only a 2 percent reduction. Following the study, placebo subjects were also offered antidepressant medication, and seven of the ten patients had a favorable response. In a follow-up evaluation, approximately eight months later, eighteen of the twenty subjects (90 percent) showed at least some improvement in their bulimic symptoms with seven (35 percent) achieving remission. Additionally, significant differences were also observed on a variety of other measures of bulimic behavior, including preoccupation with food, intensity of binges, as well as decreased depression.

The benefits of antidepressant medication and the practical features of drug therapy for bulimia are illustrated in a follow-up evaluation. Pope and Hudson (1985) continued to treat eleven of the original patients for two years. As a group, they required several additional medication trials. Seven patients continued to show symptomatic improvements on medication, three were on no medication and in remission, and one patient had relapsed.

In a more recent study with imipramine, Agras and associates (Agras, Dorian, Kirkley, Arnow, & Bachman, 1987) randomly assigned twenty-two women to imipramine or placebo over a sixteen-week study period. Similar to Pope et al. (1983), Agras observed a 72 percent reduction in vomiting, yet in contrast to prior studies, they found a far greater placebo response of 35 percent. Also, as noted in Chapter 6, the interpretation of the antidepressant effect of imipramine in this study was not straightforward, as there was no significant difference in depression at sixteen weeks between the imipramine and placebo groups.

An investigation by J.E. Mitchell and Groat (1984) studied another antidepressant by randomly assigning thirty-two bulimics to amitriptyline or placebo with all patients also receiving behavior therapy. In contrast to previous studies, patients in this study kept weekly records of their eating behavior that allowed for quantification of eating and purging. Moreover, patients were separated into two groups on the basis of a measure of depression so that nondepressed and depressed patients were equally represented in the drug and placebo conditions. As indicated in Table 9.2, Mitchell and Groat reported 79 percent reduction in bulimic episodes per week in the drug group whereas those taking placebos displayed a 53 percent reduction. While the differences favored the drug group, they were not statistically significant. While the drug therapy led to a significant reduction in the level of depression, depressed patients displayed no greater improvement in bulimic symptoms than nondepressed patients.

In contrast to the studies with imipramine, Hughes and colleagues

(Hughes, Wells, Cunningham, & Ilstrup, 1986) studied the related active metabolite desipramine with very positive results. They randomly assigned twenty-two nondepressed bulimics to 200 mg of desipramine or placebo for a six-week period. At the termination of the study, the desipramine group was superior to the placebo group on all measures of bulimic behavior and depression. For example, those taking medication displayed a 91 percent decrease in their weekly binge frequency while those on the placebo displayed a corresponding 19 percent increase. All patients who had initially taken placebo subsequently crossed over to desipramine and experienced a decrease in binge frequency of approximately 84 percent. Unfortunately, these investigators provided no separate measure of purging, and so any differential effect on bingeing or purging can not be determined.

Sabine, Yonace, Farrington, Barratt, and Wakeling (1983) investigated mianserin, and antidepressant not available in the United States. Fifty bulimic patients were randomly assigned to 60 mg/day of mianserin or to a placebo for an eight-week period. Interestingly, all patients improved significantly on measures of anxiety, depression, eating, and bulimic behavior with no difference between the mianserin and placebo groups detectable. This study has been criticized for the 60 mg dose being too low when other research indicated that 150 mg/day is necessary for an antidepressant effect. Yet, in spite of the low dose, Sabine et al. did find significant reductions in both bulimic behavior and the associated symptoms of anxiety and depression.

Monoamine oxidase inhibitors, primarily phenelzine (Nardil), are antidepressants used in treating bulimia. The antidepressant and anxiolytic effects of monoamine oxidase inhibitors have been documented and appear to be as effective as tricyclic antidepressants. There are only a few studies evaluating these drugs in bulimia nervosa. Walsh, Stewart, Roose, Gladis, and Glassman (1984) randomly assigned twenty-five patients to placebo (thirteen) and phenelzine (twelve). Ten patients had to be dropped early because of either side effects or an early placebo response from both the placebo (two) and drug (eight). A total of twenty patients completed the study, yet only 15 percent of these remained for the full eight weeks. Based on twenty patients (nine-drug; eleven-placebo), the results indicated binge frequencies of 2.6 and 10.5 per week for the drug and placebo groups, respectively.

In a subsequent publication reviewing a larger number of patients, the effects of phenelzine appear impressive (Walsh, Gladis, Roose, Stewart & Glassman, 1987). In this particular report, sixty-two patients were randomized into active drug or placebo conditions. After eight weeks on medication, the results were strongly in favor of the phenelzine group who displayed a 64 percent decrease in binge frequency over the baseline period while all patients in the placebo group showed a mere 5 percent change. Also the active medication was equally effective for depressed and nondepressed patients.

In summarizing the available literature on the effectiveness of antidepressants, Pope and Hudson (1986) note that the tricyclic antidepressants and monoamine oxidase inhibitors have been shown to reduce bulimic symptoms in a number of controlled trials. However, problems with the use of medication include compliance, toleration of side effects, and for those on monoamine oxidase inhibitors, the ability to adhere to the tyramine-free diet. Also, these drugs are only indicated on a short-term basis as their efficacy has not been established over longer durations. We noted earlier that over a two-year period, eleven patients followed by Pope and Hudson (1985) required an average of 3.5 additional medication trials. Seven of these improved and were maintained on medication, three were in remission and off medication, and one discontinued the drug and relapsed.

Hudson and Pope (1987) reviewed preliminary information on new antidepressants, including trazodone, nomifensine, and mianserin. They note that in open trials, preliminary data suggests that trazodone is effective in bulimia nervosa but perhaps not as effective as the tricyclic antidepressants. Nomifensine may be effective, but it has been withdrawn because of its potential for producing anemia (P.B. Mitchell, 1988).

Other medications have been used because of their effects on serotonin. As noted in Chapter 6, serotonin is a neurotransmitter and its accumulation in the medial hypothalamus inhibits eating. Furthermore, serotonin, via its precursor tryptophan, is influenced by carbohydrate intake. Several drugs including tryptophan, fenfluramine, and fluoxetine act to increase brain serotonin and thereby decrease eating. The use of these drugs in bulimia nervosa is designed to decrease binge eating. As summarized by Goldbloom (1987), tryptophan has been shown to decrease caloric and carbohydrate intake, yet its influence on carbohydrate craving is variable. In addition, tryptophan has yet to show a differential effect over a placebo in bulimics.

Fenfluramine increases brain serotonin levels by enhancing its presynaptic release and blocking its reuptake. Both animal and human studies indicate that fenfluramine decreases eating and has been used effectively in the treatment of obesity (Craighead, Stunkard, & O'Brien, 1981). In a controlled acute trial, Robinson, Checkley, and Russell (1985) randomly assigned fifteen patients to a counterbalanced order of placebo or a single dose of fenfluramine (60 mg). Patients receiving the drug or placebo were tested one week later in the alternate condition. As indicated, fenfluramine was specifically chosen for its ability to decrease food intake and its utility in weight control, which appears to be mediated by its serotoninergic effects. Following an overnight fast, fenfluramine was given, and patients were allowed to eat two hours later. A noneating-disordered control group received only placebo. Fenfluramine in comparison to placebo significantly decreased caloric intake in the test meal, and there was a negative correlation between blood levels of the drug and caloric intake. The bulimic patients were less likely to induce vomiting after taking fenfluramine. The results of this investigation suggest a potential therapeutic role for fenfluramine in bulimia, yet further research is needed to establish its enduring ability to suppress binge eating and determine whether the reported side effects (drowsiness, headache, unsteadiness) are well-tolerated.

Fluoxetine is another drug that increases brain serotonin by blocking its reuptake. It has shown promise as an antidepressant in trials comparing it to amitriptyline and imipramine (Hudson & Pope, 1987). Preliminary reports indicate that it may also suppress binge eating in bulimics with the drug currently being studied in a multicenter, double-blind, placebo-controlled investigation with bulimic patients (Goodbloom, 1987).

The role of drugs that alter brain neurotransmitters in the treatment of bulimia is currently unclear. Part of the problem stems from the incomplete nature of our theories of the biological regulation of food intake. While studies substantiate that drugs can alter eating behavior, it is usually unclear why these effects occur. Leibowitz (1988), in a review of the literature on drugs and neurotransmitters in eating disorders, concludes that while drugs may play a role in the treatment of bulimia nervosa, psychotherapy and behavior modification must also be an integral part of treatment.

SUMMARY

Biological therapies for anorexia nervosa include nutritional support organized for weight restoration and medication for the associated symptoms. In the majority of cases, patients eat voluntarily and gain weight. Resistance with continuing weight gain should be expected as patients often have private weight levels that they adamantly refuse to exceed. Within the context of a comprehensive behavioral treatment program, this resistance, although trying, is nonetheless temporary. In our experience in clinical treatment of eating disorders spanning some fifteen years with approximately twenty-five restricting anorexics, hyperalimentation has never been used and the nasogastric tube was required briefly on only one occasion. During the weight restoration process, it is important to utilize energy balance training (Chapter 14) so as to avoid the development of bingeing and purging, which can be an untoward side effect of weight restoration.

When body weight falls 15 percent or more below ideal and body fat is in the 10 percent range, clinicians should include weight restoration as a priority in treatment planning. When such cases fail to respond to outpatient treatment and when patients present with very low body weights, weight restoration becomes the highest priority and hospitalization in a reputable eating disorders program is necessary. To be effective in the long-term, however, weight restoration must be included within a comprehensive treatment plan. As we noted, the use of medication in anorexia nervosa is dictated on the basis of associated symptoms, which consist primarily of anxiety and depression. There appears to be a consensus favoring antianxiety agents, such as benzodiazepines rather than neuroleptics. When depression is prominent in the clinical picture, antidepressants with lower cardiotoxicity are indicated. The choice of medication, its dosage, induction of treatment response, and monitoring of side effects require careful supervision given the perilous and dramatic nature of the patient's physical condition. A psychologically oriented physician or psychiatrist with experience in the clinical management of eating disorders should assume responsibility for the pharmacological treatment.

A variety of medications have been used to treat anorexia with none demonstrating an enduring effect on weight gain, or eating disorder symptoms. Most medications target the associated symptoms of anxiety and depression and are selected on the basis of individual clinical needs. The trend in anorexia has been toward the use of drugs, such as cyproheptadine that act specifically on neurotransmitters involved in the regulation of eating behavior.

The most important features of biological therapy for bulimia nervosa are the consideration of a medication trial, nutrition information counseling (Chapter 13), and energy balance training (Chapter 14). As with anorexia, the need for medication in bulimia must be approached on the basis of individual symptoms. However, the literature clearly indicates a more prominent role for medication in bulimia as compared to anorexia. Typically, with a longer duration of bulimia, the antecedents and consequences that trigger bingeing and purging expand to include a broad array of biological and psychosocial variables. When bulimia becomes severe, dysphoric moods can both contribute to bingeing and purging and interfere with interpersonal functioning. They may serve as an indication for psychotropic medication. Adequate nutritional intake within the context of training in energy balance is very important as a means to reduce carbohydrate cravings and the likelihood of bingeing.

Patients who display large mood variations or who are moderately to severely depressed should be evaluated for psychotropic medication. In most cases, patients will be placed on an antidepressant, yet it is not unusual for lithium to be indicated when mood swings or distinct periods of manic euphoria are part of the clinical picture. Since no antidepressant has been shown to be clinically superior, choice of which to prescribe is often based on a balance between clinical response and side effects. As we noted, many physicians now favor monoamine oxidase inhibitors over tricyclic antidepressants. However, the choice of which pharmacological agent to use should be determined by a physician/psychiatrist with experience in the clinical management of patients with eating disorders.

10

Psychoanalytic and Family Therapy Approaches

IN THIS CHAPTER, we will present an overview of two of the major psychotherapy approaches to the treatment of eating disorders: psychoanalytic psychotherapy and family systems therapy. Literally hundreds of different approaches to psychotherapy are currently being practiced. It is not possible for us to review all of the approaches that have been or are being used to treat anorexia and bulimia nervosa. Instead, we have selected some of the more common approaches. The objective of this presentation will be to familiarize the reader with these approaches, their theoretical assumptions, conceptualization of eating disorders, and specifics of the therapeutic process. Other psychologically oriented treatments will be covered in separate chapters.

UNDERSTANDING PSYCHOTHERAPIES

There are few fields with as much diversity of approaches and methods as the field of psychotherapy. With so many diverse approaches and methods all legitimately falling under the category of psychotherapy, a definition is somewhat elusive. Psychotherapy is defined as a professional relationship in which one individual, by virtue of his or her expertise and training in understanding human beings, attempts to help a client overcome problems in living (McFall, 1976). In all approaches to psychotherapy, the therapist uses a theory of human behavior, experience, or emotion to understand the client's problems, then selects one or more methods of therapy to resolve the client's difficulties.

Understanding psychotherapeutic approaches to eating disorders involves three steps: appreciating the theoretical framework of the therapeutic approach, recognizing the specific conceptualization of eating disorders, and describing the methods that are selected to treat eating disorders. By approaching the psychological treatment of eating disorders in this manner, the treatment of anorexia and bulimia nervosa is placed in the broader context of psychological interventions. Such a perspective allows an appreciation of how the various approaches to treatment of eating disorders differ and how these differences are based on variations in the theory used to conceptualize the causes of eating disorders.

THE PROBLEM OF EVALUATING TREATMENT OUTCOME

When making comparisons between different therapeutic approaches to eating disorders, it is tempting to ask which therapy is most effective. Unfortunately there is no simple answer to this question. This dilemma is in part due to the theoretical basis of psychotherapies and their different conceptualizations of eating disorders. The major source of difficulty in making comparisons of efficacy is the selection of appropriate treatment outcome measures. It might seem obvious that the treatment of anorexia nervosa should result in weight gain, and the successful treatment of bulimia nervosa should result in cessation of bingeing and purging. However, a number of therapeutic approaches view these as merely symptoms of underlying psychological, emotional, or interpersonal problems. From these perspectives, successful treatment is a matter of resolving the underlying problem, rather than merely eliminating one of its symptoms.

Psychotherapy outcome studies conducted by investigators with differing theoretical orientations are often not comparable because the measures they select to evaluate the effect of treatment are very different. Thus, by one set of standards a treatment may appear very effective while by the standards of another theoretical perspective, the problem may be virtually unchanged. Bemis (1985), for example, has suggested that the goal of treatment in bulimia need not necessarily be the complete cessation of bingeing and purging. M.G. Thompson and Gans (1985) discussed the problem of comparing outcome measures between different studies. For example, the outcome of the treatment of anorexia nervosa has been evaluated in terms of weight changes, return of menses, changes in eating behavior, global ratings of recovery, mortality, psychological adjustment, vocational functioning, and psychiatric symptomatology.

Only a handful of research studies compare different methods of therapy in the treatment of eating disorders (C. Freeman, Sinclair, Turnbull, & Annandale, 1985; Kirkley, Schneider, Agras, & Bachman, 1985; G.F.M. Russell, Szmukler, Dare, & Eisler, 1987). This dearth of outcome studies is testimonial to the ethical, logical, and methodological problems characteristic of psychotherapy outcome research in general and the severity of eating disorders in particular. Because eating disorders are a severe and sometimes life-threatening problem, it is ethically difficult to justify treatment studies that employ no treatment or placebo control groups. When control groups are used, they tend to be waiting list control groups (Wolchik, Weiss, & Katzman, 1986). Even studies that include control groups are often methodologically flawed. For example, Norman, Herzog, and Chauncey (1986) compared patients receiving psychotherapy to those refusing therapy or electing only to take medication. Differences in outcome may be as much due to the factors that influenced the patient's selection of a therapy as due to the effectiveness of drugs or psychotherapy.

Typically, the numbers of patients participating in treatment outcome studies is relatively small, making it impossible to draw definitive conclusions from the results. The majority of research evaluating the impact of psychotherapies on eating disorders are studies of a single treatment used with all patients (Hsu & Holder, 1986). Differences in patient populations due to geographic location and type of treatment facility make it very difficult to compare the results of one study to another.

Research reports tend to have varying lengths of follow-up making direct comparison of studies difficult. While it is the hope of all therapists that positive changes made during treatment become permanent, the fact of the matter is that there are many relapses in the treatment of eating disorders (J.E. Mitchell, Davis, & Goff, 1985; R.J. Freeman, Beach, Davis & Solyom, 1985). Thus the answer to the question of how well a particular treatment works will depend upon the length of the follow-up period employed in a particular study.

We will not attempt to make absolute comparisons of effectiveness between treatments. Instead, we will attempt to draw attention to the strengths and weaknesses of the various psychotherapies. Given the current level of knowledge, the relatively small number of controlled research studies, and the diversity of opinion regarding what constitutes an effective treatment outcome and how to measure it, there is no way to make direct comparisons between therapeutic approaches and to choose one as superior to the others. Herzog, Hamburg, and Brotman (1987) have argued that different approaches to the psychological treatment of bulimia may be targeting different aspects of the disorder. For example, behavior therapy attempts to modify bingeing and purging while psychodynamic therapy attempts to make changes in thoughts, feelings, and underlying personality patterns. While it will become clear in later chapters that we prefer a multicomponent cognitive-behavioral approach to treatment, we are nonetheless reluctant to claim that our approach is superior to all other approaches.

PSYCHOANALYTIC THERAPY FOR EATING DISORDERS

Basic Theory

Psychoanalysis is based on the work and writings of Freud. Freud's psychoanalytic theory is a comprehensive approach to understanding and explaining human behavior. The theory has been extended, refined, and elaborated by many psychoanalytic theorists during the last forty to fifty years. One of the major distinctions in psychoanalytic theory is between different levels of conscious experiences. Anything that we could be aware of but are not paying attention to at the time is considered preconscious. The revolutionary position of psychoanalytic theory was that much of our mental activity is unconscious. That is, there are mental events that have great influence over our behavior but are not accessible to our awareness. Much of the theory of psychoanalysis involves explaining how these unconscious thought processes guide and influence our behavior.

Freud postulated that motivation arises mainly from unconscious sexual and aggressive instincts. Much of our behavior represents ways to cope with and satisfy these unconscious needs. Psychoanalysis views personality organization as resulting from the dynamic interaction of three structural components, the id, ego, and superego. The id is the source of psychic energy and is the repository of the sexual and aggressive drives. The ego is the rational, thinking part of the personality that must cope with the world and adjust behavior to the demands of reality. The superego consists of the individual's internalized beliefs about what constitutes right and wrong behavior. The job of the ego is to mediate between the desire of the id for need gratification and the demands of the superego to behave properly.

Many of the wishes and desires of the id are unacceptable to the ego and superego and would create tremendous anxiety if they were to become conscious. The sexual desires of the id get expressed indirectly through displacement and symbolization. The ego uses various defense mechanisms to prevent unacceptable unconscious desires from reaching consciousness and causing anxiety. Freud believed that all behavior has meaning, and one of the basic positions of psychoanalytic theory is that the true meaning of a behavior can only be understood in relation to the unconscious sexual or aggressive instincts.

The psychoanalytic theory is very explicit in its account of the development of personality from infancy through adulthood. The theory states that the focus of sexual gratification changes from one erotic zone to another as the child develops. Early development progresses from oral gratification (sucking and chewing) to anal gratification (holding and eliminating feces) to genital gratification. When traumatic events occur during development, the child may fixate at an early stage of development and may thus be dominated during adulthood by oral or anal rather than genital motivations. The ego is also able to act in an independent and rational manner. In the mature individual, the bulk of interpersonal and vocational behavior is a matter of autonomous ego functioning. In the individual with psychological disorder, behavior is dominated by the defensive reaction of the ego to unconscious impulses.

Psychoanalysis would probably not have developed such pervasive influence as a theory of personality had it not been for the fact that it is also a systematic methodology for the treatment of many emotional and psychophysiological disorders. In psychoanalysis, the therapist and patient develop an interpersonal relationship through which the therapist attemps to understand the unconscious dynamics of the patient's personality. The process of psychoanalysis is one in which the therapist slowly helps the patient resolve unconscious conflicts. The focus of psychoanalysis is on feelings and interpretation of feelings. The goal of psychoanalysis is the achievement of insights in order to resolve unconscious conflicts, eliminate inappropriate defense mechanisms, and generally result in the evolution of a more mature, well-adjusted personality.

The strength of psychoanalysis is its ability to offer a way of understanding and explaining almost any aspect of human experience. Psychoanalysis has become a broad and influential intellectual movement, application of which has gone well beyond the treatment of emotional disorders. Psychoanalysis is more than a scientific theory; it is a comprehensive philosophical system that offers answers to many of the great questions of life. The ability of psychoanalysis to explain is, at the same time, one of its greatest weaknesses. As a scientific theory, psychoanalysis is rich with explanatory mechanisms so far removed from measurable events that it is very difficult to derive specific, testable predictions. In fact, psychoanalytic theory is modified and extended through the use of case material from psychoanalysis rather than through the use of planned and controlled experimentation. There is no question that psychoanalysis has and continues to be an influential approach to psychotherapy and that it is widely used by mental health professionals.

Conceptualization of Eating Disorders

While most psychoanalytic thinkers share a core set of ideas and beliefs derived from Freud's theory, there are a number of contemporary variations in psychoanalytic theory. Each is associated with a slightly different conceptualization of eating disorders. Some theorists emphasize ego processes, others focus more on the development of personality through the psychosexual stages, and still others are representations. Early psychoanalytic conceptualizations of anorexia nervosa viewed the disorder as arising from the ego's defensive reaction to unconscious fantasies of oral impregnation or cannibalism. The avoidance of food (and the subsequent starvation) is seen as a way of defending against the anxiety generated by these unacceptable unconscious fears and desires. This view was the dominant psychoanalytic perspective during the 1940s and 1950s (Bruch, 1985).

More recently, Goodsitt (1985) asserted that anorexia nervosa is best conceptualized as a failure to develop appropriately internalized self-regulatory systems. These patients are passive, dependent, and helpless. The fear of fat that is a core feature of anorexia nervosa is viewed as an expression of a more generalized fear of losing control and falling apart. Food is dangerous in that eating food may lead to a loss of control. Weight loss is viewed as a desperate attempt to exert self-control in a world that is controlling and manipulative. The anorexic symptoms are thus a way of dealing with the pervasive feelings of alienation and worthlessness that arise from a failure to master the developmental task of separation and individuation. This view is also espoused by Bruch (1985).

Casper (1987) has approached the understanding of anorexia from a psychoanalytic perspective. She views anorexia as arising from the failure of the adolescent child to properly separate from the parents. The symptoms of anorexia represent an outcome of this failure to individuate and usually arises as a result of some traumatic failure to meet psychosexual needs. Anorexia is viewed as a special form of paranoia in which the fears are projected onto the body instead of into the outside world. These fears center around fatness but really represent the child's failed attempt at individuation.

Lerner (1983) analyzed bulimia nervosa from a psychoanalytic perspective and presented a formulation based on Kohut's (1971) self-psychological viewpoint. His formulation is presented as an extended interpretation of a single case. A chaotic social history centering around a turbulent mother-daughter relationship resulted in a failure to develop a viable sense of self which in turn undermined the process of self-other differentiation. The bulimic patient is a dichotomy. The very compliant, well-dressed, thin appearance that the bulimic presents to the world as a result of her over-reliance on external structure and expectation is contrasted with the chaotic bingeing and purging, sexual promiscuity, and drug and alcohol abuse that are a consequence of the failure to develop an adequate self-structure. The failure to individuate results in arrested social, sexual, and cognitive development. Food becomes symbolic of the failed mother-daughter relationship and the voracious ingestion of food represents a desire to return to an early stage of complete symbiosis between mother and infant. The binge/purge cycle represents a recurring quest for maternal need gratification and the conflicts surrounding maternal rejection (Barth & Wurman, 1986).

The question of whether patients with eating disorders have failed to individuate and develop personal autonomy was addressed in an empirical study by Strauss and Ryan (1987). Three groups of subjects were identified and matched on age, sex, race, and education: nineteen restrictor anorexics, fourteen bulimic anorexics, and seventeen normal controls. Across several measures of autonomy and individuation, anorexic patients evidenced more difficulty than the normal controls in the development of personal autonomy. However, Teusch (1988) using a different set of measures found that failure to develop autonomy was not a problem for bulimic patients, but that the bulimia was more strongly related to interpersonal difficulties and need fulfillment.

Methods of Treatment

The focus of the psychoanalytic treatment of anorexia and bulimia is on treating the underlying personality disturbance that is causing the disordered cognitions and behaviors. In the psychoanalytic method, the therapist fosters the development of a transference relationship with the client. The woman who suffers from a failure to achieve individuation is encouraged to attach herself to the therapist who functions as an empathic self-object. A self-object is perceived as external to the self yet is experienced and reacted to as part of the self. This self-object phenomenon is the basis of internalization and differentiation of a self-structure. The therapist acts as a self-object providing structure and direction to the patient. The patient is directed in such a way that she is able to regulate tension and learn self-control as she progresses towards self-growth and enhanced self-organization. The patient is able to identify needs and feelings and develop ways of satisfying them. As the patient discovers her needs and feelings, the symptoms of anorexia and bulimia become unnecessary since they are essentially ways of dealing with the failure to develop a sense of self.

Modern psychoanalytic treatments for eating disorders are more active and directive than the classic psychoanalysis used to treat neurotic disorders. While insight into unconscious motivations and needs is still of primary importance, the therapist is more active in dealing with the symptomatic behaviors than was true in classic psychoanalysis.

FAMILY THERAPY FOR EATING DISORDERS

Basic Theory

Family therapy is a term used to describe a general orientation to understanding human behavior and a school of psychotherapy (Benjamin, 1983; Hoffman, 1981; Minuchin, 1974). Family therapy is also referred to as the family systems approach and relies on General Systems Theory (von Bertalanffy, 1968) for its metatheoretical orientation. General Systems Theory is an approach to the philosophy of science that challenges traditional linear models of causality as inadequate for explaining and understanding biological, psychological, and cultural phenomena.

The idea behind systems theory is that instead of simple cause and effect models, complex phenomena should be described as systems of interrelated components that function together as a whole. The notion that the whole is greater than the sum of its parts is an example of systems thinking. Instead of trying to show that X causes Y, the systems approach views X and Y as having reciprocal influence on each other. Concepts such as homeostasis and feedback replace simple ideas of cause and effect when describing the behavior of complex systems.

In the family systems approach, the family is seen as a system composed of individuals who interact together to form a matrix of interpersonal relationships. The behavior of each family member can only be understood as it influences and is influenced by the behavior of other members of the family. Families are not capricious or random systems. The family system consists of tasks, goals, roles, organized subsystems, and recurrent patterns of interaction and behavior. The family system is organized to make adjustments in order to maintain its integrity as a unit. It is an open system and can interact and exchange information freely with other systems outside the family. It is also a self-correcting system capable of responding to changes and disruptions in a manner that tends to maintain a dynamic equilibrium.

The family systems approach holds that the psychopathology is not an isolated problem of a single individual. Instead, psychopathology is seen as arising out of the beliefs, rules, communication patterns, and feelings of the family system. The family systems approach attempts to describe family patterns that give rise to the expression of psychopathology. For example, the pattern of enmeshment characterizes some families in which psychopathology arises. In the enmeshed family, there is little differentiation of subsystems as the family members are highly involved with each other. The involvement can develop to the point where individuals within the family find their separate identities threatened.

The family systems approach emphasizes understanding patterns of communication as they reveal the structure and dynamic aspects of the family system. Communication consists not only of the overt verbal messages, but also of nonverbal messages and implied or hidden agendas. Thus, all behavior within the family context is considered to have some communication value. For example, the act of saying nothing within the family context often communicates something. By studying patterns of communication, the family therapist is able to identify the structural and dynamic patterns of interaction responsible for deviant behavior.

In practice, family therapy involves treating the entire family as the client or patient instead of focusing only on the individual who is having problems. The therapist often sees the entire family together in order to observe patterns of interaction among family members, although family therapists do at times work with individual clients using the family systems model. The therapist classifies the types of family interaction patterns and employs active interventions that will result in positive changes in the entire system. Generally, the therapeutic goal is to encourage the development and elaboration of exisiting positive patterns while helping the family eliminate destructive patterns of relating.

The family therapist often has a number of techniques that can be used to change family systems. The types of interventions include development of insight, communication skills training, behavioral contracts, and the marshalling of social support resources from outside the family.

Conceptualization of Eating Disorders

The family systems approach considers anorexia and bulimia within the context of the family. The disordered eating behavior serves some function within the family and is maintained by the behavior and communication patterns of family members. Several family interaction patterns, including enmeshment, overprotectiveness, rigidity, lack of conflict resolution, and involvement of the child in conflicts between the parents have been suggested as contributing to anorexia nervosa (Hall 1987; Stierlin & Weber, 1987; Minuchin, Rosman, & Baker, 1978; Sargent, Liebman, & Silver, 1985). The response of family members to the excessive dieting of an adolescent girl can result in establishment of behavior patterns that ultimately function to maintain the anorexic behavior. While the ideal of dieting may originally emerge from outside the family system (as a function of the cultural context), one or more of these disturbed patterns of family communication must be present in order for dieting to turn into self-starvation. For example, the adolescent dieter may desire to be thin, but when she sees that the dieting serves to unite and maintain the integrity of the parents' marriage, the dieting behaviors become more firmly established.

Bulimia is approached by examining how bingeing, purging, and weight obsession affect the entire family system (R.C. Schwartz, Barrett, & Saba, 1985). In addition to enmeshment, overprotectiveness, rigidity, lack of conflict resolution, and involvement in parental conflict, Schwartz et al. (1985) have added isolation, consciousness about appearance, and the attachment of special meaning to food and eating. While the patterns of communication are similar from one bulimic family to the next, the issues around which these patterns revolve are often very different. For example, the strong need that some families have for keeping up with the Joneses is expressed in clothing, hairstyles, home, cars, and physical appearance. In other families, the enmeshment and emphasis on appearance revolves around the maintenance of family traditions or traditional roles rather than keeping up with the Joneses.

Root, Fallon, and Freidrich (1986) have identified a number of family system problems that contribute to the development and maintenance of bulimic behavior. They point out that one of the tasks facing every child is the development of an individual identity and the eventual separation from the family. In the highly enmeshed, overprotective family, the process of individuation and separation is made difficult by the lack of appropriate boundaries regulating respect for privacy, physical space, or emotional distance. In extreme cases personal space boundaries may be violated resulting in physical and sexual abuse. Root et al. also describe families in which boundaries are impermeable (little interaction and great emotional distance) resulting in isolation, withdrawal, and impulsive behavior. The family organization seen in bulimia varies from the extremes of rigid overorganization that stifles individual growth and development to a near lack of rules and organization that gives rise to a variety of pathological behaviors.

Expression and resolution of interpersonal feelings are another problem area for families with a bulimic member. Rather than directly confront and express feelings of anger, resentment, jealously, anxiety, hostility, or depression, the bulimic family deals indirectly with these feelings through either explosive/impulsive behavior, psychosomatic illness, or compulsive eating.

Root et al. have grouped bulimic families into three classes on the basis of typical interaction patterns:

1. The *perfect family* is characterized by a strong emphasis on appearance, family reputation, family identity, achievement, and success. Enmeshment, inability to express negative feelings, strong tendency toward achievement and perfectionism, and a power structure that encourages submissive and unassertive behavior are the rule. Bulimic patients from these types of families are often successful, attractive individuals who have hidden their eating disorder for years.

2. The *overprotective family* is characterized by extreme enmeshment (especially between mother and daughter), overprotectiveness, lack of conflict resolution skills, and lack of rules for age appropriate behavior. In this type of family, the children find it difficult to develop independence and an identity of their own. The parents stifle creativity, autonomy, and achievement. In these families negative feelings have a strong impact on all family members and tend to be avoided whenever possible. While positive feelings are expressed, their method of expression is often not age appropriate or may be expressed through food. The parents find it difficult to allow the children to grow up, become independent, and leave home.

3. The *chaotic family* is characterized by absent or inconsistent rules, physical or emotional absence of at least one of the parents, physical or sexual abuse, frequent emotional outbursts and expressions of anger, and substance abuse. The eating-disordered patient in this type of family is often depressed, withdrawn, and unable to form intimate relationships. Negative emotions are often expressed explosively but positive emotions are rarely expressed. Children are often forced to take on responsibilities for which they are unprepared because of the incompetence or emotional problems of parents. Rules in these families may change constantly and discipline is inconsistent and often harsh. Bulimics from this type of family may also engage in other substance abuse, be sexually promiscuous, or engage in impulsive or delinquent behavior.

The patterns identified by family systems therapists in families of anorexic and bulimic patients are not unique but are evident in other families as well. The claim of the family systems approach is not that certain structural patterns and communication problems uniquely lead to development of bulimia. Rather, the family systems approach claims that the behavioral manifestations of bulimia must be understood in relation to the interpersonal systems in which the bulimic patient operates. Often, interaction patterns within these systems make the bulimic behavior functional and contribute to maintenance of the problem behaviors.

Broad empirical support for the family systems analysis of eating disorders is lacking. Vandereycken (1987a) notes that the family systems approach to anorexia and bulimia is based mainly on personal belief and clinical experience rather than solid empirical research. He criticized family-oriented therapists for ignoring other biological and psychological causes of eating disorders and for their failure to test the efficacy of family treatment techniques.

There has been some recent progress in family therapy research on eating disorders. G.F.M. Russell et al. (1987) reported a controlled clinical study, which included eighty anorexic and bulimic patients, comparing family therapy to individual supportive therapy. The results suggested that family therapy was more effective with younger, less chronic patients. Pole, Waller, Stewart, and Parkin-Feigenbaum (1988) compared families of fifty-six bulimic patients to thirty normal controls and reported that the bulimic families were characterized as more controlling and less caring than the normal control families. Humphrey, Apple, and Kirschenbaum (1986) showed that family interaction patterns of bulimic and anorexic patients were significantly different from normal controls when measured using two different interpersonal behavior coding systems.

Methods of Treatment

The goal in family therapy with eating-disordered patients is to intervene with the entire family system in such a way that growth occurs and the symptomatic behaviors of the eating disorder are no longer reinforced. This model is most easily applied to the treatment of adolescents living at home (R.C. Schwartz et al., 1985). In treating the older patient, husband, children, friends, extended relatives or any one else who is an important part of the patient's current social system may be included in the therapeutic endeavor. Even if the patient is seen individually, the family approach suggests that the focus of treatment is on helping this patient change her attitudes, feelings, and behaviors in relationship to her family and other important people in her interpersonal system.

Within the family system approach, there are several different approaches to treatment, including insight-oriented, structural, and strategic schools of thought (see Vandereycken, 1987a). These groups differ in emphasis and in the use of particular techniques while sharing a basic belief in the importance of treating eating disorders within the context of family relationships and interactions. None of these schools has produced substantial treatment outcome literature documenting the efficacy of their methods. However, a recent controlled clinical trial by G.F. M. Russell et al. (1987) showed that, at least for younger patients, family therapy was superior to individual supportive therapy.

Todd (1985) presented a model of structural family therapy for anorexic and bulimic patients based on the work of Minuchin et al. (1978). Eight treatment principles based on the family systems model are identified:

1. *Identifying short- and long-term goals.* The first task is to intervene with any life-threatening behaviors. Both behavioral techniques and family intervention strategies are used to stabilize the patient's behavior to enable the long-term goals of altering family interaction patterns to be addressed.

2. *Forming the therapeutic system.* The therapist must develop a

working relationship with the client family. The therapist must win their trust and establish himself or herself as a teacher and a leader.

3. *Challenging realities.* The therapist uses direct and indirect communication methods to challenge the family's view of reality. In particular, the idea that the patient is sick and that the family is helpless to do anything about it must be dispelled. The family learns to view their relationships and behaviors differently and to start analyzing how the actions of one member affect the actions of all others.

4. *Challenging enmeshment.* When enmeshment is a problem, the therapist begins to dismantle it. Three strategies are used to accomplish the objective. First, rules and patterns are modified to allow each family member sufficient personal and emotional space. Second, exisiting subsystems within the family are strengthened. Third, hierarchical organizations within the family are strengthened. The goal of challenging enmeshment is to foster the development of greater independence and autonomy.

5. *Challenging overprotection.* The therapist intervenes to lessen the effect of overprotectiveness on the patient or on any other member of the family whose creativity or identity is being stifled.

6. *Challenging conflict avoidance.* In family therapy sessions, the therapist may elicit discussions that bring up areas of family conflict. Rather than allowing the family to engage in their usual strategies for avoiding conflict, the therapist forces family members to confront the conflict and attempt to find a resolution. The therapist actively intervenes by initiating conflict and teaching new communication strategies to the family to improve conflict resolution and eliminate avoidance strategies.

7. *Challenging rigidity.* Many families are rigid and resistant to change. The therapist induces conflicts, assigns tasks, and encourages changes in family rules in order to lessen rigidity and enhance the family change process.

8. *Challenging conflict detouring.* When the eating-disordered patient is involved in triangulation with the parents, the therapist must intervene and eliminate these patterns. The boundaries between parent and child are strengthened. The therapist may also have to intervene to strengthen and modify the communication patterns between husband and wife.

A comprehensive approach to family therapy with eating disorders was described by Hedblom, Hubbard, and Andersen (1981). The process of family therapy begins with a comprehensive family assessment. The assessment consists of sessions with the entire family in which the therapist examines: (1) interactional patterns, (2) role flexibility, (3) emotional sensitivity of individual family members, (4) family supports and stresses, (5) age appropriate behaviors, and (6) family knowledge and understanding of the eating disorder. Hedblom et al. based on experience with sixty-seven family therapy cases, reported that families of eating-disordered patients fit within two general categories, highly emotionally reactive (65 percent) and emotionally unresponsive (23 percent). In addition, 12 percent of the families were functioning very well and did not appear to be contributing directly to the eating disorder.

The Hedblom et al. family therapy program was part of an inpatient unit for the treatment of anorexia nervosa. In this setting, family therapy was considered one of several important treatment approaches used with patients. The goal of family therapy was to improve the communication and interaction patterns and to enhance family structure in the emotionally reactive and emotionally unresponsive families. A number of specific problem interaction patterns were identified as targets for family intervention:

1. *Compliance and perfectionism.* This pattern, which occurred in 75 percent of the patients, involved overly dependent, submissive behavior on the part of the eating-disordered patients. These patients evidenced perfectionistic efforts to please parents, unquestioning obedience to most parental demands, and fear of risking parental displeasure. Social skills, interpersonal communication, and ability to appropriately express feelings were often a problem for this type of patient.

2. *Rebellion.* Another 15 percent of the family interaction patterns characterized the child as rebellious and unconcerned about her impact on the family. These patients were much more emotionally expressive and often their behavior engendered hostile family conflicts.

3. *Dependency.* This family interaction pattern characterized a parental behavior pattern in which the parent was overly dependent upon the child for meeting his or her psychosocial needs. Often this dependency was a result of a poor marital relationship and occured in 25 percent of the families.

4. *Unsupportiveness.* In some families (18 percent), mental illness or alcohol abuse had so impaired one parent's ability to function that the parent was unable to offer any significant support to the patient.

5. *Overprotective.* In 8 percent of the families, the parental interaction style was classified as overprotective. These parents tried to control many aspects of the patient's life and attempted to insulate them from any risk or harm.

6. *Blaming.* The parents in 8 percent of the families blamed someone outside the family or one of the other family members for the patient's problems.

Hedblom et al. articulated a series of principles, which were expanded by Andersen (1985), describing how to work with families of eating-disordered patients:

1. Approach families in a nonblaming way.
2. Assume families have done their best.
3. Recognize that families are tired from stress.
4. Assume that families want help.
5. Suggest open and direct communication among family members.
6. Discuss the patient's progress in treatment.
7. Encourage the family to become knowledgeable concerning eating disorders.
8. Set specific treatment goals for family therapy interventions.

Many family therapists also employ individual therapy techniques in their treatment of eating-disordered patients. For example, behavioral techniques, such as self-monitoring, goal setting, and contingency contracting, are often used in conjunction with family intervention techniques (Root et al., 1986; R.C. Schwartz et al., 1985; Vandereycken, 1987a). Todd (1985) discussed the use of cognitive interventions in conjunction with family therapy. Others employ psychodynamic insight-oriented individual therapies in conjunction with the family systems interventions (Weltner, 1985). However, the hallmark of the family therapy approach to the treatment of anorexia and bulimia is treating the entire family as the client rather than just the eating-disordered patient.

SUMMARY

Psychoanalytic and family systems approaches to eating disorders both offer a comprehensive framework for conceptualizing and treating anorexia and bulimia nervosa that differs from the biopsychosocial conceptualization offered in Chapters 6 and 7. At present, there is not sufficient data to conclude that any particular framework is clearly superior. However, as we argued in Chapter 7, many variables influence the development and maintenance of the core features of eating disorders. The functional analysis framework of Chapter 7 showed how the recognition of family systems influence and emotional distress is neither a complete picture of eating disorders nor mutually exclusive with the recognition of other variables, such as cognitive distortions, environmental influences, and biological motivation and reinforcement systems.

Clinicians experienced in family therapy or psychodynamic interventions should not hesitate to use their expertise in treatment of eating-disordered patients. However, they should realize that their treatment approach may only be addressing a single component of the system. As we argued in Chapter 7, we share the assumption of the family systems approach that human behavior and psychological problems are complex and that their causality must be approached using the framework of General Systems Theory. We argued that whenever one intervenes with one component of a complex system, it is likely that synergistic effects will occur, resulting in changes in other components of the system.

However, we also recommend that clinicians trained in family or psychoanalytic therapy techniques develop an awareness of the other treatment approaches that are available to intervene with different aspects of eating disorders. The use of behavioral or cognitive/behavioral techniques, for example, is not necessarily incompatible with the use of the communication training methods of family therapy. It is conceivable that the therapist could decide to help a bulimia nervosa patient stop vomiting using exposure with response prevention (Chapter 12), develop appropriate eating and exercise patterns using energy balance training (Chapter 14), and intervene with the patient's overprotective family situation using family therapy techniques.

What is happening in the practice of therapy with eating disorders is, in fact, similar to the recommendation in the preceding paragraph. Psychoanalytic and family therapists are incorporating behavior techniques into their practices to treat aspects of the eating disorders, especially the behaviors of bingeing and vomiting or to induce weight gain in anorexic patients. However, short-term intervention designed merely to stop bingeing and vomiting is not a sufficient treatment for an eating disorder (see Johnson, Schlundt, & Jarrell, 1986) since patients will relapse unless other problems that contribute to the eating disorder are addressed.

In conclusion, our clinical recommendation is that experienced psychodynamic and family therapists should employ their techniques to treat the aspects of the patient's problems for which the techniques are best suited. These therapists should also become aware of other intervention modalities that are effective in treating different components of the eating disorder and incorporate these into their practices with anorexic and bulimic patients as they prove useful.

11

Cognitive Interventions

PURPOSE AND OBJECTIVE

Eating disorders involve not only a disturbance in food intake and energy balance, but also cognitive distortions that lead to anxiety and depression. These emotional and cognitive disturbances often exacerbate and maintain the disturbed patterns of behavior (see Chapter 7). Many of the treatment procedures discussed, such as exposure with response prevention, are intended to have a rapid and substantial impact on behaviors. However, for behavior changes to be maintained over the long run, it is necessary to change cognitions.

Cognitive interventions change the way patients think about themselves, their world, the people and events in their lives, and their bodies. The objective of cognitive therapy is to replace cognitions that exacerbate the eating disorder with thoughts that promote healthy eating and exercise habits and improved emotional and interpersonal adjustment.

RATIONALE

Cognitive therapy was developed during the 1960s and 1970s in response to several converging lines of development in psychology, including the success of behavior therapy, a growing dissatisfaction with psychodynamic approaches, and the introduction of cognition into social learning theory (see Kendall & Hollon, 1979). The initial models of cognition were relatively simplistic and held that irrational beliefs or negative self-talk were at the root of many emotional problems (Ellis, 1962; Meichenbaum, 1974). Cognitive therapy, based upon these early models, involved identifying the patient's maladaptive thoughts and changing them through rational arguments combined with behavioral techniques, such as homework and role playing. The cognitive-behavioral approach has become widely accepted due at least in part to the fact that it has generated a research base demonstrating treatment efficacy (Kendall & Hollon, 1979).

COGNITIVE THERAPY FOR EATING DISORDERS

There have been numerous applications of cognitive therapy techniques to the treatment of eating-disordered patients. Garner (1986a, 1986b) described a cognitive therapy approach to anorexia and bulimia that involves simultaneous treatment of the binge/purge cycle or restrictive dieting along with identification and modification of underlying beliefs. The approach toward symptom management involves the use of written educational materials, goal setting, and directive behavior change and resembles what we call energy balance training (see Chapter 14). Garner's cognitive component involves the identification and modification of beliefs about food, body shape, and body weight based on the assumption that fundamental attitude changes are required for successful long-term treatment.

Fairburn and Cooper (1987) discussed the role of cognitive and behavioral approaches to the treatment of anorexia nervosa and bulimia nervosa. According to these authors, cognitive techniques are especially useful in the treatment of the fear of obesity and cognitive distortions related to body size and shape. They argue that bingeing and purging develop as a result of powerful and irrational beliefs about body weight and that any effective treatment plan must ameliorate these extreme concerns about body shape.

C.L. Johnson and Connors (1987) describe an integrated inpatient and outpatient treatment program for bulimia that includes cognitive/behavioral treatment components. Cognitive/behavioral techniques are used to intervene with the binge/purge cycle at four points: (1) prevention through normalization of food intake and enhancement of general emotional adjustment, (2) cognitive strategies to cope with urges to binge, (3) cognitive and behavioral strategies to avoid vomiting after a binge, and (4) intervention to restore normal eating once a binge/purge relapse has occurred. Intervention involves a combination of readings, lectures, discussion groups, and individual therapy. The cognitive interventions target the patient's beliefs about the value of thinness, dieting, and interpretation of situations that include binge eating. Johnson and Connors reported substantial reductions (70 percent) in binge/purge frequency as a result of this integrated program. However, it is not possible to attribute these results specifically to the cognitive therapy component.

Lee and Rush (1986) compared a short-term cognitive-behavioral group therapy program for bulimia nervosa to a waiting list control group. The cognitive/behavioral therapy group received relaxation therapy, directive behavior-change assignments (e.g., eat three meals/day), and group discussions during which dysfunctional attitudes and cognitions concerning weight and eating behavior were challenged. Subjects in the cognitive-behavioral group showed significantly greater reductions in bingeing and purging and more improvement in depression than the control subjects.

Fairburn (1985) provides a detailed description of a structured cognitive-behavioral program for bulimia. The program focuses first on establishing control over bingeing and purging through nutrition education and energy balance training. Once some control has been established, the focus shifts to identifying, and challenging thoughts, beliefs, and perceptions that tend to perpetuate disordered eating behavior. Fairburn (1981) reported detailed outcome data for eleven patients and Fairburn (1985) stated that similar results were obtained for a sample of fifty patients, although no specific data were provided.

Agras (1987) described a multicomponent behavior therapy program for bulimia, which included cognitive interventions along with energy balance training and exposure with response prevention. A controlled study by Kirkley, Schneider, Agras, and Bachman (1985) showed that the cognitive/behavioral program was superior to a control group that self-monitored eating and met to discuss their problems but received no specific advice.

The commonality among these different cognitive therapy programs is the assumption that the individual's knowledge, beliefs, and interpretations play an important role in maintaining eating-disordered behavior. However, it is clear from this brief review of the literature on cognitive therapy for eating disorders that all programs go well beyond the modification of attitudes and beliefs and include components of energy balance training, nutrition education, and sometimes exposure with response prevention. The beneficial results reported in controlled and uncontrolled investigations may be due to components other than the cognitive intervention.

One of the problems in the eating disorder literature has been the lumping together of a multitude of techniques under the rubric of cognitive/behavioral therapy. While one could call any therapy approach in which the therapist gives advice and talks about the patient's thoughts cognitive/behavioral, we believe that a narrower definition of cognitive intervention is preferable. Cognitive interventions are those therapeutic procedures intended specifically to change behavior by modifying the patient's mental representation of the self or the world.

Another problem evident when reviewing this literature is that little thought has been given to the relationships among cognition, affect, and behavior as they pertain to eating disorders. While we discussed the role of cognitive antecedents and consequences in Chapter 7, we did not delve deeply into the relationship between cognition and behavior.

In the remainder of this chapter, we will attempt to rectify these two problems. First, we will present an information-processing model that relates cognition, affect, and behavior. This model has heuristic value for understanding the role of cognition in the development and maintenance of the core behaviors of anorexia and bulimia and has implications for treatment. We will then separate cognitive intervention techniques from other treatment procedures providing a detailed description of intervention strategies.

AN INFORMATION-PROCESSING MODEL OF COGNITION

Recently, personality and clinical psychologists have begun to borrow the concepts and methods of modern cognitive science and apply these to the understanding of how cognitive processes contribute to emotional and behavioral disorders (Carver & Scheier, 1988). McFall (1982) suggested that an information-processing perspective could be applied to the problem of understanding social skills and interpersonal competence. Errors and distortions in information processing lead to behaviors deemed by most observers as socially incompetent. Schlundt and McFall (1985) expanded on these arguments and suggested that much of what is referred to as social skill is based on strategies of interpretation and information processing that rely on stored knowledge about the meaning of events and stimuli in the environment.

To better understand cognitive interventions, it will be useful to sketch a model of how cognitive events influence behavior. The approach is an expansion of the model that Schlundt and McFall (1985) presented. Our emphasis in this presentation is on the variables in each stage of information processing that give rise to the core behaviors of anorexia and bulimia nervosa.

Figure 11.1 presents an outline of the model. First, note that all information-processing activities occur within an environmental and biological context. The context provides a set of cues that are encoded as physical energy and become available for information processing through various sensory channels. Within the individual, information processing is conceived of as moving through a series of stages that intervene between the input of sensory information and the output of behavioral responses.

FIGURE 11.1 An Information-Processing Model of Cognition

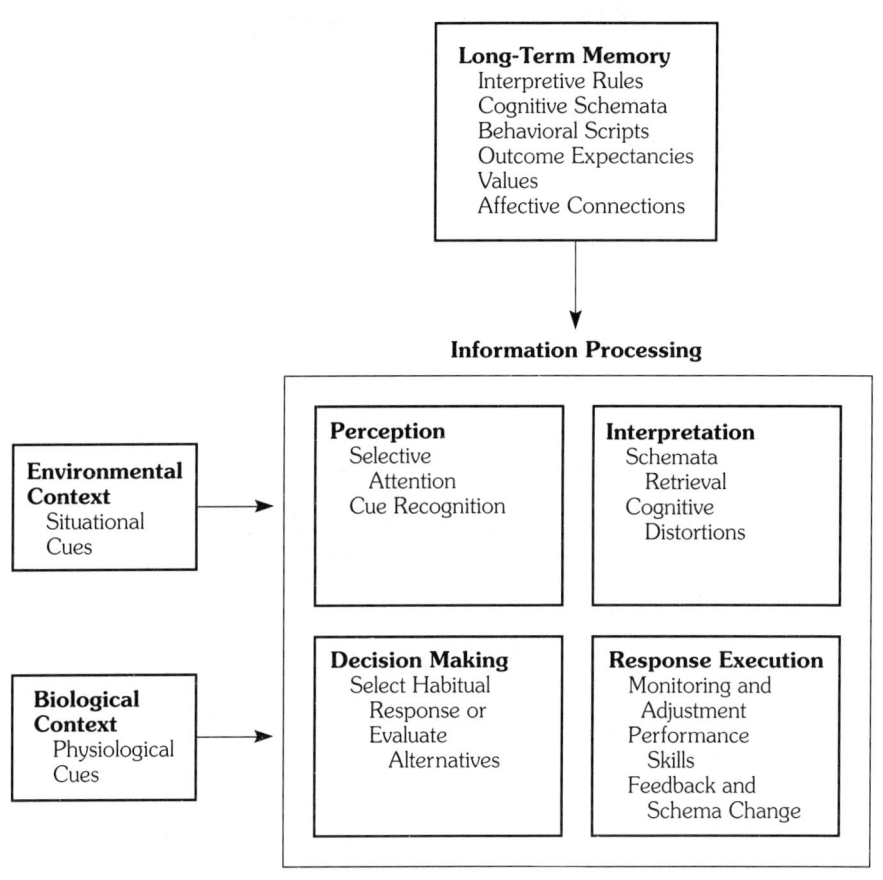

Long-Term Memory
Interpretive Rules
Cognitive Schemata
Behavioral Scripts
Outcome Expectancies
Values
Affective Connections

Information Processing

	Perception Selective Attention Cue Recognition	**Interpretation** Schemata Retrieval Cognitive Distortions
Environmental Context Situational Cues	→	
Biological Context Physiological Cues	→	
	Decision Making Select Habitual Response or Evaluate Alternatives	**Response Execution** Monitoring and Adjustment Performance Skills Feedback and Schema Change

Events within each stage are based upon the output of the previous stage, and the results are passed along to the next stage. Information processing relies heavily upon knowledge about the self and the world stored in long-term memory. The stages are perceptual processing, interpretation, decision making, response execution, and feedback.

Perceptual Processing

The first stage of processing involves attending to input from the various sensory channels and results in perception of environmental and biological cues. While defects in the sensory apparatus can give rise to maladaptive or incompetent behavior, selective attention and cue recognition are aspects of this stage that are most frequently observed and thus relevant to eating disorders.

The concept of *selective attention* involves the recognition that the capacity of the individual to process information is limited, making it impossible to perceive all of the potentially available information in the environment. The perceptual stage is organized to recognize and identify important cues and to ignore the remainder. Selective attention is guided by knowledge and experience stored in long-term memory that are used to make split-second decisions about what information to attend to and what to ignore. In addition, selective attention is affected by the salience of the cues impinging on the individual. For example, many people might not notice how tightly their clothes fit when confronted by other prepotent stimuli. However, when clothes become too tight, it becomes more difficult to ignore this sensory signal. An individual with an eating disorder, however, is more likely to attend selectively to clothing tightness and ignore other relevant stimuli. Consider two college students, one with anorexia or bulimia nervosa and the other without an eating disorder, taking an exam in class. The stress of taking the exam may be equivalent, but the stress level of the woman with the eating disorder will be compounded by her inability to ignore how her appearance compares to that of other women in the classroom, the sensory input from the tightness of her clothes, and her nutritional status. Since she is likely to have skipped a meal or purged if she ate, her ability to screen out stimuli related to her appearance and attend to the exam is severely hampered in comparison to the non-eating-disordered student.

Selective attention implies not only that people screen out irrelevant information, but also that they may miss important information while attending to nonessential features of a situation. For example, the eating-disordered patient may be attending to bodily sensations of carbohydrate craving and fail to see the stoplight turn red.

The second type of error that can occur in perceptual processing is the *misidentification of cues*. A variety of factors can contribute to the misunderstanding of environmental or biological cues. Information stored in long-term memory based on past experience may be incomplete or in error. In addition, the emotional state of the individual can influence reading of perceptual cues. Anger, anxiety, and other strong emotions influence the accessibility of information in long-term memory and may lead to misperception of cues. Misreading a cue can result in inappropriate behaviors. For example, an eating-disordered patient may misread her feelings of anxiety as a food craving and end up bingeing.

Often cue misreading occurs as a function of failing to discriminate between similar cues. The act of perceiving environmental and biological cues is not so much one of identifying isolated events. Instead, perception is a matter of pattern recognition. The meaning of the statement, "You look good today" depends upon who says it, when it was said, the previous statements made, and the nonverbal delivery of the remark. Through a combination of selective attention, failure to discriminate, and inability to take into consideration the context, the individual may misperceive the remark as a criticism of her weight.

Interpretation

Once cues in the biological and external environment have been perceived and identified, the next stage of processing involves integration of the cues into an overall interpretation of the situation. This stage of processing relies heavily upon information stored in long-term memory. Following the logic of Beck (1976), the concept of cognitive schemata is employed to conceptualize the organization of information in long-term memory and its retrieval and use in cognition.

Long-term memory is not random, but is instead hierarchically organized. The unit of organization can be referred to as cognitive schema. A schema is a bundle of rules consisting of beliefs, action scripts, expectations, and conditioned emotional responses that are linked together and are retrieved as a unit. The interpretive stage of information processing takes situational and biological cues and uses these to retrieve an appropriate schema creating an integrated interpretation of the situation that then implies the relevance of certain courses of action.

The interpretive stage of information processing is important in the analysis of modification of maladaptive behavior patterns. Most cognitive therapists have focused on how people link erroneous beliefs to specific situations and then engage in behaviors predicted on the misinterpretation. Several types of interpretive errors are commonly observed among eating-disordered patients and others experiencing emotional distress (see A. Freeman, 1987; Garner, 1986a, 1986b).

1. *All-or-none thinking.* All-or-none thinking is the tendency to see events and situations in black or white, either/or terms. Things are either very good (perfect) or very bad (terrible). In eating disorders, many bodily cues, eating behaviors, and environmental events related to food or weight are interpreted using this form of all-or-none thinking. For example, a bulimic patient may interpret her food intake as either dieting (good) or bingeing (bad) with no middle ground. It may be that all-or-none thinking involves the existence of two diametrically opposed cognitive schemata that are used on different occasions to interpret situational events.

2. *Catastrophic thinking.* In catastrophic thinking, the potential negative consequences in a situation are overexaggerated. Catastrophic thinking involves both an overestimation of the likelihood of negative consequences ("If I eat this doughnut, I will get fat") and the terribleness of the consequences ("Getting fat is the worst thing that could happen").

3. *Overgeneralization.* Past experiences are applied to the interpretation of situations in which they do not necessarily apply. An eating-disordered patient who gained a pound a day after eating a nutritious, well-balanced meal on a date may erroneously conclude that dates, regular meals, or both are too dangerous because they cause weight gain.

4. *Selective interpretation.* In many situations, there are a variety of ways of interpreting the pattern of environmental and physiological cues. Selective interpretation is a bias toward focusing exclusively on the dangers or risks involved in the situation and ignoring the potential positive outcomes. For example, the bulimic patient who is invited to a party may be able to focus only on the fact that forbidden foods will be available and fail to recognize the variety of fruits and vegetables as well as the potential of enjoying the company of others.

5. *Discounting.* Discounting involves ignoring or denying the reality of evidence of success and turning positive experiences to negative ones. For example, the bulimic who goes three days without bingeing might interpret this as due to luck and may believe that because she is such an unlucky person, she will soon binge.

6. *Arbitrary inference.* Often the conclusions that people draw from their perception of the situation are not warranted given the facts. For example, a bulimic may believe that because there is forbidden food available she will eventually binge.

7. *Minimization and magnification.* External events are seen as more important than they really are and one's own personal strengths as weak and unimportant. For example, an anorexic patient may look at another woman and see her body as slim and more beautiful while minimizing her own positive physical characteristics.

8. *Emotional Reasoning.* In emotional reasoning, a feeling is used to draw an inference about the situation. For example, feeling fat can lead to the conclusion that one has gained weight. Feeling afraid leads to the conclusion that there is danger.

9. *Absolutism.* This distortion involves rules that are viewed as absolutes. The use of words such as *should*, *ought*, and *must* are evidence of this kind of misinterpretation of the rules of conduct. For example, the individual might believe that in order to go out of the house, her hair, clothes, and makeup *must* be perfect. Another example involves the rule that one must *never* eat any forbidden foods. Many women with eating disorders spend countless hours preparing their makeup and selecting their clothes before venturing out. In fact, it is not unusual for them to become so engrossed in the process of trying to look perfect that they miss the event (e.g., call in late to work, miss class, or break a date).

10. *Mislabeling.* Mislabeling involves the use of emotionally laden words to describe situations. The words used then imply other interpretations and actions that create a maladaptive pattern of behavior. Instead of labeling one's hips as curvaceous, the person uses the word bulging, which evokes anxiety and misperception of other body parts. This leads to the decision to fast the entire day, which results in nighttime bingeing.

11. *Personalization.* Relatively innocuous events are assigned highly personal interpretations. An eating-disordered patient walking into a room and hearing people laughing, might conclude that they are laughing about how fat she looks today.

12. *Misattribution of causality.* Misattribution of causality often has profound implications for subsequent interpretations and actions. The most frequent type of misattribution is attributing one's successes to external factors and one's failure to internal weaknesses. For example, the bulimic patient who successfully resists the temptation to binge may misattribute the causality by concluding that the food really wasn't all that tempting. When she eats a forbidden food, she may interpret this as evidence of her weakness rather than the result of someone's deliberate efforts to feed her.

Schemata not only consist of rules of interpretation, they also contain information concerning affect. Affective state (e.g., depression, anxiety) may influence the retrieval of schemata during interpretive processing. For example, when a bulimic patient is experiencing fear of weight gain, the kinds of schemata retrieved to interpret biological cues (e.g., tight pants) or environmental cues (e.g., an eating situation) are most likely to be those linked to the fear of fat. In other situations (e.g., working out with weights), a very different schema might be retrieved because the affective tone differs. Likewise, stepping on the scale and observing a weight gain is capable of evoking anxiety and depression since these events, feelings, and beliefs are linked together in a consistent schema.

Decision Making

Once the individual develops an interpretation of a situation, the next phase of processing involves deciding how to behave. In this stage, the individual considers one or more response options that are usually linked to the current interpretive schema. Many schemata strongly imply habitual ways of responding. In these instances, the decision is mainly one of selecting the most easily available response, the one scripted by the schema that clearly prescribes that purging is the thing to do immediately after bingeing. The individual's behavior will appear automatic and unthinking. While it may not make sense to talk about a decision-making stage for automatic responses, a decision is made, nonetheless, since the possibility exists that the individual could override the habitual response and engage in exercise as an alternative behavioral sequence.

At other times, a clear habitual response does not exist and the individual engages in a more active process of decision making. In these instances, the individual retrieves information on several potential responses, examines the expected outcome of each response, and selects the one that is anticipated to yield the best result in terms of avoiding negative consequences and obtaining positive consequences.

People engage in maladaptive behaviors (i.e., make less than optimal response decisions) as a function of considering the wrong set of potential outcomes, placing unrealistic values on certain outcomes, or misjudging the likelihood of each outcome given a response. These three components of the behavioral decision-making process are useful in terms of suggesting ways that the therapist and patient can intervene in order to change behavior.

Response Execution

Once a response is selected, the individual translates the response strategy into a sequence of overt behaviors. This requires the use of performance skills along with monitoring and adjustment of behavior. Overt behavioral performances involve a combination of performance skills, such as motor movements, verbal articulation, coordination, and balance. As people gain experience with a behavioral performance, these skills improve and the performance of the behavior becomes quicker and smoother. Novel responses involve assembling these skills in new ways and are often slow and awkward in their appearance.

Nearly all response strategies involve an ongoing adjustment of behavior according to its impact on the environment. For example, when arguing with someone, the verbal statements made are adjusted based on the responses of the person on the other side of the debate. People differ in their ability to make these adjustments. Greater experience with a particular type of response in a specific situation leads to smoother, more effective adjustments as the automatic nature of habitual behavior begins to emerge.

Many patients make it to the execution stage and find that they are unable to translate their chosen strategy into a smooth, effective sequence of actions and words. The therapist must be aware that use of behaviors is limited by the patient's performance skills and ability to adjust the response based on its impact. Consequently, most approaches to cognitive therapy involve the use of practice and rehearsal designed to improve performance skills and increase the ease with which patients are able to translate cognitive/behavioral strategies into effective performances.

Feedback

The cognitive model of information processing and behavior is incomplete without mentioning feedback. Two types of feedback are worth noting. First, the behaviors selected and their outcomes feed back onto the cognitive schemata that were employed in interpreting the situation and selecting the behaviors. The emotions associated with a schema, the rules of interpretation, and the behavior-outcome expectancies can be altered by feedback from successful or unsuccessful performances. This feedback relationship opens the possibility of changing cognition by inducing behavior change rather than through argument and discussion. Feedback is mediated by the interpretive rules that are part of the schema, and thus may turn out to be false feedback. For example, if the person is expected to fail, then almost any outcome is interpreted as failure and is used to reinforce the negative affect and pessimism associated with that particular schema.

The second aspect of feedback is the relationship between behavior and the environment over time. Behavior is a cyclical process in which the outcome of the previous action becomes the input to the information-processing system and provides the basis for choosing the next act. As behavior changes the external or biological environment, it creates new cues that may invoke different schema, thus causing a shift in the cognitive basis of behavior. For example, when a behavior is met with a critical remark from another person, this criticism might invoke a very different schema that will exert a profound influence on subsequent behavior.

Thus, the cognitive model as presented here views the individual as an information-processing/acting system that uses information stored in long-term memory in bundles called schemata to adjust to changing circumstances in the internal and external environment over time. Errors can occur during each step of information processing, resulting in maladaptive behavior and strong negative emotions. In addition, selections of adaptive behaviors for which the individual lacks the requisite performance skills also leads to negative outcomes. The process of feedback may teach the individual to avoid use of these strategies in the future and thus force reliance on ineffective ways of coping. The information-processing system is organized to develop efficient, habitual processing and responding. This is accomplished through hierarchal organization of long-term memory around schemata and through the development of automaticity in information processing (see Shiffrin & Schneider, 1977).

Cognitive therapy is designed to alter behavior by having an impact on the way the individual processes information about the self and the environment while at the same time providing the training and experience necessary to implement new coping strategies. Repetition and practice are necessary in order to overcome the bias toward using automatic processing.

PROCEDURES

The process of cognitive therapy involves a cooperative relationship between the client and therapist. The therapist plays the role of educator and facilitator, and attempts to guide the client into changing the way he or she thinks and behaves in everyday situations. The therapist engages in assessment, diagnosis, and intervention and in doing so, structures learning experiences designed to change the patient's use of erroneous perceptions and misinterpretations and their impact on decisions.

Cognitive therapy employs several distinct procedures, each of which will be presented separately.

Teaching the System

In the first stage of cognitive therapy, the therapist's role is one of educator. The patient is taught how emotions and behaviors are influenced by thoughts and is provided with an introduction to the types of misperceptions and misinterpretations that create emotional and behavioral problems. The role of the therapist as a teacher and helper is explained. Often, the client is taught to view his or her role as that of a personal scientist who is embarking upon an empirical study of the self. The value of data, verification, and the use of personal experiments to test hypotheses about the self and the world are reviewed in detail. Above all, the rationale for cognitive therapy should clearly indicate that the client is an active participant in the process. Cognitive therapy is not an intervention that is applied to a patient. Rather, it is an active process that requires the full participation of the patient.

Assessment of Schemata and Cognitions

The patient and therapist must work at identifying the cognitive schemata that are leading to core symptoms of the eating disorder. The patient identifies problem situations related to pursuit of thinness, fear of obesity, restrictive dieting, and bingeing and purging. Next, the therapist works with the patient to help discover the different schemata that may be operating in these situations, and the kinds of interpretive rules and behavioral scripts that are part of these schemata. During this phase, the therapist helps the patient appreciate the concrete connection between perceptions, interpretations, behaviors, and emotions.

A number of strategies can be used to obtain this assessment information. Patients can be asked to keep a diary in which they record daily situations related to the eating disorder. The therapist and patient use this diary as a basis for discussing the way the patient misinterprets events. The therapist can also ask the patient to engage in role-playing exercises that simulate problem situations. During these role plays, the therapist stops the action and discusses with the patient the way he or she is thinking and feeling about the situation.

In treating bulimia, for example, the patient could be instructed to keep a diary of situations that involve the fear of gaining weight. This list of situations is examined for commonalities, and the therapist and patient develop hypotheses concerning which misperceptions or interpretations trigger the fear of fat. The patient and therapist then begin to explore how the fear of fat schemata are used to interpret these situations and decide how to respond behaviorally. The therapist uses his or her knowledge of the kinds of cognitive distortions that commonly occur and helps the patient identify them. The therapist and the patient begin to develop a list of cognitive distortions based on the patient's monitoring and the discussion that occurs during the session. As this list grows, the patterns become apparent, and the therapist may be able to identify underlying themes that unify many of the specific distortions. For example, many of the distortions may follow from the core belief that "I must be perfect in everything I do, otherwise I am a failure," the belief that "Being thin is the most important thing in the whole world," or "Losing weight will solve all my problems." Identification of these core beliefs allows cognitive therapy to progress more quickly.

Countering

Once a list of distorted perceptions and cognitions is developed, the process of countering these thoughts and beliefs begins. In countering, the patient is taught to recognize the error in thinking, and substitute more appropriate perceptions and interpretations. McMullin (1986) has compiled a comprehensive list of thought-countering strategies. Some of the most useful therapeutic strategies for countering distorted thinking are discussed in the following sections.

Alternative Interpretation

The patient learns to stop and consider other interpretations of a situation before proceeding to the decision-making stage. The patient develops a list of problem situations, evoked emotions, and interpretive beliefs. For each situation, the patient is challenged to generate at least four alternative explanations or interpretations. Once the additional interpretations have been generated, the client and therapist engage in a discussion concerning the degree to which each interpretation is logical, realistic, and supported by the data. The therapist encourages the patient to gather additional information in order to decide which interpretation is most realistic.

For example, a bulimic patient steps on the scale and sees that her weight is gone up a pound from the previous day. Her initial intepretation is that she is getting fat. She is then challenged to find four other possible explanations. She comes up with: (1) the scale is out of adjustment, (2) I am retaining water, (3) many things influence body weight and a one-pound fluctuation is not sufficient evidence to conclude that I am gaining weight, and (4) weight naturally fluctuates from day to day so that half the time it will be down one pound and half the time up a pound. The therapist and patient discuss each interpretation and if possible identify the kind of objective data that would confirm one of them as correct. If the relevant information is not available, the patient is encouraged to accept none of the interpretations and, instead, suspend judgment until persuasive data can be obtained.

Anticatastrophic Counters

As noted above, catastrophic thinking is a common cognitive distortion. Development of counters to catastrophic thinking first involves generating a list of situations in which the patient catastrophizes. The feared outcomes for each situation are then listed and the patient also lists other possible outcomes. The therapist and patient then discuss the likelihood of each outcome and their positive or negative impacts.

For example, a bulimic patient may anticipate catastrophic consequences occurring as a result of accepting a dinner date. She may anticipate losing control, overeating, and gaining weight. She is afraid that her date will notice, and think that she eats like a pig and is as big as a house. The patient is encouraged to consider how she can have a good time on the date, that her date might actually find her interesting, likeable, and attractive, and that she might not have a problem regulating her food intake. In considering past dates, she realizes the catastrophic nature of her expectations. She is encouraged to continue dating and challenge the validity of the catastrophic interpretations.

Coping Statements

People may avoid situations when they believe that the situations will be stressful or overwhelming. To counter these thoughts, the patient and therapist develop a set of coping statements that the patient uses to deal with these feared situations. A list of fearful situations is developed with the patient's active involvement. For each situation, the therapist and client write a script or dialogue of thoughts the patient can use to anticipate any problems and provide instructions for coping effectively with these problems. The dialogue should cover perception, interpretation, decision making, and enactment in the problem situation. The patient then rehearses the script out loud with the therapist. The therapist can also model the dialogue and have the patient begin by repeating it back. The patient is instructed to practice the dialogue outside the therapy context. This may involve reading a written text of the dialogue or listening to an audiotape. Another mode of rehearsal is to write various dialogues for coping with different problem situations on note cards and instruct the patient to read through the cards several times each day. For example, an eating-disordered patient may be afraid of bingeing when feeling alone and depressed at home in the evening. The therapist and patient work out a dialogue such as the following:

> I can tell that it is happening again. Here I am home by myself and starting to feel lonely and blue. In the past, I have coped with these feelings by eating. I seem to think that eating solves all of my problems. It never has and never will. What really happens when I binge is that I end up feeling guilty and really depressed. I really don't like the way I feel after bingeing, both emotionally and physically. What I need to do is first realize that being at home by myself tonight is not all that bad. I have friends, and I have family, and we enjoy each other when we are together. If I would have planned better, I could be socializing tonight. I am alone by choice, and I need to learn to live with my choices and make the best of them. Instead of feeling sorry for myself, I can find a project to work on at home this evening. If I still feel bad and working on a project doesn't help, I can always call Nancy or Ruth on the phone. Spending time by myself doesn't have to be bad, it's how I spend the time that is important. Learning to be more independent is important, and when I make it through this evening, I will feel better about myself. There really isn't anything to be upset about right now. I feel better already.

Counterattacking
Many negative thoughts are strongly linked to disruptive emotions such as fear, anxiety, guilt, and depression. Counterattacking involves defeating emotionally laden thoughts by attacking them with other thoughts that are associated with strong emotion. As with the other strategies, the therapist and patient list problem situations and disruptive thoughts and beliefs. Instead of merely developing rational counterthoughts, the patient learns to apply these counterthoughts aggressively and energetically. The more energetically the patient delivers the counterargument, the better. The energy level can be raised by having the client become physically aroused through standing up, tensing muscles, and speaking in a loud

forceful voice. In essence, the client is instructed to get angry at the unreasonable thought and to shout it down. For example, a patient might get upset and depressed whenever she walks into a room in which other attractive young women are present. She thinks that they are much prettier, thinner, and attractive than herself and starts to anticipate leading a lonely and rejected life. She then develops several counters to this thought. The therapist begins by modeling the counter, "I am a good-looking woman too. I take care of myself and have nothing to be ashamed of. Many men have found me attractive. There is nothing to feel bad about just because other women take care of themselves and try to look good, too. Getting upset about this is useless." The patient starts to imitate it first in a soft voice. Once she has learned the counterthought, she begins to repeat it in a louder and more forceful voice. The therapist encourages her to jump up out of her chair, get mad at the irrational thought, and deliver the counterthought as though it were a missile shooting down an enemy aircraft.

Label Shifting
Many times, the entire interpretation of a situation goes astray because the individual chooses to interpret the situation using an emotionally charged label, such as horrible, bad, or ugly. The patient first tries to identify the kinds of negative words she uses to interpret situations in her life, such as bad, terrible, obese, inferior, and hateful. The situations in which these labels are used are then listed. The patient and therapist replace each emotional label with two or more descriptive words. If any accurate labels have positive emotions attached, then the client is encouraged to begin to use these words instead of the negative ones. For example, a patient might get upset whenever her boyfriend comments about her clothing or hair. She considers his remarks critical and ends up hating herself for being such an ugly slob. She is encouraged to view her boyfriend as interested and concerned and react to his comments by being reflective concerning her appearance and to feel fortunate and cared for. She is instructed to write a description of each situation in which she used negative words on a note card, then list all the positive substitutes on the card. She agrees to read over the cards each morning and each evening until the new words start to come to mind automatically when the problem situations arise.

Deactivating the Illness Belief
Many patients, in part due to the well-intentioned advice of health care professionals, come to view their eating disorder as an illness. This kind of thinking encourages the patient to see herself as a victim suffering from an awful, terrible disease over which she has no control. The therapist first helps the client list her beliefs concerning anorexia or bulimia. The extent to which the illness model influences each belief is identified. The

therapist then teaches the client a cognitive/behavioral approach to interpreting maladaptive behavior and shows how bingeing, purging, and dieting can be understood from this framework. Assigning readings and other homework can facilitate the learning of an alternative framework for interpreting and understanding these behavioral problems. The patient learns to counter her use of the illness model with this alternative interpretation. For example, a patient with bulimia might have periods during which she gains control over the bingeing and purging. During these times, she insists on calling herself a recovered bulimic, a term she learned from reading an article in a popular magazine. During times of stress, she occasionally overeats. She interprets these episodes of overeating as a recurrence or flair up of her illness and tells herself there was nothing she can do about it since she is a victim of a terrible disease. The therapist teaches her to reconceptualize her response to stressful situations from a social learning framework. She is encouraged to view slips as evidence that she had been through a high-risk situation, and is told to seek for coping responses that will help her deal more effectively with the source of stress in her life. When episodes of overeating occur, she agrees to discuss them with the therapist at the next session and together they plan to analyze the behavior and develop strategies for coping more effectively the next time.

Preventing Irrational Thoughts

The problem with many countering strategies is that the patient must wait until irrational beliefs occur, then attempt to deliver counter arguments. Since irrational beliefs are often linked to strong emotions, this strategy forces the patient to endure negative emotions while struggling with countering the beliefs that lead to the emotion. A list of situations associated with strong negative emotions is constructed. The patient and therapist then develop a set of realistic rules for interpreting each situation. The beliefs should be based in fact and empirical observation as much as possible and should avoid either extremes of positive or negative emotion. The cues or events that trigger each problem situation are written on one side of a note card. On the other side of the card, the patient writes the rational and empirical interpretation of the situation. The patient uses the note cards like flash cards, practicing them several times a day for several weeks until the rational interpretations easily come to mind whenever the triggering event is considered. The patient is also encouraged to visualize the situation and to imagine responding to the situation using the new interpretations. For example, a patient had considerable difficulty forming satisfactory relationships with men because she engaged in a great deal of irrational and catastrophic thinking whenever men attempted to form a close relationship. She was encouraged to list a series of situations that were involved in the initial stages of relationship formation. The situations described the man and the way he was behaving. With the therapist's help, a realistic way of interpreting the man's behavior in each situation was developed. Each vignette was written on a note card, and the interpretation written on the other side. The patient agreed to practice the cards three times a day, while getting ready for work in the morning, during her lunch break, and just before getting into bed at night. After several weeks of practicing, she accepted a date. While she had some difficulty with irrational thinking on this date, after several more weeks of practice and discussion with the therapist, she was able to establish a friendship with this man and began to see him regularly.

Utilitarian Counters
Not all thoughts that create problems can be proven irrational or false. However, there are still more constructive ways to cope with these situations. One strategy for modifying maladaptive behaviors and cognitions is to develop counterarguments that attack the utility of a particular way of interpreting a situation and to substitute a more useful interpretation. The technique begins with a list of troublesome thoughts and the situations in which the thoughts occur. The therapist helps the patient focus on the goal or desired outcome in the situation. For each thought, the patient is asked to evaluate whether the thought contributes to reaching the goal. If not, then a more goal-directed way of thinking is identified. The patient is encouraged to practice evaluating the utility of her thinking and to begin substituting goal-directed thoughts for emotion-provoking thoughts. Whenever she had to talk to her boss, one patient found herself thinking that he was evaluating her performance. She feared a poor evaluation and being stuck in her current position in the company. The therapist helped her focus on the goal, making a favorable impression on her boss, then helped her see how her fears were not helping her achieve that goal. Instead, the patient began to focus on her boss, asking herself what kind of performance he was looking for, and encouraged herself to do her best to impress her boss favorably while still maintaining her dignity and integrity. Together, she and her therapist decided that interactions with her boss were also opportunities to make a good impression and should be sought out rather than avoided. While her fears associated with talking to her boss did not immediately subside, she gradually learned to replace them with more useful ways of interpreting the situation.

Objective Counters
Recognizing that all patients do not respond equally well to all counters, the use of objective countering can be productive in some patients. In objective countering, the problematic thoughts and beliefs are subject to a reasoned, objective, dispassionate analysis. This approach is good for dealing with core irrational beliefs, those that are common themes across many

different situations. The core beliefs are identified, broken down into their logical components, and then critically analyzed. The patient is encouraged to evaluate the logic of each belief, and to write down all the reasons that can be identified for the irrationality of any given belief. For example, an anorexic patient was afraid that eating any bread product would result immediately in becoming fat. She was sent to the library to check out books on nutrition and to read up on the bread food group and the way the body metabolizes carbohydrates. She looked critically at the assumptions underlying her fear and discovered that they were without any foundation in fact. She wrote a short report on the importance of grains in good nutrition and was able to use this knowledge to begin to include grain products in her diet.

In addition to the strategies for countering maladaptive and erroneous interpretations and beliefs, several other techniques can be quite useful in cognitive therapy with eating-disordered patients. Most of the cognitive techniques will only work if they are practiced outside of the therapy session. Several methods are available to encourage practicing. We have already mentioned use of note cards that are read repeatedly during the day as a method for practicing new ways of thinking and interpreting situations. Other techniques for practicing, such as imagery, role playing, and homework are also possible.

Imagery

The effectiveness of cognitive interventions can be enhanced through the use of imagery. Imagery involves creating scenes in which the patient sits quietly and imagines. Imagery can be enhanced though the use of audiotaped instructions. McMullin (1986) lists a number of different imagery techniques that have proven clinically useful:

1. *Coping images.* These are scenes in which the patient imagines himself or herself coping effectively with a difficult situation.
2. *Relaxation imagery.* These are scenes that are intended to induce peaceful and relaxed feelings. The scenes may be paired with training in deep muscle relaxation or meditation techniques. They are intended to counter negative emotions and return the patient to a neutral or positive affective state.
3. *Mastery images.* These involve scenes in which the patient visualizes completing a task perfectly. Mastery images can be used to overcome irrational fears of failure and as a way to learn new behaviors.
4. *Model images.* The patient tries to imagine how a model would handle a situation or perform competently. For example, the

patient might imagine how the therapist would think and behave in a certain situation then use the image as a model for her own thoughts and behaviors.
5. *Idealized images.* Idealized images are used to help patients focus on the desired long-term outcomes of their efforts. For example, an obese patient can practice imagining herself at her goal weight and use this image as an incentive to help resist temptations to binge.

Role Playing

Role playing is a very useful way to practice in cognitive therapy. The therapist takes the role of some important person in the patient's life and begins acting as if he or she were that person. The patient then practices employing new thoughts and behaviors in response to the role play. The advantage of role playing is that the patient can try new ways of thinking and behaving in a safe environment. In addition, the therapist is able to give immediate corrective feedback after a role-played interaction. At times, additional misperceptions and misinterpretations will become evident during role playing.

Homework

Once a patient has started to master the strategies for modifying irrational beliefs and maladaptive behaviors in the clinic, the next logical step is to begin practicing these new responses in everyday life. Homework assignments are one of the best ways to provide practice for patients in more realistic real-world settings. This practice is important so that new thoughts and behaviors can become incorporated into coherent schemata and so that they begin to occur at the automatic level of processing. For example, a patient who is afraid to exercise because she thinks she will look fat and grotesque in exercise clothes would first work with countering her irrational thoughts and beliefs in the clinic with the therapist. Once she was able to visualize herself wearing exercise clothing in public and feeling comfortable doing so, she would be given a homework assignment to put on exercise clothes and go out into public. The length of her initial exposure might be time-limited, but the subsequent homework assignment would increase the amount of time she spent in public in exercise garb.

SUMMARY

In this chapter, we have briefly discussed the relationship between cognition, affect, and behavior in eating disorders. Many of the core symptoms of anorexia and bulimia stem from misperceptions and misinterpretations of everyday situations. In addition, certain core beliefs act to further maintain disordered eating behavior. Cognitive therapy involves helping patients correct these misperceptions and misinterpretations thus allowing therapeutic changes in emotion and behavior. Cognitive interventions can be used alone or in conjunction with other techniques, such as exposure with response prevention or energy balance training. Cognitive therapy, however, is a lengthy, time-consuming process involving assessment, teaching, thought challenging, and repeated rehearsal of new ways of responding to a variety of everyday situations. It is unlikely that brief lectures or occasional group discussions will result in the kinds of cognitive changes that lead to long-term abandonment of the core behaviors of anorexia and bulimia.

12

Behavioral Treatment of Bingeing and Purging

IN THIS CHAPTER, two specific behavioral treatment protocols based on exposure with response prevention will be described. One is a treatment designed to rapidly reduce and eliminate self-induced vomiting. The other is a treatment approach to the cessation of binge eating that may be useful for patients who have not responded to other treatment approaches.

EXPOSURE WITH RESPONSE PREVENTION (ERP)

Purpose and Objective

Self-induced vomiting is one of the most common and most serious behavioral manifestations of bulimia. An important goal of therapy with almost any bulimic patient is to reduce or hopefully eliminate self-induced vomiting. The objective of exposure with response prevention is to rapidly decrease, then eliminate vomiting behavior.

Rationale

Rosen and Leitenberg (1982) originally proposed exposure with response prevention as a treatment for bulimia. The patient is conceptualized as having a strong fear or phobia related to gaining weight. This fear is elicited by eating. Forbidden foods, feelings of fullness, eating at the wrong time or place, and many other cues are strongly associated with increased anxiety over weight gain. At some point in the past, the patient learned that self-induced vomiting would eliminate the food, the feelings of fullness, and the fear of gaining weight. The behavior of vomiting resulted in the consequence of fear reduction. This kind of relation between behavior and consequence is referred to as negative reinforcement (the behavior removes a negative condition and is thus rewarded). When negatively reinforced behaviors become escape responses (they prevent something bad from happening), they are very difficult to change. The individual can continue to believe that the vomiting is preventing weight gain from occurring and is never exposed to any information to the contrary as long as the vomiting continues.

The use of vomiting as a way to manage the anxiety concerning weight gain is quickly established. As the disorder progresses, the individual learns to escape anxiety over weight gain altogether. This kind of progression in learning is not at all uncommon when a negatively reinforced behavior is involved. That is, the bulimic woman learns that if she simply plans to throw up after eating, she can stuff herself and never have to experience the fear of getting fat. The vomiting becomes a successful avoidance response. Rosen and Leitenberg conceptualize self-induced vomiting as an obsessive-compulsive ritual, much like checking or handwashing. The vomiting becomes a ritualized way to ward off anxieties concerning body shape and weight.

Exposure with response prevention has been used successfully in the treatment of obsessive-compulsive disorders and has been conceptualized as an extinction procedure. The idea of exposure with response prevention is to place the patient in a situation which contains all of the cues that elicit the anxiety. The compulsive behavior is prevented from occurring and the individual is allowed to experience the fact that the feared outcome never occurs. For vomiting, the person is exposed to food, eating behavior, forbidden foods, and feelings of fullness and bloatedness that come from eating. The therapist is present during the food consumption and remains with the patient to prevent her from throwing up, allowing her to experience that the expected weight gain does not occur.

Alternatively, exposure with response prevention can be seen as having a skill acquisition or behavioral training component. The person has learned to cope inappropriately with food and with sensations of fullness. By exposing the person to these cues and preventing vomiting from occurring, the therapist is in a position to teach new cognitive and behavioral responses for coping with the feelings and fears. Most likely, both views are partially correct. Exposure with response prevention results in some reduction in fear and anxiety and thus operates as an extinction procedure. In addition, the patient learns new cognitive and behavioral strategies to cope with her fears and to make it through the day without throwing up.

One other set of principles is involved in our approach to implementing exposure with response prevention. We think that the environment in which the patient lives and practices bulimia is full of cues that the person is probably not aware of. ERP will not work as well if it is only done in the safe confines of the clinic. The treatment must be extended into the natural environment. This is accomplished in two ways. Starting the first week, the patient is given homework assignments to decrease her frequency of vomiting and to start practicing exposure sessions on her own. After the patient is doing well with the exposure sessions in the clinic, further sessions are conducted in settings in the natural environment in which binge eating actually occurs.

Rosen and Leitenberg, in a preliminary study, showed that patients were able to consume foods with reduced levels of anxiety and decreased vomiting after exposure sessions with each specific type of food. In a subsequent study with five patients (Leitenberg, Gross, Peterson, & Rosen, 1984), the process of change resulting from exposure with response prevention was examined. Patients showed increases in anxiety and the urge to vomit after eating the forbidden foods, with the levels of anxiety and urge to vomit subsiding by the end of the session. The amount of food consumed increased and the levels of anxiety decreased across the subsequent sessions. By the end of treatment, four of the five subjects were completely or substantially improved.

W.G. Johnson, Schlundt, Kelley, and Ruggiero (1984) evaluated the separate and additive effects of exposure with response prevention and energy balance training in six patients with bulimia nervosa using a multiple-baseline design across behavior. The exposure with response prevention was conceptualized as a specific treatment to stop vomiting while the energy balance training was conceived of as specifically reducing binge eating. Both treatments led to substantial reductions in self-monitored rates of binge eating and vomiting with neither treatment approach appearing superior.

In a subsequent study, W.G. Johnson, Schlundt, and Jarrell (1986) used exposure with response prevention as a component in a comprehensive sixteen-week outpatient treatment program with eight bulimia nervosa patients. The treatment package consisted of exposure with response prevention, energy balance training (see Chapter 14), and personal social problem solving (see Chapter 15). An 89.9 percent reduction in the rate of self-induced vomiting was observed representing a change from twice a day to less than once a week as a result of treatment. Each treatment component added incrementally to the reduction in vomiting and excess food intake, with none of the components displaying a superiority. One-year follow-up data on six of the eight subjects showed that five of the six were symptom free or vomiting less than once a month, suggesting that the treatment effects were maintained.

In an uncontrolled trial with thirty-four patients with severe bulimia nervosa, Giles, Young, and Young (1985) tested exposure with response prevention. In subjects who completed and responded to treatment, self-induced vomiting was reduced from 19.6 episodes per week to 1.5 at the end of treatment and 1.3 follow-up. While six subjects dropped out of treatment and six did not respond to treatment, the results of this use of exposure with response prevention are encouraging.

Procedures

It is very important to first establish good rapport with a patient before attempting to undertake exposure with response prevention. The patient must learn to trust the therapist because this treatment is very uncomfortable and anxiety-provoking. Before the first session, the patient needs to be told what the treatment involves and to be given a complete rationale for the treatment.

ERP can last for various periods of time. We will present a protocol for four weeks of ERP. This protocol involves multiple sessions per week with a fading in frequency by the fourth week. This is based on our experience that ERP must be approached aggressively and with frequent contact in order to work well. Frequent contact is most important during the early stages of treatment when anxiety is high and the individual is still vomiting on a regular basis.

Each exposure session has a similar format, which is outlined below.

1. Select a food or foods for the session
   a. Use a forbidden or problem food
   b. Use sufficient quantity to elicit strong fear of weight gain and urge to vomit
   c. Do not use as much food as patient consumes in a large binge
2. Patient fills out ERP rating form (pretreatment)
3. The food is introduced and patient is asked to verbalize thoughts and feelings about eating this food
4. Patient eats until target amount of food has been consumed
   a. Therapist may have to encourage patient to eat all of the food
   b. Eating situation should approximate natural environment as closely as possible
5. During eating, patient is encouraged to verbalize any thoughts or fears
6. After food is consumed, the ERP rating form is completed (after eating evaluation)
7. Therapist enters response prevention phase of treatment
   a. Vomiting is prevented by social presence and encouragement

b. Patient's attention is focused on cues of fullness, fears she is having, and urge to throw up
c. Patient vocalizes fears of gaining weight and consequences of gaining weight, therapist engages in cognitive therapy
   (1) Basis of the fears in reality is examined. Irrational fears are identified
   (2) Therapist discusses with patient cognitive and behavioral strategies for coping with urge to vomit, weight related anxiety, and feelings of bloatedness
8. Once urge to vomit has subsided to point where patient can go at least four hours without vomiting, ERP rating form is completed (end of session evaluation)
9. Homework assignment is given. Behavioral contract for frequency of vomiting between now and next session is completed

To prepare for each session, you must first select foods for the session. In general, we try to pick foods that the patient describes as forbidden and nearly always vomited. We vary the food across sessions so that we do not use all junk food or all regular meals. It may be useful to use the Food Survey (see Chapter 8) to help identify foods that provoke anxiety.

The amount of food to use for exposure sessions must be selected carefully. If too much food is used, weight gain is more likely to occur, which will serve only to confirm the patient's worst fears. If not enough food is used too little anxiety will be evoked and the patient will not progress as quickly as possible. Our advice is to use the food that the patient binges on but to cut the amount about in half. It may be necessary to calculate the patient's typical caloric intake and to choose an amount of food that will not result in rapid weight gain.

We have developed an ERP rating form (see Figure 12.1) for keeping track of the impact of each session on the patient. The form asks the therapist to supply some information about the session, its location, and the foods eaten. The patient then completes several ratings and the patient's heart rate is recorded. The forms allow the clinician to judge whether the amount and kind of food were sufficient to induce fear of weight gain and a strong urge to vomit. In addition, the use of these forms allows the therapist to judge whether anxiety and urge to vomit is decreasing from one session to the next.

After completing the pretreatment ERP rating form, the food is introduced. At this point and throughout the session the patient is encouraged to verbalize her thoughts and feelings. The main role of the therapist in the early sessions is to encourage the patient to think out loud about her thoughts and fears. Later in the course of ERP, the therapist spends more time challenging irrational thoughts and beliefs and in helping the patient come up with new coping strategies.

FIGURE 12.1 ERP Rating Form

Name _____

Date _____ Session _____ Place _____

Phase (check one)   Foods eaten _____
_____ Pretreatment   _____
_____ After eating   _____
_____ End of session _____

How do you feel right now?

Afraid of gaining weight	1	2	3	4	5	6	7	Not afraid of gaining weight
Full	1	2	3	4	5	6	7	Hungry
Strong urge to vomit	1	2	3	4	5	6	7	No urge to vomit
Bloated	1	2	3	4	5	6	7	Not bloated
Depressed	1	2	3	4	5	6	7	Happy
Tense	1	2	3	4	5	6	7	Relaxed

Heart rate _____

Record relevant comments and observations:

Upon finishing the food, the patient fills out the ERP rating form again. The ratings for fear of weight gain and urge to vomit should be strongest at this point in the session. The response prevention portion of the session begins once the food is consumed. The patient should be encouraged not to throw up. We have found that the social presence of the therapist is usually all it takes to prevent vomiting. We typically leave a waste can in the room and instruct the patient that if she is unable to keep from vomiting to throw up in the can. For the next forty-five minutes, we do not let the patient go to the rest room alone. During the response prevention phase, the patient is still encouraged to think out loud. The therapist can facilitate this by asking questions. The questions should focus on: (1) current physical sensations, (2) current emotional reactions, (3) current thoughts, (4) anticipation of what will happen later in the day, and (5) general implications of the fear of weight gain including beliefs about the personal and social consequences of gaining weight.

At this point in the session we often repeat the rationale of the treatment, "This is how you are going to learn that you can eat and not throw up afterwards." "You will learn that most of the things that you fear do not come to pass." We also engage in cognitive therapy at this point (see Chapter 11). When the patient brings up a fear, we help her examine the fear, the assumptions that are involved, and the basis for the fear in reality. We suggest alternative ways of looking at things, and help the patient develop positive ways of coping with each anxious thought.

The response prevention phase can last anywhere from thirty to ninety minutes. After a certain amount of time has passed, the food eaten has progressed far enough in the digestive process that the individual feels it is too late to vomit. During the time it takes for the urge to vomit to subside (the fear of gaining weight may not diminish for several sessions), the patient and therapist work out plans for eating later in the day and discuss strategies for practicing ERP on her own.

Once the patient is confident that she can go at least four hours without throwing up, she completes the ERP session form again. Before the session is over, a homework assignment is given. The homework should include practicing ERP between now and the next session on her own. It is best to plan this out carefully with the patient right down to when, where, and what to eat. In addition, a goal is set with regard to reducing the number of episodes of vomiting between now and the next session. We have found that it works better not to insist that people immediately totally eliminate vomiting but instead gradually decrease the number of vomiting episodes from one session to the next. We generally start with a formula that involves reducing the number of vomits by 50 percent per week for the first three weeks then going down to one per week for several weeks. Patients sometimes find it useful to feel they can throw up one time during the week without failing to meet their goals. They save it for an occasion where they find the anxiety is unbearable. Often patients find that the week is over, and they have not used their one emergency purge.

It is useful to formalize the behavioral goal using a contract. We bring two copies of the contract form to the session (see Figure 12.2). One copy of the form is the patient's to keep, so that she does not forget what the behavioral goals were. The second copy is signed by the patient and goes into the chart so that there is never any question about the goals. It is important that at each session the patient and therapist review whether the goals from the previous session were met. Failure to meet goals should be handled in a positive way. The failure to meet goals should result in a discussion of what happened, what situation led to the extra vomiting, and what behavioral strategies could be used to handle the situation differently the next time it occurs. It is often necessary to deal directly with the patient's thoughts and feelings about herself as a failure and to challenge these thoughts, helping the patient to see herself from a slightly

FIGURE 12.2 Homework Contract

I _____ agree to the following behavioral goals for the coming week:

_____
_____
_____
_____
_____
_____
_____

I also agree to do the following homework assignment this week:

_____
_____
_____
_____
_____
_____
_____

I further agree to call _____ if I have trouble realizing these goals or completing these assignments.

_____ _____ _____
Signature   Date   Therapist

---

different perspective. Dealing with failure is facilitated if patients are given realistic expectations about the speed with which changes can be made using this approach.

Table 12.1 presents a proposed four-week schedule for ERP therapy. Many factors influence the extent to which a schedule like this can be followed in practice. The availability of the therapist's time, the expense to the patient, and the flexibility of the patient's schedule all influence whether the ambitious schedule can be met. ERP can work if done once a week over a six to eight week period as well. Some patients will respond very quickly with only one session per week while others will not. It is our experience that several sessions a week during the first two weeks helps increase the speed with which patients respond. In addition, sessions in the natural environment are encouraged, but if not possible, can be omitted. We have experimented with using imagery to help the patient imagine being in different environmental situations during exposure sessions. Imagery does not work with all patients whereas in vivo sessions are often very powerful.

TABLE 12.1 Proposed Schedule of ERP Sessions

Session Number	Week	Place	Homework	Behavior Goal
1	1	clinic	practice once	reduce 25%
2	1	clinic	practice once	reduce 25%
3	1	clinic	practice twice	hold
4	2	clinic	practice twice	reduce 50%
5	2	clinic	practice twice	hold
6	3	real world	practice twice	reduce 50%
7	3	clinic	practice 3 times	1/week
8	4	real world	practice 3 times	1/week or less

TEMPTATION EXPOSURE WITH RESPONSE PREVENTION (TERP)

Purpose and Objective

The behavioral disorder in bulimia involves both bingeing and vomiting. Exposure with response prevention was presented as a treatment technique for rapidly eliminating purging behavior. While this treatment often eliminates bingeing concomitantly, it does not always work. When binge eating is responsive to specific environmental stimuli, temptation exposure with response prevention is a method for eliminating binge episodes. TERP is also appropriate for patients who repeatedly failed to respond to other treatment modalities and for patients who initially responded but who have experienced a relapse.

Rationale

Binge eating often becomes an habitual behavior that arises in response to a wide variety of cognitive, environmental, physiological, and affective cues. We discussed in detail in Chapter 7 the evidence that binge eating is environmentally cued and outlined a number of classes of cues which may provoke binge eating.

Many approaches to the behavioral treatment of eating behavior utilize stimulus control techniques. Stimulus control techniques involve learning to control an unwanted behavior by removing or avoiding the eliciting cues in the environment. While this approach has considerable merit, it is not always possible to rid the environment of eliciting stimuli.

For these unavoidable cues, there is no alternative but to help the patient learn to respond with some other behavior beside inappropriate eating. When the bingeing response is habitual and ingrained, behavioral substitution methods (see Chapter 14) may not be powerful enough to overcome the nearly automatic response.

The individual, when confronted by binge-eating cues, often experiences feelings, such as craving and deprivation. The removal or reduction of these feelings by the act of binge eating serves to further reinforce the habitual nature of the act of bingeing. As discussed in Chapter 6, binge eating in bulimia can be conceptualized as an addictive behavior driven perhaps by endogenous opioids and/or central nervous system (CNS) serotonin levels. Environmental stimuli or past behaviors elicit craving (a withdrawal response) that leads to engaging in the addictive behavior (bingeing) that is reinforced by reduction or removal of the withdrawal syndrome. When the act of bingeing is followed by purging, the individual avoids negative consequences of the act and only derives immediate pleasure from the overconsumption of food (the high or intoxication).

The rationale of temptation exposure with response prevention is to expose the individual to the environmental, cognitive, physiological, and affective stimuli that elicit craving and binge eating and to prevent the binge-eating response from occurring. By repeating this procedure, the strength and duration of the craving is lessened through a process of behavioral extinction. Functionally, the link between eliciting stimuli and the habitual binge response is progressively weakened. Concurrently, alternative behaviors that provide more effective ways of responding to the binge stimuli are identified. These behaviors are repeatedly practiced in the presence of the eliciting stimuli and grow stronger with repetition. The eventual goal is for the individual to break the chain between specific eliciting events and binge eating and to strengthen the association between these stimuli and more positive coping responses.

Schmidt and Marks (1988) evaluated exposure to binge-eating cues with response prevention in four chronic bulimic patients using a single-subject research design. Treatment consisted of twelve exposure sessions at the rate of three per week. Patients were exposed to a series of highly preferred binge foods during these sessions. The urge to binge was created by having the patient eat a small amount of the binge food. Three of the patients appeared to have benefited from this treatment while the fourth dropped out prematurely.

The approach has also proven clinically useful in the Eating Disorders Program at the University of Mississippi Medical Center. W.G. Johnson, Corrigan, and Mayo (1987) provide further information on the theoretical rationale of TERP.

Procedures

The TERP protocol is divided into three distinct phases: (1) comprehensive assessment of eliciting stimuli, (2) temptation exposure extinction sessions, and (3) temptation exposure sessions with training in alternative responses. TERP is an intensive intervention that requires multiple sessions per week in order to have an optimal impact.

Phase 1: Assessment
The first session is devoted to administration of questionnaires, collection of physical data, such a weight and body composition, and the beginning of a comprehensive interview designed to collect data on the cues and situations that typically elicit binge-eating behavior. The interviewer should begin to collect very specific and detailed information about the kinds of situations in which binge eating or the craving to binge typically occur. The interviewer should particularly cover stress-related stimuli. If stress-related bingeing occurs, then the kinds of events (social, personal, vocational, emotional, physical) that lead to feelings of stress should be described in detail. Other eliciting stimuli, such as physical setting, time of day, use of drugs or alcohol, concurrent activities, and social context, should be covered in this initial interview.

The initial interview should also be used to obtain information on the kinds and amounts of preferred binge foods. It is important to be specific in this assessment. For example, if bingeing occurs primarily in the evening, then it is important to find out what is typically eaten for the evening meal and how this prior food intake sets the stage for the later episode of bingeing. It is also useful to learn how the client experiences the sensory qualities of the binge food. What smells, textures, or appearances are salient about the preferred binge foods.

Finally, the initial assessment interview(s) should cover the kinds of feelings and thoughts that normally accompany an eating binge. The patient can be instructed to imagine bingeing and to tell out loud what usually runs through the patient's mind at this time. Are specific thoughts about self, the foods, or feelings being experienced? What kinds of feelings accompany an urge to binge eat? Are there physical sensations of hunger or craving? What kinds of thoughts occur in response to these physical sensations? The therapist should take extensive notes and attempt to document as fully as possible the full range of antecedents that accompany eating binges.

At the end of the first session (which may last well over the usual psychotherapy hour), the client is instructed in keeping a self-monitoring diary. The patient is told that this diary is for collecting baseline information during the first week and not to attempt to change behavior yet. The diary should provide a means for documenting all eating episodes, including binges. It should provide space for recording the situational context in which each food intake occurs, and the kinds of thoughts, feelings, and sensations that accompany each binge during the coming week.

The second session should occur approximately one week after the first session. This gives the patient ample time to collect baseline data. The diary is collected at the second session and is reviewed with the therapist. Specific occurrences of binge eating should be discussed. This will allow the therapist to inquire in more detail about the antecedent thoughts, feelings, and cues associated with each eating binge along with gathering information about the kinds and amounts of food that were consumed. The patient's thoughts and feelings should be discussed, beginning with the urge to binge followed by the binge and ending with the feelings associated with purging, if it occurred. Any other information obtained from the initial interview or the administration of questionnaires that requires clarification should be discussed at the second session.

The patient should be asked whether the behavior documented in the baseline diary is representative of a typical week in terms of both the occurrence of eating behaviors and the frequency of emotional and situational antecedents. If the patient reports that it is not typical, then the therapist should find out what was atypical about this week and should attempt to gather information about what goes on in a more typical week. It is important to praise the patient for keeping an accurate diary and to stress that the diary is a very important part of the treatment program.

The second session ends with homework assignments. The patient is instructed to continue to keep the self-monitoring diary and to not try to make any major changes in eating behavior between now and the next session. The patient is also instructed to make a written list of pleasant activities or hobbies to do instead of bingeing. The emphasis is on identifying behaviors that are incompatible with binge eating and could easily be done in the kinds of settings in which binges occur. For example, if the patient binges late in the evening at home while her family is sleeping, she might identify alternative activities, such as writing letters or poetry, drawing, painting, macrame, needlepoint, embroidery, other crafts, working on a photo album, keeping a scrap book, making lists of things to be done in the future, planning for an upcoming event or vacation, studying, or reading.

The third assessment session should occur during week three. The diary is collected and reviewed again. Additional detail on the antecedents of binge eating are elicited from the patient. The patient should be asked if any important clues or situations that stimulate binge eating have been missed. At this point, the therapist should review earlier notes on the antecedents of binge eating and work with the patient in constructing a written list of all of the stimuli that elicit bingeing. The list is reviewed with the patient, and the patient indicates the relative strength of each of the antecedents on the list in terms of its ability to create craving and bingeing. The goal of the therapist is to generate several scenarios that represent strong eliciting situations that are very difficult for the patient to resist.

The list of pleasant activities is collected at the third assessment session and is reviewed with the patient. Additional items are added to the list at this time. Items that are unrealistic or potentially unworkable are removed from the list. The patient is then praised for keeping the diary and for completing the homework assignment. The basic outline of the remainder of the treatment program is presented to the patient at this time. The therapist should attempt to create a positive expectation that the procedure will be effective without creating unrealistic expectations. The patient needs to be told that the treatment procedure is difficult, but that with her active participation and cooperation it stands a very good chance of breaking the binge habit.

At the end of the third session, the patient is given a new diary to keep and again told that accurate completion of the diary is very important. An appointment later in the same week is made for the TERP assessment session. The appointment should be made during a time when binge eating is actually likely to occur. The patient is also told to eat following her usual pattern on the day of the appointment and not to engage in any compensatory behaviors (such as fasting or meal skipping) on the day of the appointment.

Between the third and fourth sessions, the therapist has two tasks to complete. The first task is to construct five minutes of audiotaped imagery induction. The tape should vividly describe a binge-eating situation that is likely to occur for the patient. The imagery should include descriptions of the physical setting, the other people (if any) who are present, the events earlier in the day leading up to the binge situation, the specific stimuli in the environment that serve as binge cues, along with a vivid description of the patient's affective and physical state at the time. The tape should include a running account of thoughts the patient typically experiences. If food is present in the situation, the foods should be described in detail including the appearance, smell, and texture of the food. The therapist should describe a strong craving to binge using the words and sensations that the patient provided during the assessment interviews. The following is an example of an imagery session that might be constructed for TERP:

> This has not been an easy day for you. You have been feeling run-down; you seem to have been experiencing a persistent, lingering, annoying cold. You wish that the cold would just go away. You are not used to being sick very often, and you don't like it. It makes everything such an effort. You hope

that it is not anything more serious than a cold. Why is it still hanging on? The *last* thing you need is some tremendous medical bills for something more serious. You wish you and your husband were both making more money so that you wouldn't have to worry so much about emergencies. It makes you mad when you think about how little concern he seems to have about the money. If it weren't up to you to worry about it, you would have been in financial ruin long ago. Anyway, why won't the cold go away? Why is it lasting so long?

Your boss seems to be under a lot of stress this week. She certainly has been fussing at you a lot. Especially today, it seemed obvious at work that a lot of things were really coming down all at once on your boss. It really has been overwhelming and stressful at work lately because of her fussing at you like this. To top it all off, you ran into one of your former professors today who asked you what you were doing in your career now. You dreaded that question, but you knew it was coming. You wish that you had not run into that professor because you really feel like you have to apologize for the job that you are doing right now. Your professor thought highly of you as a student, and really expected you to have a high-powered career. Your face was hot and your heart pounded as you talked to him about your job. Thank God he didn't ask how much you are earning. That really would have been upsetting. You keep trying to find some logical justification for what you are doing, but you know your professor was disappointed. He didn't come right out and say it, but you could tell by the tone of his voice that he was thinking it. You really ended up feeling depressed about your career situation today. You're not just bothered by your professor's disappointment, but you are really disappointed in yourself deep down inside.

After the episode with your old professor today, you start wishing you were in a better job situation. You started to think about what a struggle things have been financially and you can't imagine being able to afford more education right now. You know that more education is the only way you'll ever avoid being trapped in a horrible job working for grouchy, petty people. You really resent that your parents and your husband's parents won't help you with school. If you had more financial and moral support, you could have continued in school and you wouldn't be stuck in this awful job right now. Your husband should be more willing to help than he is. He seems to be so happy working at his worthless, low-paying job. Why can't he show some initiative? If he worked at it, he could help you go back to school and make life better for both of you. Why is he so stupid and selfish sometimes? It makes you mad thinking about it. You feel yourself getting hot, you feel the blood rushing to your face. But, as you realize there is nothing you can do about it, your heart sinks and you start to feel depressed.

When you get home, you realize how hungry you really are. You haven't been eating much the last few days because the cold has left you feeling so drained. Besides, you have been feeling so fat lately that you are glad you haven't been eating much. You have a slight headache, and your stomach is growling because you are so hungry. You walk into the kitchen to start fixing dinner for your husband who is due home in a half-hour. As you are getting the meat out of the freezer, you spot the ice cream. You have a tremendous urge to eat the ice cream. You hear yourself thinking "Only a couple of bites, it will make me feel better." You know that if you take a couple of bites, you won't be able to stop. You feel so tired, depressed, sick, and angry all at once that you say to yourself "I deserve just a little of this ice cream." Your mouth begins to water as you look at the box of ice cream. You are getting excited just thinking about how good the ice cream will taste. You are feeling a strong sense of craving that starts in your stomach and ends in your mouth. You really want some of that ice cream.

The second homework task for the therapist is to create a binge situation in the clinic. This should include obtaining ample quantities of binge food and providing other important props, such as a television set. The binge foods obtained should be highly preferred foods for the client. If beer or wine is usually present, these should be made available for the next assessment session. For the example listed above, the therapist should conduct the session in the late afternoon on a workday and have ice cream and a spoon available for the patient.

The fourth and final session of the assessment phase involves the recreation of an actual binge in the clinic. There are several purposes to this session. First, it allows the therapist to observe directly the binge-eating behavior. Second, it allows the patient to give an immediate account of the thoughts and feelings that accompanied the binge. Third, having the patient binge in the clinic helps create additional temptation during the treatment sessions. If the patient feels totally uncomfortable about eating in front of the therapist, she may have difficulty recreating the usual cravings, thoughts, and feelings that precede binge eating.

The session begins with the therapist giving instructions to the patient concerning what will happen during the session. The therapist needs to be sure that the patient understands the rationale of the session, and is given the expectation that she probably will feel uncomfortable bingeing in the clinic with the therapist present. The client is told that the session involves recreating a binge-eating episode in the clinic. If the client is reluctant to binge with the therapist present, these feelings should be acknowledged and the therapist should attempt to convince the patient that this session both provides valuable information and sets the stage for later treatment sessions. The following is an example of the instructions given to a patient before the assessment TERP session:

> We are trying to recreate an actual binge situation for you. First, we will have you make some ratings and take your heart rate. After we have left the room, turn the tape recorder on and carefully listen to the scene described. It may help you if you close your eyes and try to visualize the scene we are describing. When the tape has finished, we will come back into the room and have you repeat the ratings and take your heart rate again. When we leave the room the second time, we want you to focus on the thoughts and feelings

that were described on the tape. Think of them as your own thoughts and feelings. Try to respond as naturally as you can to these images, thoughts, and feelings. There will be some food in the room. It will be the same food described on the tape. You should give into the temptation and eat the food. Try to eat exactly the way you would if you were alone at home and really in this situation with no one else around. Feel free to eat as much as you want while you are here. Make it like a real binge. When you decide that you are not going to eat any more of the food or when the food is gone, please say "finished." We will then come back into the room and have you complete another set of ratings and take your heart rate again.

The session begins with completion of the TERP rating form, which is presented in Figure 12.3. The form is important in that it will provide a structured way for the patient to communicate feelings and responses to the procedures throughout the TERP sessions. If you want, you can take the patient's heart rate as a way to monitor the patient's level of arousal. The therapists leave the room, then imagery induction via audiotape is done. The second part of the TERP rating form is completed. The patient is then left alone to eat. If you have a room with a one-way mirror available, you may wish to observe (with informed consent) the patient through the mirror. It is also possible to monitor the patient's behavior using a closed circuit video system if this kind of equipment is available to you. If none of these alternatives are available, then the therapist may elect to remain in the room with the patient during eating in order to observe her food intake behaviors. When the patient has finished eating, the TERP rating form is completed again. Some time should then be spent discussing the experience. The feedback from the patient should be elicited concerning how realistic the tape was, and what kind of imagery can be added to increase the degree to which it is representative of the patient's actual experience with binge eating. Figure 12.4 presents a session management form that can be used to help structure and monitor the TERP sessions.

Phase 2: Temptation Exposure with Response Prevention
After completing the assessment phase of the intervention, the therapeutic sessions begin. The second phase of TERP involves a variation of the last session of the assessment phase. The basic objective of the second stage is to expose the individual to cues and situations that evoke binge eating, but to progressively train the individual to resist the urge to eat.

The TERP sessions begin with completion of the TERP rating form and assessment of heart rate. The patient is then told that a binge situation will be created in the clinic using an audiotape procedure just like the last time. The difference this time is that she is to attempt to resist the temptation to binge as long as she can. Food is made available and the patient is clearly told that she may eat as much of the food as she wishes to at any time. The tape is played, the ratings are completed again, then the exposure period begins. The patient is to remain in the presence of the food, think about the images and feelings presented on the tape, and allow herself to experience the urge to binge. She is encouraged to attempt to refrain from bingeing, or at least to delay the beginning of the binge

FIGURE 12.3 TERP Rating Form

Name _____ Date _____ Session # _____

Time 1: _____ (record time)

Circle the number that best describes your present feeling.

Very upset	1 2 3 4 5 6 7	Not upset at all
Very afraid	1 2 3 4 5 6 7	Not afraid at all
Very anxious	1 2 3 4 5 6 7	Not anxious at all
Very bloated	1 2 3 4 5 6 7	Not bloated at all
Strong urge to vomit	1 2 3 4 5 6 7	No urge to vomit at all
Very depressed	1 2 3 4 5 6 7	Not depressed at all

How sure are you that you can resist eating for the next 20 minutes?

Not at all sure	1 2 3 4 5 6 7	Very sure

Time 2: _____ (record time)

Circle the number that best describes your present feeling.

Very upset	1 2 3 4 5 6 7	Not upset at all
Very afraid	1 2 3 4 5 6 7	Not afraid at all
Very anxious	1 2 3 4 5 6 7	Not anxious at all
Very bloated	1 2 3 4 5 6 7	Not bloated at all
Strong urge to eat	1 2 3 4 5 6 7	No urge to eat at all
Strong urge to vomit	1 2 3 4 5 6 7	No urge to vomit at all
Very depressed	1 2 3 4 5 6 7	Not depressed at all

How sure are you that you can resist eating for the next 20 minutes?

Not at all sure	1 2 3 4 5 6 7	Very sure

(continued)

314 ■ Behavioral Treatment of Bingeing and Purging

FIGURE 12.3 (continued)

Time 3: _____ (record time)

Circle the number that best describes your present feeling.

Very upset	1	2	3	4	5	6	7	Not upset at all
Very afraid	1	2	3	4	5	6	7	Not afraid at all
Very anxious	1	2	3	4	5	6	7	Not anxious at all
Very bloated	1	2	3	4	5	6	7	Not bloated at all
Strong urge to eat	1	2	3	4	5	6	7	No urge to eat at all
Strong urge to vomit	1	2	3	4	5	6	7	No urge to vomit at all
Very depressed	1	2	3	4	5	6	7	Not depressed at all

How sure are you that you can resist eating for the next 20 minutes?

Not at all sure	1	2	3	4	5	6	7	Very sure

How difficult was it for you to resist eating?

Very difficult	1	2	3	4	5	6	7	Not difficult at all

How did you resist?

_____
_____
_____
_____

Time 4: _____ (if needed due to patient distress at Time 3)

Circle the number that best describes your present feeling.

Very upset	1	2	3	4	5	6	7	Not upset at all
Very afraid	1	2	3	4	5	6	7	Not afraid at all
Very anxious	1	2	3	4	5	6	7	Not anxious at all
Very bloated	1	2	3	4	5	6	7	Not bloated at all
Strong urge to eat	1	2	3	4	5	6	7	No urge to eat at all
Strong urge to vomit	1	2	3	4	5	6	7	No urge to vomit at all
Very depressed	1	2	3	4	5	6	7	Not depressed at all

How sure are you that you can resist eating for the next 20 minutes?

Not at all sure	1	2	3	4	5	6	7	Very sure

FIGURE 12.4 TERP Session Observation Form

Type of session (circle one)

Baseline   Phase I   Phase II   Post treatment   Follow-up

Tape recording: ID _____   Length _____

Target food available:

    Food 1 _____   Amount _____

    Food 2 _____   Amount _____

    Food 3 _____   Amount _____

Beverage available:

    Bev 1 _____   Amount _____

Procedure

Heart rate # 1 _____ bpm
TERP ratings
Instructional set (emphasis to tell when finished)

Play tape (and music if applicable)
Prepare food

Heart rate #2 _____ bpm
TERP ratings

Start Timing—Temptation exposure should continue for at least 20 minutes.

Start time   _____

Time of first bite   _____

Time of first sip   _____

Time of last bite   _____

Time of last sip   _____

Time "finished"   _____

Quantity of food consumed:

Food # 1 _____

Food # 2 _____

Beverage _____

Behavioral observations:

as long as she can. When the patient has finished eating or when she has resisted the urge to binge for twenty minutes, the rating forms are completed again. The patient then talks with the therapist about the experience until the end of the session. The discussion should focus on how strong the urges to binge were and the thoughts and feelings the patient had while attempting to resist the urge to binge.

During the first two TERP sessions, the therapist can remain in the room with the patient and help keep her mind focused on the images from the tape and on the urge to binge. The food should be readily accessible and should be presented in as tempting a manner as possible (e.g., the wrappers taken off and the packages open). The therapist can ask the patient to focus on the food, on its sight, smell, and texture. The goal of the therapist in these sessions is to help create maximum exposure to the stimuli that typically elicit binge eating. A different induction tape should be prepared for the second TERP session. Ideally, a new tape involving different antecedent stimuli is prepared for every other session. This exposes the patient to a wide variety of induction scenes and helps prepare her to cope with a wide range of binge situations in the natural environment.

After the first two sessions, the therapist leaves the room and the patient remains alone with the food. The TERP sessions continue at a rate of two per week until the patient is able to resist eating any of the available food for twenty minutes two sessions in a row. After each session, the therapist should discuss with the patient the extent to which the tape was able to elicit an urge to binge, and the difficulty experienced in resisting this urge. It is important that the tapes create a strong induction of food craving, that the food appear delicious and palatable, and that the patient learn to resist eating in the face of strong cravings.

During the second phase, the patient continues to keep a self-monitoring diary recording all food intakes, including binges. The patient is encouraged to begin to resist the urge to binge between sessions by progressively delaying the amount of time between craving the food and the initiation of eating. Patients who are bingeing frequently can begin to contract with the therapist for a reduction in the frequency of bingeing between sessions and/or to set goals for the length of time the patient will delay the onset of a binge. The therapist should examine the eating diaries to obtain material for constructing new temptation audiotapes.

Phase III: Temptation Exposure with Response Prevention and Alternative Activities

In the third stage of the treatment program, the patient begins to perform alternative behaviors immediately after the audiotape presentation of the binge stimuli. These behaviors were identified during the assessment phase. The patient should be presented with a variety of tapes during this stage, and should engage in behaviors that are realistic possibilities in the environmental setting being described on the tape. Ratings and heart rates are taken during these sessions just as during the last session of Phase I and the sessions of Phase II. After twenty minutes of resisting the temptation, the therapist should discuss with the patient how to use the alternative activities when faced with a similar situation in daily life.

Self-monitoring continues during this phase. The patient and therapist start working on drastically reducing the frequency of bingeing between sessions through a combined strategy or resisting temptation and alternative behaviors. The audiotapes during this phase should be based on the actual situations that cause the patient the greatest difficulty between sessions. The third phase of treatment consists of four to six sessions conducted over a two to three week period. However, if the patient has great difficulty in eliminating binge eating between sessions, it may be useful to extend the length of this treatment phase until the patient has gone two weeks without an eating binge. The frequency of sessions can be reduced to one per week and the induction tapes can be tailored to the specific situations that are still causing problems.

Follow-Up and Booster Sessions
The patient should remain in counseling following the end of Phase III for as long as necessary to insure that the strong, habitual link between daily situations and binge eating has been broken. During the follow-up period, personal/social problem solving (see Chapter 15) and/or cognitive therapy (see Chapter 11) can be used to help reduce or eliminate the kinds of problems in the patient's life that are creating negative emotions and stress. Patients will have relapses during the follow-up period. When a relapse occurs, additional TERP sessions that focus on the situation that evoked the relapse can be conducted. In addition, booster sessions can be used to help prepare the patient for difficult problems anticipated in the immediate future. For example, if binge eating on holiday foods is seen as a potential problem, the therapist can help prepare the patient to cope with the availability of holiday food and the family situations that often accompany holidays using TERP booster sessions. Booster sessions during follow-up should always emphasize the use of alternative behaviors as a way to help resist the temptation to binge. Table 12.2 presents a summary of the TERP protocol.

Clinical Recommendations

In this chapter, we have presented two very specific treatment protocols based on the exposure with response prevention treatment paradigm. We think that the ERP treatment is a valuable component in the comprehensive treatment of patients with bulimia nervosa. There are a few

TABLE 12.2 Outline of Temptation Exposure with Response Prevention

Phase	Session	Content
I	1	Questionnaires and interview.
I	2	Review of self-monitoring diary. Identify binge antecedents and incompatible behaviors.
I	3–4	Patient binges in clinic using audiotape induction.
II	5–11	Begin response prevention.
III	12–18	Add alternative behaviors to response prevention.
Follow-Up		Cognitive behavior therapy continues.

considerations, however, that must be mentioned before a clinician tries to use it. First, we do not believe that ERP is adequate as the sole treatment for bulimia nervosa. Instead, it should be one of several treatment components. Second, if ERP is used, it should be the first treatment approach applied. It is not fair to patients to use other procedures to help them gain some control over their eating behavior then require them to go through the exposure sessions. Many patients will see this as a step backwards in their progress. However, when ERP is used first, the results are often rapid and dramatic. Patients who initially did not believe they could ever stop vomiting are able to either cease entirely or else reduce the frequency to one or two times per week. These rapid changes encourage patients to stick with the treatment plan and actively participate in the other components.

The final consideration to make clear that using ERP protocol is not mutually exclusive with using other therapy techniques *simultaneously*. In fact, we strongly recommend that both cognitive intervention and behavioral problem solving be used in conjunction with ERP. There is plenty of time available while the patient is waiting for the urge to vomit to subside to work on changing beliefs and expectations or to address interpersonal or vocational issues.

With respect to TERP, we would not recommend this treatment for all or even most patients. The treatment is lengthy, time-consuming, and may address a problem that not all patients have. That is, TERP is most appropriate when the patient experiences bingeing as an uncontrollable urge or when the patient is troubled with strong food cravings. It is really more efficient to first attempt to modify binge eating using the energy balance training behavioral methods outlined in Chapter 14. Most patients will be able to learn to start eating regular meals and to use behavioral substitution strategies to avoid bingeing without the use of the elaborate exposure methodology of TERP. However, when a patient fails to respond to energy balance training because of intractable urges or strong food cravings, the TERP approach may be well worth the effort.

Both ERP and TERP require considerable effort and time on the part of the therapist. They do not necessarily lend themselves to a practice situation in which one must see a patient every hour on the hour. Both treatments involve the use of food, which requires extra effort and time for the therapist. In addition, they are emotionally powerful interventions and it is often difficult to predict how long it will take to complete a session, especially during the early sessions of the protocol. These procedures are more easily implemented when the therapist has an assistant to help.

Both ERP and TERP can be used as components of an inpatient treatment program. In fact, on an inpatient unit every meal can be treated as an ERP session. ERP can be implemented using a group format. In groups, the patients are able to help encourage each other to eat enough food to elicit a strong urge to vomit. To date, we have no experience in implementing TERP in a group. We have used forbidden foods in group settings to both teach resisting temptation and to rehearse controlled eating behavior. There is no reason theoretically that the imagery induction and exposure to binge foods could not be accomplished in a group setting. Many patients who binge have very little problem controlling their bingeing in a social context so there may be very good reasons to conduct TERP sessions individually.

SUMMARY

Exposure with response prevention, the first behavioral treatment protocol described in this chapter, is a highly effective technique for reducing or eliminating self-induced vomiting in a large proportion of bulimic patients. It can be used alone, but is probably best used as the first component of a multi-faceted intervention program. While the treatment does work, it is not clear whether the effect is due to anxiety extinction, acquisition of new cognitive and behavioral skills for coping with food, or both.

The second protocol discussed, temptation exposure with response prevention, is an innovative behavioral approach to addressing the problem of binge eating. It is an intensive, time-consuming therapy that is intended to eliminate binge eating and break the connection between environmental situations and overeating within an eight to ten-week time frame. The basic temptation exposure session involves presentation of a situational vignette via audiotape. The patient is then highly exposed to highly preferred binge foods and is encouraged to progressively delay the onset of eating until she can reliably resist for twenty minutes. The therapy then adds training in the use of alternative incompatible behaviors in order to further enhance the patient's ability to resist temptation in everyday situations. The therapist and patient begin to contract to reduce the frequency of binge eating until it is eliminated or occurring only intermittently. During follow-up, long-term behavior change is enhanced through periodic booster sessions as needed.

13

Nutrition Education and Management

PURPOSE AND OBJECTIVE

While many patients with eating disorders know a great deal about selected aspects of nutrition from voracious reading of the popular literature, a large number of patients either know very little about nutrition or have significant gaps in their knowledge. Laessle et al. (1988) administered a nutrition knowledge questionnaire to groups of bulimics, anorexics, and normal controls. They found that on the average, eating-disordered patients were more knowledgeable about calories and macronutrients than the normal controls and did not differ on knowledge of micronutrients. However, about 15 percent of the anorexic and bulimic patients showed deficits in their knowledge of nutrition.

The purpose of nutrition education and management is to educate eating-disordered patients about basic principles of good nutrition, and to help them use this information in planning healthy and appropriate patterns of food intake.

RATIONALE

While it is clear that knowledge about nutrition alone does not always result in appropriate eating behavior, it is unlikely that people will make good choices when they are not aware of the basic principles of nutrition. The behavioral procedures outlined in Chapter 12 are intended to help patients change relatively intractable patterns of behavior. However, eliminating dangerous behaviors, such as bingeing and purging, is only half of the therapist's job. The other half involves replacing these inappropriate and dangerous practices with safer more appropriate ways of eating and maintaining an ideal body weight.

The process of building good eating habits involves several components. The first step is to teach the basic principles of nutrition so that the patient has a rational and informed basis for selecting foods. This process is neither involved nor difficult, since the goal is to teach the patient a basic understanding of food and nutrition. Once the patient has the appropriate knowledge base, then behavioral procedures (see Chapter 14) can be used to help the patient translate this knowledge into a daily pattern of appropriate food choices.

Most comprehensive treatment programs address nutrition knowledge. For example, J.E. Mitchell, Hatsukami, Goff, et al. (1985) have incorporated lectures by a dietitian into their comprehensive program for bulimia treatment. The knowledge is then translated into behavior by having patients plan their meals during group sessions and receive detailed feedback on these plans. Andersen, Morse, and Santmyer (1985) include nutritional rehabilitation as the first phase of the inpatient treatment of anorexia nervosa. Rosen and Leitenberg (1985) describe the inclusion of nutrition information in their exposure with response prevention treatment. O'Connor, Touyz, and Beumont (1988) evaluated a nutrition education intervention in twenty-eight consecutive outpatients and reported that ten dropped out of treatment and that twelve of the remaining eighteen ceased all bulimic behavior. The treatment consisted mainly of the prescription of a meal plan along with self-monitoring of food intake.

PROCEDURES

This section will focus on basic nutrition information that will prove useful to patients with eating disorders. The discussion is intended to provide basic information that the counselor can use in educating patients. We have prepared handouts summarizing the information that can be copied and given to patients. Every effort has been made to make the information accurate, yet accessible to most patients. Patients who desire additional information about nutrition, can be encouraged to read an introductory text or selected popular books on nutrition.

Carbohydrates, Fats, and Proteins

Our bodies are complex machines that require energy in order to operate. Ultimately, all of our energy needs must be met by the food we eat. While food supplies other needs, it is important to communicate to eating-disordered patients that food supplies energy and that without energy, our bodies are like cars without gasoline.

Patients with eating disorders often have fears associated with the energy content in foods. While information alone may not be sufficient to overcome these fears, knowledge about energy and the body's energy needs is essential if the patient is ever to become comfortable with food.

Food can be broken down into a number of constituents on the basis of chemical composition. While different food constituents serve many functions in the body, there are four sources of energy in food: carbohydrates, proteins, fats, and alcohol. When the body needs energy to function, the source of the energy is not that important since all four constituents can be turned into energy.

When not enough energy is available from food, the body turns to its own tissue to provide energy. The body uses carbohydrates, which are stored in the liver in the form of glycogen. If these stores are not sufficient, the body turns to its fat stores, mobilizing the fat and converting it to energy. When necessary, the body can also borrow from its protein stores (usually muscle tissue and sometimes vital organs) and convert these lean tissues into usable energy.

Carbohydrates are the most important source of energy in the foods we eat. Carbohydrates are essential to proper health. It has been recommended that 50 percent to 60 percent of our energy needs should be met by carbohydrates (Senate Select Committee on Nutrition and Human Needs, 1977; Food and Nutrition Board, 1980; U.S. Departments of Agriculture and Health and Human Services, 1980). Carbohydrates consist of carbon, hydrogen, and oxygen atoms that are organized as sugars and starches. Carbohydrates constitute the major source of dietary intake, and they come primarily from plants in the form of vegetables, grains, and fruits and secondarily from dairy products. Carbohydrates are classified according to their atomic structure as simple or complex. Simple carbohydrates, referred to as mono- and disaccharides, are sugars, such as glucose, fructose, and lactose. These simple sugars provide the basic structure of which all other sugars and starches are composed, and they represent the only type of carbohydrates that are absorbed in the gastrointestinal tract.

The complex carbohydrates or polysaccharides, include starches and fibers obtained primarily from grains and legumes consumed as pasta, cereals, breads, beans, lentils and corn. Complex carbohydrates are formed in larger molecules that contain many mono and disaccharides linked in intricate chemical structures. The complex carbohydrates require longer periods to digest during which they eventually break down into mono- and disaccharides for absorption through the gastrointestinal tract.

The third type of carbohydrate is fiber. Fibers are complex carbohydrate molecules that cannot be digested by the body. The old term for fiber, roughage, indicates that its importance in the human diet has been known for a long time. Unlike the other carbohydrates, fiber provides no energy to the body yet it takes energy to move it through the digestive tract. Fiber is found in many plant sources of food such as grains, legumes, and fruits. Fiber adds bulk to the stool, which helps prevent constipation. Fiber molecules also absorb water in the intestine, which functions to keep the stool soft and easy to eliminate. Water soluble fibers (oats, bran, citrus pulp, legumes) may bind some fat molecules preventing their absorption. Fiber also decreases intestinal transit time (the time it takes food to move through the digestive tract), which may prevent the absorption of dangerous chemical contaminants in our food.

The major function of carbohydrates is to supply energy. In the process of digestion they are broken down into mono- and disaccharides, which are converted to glycogen by liver in a process called *glycogenesis* and stored in the liver and muscles. Approximately 300 grams of glycogen can be stored in the liver and muscles with trained athletes capable of storing 10 to 20 percent more. These glycogen stores constitute a readily available supply of energy that can be reconverted to glucose to be used by the cells to perform work. When the capacity of the liver and muscles to store glycogen is reached, the excess glucose can be converted to fat in a process called *lipogenesis* and stored in fat cells or adipocytes.

If for some reason dietary intake of carbohydrates is insufficient or the availability of glucose is limited, stores in the liver and muscles are utilized. When these supplies are exhausted, further glucose can be manufactured in a process called *gluconeogenesis* whereby glucose is synthesized from fatty acids, dietary protein, or lean body mass. Note that approximately 58 percent of dietary protein consists of amino acids that can be converted to glucose while only about 10 percent of dietary fat can be converted.

A reduction in caloric intake in general and carbohydrates in particular is a common dietary regimen for women. The popularity of fad diets is widespread and most of these diets severely limit carbohydrate intake. With an insufficient intake of carbohydrates, proteins and fats must be converted to glucose in order to satisfy energy requirements. Lean body mass including cardiac tissue is converted to glucose in order to meet energy demands long before the available fat stores are exhausted. Thus, nutritional intake of many dieters and those with an eating disorder can severely compromise their physical health.

Another frequent problem associated with carbohydrate restriction is diuresis. In fact, weight loss during the first few weeks of carbohydrate restricted dieting is predominately from fluid loss. The loss of fluid, along with a decreased RMR, are partly responsible for the plateau in weight reduction which occurs during the first few weeks of dieting. It is the major reason why many dieters relinquish their diet. Returning to regular meals with increased carbohydrates causes a rapid weight increase as a result of rehydration and the lower RMR.

Fats are like carbohydrates in that both contain carbon, oxygen, and hydrogen. In contrast to carbohydrates, fats have a lower ratio of oxygen to hydrogen and carbon. For example, the oxygen ratio in simple carbohydrates is approximately 1:2 as contrasted with from 1:3 to 1:7 for simple fats. This chemical structure accounts for the higher concentration of energy in fats where a gram of carbohydrate and a gram of fat provide four and nine kcal, respectively.

Fats are referred to as lipids, and they consist primarily of triglycerides, which are composed of glycerol and various types of fatty acids. Fatty acids are further grouped as saturated, monounsaturated, and polyunsaturated, depending upon the number of hydrogen atoms attached to the carbon chains. Saturated fats are solid and unsaturated fats are liquid at room temperature. Examples of saturated fats include butter and meat fat as well as hydrogenated vegetable oils. Monosaturated fat occurs primarily in vegetables and vegetable products, such as corn and olive oils and vegetable shortenings. Polyunsaturated fats have a slightly different chemical structure and are contained in the oil of seeds (e.g., sunflower, soybean) and fish.

As we noted, carbohydrates are the prime source of an energy. However, with prolonged aerobic activity, energy available in glycogen stores is exhausted in approximately one hour. During such prolonged activity, a significant amount of energy is obtained from body fat stores through the conversion of fatty acids to energy and to some extent gluconeogenesis.

As we noted, fat contains more than twice the energy per gram than carbohydrates. In addition to serving as a source of energy during prolonged activity, most fat is stored directly beneath the surface of the skin, and thereby acts to insulate the body and protect it from temperature variations. Fat stores vitamins, which are transported to the cells, and also protects many vital organs.

The most abundant sources of saturated fats include animal and milk products. While many of these saturated fats are visible in the form of meat, butter, and cream, the vast amount of fat intake is invisible in various meats, homogenized milk, yogurt, cookies, muffins, and chips to name a few. Mono- and unsaturated fats are provided in margarine, nuts, and olives. Polyunsaturated fats include fats from fish, seeds, and grains.

In addition to the storage of fat soluble vitamins, fats have an interesting and important dietary niche because of their relatively slow exit from the stomach. Since satiety appears to originate in the gastrointestinal tract, this slow release may contribute to prolonged feelings of fullness and thereby delay the onset of hunger.

During the digestive process, dietary fats are broken down into simpler glycerides and fatty acids in the intestines by bile salts secreted from the gall bladder. These monoglycerides then combine with bile salts and water compounds to be absorbed into the gastrointestinal tract. However, after this absorption is complete, the monoglycerides recombine to form triglycerides in the blood stream where they find their way to fat cells for storage. Fat cells, called adipocytes, are capable of storing up to 100,000 kcal of energy in the form of triglycerides.

While some fat in the diet is necessary in order to obtain the essential fatty acids, nutritional deficiencies related to inadequate fat intake are very rare. In fact, one of the greatest nutritional problems in the modern diet is the overconsumption of fats. Most animal sources of foods contain fats. While the proportion of fat differs from one source to the next, many animal products typically consumed are high in fat. Some yielding nearly 75 percent of their calories as fat. It has been estimated that Americans consume about 42 percent of their total calories from fats. While the ideal intake of fat is somewhat controversial, experts usually agree that fat consumption should be reduced to 30 percent or lower. The National Cancer Institute has recently recommended that Americans lower their fat consumption to 25 percent of total calorie intake in order to reduce the risk of certain forms of cancer (Greenwald, Sondik, & Lynch, 1986).

Like carbohydrates and fats, the structure of proteins also contains carbon, oxygen, and hydrogen. However, in contrast to carbohydrates and fats, proteins contain nitrogen atoms. These nitrogen atoms are characteristic of proteins, and they are not found in other nutrients. The carbon, oxygen, hydrogen, and nitrogen atoms of protein are arranged in amino acids. There are twenty-three different amino acids with eight being considered essential because they are not synthesized by the body and therefore must be obtained from dietary sources. Proteins are present in every cell and are particularly important as enzymes, hormones, and DNA and RNA. Proteins are crucial for the maintenance and regulation of cell growth, the transmission of heredity in DNA and RNA molecules, and for the structure of hormones and enzymes. They play a major role in the building and repairing of most tissues in the body and other regulatory functions as well. Several amino acids serve as precursors to brain neurotransmitters and must be obtained from dietary sources. For example, tryptophan is necessary for the synthesis of serotonin, while the catecholamines—namely, dopamine, norepinephrine, and epinephrine— are synthesized from tyrosine.

Proteins are arranged in amino acids, and it is the amino acids that are the essential nutrients and not the proteins per se. Foods vary in their amino acid composition, and before cells can grow or be maintained, they require certain amino acids. Protein deficiencies will cause a low growth rate and eventually an inability to maintain essential body tissues. Since all the cells, muscle, bone, skin, or blood, are repaired and maintained as a result of the dietary protein, adequate dietary intake of protein is essential.

The amino acids consumed in the diet are broken down in the gastrointestinal tract into a simpler structure for absorption and then they are carried in the blood for action at various tissue sites. Dietary recommendations call for an intake of protein equaling approximately one gram of protein per kg of ideal body weight. So, if a person's ideal body weight is 120 lbs or 54 kg, the person would on the average require 54 grams of protein per day.

Because amino acids consist of 16 percent nitrogen, the presence of nitrogen in the diet and excrement is used as an index for studies on protein metabolism. When nitrogen or protein intake exceeds that excreted, the individual is said to be in positive nitrogen balance. Under these conditions, tissue and vital body functions can be maintained as well as enhanced and the opportunity for growth is available. In contrast, when dietary protein is insufficient, body tissue can be broken down faster than it is replenished, and a negative nitrogen balance exists.

Protein can be utilized as energy if there is insufficient intake of carbohydrates. Since nitrogen levels represent an important index of protein metabolism, adequate caloric intake should result in the excretion of nitrogen at a relatively stable rate. However, with severe dietary restriction, protein will be transferred to energy via gluconeogenesis; so protein and lean body mass are used for energy purposes resulting in an increase in nitrogen excretion, or what is called negative nitrogen balance. During periods of caloric restriction, lean body mass used for energy comes primarily from muscle, cardiac, and liver tissue rather than nerve, connective, and other organ tissue. In restricting carbohydrates, many weight reduction diets also compromise lean body mass that is converted for energy. Carbohydrates in the diet not only supply energy, they also have a protein sparing effect.

Proteins come from a wide variety of food sources that include animal and vegetable products, and they are often classified according to their quality or completeness. High quality proteins are found in dairy products, meats, and fish. These sources provide a complete set of the eight essential amino acids. Vegetables, nuts, grains, and legumes also provide sources of protein, but they are not as biologically complete. That is, these proteins do not supply all the essential amino acids necessary for growth and vital functions. Various combinations of grains, legumes, and vegetables are necessary in order to receive the essential amino acids on a strict vegetarian diet.

Clinical Intervention

The lesson that eating-disordered patients must learn is that calories are neither good nor bad, calories are simply a way of measuring the amount of energy that is available in foods. The body needs energy to function, and one of the purposes of eating is to supply the body with the energy it needs. The goal for each patient is to develop a pattern of eating and exercise that leads to long-term energy balance and weight maintenance. Figure 13.1 summarizes the concepts involved in energy balance.

Patients with eating disorders often have ambivalent feelings about carbohydrates. Many patients think that carbohydrates are fattening and

---

FIGURE 13.1 Energy Balance

The way our bodies regulate our weight is a very simple matter of energy balance. When we talk about energy balance, we are comparing how much energy you take in (in the form of calories from the food you eat) to how much energy you burn up.

To Lose Weight: Losing weight is a matter of burning more calories than you take in. We call this a calorie deficit. A defict (burning more than you eat) of 3500 calories will result in losing about 1 pound of body weight. If you cut back by 500 calories a day, you can lose a pound a week. Running a deficit of 1000 calories per day will result in losing 2 pounds per week and so forth.

To Gain Weight: Gaining weight is a matter of consuming more calories than you burn up. We call this a calorie excess. If you eat 3500 calories more than you burn up (have a 3500 calorie excess), the energy you do not burn is stored as 1 pound of fat. Eating 500 calories a day more than you burn will result in gaining a pound a week.

To Maintain Weight: Maintaining your weight is a matter of matching your food intake to your body's energy needs. If you eat about as much as you burn up, your weight will stay the same.

How Do We Burn Calories?

For now, we can think of our body's energy needs as having two parts. First, are the calories we burn performing the activities of daily life. Every time you move, walk, lift something, or even think (yes, thinking burns a few calories), you use up energy to do the work. The heavier you are, the more energy it takes to perform work. Muscle burns more energy per pound than fat. If you lose weight, the work gets easier and you burn up fewer calories for most activities. When you build up muscle through exercise, your body needs a few more calories per pound.

The second part of our body's energy needs is called our resting metabolic rate. It takes energy to keep us alive. To breathe, pump blood, get rid of waste, digest our food, all require the use of energy. Resting metabolic rate depends on how heavy you are and on unique individual differences.

When trying to decide what you should eat and how much, your goal is to consume an amount of energy that matches your body's energy needs. We all need energy to survive. The goal of good nutrition is to eat enough energy to meet our body's needs but not so much energy that it results in getting fat.

should be avoided. Data from the Food Survey (see Chapter 8) showed that disordered eating behavior is associated with phobic fear of breads and grains. On the other hand, most eating-disordered patients can eat fruits and vegetables without much fear. In treating eating-disordered patients, it is important to assess the individual's beliefs about carbohydrates and their role in the diet and to help clear up any misconceptions that the patient has about the importance of carbohydrates as a source of food energy. In general, most eating-disordered patients will need to be counseled to increase their intake of starches in the form of breads, rice, pasta, and legumes.

While many binge foods and forbidden foods are high in carbohydrates, most of the problem foods for eating-disordered patients are also significant sources of fat. For example, many patients think that ice cream, doughnuts, and chips, and cookies are fattening because they are full of sugar. These foods, however, are also significant sources of dietary fat and should be eaten in limited quantities for that reason. Some bulimics will binge on bread or crackers. These patients will have to learn to continue to keep these kinds of foods in their diets while learning to moderate and control the amount they eat.

Counseling eating-disordered patients on protein intake usually involves helping these patients obtain adequate quantities of high quality protein while avoiding its overconsumption. Many eating-disordered patients believe that protein is good for you, and that a good diet is high in protein and low in carbohydrates. This belief is partly a function of popular myths that have been derived from ketogenic fad diets, and partly a matter of not understanding the way the body handles its need for energy.

Eating-disordered patients are critically concerned with their body weight and with the possibility of becoming obese. One possibility that must be faced when treating eating-disordered patients is that their food intake after treatment will result in weight gain. Nutrition education and counseling in eating-disordered patients must focus on reducing the intake of dietary fat to 30 percent or less of total calorie intake in order to prevent unwanted weight gain.

Most people are unaware of the fat content of the foods they eat. Even people who do not use large quantities of butter or salad oils still consume too much fat. Fat is often added during baking, frying, or processing of foods. Nearly all foods derived from animal sources contain fats. One of the major tasks of nutrition education is to sensitize people to the fat, especially hidden fats, that are contained in their diets. In counseling the patient with an eating disorder, it is important that the role of fat in weight gain be stressed, and that the patient learn to identify sources of dietary fat and replace these with foods that are high in carbohydrates. Table 13.1 presents a list of high fat foods and an alternative list of low fat foods.

TABLE 13.1 Food Substitutions

High Fat Foods		
Bread stuffing	Nut bread	Hushpuppies
French toast	Pancakes	Waffles
Granola	Fried rice	Snack crackers
Cake	Cheesecake	Doughnuts
Pastry	Cookies	Snack pies
Candy bars	Chocolate	Caramel
Fudge	Whole milk	Milk shakes
Ice cream	Cheese	Cream
Whipped cream	Sour cream	Deviled eggs
Fried eggs	Butter	Salad oil
Lard	Avocado	Hamburger
Fried meat	Ribs	Bacon
Lunch meat	Hot dogs	Sausage
Fried fish	Tuna (in oil)	Fried shrimp
Fried chicken	Chicken skin	Refried beans
Nuts	Peanut butter	Custard
Pudding	Salad dressing	Mayonnaise
Caesar salad	3-bean salad	Cheese sauce
Hollandaise sauce	White sauce	Gravy
Cheese puffs	Potato chips	Corn chips
Dips	Cheese soup	Bean with bacon soup
Chowders	Cream soups	Fried vegetables
French fries	Mashed potatoes	Au gratin potatoes

Low Fat Foods		
Coffee	Tea	Soft drinks
Alcoholic beverages	Bread	Rolls
Bagels	English muffins	Plain tortillas
Cereals	Cooked cereal	Bran
Pasta	Rice	Melba toast
Rye Krisp	Saltines	Jelly beans
Marshmallows	Jelly	Hard candy
Skim milk	Instant milk	Buttermilk
Nonfat yogurt	Sherbet	Ice milk
Egg whites	Dried beef	Well-trimmed lean beef
Lowfat lunch meats	Turkey Ham	Fish (broiled)
Tuna (water pack)	Chicken	Giblets
Legumes (dried beans)	Gelatin	Fruit salad
Low cal dressing	Steak sauce, etc.	Catsup
Pickles	Vinegar	Popcorn (no butter)
Popsicles	Pretzels	Rice cakes
Broth or bouillon	Vegetables	Potatoes (no fat added)
Vegetable juices	Fruits	Fruit juices

Fluid Balance, Minerals, and Electrolytes

The process of homeostatic compensation evident in weight regulation also extends to the regulation of body fluid. Water is the most abundant compound in the human body comprising from 55 percent to 70 percent of the body weight of adults. It is necessary for all metabolic functions including digestion, absorption of nutrients, circulation of nutrients to the cells, and excretion of waste. Water is present in all cells and body fluids where it serves primarily as a solvent, permitting a wide array of essential body functions. Cells require a fluid medium with relatively stable osmotic pressure that is partly maintained by a balance of minerals and electrolytes. Whereas the body can tolerate long periods of time without food, maintenance of water balance is essential for survival.

There are approximately thirty chemical elements in the body many of which are essential for vital function and growth. Minerals are a group of chemical elements required for the maintenance of body functions. Accordingly, the minerals include calcium, phosphorus, iron, iodine, magnesium, sulfur, zinc, and fluorine. Sodium, potassium, and chloride are minerals needed by the body for regulation of fluid balance, acid-base balance, and functioning of the nervous system. These mineral ions are needed in relatively large amounts (1,000–5,000 mg/day) and are referred to as the electrolytes. A number of other elements such as copper, molybdenum, selenium, and manganese are needed in very small amounts and are called trace elements. Minerals and trace elements are vital for body functions. For example, iron is recommended in amounts from fifteen to eighteen mg a day for adolescents and adults. An intake below this level can lead to anemia and increased susceptibility to infection. Eating a variety of foods usually provides sufficient quantities of most minerals and trace elements. However, it is not unusual for women who severely restrict their dietary intake to have dry and patchy skin, and lose large amounts of hair, as a result of low levels of essential minerals and trace elements.

Electrolytes are minerals that play a major role in the regulation of fluid balance, osmotic pressure, acid-base balance, and the electro conduction of nerve and muscle tissues. Electrolytes are dissolved in body fluids as electrically charged ions. As such, electrolytes are involved in a wide variety of regulatory physiological processes. The most important electrolytes are sodium, potassium, and chlorine with the magnesium, calcium, and phosphorus ions also playing important roles in body regulation. In addition to regulating the conduction of electrical charges, sodium conserves fluids and cell osmolarity; potassium performs functions similar to sodium but is also of major importance in the metabolic activity of muscle and cardiac tissue; chlorine participates with sodium in the maintenance of osmotic pressure of cellular fluid; and magnesium plays an important role in the function of muscle, nerve, and cardiac tissue. Calcium is necessary for blood clotting, nervous system electrical transmission, and normal cardiac function. However, 99 percent of body calcium is contained in the bones. Phosphorus is important in the utilization of cellular energy.

The concentration of electrolytes is regulated in a relatively narrow range. Some electrolytes such as sodium are stored, and thereby well-conserved in the body, while others such as potassium are not stored, and must be replenished regularly from dietary sources. Since potassium plays a major role in muscle and cardiac function, an adequate dietary intake must be maintained due to the body's poor conservation and storage of this important electrolyte. Potassium levels are often low in those with eating disorders because of insufficient nutritional intake or high rates of potassium loss due to purging. It is not unusual for patients with eating disorders to experience irregular heart beats, dizziness, fainting spells, and muscle cramps due to inadequate levels of potassium, sodium, and other electrolytes. In fact, it appears that the deaths of individuals with anorexia and bulimia nervosa can be attributed in part to low electrolyte levels.

Vitamins

Vitamins consist of organic compounds that are required by the body in very small quantities to perform specific metabolic functions. These substances must be obtained from the diet for they are not produced in the body. There are two broad categories of vitamins, namely, water and fat soluble. The fat soluble vitamins, A, D, E, and K, are stored in the fat cells throughout the body. Because of this storage, low levels of dietary intake of these vitamins are compensated for by a release of the vitamins from the fat cells, and dietary intake on a daily basis is not necessary. In contrast, water soluble vitamins circulate in body fluids and thus have a limited storage capacity. Water soluble vitamins, such as vitamin C and the B-complex, must be consumed daily. Interestingly, because of the storage capacity of fat soluble vitamins, excessive intake of these vitamins can lead to toxic reactions. In contrast, water soluble vitamins taken in excess are simply excreted in urine.

As far as the nutritional needs for vitamins are concerned, people need to have adequate amounts of vitamins but no more than that. In order to provide standards that can be used to define adequate vitamin intake, the Food and Nutrition Board of the National Research Council (1980) has established a set of recommended dietary allowances for adequate levels of vitamin intake for men and women of different ages. The Food and Drug Administration in 1973 established the U.S. RDAs for the purpose of nutrition labeling. The U.S. RDAs reflect the highest allowance of each vitamin for persons older than four, excluding pregnant or lactating women. The logic of the U.S. RDAs is that they reflect a level of vitamin intake that is adequate for the vast majority of Americans. Table 13.2 summarizes the essential vitamins, the U.S. RDAs, and typical food sources of each vitamin.

TABLE 13.2 Summary of the Essential Vitamins

Vitamin	U.S. RDA	Sources
A	5000 I.U.	Liver, sweet potatoes, carrots, greens, pumpkin, squash, broccoli, lettuce, tomatoes, melons, apricots, nectrines
D	400 I.U.	Fortified milk, exposure to sunlight
E	30 I.U.	Nuts, seeds, vegetable oils, spinach
K	70–140 μg	Chewing tobacco, turnip greens, broccoli, lettuce, beef liver, cabbage
C	60 mg	Green pepper, broccoli, greens, tomatoes, potatotes, oranges, strawberries, lemons, limes, melons
Folic Acid	.4 mg	Liver, asparagus, greens, broccoli, okra, brussels sprouts, walnuts, peanuts, almonds, orange juice, legumes
Thiamin	1.5 mg	Pork chops, ham, beef liver, Brazil nuts, pecans, barley, wheat germ, oatmeal, legumes, brewer's yeast
Riboflavin	1.7 mg	Liver, veal, beef, eggs, barley, milk, cheese, greens, broccoli, asparagus, brewer's yeast
Niacin	20 mg	Nuts, peanut butter, peas, lima beans, corn, collard greens, cottage cheese, steak, chicken
B_6	2 mg	Liver, pork, beef, chicken, fish, legumes, potatoes, greens, tomatoes, broccoli, rice, wheat germ, whole wheat bread, milk, cottage cheese, avocado, banana, raisins, walnuts
B_{12}	6 μg	Beef, liver, ham, fish, eggs, milk, cheese
Biotin	.3 mg	Beef liver, oatmeal, clams, soybeans, milk
Pantothenic Acid	10 mg	Liver, eggs, mushrooms, eggs, chicken, milk

Adequate intake of vitamins is something that patients need to be concerned about. However, there is a trend toward the use of vitamin supplements. Some sources estimate that nearly 40 percent of the American public uses vitamin supplements (Clydesdale & Francis, 1985). Large doses of vitamins that greatly exceed the RDAs have not been shown to have any nutritional benefit. Some vitamins, especially the fat soluble vitamins, can be toxic if consumed in large quantities.

The best advice that can be given to patients to insure adequate intake of vitamins is to eat a variety of foods. If an eating-disordered patient is eating a very restricted diet, or if calorie intake is low, then a multiple vitamin supplement that supplies approximately 100 percent of the U.S. RDAs can be recommended. Many eating-disordered patients are very health conscious, and some may be consuming mega-doses of vitamins. This practice should be discouraged since it has no proven benefit and places the individual at risk for vitamin overdose toxicities.

Nutrient Density

An optimal diet is a complicated goal that involves consuming adequate amounts of macro- and micronutrients without eating so much food that weight gain occurs. The achievement of this goal does not depend upon eating any one food. Instead, a variety of foods must be consumed in order to meet nutritional needs. Clydesdale and Francis point out that there is no such thing as a nutritious food since the value of any food is relative to the other foods an individual is consuming. Likewise, there is no such thing as a junk food, only junk diets.

While Clydesdale and Francis have made the important point that evaluation of a person's food intake must be based on their overall pattern and not on the consumption or failure to consume single foods, there needs to be a way of determining the potential contribution any particular food can make to an overall balanced diet. The nutrient density of a food is one way of measuring its potential for making a contribution to a healthy diet. Nutrient density refers to the ratio of nutrients in a food to the number of calories in the food. A nutrient dense food is one that contains many essential nutrients per calorie while a food with low nutrient density is essentially empty calories (it provides many calories without providing essential nutrients).

The process of nutrition education in patients with eating disorders may be facilitated by introducing the idea of nutrient densities. The main value of this concept is that it gives patients a way to evaluate some of their problem foods. Many patients are surprised to find that some of their forbidden foods, such as a vegetarian pizza, are actually foods with high nutrient density. Other forbidden foods, such as french fries, can be seen as having low nutrient densities. However, using the concept of nutrient density, the patient can be made to see that it is the frying of the potatoes that lowers the nutrient density. Potatoes, when prepared without extra fat, actually have high nutrient density for some nutrients.

Dietary Goals

A fair amount of controversy surrounds the definition of a sound and nutritious diet. A number of sources can help, such as looking at the percentage of RDAs an individual obtains from their typical food intake. Several government and scientific agencies have issued guidelines for a healthy diet that go beyond simply meeting the RDAs. These guidelines are summarized in Table 13.3.

The Basic Food Groups

While there are several different ways to group foods for the purpose of nutritional education, the use of the four food groups is simple and straightforward. The four food groups are quite useful when attempting to help patients develop an overall well-balanced diet. Other grouping systems (such at the diabetic exchange system) may be more useful for specific purposes such as controlling intake of specific macro- or micronutrients. The four food groups are milk, meats, fruits and vegetables, and grains and cereals. Table 13.4 presents the four food groups and recommendations for the number of servings each day required to obtain a nutritionally adequate diet.

CLINICAL RECOMMENDATIONS

A registered dietitian should be a key member of any multidisciplinary eating disorders treatment team. Dietitians, in order to be optimally effective, need to broaden their role from one of prescribing diets and teaching them to patients to being integrally involved in helping patients translate these recommendations into lifestyle changes. This will require training and practice in using some of the behavioral techniques described in Chapter 14.

Other health professionals, especially those practicing in a setting in which a dietitian is not routinely available, need to acquire a basic knowledge of nutrition. It is not enough to help a patient begin eating three meals a day and avoid eating binges. Instead, it is important that the nutritional adequacy of the diet also be examined. We have provided some basic

TABLE 13.3 Nutritional Guidelines

Agency	Goals
Senate Select Committee on Nutrition and Human Needs	Dietary goals for the United States (1977) 1. To avoid overweight, consume only as much energy (calories) as is expended. If overweight, decrease energy intake and increase energy expenditure. 2. Increase the consumption of complex carbohydrates and naturally occurring sugars from about 28% of energy intake to about 48% of energy intake. 3. Reduce consumption of refined and other processed sugars by about 45% to account for about 10% of total energy intake. 4. Reduce overall fat consumption from approximately 40% to about 30% of energy intake. 5. Reduce saturated fat consumption to account for about 10% of total energy intake; and balance that with polyunsaturated and monosaturated fats, which should account for about 10% of intake each. 6. Reduce cholesterol consumption to about 300 mg. per day. 7. Limit the intake of sodium by reducing the intake of salt (sodium chloride) to about 5 grams per day.
U.S. Department of Agriculture	Dietary guidelines for Americans (1980) 1. Eat a variety of foods. 2. Maintain ideal weight. 3. Avoid too much fat, saturated fat, and cholesterol. 4. Eat foods with adequate starch and fiber. 5. Avoid too much sugar. 6. Avoid too much sodium. 7. If you drink alcohol, do so in moderation.
National Research Council	Toward healthful diets (1980) 1. Select a nutritionally adequate diet from the foods available, by consuming each day appropriate servings of dairy products, meats, legumes, vegetables and fruits, and cereal and breads. 2. Select as wide a variety of foods in each of the major food groups as is practicable in order to ensure a high probability of consuming adequate quantities of all essential nutrients. 3. Adjust dietary energy intake and energy expenditure so as to maintain appropriate weight for height; if overweight, achieve appropriate weight reduction by decreasing total food and fat intake and by increasing energy expenditure.

TABLE 13.3 (continued)

Agency	Goals
	4. If the requirement for energy is low (e.g., reduce diet), reduce consumption of foods such as alcohol, sugars, fats, and oils which provide calories but few other essential nutrients. 5. Use salt in moderation; adequate but safe intakes are considered to range between 3 and 8 grams of sodium chloride daily.

National Cancer Institute	Dietary Objectives (1986)
	1. By 1990
	   i. Per capita consumption of fiber from grains, fruits, and vegetables will increase to 15 grams or more per day.
	   ii. Per capita consumption of fat will decrease to 30% or less of total calories.
	2. By 2000
	   i. Per capita consumption of fat will decrease from 40 to 25% or less of calories.
	   ii. Per capita consumption of fiber from grains, fruits, and vegetables will increase to 20–30 grams per day, from 8–12 grams per day.

TABLE 13.4 The Four Food Groups

Food Group	Servings/Day	Types of Foods	Nutrient Content
Meat	2 or more	Beef, pork, fish, poultry, nuts, legumes, eggs	Protein, iron, thiamin riboflavin, niacin, B_6, B_{12}, zinc, fats
Milk	2 or more	Milk, cheese, ice cream, yogurt	Calcium, riboflavin, protein, vitamins, carbohydrates, fats
Fruits and Vegetables	4 or more	Variety of green vegetables, yellow vegetables, citrus fruits, and other fruits	Carbohydrates, fiber, vitamins, minerals
Bread and Cereal	4 or more	Whole grain and enriched breads, rice, pasta, ready-to-eat cereals, cooked cereals, crackers	Carbohydrates, fiber, protein, vitamins, minerals

guidelines in this chapter pertaining to macronutrient composition and RDAs that health professionals who are not trained in nutrition can use to evaluate the diets of eating-disordered patients. However, if there are questions about food choice or nutritional adequacy that the clinician cannot answer, it is always appropriate to refer the patient to a registered dietitian, especially one who has experience working with eating-disordered patients.

SUMMARY

Nutrition education with eating-disordered patients involves helping these individuals develop an accurate understanding of the foods they eat, dispel myths and misconceptions about foods, and lay the foundation for the development of healthy eating patterns. Basic nutrition education can be accomplished through direct interaction supplemented by a few simple handouts. More advanced teaching can be accomplished by giving reading assignments that are appropriate to the patient's educational level. While adequate knowledge of the basic principles of nutrition is not sufficient for changing eating habits, it is usually necessary. By combining nutrition education with principles of eating behavior change, eating-disordered patients can learn to develop healthy, sensible eating patterns that result in adequate regulation of body weight without resorting to drastic methods of weight control.

The process of nutritional management in eating disorders involves three steps: (1) selection of a dietary regimen appropriate to the patient's physical status and needs, (2) educating the patient so that the patient understands the diet while insuring that food myths have been dispelled, and (3) assisting the patient in the process of integrating this new knowledge into a day-to-day lifestyle. Nutritional support is not complete until the third step has been accomplished.

14

Energy Balance Training

PURPOSE AND OBJECTIVES

Patients with anorexia and bulimia often exhibit inappropriate eating habits. These habits include skipping meals, avoiding certain nutritious foods, excessively stringent dieting, fasting, along with binge eating and self-induced vomiting. The purpose of energy balance training is to teach patients how to manage body weight at a healthy level by developing appropriate eating and exercise habits.

RATIONALE

There are a variety of ways of conceptualizing the chaotic and disordered eating behavior that is observed in bulimia (see Chapters 6 and 7). One approach is to view many of the behaviors as ineffective strategies of weight regulation. Likewise, the stringent dieting observed in restricting anorexics can be thought of as ways of coping with the fear of obesity. While there are many sources of information about healthy ways to control weight, many adolescents develop highly inappropriate ways of coping with the problem of weight management.

The problem of weight management can be viewed as a problem of developing self-management skills and of learning how to respond to a variety of different eating situations in a manner that promotes long-term energy balance (Schlundt & Zimering, 1988). Essentially, behavioral problems associated with failure to control weight are viewed as deficits in self-management skills. W.G. Johnson and Brief (1983) and W.G. Johnson, Corrigan, and Mayo (1987) have discussed the application of the energy balance model to bulimia. Many of the principles used in this chapter have been derived from behavioral programs for the treatment of obesity (e.g., W.G. Johnson & Stalonas, 1981).

The skill acquisition approach has been employed extensively in the area of interpersonal problems (Schlundt & McFall, 1985; McFall, 1982). The approach is based on the idea that interpersonal problems, such as passivity and shyness, are created by a failure to acquire the social skills needed to behave competently across a variety of interpersonal situations. This perspective has been fairly used, resulting in both assessment and intervention methods. We propose that this highly useful perspective can be applied to self-management skills in the area of weight control and eating behavior in the treatment of eating disorders.

Acceptance of the skills perspective in eating behavior has several major implications. First, it causes us to focus our assessment at the behavioral level. There are two issues to be resolved: What situations in the individual's life create problems in the area of self-regulation of eating behavior and how is the individual currently behaving in these situations (see Chapter 7). These questions are approached through the use of behavioral assessment techniques, such as the DIET questionnaire, behavioral interviews, and the use of self-monitoring diaries (see Chapter 8).

In general, the problem that energy balance training addresses is poor self-control over food intake and the mismanagement of diet and exercise. The goal is to establish eating and exercise habits that will result in the long-term maintenance of a healthy weight along with the absence of any dangerous or self-destructive behaviors. The method used is skill acquisition training in which new ways of responding to problem situations are identified and implemented.

W.G. Johnson, Schlundt, Kelley, and Ruggiero (1984) used energy balance training in conjunction with exposure with response prevention to treat a small group of patients with bulimia nervosa. The results indicated that energy balance training was effective in both normalizing eating habits and reducing the frequency of self-induced vomiting. W.G. Johnson, Schlundt, and Jarrell (1986) provided a further test of these procedures in the treatment of eight bulimia nervosa patients. Again, energy balance training helped reduce the frequency of both bingeing and vomiting and seemed to add to the efficacy of exposure with response prevention. Many other bulimia treatment programs include components of energy balance training (e.g., Agras, 1987; Fairburn, 1981, 1985; C.L. Johnson & Connors, 1987; Mitchell, Hatsukami, Goff et al., 1985; Connors, Johnson, & Stuckey, 1984; Kirkley, Schneider, Agras, & Bachman, 1985).

PROCEDURES

Energy balance training can be accomplished quite well within weekly outpatient therapy sessions. Of course, the inpatient environment offers more extensive opportunities for the supervised development of appropriate eating habits and the establishment of a regular exercise regimen. The length of time required depends on how extensive the self-control skill deficits are and on how quickly the patient is able to master new self-management strategies. Typically, we spend four to eight weeks working on energy balance in outpatient treatment with inpatient treatment taking from ten to fifteen days.

Initially, energy balance training starts with a thorough assessment involving the use of questionnaires, interview forms, eating and activity diaries, clinical interviews, and perhaps a test of physical fitness (Chapter 8). The goal of the assessment is to identify problem areas and to set goals. While the initial target of this intervention will probably be the reduction or elimination of binge eating, the goals of the treatment should go beyond the elimination of risky behavior and incorporate the acquisition of eating and exercise behaviors that will result in effective long-term weight stabilization and a healthier life style. The energy balance of many patients with bulimia nervosa is so out of control that they must totally relearn how to eat.

In the rest of this section, we will identify some of the areas in which self-control deficits are often observed. For each area, goals and suggested interventions will be discussed. We do not wish to suggest that these are the only problem areas that will be encountered. The basic methods of skill acquisition training can be used to address a problem area not included in this section.

Increasing Resistance to Temptation

Many times eating binges are provoked by situational cues (see Chapter 7). This problem can be conceptualized in general as a problem of resisting temptation. That is, when a situation occurs in which the individual is confronted with eating cues, the kind of response that is called for is a noneating response or a response that involves eating a more appropriate kind of food. The sight of food, the smell of food, seeing a TV commercial, certain activities, seeing another person eat food, and having to handle food are all examples of food cues that can create temptation. The temptation may be to binge or it may be to nibble. The problem is that nibbling often results in more nibbling which, after the person has broken the rules of dietary restraint, ends up in an eating binge.

Procedures
The first step in dealing with temptations is to identify the cues to which the patient is most responsive. This can be done by interview, by using eating diaries, or both. In general, it is best to construct a written list of temptation situations, the kinds of food that are eaten in each situation, how often the temptation situation turns into an eating binge, and the consequences of eating and not eating in that situation.

Goal setting involves determining which situations are actually appropriate eating situations and which should be responded to with noneating behavior. Temptation situations in which the goal is not to eat can be approached in one of two ways. Either the cue can be removed from the environment and the problem situation avoided or the patient can learn to substitute a noneating response for the inappropriate eating behavior.

The first approach has been referred to as stimulus control. The idea behind stimulus control is that people can learn to control their behavior by learning to control their environments. Stimulus control often involves changing the home environment, since this is the place where people have the most control over food and eating cues. Stimulus control strategies include storing food out of sight, limiting eating to certain places in the house, and removing problem foods from the house entirely. Another aspect of stimulus control strategies involves eliminating the constant pairing of eating with other activities. The idea is that if eating is often paired with television viewing, this behavior is soon established as an eating cue. By changing the relationship between behavior and the environment through eliminating the pairing of food and television, the associative link is broken, and television viewing is no longer an eating cue.

People do not have perfect control over the presence of food cues in their environments or over the actions and eating habits of other people. While certain situations can be avoided altogether, stimulus control alone will never suffice as the only self-control strategy for resisting temptation since it is impossible to remove all eating cues from the environment.

To complement stimulus control, a strategy called *behavior substitution* is used. For every situation in which inappropriate eating behavior cannot be handled using stimulus control, the individual is asked to come up with a list of alternative behaviors that she can substitute. These behaviors should be activities that occupy her attention, keep mind and hands busy, and cannot be done while eating. The following list presents a number of potential substitute behaviors patients can use to help resist temptation and to prevent binge eating.

1. Chewing sugar free gum
2. Wearing a surgical mask
3. Taking a walk
4. Working on a craft or hobby

5. Cleaning the bathroom
6. Vacuuming and other housework
7. Taking a hot bath (or cold shower)
8. Talking to someone face-to-face or on the phone
9. Writing a letter
10. Reading a book
11. Meditating or praying
12. Relaxing
13. Doing yard or garden work
14. Paying your bills or balancing your checkbook
15. Making love with your spouse
16. Exercising
17. Going for a drive in the car
18. Counting backwards from 3,000 by sevens (try it!)
19. Moving to another room in the house
20. Pounding nails into a large block of wood
21. Listening to music
22. Going to the bathroom
23. Going to a movie
24. Going shopping (not at a grocery store)
25. Running errands

Reducing the Likelihood of Binge Eating

Binge eating is often the direct focus of treatment. The problem of knowing when to inhibit eating once it has started is different from the problem of knowing when to and when not to start eating (resisting temptation).

The first step of the treatment is to conduct an assessment of the situations in which binge eating occurs for each patient. When possible, eating in some situations should be eliminated entirely. In this case the treatment becomes one of using the strategies for resisting temptation. However, in other instances, eating in the binge situation is appropriate and the goal of treatment must become helping the patient gain control over the amount and kinds of foods eaten. A functional analysis of bingeing should be conducted using interview and self-monitoring data in order to identify the emotional or interpersonal antecedents and consequences.

Binge eating can be modified into appropriate, well-controlled eating behavior by following four simple steps.

Determining Appropriate Portion Sizes

We are constantly surprised to find that many of our bulimic and anorexic patients do not have any idea what an appropriate portion of food is. They have spent most of their lives either eating next to nothing or stuffing themselves. The first step in overcoming binge eating is to develop an awareness of nutrition and of the appropriate amounts of different types of foods to eat. For each situation, the patient will need help in identifying the foods that are available, selecting which foods to eat, and determining the appropriate portion sizes (see Chapter 13).

Selecting a Stopping Rule
It is very important that bulimic patients learn never to start eating without first determining how to decide when to stop. While the easiest way is to serve just the right amount of food on a plate, then to stop when the plate is finished, there are some situations in which this is not possible. In these instances, the patient needs to learn to ask herself how much food she can eat and how she will be able to tell when to stop. At first, the therapist may have to work out the stopping rules with the patient on a situation-by-situation basis. It is important to give the patient guidance so that her stopping rules are realistic and not overly stringent.

Slowing the Rate of Eating
Binge eating is often characterized by rapid ingestion of food. The food is eaten while standing, walking, or performing other activities. One strategy for breaking the habit of binge eating is to change the topography of eating behavior. Several strategies can accomplish this, including (1) putting down the fork or spoon between bites, (2) pausing in the middle of a meal, (3) eating off plates with utensils while sitting at a table, and (4) concentrating on enjoying the taste and sensation of eating.

Limiting Second Helpings
Several tactics can be used to aid patients to avoid taking repeated helpings of food. These are often simple things like serving food and putting the leftovers away before sitting down to eat, eating in the dining room instead of the kitchen, avoiding family style meals, or positioning oneself away from the food at a party or social gathering. With some brain storming, it is always possible to find tactics that will make getting extra helpings more difficult. The rationale for making seconds more difficult is to require extra thought and effort to get seconds in order to increase the likelihood that the person can use a resisting temptation strategy between wanting seconds and actually getting them. The list that follows summarizes the strategies used to reduce the frequency of binge eating.

1. Choose the right amount of food to start with.
    a. Become familiar with portion sizes by weighing and measuring your food.
    b. Have a calorie goal for each meal and choose foods that will help you meet that goal.

c. Serve food on smaller plates to make the portions look bigger.
   d. Have someone else who knows proper portion sizes dish out your food.
   e. Never skip meals as a way to lose weight. Avoid becoming very hungry.
2. Know when to stop.
   a. Eat only what you serve.
   b. Decide when to stop before you start eating.
3. Slow down the speed of your eating.
4. Put the food away before you start to eat to make getting seconds much more difficult.

Modifying Food Choices

Eating a diet that allows for long-term maintenance of an ideal weight is a function of both the quantity of food and the kinds of foods eaten. Nearly every bulimic patient requires some nutrition counseling (see Chapter 13). For some this involves a little feedback on increasing breads and other complex carbohydrates in their diets since these foods are often phobically avoided. For others, whose eating has vacillated between stringent dieting and bingeing for years, more extensive nutrition counseling is indicated.

The basis for nutrition counseling typically involves teaching the concept of food groups and helping the patient learn to eat a balanced diet with a variety of foods. Most patients require some encouragement to increase their intake of fruits, vegetables, and high fiber grains. While many will have to decrease their intake of simple sugars, most are aware that this change needs to be made. Often, however, they are unaware of the hidden fat content of their diet. Nutritional goals attempt to achieve an ideal macronutrient intake of 55 percent to 60 percent carbohydrates, 15 percent to 20 percent protein, and 20 percent to 25 percent fat. Nobody can or should eliminate all fat from their diets. Instead, it is advisable to increase the percentage of calories from carbohydrates and lower the percentage from fats. Some strategies to accomplish this are:

1. Do not add fat to food in the form of butter, salad dressings, mayonnaise, or cream sauces.
2. Change preparation methods from frying to boiling, broiling, charcoal grilling, and baking.
3. Substitute low-fat meat and dairy products for high-fat products (e.g., chicken for beef).
4. Substitute fruits, vegetables, and breads (good carbohydrate sources) for high-fat foods like candy bars.

5. Read labels and choose processed foods lower in fat.
6. Use special low-fat formulations of certain foods like salad dressings.
7. Limit your serving size when eating high-fat foods like pizza and steak.

Learning to Eat in Positive Social Situations

Very few social events in our culture do not involve eating food. We eat at weddings, funerals, sporting events, movies, on dates, going out to celebrate, at parties, receptions, showers, business meetings, conventions, family reunions, holidays, and church socials. Not only do social events universally involve eating food, but the kinds of foods are usually prescribed by convention. Often the kinds of foods served are forbidden foods to the individual with an eating disorder.

Positive social eating can be a real problem for those who, because of their jobs, are required to attend many social functions. It is also a problem for people who have large families nearby and who have many friends who get together frequently. The eating-disordered person is no different. The data suggest that an individual with an eating disorder is more likely to binge and purge when returning home from a social event (Schlundt, Johnson, & Jarrell, 1986). While the amount of food eaten at a social event may be less than the typical binge, the kinds of foods eaten may violate self-imposed rules and elicit fear of weight gain. These perceived rule violations may result in a subsequent loss of control that culminates in bingeing and purging.

It is neither possible nor desirable to solve this problem by avoiding social situations altogether. As discussed in Chapter 7, many anorexic and bulimic individuals attempt to do so and end up socially isolated as a result. The treatment of eating disorders cannot involve advice to shun social gatherings in order to avoid having to eat at them. In treatment of eating disorders, the only realistic goal is to help the patient learn to eat at social gatherings without inducing undue weight anxiety or later binge eating.

The solution to social eating involves modifying the way the patient eats at these gatherings and planning ahead to accommodate the extra calories that are often consumed. Eating-disordered patients must accept that social eating is part of life and must learn to live with it. Not only must they learn to eat comfortably at social gatherings, but they must also learn to do so without bingeing and purging afterwards.

Eating appropriately at social gatherings involves both avoiding overeating and undereating. Overeating should be avoided in order to help maintain an appropriate energy balance. Yet, the patient must learn to accept that overeating may occur and if so, understand that a single episode of overeating does not indicate a return to old habits or call for purging. Undereating should be avoided because it may trigger further inappropriate dieting behaviors or create conditions that eventuate in later binge eating.

Meal Planning

Planning ahead is a critical factor in learning to live comfortably with social eating. People usually know when a social event is on their calendar. The patient should determine a calorie intake that will result in weight maintenance and should use this figure as a goal in planning. When the patient enters a social setting with an unrealistically low idea of how much food should be eaten, the chances of stimulating binge eating afterwards are much increased.

The bulimic woman is encouraged to plan all meals for the day around the social event. If she must attend a social function in the evening (for example eating dinner with friends at a favorite deli or expensive French restaurant), the therapist can help her estimate how many calories she will probably eat. It is very important to be realistic in this planning and appraisal process. The patient can use a few calorie-reducing strategies to avoid overeating, but should not fool herself into thinking that she will just order a salad when everyone else is ordering full meals.

Once the patient has estimated her calorie budget for the social event, the remaining calories for the rest of the day can be budgeted. Even if it is as low as 300 or 400 calories, low-calorie/low-fat foods can be found that will not promote inappropriate dieting. Eating a variety of vegetables, breads, low-fat dairy products, and fruits can be used to manage caloric intake.

Once the patient has developed a calorie budget for the day of the social event, she should attend the event and eat within her budget. This is where training in self-control strategies is useful. First, it is important to have accurate knowledge about food and nutrition. The more knowledgeable the patient is about portion sizes and calorie values of foods, the more successful she will be at living within her budget. Another strategy is to plan the meal around the entree. It is most important to be able to estimate the calorie content of various entrees. A little assertiveness training with role playing can be useful. If the patient does not know portion sizes, then she should be able to ask the waiter or waitress. At a buffet style meal, the patient controls the portion size. The patient begins by choosing an entree she likes, but chooses one that is moderate to low in fat to allow more room for building the rest of the meal. If vegetables are available, these will add food to the meal with a relatively low cost in calories unless they are creamed or seasoned with fat. Bread adds some calories, but not as much as the butter. If the patient can avoid the butter, gravy, sauce, creamed soups, oil-based salad dressings, and other high-fat foods she will be able to have a satisfying meal and still stay within her calorie budget. Some modeling, coaching, and rehearsal may be needed to help the patient learn to ask for food prepared and served the way she wants it. It is often useful to take patients out to eat in restaurants in order to provide in vivo practice at social eating.

Being Assertive

The bulimic who is normal weight or slightly underweight may be the recipient of offers of high-fat foods in social situations. The normal weight person is sometimes viewed as being able to eat anything and as not having a good excuse to turn down food. People who are overeating do not want to be alone and may attempt to involve others. Often, offering food is just the polite thing for a host or hostess to do. It is important to be able to turn down food effectively when desired. Some patients will need to be taught how to say no appropriately. A simple, polite "No, thank you" with perhaps the addition of a compliment is the best way to turn down food. There is no need to go into elaborate explanations about diet, recovery from an eating disorder, or how much food has already been eaten. Such explanations invite further inquiry and are counterproductive.

Reducing Food Anxiety

While the first phase of dealing with social eating is to teach the patient self-control strategies so that over- and undereating can be avoided, the next step is to help the person become comfortable with eating an appropriate amount of food in social situations. This involves both cognitive therapy, in which the patient's thoughts and feelings about eating in public are examined and challenged, and guided exposure.

Helping the patient become comfortable with social eating will take more than one session of cognitive intervention. The cognitions that lead to fear of weight gain after social eating cannot be modified by simply talking about them once or twice. Instead, the cognitive techniques presented in Chapter 11 can be used.

Guided exposure involves accompanying the patient to a social setting where social eating can be practiced. Much like the exposure with response prevention sessions described earlier, it is possible to deal with the cognitions and emotions more directly by having the patient eat and then verbalize feelings. This type of intervention violates the usual practice of office psychotherapy. However, it may be quite worthwhile as a method of helping the patient learn to be comfortable with social eating. If it is not possible to accompany the patient, social eating can be prescribed as a homework assignment. The experiences of doing the homework assignment can be the basis for discussion and cognitive therapy at the next session. The following list summarizes some of the behavioral strategies that are useful for self-control in social eating situations.

1. Establish a calorie budget for the social event.
2. Plan to modify your intake during the rest of the day to increase the calories available for the social event.
3. Anticipate the foods that will be available and plan ahead.
4. Choose your foods to stay within your budget. Be realistic about portion sizes and choose carefully.
5. Be careful with salads and salad bars. Dressings and toppings are often high in fat.
6. Moderate your alcohol intake. It adds extra calories and reduces your ability to make good eating decisions.
7. Learn ways to refuse foods when they are offered.

Moderating Alcohol Consumption
In our society, alcohol is often consumed at social gatherings. It has been reported that many bulimics have considerable difficulty with alcohol abuse (Hatsukami, Eckert, Mitchell, & Pyle, 1984). Even if abusive drinking is not an issue, alcohol can loosen inhibitions and function as an antecedent to binge eating. Each patient should be counseled on alcohol use and on regulating both alcohol intake and food intake while under the influence of alcohol.

Negative Emotions

As discussed in detail in Chapter 7, negative emotions are a strong antecedent to binge eating in bulimia. The use of eating as a way to cope with negative affect may have several sources. Early childhood experiences with feeding may be one contributing factor. It is common practice to quiet a fussy infant by giving the baby something to eat or suck. In young children as well, food is used as a way to soothe hurts, both emotional and physical. In addition, food may be paired with physical comforting, holding, and touching, all of which have a soothing effect. Through classical conditioning, food becomes a conditioned stimulus that elicits tension reduction and feelings of comfort.

In addition, there is growing evidence that food may serve as a tension reducer on a physiological as well as a psychological level. Intake of foods high in carbohydrates and low in protein (which describes many of the junk foods eaten during binges) causes a change in the ratio of tryptophan to other amino acids crossing the blood-brain barrier. This influx in tryptophan increases synthesis of serotonin in the brain. Increased serotonin has been associated with feelings of calmness and drowsiness and for many bulimics, may provide a physiological basis for the tension-reducing effect of food (see Chapter 6).

Emotions like anger, fear, frustration, anxiety, sadness, depression, rejection, guilt, and boredom can serve as cues to trigger binge eating. In terms of treatment, there is a real difference between emotional eating and resisting temptation. In resisting temptation, the connection between cues and eating have developed over the years. However, the eating doesn't have the same immediate reinforcing payoff as emotional eating. In emotional eating, food is being used as a way to solve a problem or as a way to deal with the negative affect that is created by a life-problem. Not only is there an habitual connection between the cue and the eating, there is also an immediate negative reinforcement for bingeing. Food actually works in the short run as a source of comfort. Figure 14.1 presents a representation of the typical chain of events that occur in an emotional eating episode. The episode begins with some sort of stressful situation or difficult life-event. The individual may engage in an ineffective coping response, or uncontrollable stress may occur. The stressful situation gives rise to negative affect that disregulates eating, resulting in a binge/purge episode. The result is temporary escape or relief of the negative affect. If the life-event is never addressed, the person's emotional state may worsen and a cycle of repeated binge/purge episodes may occur.

As a way to solve emotional problems, food is not an effective long-term solution. In the first place, the source of the problem is not changed in any way by bingeing. If a patient is depressed about having a fight with her boyfriend, binge eating will not change the situation in the least and whatever the fight was about will remain after the binge. All that the patient has accomplished is to take a very short vacation from her bad feelings.

The relief from negative affect is often short-lived. Soon after the binge

FIGURE 14.1 Emotional Eating Behavior Chain

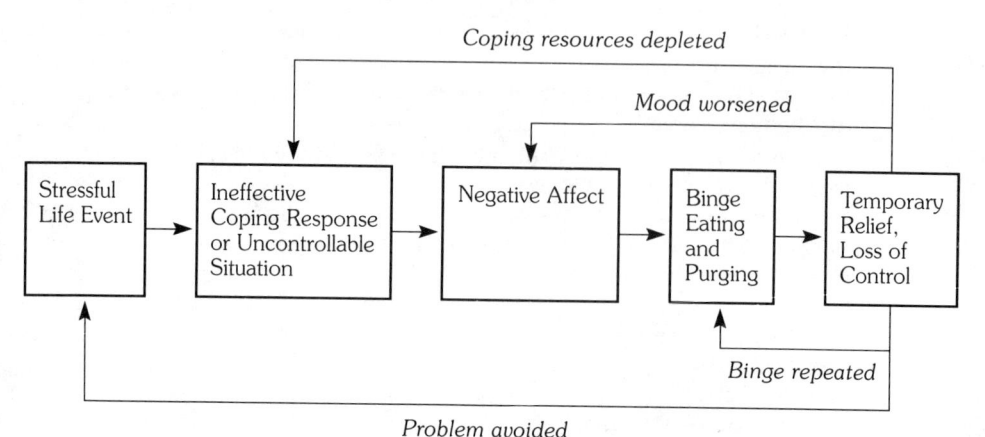

is over, the person will start to feel anxious about weight, guilty over having binged, and depressed about being unable to exercise self-control. The anxiety over weight can be eliminated by purging, but the guilt and depression may only be worsened by throwing up. Because of the guilt and depression experienced after the binge/purge episode is over, emotional eating can set up a positive feedback system in which the more a patient eats, the worse the patient feels, and the worse the patient feels, the more the patient eats. This feedback system may be mediated by endogenous opiates and insulin (see Chapter 6).

There is one other way in which stress and bad feelings affect the bulimic's ability to refrain from bingeing and vomiting. Maintaining appropriate control over food intake requires a considerable investment of time and energy. When a bulimic female enters into a stressful period in her life, she is forced to cope with the problems, even if her style of coping is ineffective. Coping takes time and energy. Time spent coping with a financial set back, for example, is time unavailable for planning meals and preparing nutritionally balanced foods. Each person has a fixed amount of time and energy resources to solve the problems of daily living. When these problems get difficult, these resources must be used to cope. Stress creates negative feelings that may trigger uncontrolled eating behavior creating further stress. Stress also takes the time and energy resources that were previously devoted to self-control efforts and may thus precipitate a relapse.

Problem Solving
Three intervention methods can be used in treating emotional eating. First, the patient is taught to engage in active, effective problem solving. The source of the bad feelings is identified and action is taken to rectify the problem. Negative moods can be controlled to a certain extent by active and effective efforts aimed at reducing the source of the stress. If the patient only copes with problems by eating, the problems will not be solved and the patient has created an additional problem, namely uncontrolled bingeing. Chapter 15 discusses techniques of personal social problem solving designed to help patients deal directly with the situations in their lives that are creating stress. Figure 14.2 depicts the problem-solving approach to interrupting emotional eating. This approach has the advantage of avoiding binge eating and loss of control, neutralizing the negative mood, either solving or accepting the problem, and strengthening the individual's personal resources for coping with life-problems.

Coping Effectively with Negative Feelings
The second intervention method is to find alternative, nondestructive ways of coping with negative emotions. Substituting alcohol or drugs for food is still a destructive way to cope. Flying into a fit of anger or rage, doing

FIGURE 14.2 Strategy 1: Problem Solving

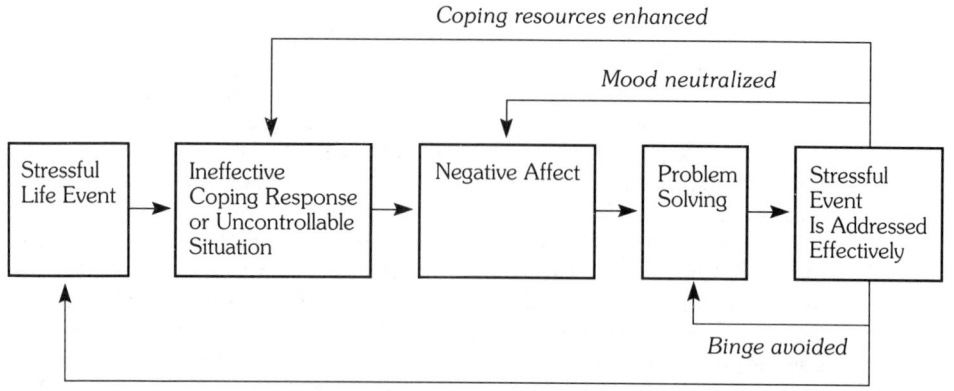

```
                    Coping resources enhanced
        ┌─────────────────────────────────────────────────┐
        │              Mood neutralized                    │
        │       ┌──────────────────────────┐              │
        ▼       ▼                          │              │
┌──────────┐ ┌──────────────┐ ┌──────────────┐ ┌─────────┐ ┌──────────────┐
│Stressful │ │Ineffective   │ │Negative Affect│ │Problem  │ │Stressful     │
│Life Event│→│Coping Response│→│              │→│Solving  │→│Event         │
│          │ │or Uncontrollable│ │            │ │         │ │Is Addressed  │
│          │ │Situation     │ │              │ │         │ │Effectively   │
└──────────┘ └──────────────┘ └──────────────┘ └─────────┘ └──────────────┘
     ▲                                              ▲
     │                                      Binge avoided
     └──────────────────────────────────────────────┘
                    Problem solved or accepted
```

things that will hurt oneself or other people are also destructive ways of coping. A constructive method for coping with negative affect is a strategy that works in the short run to relieve the emotional distress and does not have appreciable long-term negative consequences. Some methods of coping, such as exercise, may have positive long-term consequences. Some examples of positive ways of coping with bad feelings are:

1. Take a walk.
2. Do something that will keep your hands and mind busy.
3. Work on a hobby.
4. Meditate or pray.
5. Relax, especially if you use deep muscle relaxation exercises.
6. Call a friend or family member on the phone for support.
7. Visit a friend or a relative.
8. Talk to your spouse or boyfriend about the problem, ask him for help.
9. Go for a drive.
10. Go shopping.
11. Participate in an active sport activity.
12. Do something you haven't done for a long time but really enjoy.
13. Read a book or a magazine.
14. Go see a good movie (a comedy perhaps).
15. Cuddle or make love.
16. Talk to your minister or counselor.
17. Talk to a co-worker or friend you trust.

18. Go visit the zoo.
19. Go to the art museum.
20. Take a hot bath.

There are many constructive ways of coping. What separates the good strategies from the bad strategies is that positive ways of coping focus the patient's attention on something besides her problems for a while. Once she has calmed down, the patient can apply herself to ameliorating the source of stress. This strategy is illustrated in Figure 14.3.

Food Substitution
It may be unrealistic to expect patients to always refrain from eating when they are experiencing stress and negative emotions. The goal of treatment is not necessarily to have the patient never eat when feeling bad. Rather, the goal is to prevent emotional eating from triggering bingeing and purging. One strategy for accomplishing this objective is to have the patient substitute low-fat foods for the calorically dense foods that are usually consumed during a binge. Instead of eating ice cream, potato chips, or candy bars, the patient can learn to eat air-popped popcorn, sugar-free popsicles, pretzels, toast with jam, fruit, raw vegetables, or fat-free yogurt. While these foods can contribute extra unplanned calories to the patient's diet, they are unlikely to result in the creation of excess body fat. For this strategy to work, the patient must learn to view these fat-free foods as safe alternatives, to accept that occasional emotional eating is normal, and not to allow this kind of eating to disrupt her food intake at subsequent meals. When this strategy is combined with problem solving and alternative

FIGURE 14.3 Strategy 2: Coping Effectively with Negative Feelings

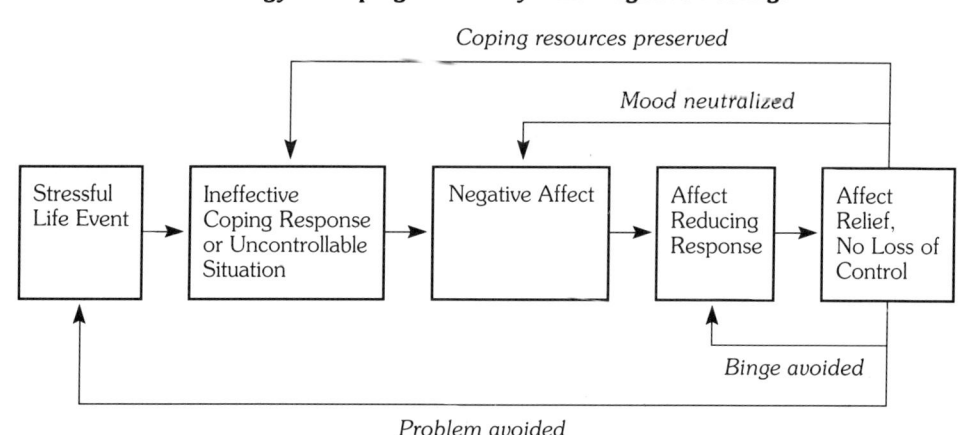

methods for coping with negative feelings, the patient is fully prepared to deal with emotions without resorting to eating binges. Figure 14.4 depicts this strategy along with its impact on the emotional eating behavior chain.

Treating Emotional Eating

The first step in therapy is to assess the kinds of interpersonal conflict situations and negative emotional reactions that trigger binge eating. A list of these situations is written together with the patient and each is described in as much detail as possible. The therapist selects a problem situation and helps the patient develop a detailed plan for how to cope with the situation and the negative emotion when it arises. The plan should include both behavioral and cognitive coping strategies. The patient may even be helped to identify safe foods that can be eaten if the patient is unable to engage in problem solving or otherwise cope with negative emotions constructively. In many cases role playing and homework assignments can be used to help the patient practice or rehearse the substitute responses. For example, if the strategy for coping with feeling depressed involves taking a walk, then the patient is assigned a homework task that involves imagining that she feels depressed then coping with the feeling by walking. Because emotional eating is so overlearned, imagery and rehearsal are necessary to help the patient develop positive coping responses.

There are apt to be many different situations in which emotions evoke binge eating. It may be necessary to work with the patient one situation at a time starting with the emotions and situations creating the most

FIGURE 14.4 Strategy 3: Food Substitution

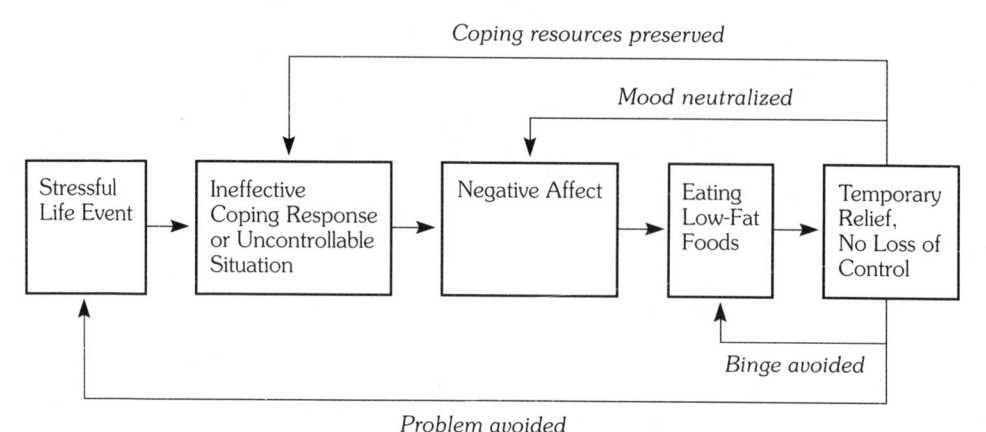

immediate difficulty. As the patient learns to use positive coping behaviors for one situation, transfer of learning to other situations will begin to occur.

If the emotional problems are overwhelming, or if the patient is clinically depressed, then adjunct pharmacological treatment may be necessary (see Chapter 9). Even if antianxiety or antidepressant medications are used, behavioral treatment designed to facilitate problem solving and teach more adaptive strategies for coping with negative emotions is still strongly indicated.

Exercise

There is considerable variability in the exercise habits of eating-disordered patients when they initially seek treatment. Part of energy balance training is to help the patient integrate appropriate exercise into his or her lifestyle. There is much we do not know about the role of exercise in weight maintenance, especially when it comes to understanding the mechanisms involved. However, the available evidence indicates that regular aerobic activity is an important element of maintaining energy balance and that the individual may derive additional psychological benefits from exercise. In this section, we will discuss exercise in energy balance training. We include basic information on exercise physiology and on aerobic activity that patients need to know along with some behavioral issues involved in maintenance of the exercise habit.

Exercise is not immediately appropriate for all patients. An anorexic with a low body weight or patients who experience chest pain or heart palpitations must be prohibited from engaging in any strenuous activity until lean weight is restored. Only after lean body weight increases or physical status improves can the patient begin to exercise, and then only at low levels of intensity.

Patients with anorexia nervosa or bulimia nervosa can be categorized into two groups with respect to their pretreatment exercise. One type of patient will be sedentary or exercise only intermittently. Most of the following material deals with helping these individuals develop regular physical activity as part of their life-style. The second group of patients is already active and may be using exercise as a way of purging.

The excessive exerciser is encouraged to continue to be active on a regular basis. However, the therapist must work to modify how these patients view the role of exercise in their lives, and help them overcome anxieties experienced as a result of reducing the frequency, intensity, or duration of activity to more appropriate levels.

It is difficult to give a good definition of what constitutes appropriate exercise. This will vary a great deal depending on the individual's genetic makeup, her interpersonal situation, and her vocational responsibilities.

As a starting point, we can define inappropriate exercise as an amount or intensity of physical activity that has negative physical, social, or vocational consequences. Exercise that results in either frequent acute injuries or chronic physical disabilities is excessive. Likewise, if the individual is spending so much time exercising that she neglects responsibilities to her family, does not have time for meaningful social relationships, or is adversely affected in her job performance then the exercise is excessive.

The second criteria for judging the appropriateness of a patient's physical activity involves identifying the reasons for exercising. If the exercise is being used as a way to compensate or punish for overeating, then the therapeutic goal is to learn to view exercise as a way of maintaining a healthy life-style. However, if the patient is training for endurance events such as triathalons, then a high level of activity may be perfectly appropriate. Again, the patient should be encouraged to view the purpose of exercise as enhancing health and well-being and to focus on the long-term benefits rather than on the short-term expenditure of calories. Accomplishing these goals with a patient may involve a number of sessions of cognitive therapy along with writing behavioral contracts to alter the timing of exercise in relation to meals and to decrease the amount of exercise to a reasonable level.

Any exercise prescription has several components: the type of exercise, its frequency, its duration, and its intensity. The maximum benefits from exercise are derived from aerobic training at least four times a week with a duration of thirty to sixty minutes each session. Aerobic activity can be interspersed with lower intensity activity, such as competitive sports, strength training using weights, or activities like yoga that enhance flexibility, on different days.

The patient needs to be taught what the term aerobic means. Whenever we exercise or do any kind of work, our bodies have to burn calories in order to turn food energy into kinetic energy (movement and heat). Burning glucose, like a burning flame, requires oxygen, which enters the blood in the lungs and then circulates in the blood stream where it is used to oxidize glucose in the cells of the body. Carbon dioxide, the waste product, passes through the body in the blood and exits in the lungs where it is exhaled (see Katch & McArdle, 1977 for a detailed description of exercise physiology).

Most of the activity of the body, including the beating of the heart and functioning of the brain, involves turning calories into energy by burning them with oxygen. This process is called aerobic metabolism. The body has a limit to the amount of oxygen that it can process and deliver to the cells. This limit is called maximum oxygen uptake, or vO_2 max.

In extreme emergencies, the body may need to burn more energy than the available oxygen will allow. For example, someone running from a wild animal would respond with all of the emergency energy available. The body is able to utilize energy without oxygen during a crisis for a relatively short period of time. This type of metabolism is called anaerobic metabolism. Anaerobic metabolism creates waste products that collect in the muscles and cause a painful burning sensation (lactic acid). If you have ever tried to sprint as fast as you could, you discovered that you could not keep it up very long because your muscles became painfully fatigued. As long as the body is burning calories using aerobic metabolism, the activity can be continued for long periods of time since aerobic metabolism is clean and sustainable.

During exercise, the body's need for oxygen increases. To supply the muscles with the oxygen they need, breathing becomes deeper and more rapid while heart rate and cardiac output increase. There is an absolute limit to how fast the heart can pump, which decreases as people age. The age-predicted maximum heart rate can be estimated by subtracting one's age from 220. A 40-year-old individual would have a predicted maximum heart rate of 180 beats per minute while a twenty-year old would have a predicted maximum heart rate of 200 beats per minute.

The heart and the lungs are like any other set of muscles. The more they are used, the stronger and more efficient they become. Certain kinds of exercise are best for strengthening the heart and lungs. This kind of exercise is called aerobic exercise or aerobic training. Aerobic training involves activities that use the large muscles of the body to sustain rhythmic and coordinated movements over time. Walking, running, riding a bicycle, using a rowing machine, and swimming are examples of these kinds of activities. When these activities are performed for thirty to sixty minutes at a time, and when they are done at an intensity that makes the heart beat at 65 percent to 85 percent of its age-predicted maximum, then the heart and lungs receive maximum benefit. Thus, a forty-year-old should work hard enough to achieve a sustained heart rate between 117 and 153 beats per minute.

When starting an exercise program, the first task is to decide on an activity that the patient will perform regularly and that will not be harmful. For someone who has been sedentary and who is not in good physical condition, walking is an excellent form of exercise. Heart rate can be increased in order to keep within the aerobic training range by increasing the speed of walking.

Patients starting an exercise program are encouraged to begin slowly and to increase intensity and duration gradually. They will like exercising more and will stick with it longer if they do not injure themselves from overexertion. Finally, the most important goal is to encourage the sedentary patient to exercise for twenty to thirty minutes at a time at low intensity. It does not matter if the heart rate does not rise to the aerobic training range.

A major obstacle in beginning an exercise program is finding the time for it. Patients should rearrange daily routines to make exercise a permanent part of their life-style. This often involves making some compromises and giving up other highly preferred activities. Advising patients to pick one time every day and to exercise at that time is a good strategy to facilitate making daily exercise habitual.

Achieving a balance between rigidly exercising at the same time each day and being flexible in order to work physical activity into a busy schedule is a challenge. Patients are encouraged to establish an habitual exercise time. However, for some patients who work flexible hours or whose schedule varies a great deal from day to day, a more flexible approach is required. Patients can use a calendar to schedule their time for an entire week first indicating their work and other required activities, such as meals and business meetings. Then, time for exercise is written into the schedule. Instruct patients to treat scheduled exercise time like any other commitment they have made. Other nonessential events and activities are scheduled around exercise times.

Unless exercise is given a high priority, it easily disappears from one's life-style. There are times in everyone's life when social events, stress, illness, or work demands, interfere with the desire or ability to exercise. No matter how many days have been missed due to these competing demands, starting to exercise again at the very first opportunity is important. The longer the person waits, the harder it is to reestablish the exercise routine.

Making exercise a social activity can help with adherence. Rather than walking alone, patients can arrange to walk with a friend or family member at regular times. This will help adherence by establishing a commitment to another person, allowing friends and family to give each other encouragement and support, and making exercise more fun. Exercise groups can be conducted with other patients, especially when inpatient treatment is involved.

Obstacles that might interfere with daily exercise can be anticipated and a plan developed for addressing each obstacle. For example, if clean clothes are needed for exercise, then a plan should be devised to make sure they are ready. If the person does not like to walk in the rain or snow, then bad weather alternatives, such as walking in an enclosed mall or riding an exercise bicycle, can be identified. The patient lists the kinds of obstacles that interfere with exercise adherence, then is helped to identify a coping strategy for each obstacle.

SUMMARY

Energy balance training involves identifying inappropriate eating and activity patterns and replacing these with more appropriate self-management skills. Both anorexic restrictors and bulimic patients will need intervention in this area, although the kinds of changes to be made will differ. With an eating-disordered patient, it is important to break the cycle of alternating between extreme restraint and uncontrolled eating. Any diet or exercise regimen that is developed should be flexible and adaptive. Patients should be encouraged to approach self-management with a degree of moderation rather than replacing one set of restrictive rules with another.

The goal of this phase of treatment is to establish a stable life-style in which nutritious eating and regular physical activity allow the patient to remain in energy balance and avoid unhealthy weight gain without resorting to dangerous practices such as purging. This component of therapy can be used by clinicians of any theoretical persuasion since it involves practical, straightforward behavioral advice.

■ 15
Personal Social Problem Solving

PURPOSE AND OBJECTIVE

We showed in Chapter 7 that many family, interpersonal, and vocational events have a direct or indirect influence on the eating behavior of anorexic and bulimic patients. The interventions described in this chapter identifies and addresses the patient's critical interpersonal problems that create stress and exacerbate the eating disorder. The objective of personal social problem solving (PSPS) is to reduce the patient's level of emotional distress by helping the patient find effective solutions to interpersonal and vocational problems.

RATIONALE

The rationale behind this treatment is twofold. First, as we showed in Chapter 7, emotional problems disrupt eating behavior and exacerbate an eating disorder. The principle objective of PSPS is to eliminate the source of emotional distress. The second assumption is that many emotional problems arise from learned deficits in coping skills and many of these deficits relate to handling social and interpersonal problems.

PSPS has arisen from a school of psychotherapy that has been called assertiveness training, social skills training, or more generally behavioral training (L'Abate & Milan, 1985; McFall, 1976, 1982). The common assumption of these approaches is that psychological difficulties arise from the interaction between an individual and his or her environment. While the physical environment is not unimportant, this perspective emphasizes the overriding importance of the social environment. There are several consistent themes in social skills training that underlie the treatment approach we will describe.

The Situational Specificity of Behavior

A long-standing debate in personality psychology concerns the empirical failure of trait theories of personality (Mischel, 1968). While the theory that human behavior can be explained in terms of generalized personality traits, such as aggressiveness or shyness, is intuitively appealing, a considerable body of empirical literature has led many personality psychologists to the conclusion that the traits displayed in a person's behavior vary from one situation to the next. The idea that the kind and quality of a person's behavior varies from one situation to the next has been referred to as the situational specificity of behavior. There are several implications of this position. One implication is that in order to make accurate predictions concerning behavior, the scientist should have information on the situational context in which that behavior occurs. Another implication is that psychological interventions must focus on the way people behave in specific situations rather than trying to restructure or modify deep-seated personality traits or structures. Thus, the emphasis of the behavioral training approach is on how people cope with the day-to-day situations that make up their lives and the implications that coping has for emotional adjustment.

The Importance of Learning in the Development of Psychological Problems

Researchers in the social skills tradition rarely argue that genetic factors are not important in emotional disorders. Instead, they contend that most social behavior is learned (see Bandura, 1969). The idea that social behavior is learned is both simple and far-reaching. The simple aspect is that a theory of social learning can provide a basis for understanding a broad array of diverse psychological problems. In addition, by understanding the laws that govern the acquisition and maintenance of social behavior, we thereby develop a basis for behavior change. A focus on learning moves our attention away from intrapsychic phenomenon and toward the study of behavior-environment interactions. Learning is an inherently adaptive process whereby the organism makes long-lasting modifications in behavior in order to accommodate to the social and physical environment. The social skills approach is a functionalist approach that views the individual's current repertoire of interpersonal behavior as representing the person's best effort to maximize reward and minimize punishment in the myriad array of day-to-day situations.

An Emphasis on Competence

The behavioral training approach is positive and optimistic. Behavior is judged according to its competence or effectiveness in coping with the tasks of everyday living. Competence refers to a value-based judgment by an observer as to how effective a particular behavior is at solving some problem in living (see Schlundt & McFall, 1985). The emphasis on competence creates a positive view of mental health. By focusing on competence rather than pathology, the skills approach emphasizes what people can do and how well they do it. When the individual's attempt to cope with a problem is judged ineffective, the behavioral training approach explores how the individual can modify his or her behavior to make it more effective. The competence orientation shifts our focus from understanding pathology to searching for solutions.

The Problem-Solving Approach

D'Zurilla and Goldfried (1971) and McFall (1976) have shown how psychological interventions from a behavioral training perspective can be framed in terms of a general problem-solving approach. Problem solving is a methodology that has been applied not only to psychotherapy, but also to nursing, engineering, business management, and many other areas of human endeavor. The problem-solving approach is a step-by-step method for generating and implementing strategies for optimizing performance within complex environments. The problem-solving process involves five discrete steps:

   1. *Problem identification and description.* The first step in solving any problem involves developing a thorough understanding of the problem. In psychotherapy, this means identification of the problem situation, the current behavioral solutions the patient is using, and the short- and long-term consequences of these solutions. It involves understanding the patient's perception of the situation, and perceptions of the current behavior and its consequences. In general, the functional analysis of Chapter 7 can be used as a framework for analyzing problems with interpersonal behavior.

   2. *Identification of goals.* Once a conceptual understanding of the problem has been developed, the next step is to describe the general

parameters of the solution. Goal specification is oriented toward identifying changes in consequences that will result from having solved the problem.

3. *Brainstorming solutions.* This aspect of problem solving is focused on generating as many alternative ways of achieving the stated goal as possible. In brainstorming, judgment and evaluation are suspended in order to arrive at a large number of alternative strategies. This is a creative step and involves cooperation between the therapist and the patient.

4. *Strategy evaluation and selection.* Once a wide range of alternatives has been identified, the next step in the problem-solving process is to evaluate the proposed solutions. Here the focus is on eliminating ineffective strategies and on choosing those strategies that have the greatest probability of working with the minimum of negative consequences.

5. *Implementation and follow-up.* Once a strategy has been selected for addressing a problem, the final step is to implement the solution and to monitor the results. This may involve additional plans for collecting data that will be used later to decide if the intervention has been effective. If the strategy does not have the intended result, then the problem-solving process is repeated in order to generate further understanding of the problem and to select alternative goals or strategies.

W.G. Johnson, Schlundt, and Jarrell (1986) included PSPS as a component of their comprehensive behavioral treatment for bulimia nervosa. This component was added to the treatment program after noting that patients who initially responded to exposure with response prevention and energy balance training tended to relapse during periods of stress and emotional crisis (W.G. Johnson, Schlundt, Kelley, & Ruggiero, 1984). In the Johnson, Schlundt, and Jarrell (1986) report, patients continued to show improvement in their eating behavior during the final PSPS phase of treatment. However, the design of the study did not allow an independent evaluation of this treatment component.

Many other eating disorder programs contain elements similar to the PSPS techniques described in this chapter. They are often labeled as assertiveness training (Weiss, Katzman, & Wolchik, 1985), coping with the antecedents of bingeing (Agras, 1987), individual psychotherapy (C.L. Johnson & Connors, 1987), and teaching adaptive skills (J.E. Mitchell, Hatsukami, Goff, et al., 1985). Other programs include a psychotherapy component that is more psychodynamic or eclectic. However, there seems to be a wide recognition in the field that treatment of anorexia and bulimia requires intervention with problems in the area of interpersonal relationships, education, and vocational function.

PROCEDURES

The procedures involved in PSPS generally follow the problem-solving model described above. In presenting the procedures, we will structure the discussion accordingly.

Problem Definition and Description

To understand a patient's social and vocational problems and how these interact with an eating disorder involves use of a variety of sources of information. In working with a patient, the therapist begins to develop a list of problem areas requiring intervention.

Some psychological or behavioral assessment procedures may be useful in the problem identification stage. However, most assessment methods are either oriented toward measuring global personality traits or are quite specific to a single area of concern, such as assertiveness.

The interview is the best source of information available for generating a list of problem areas that must be addressed by PSPS. The interview strategy should be a combination of asking the patient to volunteer problem areas and presenting a problem and asking the individual to judge the extent of difficulties in that area. The first phase of assessment is to determine a broad outline of the individual's competencies and difficulties. A checklist for the therapist to use in conducting a broad-based assessment of areas of difficulty can be found in Appendix B.

Once areas of difficulty have been identified, the next step is to prioritize the problem areas. The objective is to find the most pressing problems that require initial intervention and, if time allows, to hold less pressing problems for a later date. The problem area or areas picked for intervention should then be assessed in much greater detail. The assessment process involves delving into the situations in which the problems occur, the behaviors currently being used to cope with these situations, the cognitions and affect that accompany or elicit the behaviors, and the short- and long-term consequences of the patient's current style of coping. This phase of the assessment and problem definition process involves the collection of detailed information from the patient. It is often necessary to help patients learn to provide this kind of information through repeated prompting and feedback. For example, if the patient is describing conflict with a spouse, the therapist needs to learn about the times and places at which the conflicts occur, the issues involved, the kinds of verbal interchanges that occur, the nonverbal behavior of both parties, the kinds of thoughts and feelings that precede and accompany the conflict, and the eventual outcomes of the conflict. It may take several sessions to elicit this kind of detail from many patients who are not used to paying attention to and describing their behavior.

Finally, the interconnections among important problem areas should be elaborated. Poor handling of certain problem situations creates other situations that may also prove difficult. It is especially important to draw the connections between social/personal problems and the eating disorder. In many instances, as we showed in Chapter 7, social/personal problem situations generate negative emotions and stress that serve as an antecedent to bingeing and purging. The interaction between eating disorders and personal/social problems goes in the other direction as well. In many instances the disordered eating behavior helps create difficult interpersonal situations or may serve as a mechanism for avoiding other difficult situations. Figure 15.1 presents a flowchart outlining the process of problem identification in PSPS.

Setting Intervention Goals

The second phase of PSPS involves selecting appropriate intervention goals. The objective of this phase is not to solve all of the individual's problems and difficulties in living. Rather, the desired outcome is to improve the patient's ability to cope to the point that personal/social problems no longer create instability in the individual's eating behavior, body image, or comfort with current body weight.

The work in this phase is actually made easy if a thorough problem assessment has been completed. The goals of intervention involve addressing the high priority problems that were identified and analyzed in the problem assessment phase. The statement of intervention goals involves describing changes in outcomes that will represent a solution of each of the problems. For example, if completion of formal education is identified as a priority problem, then an appropriate goal might be to become enrolled in an educational or vocational training program. If friction between the patient and the patient's parents over issues of independence are identified as a priority problem area, then an intervention goal might be to decrease the level of conflict and to obtain resolution of key issues, such as curfew, financial independence, completion of household chores, or selection of friends and associates.

Intervention goals, however, are not always easy or straightforward to describe. For example, it is easy to state that cessation of conflict is the goal of intervention. However, this is an incomplete goal since some other quality of social interaction must take the place of interpersonal conflict. Thus, the removal of negative consequences must be accompanied by a statement describing the kinds of interpersonal or vocational outcomes that should occur instead. In addition, goals that are vague or stated only generally are sometimes hard to achieve and almost always difficult to

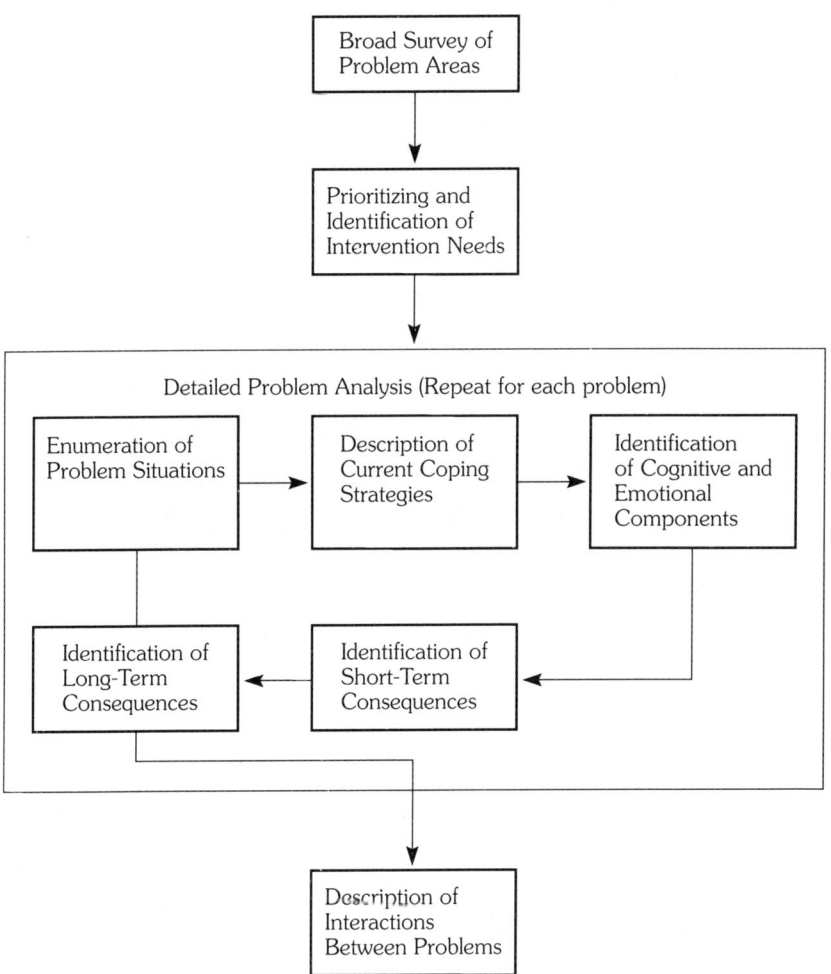

FIGURE 15.1 Flowchart Model of the Problem Identification Process

```
         ┌─────────────────────┐
         │   Broad Survey of   │
         │   Problem Areas     │
         └──────────┬──────────┘
                    ▼
         ┌─────────────────────┐
         │  Prioritizing and   │
         │  Identification of  │
         │ Intervention Needs  │
         └──────────┬──────────┘
                    ▼
┌───────────────────────────────────────────────────────────┐
│   Detailed Problem Analysis (Repeat for each problem)     │
│                                                           │
│  ┌────────────┐    ┌────────────┐    ┌─────────────┐      │
│  │Enumeration │    │Description │    │Identification│     │
│  │of Problem  │───▶│of Current  │───▶│of Cognitive │      │
│  │Situations  │    │Coping      │    │and Emotional│      │
│  │            │    │Strategies  │    │Components   │      │
│  └─────┬──────┘    └────────────┘    └─────────────┘      │
│        │                                                  │
│  ┌─────▼──────┐    ┌────────────┐                         │
│  │Identification│  │Identification│                       │
│  │of Long-Term │◀─│of Short-Term│◀──                      │
│  │Consequences │   │Consequences│                         │
│  └────────────┘    └────────────┘                         │
└──────────────────────────┬────────────────────────────────┘
                           ▼
              ┌─────────────────────┐
              │   Description of    │
              │    Interactions     │
              │  Between Problems   │
              └─────────────────────┘
```

determine when they have been reached. Goals should be described in specific terms, should be directly related to the problem situations, and should be stated in a manner that establishes an unambiguous criteria of success.

Goals for intervention can be stated not only in terms of specific outcomes but may also involve the occurrence of behaviors. For example, someone who is troubled by shyness and social withdrawal may establish an intervention goal of joining a social organization and initiating conversations with other people at the organization's social events. In many cases it is possible to take rather general long-term goals, such as increased income and job satisfaction, and generate a list of short-term subgoals involving outcomes and behaviors that will lead to ultimate success.

The process of goal setting is often a process of negotiation. Many different goals are possible as solutions of some problems. The goals that the therapist sees as relevant may not always fit with the patient's needs and values. Often, the goals that a patient initially chooses will create further problems or may represent inefficient or ineffective solutions to personal/social problems. In these instances, a process of negotiation must occur during which the therapist and patient are both willing to modify their ideas of what the appropriate goals of intervention should be.

There are several traps that must be avoided in setting intervention goals. The major trap is selection of a goal that will create additional stress and ultimately exacerbate the patient's eating disorder if it is pursued. Another version of this trap is selection of a goal that is mutually exclusive with some other important area of current satisfaction in the patient's life. When this occurs, achievement of the intervention goal will eliminate a source of life-satisfaction creating stress and emotional disequilibrium. A rather obvious example is the choice to go back to school and complete one's education, which may compromise one's ability to enjoy an active social life and stretch one's ability to generate enough income to meet current financial obligations. Before selecting an intervention goal, the interaction of the goal with other areas should be anticipated so that unintended negative consequences do not occur.

Brainstorming Potential Intervention Strategies

The focus of the brainstorming stage of the problem-solving process is to generate an extensive list of behaviors that may lead to achievement of the intervention goal. The brainstorming phase is one in which the options available are enumerated so that the individual has a wide range of choices available for achieving the desired goals.

The responsibility in this phase is divided between the patient and the therapist. The therapist should be willing to serve as an expert in human relations and apply his or her knowledge of how to solve real world problems in order to suggest intervention alternatives. However, the patient is the one whose problems are being addressed and should be encouraged to work at generating comfortable alternatives.

In this phase of problem solving, it is very useful to use paper or a blackboard to generate a written list of alternatives. This allows the patient to gain a sense that there are many possibilities and avoids the problem of poor memory on the part of both the patient and the therapist.

Alternative solutions should focus on specific thoughts and behaviors that may lead to the desired intervention goals. The more explicit the description of behaviors the better. While most problems require specific actions to be solved, there are some instances where the intervention strategy may be completely cognitive. For example, sometimes it is possible to solve a problem by reinterpreting a situation or changing the extent to which one values certain consequences. However, even when the solution to a problem involves a change in thinking rather than a prescription for behaving differently, it is important to describe the new way of thought in a specific and detailed manner.

Strategy Evaluation and Selection

After generating a generous list of potential ways of acting or thinking in order to achieve intervention goals, the next step is to evaluate each of the alternatives and to piece together a plan of action. The evaluation of an option involves several judgements:

1. Is the behavioral strategy likely to lead to the desired consequences?
2. Might there be unintended negative consequences if this plan is accepted?
3. Is the patient capable of performing the response or is learning to perform the response a realistic possibility?
4. How difficult is the option and can an easier, more realistic option be identified?

In some instances, these judgements will be difficult to make. Often it is not possible to know how a particular strategy will work without trying. Also, the individual's skills, capabilities, and capacity to learn are often not readily apparent. Nevertheless, an attempt must be made to evaluate and ultimately rank order the solutions.

The options generated during brainstorming are not always mutually exclusive. The goal of this stage of PSPS is to formulate an intervention plan. This may involve the selection of several strategies that will be implemented simultaneously or sequentially in order to meet the stated goals and improve the extent to which the individual is coping effectively with the problem situation(s). The formulation of a viable plan may take some time and require several revisions before completion. The eventual outcome is the development of a list, preferably written, of things that will be done, when they will be done, and the situations in which they will occur in order to solve the problem.

It is sometimes difficult for patients to accept the inherent risk involved in trying out new behaviors. Patients often balk at trying one of the better strategies that has been identified out of fear of the unknown. There are several solutions to this problem. The first solution is to help the patient become aware of the fear, the origin of the fear, and the irrationality of the fear (see Chapter 11). Another method that may work is to have the patient agree to try a new behavior as an experiment. That is, the patient does not commit to behaving in a new way on a permanent basis because of fears that this way will ultimately be too painful to fail to work. Instead, the patient and therapist form a contract to try a new behavior on one or two occasions and to see how well it works. If the patient is well prepared, then the experiment will turn out to be a success, and the patient will become increasingly enthusiastic about trying out new ways of thinking and behaving.

Implementation and Follow-Up

There are two important aspects of this phase of PSPS. The first aspect is the provision of appropriate learning experiences that will teach the patient new ways of behaving. The second is monitoring the success of the behavior change attempts and refining the plan as needed.

The provision of learning experiences is a crucial step in insuring the success of a behavioral intervention. If behavior change were as easy as suggesting that a person act differently, then few of us would have behavioral problems since this kind of information is often readily available to us. As we discussed earlier, one of the basic assumptions of the PSPS approach is that most social behavior is learned and that new behaviors can be acquired through learning. However, verbal learning alone is not sufficient. Certainly it is important that the patient acquire a cognitive knowledge of the solutions the patient plans to implement. If the person is not able to even remember or describe the plan, there is little hope that the plan will succeed. However, many social, intellectual, and vocational skills require the provision of structured learning experiences because the amount of knowledge to be learned is extensive or, more frequently, because they involve the acquisition of performance skills. Let us consider the learning of a complex cognitive and motor skill, such as learning to play a musical instrument. To learn a musical instrument, one must listen to music, take musical lessons from an experienced musician, practice, then receive feedback from the teacher in order to perfect performance on the instrument. The acquisition of a social skill, such as engaging in conversation or defusing an argument, is not much different from learning to play a musical instrument in the amount of effort and feedback required to achieve mastery.

McFall (1976) provided a useful outline of social skills training. He construed the learning process as involving a series of steps:

1. *Modeling.* In the first step, the therapist models the skill or behavior to be learned. This involves demonstration of the performance under simulated conditions. For example, if the behavior to be learned is how to stop unwanted sexual advances from a date, the therapist uses role playing to show the exact sequences of behavior that would be used. Models do not need to be confined to role-played demonstrations on the part of the therapist. Videotapes, audio recording, and observation of other people's performance in the real world can all serve as models to an individual trying to learn a new skill. It may be necessary to repeat the modeling experience several times. The first few times, the individual becomes familiar with the behavior and able to recognize it. After a few times, the individual is ready to begin to learn by imitating the model.

2. *Coaching.* The observation of a competent model performing the target behavior is then supplemented through the use of verbal instruction. The therapist explains the behavior and any general principles involved in performing the response. Coaching involves explanation of any cognitive aspects of coping with the problem situation. For example, the therapist may instruct the patient on how to interpret another person's behavior or what to expect as a result of various response options. Coaching may also involve explaining how to respond to various contingencies that may arise during a performance. For example, what should you do when someone does not respond to your first attempt to refuse an unreasonable request. Verbal coaching can be supplemented through the use of written materials that explain in detail how to handle certain situations. The objective of coaching is to provide the individual with the information needed to successfully perform the modeled behaviors.

3. *Rehearsal.* After modeling and coaching, the individual is given a chance to try out the new behaviors. This involves constructing a safe climate in which the patient is able to try out new behaviors without fear of embarrassment or failure. One of the main methods of rehearsal involves role playing. This means that the patient is asked to behave as if she were in the actual situation while the therapist plays the role of the other person involved. For example, if the situation involves having a discussion with one's mother and asking her to stop interfering in one's social life, the patient tries out the interaction with the therapist playing the role of mother. The therapist attempts to respond in a realistic manner that allows the patient to try out new behaviors to see if she can imitate the responses she has observed and follow the coaching instructions. Often, homework assignments are given as a way to foster rehearsal. If the intervention involves learning how to meet people and make friends, the homework assignment might involve going to the health club and starting a conversation with someone there. Devising innovative ways of

providing opportunities for behavioral rehearsal is one of the greatest challenges to the therapist doing PSPS.

4. *Feedback.* The therapist observes the patient's attempt to rehearse the behavior or listens to the patient recount the results of a homework assignment, then offers constructive feedback. Feedback is very important when trying to learn a complex social or motor skill. The patient's early attempts may appear clumsy and incompetent. The performance can only be improved by offering constructive feedback. By constructive, we mean that the feedback focuses on what the patient can do to improve the performance and make it more effective.

While the process of behavioral training using modeling, coaching, rehearsal, and feedback is a primary method of educational intervention, it is not the only method. McFall (1976) points out that any educational intervention designed to teach new ways of thinking and behaving is a valid technique in behavioral training. Thus, programmed learning texts or interactive computer programs could be used as ways to teach someone how to implement a new strategy. The identification of teaching methods is only limited by the therapist's creativity and willingness to experiment with different teaching approaches.

The second aspect of implementation is to monitor the success of the plan. Having the patient keep a diary or a self-monitoring record may be a useful way to collect information that will allow the therapist and the patient to judge whether or not the intervention is working. At the very least, the results of an intervention need to be discussed with the patient at the next interview.

If the intervention plan works as desired, then the patient and therapist are ready to move on to the next treatment goal. However, plans sometimes do not work for a variety of reasons. The problem identification and assessment may not have been sufficiently thorough and unanticipated problems may arise. The goals selected may be inappropriate or the patient may not have acquired sufficiently well developed performance skills to insure success. The therapist needs to be willing to be flexible when evaluating the impact of a treatment plan. The plan may simply need some fine tuning and a little more practice in order to make it successful or the plan may need to be abandoned and the entire problem-solving process repeated.

It is worth adding at this point a note about what to expect when conducting PSPS. The method is a behavioral intervention technique and as such is designed to achieve results quickly. However, interpersonal problems are rarely simple. It may take considerable time and require many repeated uses of the problem-solving process to achieve a significant impact on the patient's style of coping with difficult interpersonal problems.

This is especially true when the problems to be addressed involve long-standing interactions with family members. In many cases there are strong contingencies that reward incompetent/maladaptive behaviors in the short term, which will be difficult to overcome using behavioral training. This does not mean that the PSPS approach should necessarily be abandoned if immediate results are not achieved. Rather, the therapist and the patient must endure a lengthy process of attempting different strategies for overcoming these difficult and long-standing interpersonal problems. We assume that social behavior is learned and that new social behaviors can be acquired, but we do not assume that the process is necessarily easy or quick.

At other times, newly acquired behaviors will stop being performed during times of stress and crises. It is not possible to control one's environment completely, nor is it possible to avoid all stressful situations. When the patient regresses to old ways of coping, a thorough review of the situation is in order. The solution may be to begin the problem-solving process again, set new goals, and formulate new intervention plans. The therapist must be willing to tolerate frustration and setbacks and to approach the process of PSPS with enthusiasm over and over again.

There are situations in which PSPS alone will probably not work. For example, if a patient is suffering from a profound depression, it may be that a pharmacological treatment is necessary as an adjunct to behavior therapy. Patients who are severely depressed do not learn as readily nor are they as willing to take the necessary risks to change the way they cope with difficult interpersonal situations.

SUMMARY

The personal social problem solving (PSPS) approach is a behavior change technique that can be used to intervene with the myriad of problems that feed into and exacerbate an eating disorder. The approach is derived from a social learning conception of personality. It is structured around a process of problem solving that involves problem identification, goal setting, brainstorming options, evaluation and selection of an intervention plan, and implementation and follow-up. PSPS relies heavily on educational methods for teaching patients new ways of acting and thinking. It requires knowledge, creativity, and patience on the part of the therapist. It is designed to produce quick and satisfying changes in behavior, but may be a lengthy process when the patient has complex interpersonal problems.

The use of PSPS is not mutually exclusive with many of the other techniques described in this volume. In fact, PSPS is best used in conjunction with other intervention methods, such as exposure with response prevention, nutrition education, and energy balance training. In this volume, we have separated cognitive interventions from PSPS for clarity of presentation. It should be evident that PSPS is a variant of cognitive behavior therapy. The cognitive interventions presented in Chapter 11 focus on changing ways of thinking and interpreting situations. PSPS focuses more on changing the ways patients behave in problem situations. In practice, these two methods are combined by many cognitive behavior therapists. Both emphasize the importance of coping with day-to-day situations. In practice, some problem situations will involve making changes in patterns of thinking and feeling, others will involve learning new ways to behave, while others will involve some combination of cognitive restructuring and behavioral training.

■ 16
Body-Image Treatment

BODY-IMAGE DISTURBANCE is widely recognized as a major feature of eating disorders with many authorities considering it to be of central importance in the origin and maintenance of both anorexia and bulimia nervosa. Casper (1986) reviewed the similarity between subjects who have been exposed to experimental semistarvation diets and women with low body weights as a result of anorexia nervosa. In spite of the many similarities in the clinical profiles of these two groups, Casper noted that the body-image disturbance is unique to anorexia and is not obvious in participants in experimental starvation studies.

In our discussion in Chapters 3 and 8, we noted that the literature on body image and its disturbance is confusing in both conception and measurement. In contrast, the clinical descriptions of body-image disturbance are surprisingly uniform. Women with anorexia and bulimia nervosa view themselves as larger than they are, express a desire to be thinner, and are dissatisfied with various body parts. There are several notable exceptions, the most prominent being the restricting anorexic who has achieved a low body weight and who displays little or no distortion or dissatisfaction. These young girls view themselves accurately, display no desire for a lower body weight, and admire their emaciated figure. They have achieved the lower body weight sought so fervently and are pleased with the results of their dieting efforts.

UNDERSTANDING BODY-IMAGE DISTURBANCE

Several crucial questions are raised by the clinical phenomenon of body-image disturbance and their answers will allow for an understanding of the construct of body-image disturbance. These questions are important not only to delineating the construct but also as an aid in structuring treatment efforts. These questions include the following:

1. Is body-image disturbance a basic perceptual distortion? That is, do women with body-image disturbance actually perceive themselves as larger or smaller than they actually are? Does the perceptual distortion generalize to estimates of other animate or inanimate objects, or are they specific to the individual's body?
2. Is the concept of body image and its disturbance simple and unidimensional as clinical description suggests or is the concept multidimensional?
3. How can we measure body image and its disturbance? What procedures and techniques have adequate psychometric properties, including reliability and validity, and which techniques are useful in body-image therapy?
4. What is the relationship between changes in body-image disturbance and clinical improvement in anorexia and bulimia nervosa?
5. How can we best structure treatment for body-image disturbance? Are there specific targets that should be the focus of treatment? Do such targets differ depending on whether the patient is anorexic or bulimic? What specific procedures should be implemented and for how long?

Body-Image Distortion

A partial answer to the first question concerning whether body-image disturbance represents a basic perceptual distortion is provided in the research of Barrios and his colleagues (Barrios, Ruff, & York, 1989). These investigators utilized the Body Image Detection Device (BIDD) and compared estimates of body image with size estimates of inanimate, unrelated objects. They found that even normal-sized, non-eating-disordered women judged themselves as heavier and larger than they really are. In comparing normal women to bulimic subjects, the bulimics judged themselves as heavier than normals. Interestingly, there was no relationship between body size estimates for the self and estimates of the body size of another person or the size of an inanimate object. Based on these data, Barrios et al. suggested that body-image disturbance is confined to the self and is not a generalized perceptual distortion involving other physical objects. Thus, the oversized estimates of body size displayed by eating-disordered women, while distorted, are not indicative of a perceptual defect. As suggested in

Chapter 3, the disturbance in body image consists of an overestimation of body features and parts that deviate from an ideal. These deviations appear to originate as a fear of fat and weight gain.

As noted in Chapter 3, the conceptualization of body image and its disturbance is more complex than originally thought. The multidimensional nature of body image was elucidated by Garner and Garfinkel (1981), who differentiated the perceptual from the cognitive-affective dimension. The perceptual component of body image refers to the ability to make accurate judgments of body size in comparison with other judges or external criteria. Size misestimation is present in both eating-disordered and normal women, may be more exaggerated in women with an eating disorder, and is confined to estimates of the self.

In Chapter 3, we extended the body-image construct by organizing it around cognitive schemata. We suggest that multiple body-image schemata are employed to perceive and interpret bodily information, that these schemata are contextually sensitive, and that they consist of perceptual, cognitive, affective, and behavioral information that is retrieved from memory as a unit. Body-image distortion arises from errors in perceptually based information stored with body schemata. At this point, we understand very little about body-image distortion since none of the assessment procedures have been independent of the cognitive and affective components of body schemata.

Body-Image Dissatisfaction

The second component of body image is referred to as body-image dissatisfaction and represents the cognitive-affective dimension. This cognitive-affective component appears to be intimately related to a fear of fat or weight gain and a drive for a thin, often emaciated figure. Body-image dissatisfaction can be congruent with body-image distortion or can display no correspondence with perceptual judgments. Thus, a young woman can display body-image distortion yet may be perfectly satisfied with her body size and shape. For example, a restricting anorexic who is below ninety pounds may perceive her body as heavier and fatter than its actual dimensions. She may, however, be completely satisfied with the different parts of her body, no doubt because of their emaciated look. Also, it is not unusual to see a young woman whose body weight is well below ideal and who accurately perceives her thinness, yet is completely dissatisfied with one or more specific areas of her body. Typically, the basis of the dissatisfaction centers around the belief that there is too much fat associated with certain body parts.

Body-image dissatisfaction varies considerably, with some patients being completely dissatisfied with their whole body while others focus their distress on isolated parts. Most often, dissatisfaction is centered on areas of the body that are prone to accumulate subcutaneous fat. These areas include the hips, waist, stomach, buttocks, and thighs. Many patients regularly monitor these body parts by frequent weighing, observations in a mirror, and trying on certain articles of clothing. These patients often have idiosyncratic standards against which they assess particular body areas. Some patients regularly view their face in the mirror and are attuned to any puffiness or swelling, others examine the size of their waist, hips, and thighs in a full-length mirror, while others try on various articles of clothing and use the fit of the clothes as a standard for evaluation. Patients utilize these self-tests to regulate the severity of dieting and/or purging.

In Chapter 8 we described various approaches to the measurement of body image. As was evident, there are several different measurement approaches, some of which emphasize perceptual distortion while others assess body satisfaction. Additional reviews of the methodology of body-image assessment are provided by Cash and Brown (1987) and Barrios et al. (1989).

Cognitive Distortions

A variety of cognitive distortions occur in patients with body-image problems. These include:

1. *Unrealistic ideal body.* The patient has an ideal body image that is based on cultural stereotypes, such as magazine models or movie stars. Given her body build, there is no chance she will ever achieve this ideal appearance.
2. *Social comparison.* This problem involves focusing on the positive features of other women's appearance and comparing them to one's own perceived negative features. Often, other women's beauty, thinness, or attractiveness is exaggerated while one's own attractiveness is denigrated.
3. *Obsession with certain body parts.* Often, certain body parts are identified as being too fat or unattractive. The individual's evaluation of her appearance is based on her thoughts and feelings about this single body part. Often the perceived negative features of the body part are greatly exaggerated.
4. *Failure to attend to positive features.* The woman who is obsessed with the unattractiveness of a particular body part often fails to attend to or perceive the strength of her other physical features.
5. *Misattributions.* Unpleasant experiences, failures, and other

negative outcomes are misattributed to one's physical features. For example, breaking up with a boyfriend could be perceived as being caused by a weight problem when in fact it was caused by factors completely unrelated to body weight.
6. *Magical belief in the power of weight loss.* The patient believes that losing weight or changing the shape or size of certain body parts will result in solving all of her problems. This intensifies the perceived need for weight loss and tends to cause the individual to become even more obsessed with body weight.

Problem Situations

Unhappy feelings and illogical thoughts about one's body do not just arise in a vacuum. These thoughts and feelings are elicited by events that occur in daily life. In order to gain a better understanding of the kinds of problems, a list of potential problem areas was presented to fifty female college undergraduates at Vanderbilt University. The areas were:

1. Dating or sexual situations,
2. Parties and social events,
3. Seeing an old friend,
4. Trying on clothes, shopping,
5. Exercising and locker rooms,
6. Meal situations,
7. Comparing yourself to other women,
8. Comments people make about your body,
9. Seeing yourself in the mirror, and
10. Interacting with people in job and professional situations.

The students were asked to provide specific examples of situations in each category in which they felt self-conscious about their body shape or size. They were also asked to describe how they thought, felt, and behaved in the situation. Here are several examples of the kinds of situational descriptions that were provided:

> You are at a party and you spy a girl who has the same dress that you have on. You wonder if the dress is more flattering to your figure or to hers. You notice your boyfriend is glancing at her.

> You are in the shower and you don't want to look down because you're afraid your stomach will be sticking out. You can't stand the suspense anymore and you look down. Sure enough, it's sticking out.

Your friend, who is beautiful and has a perfect figure, goes shopping for bathing suits with you. You each try on a number of suits. Hers all look perfect and you will not model yours because they don't look as good as hers. She becomes depressed and says they all make her look so fat. You don't feel so good about the shopping trip either since if she looks fat you must look positively obese.

The first phase of this research project led to the identification and description of 120 specific problem situations related to body dissatisfaction in college-aged women. We are currently in the process of collecting data on how different people cope with these situations in order to identify effective and ineffective coping strategies. Once these strategies have been identified, we will use this information to develop a behavioral training program for the treatment of body-image problems that will involve teaching patients effective strategies for dealing with these day-to-day problem situations.

IMPACT OF THERAPY ON BODY-IMAGE DISTURBANCE

Given the findings that body-image disturbance is exclusive to the self and that it appears to consist of both a perceptual distortion and affect-dissatisfaction dimension, an important question is the degree to which each aspect of body image changes as a result of therapeutic intervention. Several studies have reported the relationship of treatment and body image. Recently, Button (1986) measured body-image size estimates in a sample of anorexics who were undergoing inpatient treatment. Measures of body size estimation were attained at admission, one week later, at near maximum weight, and after discharge. The relationship of body size estimates obtained on admission and one week later suggested that body size overestimation decreased during the first week of treatment. Increases in body size estimates at the other assessment points were congruent with the degree of weight gain the patients experienced. In general, patients who had a lower percentage of ideal body weight at admission tended to overestimate body size to a greater extent. Greater body size overestimation was associated with poor clinical outcome.

With several exceptions, body image per se has not been explicitly targeted for intervention in most treatment programs. Thus, while inpatient and outpatient programs may monitor body-image disturbance as an important indicator of progress, few programs provide direct treatment. In spite of this lack of explicit treatment focus, the majority of treatment programs seem to provide some form of direct albeit nonsystematic feedback to patients as they progress through treatment. Given the extent of body-image disturbance in eating-disordered patients and the potential importance of body perception and satisfaction in the origin and maintenance of eating disorders, therapy should actively address body image in an explicit, systematic fashion.

ASSESSMENT OF BODY-IMAGE DISTURBANCE

Prior to intervention, the assessment of body-image disturbance and its controlling variables is necessary. The assessment of body-image disturbance should be approached using multiple measures that tap both perceptual distortion and cognitive/affective dissatisfaction (see Chapter 8). The clinician should be able to articulate whether the patient sees herself as heavier or fatter than she actually is, or whether there is no indication of the disturbance. Similarly, the relative satisfaction-dissatisfaction with overall body shape, and more specifically various body parts, should be determined.

After determining the nature, extent, and magnitude of the body-image disturbance, attention shifts to its controlling variables. Accordingly, antecedents and consequences of body-image disturbance should be investigated and these controlling variables should be utilized in formulating a treatment program. Unfortunately, no studies have been reported in which a functional analysis of body distortion or dissatisfaction has been conducted. However, elucidating these variables on an individual, clinical basis is very informative and helpful in developing a therapeutic intervention. Many situations can elicit concerns about the body including (1) self-monitoring using mirrors and clothing, (2) eating, (3) social comparisons, (4) comments and remarks from other individuals, (5) shopping for clothes, (6) attending parties and social functions, and (6) sexual interactions. When bodily concerns are elicited, either dieting or bingeing may be stimulated as a result.

INTERVENTION

An important clinical and empirical question is whether changes in body image will correlate with general clinical improvement or whether such change requires an explicit focus on body image. Garner and Garfinkel (1981) recommended that clinicians consider body-image disturbance within the context of semistarvation/malnutrition syndrome, individual personality, psychopathology and family interaction patterns. They suggested that body-image disturbance may resolve with general clinical improvement. They stated for example, that body-image disturbance is self-correcting in most patients and improves along with changes in the eating disorder.

Garner and Garfinkel argued against direct modification of patients' inaccurate body percepts. Instead, they recommended that body-image disturbance should be addressed by focusing on the patient's interpretation of her experience. Accordingly, the patient's experience of body-image disturbance should not be denied, rather, the patient should be told that others do not have the same impression of the patient's size and shape, that perceptual distortions and body dissatisfaction are common in eating-disordered patients, and that subjective experiences of one's body shape and size are influenced by a number of variables, including standards of personal attractiveness. Patients should be encouraged to challenge their own percepts of body size and shape as well as levels of satisfaction. They should, for example, be encouraged to challenge the impression that they are overweight and instead begin to appreciate aspects of their body that are healthy. While these recommendations share much in common with methods of cognitive therapy, they are not part of a systematic program designed to target body-image problems.

In contrast to Garner and Garfinkel, other clinical programs have focused systematic attention on the treatment of body image. For example, Wooley and Wooley (1985) outlined an extensive treatment for body image. They suggested that body-image disturbance begins in early life and intensifies during the physical maturation of puberty. Soon thereafter, body dissatisfaction leads to the dieting and weight control attempts that most teenagers embark upon. According to Wooley and Wooley (1985), the first goal of body-image therapy is to develop an awareness of the distortion. This is approached by a number of techniques including the presentation of feedback regarding one's self-image as it compares to the objective information provided by others. The Wooleys describe an exercise in which the patient draws an image of her shape on a piece of paper attached to the wall. Other patients are asked to draw an outline of this patient after which the patient is requested to stand against the wall while the therapist draws an actual outline of her shape on the paper. The three representations of body shape—patient, other, and therapist—provide material for a group discussion of accuracy and body dissatisfaction. The group context provides an excellent medium for addressing body-image disturbance. The feedback from objective data and other patients provides a way to confront body-image disturbance and target any denial by the patient.

Videotape feedback has also been used to help patients develop an awareness of body-image distortion. Patients are videotaped engaging in a range of activities. The videotape will show a talking head, partial body exposure while seated, and full body exposure with movement. In addition, the patient can be videotaped wearing a wide variety of clothing that provides varying degrees of accentuation of body shape.

Wooley and Wooley also describe exercises designed to make patients aware of their body image, utilizing art, imagery, and movement to accentuate feelings and impressions about their body. Initially, an attempt is made to teach patients that body image is changeable and that women can reorganize the perceptions and feelings they have about their body. Specifically, Wooley and Wooley described a procedure in which the patients are instructed to imagine themselves as different on several dimensions including size, race, and being larger or smaller in particular areas. They also are asked to imagine themselves as younger, older, what they look and feel like before and after eating, as well as before and after academic-vocational and social successes and failures. Wooley and Wooley believe that in order to recover from eating disorders, women must develop a broader range of concepts regarding their bodies in addition to the dichotomous "good" and "bad" size. While they offer anecdotal, clinical comments regarding the efficacy of these interventions, unfortunately no objective data are available to evaluate the contribution of these techniques to changes in body-image distortion or general clinical improvement.

Butters and Cash (1987) described the implementation of a cognitive-behavioral treatment program for body dissatisfaction. Thirty-two female college students were selected on the basis of their scores on a variety of scales, including those measuring body-image dissatisfaction. Individual treatment consisted of one-hour sessions during which the therapist met briefy with the students to establish rapport. The students then sat in a room and listened to audio and visual presentations. These interventions lasted for approximately thirty minutes, following which the students reviewed the major features of the intervention with the therapists. Over six sessions, subjects received information concerning body-image dissatisfaction, its possible causes, and how it can affect individual functioning. They also received relaxation training and constructed a hierarchy of body parts ranging from moderate to least satisfied. They were then guided through imagined desensitization for each body part by pairing imagery with relaxation. Subjects were given homework consisting of tactics for the adoption of more positive approaches to appearance. These cognitive techniques included challenging irrational beliefs, viewing their body's positive features, and relapse prevention strategies. The students were also instructed to apply the desensitization procedure at home while clothed and unclothed before a mirror.

In comparison to a waiting list control, the cognitive-behavioral intervention subjects experienced significant pre- to post-test changes in overall body parts satisfaction and reduced stress while viewing themselves in a mirror. Specifically, in comparison to the waiting list control, students receiving therapy reported greater satisfaction with their face, extremities, breasts, and midtorso and marginal levels of satisfaction with their lower torso. These changes were also evident at a seven-week follow-up. Moreover, the treatment program enhanced student self-esteem, improved interest in sexuality and promoted a more positive overall evaluation of physical appearance. These positive changes in body satisfaction were also associated with changes in body-image distortion. Students judged their body size as smaller and closer to the norm after treatment. An abbreviated three-week program was delivered to the waiting list control subjects and resulted in changes similar to those observed in the more extensive six-week program.

Body-image therapy sessions are routinely conducted for anorexic and bulimic patients at the University of Mississippi Medical Center. In an assessment phase, patients complete the BIATQ, silhouette rating, the BPSS, and seven-site skinfolds thickness measures. The therapist then meets with the patient in a feedback session. If the therapist is male, a female must be an active cotherapist in the feedback session. This assessment-feedback session is used to set body satisfaction goals that are targeted in group and individual therapy sessions. The patient comes to the session wearing a bathing suit or other form fitting clothing underneath regular apparel. The objective of the session is to review the measures of body-image disturbance with the patient and to relate these data to actual body parts. These objectives are explained to the patient prior to the session. The patient removes her outer clothing with the male therapist leaving the room until the outer clothing is removed. Thereafter, the BIATQ is reviewed and the patient's negative and positive scores are compared with those of the normative sample of women. Silhouette ratings are then discussed including the *current body size* choice, the *ideal body size,* and the discrepancy between the two. Patients typically perceive current body sizes as heavier than their ideal body size. Data on a sample of twenty-two inpatients indicates a mean of 6.5 on a 1 to 9 scale for *current body size* and *an ideal body size* average of 2.3. Patients are asked to reflect on the relationship between their current body size estimates and how significant others may rate them. In this exercise, it is not unusual for patients to generate a lower body size that corresponds more closely to their actual shape. In discussing an ideal body size, the patient is encouraged to anticipate what their life would be like if in fact they weighed or looked like the smaller silhouette. The therapist attempts to help the patient realize that the low body weight per se does not resolve personal problems and that the low body weight may be associated with adverse health consequences.

The next phase of the feedback session involves a review of the BPSS. The patient is first directed toward those body areas she has rated as positive. In most cases, patients are much more positive regarding their extremities (e.g. feet, hands), face, hair, and often their height. Patients are asked to reveal specifics about those body parts that are pleasurable, and how they regularly come in contact with them. For example, a patient may be asked to explain why it is that her hands are rated as 5 on a scale of 1 to 6, and how she comes into contact with hands on a regular basis. Patients typically comment positively on the structure of their bones, the size of their hands, their fingernails, and wrists. They also indicate that they see their hands regularly while washing and brushing their teeth as well as while talking, working, and studying.

The discussion then shifts to those areas rated negatively on the BPSS. These areas are more likely to include the midtorso, waist, and occasionally the upper body and face. In each instance, the patient is encouraged to discuss what it is about the particular body part that is not satisfactory, what she could do to change it, how she would feel if it were changed accordingly, and how such changes would influence her life. This discussion constitutes a rational-therapeutic interchange in which efforts are made to identify and challenge beliefs and myths regarding fat, muscle, and bone. Many patients are concerned with subcutaneous fat on their upper legs, waists, and buttocks, which they mistakenly refer to as cellulite. Many also believe that loose flesh is fat rather than untoned muscle. They may also believe that particular dieting practices and exercises, many of which are misinformation supplied by the popular media, can reduce the cellulite.

Patients are also asked how they come in contact with each particular body area. It is typical for patients to focus attention on a disliked body part such as their midtorso, for example, without viewing the body part in the context of their whole body structure. This response seems to be characteristic of patients with bulimia nervosa and has the effect of magnifying the dissatisfaction and misperception of the particular body part as it is experienced in isolation from the body.

Patients are engaged in a discussion of realistic changes that can be made, including exercise, and unrealistic expectations, such as changes in their height, frame, torso, and leg length. These procedures are repeated for each part of the body accordingly.

Most recently, we have begun to utilize videotaping of patients in various clothing as they engage in various body movements much like that described by Wooley and Wooley (1985). Unfortunately, we are not able to evaluate the influence of our body-image therapy independent of the overall therapeutic program. Our inpatient and outpatient programs generate clinically significant improvements on all measures of body distortion and dissatisfaction. Our impression is that the body-image sessions have a definite impact on distortion and dissatisfaction.

The following procedures are used for the videotape exercise:

1. The taping should occur in a large, open room containing at least two plain chairs.

2. The camera should be set up and ready to tape before the patient arrives.

3. The patient should wear close-fitting clothing that reveals her body size and shape (e.g., leotard, tank top, and shorts).

4. When the patient arrives, the following instructions are given: "I am going to ask you to move around the room while I film you. As we have already discussed, I will be filming you from various angles and later you will be able to observe the tape. Occasionally, I may ask you to pause. So, just relax and follow my instructions."

5. The patient is then instructed to perform the following movements.

- First, turn around and write today's date on the blackboard.
- Now have a seat in one of the chairs. Cross your legs. Now uncross your legs.
- Turn to the side while remaining seated. Cross your legs. Now uncross your legs.
- Now move to the next seat and cross and uncross your legs in a front and side position again.
- Stand up and walk over to the window and look out.
- Turn and walk across the room toward the door as if you were going to open it.
- Move back to the center of the room. Face me. Now hold your arms out from your sides (about ten inches) and slowly do a full turn.
- Now walk straight toward me.

6. The taping exercise can be conducted with groups of patients following these procedures:

- Turn around and write today's date on the blackboard.
- Turn and face me.
- Turn one quarter turn to the right.
- Keep turning one quarter to the right until a complete circle has been made.
- Now walk freely around the room, talking to one another.
- One by one, come straight toward the camera, then veer to the left.

7. The camera operator gets full length and zoom shots of each position. Zoom shots should focus on problem areas, such as buttocks, hips, legs, stomach, and face. Occasionally, the patient may have to be asked to pause during the zoom shots.

8. Later, the tape is replayed while the patient and the therapist discuss the patient's reactions to seeing herself from the different angles performing the different activities.

SUMMARY

Body image is not a simple construct. We have seen that body-image problems can refer to misperception of one's body, dissatisfaction with one's body, irrational cognitive beliefs about the body, and ineffective ways of coping with problem situations. The treatment of body-image problems is not well defined, nor is there a large body of treatment-outcome research. Most clinicians, however, agree that some component of the patient's therapy must address issues related to body satisfaction or perception. We reviewed several ways the treatment of body-image problems has been approached and provided a detailed protocol for using videotaped feedback. This is an area in which much innovative work remains to be done.

17

Group and Inpatient Treatment

OTHER CHAPTERS DEAL with specific types of treatment for eating disorders. Much of the material in these chapters was presented as though treatment consists of individual outpatient therapy sessions. While a great deal of the treatment for eating disorders is delivered using the individual outpatient psychotherapy modality, this is not the only approach available. In this chapter, we review two additional models for treatment delivery: group therapy and inpatient hospitalization. Our approach to this presentation involves describing the basic theory behind these modalities, discussing specific practical issues that must be considered in their use, then presenting detailed descriptions of published eating disorder treatment programs that have employed group or inpatient modalities. In reviewing these various programs, it will become clear to the reader that group and inpatient modalities can be used in conjunction with almost all of the treatment approaches that have been discussed. In fact, the two modalities are not incompatible since most inpatient treatment programs offer at least part of the treatment through therapy groups.

GROUP THERAPY FOR EATING DISORDERS

Basic Theory

Unlike psychoanalysis, family systems therapy, or cognitive/behavior therapy, group therapy is a modality of treatment rather than a theoretical/clinical perspective. Group therapy differs from the usual forms of psychotherapy in that several patients meet together with one or more therapists to work on a common behavioral or emotional problem (Klein, 1983; Leiberman, 1976; Parloff & Deis, 1977). Therapists from nearly all orientations have used group approaches to treatment. Generally, group approaches employ the same techniques that are used in individual therapy. For example, a psychoanalytically oriented therapy group would employ insight, interpretation, and transference in order to help members resolve unconscious emotional conflicts (Kauff, 1979). Behavioral groups tend to focus on identification of behavior patterns and strategies for behavior change (Harris, 1979). Cognitive/behavior therapy groups encourage participants to identify maladaptive cognitions and to substitute more appropriate and rational ways of thinking and acting.

To a certain extent, the group mode of treatment has been adopted in many settings out of concerns over resources and cost effectiveness. A single therapist can serve more clients in less time at a lower cost per patient using group therapy. Groups are particularly common in psychiatric inpatient settings.

Group therapy may provide other benefits beside cost reduction. A number of group process variables are presumed to make a direct contribution to a positive treatment outcome (Klein, 1983; Yalom, 1975). These variables include the following:

1. Feelings of belongingness and acceptance that develop within a therapy group.
2. Opportunities for interpersonal learning that occur as a result of the interactions among group members and the feedback from the group leader.
3. A chance to learn behaviors through imitation and modeling.
4. The opportunity to expand one's behavioral repertoire and to try out new behaviors in a safe setting.
5. The opportunity to experience qualities of interpersonal relationships (e.g., unconditional positive regard, trust) that have been absent or unavailable to the individual previously.

In spite of its widespread use, there is a lack of empirical research showing that the group treatment provides benefits that cannot be obtained from individual psychotherapy. Klein (1983) summarized the research literature on group psychotherapy drawing the following conclusions:

1. Group therapy approaches have been shown to be more effective than no treatment or placebos but have not produced uniformly beneficial results.
2. There may be many nonspecific changes in self-concept and attitude as a result of a group therapy experience that are unrelated to therapeutic behavior changes.

3. The presumed curative properties of the group experience have not been documented through systematic empirical research.
4. The lack of a conceptual framework for understanding the group process and its impact on the individual has hampered the development of an understanding of the specific benefits of group psychotherapy.
5. There are studies that demonstrate the benefits of group psychotherapy in specific populations such as schizophrenics, neurotics, alcoholics, and juvenile delinquents.
6. In spite of the widespread use of group psychotherapy, our understanding of its effectiveness and mechanism of action is quite limited.

Conceptualization of Eating Disorders

As with the types of interventions employed in group therapy, the specific conceptualization of eating disorders varies widely. There do not appear to be any compelling theoretical reasons for choosing a group as opposed to an individual format for therapy with eating disorders. In fact, some have argued that selection of anorexic patients for therapy groups must be done with great care (Hall, 1985). That is, the selection of group therapy treatment for eating disorders is either based on practical and cost considerations or is based on the presumed therapeutic benefits of the group treatment modality in general.

Methods of Treatment

In this section, we will describe the outline of several published descriptions of group therapy programs for eating-disordered patients.

Intensive Outpatient Group Treatment for Bulimia

J.E. Mitchell, Hatsukami, Goff, et al. (1985) have described a two-month intensive group therapy program for bulimia. The theoretical orientation of the program combines the Alcoholics Anonymous approach to chemical dependency with cognitive/behavior therapy. Abstinence from the addictive behaviors upon entry into the program, the use of group pressure and confrontation to reinforce abstinence, and the view that bulimia is a disease are the major components of the AA model. The behavioral focus has led to the inclusion of other techniques, including education and informational interventions, self-monitoring of eating behavior, the analysis of situational and emotional antecedents to bulimic behavior, direct advice to change eating patterns, stimulus control strategies, stress management, assertiveness training, self-reinforcement, and cognitive restructuring.

There are usually about ten patients in each group with weekly meetings declining from five times a week during the first week, four times a week the second week, three times the third and fourth weeks, to twice a week for the remainder of the program. The group meetings take place in the evenings when bingeing and vomiting are most likely to occur. The meetings combine lectures, discussions, support groups, and supervised dinners.

The program focuses directly on eating behavior and begins to intervene at the first session. Meal planning is done as a group exercise. Patients are instructed to eat three meals each day, to avoid forbidden foods that might trigger binge eating, and to refrain from trying to lose weight during the program. The meal plans contain at least 1,200 calories a day and may be higher depending upon the individual's calorie needs for weight maintenance.

The schedule of most group meetings is similar with sessions lasting for three hours. Each session begins with a lecture on a topic such as behavioral cues, stress management, self-help groups, or relapse prevention. The patients then have a group therapy session in which they begin by discussing whether they have been abstinent since the last session. Those who have had slips are encouraged to find ways to avoid them in the future. Those patients who have done well are given praise and encouragement. The lecture topic is then discussed, and its application to problems of individual members is considered. The last portion of the group session involves meal planning and feedback from the therapist and other group members on the appropriateness of the plan. Group members are required to have contact with each other outside the group session and are strongly encouraged to seek each other's support whenever they are tempted to binge and purge.

The program uses a strong contingency management procedure to further enhance abstinence. Patients are told that if they do not become abstinent, if they miss sessions, or if they do not cooperate with other aspects of the program such as meal planning, they will be terminated from the program. While the threat of termination is frequently used, only a small percentage of the patients entering this program have actually been asked to leave.

At the end of the two-month intensive program, patients are encouraged to join an ongoing bulimia support group. Some patients become volunteers to the program and assist new patients in overcoming their problem with bulimia. Preliminary results reported by Mitchell et al. appear encouraging.

Psychoeducational Group Treatment of Bulimia

Weiss, Katzman, and Wolchik (1985) described a brief group therapy program for bulimia. The program lasts seven weeks and is designed to address the interpersonal and emotional concomitants of bulimia. Behavioral procedures are used to reduce the frequency of the binge/purge cycle. However, the major emphasis of the program is to enhance interpersonal competence, assertiveness, and coping styles rather than the modification of eating behavior per se. The therapeutic program consists of group sessions, assigned readings, homework assignments, and a participant workbook.

The program begins with a complete diagnostic and assessment interview with one of the program leaders to determine if the patient meets the diagnostic criteria for bulimia. The purpose and format of the program is described and the acquisition of coping skills as the goal of the program is emphasized.

The outline of the group program is as follows:

Session 1: Education and overview. This session is used to establish group rapport and provide an informational overview of bulimia. Group members discuss their reasons for joining the group. The group leaders attempt to focus the discussion away from bingeing and purging and toward feelings, interpersonal behaviors, and coping strategies. Instead of lecturing, information is presented through question and answer techniques. Group members are encouraged to talk and actively participate in all phases of the group experience. The first session covers the definition of bulimia, its incidence, and complications. The homework assignment for the first week is to read about bulimia and keep a diary documenting binge-eating episodes.

Session 2: Eating as coping: developing alternative coping strategies. Participants identify the environmental and emotional cues that elicit binge eating through discussion and review of the binge diaries. Appropriate eating habits and methods of weight control are discussed. The participants are encouraged to refrain from purging for a single week. Patients are taught to identify sources of stress, learn to communicate more effectively, become better organized, modify distorted cognitions, and begin to alter other habits that may be negatively impacting health or well-being. The homework assignment is to develop a list of alternative coping strategies that can be used in place of binge eating.

Session 3: Self-esteem, perfectionism, and depression. Group participants read an article on the pitfalls of perfectionistic thinking and then spend time discussing how this applies to their own lives. The relationship between perfectionism, achievement, and depression is discussed. Participants are encouraged to review their personal goals periodically to make sure they are realistic and attainable. The session also includes an exercise designed to raise self-esteem. Participants are encouraged to identify nourishing activities, behaviors that will enhance well-being and self-esteem, while not involving eating. The homework is to develop a list of positive qualities and to ask at least three friends to describe the participant's positive qualities.

Session 4: Anger and assertiveness. The role of interpersonal conflict and anger as an antecedent to binge eating is discussed. The remainder of the session involves assertiveness training. The goal is to teach the participants to respond to conflict by appropriately standing up for themselves instead of binge eating. Exercises for expressing anger and saying no are used to rehearse assertive responses. The homework assignment is to say no to three things the participant really does not want to do and to engage in three nourishing activities during the coming week. Participants are also told to keep track of situations in which they become angry and to write a description of how they handled the situations.

Session 5: Cultural expectations of thinness for women. Three exercises are used in this session to help participants develop an awareness of the cultural expectations of thinness for women and their own feelings and responses to these expectations. First, participants are encouraged to write a description of the perfect woman and to try to visualize what this woman would look like. The unrealistic nature of this perfect woman is discussed to show that the cultural ideal is unattainable. The second exercise involves the group generating a list of the payoffs and disadvantages of trying to live up to this image of the perfect woman. The third exercise involves a detailed examination of how the group members behave when they are with men whom they find attractive. The women are encouraged to be themselves around men and to avoid the pursuit of an unattainable stereotype of the perfect woman. The homework for the week involves generating a list of parts of their bodies they do not like, talking to three men about what they look for in an attractive woman, and finding a picture from a magazine of a woman whose body is like their own and another picture which corresponds to their ideal body image.

Session 6: Enhancing body image. The goal of this session is to help participants view their own bodies more realistically and to become more comfortable with their bodies as they currently appear. The women are encouraged to see that there are aspects of appearance beside body weight that are involved in being attractive. The role of behavior in attractiveness is discussed. Areas of body-image distortion are identified for each participant. The homework assignments are reviewed so that a comprehensive list of what men look for in an attractive woman is generated. The homework is to generate a list of attractive aspects of the participant's appearance and behavior. One of the attractive behaviors is to be chosen for exaggeration during the coming week. Participants are encouraged to make some positive change in appearance other than losing weight and to note how people react to the change.

Session 7: Summary. This session is used to review progress, set further goals for change, and to prepare participants for the possibility of relapse.

Wolchik, Weiss, and Katzman (1986) reported the results of a controlled evaluation of this program. The results showed greater improvement in eating behavior, depression, self-esteem, and body image in the treated group as compared to a control group. While improvements were shown, many of the patients were still bingeing and purging at a reduced rate at the end of treatment and several showed no change at all.

Brief Psychoeducational Group Treatment

Connors, Johnson, and Stuckey (1984) and C.L. Johnson and Connors (1987) have described a twelve-session structured group program for the treatment of bulimia. The program is eclectic and involves reading, presentations, group discussions, disclosure of personal feelings, self-monitoring, individual feedback, goal setting, nutrition counseling, assertiveness training, and behavior modification. Johnson and Connors also describe a bulimia self-help group and several other treatment groups used at the Northwestern Memorial Hospital inpatient treatment program. Follow-up data on twenty patients participating in the psychoeducational group was presented showing a substantial reduction in binge/purge frequency that was maintained at one- to two-year follow-up.

Other Group Therapy Programs for Eating Disorders

Other writers have reported descriptions of group therapy interventions for eating disorder in more or less detail. Schneider and Agras (1985) provided a brief description of a sixteen-week cognitive/behavioral group treatment program for bulimia. Roy-Byrne, Lee-Benner, and Yager (1984) describe a group therapy program for bulimics that combined behavioral and psychoanalytic elements. The program was tested on eleven patients over a one-year period with apparently good results. Brisman and Siegel (1985) described a group treatment for bulimia that begins with an intensive weekend workshop, followed by weekly group therapy sessions, and culminates in a support group attended only by the patients. The program also combines elements of behavioral and traditional psychodynamic therapy approaches. Huon and Brown (1985) described a twelve-week group therapy program for bulimia that utilized cognitive/behavioral treatment methods. Follow-up data on forty patients indicated that at eighteen months 68 percent had ceased bingeing and purging with another 22 percent showing improvement.

General Considerations in Forming Therapy Groups

A number of decisions must be made in developing a therapy group for eating disordered patients. These considerations include the following:

1. *Patient selection.* All patients should be carefully screened against explicit inclusion and exclusion criteria before entry into a group therapy program. For anorexic patients, no patients who are severely emaciated or who may require hospitalization because of life-threatening complications should be allowed in a therapy group. Patients should only be allowed into therapy groups for eating disorders if their participation is voluntary. Hall (1985) states that patients who are psychotic, or who are extremely shy and withdrawn are also not good candidates for group therapy. It is important to screen patients carefully to insure that they will be able to attend the sessions at the scheduled time before allowing them to start a group.

Homogeneity of eating disorders among group members is an issue that must be resolved in patient selection. Most experienced group therapists agree (Hall, 1985; Roy-Byrne, et al., 1984; Neuman & Halverson, 1983) that anorexic restrictor and bulimic patients should not be mixed together in the same group. Likewise, patients who binge and purge should not be mixed with obese binge eaters who do not purge.

2. *Degree of therapist directiveness.* Therapist styles are often quite different and these differences are a matter of therapist personality, theoretical orientation, experience, and training. At the one extreme is the client-centered, nondirective therapist who takes the role of facilitator rather than leader. At the other extreme is the highly directive behavior therapist who has a planned lesson for each group session, sets behavior change goals for the patients, and gives homework assignments each week (Johnson, 1975). While extremes of directiveness bordering on domination should be avoided, the therapist who will not take an active role in facilitating behavior change will probably be frustrated with group therapy for anorexia or bulimia. Mitchell, Hatukami, Goff, et al. (1985) reported having experimented informally with many different leadership styles. They concluded that therapy groups for eating disorders should be directive in addressing changes in the symptomatic behavior patterns. White (1985) advocates that the focus of group treatment of bulimia should be on the direct modification of bingeing and purging via the use of directive goal setting and behavioral homework assignments.

3. *Group size.* Most group therapy programs attempt to enroll between five and fifteen members. Generally, it takes five or more members for group cohesion and the other benefits of the group process to occur. However, when there are too many people in a therapy group, each individual has little chance for direct participation. In larger groups, the members can be divided into dyads or triads for exercises and mini-discussions in order to ensure a high level of involvement from each member.

4. *Focus of the group.* The theoretical orientation of the therapist determines which of the many possible forms a therapy group might follow. Thus, the focus of the group can be on developing insight into the origin of the eating disorder, understanding and solving the emotional and interpersonal problems that accompany eating disorders, or making changes in patterns of eating and food-related behavior. In addition, groups can rely on lectures and presentation of information, or they can be less structured, focusing on individual problems of the group members. Some groups will focus more on behaviors and actions while others emphasize thoughts and still others emphasize feelings.

5. *Format of the group session.* Formats for conducting group sessions vary widely. In part, the format used will depend on the focus and objectives of the group. A group that is oriented toward insight and whose group leader is nondirective can follow a relatively flexible and unstructured format. Groups that involve lectures and weekly agendas will follow a more fixed and structured format. However, even when the focus of the group is very educational, there should be time at each session for group members to share problems and receive feedback. Typically, the format of the group changes as group members become comfortable with the group and begin to share problems and feelings with other group members. Mitchell, Hatsukami, Goff, et al. (1985) provide an example of a program in which the group sessions had schedules, agendas, and a fixed format. The format allowed plenty of time for discussion and group interaction. The time allowed for this activity was scheduled around lectures and other more structured exercises. Roy-Byrne et al. (1984) described a much less structured group format. While group sessions tended to focus on specific themes, the themes were dictated by the needs and reactions of the patients rather than the plans of the therapists.

6. *Length and frequency of sessions.* The typical therapy group meets once a week for ninety minutes each session. Few groups meet less frequently or for shorter periods. The major variations are toward longer and more frequent sessions. Mitchell et al. had their groups meet three hours a day five days a week initially, tapering to three hours a day twice a week by the second month. Brisman and Siegel (1985) described a variation in timing in which the group therapy program began with an intensive weekend workshop.

7. *Number of therapists.* Typically, the decision that must be made about number of group leaders is to decide between one or two. Neuman and Halverson (1983) argued that groups with two leaders are generally preferable. Two leaders can share the stress and emotional strain that results from running a therapy group and will usually have different styles, which may allow a greater proportion of the group members to benefit. Planning between sessions is made easier when there are two leaders who can discuss the progress of the patients and the events of the previous group session. If two leaders are used to treat eating-disordered patients, they should either be a male and a female or two females. The inclusion of at least one female therapist is desireable so that the eating-disordered patients can observe a competent female role model.

8. *Attendance.* Attendance and dropouts are frequently a problem in therapy groups. Before initiating group therapy, the patient needs to make a definite commitment to attend every group session over a specified period of time. In addition, it is useful to have the therapist or another group member contact participants who unexpectedly miss a group session. Often a missed session is an indication that a slip or relapse has occurred, with the participant feeling reluctant to face the therapists and other group members and admit problems. When a member must miss a session because of scheduling conflicts, such as work or family vacations, the member should be encouraged to inform the leader ahead of time and obtain an excused absence. Dropouts can be quite disruptive to the formation of a cohesive and effective therapy group. Merrill, Mines, and Starkey (1987) reported on a sample of fifty-three bulimic patients entering various group therapy programs. By the twentieth week of therapy, 38 percent of the patients had dropped out with three of the therapy groups having a 50 percent dropout rate. Dropouts were more likely to be younger, single, unemployed, and experiencing greater somatic distress than those who remained in therapy. The major conclusion that Merrill et al. drew from this study was that attendance and dropout problems can be best dealt with by having time-limited groups that focus on cognitive/behavior modification of the bulimic symptoms.

9. *Contact between group members outside the group.* There are differences in opinion as to whether members of a therapy group should be encouraged to have contact with each other outside the therapy session. On the one hand, forcing patients to have contact with each other may violate their rights to privacy and confidentiality. In addition, the advice given by other group members in time of crisis may end up exacerbating rather than helping the problem. However, many experienced therapists encourage patients to contact each other outside the session (Hall, 1985; Neuman & Halverson, 1983). In fact, Mitchell et al. required as a homework assignment daily contact with each other by telephone between sessions. White (1985) reported that group members are encouraged to eat and practice homework assignments together between sessions. The strategy of turning to others for help and support during a crisis is much more adaptive than coping with a crisis by bingeing and vomiting. However, Roy-Byrne et al. (1984) reported that most of the between-session phone calls between group members occurred after rather than before slips and relapses.

Group therapy for eating disorders can take on many different forms. Many variations in group composition, leadership, and format have been used. In addition, the leader's theoretical orientation has a profound influence on the activities that occur within a therapy group. There is no doubt that many patients are currently receiving group treatment for eating disorders, especially bulimia nervosa. It is likely that groups will continue to be an important tool in the treatment of eating disorders. This is an area in which much more research is needed. We do not know how effective different types of group therapy are, what format the optimal group should take, how long the group should last, and what the focus of the groups should be.

INPATIENT TREATMENT PROGRAMS

Basic Theory

The earliest approaches to treating anorexia and bulimia nervosa involved lengthy hospital admissions. George, Weiss, Gwirtsman, and Blazer (1987) have traced the history of the inpatient treatment of anorexia nervosa from 1958 to 1982. They observed a strong trend toward increased use of psychotherapy and behavior therapy and a shift from treatment of anorexics on general medical wards toward specialized psychiatric units. While data on trends in treatment delivery are rare, there appears to be an increased utilization of inpatient treatment for bulimia nervosa.

There are two basic approaches to the use of hospitalization in the treatment of eating disorders. There are times when patients must be hospitalized in order to prevent a life-threatening medical emergency. The fact that anorexia nervosa has a relatively high mortality rate has led to the use of hospitalization as a way to avoid death from starvation or electrolyte imbalances.

Hospitalization may also be a way of offering intensive therapy in a controlled environment that may be more beneficial to some patients than prolonged outpatient treatment (Garner, Garfinkel, & Irvine, 1986). Halmi (1983c, p. 47) has argued that the inpatient treatment of anorexia nervosa "... occurs most efficiently and rapidly in a structured hospitalized treatment program." The constant supervision and controlled environment of the hospital facilitate interruption of bingeing and vomiting in patients with bulimia nervosa. The hospital setting allows for simultaneous medical management, nutritional counseling, individual psychotherapy, and group therapy. All of the patient's meals are provided in the hospital where food intake can be carefully monitored and observed. Separation of patients from their families interrupts interaction patterns and family conflicts that may have been exacerbating or maintaining the patient's disordered eating behavior.

As with the comparison of different schools of psychotherapy, there are no data for evaluating the role and importance of inpatient treatment of eating disorders. As suggested above, the question is not whether patients with life-threatening medical conditions should be hospitalized. The real issue is whether anorexic patients whose weight loss is not currently life-threatening and normal weight bulimics should be treated as inpatients.

The superiority of inpatient treatment hinges on three assumptions:

1. Patients who are hospitalized receive more intensive, multidisciplinary treatment. The increased intensity and breadth of treatment may reduce the amount of time required to achieve symptom change and may be the only way to treat difficult cases. However, there is little evidence that these parameters are important in determining treatment outcome for either anorexia or bulimia nervosa.

2. The controlled environment of the hospital allows greater and quicker therapeutic impact on the eating patterns of anorexic and bulimic patients. The control over eating behavior is made possible by regulating access to foods, serving carefully planned nutritionally balanced meals, and providing the treatment staff an opportunity to monitor and treat patient eating behavior. In the outpatient setting, the therapist must rely on the patient's self-report or entries in an eating diary in order to monitor food intake. By establishing environmental control over eating behavior in the hospital, the therapist may have a better chance of teaching the patient self-control skills that will generalize to the natural environment. There is little question that most patient's eating behavior can be managed in the controlled environment of the hospital. However, it is not clear that hospitalization leads to greater changes in food intake after discharge than outpatient treatment.

3. The hospital environment is a safe, quiet, stress-free environment that often contrasts with the patient's home, school, or work environments. By removing the patient from the environmental stresses and conflicts, therapy can be quickly implemented with few distractions. The idea that the hospital milieu contributes to the treatment of emotional problems is a common idea in the mental health community. However, like the other two assumptions, there are few data to support or refute the argument that removing patients from their stressful environments positively impacts their treatment outcome. In fact, hospitalization can have a disruptive influence on the patient's family, vocational situation, or education. In addition, financial and interpersonal problems may get worse following an extended inpatient hospitalization.

Most of the early inpatient eating disorder programs were established at regional medical centers associated with major medical schools. The programs were initially established for the treatment of anorexia nervosa. The serious and often fatal course of anorexia nervosa dictated the need for inpatient treatment. As time progressed, more patients with anorexia and bulimia were being treated. Many of these institutions began to relax their admissions criteria and admit normal weight patients with bulimic symptoms for inpatient treatment. Much of what we currently know about the characteristics and treatment of anorexia and bulimia nervosa are due to the fact that these medical school treatment programs usually had a strong research emphasis.

More recently, inpatient eating disorder programs have been established in small private medical and psychiatric hospitals typically managed by large medical holding corporations. These programs were established by corporate executives for the purpose of making money. The use of inpatient treatment facilities may have many economic advantages for these private hospitals over the establishment of an outpatient program. Inpatient programs generate much more revenue than outpatient treatment of eating disorders, may provide advantages in obtaining third party payment, and provide a highly visible focal point for the marketing efforts of the parent corporation. When a patient is clearly a candidate for either inpatient or outpatient treatment, the final decision may rest more upon economic considerations than the presumed psychological or medical superiority of one treatment approach over the other.

In summary, hospitalization should always be considered the appropriate response to life-threatening medical complications in patients with eating disorders. There are theoretical arguments in favor of inpatient treatment that unfortunately cannot be evaluated given the current state of our knowledge. Much of what we know about eating disorders has come from the large inpatient programs that were established early in regional medical research centers. Recently, many private hospitals have established inpatient eating disorder units. The comparability of these programs to the medical center research programs cannot be assessed.

Conceptualization of Eating Disorders

A variety of theoretical approaches to eating disorders have been employed in inpatient programs including the following:

1. Psychoanalytic models that view bulimia as a problem arising from an underlying personality disorder (Herzog, Hamburg, & Brotman, 1987)
2. Medical notes that view anorexia and bulimia as neuroendocrine problems (Mitchell, 1986)
3. Behavioral models that view anorexia and bulimia as learned patterns of behavior that are reinforced by the environment (Levendusky & Dooley, 1985)
4. Models that emphasize the similarities between bulimia and alcoholism and treat bulimia as a substance abuse problem (Hardy & Waller, 1988)
5. Psychiatric models that view eating disorders as an expression of an underlying biologically based major affective disorder (Hudson, Pope, & Jonas, 1985)

Many programs, due to their multidisciplinary nature, involve a mixture of several of these models (Garner, Garfinkel, & Irvine, 1986).

Methods of Treatment

In this section, we will provide a brief description of several inpatient eating disorder programs. While these examples will not exhaust the possibilities nor the published descriptions for the inpatient management of eating disorders, many of the therapeutic options will be covered.

Therapeutic Contract Program

Levendusky and Dooley (1985) described an inpatient treatment program for anorexia nervosa based on behavioral contracting.

1. *The treatment team.* Each patient in the program is served by a team of health professionals that includes an individual therapist, a contingency manager, a family therapist, a nurse coordinator, and an administrator. The individual therapist begins the process of psychotherapy during the hospitalization phase of treatment. A contingency manager negotiates behavioral contracts with the patient and oversees the administration of the rewards and punishments specified by the contract. The role of the contingency manager is to intervene directly with the disordered eating behavior in order to promote appropriate weight gain and cessation of dangerous behaviors such as laxative abuse. A family therapist begins the outpatient treatment of the patient's family while the patient is hospitalized. These treatment sessions later evolve into family systems therapy and include the patient, parents, and other family members as deemed appropriate. Each patient has a nurse coordinator

who provides support, guidance, and contingency management as specified in the behavioral contracts. The nurse coordinator has extensive daily contact with the patient during the period of hospitalization. Finally, each treatment team is headed by an administrator who insures that the appropriate assessment and treatment tasks are being accomplished.

   2. *Treatment contracts.* The goal of the treatment contract program is to achieve medical and behavioral stabilization and teach effective problem-solving skills to the patient. Weekly contracts are developed through the interaction of the patient with staff members and with other patients in the program. The contract specifies long-term goals along with a set of specific short-term behavioral goals. For example, the long-term goal might be to normalize eating patterns. The relevant short-term goals might include the following:

- Limit conversations about food
- Follow prescribed behavioral eating program
- Monitor mood after meals
- Use only two occasions during the day to verbalize fears and concerns about food, body size, and body weight

The patient takes primary responsibility for writing the behavioral contract. Early in the program, the staff provides much guidance. As the patient progresses, she takes increasing responsibility for setting both short- and long-term goals. The treatment contracts deal both with anorexia and bulimic behaviors and with psychological issues, such as social skills, physical appearance, family relations, and self-esteem. Through the use of contracts, patients learn to approach problems by analyzing them and by setting a series of short-term, realistic behavioral goals.

   3. *Group therapy.* Patients are involved in a variety of groups during hospitalization spending as much as fifteen hours a week in group therapy. The various therapies include contract writing, assertiveness training, relaxation, body awareness, vocational planning, patient government, and sexual identity. The groups utilize a similar behavioral intervention model but differ in their topical focus.

   4. *Integrated treatment program.* The treatment of anorexia is structured into a three-phase program. Each phase increases the degree of environmental control required to modify the disordered eating behavior. The first phase involves introducing the patient to the treatment setting, the therapy groups, and regular meals in a supervised setting. The second phase involves greater staff supervision but emphasizes patient responsibility in developing self-control and conforming to the limits placed on behavior. When patients do not respond to either the general therapeutic routine or to the self-control program, the staff-control program is initiated. Patients are restricted to their rooms during this phase, and access to social contact and recreational diversions is made contingent upon conforming to the behavioral goals of the program. Noncompliance with the program is met with well-defined contingencies that typically involve immediate return to quiet isolation. As patients begin to comply with the strict behavioral program, the self-control aspects are gradually introduced with the patient assuming increasing responsibility for setting goals and establishing limits.

5. *Aftercare.* Patients are discharged when they have acquired self-control skills within the hospital setting, reach target weight, and arrange satisfactory living arrangements. Treatment continues on an outpatient basis until the patient has become well-adjusted in her family and vocational roles and has maintained a steady weight. Behavioral contracts continue to be written on a weekly basis.

Interdisciplinary Inpatient Program
Collins, Hodas, and Leibman (1983) described an interdisciplinary treatment program for adolescents with anorexia nervosa. The program had four primary goals: improvement of eating habits, increased socialization, initiation of family-oriented psychotherapy, and weight gain. Only 15 percent to 20 percent of anorexia patients treated in this facility required hospitalization. The criteria for hospitalization usually consist of either medical problems that require inpatient treatment or failure of previous outpatient therapy. Hospitalization is short-term, lasting usually about three weeks. The setting is an adolescent medical unit that also houses adolescents with other medical, surgical, or psychiatric problems. The treatment team is large, consisting of nurses, resident and staff physicians, social workers, psychiatrists, and recreational therapists. The staff meets twice weekly to establish treatment plans for patients. Each staff member assumes a slightly different role with the patient, as teacher, therapist, or program manager. Patients are encouraged to gain weight by making privileges contingent upon daily weight gain. Family therapy is initiated in the hospital and once weight gain goals are reached, the patient is discharged and enters into outpatient family therapy.

Johns Hopkins Inpatient Treatment Program
Andersen (1985) provided a detailed description of the inpatient treatment program for anorexia nervosa at Johns Hopkins University. There are five specific criteria for inpatient admission: (1) low weight (25 percent or more below ideal body weight), (2) hypokalemia from vomiting, laxative, or diuretic abuse, (3) severe depression or suicidal ideation, (4) failure to

respond to an intensive, well-organized outpatient treatment program, and (5) family request for hospitalization due to extreme discouragement or lack of appropriate facilities nearby.

The patient is carefully and gradually introduced to the treatment program through a structured orientation process and by signing a specific treatment contract. A complete medical, psychological, social, nutritional, and educational evaluation is conducted. The evaluation process includes numerous medical tests, psychological questionnaires, and interviews with different members of the treatment team.

Treatment progresses in four stages: (1) nutritional rehabilitation, (2) intensive psychotherapy, (3) maintenance phase, and (4) follow-up. The nutritional rehabilitation phase has as its goals the restoration of body weight and the establishment of appropriate eating habits. Patients are carefully supervised to insure that self-induced vomiting does not occur. Andersen offered very specific advice on solving difficult patient management problems that occur during nutritional rehabilitation, such as the refusal to eat, self-induced vomiting, and preoccupation with food and weight.

The intensive psychotherapy phase involves a multimodal intervention delivered by a team of therapists. It includes a relaxation group, an assertiveness training group, a support group oriented toward talking about feelings, family systems therapy, and individual psychodynamic psychotherapy.

During the maintenance phase, the patient is encouraged to begin to exercise more choice and autonomy in food selection. Psychotherapy and group therapy continue during this phase. The final follow-up phase begins when the patient is discharged from the hospital. During this phase, group therapy and individual therapy continue on an outpatient basis.

Behavioral Medicine Unit

At the University of Mississippi Medical Center, anorexic and bulimic patients are treated on a special behavioral medicine unit. The treatment program is primarily administered by psychology with close consultation and support from medicine, psychiatry, nursing, and nutrition. Treatment consists of a progression through three to four separate phases that may last from two to eight weeks as inpatients and up to twelve months as outpatients. Figure 17.1 presents an outline of the five-phase treatment inpatient program for anorexia and Figure 17.2, the three-phase program for bulimia.

The inpatient programs are for chronic anorexia and bulimia patients who are at low body weight or have failed to benefit from previous outpatient treatment. The basic principles involved in the design of the program are (1) multidimensional treatment interventions are necessary to modify anorexic and bulimic behavior, (2) treatment goals progress in a stepwise

FIGURE 17.1 Mississippi Behavioral Medicine Unit Anorexia Treatment Program

I. Inpatient diagnostic studies (1-2 days)
   A. Patient is confined to room except for meals and testing
   B. Goals
      1. Establish diagnosis of anorexia nervosa
      2. Determine whether concurrent diagnosis of bulimia nervosa is warranted
      3. Assessment of eating, nutrition, body image, psychopathology, and health habits
      4. Identify concurrent conditions such as alcohol or drug use
      5. Rule out other disorders such as schizophrenia and major affective disorder
      6. Assess nutritional and medical status
      7. Evaluate for psychotropic medication
      8. Establish weight goals for phases 1,2,3 and discharge
   C. Laboratory studies
      1. Routine blood and urine chemistries
      2. Endocrine profiles (LH, FSH, prolactin)
      3. Other lab tests as indicated (e.g., MHPG, DMST, insulin)
      4. Psychological testing (e.g., SCL90, Health Habit Survey, Beck depression inventory)
   D. Begin to self-monitor eating and exercise behavior
II. Stage I. Inpatient treatment (5-15 days)
   A. Patient is confined to unit
   B. General goals
      1. Improved nutrition and physical status
      2. Weight gain of .5 to 1.0 kg per 5 days
      3. Development of appropriate eating habits
      4. Establishment of therapeutic alliance
   C. Specific Goals
      1. 1,200-2,000 kcal diet per day in three meals plus snacks
      2. Prevention of vomiting in bulimia patients
      3. Nutritional consultation for meal planning
      4. Family education
   D. Treatment procedures
      1. Continued self-monitoring of eating and activity
      2. Meals become exposure with response prevention sessions for bulimic patients
      3. Entry into Stage II is contingent upon meeting a weight goal
      4. Daily psychotherapy sessions are initiated. Initial goal is to establish a working interpersonal relationship.
      5. Daily group psychotherapy
      6. Family therapy when indicated
III. Stage II. Inpatient treatment (5-15 days)
   A. Social and recreational privileges increased contingent upon program compliance
   B. General goals
      1. Further improvement in eating habits and nutritional status

FIGURE 17.1 (continued)

   2. Weight gain of 1.0 to 1.5 kg per five days
   3. Improvement in body image and acceptance of weight gain
   C. Specific goals
      1. Ingestion of 1,800-3,200 kcal in three meals per day plus snacks
      2. Decrease amount of time spent talking about weight, figure, and attractiveness
   D. Treatment procedures
      1. Begin to develop self-regulation of eating behavior
      2. Nutritional education
      3. Cognitive/behavior therapy oriented toward more appropriate evaluation of oneself and others using attributes other than body weight
      4. Therapeutic day passes
IV. Stage III. Inpatient treatment (5-15 days)
   A. Social and recreational privileges increased contingent upon program compliance
   B. General goals
      1. Continued development of nutritionally sound eating habits
      2. Stable weight approaching 90% of ideal body weight
      3. Continued improvement in body image
      4. Improvement in social/interpersonal skills
      5. Enhanced sense of self-efficacy and personal competence
   C. Specific goals
      1. 1,800-3,200 kcal diet in three meals per day
      2. Decrease amount of time spent talking and thinking about weight and appearance
      3. Evaluation of social skills strengths and deficits and setting of goals for improvement
      4. Increased self-regulation of food intake
   D. Treatment procedures
      1. Continue to allow patient to take increased responsibility for food intake
      2. Further nutritional education on planning, shopping, and cooking
      3. Social skills training using modeling, coaching, rehearsal, and feedback
      4. Cognitive behavior therapy focusing on body image
      5. Therapeutic overnight passes
   E. Discharge when weight goals have been achieved
V. Outpatient treatment and follow-up (3-9 months)
   A. Goals
      1. Adjustment of eating habits to natural environment
      2. Maintenance of weight at or above 90% of ideal body weight
      3. Improved social interactions and adjustment
      4. Continued improvement in body image
   B. Treatment procedures
      1. Weekly group therapy
      2. Weekly individual therapy

FIGURE 17.2 Mississippi Behavioral Medicine Unit Bulimia Treatment Program

I. Inpatient diagnostic studies (1-2 days)
   A. Patient is confined to room except for meals and testing
   B. Goals
      1. Establish diagnosis of bulimia nervosa
      2. Assessment of eating, nutrition, body image, psychopathology, and health habits
      3. Identify concurrent conditions such as alcohol or drug use
      4. Rule out other disorders such as schizophrenia and major affective disorder
      5. Assess nutritional and medical status
      6. Evaluate for psychotropic medication
      7. Establish treatment goals for inpatient and outpatient therapy
   C. Laboratory studies
      1. Routine blood and urine chemistries
      2. Other lab tests as indicated (e.g., MHPG, DMST, insulin)
      3. Psychological testing (e.g., SCL90, Health Habit Survey, Beck depression inventory)
   D. Begin to self-monitor eating and exercise behavior

II. Inpatient treatment (5-15 days)
   A. Patient is confined to unit
   B. General goals
      1. Improved nutrition and physical status
      2. Prevention of self-induced vomiting
      3. Development of appropriate eating and exercise habits
      4. Establishment of therapeutic alliance
   C. Specific Goals
      1. 1,200-2,000 kcal diet per day in three meals plus snacks
      2. Prevention of vomiting
      3. Nutritional consultation for meal planning
      4. Family education
   D. Treatment procedures
      1. Continued self-monitoring of eating and activity
      2. Meals become exposure with response prevention sessions
      3. Patients eat and remain together for a two-hour period
      4. Daily psychotherapy sessions are initiated. Initial goal is to establish a working interpersonal relationship.
      5. Daily group psychotherapy
      6. Family therapy when indicated
      7. Energy balance training
      8. Temptation exposure with response prevention
      9. Body-image therapy

III. Outpatient treatment and follow-up (3-12 months)
   A. Goals
      1. Adjustment of eating habits to natural environment
      2. Assessment and evaluation of body image

FIGURE 17.2 (continued)

    3. Improved social interactions and adjustment
    4. Improvement of physical fitness
B. Treatment procedures
    1. Weekly group therapy
    2. Energy balance training
    3. Cognitive therapy for body image and social comparison problems
    4. Personal social problem solving to improve coping skills
    5. Nutrition education, cooking demonstration, shopping trips, group meals at restaurants
    6. Exposure with response prevention as needed
    7. Temptation exposure with response prevention as needed

fashion, and (3) treatment procedures used for anorexia and bulimia should be integrated into a single program. The basic emphasis of the program is on helping patients develop self-control over their eating and to replace their previously dangerous weight control strategies with sensible, well-balanced eating plans. Control over the anorexic and bulimic behaviors then allows therapy to address body-image, family, and interpersonal problems. The program begins with a comprehensive assessment and then progresses through a sequence of phases with slightly different goals for anorexics and bulimics. Patients begin the first phase by following a daily eating, therapy, exercise, and bathroom schedule with a high level of staff supervision. The behavioral requirements remain constant during each phase. The patients eat meals together and are encouraged to select and eat something from each of the four food groups. The patients also complete scales in which they rate their level of anxiety, tension, bloatedness, fear of weight gain, and urge to vomit. The patients remain in the dining room for approximately one hour after eating or until the urge to vomit subsides. These meals constitute exposure with response prevention sessions for bulimic patients. Psychotherapy and sometimes pharmacotherapy are initiated during the first phase of treatment, and eating and weight goals are established.

    In the second phase, weight change goals are revised if necessary and food intake is adjusted in relationship to the weight goals. Patients begin to plan their own meals while living in the hospital ward and are also exposed to junk food during exposure with response prevention sessions in order to blur the distinction between good foods and forbidden foods. Strategies for dealing with snacking and social eating are developed and practiced in the hospital. The program is structured so that patients interact with each other and provide both support and modeling of appropriate behaviors.

During the second phase of hospitalization, therapy for body image is initiated (see Chapter 16). Patients are given educational sessions on physiology and body function, especially as it relates to digestion. An individually tailored exercise program for conditioning or strengthening is developed and initiated while in the hospital. Sexuality and body shape are addressed through discussion, verbal, and nonverbal exercises. Also, cognitive therapy is used to eliminate harmful social comparisons that elicit negative moods of fear of weight gain. Upon completing the inpatient phase, patients continue in outpatient psychotherapy using a variety of cognitive and behavioral techniques depending upon need.

Clinical Recommendations

There is no clear basis for claiming that any particular modality of treatment (inpatient versus outpatient; individual versus group) is superior. When there is a medical emergency, inpatient treatment may be clearly indicated. However, when the condition is not life-threatening, as is often the case in normal weight bulimia, the choice of treatment modality must be dictated by clinical judgement and practical considerations rather than hard and fast evidence.

In our own work, we prefer an individual outpatient approach in most cases. Some patients are briefy hospitalized for intensive medical and psychological evaluations, but the bulk of treatment occurs on an outpatient basis. There are advantages to inpatient programs in some cases, such as failure to respond to outpatient therapy. For most practicing therapists, the choice of inpatient or outpatient treatment will in part depend upon the therapist's work setting. A therapist who works for an inpatient eating disorders unit is most likely to prefer to treat most patients in that setting. A therapist with an outpatient private practice is most likely to try outpatient treatment first before attempting to hospitalize a patient.

Those who choose to affiliate with an inpatient treatment program should strive to emulate one or more of the programs we have described. The inpatient treatment should be intensive, well-structured, time-limited, and multidisciplinary. Inpatient treatment should combine group and individual therapy. It should provide a definite follow-up plan for continued treatment after discharge.

Group therapy is an excellent choice as a component in the overall treatment of patients. Patients with mild cases of bulimia without serious complications may be treated effectively with a structured group program alone. However, it is our experience that individual therapy can be more flexible and intensive in addressing patients' needs. For example, outpatient treatment can begin with an individual program. Once the patient has progressed and entered a stable maintenance phase, it is often helpful to join an ongoing therapy group. Patients need less intensive intervention and more social support during maintenance than during initial efforts at making behavior changes.

Certain types of treatments lend themselves to group implementation more easily than others. Family therapy, for example, probably would not work in a group of unrelated individuals. Cognitive behavior therapy, energy balance training, nutrition education, and social problem solving all lend themselves well to a group format. It is not clear that psychoanalytic treatments lend themselves well to group implementation, although many therapists have attempted to run such groups. Our preference is for structured groups with co-therapists who are fairly directive. This is easier with behavioral than with psychodynamic approaches.

SUMMARY

Inpatient therapy is widely used for the treatment of anorexia and bulimia. Inpatient units tend to be multidisciplinary, highly structured programs to achieve rapid impact on eating behavior and body weight. When used with patients who are medically compromised or who have failed to respond to outpatient therapy, inpatient treatment programs may be the only reasonable approach. But, there is at this point no evidence that favors routine hospitalization of all or even most patients with eating disorders. Hospitalization is expensive and often interferes with jobs or educations. Routine hospitalization for a brief but intensive diagnostic workup may be justifiable in many cases. However, in order for any changes made in the hospital to be maintained, patients must be seen at least on a weekly basis for several months after discharge. The outpatient program can consist of group and/or individual psychotherapy or behavior therapy.

18

Therapeutic Programming: Integrating Assessment and Treatment

IN THE PREVIOUS CHAPTERS, we described assessment techniques and treatment procedures useful in the treatment of eating-disordered patients. Attention was devoted to the specific behaviors displayed by these patients and to treatment procedures intended to change them. In the present chapter, we will illustrate how therapeutic programming naturally follows from the selective use of assessment techniques and their integration with treatment procedures.

Over the past fifteen years, assessment techniques have become more specialized and thereby more useful in treatment planning. Initially, psychological testing and assessment techniques were oriented primarily to diagnostic questions. The results of tests were utilized to develop a generalized personality description that was then related to a psychiatric diagnosis. The empirical difficulties with this approach, including low reliability and validity, posed severe problems for clinical utility of behavioral classification. Specifically, a major problem has been the lack of a relationship between diagnostic categories and treatment. Thus, the assignment of a psychodiagnostic label, such as anorexia nervosa, often provides little information for treatment since there is often wide variation between individuals in the same diagnostic category. While the criteria for diagnoses in DSM-III-R are more empirically sound the diagnoses of anorexia nervosa and bulimia nervosa as well as other disorders still suffer from the problem of heterogeneity. So, while there is some convenience associated with assigning a diagnostic label, the degree to which this assignment has utility for treatment planning is open to question.

In contrast to this approach, the current trend in the assessment of personality and clinical problems is toward a description of specific behaviors, behavior patterns, and the variables influencing them. This approach developed as a result of the logical and empirical difficulties associated with traditional psychological assessment. The targets of treatment in current psychological assessment are not generalized disorders or diagnostic categories per se, such as anorexia nervosa or bulimia nervosa, but idosyncratic, measurable behaviors and cognitions displayed by specific patients. This current approach to behavioral classification is typified in the functional analysis of eating disorders presented in Chapter 7.

THE OUTCOME OF THE ASSESSMENT PROCESS

In the selection of assessment techniques for eating disorders, the therapist is guided by several questions organized to provide a description of the problem behaviors and cognitions. Taken together, the answers to these questions carry direct implications for treatment. The first set of questions typically posed is: What behaviors and cognitions require therapeutic intervention? For anorexia nervosa and bulimia nervosa, these behaviors and cognitions include binge eating, restrictive dieting, purging, body-image disturbance, and nutritional knowledge.

A second set of questions is oriented toward the antecedent and consequent events that influence these behaviors. The functional analysis developed in Chapter 7 provides an excellent model of the behaviors and possible variables affecting them. While the first question seeks the specific problem behaviors and their characteristics, the second set of questions considers these behaviors in terms of their antecedents and consequences. A third and final set of questions concerns the implementation of a therapeutic program. These questions cover a wide array of tactical issues in therapeutic planning including decisions concerning inpatient versus outpatient treatment, the selection of behaviors requiring immediate intervention, the inclusion of family members in the treatment process, and the use of medication. This third set of questions utilizes information developed from the functional analysis of the problem behavior, yet it focuses on the many choice points and tactical issues that must be addressed prior to the initation of therapy. For example, it is not unusual that binge eating is precipitated by negative affect subsequent to parental conflict and concomitant feelings of rejection. Given an adequate description of the behavior and cognitions as well as a comprehensive functional analysis, several tactical questions emerge. For example, should the therapist focus the initial phase of treatment on bingeing and vomiting using ERP? Given the role of parents as antecedents to the binge/purge cycle, should family therapy be considered, and if so, when? Recognizing that the patient must eventually deal with rejection more effectively, should therapy be directed at improving coping skills, and if so, when should this therapy be initiated? Obviously introducing and maintaining the change process requires clinical skill and should not be taken lightly. Based in part upon the experimental and applied analysis of behavior and our clinical trials (Johnson, Schlundt, & Jarrell, 1986; Johnson, Schlundt, Kelley, & Ruggiero, 1984), we initiate treatment on those behaviors occurring last in the behavioral sequence. For bulimia nervosa, this involves targeting purging for immediate attention, and then working backwards in the chain to the erratic eating habits, negative affect, and so on.

While the prime focus of assessment is to describe the difficulties in eating and eating-related behaviors and the variables that influence them, other aspects of the individual are important and influence therapeutic programming. In addition to selecting assessment procedures that focus on deviant behavior, a feature of state-of-the-art psychological assessment is an emphasis on assets or *what the individual does well*. These assets can be crucial in aiding the patient's clinical progress and appear particularly important in the early phase of therapy. In fact, many therapists attempt to enhance existing assets and utilize them to assist the individual with problems. A great deal of attention, then, is devoted to what the individual does well. The possibility of skills and competencies in social, intellectual, personal, family, and other areas requires careful attention as resources for therapeutic programming.

The outcome of the assessment process, then, is an exact description of the problem eating and related behavior and its controlling variables. This information is obtained through psychological tests, questionnaires, diaries, and interviews that assess eating and related behaviors, such as body image. Personality and psychopathological characteristics represent a second category of relevant information identified in the literature as correlated with eating disorders. These variables include anxiety, compulsivity, depression, fear of rejection, and social avoidance. Another category of information includes measures of physical fitness, nutritional status, body fat composition, and overall health status. The information provided by measures of personality, psychopathology, and physical fitness plays a major role in structuring each patient's treatment program. Data on the patient's physical status are useful in decisions regarding outpatient versus inpatient treatment, the establishment of a goal weight range, and exercise recommendations. Measures of personality and the degree of psychopathology also serve to direct the therapist to a more detailed assessment of problems that require treatment in their own right and, if left untreated, could interfere with therapy or eventually lead to relapse.

To develop a profile of the patient's eating behavior, the clinician can utilize questionnaires, including the three-factor eating questionnaire, the Binge Scale, the BULIT, and the Food Survey. These self-report questionnaires are supplemented by a comprehensive structured interview with questions regarding eating habits and the self-monitoring of eating in the natural environment (Chapter 8). Here, the patient records each eating episode over 25 k calories, indicating the time, place, mood, degree of hunger, and purging as well as a description of the food eaten, the amount, and its caloric content. Bulimic patients can also provide descriptions or scripts of several typical binge/purge episodes. These scripts are reviewed with the patient and organized for use in the overall therapeutic plan and more specifically, in TERP sessions.

Particular attention is devoted to body-image disturbance. Measures include the Body Image Automatic Thoughts Questionnaire (BIATQ), the Body Parts Satisfaction Scale (BPSS) and silhouette ratings. The BIATQ estimates the extent of negative and positive automatic body-related thoughts. The BPSS focuses on the degree of dissatisfaction over specific body parts. Additionally, nine silhouettes ranging from lean to obese are arranged randomly for the individual, and ideal and real body shape ratings are obtained. These ideal and real ratings provide information regarding the degree of distortion and dissatisfaction. Other instruments, such as the Body Image Testing System and the Body Satisfaction Questionnaire, could be employed with the same results.

As noted, data on eating behavior is augmented by other sources of information regarding behavior, personality, psychology, and pathology, and physical status. Many individuals with eating disorders display social skill deficits due to fears of rejection and negative evaluation as evidenced by the Social Avoidance and Distress Scale (SAD) and the Fear of Negative Evaluations Scale (FNE). Information provided by these measures is very helpful in organizing interventions to overcome social problems. The Beck Depression Inventory and the SCL-90 serve as general psychopathological screening inventories. The BDI is a widely used, face-valid measure of depression. The SCL-90 is a quickly administered, psychopathological screening technique, described in Chapter 8, which quickly ascertains the presence or absence of associated psychopathology ranging from paranoid ideation to obsessions and compulsions.

Measures of physical fitness are also important in therapeutic programming and include a modified Harvard Step Test, nutritional status determined by use of a computerized nutritional survey, and skinfolds thickness measures of body fat.

THERAPEUTIC PROGRAMMING

The process of therapeutic programming begins with a review of all the information gathered, the organization of this information as targets for change, controlling variables, behavioral assets, tactics for implementing change, and a presentation of this information in a feedback session with the patient. The therapist should develop a tentative therapeutic plan on the basis of the assessment information, yet it is often a discussion of this plan with the patient that is crucial for development of mutual therapeutic goals. This feedback session helps insure the patient's participation in the development of goals and greatly aids therapeutic programming and patient compliance.

As may be expected, not all patients are able to participate in such feedback sessions. Some patients are hostile and belligerent, others are extremely depressed. Many restricting anorexics with low body weight cannot process the information, and they are also resistent to the development of any therapeutic programming. In our experience, this resistance is temporary, resolving with improved nutrition and weight gain. However, resistance frequently reappears as the patient reaches milestone weights.

THERAPEUTIC TECHNIQUES

The therapeutic techniques described in the preceding chapters provide a set of formidable clinical methods, many of which have been proven effective in the treatment of eating disorders. We will briefly review these procedures, their rationale, and then discuss how they can be implemented in an overall treatment program. As noted, *exposure with response prevention* is a technique designed to teach individuals how to cope with urges to induce vomiting after eating binges (see Chapter 12). In this intervention, patients eat foods they have identified as binge foods or foods that they would otherwise purge. The therapist remains with the patient until the urge to purge subsides. During this time, constructive cognitive coping tactics are reviewed.

Other interventions are organized to deal with binges and episodes of inappropriate eating. *Training in energy balance* (Chapter 14) and *temptation and exposure with response prevention* (Chapter 12) focus on eliminating bingeing and other inappropriate eating behaviors and replacing them with more appropriate eating habits. More specifically, *TERPS* targets bingeing behavior by exposing the patient to situations and associated moods that are typically antecedent to binge episodes. Training in energy balance deals with the broader issues involved in weight regulation. This more comprehensive intervention focuses on normalizing eating of two or three nutritionally balanced meals per day and the incorporation of regular aerobic exercise. A necessary component of training in energy balance is nutritional education and counseling, which develops knowledge regarding recommended dietary allowances, reviews selections from the four food groups to insure variety in diet, and in the process deals explicitly with food myths and distortions often entertained by those with eating disorders (see Chapter 13).

As we discussed in Chapter 11, thought patterns are intimately involved as maintaining or precipitating factors in eating disorders. Some of the most prominent thought patterns identified in eating disorders include dichotomous reasoning, overgeneralization, personification, and selective interpretation. These thought patterns are explicitly addressed through various *cognitive interventions* (see Chapter 11). Also, body image and its disturbances are intimately related to the development and maintenance of eating disorders. Patients with anorexia nervosa typically perceive themselves as normal size or heavy when, in fact, they are underweight. Those with bulimia nervosa often perceive themselves as heavy when they have weights that are normal or slightly above normal for their height. It is not unusual, however, for some restricting anorexics to display little or no body-image distortion. They accurately perceive themselves as appreciably underweight and emaciated. These women have realized their goal of a low body weight and so display little or no body-image distortion. They take pride in their emaciated appearance and some even enjoy their protruding pelvis, ribs, and clavicle bones.

Dissatisfaction with body image is often coupled with body-image distortion. In most cases, dissatisfaction is focused on the midtorso and appears more pronounced in patients who perceive themselves as being heavy in spite of their actual weight. Thus, regardless of whether they are emaciated or within the normal weight range, patients who perceive themselves as heavy will display a great deal of dissatisfaction with their thighs, hips, stomach, waist, and buttocks. They accentuate the degree of subcutaneous fat in these areas.

Personal social problem solving deals with the inadequate coping efforts that are often antecedent to negative affect, inappropriate eating, and subsequent self-induced vomiting. The problem-solving approach adapted from D'Zurilla and Goldfried (1971) elucidates personal problems, evaluates typical responses, and then develops more appropriate and effective coping strategies leading to more favorable outcomes.

CASE DESCRIPTIONS

Nancy, a Case of Bulimia Nervosa

Nancy is a nineteen-year-old female at 5'1" and approximately 100 pounds with 20 percent body fat. She displayed high rates of bingeing and self-induced vomiting, ranging from six to eight times per day, and experienced concomitant physical symptoms of generalized weakness, dizziness, irregular menses, and amenorrhea. In an attempt to cope with her high rate of bingeing, she would severely limit her caloric intake, consuming only 300 kcal for several consecutive days. All measures of eating behavior corresponded with her reports of the extent of binge/purge episodes and a lack of control over her eating. Nancy's body perception was accurate, yet she desired a much lower body weight than her present 100 lbs. She was dissatisfied with her body generally, and in particular, her waist and thighs were disgusting to her. Nancy regularly monitored her shape by observing herself in a full-length mirror wearing a pair of tight blue shorts. Figure 18.1 presents the test results for Nancy.

Nancy's parents divorced when she was twelve years old. Her mother managed and taught aerobic classes at a fitness center. Nancy had been active, beginning with dance and gymnastics, through her high school years. She was a cheerleader in high school and college and taught aerobic classes four to six hours per week for her mother. Interestingly, when she was eight years old, Nancy's gymnastic instructor cautioned her repeatedly not to gain weight. As a result of this admonishment, she became sensitized to her weight and at this early age began to practice restrictive dietary practices.

Because of her physical symptoms, the level of caloric intake and the frequency of binge/purge episodes, Nancy was hospitalized. The initial hospital goals for Nancy were to normalize her eating with three meals a day and an occasional planned snack. She displayed little or no body-image distortion but did have considerable areas of dissatisfaction, and these were addressed directly in body-image therapy sessions. Specific attention was devoted to her waist, thighs, and buttocks, and she was given a routine of regular aerobic and figure toning exercise.

Nancy avoided social activities, preferring to spend time with her boyfriend. This avoidance was in part attributed to her extensive fear of negative evaluation. She was also depressed primarily over her inability to control the binge/purges episodes. Her social activities were limited to around-the-clock involvement with a boyfriend who is independently wealthy. She eventually dropped out of school and had no vocational or

FIGURE 18.1 Test Results: Nancy

Diagnosis:
   Bulimia Nervosa
   Nancy
   19-year-old female
   5' 1", 100 pounds
   20% body fat
Measures of Eating Behavior
   BULIT   128
   Restraint Scale   22
   Binge Scale   20
Body Image
   BIATQ:
      Negative — 2.8
      Positive — 2.2
   Silhouettes:
      Ideal — 2
      Real — 4
   BPRS:
      Face   5.0
      Extremities   4.5
      Lower torso   2.6
      Mid torso   2.2
      Breasts   3.2
      Height   3.6
      Overall   2.0
Social Function
   SAD — 24
   FNE — 29
Psychopathology
   BDI — 28
   SCL-90:
      Interpersonal sensitivity: obsessive-compulsive, anxiety, paranoid ideation, depression, somatization, phobic anxiety

educational goals. Her fear of negative evaluation and social avoidance were addressed during individual and group therapy sessions. Nancy and her therapist reviewed her past social activities and how she enjoyed each. While still in the hospital, she began to reenter her past social realm and directly confronted her fears of negative evaluation by relying on her newly developed coping tactics rather than withdrawing to the comfort of her boyfriend. Her educational and vocational interests were rekindled, and Nancy returned to college determined to be a professional, career-oriented woman.

Leigh's Treatment Plan

In addition to the test information, the results of the semistructured interview indicated that Leigh suffered from periodic dizziness and that she had come close to fainting on several occasions. She also experienced heart palpitations while exercising and had not menstruated for approximately fourteen months. She was hypothermic in the extremities with her hands and feet being cold most of the time. Figure 18.2 presents the test results for Leigh.

Together, Leigh and the therapists developed goals over the following areas: eating and weight regulation, body image, social interpersonal, and psychopathological. In Leigh's case, a primary goal was to increase her nutritional status by developing regular patterns of meal intake starting out at approximately 1,000 kcal per day. She was encouraged to eat a variety of foods, in particular fruits, vegetables, meat, and pasta, which would have been a marked departure from her habitual intake of salad and crackers. Additionally, she was restricted from exercising and her activity limited so as not to increase her heart rate and risk arrhythmias.

Efforts were also made to improve her body image. She was instructed to cease weighing herself and to refrain from looking in the mirror other than to dress herself and apply makeup. Weight goals were developed that would increase her weight in a stepwise fashion to over 130 pounds. The therapeutic message regarding the weight and body-image goals was that a higher weight would be healthier and allow her to work as a teacher without experiencing weakness and fatigue. She was informed that she was not in a position to evaluate her weight status, and that her perceptions of her weight (silhouette = 6) were distorted. Her desired lower body weight (silhouette = 2) was actually close to what she looked like at the time but was definitely not a healthy body weight to maintain as it would be associated with continuing problems in eating, weight control, and its associated physical symptoms, such as amenorrhea. Leigh had considerable difficulty in accepting these weight standards and the evaluation of her body shape. However, the elimination of weighing and looking in the mirror, and the resolution of the physical symptoms associated with her poor physical status gradually called her to question how she perceived her body. Group therapy also aided this process considerably. Group participants were able to give her more accurate, objective, and realistic feedback on the way she looked even though they could not apply the same realistic standard to their own bodies.

FIGURE 18.2 Test Results: Leigh

Diagnosis:
    Anorexia Nervosa — Restrictor type
        Leigh
        20-year-old female
        5' 11", 116 pounds
        12% body fat
Measures of Eating Behavior
    BULIT   82
    Restraint Scale 20
    Binge Scale   8
Body Image
    BIATQ:
        Negative — 2.53
        Positive — 1.56
    Silhouettes:
        Ideal — 2
        Real — 6
    BPRS:
        Face   2.4
        Extremities   4.6
        Lower torso 2.0
        Mid torso   1.0
        Breasts   5.0
        Height   4.0
        Overall   1.6
Social Function
    SAD — 26
    FNE — 22
Psychopathology
    BDI — 14
    SCL-90:
        Interpersonal sensitivity: somatization, anxiety

Assessment of Leigh's social and personal functioning indicated that she had a well-established repertoire of small talk and interpersonal skills, yet the initiation of social behavior was almost completely lacking. Accordingly, Leigh and the therapist devised a graded sequence of social interactions beginning with spending time with peers and colleagues and progressively extending the duration and variety of social contacts.

Following a course of approximately six months of outpatient therapy, Leigh had made substantial changes in her nutritional intake, increasing from 1,200 to 1,500 kcal per day. She was more sociable. However, her body weight remained relatively constant and it was difficult for her to refrain from exercising. She had continuing physical symptoms of generalized weakness and dizziness and remained amenorrheic. She finally consented to enter the hospital, and, during a twenty-one day stay, she was able to increase her weight from 116 to 122 pounds on restricted activity and progressive increase in her diet to 2,800 kcal per day. Leigh also developed an ability to initiate social interaction beyond the mere exchange of small talk in daily group therapy. Her physical symptoms subsided and she began menstruating at approximately 120 pounds and 16 percent body fat.

Andi's Treatment Program

The goals for Andi were similar to those developed for Leigh. As previously indicated, Andi had a history of a very low body weight. She continued to have distortions in her body image and display a desire for body weight much lower than her 102 pounds. In contrast to Leigh, however, Andi binged and purged. A goal weight range between 106 to 110 was set, which would have increased her weight slightly yet provided more body weight than she was accustomed to. A pattern of nutritious meals and preventing self-induced vomiting was initiated. The regular meals remarkably decreased any tendency to binge and during her hospital stay, each meal actually consisted of an exposure session as a therapist remained with her for up to 1½ hours following completion of the meal or until any urge to self-induce vomiting dissipated. Figure 18.3 presents the test results for Andi.

Andi was also placed on restricted activity. As her weight gradually increased, she was allowed to exercise again, beginning with a nonaerobic walk akin to a stroll. As her weight gain progressed and her body fat increased, she was allowed to begin an exercise regimen, which was pursued for its health and cardiovascular benefits rather than to burn off calories. Andi was instructed not to look at herself in the mirror or weigh herself and to challenge negative thoughts about her body appearance. Since she was very physically fit, efforts were made to impress upon her how weight loss would mean reductions in lean body mass and that she would be considerably less healthy and unable to do the types of strenuous exercise she enjoyed.

Andi also had considerable apprehension in social situations and a very pronounced fear of negative evaluation. These fears were based primarily on her perception of her body as fat. Invariably entering any social situation with other women triggered fears. Women and young girls whom Andi considered smaller were envied for their lower body weight, whereas those she considered heavier evoked a fear of weight gain. She

FIGURE 18.3 Test Results: Andi

Diagnosis:
  Anorexia Nervosa — Bulimic type
    Andi
    20-year-old female
    5' 3", 102 pounds
    16% body fat
Measures of Eating Behavior
  BULIT   122
  Restraint Scale 26
  Binge Scale   18
Body Image
  BIATQ:
    Negative — 2.8
    Positive — 1.6
  Silhouettes:
    Ideal — 2
    Real — 6
  BPRS:
    Face   5.0
    Extremities 3.6
    Lower torso 2.2
    Mid torso   1.0
    Breasts   4.0
    Height   2.0
    Overall   2.2
Social Function
  SAD — 12
  FNE — 26
Psychopathology
  BDI — 24
  SCL-90:
    Interpersonal sensitivity: obsessive
    compulsive, paranoid ideation

was challenged to see herself from the eyes of others, in order to help her entertain alternate ideas about her body shape and size. This therapeutic goal was augmented by feedback from others in group therapy.

During the course of Andi's evaluation it was obvious that there were significant family interactional patterns, particularly with her parents, that precipitated binge/purge cycles. These difficulties were identified and dealt with individually as well as within the context of family therapy. Her mother had been overprotective of her and developed a very dependent relationship that was accentuated when Andi was anorexic. Her mother continued this pattern of behavior, treating Andi as if she were sick and frail. This maternal overprotection was often directly antecedent to binge/purge episodes. Temptation scenes (TERPS) were developed involving actions of her mother. These mood induction exercises appeared to have a dramatic impact by helping Andi cope with her problems with her mother directly rather than allowing them to influence her eating behavior.

SUMMARY

These three cases illustrate the use of a multimodal, cognitive/behavioral approach to the treatment of eating disorders. We have presented the treatment components in separate chapters in this volume. It should be clear, however, that their separation was for purposes of exposition and description rather than implying that they represent mutually exclusive approaches to treatment. The therapist's task is to evaluate the patient and select the best combination of treatment approaches available for addressing each patient's unique set of circumstances.

■ References

Abelson, R., & Black, J. (1986). Introduction. In J. Galabamos, R. Abelson, & J. Black (Eds.), *Knowledge structures*. Hillsdale, NJ: Lawrence Erlbaum Associates.

Abou-Saleh, M.T., Oleesky, D.A., & Crisp, A.H. (1985). Dexamethasone suppression in energy balance: A study of anorexia patients. *Journal of Psychiatric Research, 19*, 203-206.

Abraham, S.F., & Beumont, P.J.V. (1982). How patients describe bulimia or binge eating. *Psychological Medicine, 12*, 625-635.

Adams, C.F. (1975). *Nutritive values of American foods in common units*, (Handbook no. 456). Washington, DC: U.S. Department of Agriculture.

Agras, W.S. (1987). *Eating disorders: Management of obesity, bulimia, and anorexia nervosa*. New York: Pergamon Press.

Agras, W.S., Dorian, B., Kirkley, B.G., Arnow, B., & Bachman, J. (1987). Imipramine in the treatment of bulimia: A double-blind controlled study. *International Journal of Eating Disorders, 6*, 29-38.

Agras, W.S., & McCann, U. (1987). The efficacy and role of antidepressants in the treatment of bulimia nervosa. *Annals of Behavioral Medicine, 9*, 18-22.

Altschuler, S., Conte, A., Sebok, M., Marlin, R.L., & Winick, C. (1982). Three controlled trials of weight loss with phenylpropanolamine. *International Journal of Obesity, 6*, 549-556.

American College of Sports Medicine. (1980). *Guidelines for graded exercise testing and exercise prescription*. Philadelphia: Lea & Febiger.

American Psychiatric Association. (1980) *Diagnostic and statistical manual of mental disorders*. Washington, DC: Author.

American Psychiatric Association. (1987). *Diagnostic and statistical manual of mental disorders*. Washington, DC: Author.

Andersen A.E. (1983). Anorexia nervosa and bulimia: A spectrum of eating disorders. *Journal of Adolescent Health Care, 4*, 15-21.

Andersen, A.E. (1985). *Practical comprehensive treatment of anorexia nervosa and bulimia*. Baltimore: Johns Hopkins Press.

Andersen, A.E. (1987). Uses and potential misuses of anxiety agents in the treatment of anorexia nervosa and bulimia nervosa. In P.E. Garfinkel & D.M. Garner (Eds.), *The role of drug treatments for eating disorders*. (pp. 59-73). New York: Brunner/Mazel.

Andersen, A.E., & Ebert, M. (1983). Anorexia nervosa and major affective disorders associated in families: A preliminary report. In S. Guze, F. Earls, & J. Barrett (Eds.), *Childhood psychopathology and development.* New York: Raven Press.

Andersen, A.E., Morse, C., & Santmyer, K. (1985). Inpatient treatment or anorexia nervosa. In D.M. Garner & P.E. Garfinkel (Eds.), *Handbook for psychotherapy for anorexia nervosa and bulimia* (pp. 311–343). New York: Guilford Press.

Anderson, J. (1985). *Cognitive psychology and its implications* (2nd edition). New York: W.H. Freeman.

Apfelbaum, M., Fricker, J., & Igoin-Apfelbaum, L. (1987). Low- and very low-calories diets. *American Journal of Clinical Nutrition, 45,* 1126–1134.

Askevold, F. (1975). Measuring body image. *Psychotherapy and Psychosomatics, 26,* 71–77.

Asp, E.H., Buzzard, I.M., Chlebowski, R.T., Nixon, D., Blackburn, G., Jochimsen, P., Scanlon, W., Insul, W., Elashoff, R., Butrum, R., & Wynder, E. (1987). Reducing total fat intake: Effect on body weight. *International Journal of Obesity, 11,* 397A–398A. (Abstract #5).

Astrand, P.O., & Rodhal, K. (1977). *Textbook of work physiology.* New York: McGraw-Hill.

Baer, D.M., Wolf, M.M. & Risely, T.R. (1968). Some current dimensions of applied behavior analysis. *Journal of Applied Behavior Analysis, 1,* 91–97.

Bandura, A. (1969). *Principles of behavior modification.* New York: Holt, Rinehart and Winston.

Barker, R.G. (1968). *Ecological psychology: Concepts and methods for studying the environment of human behavior.* Stanford: Stanford University Press.

Barrios, B.A., Ruff, G., & York, C. (1989). Bulimia and body image: Assessment and explication of a promising construct. In W.G. Johnson (Ed.), *Advances in eating disorders Vol. II.* New York: JAI Press.

Barth, D., & Wurman, V. (1986). Group therapy with bulimic women: A self-psychological approach. *International Journal of Eating Disorders, 5,* 735–745.

Beck, A.T. (1976). *Cognitive therapy and emotional disorders.* New York: International Universities Press.

Beck, A.T. & Beck, R.W. (1972). Screening depressed patients in family practice: A rapid technique. *Postgraduate Medicine,* December, 81–85.

Beiderman, J., Bladessarini, R.J., Harmatz, J.S., Rivinus, T.M., Arana, G.W., Herzog, D.B., & Schildkraut, J.J. (1986). Heterogeneity in anorexia nervosa. *Biological Psychiatry, 21,* 213–216.

Beiderman, J., Herzog, D.B., Rivinus, T.N., Harper, G.P., Ferber, R.A., Rosenbaum, J.F., Harmatz, J.S., Tondorf, R., Orsulak, P., & Schildkraut, J.J. (1985). Amitriptyline in the treatment of anorexia nervosa. *Journal of Clinical Psychopharmacology, 5,* 10–16.

Bemis, K.M. (1978). Current approaches to the etiology and treatment of anorexia nervosa as a disease. *Psychological Bulletin, 85,* 593–617.

Bemis, K.M. (1985). "Abstinence" and "nonabstinence" models for the treatment of bulimia. *International Journal of Eating Disorders, 4,* 407–437.

Benjamin, M. (1983). General systems theory, family systems theory, and family therapy: Towards an integrative model of family process. In A. Bross (Ed.), *Family therapy.* (pp. 34–38). New York: Guilford.

Berscheid, E., Walster, W., & Bohrnstedt, G. (1973). The happy American body: A survey report. *Psychology Today, 7,* 119–131.

Beumont, P.J.V. (1988). Bulimia: Is it an illness entity? *International Journal of Eating Disorders, 7,* 167–176.

Beumont, P.J.V., Bearwood, C.J., & Russell, G.F.M. (1972). The occurrence of the syndrome of anorexia nervosa in male subjects. *Psychological Medicine, 2,* 216–231.

Beaumont, P.J.V., George, G.C.W., & Smart, D.E. (1976). "Dieters" and "vomiters and purgers" in anorexia nervosa. *Psychological Medicine, 6,* 617–622.

Bhanji, S., & Mattingly, D. (1981). Anorexia nervosa: Some observations on dieters an vomiters, cholesterol and carotene. *British Journal of Psychiatry, 139,* 238–241.

Blackburn, G.L., Lynch, M.E. & Wong, S.L. (1986). The very-low-calorie-diet: A weight reduction technique. In K.D. Brownell & J.P. Foreyt (Eds.), *Handbook of eating disorders* (pp. 198–212). New York: Basic Books.

Blatt, S.J., & Lerner, H. (1983). Psychodynamic perspectives on personality theory. In M. Hersen, A.E. Kazdin, & A.S. Bellack (Eds.), *The clinical psychology handbook,* (pp. 87–106). New York: Pergamon Press.

Block, G.A. (1982). A review of dietary assessment methods. *American Journal of Epidemiology, 115,* 392–405.

Blundell, J.E., & Hill, A.J. (1986). Behavioral pharmacology of feeding: Relevance of animal experiments for studies in man. In M.O. Carruba & J.M. Blundell (Eds.), *Pharmacology of eating disorders: Theoretical and clinical developments* (pp. 51–70). New York: Raven Press.

Bo-Linn, G.W., Santa Ana, C.A., Morawski, S.G., & Fordtran, J.S. (1983). Purging and calories absorption in bulimic patients and normal women. *Annals of Internal Medicine, 99,* 14–17.

Boone-O'Neill, C. (1982). *Starving for attention.* New York: Continuum.

Boskind-Lodahl, M. (1976). Cinderella's stepsisters: A feminist perspective on anorexia and bulimia. *Signs, the Journal of Women in Culture and Society, 2,* 324–356.

Boskind-Lodahl, M., & White, W.C. (1978). The definition and treatment of bulimarexia in college women–a pilot study. *Journal of the American College Health Association, 2,* 27–29.

Boskind-White, M. (1985). Bulimarexia: A sociocultural perspective. In S.W. Emmett (Ed.), *Theory and treatment of anorexia nervosa and bulimia* (pp. 113–126). New York: Brunner/Mazel.

Boskind-White, M., & White, W.C. (1983). *Bulimarexia: The binge/purge cycle.* New York: W.W. Norton.

Boskind-White, M., & White, W.C. (1986). Bulimarexia: A historical-sociocultural perspective. In K.D. Brownell & J.P. Foreyt (Eds.), *Handbook of eating disorders* (pp.353–366). New York: Basic Books.

Bouchard, C., Perusse, L., Leblanc, C., Tremblay, A., & Theriault, G. (1988). Inheritance of the amount and distribution of human body fat. *International Journal of Obesity, 12,* 205–215.

Bray, G. (1982). Management options in obesity. *Hospital Practice, 27,* 104–112.

Bray, G. (1986). Effects of obesity on health and happiness. In K.D. Brownell & J.P. Foryt (Eds.), *Handbook of eating disorders: Physiology, psychology, and treatment of obesity, anorexia, and bulimia.* (pp. 3–44). New York: Basic Books.

Brisman, J., & Siegel, M. (1985). The bulimia workshop: A unique integration of group treatment approaches. *International Journal of Group Psychotherapy, 35,* 585–601.

Brooks-Gunn, J., Burrow, C., & Warren, M.P. (1988). Attitudes toward eating and body weight in different groups of female adolescent athletes. *International Journal of Eating Disorders, 7,* 749–757.

Brown, G.D., Whyte, L., Gee, M.I., Crockford, P.M., Grace, M., Oberle, M.N., Williams, M.B., & Hutchinson, K.J. (1984). Effects of two "lipid lowering" diets on plasma lipid levels of patients with peripheral vascular disease. *Journal of the American Dietetic Association, 84,* 546–550.

Brownell, K.D., Greenward, M.R., Stellar, E., & Shrager, E.E. (1986). The effects of repeated cycles of weight loss and regain in rats. *Physiology and Behavior, 38,* 459–464.

Bruch, H. (1962). Perceptual and conceptual disturbances in anorexia nervosa. *Psychosomatic Medicine, 24,* 187–194.

Bruch, H. (1973). *Eating disorders: Obesity, anorexia, and the person within.* New York: Basic Books.

Bruch, H. (1985). Four decades of eating disorders. In D.M. Garner & P.E. Garfinkel (Eds.), *Handbook of psychotherpay for anorexia and bulimia.* New York: Guilford Press.

Burchard, J.D., & Tyler, V.O. (1965). The modification of delinquent behavior through operant conditioning. *Behaviour Research and Therapy, 2,* 245–250.

Burton, B.T., Foster, W.R., Hirsch, J., & Van Itallie, T.B. (1985). Health implications of obesity: An NIH consensus development conference. *International Journal of Obesity, 9,* 155–169.

Butters, J.W., & Cash, T.F. (1987). Cognitive-behavioral treatment of women's body-image satisfaction: A controlled outcome study. *Journal of Consulting and Clinical Psychology, 55,* 889–897.

Button, E. (1986). Body size perception and response to inpatient treatment in anorexia nervosa. *International Journal of Eating Disorders, 5(4),* 617–629.

Calloway, P., Fonagy, P., & Wakeling, A. (1983). Autonomic arousal in eating disorders: Further evidence for the clinical subdivision of anorexia nervosa. *British Journal of Psychiatry, 12,* 38–42.

Carruba, M.O., & Blundell, J.E. (1986). *Pharmacology of eating disorders: Theoretical and clinical developments.* New York: Raven Press.

Carver, C.S., & Scheier, M.F. (1988). *Perspectives on personality.* New York: Allyn and Bacon.

Cash, T.F., & Brown, T.A. (1987). Body image in anorexia nervosa and bulimia nervosa: A review of the literature. *Behavior Modification, 11,* 487–521.

Cash, T.F., & Green, G.K. (1986). Body weight and body image among college women: Perception, cognition, and affect. *Journal of Personality Assessment, 50,* 290–301.

Cash, T.F., Winstead, B.A., & Janda, H.L. (1986). The great American shape-up: Body image survey report. *Psychology Today, 20,* 30–37.

Casper, R.C. (1984). Hypothalamic dysfunction and symptoms of anorexia nervosa. *Psychiatric Clinics of North American, 7,* 201.

Casper, R.C. (1986). The pathophysiology of anorexia and bulimia nervosa. *Annual Review of Nutrition, 6,* 299–316.

Casper, R.C. (1987). The psychopathology of anorexia nervosa: The pathological psychodynamic processes. In P.J.V. Beumont, G.D. Burrows, & R.C. Casper (Eds.) *Handbook of eating disorders part 1: Anorexia and bulimia nervosa.* (pp. 159-169). New York: Elsevier.
Casper, R.C., Eckert, E.D., Halmi, K.A., Goldberg, S.C., & Davis, J.M. (1980). Bulimia: Its incidence and clinical importance in patients with anorexia nervosa. *Archives of General Psychiatry, 37,* 1030-1035.
Cattanach, L., & Rodin, J. (1988). Psychosocial components of stress process in bulimia. *International Journal of Eating Disorders, 7,* 75-88.
Chaiken, S., & Pilner, P. (1987). Women, but not men, are what they eat: The effect of meal size and gender on perceived femininity and masculinity. *Personality and Social Psychology Bulletin, 13,* 166-176.
Clydesdale, F.M., & Francis, F.J. (1985). *Food, nutrition, and health.* Westport, CT: AVI Publishing.
Collins, J.K. (1987). Methodology for the objective measurement of body image. *International Journal of Eating Disorders, 6,* 393-399.
Collins, J.K., Beumont, P.J.V., Touyz, S.W., Krass, J., Thompson, P., & Phillips, T. (1987). Variability in body shape perception in anorexic, bulimic, obese, and control subjects. *International Journal of Eating Disorders, 6,* 633-638.
Collins, M., Hodas, G.R., & Leibman, R. (1983). Interdiciplinary model for the inpatient treatment of adolescents with anorexia nervosa. *Journal of Adolescent Health Care, 4,* 3-8.
Committee on Exercise and Physical Fitness. (1967). Is your patient fit? *Journal of the American Medical Association, 201,* 131-132.
Cone, J.D. (1986). Idiographic, nomothetic, and related perspectives in behavioral assessment. In R.O. Nelson & S.C. Hays (Eds.). *The conceptual framework of behavioral assessment.* New York: Guilford Press.
Connors, M.E., Johnson, C.L., & Stuckey, M.K. (1984). Treatment of bulimia with brief psychoeducational therapy. *American Journal of Psychiatry, 141,* 1512-1516.
Cooper, J.L., Morrison, T.L., Bigman, O.L., Abramowitz, S.I. Blunden, D., Nassi, A., & Krener, P. (1988). Bulimia and borderline personality disorder. *International Journal of Eating Disorders, 7,* 43-49.
Cooper, J.L., Morrison, T.L. Bigman, O.L., Abramowitz, S.I., Levin, S., & Krener, P. (1988). Mood changes and affective disorder in the bulimic binge-purge cycle. *International Journal of Eating Disorders, 7,* 469-474.
Cooper, K.H. (1977). *The aerobics way: New data on the world's most popular exercise program.* New York: J.B. Lippincott.
Cooper, P.J., & Fairburn, C.G. (1986). The depressive symptoms of bulimia nervosa. *British Journal of Psychiatry, 148,* 268-274.
Cooper, P.J., Taylor, M.J., Cooper, Z., & Fairburn, C.G. (1987). Develoment and validation of the body shape questionnaire. *International Journal of Eating Disorders, 6,* 485-494.
Craighead, L.W., Stunkard, A.S., & O'Brien, R.M. (1981). Behavior therapy and pharmacotherapy for obesity. *Archives of General Psychiatry, 52,* 190-199.
Crisp, A.H. (1970). Anorexia nervosa: "Feeding disorder", "nervous malnutrition", or "weight phobia"? *World Review of Nutrition and Diet, 12,* 542-544.

Crisp, A.H. (1980). *Anorexia nervosa: Let me be me.* London: Academic Press.
Crisp, A.H. (1981). Anorexia nervosa at normal body weight!—The abnormal weight control syndrome. *International Journal of Psychiatry in Medicine, 11,* 203-233.
Crisp, A.H., & Toms, D. (1972). Primary anorexia nervosa or a weight phobia in the male: Report of thirteen cases. *British Medical Journal, 1,* 334-337.
Crowther, J.H., Lingswiler, V.M., & Stephens, M.A. (1984). The topography of binge eating. *Addicitive Behaviors, 9,* 299-303.
Crowther, J.H., Post, G., & Zaynor, L. (1985). The prevalence of bulimia and binge eating in adolescent girls. *International Journal of Eating Disorders, 4,* 29-42.
Dahlstrom, W.G., Welsh, G.S., & Dahlstrom, L.E. (1972). *An MMPI handbook volume I: Clinical interpretations.* Minneapolis: University of Minnesota Press.
Danforth, E. (1985). Diet and obesity. *The American Journal of Clinical Nutrition, 41,* 1132-1145.
Darby, P.L., Garfinkel, P.E., Garner, D.M., & Coscina, D.V. (Eds.). (1983). *Anorexia nervosa, recent developments in research.* New York: Alan R. Liss.
Davis, J.M., Lowrey, M.T., Yim, G.K., Lamb R., & Malven, P.V. (1983). Relationship between plasma concentrations of immunoreactive beta endorphin and food intake in rats. *Peptides, 4,* 79-83.
Davis, R., Freeman, R., & Solyom, L. (1985). Mood and food: An analysis of bulimic episodes. *Journal of Psychiatric Research, 19,* 333-335.
Derogatis, L.R., Lipman, R.S., & Covi, L. (1973). SCL-90: An outpatient psychiatric rating scale—preliminary report. *Psychopharmacology Bulletin, 9,* 13-27.
Doer, P., Fichter, M., Pirke, K.M., & Lund, R. (1980). Relationship between weight gain and hypothalamic pituitary adrenal function in patients with anorexia nervosa. *Journal of Steroid Biochemistry, 13,* 329-537.
Dum, J., Gramsch, C., & Herz, A. (1983). Activation of hypothalamic B-endorphin pools by reward induced by highly palatable food. *Psychopharmacology, Biochemistry, & Behavior, 18,* 443-447.
Dwyer, J. (1985). Nutritional aspects of anorexia nervosa and bulimia. In S.W. Emmett (Ed.), *Theory and treatment of anorexia nervosa and bulimia: Biomedical, sociocultural, and psychological perspectives* (pp. 25-50). New York: Brunner/Mazel.
D'Zurilla, T., & Goldfried, M.R. (1971). Problem solving and behavior modification. *Journal of Abnormal Psychology, 78,* 107-126.
Elder, G.H. (1969). Appearance and education in marriage and mobility. *American Sociological Review, 34,* 519-533.
Ellis, A. (1962). *Reason and emotion in psychotherapy.* New York: Stuart.
Enright, A.B., & Sansone, R.B. (in press). Treating the patient with borderline personality disorder. In W.G. Johnson (Ed.), *Advances in eating disorders,* Vol. ii. New York: JAI Press.
Epling, W.F., & Pierce, W.D. (1988). Activity-based anorexia: A biobehavioral perspective. *International Journal of Eating Disorder, 7,* 475-485.
ESHA Research (1987). *The food processor II user's manual.* Salem, OR: ESHA Research.
Fairburn, C.G. (1981). A cognitive behavioral approach to the treatment of bulimia. *Psychological Medicine, 11,* 707-711.
Fairburn, C.G. (1985). Cognitive-behavioral treatment for bulimia. In D.M. Garner

& P.E. Garfinkel (Eds.), *Handbook of psychotherapy for anorexia nervosa and bulimia* (pp. 160-192). New York: Guilford Press.

Fairburn, C.G., & Cooper, P.J. (1982). Self-induced vomiting and bulimia nervosa: An undetected problem. *British Medical Journal, 284,* 1153-1155.

Fairburn, C.G., & Cooper, P.J. (1983). The epidemiology of bulimia nervosa. *International Journal of Eating Disorders, 2,* 61-67.

Fairburn, C.G., & Cooper, P.J. (1984). The clinical features of bulimia nervosa. *British Journal of Psychiatry, 144,* 238-246.

Fairburn, C.G. & Cooper, Z. (1987). Behavioral and cognitive approaches to the treatment of anorexia and bulimia nervosa. In P.J. V. Beumont, G.D. Burrows, & R. C. Casper (Eds.), *Handbook of eating disorders part I: Anorexia and bulimia nervosa* (pp.271-298). New York: Elsevier.

Fairburn, C.G., Cooper, Z., & Cooper, P.J. (1986). The clinical features and maintenance of bulimia nervosa. In K.D. Brownell & J.P. Foryet (Eds.). *Handbook of eating disorders.* (pp. 389-404). New York: Basic Books.

Fairburn, C.G., & Garner, D.M. (1986). The diagnosis of bulimia nervosa. *International Journal of Eating Disorders, 5,* 403-419.

Fallon, A.E., & Rozin, P. (1985). Sex differences in perceptions of desirable body shape. *Journal of Abnormal Psychology, 94,* 102-105.

Feighner, J.P., Robins, E., Guze, S.B., Woodruff, R.A., Winokur, G., & Munoz, R. (1972). Diagnostic criteria for use in psychiatric research. *Archives of General Psychiatry, 26,* 57-63.

Felixbrod, J.J., & O'Leary, K.D. (1973). Effects of reinforcement of children's academic behavior as a function of self-determinant and externally imposed contingencies. *Journal of Applied Behavior Analysis, 6,* 241-250.

Fernandez, R.C. (1984). Group therapy of bulimia. In P.S. Powers & R.C. Fernandez (Eds.) *Current treatments of anorexia nervosa and bulimia,* (pp. 277-291). New York: Karger.

Fine, R. (1973). Psychoanalysis. In R.J. Corsini (Ed.), *Current Psychotherapies* (pp. 1-34). Itasca, IL: F.E. Peacock.

Fisher, S., & Cleveland, S. (1958). *Body Image and Personality.* New York: Dover Press.

Fichter, M.M., Pirke, K.M., & Holsber, F. (1986). Weight loss causes neuroendocrine disturbances: Experimental study in healthy starving subjects. *Journal of Psychiatric Research, 17,* 61-72.

Flatt, J.P. (1987). Dietary fat, carbohydrate balance, and weight maintenance: Effects of exercise. *American Journal of Clinical Nutrition, 45,* 296-306.

Fong, G., & Markus, H. (1982). Self-schemas and judgements about others. *Social Cognition, 1,* 191-205.

Food and Nutrition Board, National Research Council. (1980). *Toward healthful diets.* Washington, DC: National Academy of Sciences.

Franzoi, S.L., & Herzog, M.E. (1987). Judging physical attractiveness: What body aspects do we use? *Personality and Social Psychology Bulletin, 13,* 19-33.

Freeman, A. (1987). Cognitive therapy: An overview. In A. Freeman & V.B. Greenwood (Eds.), *Cognitive therapy: Applications in psychiatric and medical settings.* New York: Human Sciences Press.

Freeman, C., Sinclair, F., Turnbull, J., & Annandale, A. (1985). Psychotherapy for bulimia: A controlled study. *Journal of Psychiatric Research, 19,*473-478.

Freeman, R., Thomas, C., Solyom, L., & Koopman, R. (1985). Clinical and personality correlates of body size overestimation in anorexia and bulimia nervosa. *International Journal of Eating Disorders, 4,* 439–556.

Freeman, R.J., Beach, B., Davis, R., & Solyom, L. (1985). The prediction of relapse in bulimia nervosa. *Journal of Psychiatric Research, 19,* 349–353.

Friedman, C.I., & Kim, M.H. (1985). Obesity and its effect on reproductive function. *Clinical Obstetrics and Gynecology, 28,* 645–663.

Fullerton, D.T., Getto, C.J., Swift, W.J., & Carlson, I.H. (1985). Sugar, opiods, and binge eating. *Brain Research Bulletin, 14,* 673–680.

Fullerton, D.T., Swift, W.J., Getto, C.J., & Carlson, I.H. (1986). Plasma immunoreactive beta-endorphin in bulimics. *Psychological Medicine, 11,* 59–63.

Fullerton, D.T., Swift, W.J., Getto, C.J., Carlson, L.H. & Gutzmann, L.D. (1988). Differences in the plasma beta-endophin levels of bulimics. *International Journal of Eating Disorders, 7,* 191–200.

Ganley, R.M., (1988). Emotional eating and how it relates to dietary restraint, disinhibition, and perceived hunger. *International Journal of Eating Disorders, 7,* 635–647.

Garfinkel, P.E., & Garner, D.M. (1982). *Anorexia nervosa: A multidimensional Perspective.* New York: Brunner/Mazel.

Garfinkel, P.E., Moldofsky, H., & Garner, D.M. (1979). The heterogeneity of anorexia nervosa: Bulimia as a distinct subgroup. *Archives of General Psychiatry, 37,* 1036–1040.

Garner, D.M. (1981). Body image in anorexia nervosa. *Canadian Journal of Psychiatry, 26,* 224–227.

Garner, D.M. (1986a). Cognitive therapy for bulimia nervosa. *Annals of the American Society for Adolescent Psychiatry, 13,* 358–390.

Garner, D.M. (1986b). Cognitive therapy for anorexia nervosa. In K.D. Brownell & J.P. Foreyt (Eds.), *Handbook of eating disorders: Physiology, psychology, and treatment of obesity, anorexia, and bulima* (pp. 301–327). New York: Basic Books.

Garner, D.M., & Garfinkel, P.E. (1979). The eating attitude test: An index to the symptoms of anorexia nervosa. *Psychological Medicine, 9,* 237–279.

Garner, D.M., & Garfinkel, P.E. (1981). Body image in anorexia nervosa: Measurement, theory, and clinical implications. *International Journal of Psychiatry in Medicine, 11,* 263–284.

Garner, D.M., Garfinkel, P.E., & Irvine, M.J. (1986). Integration and sequencing of treatment approaches for eating disorders. *Psychotherapy and Psychosomatics, 46,* 67–75.

Garner, D.M., Garfinkel, P.E., & Moldofsky, H. (1978). Perceptual experiences in anorexia nervosa and obesity. *Canadian Psychiatric Association Bulletin, 23,* 249–263.

Garner, D.M., Garfinkel, P.E., & O'Shaughnessy, M. (1985). The validity of the distinction between bulimia with and without anorexia nervosa. *American Journal of Psychiatry, 142,* 581–587.

Garner, D.M., Garfinkel, P.E., Schwartz, D., & Thompson, M. (1980). Cultural expectations of thinness in women. *Psychological Reports, 47,* 483–491.

Garner, D.M., Olmstead, M.P., & Garfinkel, P.E. (1983). Does anorexia nervosa occur on a continuum? Subgroups of weight-preoccupied women and their relationship to anorexia nervosa. *International Journal of Eating Disorders, 2*, 11-19.

Garner, D.M., Olmstead, M.P., & Garfinkel, P.E. (1985). Similarities among bulimic groups selected by different weights and weight histories. *Journal of Psychiatric Research, 19*, 129-134.

Garner, D.M., Olmstead, M.P., & Polivy, J. (1983). Development and validation of a multidimensional eating disorder inventory for anorexia and bulimia. *International Journal of Eating Disrorders, 2*, 15-34.

Garner, D.M., Rockert, W., Olmstead, M.P., Johnson, C., & Coscina, D.V. (1985). Psychoeducational principles in the treatment of bulimia and anorexia nervosa. In D.M. Garner & P.E. Garfinkel (Eds.), *Handbook of psychotherpay for anorexia nervosa and bulimia.* (pp. 513-572). New York: Guilford Press.

Garrow, J.S. (1986). Physiological aspects of obesity. In K.D. Brownell & J.P. Foreyt (Eds.), *Handbook of eating disorders.* New York: Basic Books.

George, D.T., Weiss, S.R., Gwirtsman, H.E., & Blazer, D. (1987). Hospital treatment of anorexia nervosa: A 25-year retrospective study from 1958 to 1982. *International Journal of Eating Disorders, 2*, 321-329.

George, V., Tremblay, A., Despres, J.P., Leblanc, C., Perusse, L., & Bouchard, C. (1989). Evidence for the existence of small eaters and large eaters of similiar fat-free mass and activity level. *International Journal of Obesity, 13*, 43-53.

Gershon, E., Hamovit, J.R., Schreiber, J.L., Dibble, E., Kaye, W., Nurnberger, J., Giles, T.R., Young, R.R., & Young, D.E. (1985). Behavioral treatment of severe bulimia. *Behavior Therapy, 16*, 393-405.

Gershon, E.S., Schrieber, J.L., Hamovit, J.R., Dibble, E.D., Kaye, W., Nurnberger, J.I. Jr., Andersen, A.E., & Ebert, M. (1984). Clinical findings in patients with anorexia nervosa and affective illness in their relatives. *American Journal of Psychiatry, 141*, 1419-1422.

Giles, T.R., Young, R.R., & Young, D.E. (1985). Behavioral treatment of severe bulimia. *Behavior Therapy, 16*, 393-405.

Glucksman, M.L., & Hirsch, J. (1969). The response of the obese patient to weight reduction. *Psychosomatic Medicine, 31*, 1-7.

Gold, P.W., Girtsman, H., Avgerinos, P.C., Niemen, L.K., Gallucci, W.E., Kaye, W., Jimerson, D., Ebert, M., Rittmaster, R., Loriaux, D.L., & Chrousos, G.P. (1986). Pathophysiologic mechanisms in underweight and weight-corrected patients. *New England Journal of Medicine, 314*, 1335-1342.

Goldberg, S.C., Halmi, K.A., Eckert, E.D., Casper, R.C., & Davis, J.M. (1979) Cyproheptadine in anorexia nervosa. *British Journal of Psychiatry, 134*, 67-170.

Goldberg, S.C., Halmi, K.A., Eckert, E.D., Casper, R.C., Davis, J., & Roper, M. (1980). Attitudinal dimension in anorexia nervosa. *Journal of Psychiatric Research, 15*, 239-251.

Goldbloom, D.S. (1987). Serotonin in eating disorders: Theory and therapy. In P.E. Garfinkel & D.M. Garner (Eds.), *The role of drug treatments for eating disorders* (pp. 59-73). New York: Brunner/Mazel.

Goodman, J.I., Richardson, S.A., Dornbusch, S.M., & Hastorf, A.H. (1963). Variant reactions to physical disabilities. *American Sociological Review, 28*, 429-435.

Goodsitt, A. (1985). Self psychology and the treatment of anorexia nervosa. In D.M.

Garner & P.E. Garfinkel (Eds.), *Handbook of psychotherapy for anorexia nervosa and bulimia.* (pp. 55-82). New York: Guilford Press.

Green, R.S., & Rau, J.H. (1974). Treatment of compulsive eating disturbances with anticonvulsant medication. *American Journal of Psychiatry, 131,* 428-432.

Greenberg, B.R. (1986). Predictors of binge eating in bulimic and nonbulimic women. *International Journal of Eating Disorders, 5,* 269-284.

Greenwald, P., Sondik, E., & Lynch, B.S. (1986). Diet and chemoprevention in NCI's research strategy to achieve national cancer control objectives. *Annual Review of Public Health, 7,* 267-291.

Gross, J., & Rosen, J.C. (1988). Bulimia in adolescents: Prevalence and psychosocial correlates. *International Journal of Eating Disorders, 7,* 51-61.

Grunewald, K.K. (1985). Weight control in young college women: Who are the dieters? *Journal of the American Dietetic Association, 85,* 1445-1450.

Guiora, A.Z. (1967). Dysorexia: A psychopathological study of anorexia and bulimia. *American Journal of Psychiatry, 124,* 391-393.

Hall, A. (1985). Group psychotherapy for anorexia nervosa. In D.M. Garner & P.E. Garfinkel (Eds.), *Handbook of psychotherapy for anorexia nervosa and bulimia.* (pp. 213-239). New York: Guilford Press.

Hall, A. (1987). The patient and the family. In P.J.V. Beumont, G.D. Burrows, & R.C. Casper (Eds.), *Handbook of eating disorders part 1: Anorexia and bulimia nervosa.* (pp. 189-200). New York: Elsevier.

Halmi, K.A. (1983a). Classification of eating disorders. *International Journal of Eating Disorders, 2,* 21-26.

Halmi, K.A. (1983b). The state of research in anorexia and bulimia. *Psychiatric Developments, 3,* 247-262.

Halmi, K.A. (1983c). Treatment of anorexia nervosa: A discussion. *Journal of Adolescent Health Care, 4,* 47-50.

Halmi, K.A. (1985a). Classification of the eating disorders. *Journal of Psychiatric Research, 19,* 113-119.

Halmi, K.A. (1985b). Rating scales in the eating disorders. *Psychopharmacology Bulletin, 21,* 1001-1003.

Halmi, K.A., Broadland, G., & Rigas, C. (1975). A follow-up study of 79 patients with anorexia nervosa: An evaluation of prognostic factors and diagnostic criteria. *Life History Research in Psychopathology, 4,* 290-298.

Halmi, K.A., Eckert, E.D., LaDu, T.J., & Cohen, J. (1986). Anorexia nervosa: Treatment efficacy of cyproheptadine and amitriptyline. *Archives of General Psychiatry, 43,* 177-181.

Halmi, K.A., & Falk, J.R. (1982). Anorexia nervosa: A study of outcome discriminators in exclusive dieters and bulimics. *Journal of the American Academy of Child Psychiatry, 21,* 369-375.

Halmi, K.A., Falk, J.R., & Schwartz, E. (1981). Binge eating and vomiting: A survey of college populations. *Psychological Medicine, 11,* 697-706.

Hamilton, L.H., Brooks-Gunn, J., & Warren, M.P. (1985). Sociocultural influences on eating disorders in professional female ballet dancers. *International Journal of Eating Disorders, 4,* 465-477.

Hardy, B.W., & Waller, D.A. (1988). Bulimia as substance abuse. In W.G. Johnson (Ed.), *Advances in Eating Disorders (Vol II).* New York: JAI Press.

Harris, F. (1979). Behavioral approach to group therapy. *International Journal of*

Group Psychotherapy, 29, 453–470.
Hart, K.J., & Ollendick, T.H. (1985). Prevalence of bulimia in working and university women. *American Journal of Psychiatry, 142,* 851–854.
Hatsukami, D., Eckert, E., Mitchell, J.E., & Pyle, R. (1984). Affective disorders and substance abuse in women with bulimia. *Psychological Medicine, 14,* 701–704.
Hawkins, R.C., & Clement, P.F. (1980). Development and construct validation of a self-report measure of binge eating tendencies. *Addictive Behaviors, 5,* 219–226.
Healy, K., Conroy, R.M., & Walsh, N. (1985). The prevalence of binge-eating and bulimia in 1063 college students. *Journal of Psychiatric Research, 19,* 161–166.
Hedblom, J.E., Hubbard, F.A. & Andersen, A.E. (1981). Anorexia nervosa: A multidisciplinary treatment program for patient and family. *Social Work in Health Care, 71,* 67–86.
Henderson, M., & Freedman, C.P.L. (1987). A self-rating scale for bulimia: The BITE. *British Journal of Psychiatry, 150,* 18–24.
Henley, K.M., & Vaitukaitis, J.L. (1985). Hormonal changes associated with changes in body weight. *Clinical Obstetrics and Gynecology, 28,* 615–631.
Herman, C.P., & Mack, D. (1975). Restrained and unrestrained eating. *Journal of Abnormal Psychology, 43,* 647–660.
Herman, C.P., & Polivy, J. (1975). Anxiety, restraint, and eating behavior. *Journal of Abnormal Psychology, 84,* 666–672.
Hernandez, L., & Hobel, B.G. (1980). Basic mechanisms of feeding and weight regulation. In A.J. Stunkard (Ed.), *Obesity.* Philadelphia: W.B. Saunders.
Herzog, D.B., Hamburg, P., & Brotman, A.W. (1987). Commentry: Psychotherapy and eating disorders: An affirmative view. *International Journal of Eating Disorders, 6,* 545–550.
Herzog, D.B., Pepose, M., Norman, D.K., & Rigotti, N.A. (1985). Eating disorders and social maladjustment in female medical students. *The Journal of Nervous and Mental Disease, 173,* 734–737.
Hill, A.J., & Blundell, J.E. (1982, 1983). Nutrients and behavior: The investigation of taste characteristics and food preferences, hunger sensations, and eating patterns in man. *Journal of Psyciatric Research, 17,* 203–212.
Hill, J.O., Schlundt, D.G., Sbrocco, T., Sharp, T., Pope, J., Stetson, B.A., Kaler, M., & Heim, C. (1988). Food restriction in obese women: Effects of alternating low and moderate calorie intake. *American Journal of Clinical Nutrition,* in press.
Hill, J.O., Sparling, P.B., Shields, T.W., & Heller, P.A. (1987). Effects of exercise and food restriction on body composition and metabolic rate in obese women. *American Journal of Clinical Nutrition, 46,* 622–630.
Hoebel, B.G. (1985). Brain and neurotransmitters in food and drug reward. *American Journal of Clinical Nutrition, 42,* 1133–1150.
Hoek, H.W., & Brook, F.G. (1985). Patterns of care of anorexia nervosa. *Journal of Psychiatric Research, 19,* 155–160.
Hoffman, L. (1981) *Foundations of family therapy.* New York: Basic Books.
Holland, A.J., Hall, A., Murray, R., Russell, G.F.M., & Crisp, A.H. (1984). Anorexia nervosa: A study of 34 twin pairs and one set of triplets. *British Journal of Psychiatry, 145,* 414–419.

Holmgren, S., Humble, K., Norring, C., Roos, B., Rosmark, B., & Sohlberg, S. (1983). The anorectic bulimic conflict: An alternative diagnostic approach to anorexia nervosa and bulimia. *International Journal of Eating Disorders, 2,* 3–15.

Holmgren, S., Sohlberg, S., Berg, E., Johansson, B., Norring, C., & Rosmak, B. (1984). Phase I treatment for the chronic and previously treated anorexia and bulimia nervosa patient. *International Journal of Eating Disorders, 3,* 17–36.

Hoover, W. (1983). Computerized nutrient data bases: I. Comparison of nutrient analysis systems. *Journal of the American Dietetic Association, 82,* 501.

Hsu, L.K.G. (1980). Outcome of anorexia nervosa: A review of the literature. *Archives of General Psychiatry, 37,* 1041–1046.

Hsu, L.K.G. (1983). The aetiology of anorexia nervosa. *Psychological Medicine, 13,* 231–238.

Hsu, L.K.G. (1987). Lithium in the treatment of eating disorders. In P.E. Garfinkel & D.M. Garner (Eds.), *The role of drug treatments for eating disorders* (pp. 90–95). New York: Brunner/Mazel.

Hsu, L.K.G., Crisp, A.H., & Harding, B. (1979). Outcome of anorexia nervosa. *Lancet, 1,* 61–65.

Hsu, L.K.G., & Holder, D. (1986). Bulimia nervosa: Treatment and short-term outcome. *Psychological Medicine, 16,* 65–70.

Hudson, J.I., Katz, D.L., Pope, H.G., Hudson, M.S., Griffing, G.T., & Melby, J.C. (1987). Urinary free cortisol and response to the dexamethasone suppression test in bulimia: A pilot study. *International Journal of Eating Disorders, 6,* 191–198.

Hudson, J.I., & Pope, H.G. (1987). Newer antidepressants in the treatment of bulimia nervosa. *Psychopharmacology Bulletin, 23,* 52–57.

Hudson, J.I., Pope, H.G., & Jonas, J.M. (1984a). Psychosis in anorexia nervosa and bulimia. *British Journal of Psychiatry, 145,* 420–423.

Hudson, J.I., Pope, H.G., & Jonas, J.M. (1984b). Treatment of bulimia with antidepressants: Theoretical considerations and clinical findings. In A.J. Stunkard & E. Steller (Eds.), *Eating and its disorders.* New York: Raven Press.

Hudson, J.I., Pope, H.G., & Jonas, J.M. (1985). Antidepressant treatment of bulimia. *Advances in Behavior Research and Therapy, 7,* 173–179.

Hudson, J.I., Pope, H.G. Jonas, J.M., & Yurgelun-Todd, D. (1983). Family history study of anorexia nervosa and bulimia. *British Journal of Psychiatry, 142,* 133–138.

Hughes, P.L., Wells, L.A., Cunningham, C.J., & Ilstrup, D.M. (1986). Treating bulimia with desipramine: A placebo-controlled double-blind study. *Archives of General Psychiatry, 43,* 182–186.

Humphrey, L.L. (1983). A sequential analysis of family processes in anorexia and bulimia. *Report of the 4th Ross Conference on Medical Research,* (pp. 37–45).

Humphrey, L.L., Apple, R.F., & Kirschenbaum, D.S. (1986). Differentiating bulimic-anorexic from normal families using interpersonal and behavioral observational systems. *Journal of Consulting and Clinical Psychology, 54,* 190–195.

Huon, G.F., & Brown, L.B. (1985). Evaluating a group treatment for bulimia. *Journal of Psychiatric Research, 19,* 479–483.

Israel, A.C., Stolmaker, L., & Andrian, C.A.G. (1985). Thoughts about food and their relationship to obesity and weight control. *International Journal of*

Eating Disorders, 4, 549–558.
Johnson, C. (1985). The initial consultation for patients with bulimia and anorexia nervosa. In D.M. Garner & P.E. Garfinkel (Eds.), *Handbook of psychotherapy for anorexia and bulimia* (pp. 19–51). New York: Guilford Press.
Johnson, C.L., & Berndt, D.J. (1983). Preliminary investigation of bulimia and life adjustment. *American Journal of Psychiatry, 140,* 774–777.
Johnson, C.L., & Connors, M.E. (1987). *The etiology and treatment of bulimia nervosa: A biopsychosocial perspective.* New York: Basic Books.
Johnson, C.L., Lewis, C., Love, C., Stuckey, M., & Lewis, L. (1983). A descriptive survey of dieting and bulmic behavior in a female high school population. *Report of the 4th Ross Conference on Medical Research,.*
Johnson, C.L., & Love, S.Q. (1985). Bulimia: Multivariate predictors of life impairment. *Journal of Psychiatric Research, 19,* 343–347.
Johnson, C.L., Stuckey, M.K., Lewis, L.D., & Schwartz, D.M. (1983). Bulimia: A descriptive survey of 316 cases. *International Journal of Eating Disorders, 2,* 3–19.
Johnson, W.G., (1975). Group therapy: A behavioral perspective. *Behavior Therapy, 6,* 30–38.
Johnson, W.G. (1989). Influence of exercise on appetite and insulin. Unpublished manuscript, University of Mississippi Medical School.
Johnson, W.G., & Brief, D.J. (1983). Bulimia. *Behavioral Medicine Update, 4,* 16–21.
Johnson, W.G., Corrigan, S.A., Crusco, A.H., & Jarrell, M.P. (1987). Behavioral assessment and treatment of postprandial regurgitation. *Journal of Clinical Gastroenterology, 9,* 679–684.
Johnson, W.G., Corrigan, S.A., Crusco, A.H., & Schlundt, D.G. (1986). Restraint among bulimic women. *Addictive Behaviors, 11,* 351–354.
Johnson, W.G., Corrigan, S.A., & Mayo, L.L. (1987). Innovative treatment approaches to bulimia nervosa. *Behavior Modification, 11,* 373–388.
Johnson, W.G., & Jarrell, M.P. (1988). The effect of self-induced vomiting on insulin/glucose levels. Unpublished manuscript, University of Mississippi Medical Center, Jackson.
Johnson, W.G., Schlundt, D.G., & Jarrell, M.P. (1986). Exposure with response prevention, training in energy balance, and problem-solving therapy for bulimia nervosa. *International Journal of Eating Disorders, 5,* 35–45.
Johnson, W.G., Schlundt, D.G., Kelloy, M.L., & Ruggiero, L. (1984). Exposure with response prevention and energy regulation in the treatment of bulimia. *International Journal of Eating Disorders, 3,* 37–46.
Johnson, W.G., & Stalonas, P.M. (1981). *Weight no longer.* Gretna, LA: Pelican Press.
Johnson, W.G., & Wildman, H. (1980). Influence of external and covert food stimuli on insulin secretion in obese and normal persons. *Behavioral Neuroscience, 97,* 1025–1028.
Johnson-Sabine, E.C., Wood, K.H., & Wakeling, A. (1984). Mood changes in bulimia nervosa. *British Journal of Psychiatry, 145,* 512–516.
Jonas, J., & Gold, M. (1986). Naltexone reverses bulimic symptoms. *Lancet, 1,* 807.
Jonas, J., & Gold, M. (1987). Treatment of anti-depressant resistant bulimia with naltrexone. *International Journal of Psychiatry in Medicine, 16,* 305–309.
Jones, D.A., Cheshire, N., & Moorhouse, H. (1985). Anorexia and nervosa and alcoholism—Association of eating disorder and alcohol. *Journal of Psychiatric*

Research, 19, 377–380.
Jourard, S.M., & Secord, P.F. (1955). Body cathexis and the ideal female figure. *Journal of Abnormal and Social Psychology, 50,* 243–246.
Judd, F.K., Norman, T.R., & Burrows, G.D., (1987). Pharmacotherpay in the treatment of anorexia and bulimia nervosa. In P.J.V. Beumont, G.D. Burrows, R.C. Casper (Eds.), *Handbook of eating disorders part I: Anorexia and bulimia nervosa* (pp. 361–370). New York: Elsevier.
Katch, F.I., & McArdle, W.D. (1977). *Nutrition, weight control, and exericse.* Boston: Houghton Mifflin.
Katzman, M.A., Wolchik, S.A., & Braver, S.L. (1984). The prevalence of frequent binge eating and bulimia in a nonclinical college sample. *International Journal of Eating Disorders, 3,* 53–64.
Kauff, P.F. (1979). Diversity in analytic group psychotherapy: The relationship between theoretical concepts and techniques. *International Journal of Group Psychotherapy, 29,* 51–65.
Kaye, W.H., Gwirtsman, H., George, T., Ebert, M.H., & Petersen, R. (1986). Caloric consumption and activity levels after weight recovery: A prolonged delay in normalization. *International Journal of Eating Disorders, 5,* 489–502.
Kazdin, A.E. (1973). The effect of vicarious reinforcement on attentive behavior in the classroom. *Journal of Applied Behavior Analysis, 6,* 71–78.
Keesey, R.E. (1986). A set-point theory of obesity. In K.D. Brownell & J.P. Foreyt (Eds.), *Handbook of eating disorders* (pp. 63–88). New York: Basic Books.
Keesey, R.E., & Corbett, S.W. (1984). Metabolic defense of the body weight setpoint. In A.J. Stunkard & E. Stellar (Eds.), *Eating and its disorders.* New York: Raven Press.
Keesey, R.E., & Powley, T.L. (1986). The regulation of body weight. *Annual Review of Psychology, 37,* 109–133.
Kendall, P.C., & Hollon, S.D. (1979). Cognitive-behavioral interventions: Overview and current status. In P.C. Kendall & S.D. Hollon (Eds.), *Cognitive-behavioral interventions: Theory, research, and procedures.* New York: Academic Press.
Keys, A., Brozek, J., Henschel, A., Mickelsen, O., & Taylor, H.L. (1950). *The biology of human starvation.* Minneapolis: University of Minnesota Press.
Killen, J.D., Taylor, C.B., Telch, M.J., Saylor, K.E., Maron, D.J., & Robinson, T.N. (1986). Self-induced vomiting and laxative and diuretic use among teenagers. *Journal of the American Medical Association, 255,* 1447–1449.
Kirkley, B.G., Burge, J.C., & Ammerman, A. (1988). Dietary restraint, binge eating, and dietary behavior patterns. *International Journal of Eating Disorders, 7,* 771–778.
Kirkley, B.G., Schneider, J.A., Agras, W.S., & Bachman, J.A. (1985). Comparison of two group treatments for bulimia. *Journal of Consulting and Clinical Psychology, 53,* 43–48.
Klanjer, F., Herman, C.P., Polivy, J. & Chhabra, R. (1981). Human obesity, dieting, and anticipatory salivation to food. *Physiology and Behavior, 27,* 195–198.
Klein, R.H. (1983). Group treatment approaches. In M. Hersen, A.E. Kazdin, & A.S. Bellack (Eds.), *The Clinical Psychology Handbook* (pp. 593–610). New York: Pergamon.
Kog, E., & Vandereycken, W. (1985). Family characteristics of anorexia nervosa

and bulimia: A review of the research literature. *Clinical Psychology Review, 5,* 159-180.

Kog, E., & Vandereycken, W. (1989). Family interaction in eating disorder patients and normal controls. *International Journal of Eating Disorders, 8,* 11-23.

Kohut, H. (1971). *The analysis of the self.* New York: International Universities Press.

Krall, E.A., & Dwyer, J.T. (1987). Validity of a food frequency questionnaire and a food diary in a short-term recall situation. *Journal of the American Dietetic Association, 87,* 1374-1377.

Kuldau, J.M., & Rand, C.S.W. (1986). The night eating syndrome and bulimia in the morbidity obese. *International Journal of Eating Disorders, 5,* 143-148.

L'Abate, L.L., & Milan, M.A. (1985). *Handbook of social skills training and research.* New York: Wiley.

Lacey, J.H. (1982). The bulimic syndrome at normal body weight: Reflections on pathogenesis and clinical features. *International Journal of Eating Disorders, 1,* 59-65.

Lacey, J.H., Coker, S., & Birtchnell, S.A. (1986). Bulimia: Factors associated with its etiology and maintenance. *International Journal of Eating Disorders, 5,* 475-487.

Lacey, J.H., & Gibson, E. (1985). Does laxative abuse control body weight? A comparative study of purging and vomiting in bulimia. *Human Nutrition/Applied Nutrition, 39,* 36-42.

Laessle, R.G., Schweiger, U., Daute-Herold, U. Schweiger, M., Fichter, M.M., & Pirke, K.M. (1988). Nutritional Knowledge in patients with eating disorders. *International Journal of Eating Disorders, 7,* 63-73.

Larson, R., & Johnson, C. (1985). Bulimia: Disturbed patterns of solitude. *Addictive Behaviors, 10,* 281-290.

Lee, N.F., & Rush, A.J. (1986). Cognitive-behavioral group therapy for bulimia. *International Journal of Eating Disorders, 5,* 599-616.

Leiberman, H.R., Wurtman, J.J., & Chew, B. (1986). Changes in mood after carbohydrate consumption among obese individuals. *American Journal of Clinical Nutrition, 44,* 772-778.

Leiberman, M.A. (1976). Change induction in small groups. In M.R. Rozenweig & L.W. Porter (Eds.), *Annual Review of Psychology.* Palo Alto: Annual Reviews.

Leibowitz, S.F. (1983). Hypothalamic catecholamine systems controlling eating behavior: A potential model for anorexia nervosa. In P.L. Darby, P.E. Garfinkel, D.M. Garner, & D.V. Corsica (Eds.), *Anorexia nervosa: Recent developments in research* (pp. 221-229). New York: Allen R. Liss.

Leibowitz, S.F. (1988). Brain neurotransmitters and drug effects on food intake and appetite: Implications for eating disorders. In B.T. Walsh (Ed.), *Eating behavior in eating disorders* (pp. 21-35). Washington, DC: American Psychiatric Press.

Leibowitz, S.F., & Shor-Posner, G. (1986). Hypothalamic monoamine systems for control of food intake: Analysis of meal patterns and macronutrient selection. In M.O. Carruba & J.E. Blundell (Eds.), *Pharmacology of eating disorders: Theoretical and clinical developments* (pp. 29-49). New York: Raven Press.

Leitenberg, H., Gross, J., Peterson, J., & Rosen, J.C. (1984). Analysis of an anxiety model and the process of change during exposure with response prevention treatment of bulimia nervosa. *Behavior Therapy, 15*, 3–20.

Leon, G.R. (1984). Anorexia and sports activities. *The Behavior Therapist, 7*, 9–10.

Leon, G.R., Carroll, K., Chernyk, B., & Finn, S. (1985). Binge eating and associated habit patterns within college student and identified bulimic populations. *International Journal of Eating Disorders, 4*, 43–57.

Lerner, H.D. (1983). Contemporary psychoanalytic perspectives on gorge-vomiting: A case illustration. *International Journal of Eating Disorders, 3*, 47–63.

Levendusky, P.G., & Dooley, C.P. (1985). An inpatient model for the treatment of anorexia nervosa. In S. Emmett (Ed.), *Eating disorders: Research, theory, and treatment* (pp. 211–233). New York: Brunner/Mazel.

Levine, A.S., Morley, J.E., Gosnell, B.A., Billington, C.J., & Bartness, T.J. (1985). Opiods and consummatory behavior. *Brain Research Bulletin, 14*, 663–672.

Lisner, L., Levitsky, D.A., Strupp, B.J., et al. (1987). Dietary fat and the regulation of energy intake in human subjects. *American Journal of Clinical Nutrition, 46*, 886–892.

Lowenkopf, E.L. (1982). Anorexia nervosa: Some nosological considerations. *Comprehensive Psychiatry, 23*, 233–240.

Lucas, A.R., Beard, C.M., Kranz, J.S., & Kurland, L.T. (1983). Epidemiology of anorexia nervosa and bulimia: Background of the Rochester project. *International Journal of Eating Disorders, 2*, 85–89.

Machover, K. (1957). *Personality projection in the drawing of the human figure.* Springfield: C.C. Thomas.

Maddox, G.L., Back, K.W., & Liederman, V.R. (1968). Overweight and social deviance and disability. *Journal of Health and Social Behavior, 9*, 287–298.

Magnusson, D., & Endler, N.S. (1977). *Personality at the crossroads: Current issues in interactional psychology.* Hillsdale, NJ: Lawrence Erlbaum.

Maloney, M.J., & Farrell, M.K. (1980). Treatment of severe weight loss in anorexia nervosa with hyperalimentation and psychotherapy. *American Journal of Psychiatry, 137*, 310–314.

Marks, J., Sonoda, B., & Schalock, R. (1968). Reinforcement vs. relationship therapy for schizophrenics. *Journal of Abnormal Psychology, 73*, 397–402.

Markus, H. (1977). Self-schemata and processing information about the self. *Journal of Personality and Social Psychology, 35* (2), 63–78.

Markus, H., Crane, M., Bernstein, S., & Siladi, M. (1982). Self-schemas and gender. *Journal of Personality and Social Psychology, 42* (1), 38–50.

Markus, H., Hamil, R., and Sentis, K.P. (1987). Thinking fat: Self-schemas for body weight and the processing of weight relevant information. *Journal of Applied Social Psychology, 17*, 50–71.

Markus, H., & Smith, J. (1981). The influence of self-schemata on the perception of others. In N. Cantor & J. Kihlstrom (Eds.), *Personality, cognition and social interaction.* Hillsdale, NJ: Lawrence Erlbaum.

Marlat, G.A., & Gordon, J.R. (1980). Determinants of relapse: Implications for the maintenance of behavior change. In P.O. Davison & S.M. Davison (Eds.), *Behavioral medicine: Changing health lifestyles.* New York: Brunner/Mazel.

Marrazzi, M.A., & Luby, E.D. (1986). An auto-addiction model of chronic anorexia nervosa. *International Journal of Eating Disorders, 5*, 191–208.

Martin, J.R., & Wollitzer, A.O. (1988). The prevalence, secrecy, and psychology

of purging in a family practice setting. *International Journal of Eating Disorders, 7,* 515–519.
Matusewich, E. (1983). Labor relations: Employment discrimination against the overweight. *Personel Journal,* (June), 446–450.
McArdle, W.D., Katch, F.I., & Katch, V.L. (1986). *Exercise physiology: Energy, nutrition, and human performance.* Philadelphia: Lea & Febiger.
McFall, R.M. (1976). *Behavioral training: A skill acquisition approach to clinical problems.* Morristown, NJ: General Learning Press.
McFall, R.M. (1982). A review and reformulation of the concept of social skills. *Behavioral Assessment, 4,* 1–33.
McGowen, C.R., Epstein, L.H., Kupfer, D.J., & Bulik, C.M. (1986). The effect of exercise on nonrestricted caloric intake in male joggers. *Appetite, 7,* 97–105.
McMullin, R.E. (1986). *Handbook of cognitive therapy techniques.* New York: Norton.
McNeill, G., Bruce, A.C., Ralph, A., & James, W.P.T. (1988). Interindividual differences in fasting nutrient oxidation and the influence of diet composition. *International Journal of Obesity, 12,* 455–463.
Meichenbaum, D. (1974). *Cognitive behavior modification.* Morristown, NJ: General Learning Press.
Merrill, C.A., Mines, R.A., & Starkey, R. (1987). The premature dropout in the group treatment of bulimia. *International Journal of Eating Disorders, 6,* 293–300.
Mickalide, A.D., & Andersen, A.F. (1985). Subgroups of anorexia nervosa and bulimia: Validity and utility. *Journal of Psychiatric Research, 19,* 121–128.
Miller, J.G. (1978). *Living systems.* New York: McGraw Hill.
Minuchin, S. (1974). *Families and family therapy.* Cambridge, MA: Harvard University Press.
Minuchin, S., Rosman, B., & Baker, L. (1978). *Psychosomatic families: Anorexia nervosa in context.* Cambridge, MA: Harvard University Press.
Mischel, W. (1968). *Personality and Assessment.* New York: Wiley.
Mischel, W. (1973). Toward a cognitive social learning reconceptualization of personality. *Psychological Review, 80,* 252–283.
Mitchell, J.E. (1986). Anorexia nervosa: Medical and physiological aspects. In K.D. Brownell & J.P. Foreyt (Eds.), *Handbook of eating disorders.* New York: Basic Books.
Mitchell, J.E., & Boutacoff, M.A. (1986). Laxative abuse complicating bulimia: Medical and treatment implications. *International Journal of Eating Disorders, 5,* 325–334.
Mitchell, J.E., Davis, L., & Goff, G. (1985). The process of relapse in patients with bulimia. *International Journal of Eating Disorders, 4,* 457–463.
Mitchell, J.E., & Groat, R.A. (1984). A placebo-controlled double-blind trial of amitriptyline in bulimia. *Journal of Clinical Psychopharmacology, 4,* 186–193.
Mitchell, J.E., Hatsukami, D., Eckert, E.D., & Pyle, R.L. (1985). Characteristics of 275 patients with bulimia. *American Journal of Psychiatry, 142,* 482–485.
Mitchell, J.E., Hatsukami, D., Goff, G., Pyle, R.L., Eckert, E.D., & Davis, L.E. (1985). Intensive outpatient group treatment for bulimia. In D.M. Garner & P.E. Garfinkel (Eds.), *Handbook of psychotherapy for anorexia nervosa and bulima* (pp. 240–253). New York: Guilford Press.

Mitchell, J.E., & Laine, D.C. (1985). Monitored binge-eating behavior in patients with bulimia. *International Journal of Eating Disorders, 4,* 177–183.

Mitchell, J.E., Laine, D.C., Morely, J.E., & Levine, A.S. (1986). Naloxone but not CCK-8 may attenuate binge-eating behavior in patients with the bulimia syndrome. *Biological Psychiatry, 21,* 1339–1406.

Mitchell, J.E., Pomeroy, C., & Huber, M. (1988). A clinician's guide to the eating disorders medicine cabinet. *International Journal of Eating Disorders, 7,* 211–223.

Mitchell, J.E., Pomeroy, C., Seppala, M., & Huber, M. (1988). PseudoBartter's syndrome, diuretic absued, ideopathic edema, and eating disorders. *International Journal of Eating Disorders, 7,* 225–237.

Mitchell, J.E., Pyle, R.L., & Eckert, E.D. (1981). Frequency and duration of binge-eating episodes in patients with bulimia. *American Journal of Psychiatry, 138, 835–836.*

Mitchell, J.E., Pyle, R.L., Hatsukami, D., & Eckert, E.D. (1986). What are atypical eating disorders? *Psychosomatics, 27,* 21–27.

Mitchell, P.B. (1988). The pharmacological management of bulimia nervosa: A critical review. *International Journal of Eating Disorders, 7,* 29–41.

Mori, D., Chaiken, S., & Pliner, P. (1987). "Eating lightly" and the self-presentation of femininity. *Journal of Personality and Social Psychology, 53,* 693–702.

Morley, J.E., Levine, A.S., Gosnell, B.A., & Billington, C.J. (1984a). Neuropeptides and appetite: Contributions of neuropharmacological modeling. *Federation Proceedings, 43,* 2903–2907.

Morley, J.E., Levine, A.S., Gosnell, B.A., & Billington, C.J. (1984b). Which opiod receptor modulates feeding? *Appetite, 5,* 61–68.

Morley, J.E., Levine, A.S., & Willenbring, M.L. (1986). Stress-induced feeding disorders. In M.O. Carruba & J.E. Blundell (Eds.), *Pharmacology of eating disorders: Theoretical and clinical developments* (pp. 71–99). New York: Raven Press.

Neilsen, S. (1985). Evaluation of growth in anorexia nervosa from serial measurements. *Journal of Psychiatric Research, 19,* 227–230.

Neuman, P.A., & Halverson, P.A. (1983). *Anorexia nervosa and bulimia: A handbook for counselors and therapists.* New York: Van Nostrand Reinhold.

Nevo, S. (1985). Bulimic symptoms: Prevalence and ethnic differences among college women. *International Journal of Eating Disorders, 4,* 151–168.

Nicholas, P., & Dwyer, J. (1986). Diets for weight reduction: Nutritional considerations. In K.D. Brownell & J. P. Foreyt (Eds.), *Handbook of eating disorders* (pp. 122–144). New York: Basic Books.

Nisbett, R.E. (1972). Hunger, obesity, and the ventromedial hypothalamus. *Psychological Reviews, 79,* 433–453.

Nisbett, R.E., & Temoshok, L. (1976). Is there an external cognitive style? *Journal of Personality and Social Psychology, 33,* 36–47.

Nishita, J.K., Knopes, K.D., Ellinwood, E.H., & Rockwell, W.J.K. (1986). Hypothermia and abnormalities in thermoregulation with anorexia nervosa. *International Journal of Eating Disorders, 5,* 713–725.

Noles, S.W., Cash, T.F., & Winstead, B.A. (1985). Body image, physical attractiveness, and depression. *Journal of Consulting and Clinical Psychology, 53,* 88–94.

Norman, D.K., & Herzog, D.B. (1984). Persistant social maladjustment in bulimia: A 1-year follow-up. *American Journal of Psychiatry, 141,* 444–446.

Norman, D.K., Herzog, D.B., & Chauncey, S. (1986). A one-year outcome study of bulimia: Psychological and eating symptom changes in a treatment and nontreatment group. *International Journal of Eating Disorders, 5,* 47–57.

Norris, P.D., O'Malley, B.P., & Palmer, R.L. (1985). The TRH test in bulimia and anorexia nervosa: A controlled study. *Journal of Psychiatric Research, 19,* 215–219.

Norton, K.R.W., Crisp, A.H., & Bhat, A.V. (1985). Why do some anorexics steal? Personal, social, and illness factors. *Journal of Psychiatric Research, 19,* 385–390.

Nudelman, S., Rosen, J.C., & Leitenberg, H. (1988). Dissimilarities in eating attitudes, body image distortion, depression, and self-esteem between high-intensity male runners and women with bulimia nervosa. *International Journal of Eating Disorders, 7,* 625–643.

Nylander, I. (1971). The feeling of being fat and dieting in a school population: Epidemiologic, interview investigation. *Acta Sociomedica Scandinavia, 3,* 17–26.

O'Connor, M., Touyz, S., & Beumont, P. (1988). Nutritional management and dietary counseling in bulimia nervosa: Some preliminary observations. *International Journal of Eating Disorders, 1,* 657–662.

Oppenheimer, R., Howells, K., Palmer, R.L., & Chaloner, D.A. (1985). Adverse sexual experience in childhood and clinical eating disorders: A preliminary description. *Journal of Psychiatric Research, 19,* 357–361.

Orbach, S. (1978). Social dimensions in compulsive eating in women. *Psychotherapy Research and Practice, 15,* 180–189.

Orbach, S. (1985). Visibility/invisibility: Social considerations in anorexia nervosa—A feminist perspective. In S.W. Emmett (Ed.), *Theory and treatment of anorexia nervosa and bulimia.* New York: Brunner/Mazel.

Ordman, A.M., & Kirschenbaum, D.S. (1986). Bulimia: Assessment of eating, psychological adjustment, and familial characteristics. *International Journal of Eating Disorders, 5,* 865–878.

Oyebode, F., Boodhoo, J.A., & Schapira, K. (1988). Anorexia nervosa in males: Clinical features and outcomes. *International Journal of Eating Disorders, 7,* 121–124.

Palmer, R.L. (1979). The dietary chaos syndrome: A useful new term? *British Journal of Medical Psychology, 52,* 187–190.

Parloff, M.B., & Deis, R.R. (1977). Group psychotherapy outcome researc 1966–1975. *International Journal of Group Psychotherpay, 28,* 281–319.

Pasman, L., & Thompson, J.K. (1988). Body image and eating disturbance i obligatory runners, obligatory weightlifters, and sedentary individuals. *I ternational Journal of Eating Disorders, 7,* 759–769.

Pendergrass. V.E. (1972). Timeout from positive reinforcement following persi tent, high-rate behavior in retardates. *Journal of Applied Behavior Analysi 5,* 85–91.

Pertschuk, M., Collins, M., Kreisberg, J., & Fager, S.S. (1986). Psychiatric sym] toms associated with eating disorder in a college population. *Internationc Journal of Eating Disorders, 5,* 563–568.

Pertschuk, M.J., Forster, J., Buzby, G., & Mullen, D. (1981). The treatment of anorexia nervosa with total parenteral nutrition. *Biological Psychiatry, 16,* 539–550.

Pierloot, R., & Houben, M. (1978). Estimation of body dimensions in anorexia nervosa. *Psychological Medicine, 8,* 317–324.

Piran, N., Kennedy, S., Garfinkel, P.E., & Owners, M. (1985). Affective disturbance in eating disorders. *The Journal of Nervous and Mental Disease, 173,* 395–400.

Piran, N., Lerner, P., Garfinkel, P.E., Kennedy, S.H., & Brouillette, C. (1988). Personality disorders in anorexic patients. *International Journal of Obesity, 7,* 589–600.

Pole, R., Waller, D.A., Stewart, S.M., & Parkin-Feigenbaum, L. (1988). Parental caring versus overprotection in bulimia. *International Journal of Eating Disorders, 7,* 601–606.

Polivy, J., & Herman, C.P. (1985). Dieting and binging: A causal analysis. *American Psychologist, 40,* 193–201.

Polivy, J., & Herman, C.P. (1987). Diagnosis and treatment of normal eating. *Journal of Consulting and Clinical Psychology, 55,* 635–644.

Pope, H.G., Champoux, R.F., & Hudson, J.I. (1987). Eating disorder and socioeconomic class: Anorexia nervosa and bulimia in nine communities. *Journal of Nervous and Mental Disease, 175,* 620–623.

Pope, H.G., & Hudson, J.I. (1985). Biological treatment of eating disorders. In S.W. Emmett (Ed.), *Theory and treatment of anorexia nervosa and bulimia* (pp. 73–92). New York: Brunner/Mazel.

Pope, H.G., & Hudson, J.I., (1986). Antidepressant drug therapy of bulimia: Current status. *Journal of Clinical Psychiatry, 47,* 339–345.

Pope, H.G., & Hudson, J.I. (1988). Is bulimia nervosa a heterogeneous disorder? Lessons from the history of medicine. *International Journal of Eating Disorders, 7,* 155–166.

Pope, H.G., & Hudson, J.I. (1989). Are eating disorders associated with borderline personality disorder? A critical review. *International Journal of Eating Disorders, 8,* 1–9.

Pope, H.G., Hudson, J.I., Jonas, J.M., & Yurgelun-Todd, D. (1983). Bulimia treated with imipramine: A placebo-controlled double-blind study. *American Journal of Psychiatry, 35,* 811–828.

Pope, H.G., Hudson, J.I., & Yurgelun-Todd, D. (1984a). Anorexia nervosa and bulimia among 300 suburban women shoppers. *American Journal of Psychiatry, 141,* 292–294.

Pope, H.G., Hudson, J.I., Yurgelun-Todd, D., & Hudson, M. (1984b). Prevalence of anorexia nervosa and bulimia in three student populations. *International Journal of Eating Disorders, 3,* 45–54.

Powers, P.S. (1984). Therapeutic use of symptoms, signs, and laboratory data. In P.S. Powers & R.C. Fernandez (Eds.), *Current treatment of anorexia nervosa and bulimia.* (pp. 215–239). New York: Karger.

Powers, P.S., & Fernandez, R.C. (1984). Appendix. In P.S. Powers & R.C. Fernandez (Eds.), *Current treatment of anorexia nervosa and bulimia* (pp. 302–325). New York: Karger.

Price, J.M., & Grinker, J. (1973). Effects of degree of obesity, food deprivation, and palatability on eating behavior of humans. *Journal of Comparative and*

Physiological Psychology, 85, 68-78.
Pyle, R.L., Halvorson, P.A., Neuman, P.A., & Mitchell, J.E. (1986). The increasing prevalence of bulimia in freshman college students. *International Journal of Eating Disorders, 5,* 631-647.
Pyle, R.L., Mitchell, J.E., & Eckert, E.D. (1981). Bulimia: a report of 34 cases. *Journal of Clinical Psychiatry, 42,* 60-64.
Pyle, R.L., Mitchell, J.E., & Eckert, E.D. (1986). The use of weight tables to categorize patients with eating disorders. *International Journal of Eating Disorders, 5,* 377-383.
Pyle, R.L., Mitchell, J.E., Eckert, E.D., Halvorson, P.A. Neuman, P.A., & Goff, G.M. (1983). The incidence of bulimia in freshman college students. *International Journal of Eating Disorders, 2,* 75-85.
Raciti, M.C., & Norcross, J.C. (1987). The EAT and the EDI: Screening interrelationships, and psychometrics. *International Journal of Eating Disorders, 6,* 579-586.
Rand, C.S.W., & Kuldau, J.M. (1986). Eating patterns in normal weight individuals: Bulimia, restrained eating, and the night eating syndrome. *International Journal of Eating Disorders, 5,* 75-84.
Reid, L.D., (1985). Endogenous opiod peptides and regulation of drinking and feeding. *The American Journal of Clinical Nutrition, 42,* 1099-1132.
Reitman, E.E., & Cleveland, S.E. (1969). Changes in body image following sensory deprivation in schizophrenia and control groups. *Journal of Abnormal and Social Psychology, 68,* 169-176.
Richardson, S.A., Hastorf, A.H., Goodman, N., & Dornbusch, S.M. (1961). Cultural uniformity in reaction to physical disabilities. *American Sociological Review, 90,* 44-54.
Richert, A.J., & Hummers, J.A. (1986). Patterns of physical activity in college students at possible risk for eating disorder. *International Journal of Eating Disorders, 5,* 757-763.
Rippon, C., Nash, J., Myburgh, K.H., & Noakes, T.D. (1988). Abnormal eating attitude test scores predict menstrual dysfunction in lean females. *International Journal of Eating Disorders, 7,* 617-624.
Robinson, P., & Andersen, A. (1985). Anorexia nervosa in American Blacks. *Journal of Psychiatric Research, 19,* 183-188.
Robinson, P.H., Checkley, S.A., & Russell, G.F.M. (1985). Suppression of eating by fenfluramine in patients with bulimia nervosa. *British Journal of Psychiatry, 146,* 169-176.
Rockwell, W.J.K., Ellingwood, E.H., Dougherty, G.G., & Brodie, H.K.H. (1982). Anorexia nervosa: Review of current treatment practices. *Southern Medical Journal, 75,* 1101-1107.
Rodin, G.M., Daneman, D., Johnson, L.E., Kenshole, A., & Garfinkel, P. (1985). Anorexia nervosa and bulimia in female adolescents with insulin dependent diabetes mellitus: A systematic study. *Journal of Psychiatric Research, 19,* 381-384.
Rodin, J. (1981). The current status of the internal-external obesity hypothesis: What went wrong. *American Psychologist, 36,* 361-372.
Rodin, J., Silberstein, L.R., and Streigel-Moore, R.H. (1985). Women and weight: A normative discontent. In T.B. Sonergger (Ed.), *Nebraska Symposium on*

Motivation: Vol 32. Psychology and Gender (pp. 267–307). Lincoln: University of Nebraska Press.

Rodin, J., Slochower, J., & Fleming, B. (1977). The effects of degree of obesity, age of onset, and energy deficit on external responsiveness. *Journal of Comparative and Physiological Psychology, 91,* 586–597.

Root, A.W. (1984). Biological aspects of eating behaviors. In P.S. Powers & R.C. Fernandez (Eds.), *Current treatment of anorexia nervosa and bulimia* (pp. 158–165). New York: Karger.

Root, M.P.P. (1983). *Bulimia: A descriptive and treatment outcome study.* Doctoral dissertation, University of Washington, Seattle.

Root, M.P.P., Fallon, P., & Freidrich, W.N. (1986). *Bulimia: A systems approach to treatment.* New York: W.W. Norton.

Rosen, J.C. (1988). Test meals in the assessment of bulimia. In M.Hersen & A.S. Bellack (Eds.), *Dictionary of Behavioral Assessment* (pp. 473–474). New York: Pergamon Press.

Rosen, J.C., & Gross, J. (1987). The prevalence of weight reducing and weight gaining in adolescent girls and boys. *Health Psychology, 6,* 131–147.

Rosen, J.C., & Leitenberg, H. (1982). Bulimia nervosa: Treatment with exposure and response prevention. *Behavior Therapy, 13,* 117–124.

Rosen, J.C., & Leitenberg, H. (1985). Exposure plus response prevention treatment of bulimia nervosa. In D.M. Garner & P.E. Garfinkel (Eds.), *Handbook of psychotherapy for anorexia nervosa and bulimia* (pp. 193–212). New York: Guilford Press.

Rosen, J.C., Leitenberg, H., Fisher, C., & Khazam, C. (1986). Binge-eating episodes in bulimia nervosa: The amount and type of food consumed. *International Journal of Eating Disorders, 5,* 255–267.

Rosen, J.C., Leitenberg, H., Fondacaro, K.M., Gross, J., & Wilmuth, M. (1985). Standardized test meals in assessment of eating behavior in bulimia nervosa: Consumption of feared foods when vomiting is prevented. *International Journal of Eating Disorders, 4,* 59–70.

Rosen, L.W., Shafer, C.L., Drummer, G.M., Cross, L.K., Deuman, G.W., & Malmberg, S.R. (1988). Prevalence of pathogenic weight-control behaviors among Native American women and girls. *International Journal of Eating Disorders, 7,* 807–811.

Rothblum, E.D., Miller, C.T., & Garbutt, B. (1988). Stereotypes of obese female job applicants. *International Journal of Eating Disorders, 7,* 277–283.

Rothwell, N.J., & Stock, M.J. (1988). Insulin and thermogenesis. *International Journal of Obesity, 12,* 93–102.

Roy-Byrne, P., Lee-Benner, K., & Yager, J. (1984). Group therapy for bulimia: A year's experience. *International Journal of Eating Disorders, 3,* 97–116.

Ruderman, A.J. (1986). Dietary restraint: A theoretical and empirical review: *Psychological Bulletin, 99,* 247–262.

Ruderman, A.J. & Wilson, G.T. (1979). Weight, restraint, cognitions, and counterregulation. *Behavior Research and Therapy, 17,* 581–590.

Ruff, G., & Barrios, B. (1986). Realistic assessment of body image. *Behavioral Assessment, 8,* 237–252.

Ruggiero, L., Williamson, D.A., Davis, C.J., Schlundt, D.G., & Carey, M.P. (1988). Forbidden food survey: Measure of bulimic's anticipated emotional reactions

to specific foods. *Addictive Behaviors, 13,* 267–274.
Russell, G. (1970). Anorexia nervosa: Its identity as an illness and its treatment. In J.H. Price (Ed.), *Modern trends in psychological medicine* (pp. 131–164). London: Buttersworth.
Russell, G. (1979). Bulimia nervosa: an ominous variant of anorexia nervosa. *Psychological Medicine, 9,* 429–488.
Russell, G.F.M. (1983). Anorexia nervosa and bulimia nervosa. In G.F.M. Russell & L.A. Hersov (Eds.), *Handbook of psychiatry vol IV: The neuroses and personality disorders* (pp. 285–298). Cambridge: Cambridge University Press.
Russell, G.F.M., Checkley, S.A., & Robinson, P.H. (1986). The limited role of drugs in the treatment of anorexia nervosa and bulimia. In M.O. Carruba & J.E. Blundell (Eds.), *Pharmacology of eating disorders: Theoretical and clinical developments.* New York: Raven Press, 151–167.
Russell, G.F.M., & Mezey, A.G. (1962). An analysis of weight gain in patients with anorexia nervosa treated with high calorie diets. *Clinical Science, 23,* 449–461.
Russell, G.F.M., Szmukler, G.I., Dare, C., & Eisler, I. (1987). An evaluation of family therapy in anorexia nervosa and bulimia nervosa. *Archives of General Psychiatry, 44,* 1047–1056.
Sabine, E. J., Yonace, A., Farrington, A.J., Barratt, K.H., & Wakeling, A. (1983). Bulimia nervosa: A placebo-controlled double-blind trial of mianserin. *British Journal of Clinical Psychopharmacology, 15,* 195S–202S.
Sargent, J., Liebman, R., & Silver, M. (1985). Family therapy for anorexia nervosa. In D.M. Garner & P.E. Garfinkel (Eds.), *Handbook of psychotherapy for anorexia nervosa and bulimia* (pp. 257–279). New York: Guilford Press.
Schachter, S. (1971). *Emotion, obesity, and crime.* New York: Academic press.
Schachter, S., & Gross, L. (1968). Manipulated time and eating behavior. *Journal of Personality and Social Psychology, 10,* 98–106.
Schachter, S., & Rodin, J. (1974). *Obese humans and rats.* Washington, DC: Erlbaum/Halstead.
Schlesier-Stroop, B. (1984). Bulimia: A review of the literature. *Psychological Bulletin, 95,* 247–257.
Schlundt, D.G. (1985). An observational method for functional analysis. *Bulletin of the Society for Psychologists in Addictive Behaviors, 4,* 234–249.
Schlundt, D.G. (1986a). *The DIET lifestyle and behavior change workbook.* Nashville, TN: Vanderbilt University Weight Management Program.
Schlundt, D.G. (1986b). *Helping others lose weight: A step-by-step behavior change program.* Nashville, TN: Vanderbilt University Weight Management Program.
Schlundt, D.G. (1988). Accuracy of nutrient intake estimates. *Journal of Nutrition,* in press.
Schlundt, D.G. (in press). Behavioral assessment of eating behavior in bulimia: The self-monitoring analysis system. In W.G. Johnson (Ed.), *Advances in eating disorders Vol II.* New York: JAI Press.
Schlundt, D.G., & Bell, C. (1987). Behavioral assessment of eating patterns and blood glucose in diabetes using the self-monitoring analysis system. *Behavior Research, Methods, Instruments, and Computers, 19,* 215–223.
Schlundt, D.G., & Bell, C. (1988). Body Image and Testing System: Preliminary validation of a computerized approach to body image assessment. Paper

presentation at the Association for Advancement of Behavior Therapy, November, New York.

Schlundt, D.G., Hill, J.O., Sbrocco, T., Pope-Cordle, J., & Kasser, T. (1988). Behavioral assessment of eating in obese women. Under editorial review.

Schlundt, D.G., Johnson, W.G., & Jarrell, M.P. (1985). A naturalistic functional analysis of eating behavior in bulimia and obesity. *Advances in Behavior Research and Therapy, 7,* 149–162.

Schlundt, D.G., Johnson, W.G., & Jarrell, M.P. (1986). A sequential analysis of environmental, behavioral, and affective variables predictive of vomiting in bulimia nervosa. *Behavioral Assessment, 8,* 253–269.

Schlundt, D.G., & McFall, R.M. (1985). New directions in the assessment of social competence and social skills. In M.A. Milan & L.L. L'Abate (Eds.), *Handbook of social skills training and research.* New York: Pergamon Press.

Schlundt, D.G., & McFall, R.M. (1987). Classifying social situations: A comparison of five methods. *Behavioral Assessment, 9,* 21–42.

Schlundt, D.G., & Pope, J. (1988). *The Vanderbilt Food Inventory users manual.* Nashville, TN: Vanderbilt University Weight Management Program.

Schlundt, D.G., Sbrocco, T., & Bell, C. (in press). A sequential analysis of dietary slips. *International Journal of Obesity.*

Schlundt, D.G., & Zimering, R.T. (1988). The dieter's inventory of eating temptations: A measure of weight control competence. *Addictive Behaviors, 13,* 151–164.

Schmidt, U., & Marks, I. (1988). Cue exposure to food plus response prevention of binges for bulimia: A pilot study. *International Journal of Eating Disorders, 7,* 663–672.

Schneider, J.A., & Agras, W.S. (1985). A cognitive behavioral group treatment of bulimia. *British Journal of Psychology, 146,* 66–69.

Schotte, D.E., & Stunkard, A.J. (1987). Bulimia vs. bulimic behaviors on a college campus. *Journal of the American Medical Association, 258,* 1213–1215.

Schulman, R.G., Kinder, B.N. Powers, P., Prange, M., & Gleghorn, A. (1986). The development of a scale to measure cognitive distortions in bulimia. *Journal of Personality Assessment, 50,* 630–639.

Schutz, Y., & Bessard, T. (1984). Diet induced thermogenesis measured over a whole day in obese and nonobese women. *American Journal of Clinical Nutrition, 40,* 542–552.

Schwartz, D.M., Thompson, M.G., & Johnson, C.L. (1981). Anorexia nervosa and bulimia: The socio-cultural context. *International Journal of Eating Disorders, 1,* 20–36.

Schwartz, G.E. (1982). Testing the biopsychosocial model: The ultimate challenge facing behavioral medicine? *Journal of Consulting and Clinical Psychology, 50,* 1040–1053.

Schwartz, R.C., Barrett, M.J., & Saba, G. (1985). Family therapy for bulimia. In D.M. Garner & P.E. Garfinkel (Eds.), *Handbook of psychotherapy for anorexia nervosa and bulimia* (pp. 257–279). New York: Guilford Press.

Scott, D.W. (1986). Anorexia nervosa: A review of possible genetic factors. International Journal of Eating Disorders, 5, 1–20.

Secord, P., & Jourard, S. (1953). The appraisal of body cathexis and the self. *Journal of Consulting and Clinical Psychology, 17,* 343–347.

Senate Select Committee on Nutrition and Human Needs. (1977). *Dietary goals for the United States, 2nd Edition.* Washington, DC: U.S. Government Printing Office #052-070-04376-8.

Shangold, M.M. (1985). Athletic amenorrhea. *Clinical Obstetrics and Gynecology, 28,* 664-669.

Shiffrin, R.M., & Schneider, W. (1977). Controlled and automatic human information processing: II. Perceptual learning, automatic attending, and a general theory. *Psychological Review, 84,* 127-190.

Silber, T.J. (1986). Anorexia nervosa in Blacks and Hispanics. *International Journal of Eating Disorders, 5,* 121-128.

Silverstone, T., & Goodall, E. (1986). A pharmacological analysis of human feeding: Its contribution to the understanding of affective disorders. In M.O. Carruba & J.E. Blundell (Eds.), *Pharmacology of eating disorders: Theoretical and clinical developments.* (pp.141-150). New York: Raven Press.

Simms, E.A.H., & Horton, E.H. (1968). Endocrine and metabolic adaptation to obesity and starvation. *American Journal of Clinical Nutrition, 21,* 1455-1470.

Slade, P. (1985). A review of body image studies in anorexia nervosa and bulimia nervosa. *Journal of Psychiatric Research, 19*(2/3), 255-265.

Slade, P.D., & Dewey, M.E. (1986). Development and preliminary validation of the SCANS: A screening instrument for identifying individuals at risk of developing anorexia and bulimia nervosa. *International Journal of Eating Disorders, 5,* 517-538.

Slade, P.D., & Russell, G.F.M. (1973). Experimental investigations of body perception in anorexia nervosa and obesity. *Psychotherapy and Psychosomatics, 22,* 359-363.

Smith, M.C., & Thelen, M.H. (1984). Development and validation of a test for bulimia. *Journal of Consulting and Clinical Psychology, 52,* 863-872.

Smith, M.C., Pruitt, J.A., Mann, L.M., & Thelen, M.H. (1986). Attitudes and knowledge regarding bulimia and anorexia nervosa. *International Journal of Eating Disorders, 5,* 545-553.

Spitzer, L., & Rodin, J. (1987). Effects of fructose and glucose preloads on subsequent food intake. *Appetite, 8,* 135-145.

Stein, D.M., & Laakso, W. (1988). Bulimia: A historical perspective. *International Journal of Eating Disorders, 7,* 201-210.

Stern, S.L., Dixon, K.N. Jones, D., Lake, M., Nemzer, E., & Sansone, R. (1989). Family environment in anorexia nervosa and bulimia. *International Journal of Eating Disorders, 7,* 25-31.

Stierlin, H., & Weber, G. (1987). Anorexia nervosa: Family dynamics and family therapy. In P.J.V. Beumont, G.D. Burrows, & R.C. Casper (Eds.), *Handbook of eating disorders part 1: Anorexia and bulimia nevosa.* (pp.319-348). New York: Elsevier.

Strauss, J., & Ryan, R.M. (1987). Autonomy disturbances in subtypes of anorexia nervosa, *Journal of Abnormal Psychology, 96,* 254-258.

Striegel-Moore, R., McAvay, G., & Rodin, J. (1986). Psychological and behavioral correlates of feeling fat in women. *International Journal of Eating Disorders, 5,* 935-947.

Strober, M., & Humphrey, L.L. (1987). Familial contribution to the etiology and course of anorexia nervosa and bulimia. *Journal of Consulting and Clinical*

Psychology, 55, 654–659.
Strober, M., & Katz, J.L. (1987). Do eating disorders and affective disorders share a common etiology? A dissenting opinion. *International Journal of Eating Disorders, 6,* 111–122.
Strober, M., Morrell, W., Burroughs, J., Salkin, B., & Jacobs, C. (1985). A controlled family study of anorexia nervosa. *Journal of Psychiatric Research, 19,* 239–246.
Strober, M., Salkin, B., Burroughs, J. & Morrell, W. (1982). Validity of the bulimia-restricter distinction in anorexia nervosa: parental personality characteristics and family psychiatric morbidity. *The Journal of Nervous and Mental Disease, 170,* 345–351.
Stunkard, A. (1959). Obesity and the denial of hunger. *Psychosomatic Medicine, 21,* 281–289.
Stunkard, A.J., & Messick, S. (1985). The three-factor eating questionnaire to measure dietary restraint, disinhibition, and hunger. *Journal of Psychosomatic Research, 29,* 71–83.
Stunkard, A.J., Sorensen, T.I.A., Hanis, C., Teasdale, T.W., Chakraborty, R., Schull, W.J., & Schulsinger, F. (1986). An adoption study of human obesity. *The New England Journal of Medicine, 314,* 193–198.
Suitor, C.J.W., & Crowley, M.F. (1984). *Nutrition principles and application in health promotion.* Philadelphia: J.B. Lippincott.
Surgeon General. (1979). *Healthy people: The surgeon general's report on health promotion and disease prevention.* (017-001-00416-2). Washington, DC: Public Health Service, U.S. Department of Health, Education, and Welfare.
Swift, W.J., Andrews, D., & Barklage, N.E. (1986). The relationship between affective disorder and eating disorders: A review of the literature. *American Journal of Psychiatry, 143,* 290–299.
Swift, W.J., Kalin, N.H., Wambolt, F.S. Kaslow, N., and Ritholz, M. (1985). Depression in bulimia at 2 to 5 year follow-up. *Psychiatric Research, 16,* 111–122.
Szmukler, G.I. (1983). Weight and food preoccupation in a population of English school girls. *Report of the 4th Ross Conference on Medical Research,* (pp. 21–27).
Szmukler, G.I., Eisler, I., Gillies, C., & Hayward, M.E. (1985). The implications of anorexia nervosa in a ballet school. *Journal of Psychiatric Research, 19,* 177–181.
Szmukler, G.I., McCance, C., McCrone, L., & Hunter, D. (1986). Anorexia nervosa: A psychiatric case register study from Aberdeen, *Psychological Medicine, 16,* 49–58.
Telch, C.F., Agras, W.S., & Rossiter, E.M., (1988). Binge eating increases with increasing adiposity. *International Journal of Eating Disorders, 7,* 115–119.
Teusch, R. (1988). Level of ego development and bulimic's conceptualization of their disorder. *International Journal of Eating Disorders, 7,* 607–615.
Tharp, R.G., & Wetzel, R.J. (1969). *Behavior modification in the natural environment.* New York: Academic Press.
Theander, S. (1970). Anorexia nervosa: A psychiatric investigation of 94 female patients. *Acta Psychiatrica Scandinavia, 214,* 1–194.
Thompson, J.K. (1986). Larger than life. *Psychology Today, 20,* 39–44.
Thompson, J.K. (1987). Body size distortion in anorexia nervosa: Reanalysis and reconceptualization. *International Journal of Eating Disorders, 6,* 379–384.

Thompson, J.K. (1988). Similarities among bulimia nervosa patients categorized by current and historical weight: Implications for the classification of eating disorders. *International Journal of Eating Disorders, 7,* 185–189.

Thompson, J.K., Berland, N.W., Linton, P.H., & Weinsier, R.L. (1986). Utilization of a self-adjusting light beam in the objective assessment of body image distortion in seven eating disorder groups. *International Journal of Eating Disorders, 5,* 113–120.

Thompson, J.K., Dolce, J.J., Spana, R.E., & Register, A. (1987). Emotional versus intellectually based estimates of body size. *International Journal of Eating Disorders, 6,* 507–514.

Thompson, M.G., & Gans, M.T. (1985). Do anorexics and bulimics get well? In S.W. Emmett (Ed.), *Theory and treatment of anorexia nervosa and bulimia: Biomedical, sociocultural, and psychological perspectives* (pp. 291–303). New York: Brunner/Mazel.

Todd, T.C. (1985). Anorexia nervosa and bulimia: Expanding the structural model. In M.P. Mirkin & S.L. Koman (Eds.), *Handbook of adolescents and family therapy,* (pp. 39–50). New York: Gardner Press.

Toner, B., Garfinkel, P.E., & Garner, D.M. (1987). Cognitive style of patients with bulimic and diet-restricting anorexia nervosa. *American Journal of Psychiatry, 144,* 510–512.

Touyz, S.W., Beumont, P.J.V., Collins, J.K., McCabe, M.P., & Jupp, J.J. (1984). Body shape perception and its disturbance in anorexia nervosa. *British Journal of Psychiatry, 144,* 167–171.

Tremblay, A., Fountaine, E., Poehlman, E.T., Mitchell, D., Perron, L., & Bouchard, C. (1986). The effect of exercise-training on resting metabolic rate in lean and moderately obese individuals. *International Journal of Obesity, 10,* 511–517.

U.S. Department of Agriculture. (1980). Nutrition and your health: Dietary guidelines for Americans. *Home and Garden Bulletin* (# 232). Washington, DC: U.S. Department of Agriculture and Department of Health and Human Services.

Van Buren, D.J., & Williamson, D.A. (1988). Marital relationships and conflict resolutions skills of bulimics. *International Journal of Eating Disorders, 7,* 735–741.

Vandereycken, W. (1984). Neuroleptics in the short-term treatment of anorexia nervosa: A double-blind placebo-controlled study with sulpiride. *British Journal of Psychiatry, 144,* 288–292.

Vandereycken, W. (1987a). The constructive family approach to eating disorders: Critical remarks on the use of family therapy in anorexia and bulimia nervosa. *International Journal of Eating Disorders, 6,* 455–467.

Vandereycken, W. (1987b). The use of neuroleptics in the treatment of anorexia nervosa patients. In P.E. Garfinkel & D.M. Garner (Eds.), *The role of drug treatments for eating disorders* (pp. 74–89). New York: Brunner/Mazel.

Vandereycken, W., & Pierloot, R. (1982). Pimozide combined with behavior therapy in the short-term treatment of anorexia nervosa: A double-blind placebo-controlled cross-over study. *Acta Psychiatrica Scandinavica, 66,* 445–450.

Vandereycken, W., & Pierloot, R. (1983). The significance of subclassification in anorexia nervosa: A comparative study of clinical features in 141 patients.

Psychological Medicine, 13, 543–549.
Vigersky, R.A., & Loriaux, D.L. (1977). The effect of cyproheptadine in anorexia nervosa: A double-blind trial. In R.A. Vigersky (Ed.), *Anorexia nervosa.* New York: Raven Press.
von Bertalanffy, L. (1968). *General systems theory.* New York: Braziller.
Wakeling, A. (1985). Neurobiological aspects of feeding disorders. *Journal of Psychiatric Research, 19,* 191–201.
Waller, D.A., Kiser, S., Hardy, B.W., Fuchs, I., Feigenbaum, L.P., & Uauy, R. (1986). Eating behavior and plasma beta-endorphin in bulimia. *The American Journal of Clinical Nutrition, 4,* 20–23.
Waller, J.V., Kaufman, M.R., & Deutsch, F (1940). Anorexia nervosa: a psychosomatic entity. *Psychosomatic Medicine, 2,* 3.
Walsh, B.T., Gladis, M., Roose, S.P., Stewart, J.H., & Glassman, A.H. (1987). A controlled trial of phenelzine in bulimia. *Psychopharmacology Bulletin, 23,* 49–51.
Walsh, B.T., Stewart, J., Roose, S.P., Gladis, M., & Glassman, A.H. (1984). Treatment of bulimia with phenelzine: A double-blind placebo-controlled study. *Journal of Psychiatric Research, 19,* 485–489.
Walster, E., Aronson, V., Abrahams, D., & Ratlmann, L. (1966). Importance of physical attractiveness in dating behavior. *Journal of Personality and Social Psychology, 4,* 508–516.
Warren, M.P. (1985). Anorexia nervosa and related eating disorders. *Clinical Obstetrics and Gynecology, 28,* 588–597.
Watson, D., & Friend, R. (1969). Measurement of social-evaluative anxiety. *Journal of Consulting and Clinical Psychology, 33,* 448–557.
Weiner, H. (1983). Abiding problems in the psychoendocrinology of anorexia nervosa. *Report of the 4th Ross Conference on Medical Research,* (pp. 47–53).
Weiss, L., Katzman, M., & Wolchik, S. (1985). *Treating bulimia: A psychoeducational approach.* New York: Pergamon Press.
Weiss, S.M., & Schwartz, G.E. (1982). Behavioral medicine: The biobehavioral perspective. In R. Williams & R. Surwitt (Eds.), *Proceedings of the NATO Symposium on Behavioral Medicine.* New York: Plenum Press.
Weiss, S.R., & Ebert, M.H. (1983). Psychological and behavioral characteristics of normal-weight bulimics and normal-weight controls. *Psychosomatic Medicine, 45,* 293–303.
Weits, T., Van Den Beer, E.J., & Wedel, M. (1986). Comparison of ultrasound and skinfolds caliper measurement of subcutaneous fat tissue. *International Journal of Obesity, 10,* 161–168.
Weltner, J.S. (1985). Matchmaking: Choose an appropriate therapy for families at various levels of pathology. In M.P. Mirkin & S.L. Koman (Eds.), *Handbook of adolescents and family therapy* (pp. 39–50). New York: Gardner Press.
Wermuth, B.M., Davis, K.L., Hollister, L.E., & Stunkard, A.J. (1977). Phynytoin treatment of the binge-eating syndrome. *American Journal of Psychiatry, 134,* 1249–1253.
White, W.C. (1985). Bulimarexia: Intervention strategies and outcome considerations. In S. Emmett (Ed.), *Eating disorders: Research, theory, and treatment* (pp. 211–233.). New York: Brunner/Mazel.

Whitehouse, A.M., & Button, E.J. (1988). The prevalence of eating disorders in a U.K. college population: A reclassification of an earlier study. *International Journal of Eating Disorders, 7,* 393–397.

Willard S.G., & Winstead, D.K. (in press). Laxative abuse in bulimia. In W.G. Johnson (Ed.), *Advances in eating disorders vol II.* New York: JAI press.

Williams, R.L., Schaefer, C.A., Shisslak, C.M., Gronwaldt, V.H., & Comerci, G.D. (1986). Eating attitudes and behaviors in adolescent women: Discrimination of normals and suspected bulimics using the eating attitudes tests and eating disorder inventory. *International Journal of Eating Disorders, 5,* 879–894.

Williamson, D.A., Kelley, M.L., Davis, C.J., Ruggiero, L., & Veitia, M.C. (1985). The psychophysiology of bulimia. *Advances in Behavior Research and Therapy, 7,* 163–172.

Williamson, D.A., Kelley, M.L., Ruggiero, L., & Blouin, D.C. (1985). Psychopathology of eating disorders: A controlled comparison study. *Journal of Consulting and Clinical Psychology, 53,* 161–166.

Williamson, D.A., Kelley, M.L., Davis, C.J., Ruggiero, L., & Blouin, D.C. (1985). Psychopathology of eating disorders: A controlled comparison of bulimic, obese, and normal subjects. *Journal of Consulting and Clinical Psychology, 53,* 161–166.

Williamson, D.A., Prather, R.C., Goreczy, A.J., Davis, C.J., & McKenzie, S.J. (in press). Psychopathology of bulimia. In W.G. Johnson (Ed.), *Advances in eating disorders.* Greenwich, CN: JAI Press.

Wilmuth, M.E.,Leitenberg, H., Rosen, J.C., & Cado, S. (1988). A comparison of purging and nonpurging normal weight bulimics. *International Journal of Eating Disorders, 7,* 823–835.

Wilmuth, M.E., Leitenberg, J., Rosen, J.C., Fondacaro, K.M., & Gross, J. (1985). Body size distortion in bulimia nervosa. *International Journal of Eating Disorders, 4,* 71–78.

Wilson, G.T., & Lindholm, L. (1987). Bulimia nervosa and depression. *International Journal of Eating Disorders, 6,* 725–732.

Wingate, B., & Christie, M. (1978). Ego strength and body image in anorexia nervosa. *Journal of Psychosomatic Research, 22*(3), 201–204.

Witkin, H.A. (1965). Development of the body concept and psychological differentiation. In S. Wampner & H. Werner (Eds.), *The body percept* (pp. 82–106). New York: Random House.

Wolchik, S.A., Weiss, L., & Katzman, M.A. (1986). An empirically validated, short-term psychoeducational group treatment for bulimia. *International Journal of Eating Disorders, 5,* 21–34.

Wolfe, E.M., & Crowther, J.H. (1983). Personality and eating habit variables as predictors of severity of binge eating and weight. *Addictive Behaviors, 8,* 335–344.

Wooley, S.C., & Wooley, O.W. (1985). Intensive outpatient and residential treatment for bulimia. In D.M. Garner & P.E. Garfinkel (Eds.), *Handbook of psychotherapy for anorexia and bulimia* (pp. 391–430). New York: Guilford.

Wooley, O.W., Wooley, S.C., & Dryenforth, S.R. (1979). Obesity and women II: A neglected feminist topic. *Women's Studies Institute Quarterly, 2,* 81–92.

Wurtman, J. (1984). The involvement of brain serotonin in excessive carbohydrate snacking by obese subjects. *Journal of the American Dietetic Association, 84,* 1004–1007.

Wurtman, J.J. (1986). Abnormal regulation of carbohydate consumption. In M.O. Carruba & J.E. Blundell (Eds.), *Pharmacology of eating disorders: Theoretical and clinical developments.* New York: Raven Press, 133–139.

Wurtman, J.J., & Wurtman, R. J. (1982). Studies on the appetite for carbohydrates in rats and humans. *Journal of Psychiatric Research, 17,* 213–221.

Wurtman, J.J., Wurtman, R.J., Growdon, J.H., Henry, P., Lipscomb, A., & Zeisel, S.H. (1981). Carbohydrate craving in obese people: Suppression by treatments affecting serotoninergic transmission. *International Journal of Eating Disorders, 1,* 2–15.

Yalom, I.D. (1975) *The theory and practice of group psychotherapy.* New York: Basic Books.

Yates, A., Lechey, K., & Shisslak, C.M. (1983). Running–An analogue of anorexia? *New England Journal of Medicine, 308,* 251–255.

Yellowlees, A.J. (1985). Anorexia and bulimia in anorexia nervosa: A study of psychosocial functioning and associated psychiatric symptomatology. *British Journal of Psychiatry, 146,* 648–652.

APPENDIX A

Tabular Summary of Studies Describing Eating Disorders

APPENDIX A.1 Epidemiology of Anorexia Nervosa

Study	Population	N	Ages	Incidence
Szmukler et al. (1985)	Ballet dancers	100	15.6	9.0%
Herzog et al. (1985)	Medical students	121	25.1	3.3%[a]
Pope et al. (1984b)	College students	544	20.3	3.5%
Szmukler (1983)	English day school students	1331	16.2	0.8%
Rodin et al. (1985)	Diabetics	46	17.2	6.5%
Hoek & Brook (1985)	Psychiatric patients	–	–	0.04%
Szmukler et al. (1986)	Psychiatric patients	–	–	0.004%
Pope et al. (1984a)	Urban shoppers	300	12–65	0.7%[a]

[a]Indicates lifetime history of anorexia

APPENDIX A.2 Restricting versus Bulimic Anorexics

Study	Population	N	Ages	% Restrictor	% Bulimic
Beumont et al. (1976)	Hospital	31	17.6	55%	45%
Garner et al. (1985)	Hospital	126	22	50%	50%
Mickalide & Andersen (1985)	Hospital	165	22.7	77%	33%
Vandereycken & Pierloot (1983)	Hospital	145	20.9	45%	55%
Halmi & Falk (1982)	Hospital	40	19.3	53%	47%
Casper et al. (1980)	Hospital	105	19.9	53%	47%
Garfinkle et al. (1979)	Hospital	135	21.3	51%	49%

APPENDIX A.3 Epidemiology of Bulimia—Diagnosis of Bulimia

Study	Population	Sample Size	Age	Criteria	N	Percentage
Herzog et al. (1985)	Medical students	212	25.1	Modified DSM-III	5	4.1
Healy et al. (1985)	Dublin students	701	17–24	DSM-III CHEQ	21	2.8
Hart et al. (1985)	Working women	139	24.0	DSM-III	2	1.0
Hart et al. (1985)	College	234	18.9	DSM-III	12	5.0
Johnson et al. (1983)	High school	1268	13–19	Modified DSM-III	62	4.9
Halmi et al. (1981)	College	355	25.6	DSM-III	46	13.0
Pyle et al. (1983)	College	1355	–	DMS-III	56	4.1
Nevo (1985)	College	505	17–30	EDI Scores	70	11.0
Fairburn & Cooper (1983)	Medical clinic	369	24.1	Bulimia nervosa ever	7	1.9
				Bulimia nervosa Weekly	2	0.5
Katzman et al. (1984)	College	485	–	DSM-III	19	3.9
Pope et al. (1984b)	College A	287	22.0	DSM-III	36	12.5
Pope et al. (1984b)	College B	102	22.0	DSM-III	19	18.6
Pope et al. (1984b)	High school	155	17.0	DSM-III	10	6.5
Williams et al. (1986)	Grade 7–12	72	15.5	Interview	9	12.5
Pyle et al. (1986)	College 1983	722	–	DMS-III	54	7.5
Pyle et al. (1986)	College 1980	575	–	DSM-III	45	7.8
Pertschuk (1986)	College	957	–	Binge or Purge	207	21.6
Rand et al. (1986)	Community volunteers	232	35.5	DSM-III	1	0.4
Kuldau et al. (1986)	Obese	100	36.0	DSM-III	2	2.0
Hamilton et al.(1985)	Ballet dancers	66	24.9	Self-report	10	15.2
Rodin et al. (1985)	Diabetic	46	17.2	DSM-III	3	6.5
Pope et al. (1984a)	Shoppers	300	30.4	DSM-II	31	10.3

APPENDIX A.4 Epidemiology of Bulimia—Binge Eating

Study	Population	Sample Size	Age	Frequency	N	Percentage
Herzog et al. (1985)	Medical students	212	25.1	1/month	23	19.2
				2–3/month	16	13.3
				1/week	8	6.7
				daily	3	2.5
				2+/day	2	1.7
Healy et al. (1985)	Dublin students	701	17–24	Weekly	98	14.0
Hart et al. (1985)	Working women	139	24.0	Ever	57	41.0
Hart et al. (1985)	College	234	18:9	Ever	161	69.0
Johnson et al. (1983)	High school	1268	13–19	Monthly	343	27.3
				Weekly	213	17.0
				Daily	50	4.0
Leon et al. (1985)	College	141	19	Ever	47	33.6
Pyle et al. (1983)	College	1355	–	Ever	675	50.0
Nevo (1985)	College	505	17–30	At least monthly	213	42.2
Fairburn & Cooper (1983)	Medical clinic	369	24.1	Ever	97	26.4
				Weekly	27	7.3
				Daily	2	0.5
Crowther et al. (1985)	High school	363	16.0	1/month	77	27.3
				2–3/month	49	13.5
				Weekly	24	6.6
				Daily	13	3.6
Katzman et al. (1984)	College	485	–	Ever	21	4.3
Williams et al.(1986)	Grade 7–12	72	15.5	Ever	16	22.0
Pyle et al. (1986)	College	722	–	Current	104	14.4
Pertschuk (1986)	College	957	–	Current	137	14.3
Rand et al. (1986)	Community volunteers	232	35.3	Ever	130	56.0
				Past Month	97	42.0
Kuldau et al. (1986)	obese	100	36.0	Ever	42	42.0

APPENDIX A.5 Bingeing and Tasting in Bulimic Patient Samples

Study	N	Binge		Tasting Spitting	
Fairburn & Cooper (1984)	35	Daily	49%	Ever	37%
		2/day	17%	Now	20%
Calloway et al. (1983)	24	Now	95.8%		
Johnson et al. (1983)	316		100%		
Johnson & Love (1985)	544	2/day	26%		
		Daily	23%		
		Week	42%		
		Month	8%		
		Less	2%		
Garner et al. (1985)	130	Daily	85%		
Ordman & Kirschenbaum (1986)	25	—			
Lacey et al. (1986)	50		100%		
Johnson & Berndt (1983)	80	Daily	51%		
		Week	41%		
		Month	8%		
Pyle et al. (1981)	34	Daily	56%		
		Week	44%		
		Less	0%		
Casper et al. (1980)	105	Ever	47%		
		Week	67%		
		Daily	16%		
Fairburn & Cooper (1982)	499	Daily	27%		
		Week	33%		
Mitchell et al. (1981)	40	11.7/week			
Garner et al. (1985)	177	Daily	51%		
		Week	93%		
Mitchell et al. (1985)	275	Daily	82%	Ever	64%
		Week	16%		
		Less	2%		
Johnson-Sabine et al. (1984)	50	4.1/week			
Beumont et al. (1976)	31		43%		
Russell (1979)	30		100%		

APPENDIX A.6 Epidemiology of Bulimia—Vomiting

Study	Population	Sample Size	Age	Frequency	N	Percentage
Herzog et al. (1985)	Medical students	212	25.1	1–3/month	6	5.0
Hart et al. (1985)	Working women	139	24.0	Weekly	2	1.0
Hart et al. (1985)	Students	234	18.9	Weekly	12	5.0
Johnson et al. (1983)	High school	1268	13–19	Monthly	83	6.6
				Weekly	26	2.1
				Daily	20	1.6
Halmi et al. (1981)	College	355	25.6	Monthly	3	0.8
				Weekly +	6	1.7
Leon et al. (1985)	College	141	19	Ever	13	9.2
Killen et al. (1986)	10th grade	1728	15	Monthly	71	8.6
				Weekly	9	1.1
				Daily	7	0.9
Nevo (1985)	College	505	17–30	Sometimes	55	10.9
Fairburn & Cooper (1983)	Medical clinic	369	24.1	Ever	24	6.5
				Weekly	2	0.5
				Daily	2	0.5
Crowther et al. (1985)	High school	363	16.0	1/month	21	5.8
				2–3/month	10	2.7
				Weekly	5	1.4
				Daily	4	1.1
Katzman et al. (1984)	College	485	—	Ever	274	56.0
Williams et al. (1986)	Grade 7–12	72	15.5	Ever	6	8.0
Pyle et al. (1986)	College	722	—	Present	21	2.9
				Weekly	11	1.5
				Daily	5	0.7
Pyle et al. (1986)	College 1980	575	—	Present	8	1.4
				Weekly	5	0.9
				Daily	4	0.7
Rand et al. (1986)	Community volunteers	232	35.3	Ever	4	1.7
Kuldau et al. (1986)	Obese	100	36.0	Ever	6	6.0

APPENDIX A.7 Epidemiology of Bulimia—Laxative Abuse

Study	Population	Sample Size	Age	Frequency	N	Percentage
Johnson et al. (1983)	High school	1268	13–19	Monthly	58	4.6
				Weekly	21	1.7
				Daily	12	1.0
Halmi et al. (1981)	College	355	25.6	Monthly	5	1.4
				Weekly +	1	0.3
Killen et al. (1986)	10th grade	1728	15	Monthly	50	6.1
				Weekly	5	0.5
				Daily	2	0.2
Fairburn & Cooper (1983)	Medical clinic	369	24.1	Ever	18	4.9
				Weekly	2	0.5
Crowther et al. (1985)	High school	363	16.0	1/Month	12	3.3
				2–3/Month	3	0.8
				Weekly	2	0.6
Williams et al. (1986)	Grade 7–12	72	15.5	Ever	1	1.0
Pyle et al. (1986)	College	722	—	Present	6	0.8
				Weekly	1	0.1
				Daily	0	0.0
Pyle et al. (1986)	College 1980	575	—	Present	10	1.7
				Weekly	4	0.7
				Daily	2	0.3
Rand et al. (1986)	Community volunteers	232	35.3	Ever	8	3.6

APPENDIX A.8 Epidemiology of Bulimia—Diuretic Abuse

Study	Population	Sample Size	Age	Frequency	N	Percentage
Johnson et al. (1983)	High school	1268	13–19	Monthly	26	2.1
				Weekly	9	0.7
				Daily	15	1.2
Halmi et al. (1981)	College	355	25.6	Monthly	3	0.8
				Weekly +	2	0.6
Killen et al. (1986)	10th grade	1728	15	Monthly	26	3.1
				Weekly	1	0.1
				Daily	3	0.2
Pyle et al. (1986)	College 1983	722	—	Present	9	1.2
				Weekly	3	0.4
				Daily	1	0.1
Pyle et al. (1986)	College 1980	575	—	Present	7	1.2
				Weekly	5	0.9
				Daily	2	0.3

APPENDIX A.9 Epidemiology of Bulimia—Excessive Dieting and Fasting

Study	Population	Sample Size	Age	Frequency	N	Percentage
Healy et al. (1985)	Dublin students	701	17–24	Fasting Ever	56	8%
Johnson et al. (1983)	High school students	1268	13–19	Dieting Now	456	36%
				Ever	875	69%
				Chronic	178	14%
Halmi et al. (1981)	College students	355	25.6	Dieting Ever	28	8%
Pyle et al. (1983)	College students	1355	—	Fasting Ever	34	6%
				Weekly	12	2%
Nevo (1985)	College	505	17–30	Dieting Monthly	263	52%
				Crash diet Monthly	77	15%
				Fasting Monthly	81	16%
Crowther et al. (1985)	High school	363	16.0	Fasting Ever	132	59%
				Monthly	92	25%
				Weekly	40	11%
Williams (1986)	Grade 7–12	72	15.5	Dieting	18	25%
				Meal skip	43	60%
				Avoid Carb.	14	19%
Pyle et al. (1986)	College 1983	722	—	Fasting Present	25	3%
				Weekly	13	2%
Pyle et al. (1986)	College 1980	575	—	Fasting Present	34	6%
				Weekly	17	3%
Rand et al. (1986)	Community volunteers	232	35.2	Dieting	—	47%

APPENDIX A.10 Epidemiology of Bulimia—Excessive Exercise

Study	Population	Sample Size	Age	Frequency	N	Percentage
Halmi et al. (1981)	College	355	25.6	Current	16	5%
Fairburn & Cooper (1983)	Medical clinic	369	24.1	Current	27	7%

APPENDIX A.11 Purging in Bulimic Patient Samples

Study	N	Vomit		Laxatives		Diuretics		Exercise	
Fairburn & Cooper (1984)	35	Daily	74%	Ever	31%			Ever	29%
		2/day	40%	Mean	17.4%				
Calloway et al. (1983)	24	Now	87.5%	Now	50.0%				
Johnson et al. (1983)	316		81%		63%				
Johnson & Love (1985)	544	2/day	35%	2/day	9%				
		Daily	24%	Daily	14%				
		Week	28%	Week	33%				
		Month	6%	Month	24%				
		Less	7%	Less	2%				
Garner et al. (1985)	130	Daily	69%						
Ordman & Kirschenbaum (1986)	25	Mean 11.3/week							
Lacey et al. (1986)	50		78%		56%				
Johnson & Berndt (1983)	80	Now	77%	Now	33%				
		Daily	59%	Daily	24%				
		Week	29%	Week	30%				
		Month	12%	Month	46%				
Pyle et al. (1981)	34	Daily	50%	Daily	6%	Ever	29%	Daily	76%
		Week	44%	Week	22%				
		Less	6%	Less	72%				
Casper et al. (1980)	105	Ever	57%	Ever	37%				
		Week	67%						
		Daily	16%						
Fairburn & Cooper (1982)	499	Daily	56%	Ever	19%			Ever	61%
		Week	18%						
Mitchell et al. (1981)	40	11.7/week							
Garner et al. (1985)	177	Ever	77%	Ever	53%	Ever	12%	Daily	57%
Mitchell et al. (1985)	275	Daily	72%	Daily	20%	Daily	10%	Week	28%
		Week	12%	Week	27%	Week	14%	Less	6%
		Less	2%	Less	14%	Less	10%		
Johnson-Sabine et al. (1984)	50	4.4/week		2.2/week					
Beumont et al. (1976)	31		64%		79%		86%		
Russell (1979)	30		90%		43%				

APPENDIX B
Assessment Instruments

APPENDIX B.1 Eating Disorder Functional Analysis Form

What antecedents and consequences affect bingeing, dieting, body image/body weight concerns, or purging?

Environmental Antecedents   *Environmental Consequences*

A. Situational Cues

_____

_____

_____

1. Physical Setting

_____

_____

_____

2. Time of Day

_____

_____

_____

3. People

_____

_____

_____

4. Behavior Setting

_____

_____

_____

B. Environmental Systems
1. Family

1. Family

2. Friendships

2. Friendships

3. Vocational (School)

3. Vocational (School)

4. Financial Resources

4. Financial Resources

5. Sexual/Intimate Relationships

5. Sexual/Intimate Relationships

6. Health Care Systems

6. Health Care Systems

Behavioral Antecedents

1. Ongoing Activity

2. Previous Activity

3. Dieting Behavior

Cognitive Antecedents

1. Knowledge of Food

2. Rules of Dieting

3. Outcome Expectancies

Behavioral Consequences

1. Competing Activities

2. Behavioral Chaining

3. Dieting Behavior

Cognitive Consequences

1. Self-Evaluation

2. Rules of Dieting

3. Outcome Expectancies

Cognitive Antecedents

4. Body Image

Cognitive Consequences

4. Body Image

Emotional Antecedents

1. Transient mood changes

Emotional Consequences

1. Guilt

2. Psychopathology

2. Depression

3. Fear of Fat

3. Anxieties

4. Body Dissatisfaction

4. Body Dissatisfaction

5. Food Phobia

5. Food Phobia

Physiological Antecedents

1. Insulin/Glucose

2. Starvation Response

3. Hunger

4. Hypokalemia

5. Reproductive Hormones

6. Neurotransmitters

Physiological Consequences

1. Insulin/Glucose

2. Starvation Response

3. Hunger

4. Hypokalemia

5. Reproductive Hormones

6. Neurotransmitters

Physiological Antecedents

7. Endogenous Opiates

Physiological Consequences

7. Endogenous Opiates

APPENDIX B.2 Dieter's Inventory of Eating Temptations (DIET)

Each item in this questionnaire describes a situation and a behavior that promotes weight loss or weight control. Imagine that you are in the situation described and rate the percent of the time you would behave in the way described. If you would always act in the way described then give a rating of 100%. If you would never act that way give a rating of 0%. If you would sometimes act that way then mark an "X" at the point on the scale that shows how often you would act as described. If you feel that you never get into a situation like the one described (it does not apply to you), then rate how often you engage in the kind of behavior described in general.

1. You're having dinner with your family and your favorite meal has been prepared. You finish the first helping and someone says, "Why don't you have some more?" What percent of the time would you turn down a second helping?

    0----10----20----30----40----50----60----70----80----90----100

2. You would like to exercise every day but it is hard to find the time because of your family and work obligations. What percent of the time would you set aside a daily time for exercise?

    0----10----20----30----40----50----60----70----80----90----100

3. You like to eat high calorie snack food (e.g., cookies, potatoes chips, crackers, cokes, beer, cake) while watching television. What percent of the time would you watch TV without eating a high calorie snack?

    0----10----20----30----40----50----60----70----80----90----100

4. When you eat in a good restaurant, you love to order high calorie foods. What percent of the time would you order a low calorie meal?

    0----10----20----30----40----50----60----70----80----90----100

5. When planning meals, you tend to choose high calorie foods. What percent of the time would you plan low calorie meals?

    0----10----20----30----40----50----60----70----80----90----100

6. You are at a party and there is a lot of fattening food. You already have eaten more than you should and you are tempted to continue eating. What percent of the time would you stop with what you have already eaten?

    0----10----20----30----40----50----60----70----80----90----100

7. You like to flavor your vegetables with butter, margarine, ham, or bacon fat. What percent of the time would you choose a low calorie method of seasoning?

    0----10----20----30----40----50----60----70----80----90----100

8. You often prepare many of your foods by frying. What percent of the time would you prepare your food in a way that is less fattening?

    0----10----20----30----40----50----60----70----80----90----100

9. You allow yourself a snack in the evening but you find yourself eating more than your diet allows. What percent of the time would you reduce the size of your snack?

0----10----20----30----40----50----60----70----80----90----100

10. Instead of putting foods away after finishing a meal, you find yourself eating the leftovers. What percent of the time would you put the food away without eating any?

0----10----20----30----40----50----60----70----80----90----100

11. You are asked by another person to go for a walk but you feel tired and kind of low. What percent of the time would you overcome these feelings and say "yes" to the walk?

0----10----20----30----40----50----60----70----80----90----100

12. You often overeat at supper because you are tired and hungry when you get home. What percent of the time would you not overeat at supper?

0----10----20----30----40----50----60----70----80----90----100

13. When you have errands to run that are only a couple of blocks away you usually drive the car. What percent of the time would you walk on an errand when it only involves a couple of blocks?

0----10----20----30----40----50----60----70----80----90----100

14. You are invited to someone's house for dinner and your host is an excellent cook. You often overeat because the food tastes so good. What percent of the time would you not overeat as a dinner guest?

0----10----20----30----40----50----60----70----80----90----100

15. You like to have something sweet to eat on your coffee break. What percent of the time would you only have coffee?

0----10----20----30----40----50----60----70----80----90----100

16. When you cook a meal you snack on the food. What percent of the time would you wait until the meal is prepared to eat?

0----10----20----30----40----50----60----70----80----90----100

17. You planned to exercise after work today but you feel tired and hungry when the time arrives. What percent of the time would you exercise anyway?

0----10----20----30----40----50----60----70----80----90----100

18. There is a party at work for a co-worker and someone offers you a piece of cake. What percent of the time would you turn it down?

0----10----20----30----40----50----60----70----80----90----100

19. You would like to climb the stairs instead of taking the elevator. What percent of the time would you take the stairs to go one or two flights?

0----10----20----30----40----50----60----70----80----90----100

APPENDIX B.2 (continued)

20. You are happy and feeling good today. You are tempted to treat yourself by stopping for ice cream. What percent of the time would you find some other way to be nice to yourself?

        0----10----20----30----40----50----60----70----80----90----100

21. You are at a friend's house and your friend offers you a delicious looking pastry. What percent of the time would you refuse this offer?

        0----10----20----30----40----50----60----70----80----90----100

22. You feel like celebrating. You are going out with friends to a good restaurant. What percent of the time would you celebrate without overeating?

        0----10----20----30----40----50----60----70----80----90----100

23. You finished your meal and you still feel hungry. There is cake and fruit available. What percent of the time would you choose the fruit?

        0----10----20----30----40----50----60----70----80----90----100

24. You are at home feeling lonely, blue, and bored. You are craving something to eat. What percent of the time would you find another way of coping with these feelings besides eating?

        0----10----20----30----40----50----60----70----80----90----100

25. Today you did something to hurt your ankle. You want to get something to eat to make yourself feel better. What percent of the time would you find some other way to take your mind off your mishap?

        0----10----20----30----40----50----60----70----80----90----100

26. When you spend time alone at home you are tempted to snack. You are spending an evening alone. What percent of the time would you resist the urge to snack?

        0----10----20----30----40----50----60----70----80----90----100

27. You are out with a friend at lunch time and your friend suggests that you stop and get some ice cream. What percent of the time would you resist the temptation?

        0----10----20----30----40----50----60----70----80----90----100

28. You just had an upsetting argument with a family member. You are standing in front of the refrigerator and you feel like eating everything in sight. What percent of the time would you find some other way to make yourself feel better?

        0----10----20----30----40----50----60----70----80----90----100

29. You are having a hard day at work and you are anxious and upset. You feel like getting a candy bar. What percent of the time would you find a more constructive way to calm down and cope with your feelings?

        0----10----20----30----40----50----60----70----80----90----100

30. You just had an argument with your (husband, wife, boyfriend, girlfriend). You are upset, angry, and you feel like eating something. What percent of the time would you talk the situation over with someone or go for a walk instead of eating?

0----10----20----30----40----50----60----70----80----90----100

APPENDIX B.3 DIET Profile

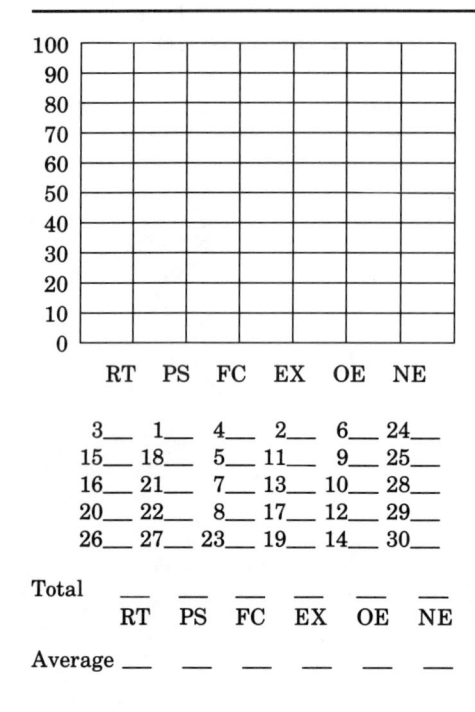

[Profile chart with y-axis 0–100 in increments of 10, and x-axis labels: RT PS FC EX OE NE]

Scoring Instructions:

1. Write the rating for each item beside the item number at the bottom of the chart.
2. Add the ratings for each scale to get the total.
3. Divide the total by 5 to get the average.
4. Plot the average score for each scale on the profile chart.

RT	PS	FC	EX	OE	NE
3__	1__	4__	2__	6__	24__
15__	18__	5__	11__	9__	25__
16__	21__	7__	13__	10__	28__
20__	22__	8__	17__	12__	29__
26__	27__	23__	19__	14__	30__

Total __ __ __ __ __ __
      RT PS FC EX OE NE

Average __ __ __ __ __ __

Interpretations: High scores indicate areas of strength; low scores indicate areas of weakness. The scales are:

RT – Resisting Temptation
PS – Positive Social
FC – Food Choice
EX – Exercise
OE – Overeating
NE – Negative Emotions

APPENDIX B.4   DIET Profile—Normative Scoring

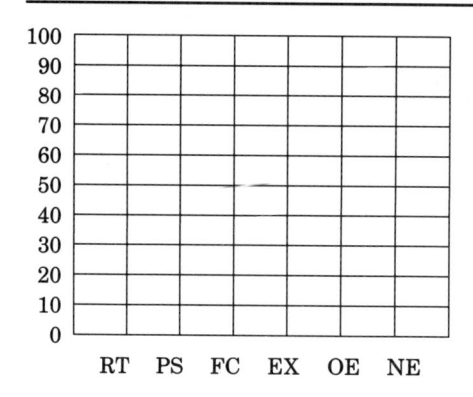

Scoring Instructions:

1. For each scale, look up M and S in the following table. If you can categorize the person as overweight, use the overweight columns, otherwise use the normal weight columns.

	Overweight M	Overweight S	Normal M	Normal S
RT	56	23	56	22
PS	44	23	46	21
FC	48	21	49	23
EX	50	20	58	21
OE	54	23	61	21
NE	57	25	67	21

2. Take each scale average and apply the following equation using M and S for that scale:

   $T = [\{(M - AVG)/S\} \times 10] + 50$

3. Plot the value of T on the profile chart.
4. T-scores represent the extent to which people deviate from the typical or usual response. T-scores have a mean of 50 and a standard deviation of 10. Each 10 points below 50 represents 1 standard deviation below the mean. Each 10 points above 50 represents 1 standard deviation above the mean. The following chart will aid in interpreting T-scores:

T-score From	To	Interpretation
0	30	An extreme problem in this area. Less than 2% of the people will score this low.
31	40	This area is very difficult for this person to handle. About 14% of the people experience this much difficulty.
41	50	Moderate difficulty. About 34% of the people will fall into this range.
51	60	Moderate competent. About 34% of the people will do this well.
61	70	Very competent. About 14% of the people do this well.
71	100	Extremely competent. Less than 2% of the people do this well.

APPENDIX B.5 Food Survey

Rate how you would feel about yourself after eating each food.

1 = I would feel very good about myself
2 = I would feel good about myself
3 = I would feel neither good nor bad about myself
4 = I would feel bad about myself
5 = I would feel very bad about myself

1. English muffin	1	2	3	4	5	24. Shrimp	1	2	3	4	5
2. Jello	1	2	3	4	5	25. Wine	1	2	3	4	5
3. Apple	1	2	3	4	5	26. Popcorn	1	2	3	4	5
4. Corn	1	2	3	4	5	27. Spinach	1	2	3	4	5
5. Hot fudge sundae	1	2	3	4	5	29. Lima beans	1	2	3	4	5
7. Carrots	1	2	3	4	5	30. Diet soda	1	2	3	4	5
8. Cheddar cheese	1	2	3	4	5	31. Waffles with syrup	1	2	3	4	5
9. Beer	1	2	3	4	5	32. Swiss cheese	1	2	3	4	5
10. Corn bread	1	2	3	4	5	33. Hot dog	1	2	3	4	5
11. Skim milk	1	2	3	4	5	34. Peanut butter	1	2	3	4	5
12. Sweet potato	1	2	3	4	5	35. Coke	1	2	3	4	5
13. Boiled ham	1	2	3	4	5	36. Saltines	1	2	3	4	5
14. Pizza	1	2	3	4	5	37. Sour cream	1	2	3	4	5
15. Spare ribs	1	2	3	4	5	38. Veal cutlet	1	2	3	4	5
16. Cantaloupe	1	2	3	4	5	39. Ice cream	1	2	3	4	5
17. Fried chicken	1	2	3	4	5	40. Liquor	1	2	3	4	5
18. White bread	1	2	3	4	5	41. Biscuits	1	2	3	4	5
19. Orange juice	1	2	3	4	5	42. Plain yogurt	1	2	3	4	5
20. Doughnuts	1	2	3	4	5	43. Tomato juice	1	2	3	4	5
21. Potato	1	2	3	4	5	44. Cottage cheese	1	2	3	4	5
22. Milk shake	1	2	3	4	5	45. Apple Juice	1	2	3	4	5
23. Banana	1	2	3	4	5						

APPENDIX B.6 Food Survey Profile Chart

[Profile chart grid: y-axis 0 to 100 in increments of 10, with columns for Meat, Milk, Fruits & Vegetables, Grain, Beverage, Low, Medium, High]

		Meat	Milk	Fruits & Vegetables	Grain	Beverage	Low	Medium	High	
Items	L	13	11	7		8	19			Meat
Items	O	24	42	16	26	30				Milk
Items	W	33	44	27	36	43				Fruit & Vegetables
Items	M E D	6	8	3	1	2				Grain
Items	I	17	32	21	10	25				Beverage
Items	U M	38	39	23	41	45				Total
Items		15	22	4	14	9				Average
Items	H I	28	25	12	20	35	2.32	2.78	3.42	M
Items	G H	34	37	29	31	40	0.49	0.38	0.65	S
Total										T
Average										
M		3.10	2.92	2.16	3.12	2.79				
S		0.52	.041	0.69	0.55	0.45				
T										

Instructions for Scoring the Food Survey

1. The item numbers are listed in the boxes under each of the food groups on the left side of the workspace. Write the rating given for each item in the appropriate box.
2. Add the items down each column to get a total score for each food group. Divide this score by nine to get the average rating.
3. Using M and S from each column, apply the following formula to get T:

$$\left[\frac{(\text{Average} - M)}{S} \times 10 \right] + 50 = T$$

4. Plot the value of T on the profile chart.

(continued)

APPENDIX B.6 (continued)

5. You are now ready to figure the scores for the calorie levels. There are three calorie levels at the right side of the worksheet. Under each calorie level is a box for each food group. Add the three numbers for each calorie level for each food group and record in the appropriate box. For example, low calorie meats are items 13, 24, and 33. The legend at the left of the worksheet indicates the calorie level of each item.

6. Add the numbers down the columns for each calorie level to get the total score. Divide this number by 15 to get the average.

7. Using M and S from each column, apply the following formula to get T:

$$\left[\frac{(\text{Average} - M)}{S} \times 10 \right] + 50 = T$$

8. Plot the value on the profile chart.

9. T-scores represent the extent to which people deviate from the typical or usual response. T-scores have a mean of 50 and a standard deviation of 10. Each 10 points below 50 represents 1 standard deviation below the mean. Each 10 points above 50 represents 1 standard deviation above the mean. Higher T-scores indicate a food phobia. Lower T-scores indicate an insensitivity to the caloric value of the foods. The following chart will aid in interpreting T-scores.

T-score From	To	Interpretation
0	30	An extreme insensitivity to caloric value of foods. Less than 2% of the people will score this low.
31	40	This person is moderately unconcerned about calories. About 14% of the people show this little concern.
41	50	Typical person who watches calories somewhat. About 34% of the people will show this degree of concern.
51	60	Moderately concerned about calories. About 34% of the people show this degree of concern.
61	70	Mild food phobia. About 14% of the people show this degree of fear and avoidance of calories.
71	100	Severe food phobia. Less than 2% of the people show this extreme degree of concern about calories.

APPENDIX B.7 Health Habit Survey

PLEASE PRINT   Date _____

Name: _____
        (Last)   (First)   (Middle initial)

Date of birth: _____ Age _____

Sex (Circle)   Male   Female

Permanent Address: _____
                              (Rt. or Street)

        _____
              (City)   (State)   (Zip)

Weight _____ lbs.   Height _____ ft. _____ inches

Ideal Weight _____ lbs.

Frame Size (Circle)   Small   Medium   Large

Highest Grade Completed _____

Mother's Education _____ Occupation _____

Father's Education _____ Occupation _____

If self-supporting, your occupation _____

Are you employed? (Circle)   Full-time   Part-time   Unemployed

Are you a student? (Circle)   Full-time   Part-time   No

Marital Status (Circle)   Single   Married   Separated   Divorced   Widowed

I. <u>MEDICAL HISTORY</u> Instructions: Circle any of the following which apply to you either now or in the past and indicate the age when you first became aware of the problem.

<u>Heart and Lung</u>
Fast heart rate   Slow heart rate
Low blood pressure   High blood pressure
Irregular heart beat   Rheumatic fever
Murmurs   Shortness of breath on exertion
Fainting spells   Shortness of breath while resting
Others: (please specify) _____
_____
_____

(continued)

APPENDIX B.7 (continued)

Kidney
Urinate more than 5 times per day on the average
Kidney stones
Wake up to urinate every night
Kidney or bladder infections
Blood in urine
Others: (please specify) _____

_____
_____
_____

Stomach, Intestines, and Liver
Ulcers
Frequent or persistent pain in the stomach
Frequent of persistent nausea and vomiting
Discomfort or pain after eating fatty foods
Diarrhea (more than two bowel movements per day)
Constipation (fewer than one bowel movement per two days)
Blood in stool
Inflammation at colon
Others: (please specify) _____

_____
_____
_____

Endocrine (Hormone disorders)
Diabetes (high blood sugar or sugar in urine)
Increased thirst and frequent urination
Thyroid disease (large gland, underactive or overactive gland)
Hypoglycemia (low blood sugar)
Gout
Others: (please specify) _____

_____
_____
_____

Gynecological and Reproductive Systems (Females)
Irregular cycle
Excessive or reduced flow
No menstrual periods
Excessive lactation in the absence of previous pregnancy
Others: (please specify) _____

_____
_____

Gynecological and Reproductive Systems (Males)
Never had a nocturnal emission
Never had or can't have erections
Others: (please specify) _____

_____
_____

Nervous System
Dizziness
Abnormal taste or smell sensations
Inability to taste and/or smell food
Frequent fainting spells
Weakness in legs or arms on climbing stairs or lifting objects
Seizures
Frequent headaches
Decreased hearing or vision
Head trauma resulting in loss of consciousness or disability
Emotional or mental illness requiring hospitalization or long-term out-
    patient treatment (more than three follow-up visits to the therapist)
Others: (please specify) _____

_____
_____
_____

Other
Fluid retention (swelling of fingers or feet and ankles)
Skin problems (too dry, rashes, too sweaty, too oily)
Hair problems (loss of hair anywhere, growth disturbances)
Rapid weight changes (3–5 pounds in 1–2 days)
Others: (please specify) _____

_____
_____
_____

Medications
List ALL medications, including vitamins, birth control pills, thyroid
medications, weight reduction medications, and hormones such as
steroids. Indicate what each one is prescribed for:

_____
_____
_____
_____
_____
_____
_____

(continued)

APPENDIX B.7 (continued)

Social History
Do you smoke?
How many cigarettes per day?
Do you drink alcoholic beverages?
How much and how often?

_____
_____
_____

Past History
1. List all hospital admissions giving date and reason
2. Birth weight if known
3. Underweight in the past

_____
_____
_____
_____
_____

Family History
Problems with weight, diabetes, thyroid disease, heart disease or high blood pressure in: father, mother, brothers, sisters, children, aunts and uncles.

_____
_____
_____

II. EATING PATTERNS

1. What would a typical meal consist of for you?
    a. Breakfast _____

    b. Lunch _____

    c. Supper _____

2. How many of your daily meals usually include a dessert? (circle number per day)

                0   1   2   3   4+

3. How fast do you eat in comparison to most people? (Check one.)
    _____ Much slower than most people
    _____ A little slower than most people
    _____ About the same as most people
    _____ A little faster than most people
    _____ Much faster than most people

4. Do you ever find yourself eating or snacking more than you should, or more than you planned to? (Circle one).
   YES   NO

If yes, approximately how many times a day? (Circle one.)
   1-2   3-4   5-6   7-8   9-10+

5. How many regular meals do you eat on most days?
   1-2   3-4   5-6   7-8   9-10+

6. At what times do you usually eat? (Enter 0 if you don't regularly eat the meal in question.)
   _____ Breakfast
   _____ Morning snack #1
   _____ Morning snack #2
   _____ Lunch
   _____ Afternoon snack #1
   _____ Afternoon snack #2
   _____ Supper
   _____ Evening snack #1
   _____ Evening snack #2

7. Do you usually clean your plate? Circle the most appropriate answer:
   Never   Seldom   Sometimes   Often   Always

8. Do you eat anything at all between meals? (Exclude black coffee, boullion, and water). Circle the number of times per day.
   0-1   1-2   3-4   5-6   6-7   8-9+

9. How frequently do you eat anything after 9:00 pm? Circle the number of times per day.
   0   1   2   3   4+

10. Do you tend to eat a lot more on some days than others? (Circle one.)
    YES   NO

11. Would you characterize yourself as a (check any appropriate choices):
    _____ non-snacker
    _____ morning snacker
    _____ afternoon snacker
    _____ evening snacker
    _____ night snacker
    _____ all the time snacker

12. Do you ever eat even when you don't really feel hungry? Circle the number of times per week.
   0-2   3-5   6-8   9-11   12+

(continued)

APPENDIX B.7 (continued)

13. Are you likely to overeat (check all appropriate choices):
    _____ when you serve yourself
    _____ when food is on display
    _____ when food is served by others
    _____ when parents or family urge you to eat more
    _____ when friends urge you to eat more
    _____ when others (non-family members) are present
    _____ when others (e.g., friends) are eating with you
    _____ when you feel "nervous"
    _____ in a compulsive fashion

14. With favorite foods (such as cakes, pies, or ice cream) do you ever eat directly from the container rather than removing a slice or scoop and eating from a plate or bowl? Circle the number of times per week.
                        0–1   2–3   4–5   6–7   8–9+

15. Do you ever find yourself eating from the pot or container that something was cooked in rather than from a plate, bowl, or cup? Circle the number of times per week.
                        0–1   2–3   4–5   6–7   8–9+

16. Do you ever find yourself eating directly from the refrigerator? Circle the number of times per day.
                        0–1   2–3   4–5   6–7   8–9+

17. Do you sometimes eat from other people's dishes (such as family members)? Include while cleaning up, serving, etc. Circle the number of times per week.
                        0–1   2–3   4–5   6–7   8–9+

18. If you wanted a snack, which of the following would you be most likely to do?
    _____ Eat something available, but not very good
    _____ Eat something better that took 5–10 minutes to prepare
    _____ Make a trip to the store to buy something still better to eat

19. If you finished what's on your plate, and you're not really hungry anymore but there's still plenty of good food on the table, are you more likely to: (Check one.)
    _____ Not eat anymore
    _____ Eat just a little bit more
    _____ Eat more
    _____ Eat quite a bit more
    _____ Eat almost until you can't eat anymore

20. If a mealtime arrives and you don't feel particularly hungry, are you more likely to: (Check one.)
　　　　　＿＿＿＿＿ Eat the meal then
　　　　　＿＿＿＿＿ Eat the meal later

21. If you were going to have a snack (not at mealtime) please check how likely you would be to eat each of the following foods:

	Never	Seldom	Sometimes	Often	Very Often
Fruit					
Candy					
Cookies					
Vegetables					
Cold cuts					
Meat					
Chicken					
Cake					
Ice cream					
Pie					
Potato chips					
Pizza					
Hot dog					
Milkshake					
Beer					
Liquor					
Liquer					
Mixed (alcoholic)					
Coffee					
Tea					
Cocoa					
Milk					
Bread, toast					
Muffins					
Soup					
Non-diet drinks					
Diet soft drinks					
Ice cream soda					
Sandwich					
Others: specify					

(continued)

APPENDIX B.7 (continued)

III. ACTIVITY PATTERNS

1. What time do you usually go to bed at night? _____

2. How long does it usually take you to fall asleep? _____

3. Do you usually have difficulty falling asleep at night? (Circle one.)
   YES   NO

4. Approximately how many hours do you sleep each night? Include daytime naps.
   3–4   5–6   7–8   9–10   11–12+

5. At what time do you usually arise in the morning? _____

6. How frequently do you engage in an activity requiring more than your normal rate of energy expenditure, such as swim, jog, play volleyball, bowl, walk, individual exercise, dance, strenous work, etc. (Check one.)
   _____ 5 or more times per week
   _____ 3 to 4 times per week
   _____ 1 to 2 times per week
   _____ 1 to 3 times per month
   _____ less than once per month

7. Would you characterize your usual daily physical activity level as: (Check one.)
   _____ Inactive
   _____ Less active than average
   _____ More active than average
   _____ Very active

8. Have you engaged in a regular activity or exercise which you no longer perform? (Circle one.)
   YES   NO

If yes, please list the activity or activities: _____

9. Have you attempted to increase your activity/exercise level in the last 12 months? If so, what did you do? With what results (e.g., felt better, lost weight, gave it up)?_____

IV. WEIGHT AND DIET HISTORY
Check where appropriate:

	Very Thin −20% or more	Thin −10% to −20%	Normal −10% to +10%	Overweight +10% to +20%	Very Overweight +20% or more
Your own weight					
Father					
Mother					
Father's Mother					
Father's Father					
Mother's Mother					
Mother's Father					
Your brother #1					
Your brother #2					
Your sister #1					
Your sister #2					
Your spouse					
Best friend #1					
Best friend #2					

If you are or have been overweight, answer questions 1–6. If you are not overweight or have never been overweight, skip to question 7.

1. What was the highest that your weight has ever been? _____ lbs.

2. When was that? _____

3. Have you been overweight (i.e., had a weight problem) for at least: (Check one.)
    _____ 1–3 years
    _____ 4–6 years
    _____ 7–9 years
    _____ 10–12 years
    _____ more than 12 years

4. At what age did you first have a problem with overweight? (Circle one.)
    1–7 years   8–14 years   15–21 years   22–28 years   29–35 years

(continued)

APPENDIX B.7 (continued)

5. My weight could be described as: (Check each one that is appropriate.)
   _____ no problem
   _____ up and down (in cycles)
   _____ gradually getting heavier
   _____ weight stays about the same but is too high
   _____ long-term problem (more than 1 year)
   _____ short-term problem (less than one year)

6. If you are overweight, please check which of the following statements characterize your situation: (Check all that apply.)
   _____ while overweight I have never attempted to diet
   _____ while overweight I have tried to diet, but have been unsuccessful
   _____ while overweight I have sometimes dieted successfully, but never lost much weight
   _____ always put the weight back on

7. How many weight-loss diets have you begun or undertaken in the past?
   1–2   3–4   5–6   7–8   9–10+

8. Please list the kinds of diets you've been on, how long were you on each diet, the amount of weight lost, and the amount of time you kept most of the weight off. Please print clearly.

_____

_____

_____

_____

_____

_____

_____

9. Are you currently on a diet? (Circle one.)
   YES   NO

10. If yes, which one?_____

11. What is the lowest you have weighed? _____ the highest _____?

12. Have you ever:
    a. Binged or eaten a lot of food in a short period of time?
               YES   NO

     Is this a problem for you now?
               YES   NO

    b. Purged?
               YES   NO

     Is this a problem for you now?
               YES   NO

     Method of purging: (Check all that apply.)
     _____ exercise
     _____ diuretics
     _____ self-induced vomiting
     _____ laxatives

APPENDIX B.8 Problem Checklist for Personal Social Problem Solving

Rate the patient's difficulty in coping with each type of problem situation using a seven-point scale:
1 = Extremely difficult to handle
2 = Very difficult to handle
3 = Difficult to handle
4 = Slightly difficult to handle
5 = Moderately competent
6 = Very competent
7 = Extremely competent

Rating	Problem Description
_____	Communicating with parents
_____	Communicating with same-sex friends
_____	Communicating with spouse/lover
_____	Sexual relations
_____	Meeting people and making friends
_____	Shyness in social interactions
_____	Speaking in front of groups of people
_____	Talking on the telephone
_____	Planning social activities
_____	Saying no to unreasonable requests
_____	Expressing positive feelings to other people
_____	Expressing negative feelings to other people
_____	Taking constructive criticism
_____	Giving feedback to other people
_____	Asking for help when it is needed
_____	Using other people to obtain information
_____	Seeking emotional comfort from others when upset
_____	Dealing with peer pressure to behave inappropriately
_____	Appropriate use of alcohol and/or drugs
_____	Managing personal finances
_____	Paying bills and meeting other obligations on time
_____	Keeping one's living space clean and tidy
_____	Dressing appropriately for various occasions
_____	Able to get places on time
_____	Setting priorities in daily tasks and errands
_____	Taking care of insurance business
_____	Participation in religious/spiritual activities
_____	Participation in community/civic affairs
_____	Personal record keeping
_____	Completion of formal education
_____	Pursuit of informal adult educational experiences
_____	Career advancement
_____	Job satisfaction
_____	Earning adequate income
_____	Getting married
_____	When to have children and start a family
_____	Raising children
_____	Coping with children's behavior problems

Name Index

Abelson, R., 68
Abraham, S.F., 79, 143, 145, 159, 163
Abrahams, D., 59
Abramowitz, S.I., 164, 167
Adams, C.F., 230
Agras, W.S., 30, 131, 132, 253, 261, 277, 340, 364
Altschuler, S., 106
American College of Sports Medicine, 213
American Psychiatric Association, 5, 7, 10–15, 17, 50, 78
Ammerman, A., 29, 35
Andersen, A.E., 16, 21, 22, 147, 246, 271, 273, 322, 404
Andrews, D., 166
Andrian, C.A.G., 161
Annandale, A., 261
Apple, R.F., 270
Arnow, B., 131, 253
Aronson, V., 59
Askevold, F., 218
Astrand, P.O., 214
Avgerinos, P.C., 117

Bachman, J., 131, 253, 261, 277, 340
Back, K.W., 59
Baer, D.M., 135
Baker, L., 267, 270
Bandura, A., 62, 135, 362
Barker, R.G., 145
Barklage, N.E., 166
Barrett, K.H., 132, 254

Barrett, M.J., 268, 270, 273
Barrios, B.A., 66, 162, 163, 220, 221, 376, 378
Barth, D., 265
Beach, B., 261
Beard, C.M., 19
Beck, A.T., 66, 191
Beck, R.W., 191
Beiderman, J., 246
Bell, C., 157, 233
Bemis, K.M., 16, 260
Benjamin, M., 266
Berg, E., 23
Berland, N.W., 64, 220
Berndt, D.J., 85, 145, 164
Bernstein, S., 69
Berscheid, E., 216
Bessard, T., 43
Beumont, P.J.V., 10, 16, 79, 85, 103, 143, 145, 153, 159, 163, 221, 322
Bhanji, S., 22
Bhat, A.V., 152, 153
Bigman, O.L., 164, 167
Billington, C.J., 37, 118
Birtchnell, S.A., 85, 151, 153, 159
Black, J., 68
Blazer, D., 399
Block, G.A., 228
Blouin, D.C., 165, 189, 190, 222
Blundell, J.E., 34, 168
Blunden, D., 167
Bo-Linn, G.W., 100
Bohrnstedt, G., 216
Boodhoo, J.A., 16

497

Boone-O'Neill, C., 105
Boskind-Lodahl, M., 5, 6
Boskind-White, M., 5, 6, 59
Bouchard, C., 27, 30, 39
Boutacoff, M.A., 100
Braver, S.L., 97
Bray, G., 58
Brief, D.J., 178, 340
Brisman, J., 395, 397
Brodie, H.K.H., 245
Brook, F.G., 19, 20
Brooks-Gunn, J., 19, 106
Brotman, A.W., 261, 402
Brouillette, C., 166
Brown, L.B., 64, 395
Brown, T.A., 378
Brownell, K.D., 125
Brozek, J., 40, 49, 52–53, 114, 124, 243
Bruce, A.C., 43
Bruch, H., 147, 152, 264
Bulik, C.M., 39
Burge, J.C., 29, 35
Burroughs, J., 120
Burrow, C., 107
Burton, B.T., 58
Butters, J.W., 218, 383
Button, E.J., 21, 380
Buzby, G., 242, 243

Cado, S., 9, 15
Carey, M.P., 73, 197
Carlson, I.H., 126
Carrol, K., 81, 96
Carver, C.S., 135, 278
Cash, T.F., 64, 216, 378, 383
Casper, R.C., 2, 12, 86, 118, 165, 182, 246, 264
Cattanach, L., 164
Chaiken, S., 155
Chakraborty, R., 27
Chaloner, D.A., 22, 153
Champoux, R.F., 147
Chauncey, S., 261
Checkley, S.A., 255
Chernyk, B., 81, 96
Chew, B., 47
Chhabra, R., 45, 125

Christie, M., 218
Chrousos, G.P., 117
Clement, P.F., 184
Cleveland, S.E., 215, 218
Clyesdale, F.M., 334
Cohen, J., 246
Coker, S., 85, 151, 153, 159
Collins, J.K., 221
Collins, M., 20, 404
Comerci, G.G., 20, 96, 97, 101, 182
Committee on Exercise and Physical Fitness, 214
Cone, J.D., 140
Connors, M.E., 276, 340, 364, 395
Conte, A., 106
Cooper, J.L., 164, 167
Cooper, K.H., 214
Cooper, P.J., 9, 19, 22, 83, 85, 86, 94, 96, 97, 101, 107, 108, 122, 127, 149, 151, 165, 216, 276
Cooper, Z., 151, 216
Corbett, S.W., 115
Corrigan, S.A., 18, 29, 201, 306, 340
Corscina, D.V., 16, 108
Covi, L., 188
Craighead, L.W., 255
Crane, M., 69
Crisp, A.H., 16, 86, 117, 121, 152, 153, 244
Cross, L.K., 16
Crowley, M.F., 231
Crowther, J.H., 78, 80, 101, 164
Crusco, A.H., 18, 29, 201
Cunningham, C.J., 132, 254

D'Zurilla, T., 363
Dahlstrom, L.E., 191
Dahlstrom, W.G., 191
Daneman, D., 19
Danforth, E., 43
Darby, P.L., 16
Dare, C., 261, 269, 270
Daute-Herold, U., 321
Davis, C.J., 73, 177, 190, 197, 222, 234
Davis, J.M., 2, 12, 86, 165, 182, 246, 261
Davis, K.L., 123

Davis, L.E., 322, 340, 364, 391, 397
Davis, R., 158, 163, 261
Deis, R.R., 390
Department of Health and Human Services, 323
Derogatis, L.R., 188
Despres, J.P., 30
Deuman, G.W., 16
Deutsch, F., 6
Dewey, M.E., 184
Dibble, E., 119, 147
Doer, P., 117
Dolce, J.J., 223
Dooley, C.P., 402
Dorian, B., 131, 253
Dornbusch, S.M., 59
Dougherty, G.C., 245
Drummer, G.M., 16
Dryenforth, S.R., 155
Dum, J., 126
Dwyer, J., 48, 49, 55, 95, 100, 230

ESHA research, 230
Ebert, M., 117, 147, 165, 189, 244
Eckert, E.D., 2, 12, 27, 30, 80, 85, 86, 87, 103, 104, 105, 108, 144, 153, 158, 163, 164, 165, 166, 182, 203, 246, 322, 340, 349, 364, 391, 397
Eisler, I., 19, 261, 269, 270
Elder, G.H., 59
Ellingwood, E.H., 49, 245
Ellis, A., 276
Endler, N.S., 135
Enright, A.B., 167
Epling, W.F., 41, 244
Epstein, L.H., 39

Fager, S.S., 20
Fairburn, C.C., 8, 9, 19, 22, 83, 85, 86, 94, 96, 97, 101, 107, 108, 122, 127, 149, 151, 161, 165, 216, 276, 277, 340
Falk, J.R., 20, 22, 98, 108, 184
Fallon A.E., 59
Fallon, P., 147, 268, 273
Farrell, M.K., 241
Farrington, A.J., 132, 254

Feigenbaum, L.P., 126
Ferber, R.A., 246
Fichter, M.M., 49, 53, 117, 124, 129, 321
Finn, S., 81, 96
Fisher, C., 78
Fisher, S., 215
Flatt, J.P., 43
Fleming, B., 143
Fondacaro, K.M., 162, 222, 233
Fong, G., 69
Food and Nutrition Board, 323, 332
Fordtran, J.S., 100
Forster, J., 242, 243
Foster, W.R., 58
Fountaine, E., 39
Francis, F.J., 334
Franzoi, S.L., 59
Freedman, C.P.L., 187
Freeman, A., 281
Freeman, C., 261
Freeman, R.J., 63, 158, 163, 223, 261
Freidrich, W.N., 147, 268, 273
Friend, R., 192, 193
Freud, S., 264
Fuchs, I., 126
Fullerton, D.T., 126

Gallucci, W.E., 117
Ganley, R.M., 29, 200
Gans, M.T., 260
Garbutt, B., 59
Garfinkel, P.E., 12, 16, 19, 22, 63, 106, 117, 147, 148, 151, 152, 153, 155, 165, 166, 182, 220, 221, 245, 381, 399
Garner, D.M., 8, 12, 16, 22, 63, 106, 108, 117, 147, 148, 151, 152, 153, 155, 162, 182, 220, 221, 245, 276, 281, 381, 399
Garrow, J.S., 29, 212
George, D.T., 399
George, G.C.W., 85, 103, 153
George, T., 244
George, V., 30
Gershon, E., 119, 147
Getto, C.J., 126

Name Index

Gibson, E., 80, 95, 100
Giles, T.R., 300
Gillies, C., 19
Girtsman, H., 117
Gladis, M., 202, 254
Glassman, A.H., 254
Gleghorn, A., 162, 184
Glucksman, M.L., 221
Goff, G.M., 103, 261, 322, 340, 364, 391, 397
Gold, M., 126
Gold, P.W., 117
Goldberg, S.C., 2, 12, 86, 165, 182, 246
Goldbloom, D.S., 255, 256
Goldfried, MR., 363
Goodall, E., 48
Goodman, N., 59
Goodsitt, A., 264
Gorceczy, A.J., 73, 177
Gordon, J.R., 158
Gosnell, B.A., 37, 118
Gramsch, C., 126
Green, G.K., 216
Green, R.S., 123
Greenberg, B.R., 164
Greenwald, P., 326
Greenward, M.R., 125
Grinker, J., 143
Groat, R.A., 253
Gronwalt, V.H., 20, 96, 97, 101, 182
Gross, J., 20, 57, 162, 222, 233
Gross, L., 144
Grunewald, K.K., 56, 150
Guiora, A.Z., 6, 21
Gutzmann, L.D., 126
Gwirtsman, H., 244, 399

Hall, A., 120, 267, 391, 396, 398
Halmi, K.A., 2, 11, 12, 14, 19, 22, 50, 86, 98, 108, 165, 182, 184, 202, 203, 246, 399
Halverson, P.A., 29, 101, 103, 396, 397, 398
Hamburg, P., 261, 402
Hamil, R., 69
Hamilton, L.H., 19, 20
Hamovit, J.R., 119, 147
Hanis, C., 27

Harding, B., 244
Hardy, B.W., 126, 402
Harmatz, J.S., 246
Harper, G.P., 246
Harris, F., 390
Hart, K.J., 19, 97
Hastorf, A.H., 59
Hatsukami, D., 85, 87, 104, 105, 108, 144, 158, 163, 166, 203, 322, 340, 349, 364, 391, 397
Hawkins, R.C., 184
Hayward, M.E., 19
Hedblom, J.E., 271, 273
Heim, C., 124
Heller, P.A., 124
Henderson, M., 187
Henley, K.M., 12, 50
Henschel, A., 40, 49, 52–53, 114, 124, 243
Herman, C.P., 28, 29, 45, 51, 124, 125, 184, 201
Hernandez, L., 36, 203
Herz, A., 126
Herzog, M.E., 59, 83, 97, 246, 261, 402
Hill, A.J., 34, 168
Hill, J.O., 124, 231
Hirsch, J., 58, 221
Hobel, B.G., 36
Hodas, G.R., 404
Hoek, H.W., 19
Hoffman, L., 266
Holder, D., 261
Holland, A.J., 120
Hollister, L.E., 123
Hollon, S.D., 275, 276
Holmgren, S., 23
Holsber, F., 49, 53, 114, 124, 129
Hoover, W., 230
Horton, E.H., 40, 42
Houben, M., 218
Howells, K., 22, 153
Hsu, L.K.G., 28, 64, 244, 246, 261
Hubbard, F.A., 271, 272
Huber, M., 100, 103, 106
Hudson, J.I., 10, 19, 20, 129, 130, 131, 132, 147, 167, 252, 253, 255, 256, 402
Hudson, M., 20

Hughes, P.L., 132, 254
Humble, K., 23
Hummers, J.A., 106
Humphrey, L.L., 147, 148, 270
Hunter, D., 19
Huon, G.F., 64, 395

Ilstrup, D.M., 132, 254
Irvine, M.J., 399
Isreal, A.C., 161

Jacobs, C., 120
James, W.P.T., 43
Janda, H.L., 64
Jarrell, M.P., 14, 18, 34, 48, 124, 135, 136, 143, 144, 145, 153, 156, 158, 163, 168, 232, 233, 244, 274, 299, 340, 346, 364, 415
Jimerson, D., 117
Johansson, B., 23
Johnson, C.L., 56, 83, 85, 97, 101, 108, 145, 150, 153, 155, 158, 164, 202, 276, 340, 364, 395
Johnson, L.E., 19
Johnson, W.G., 14, 18, 29, 33, 34, 39, 45, 48, 124, 125, 135, 136, 143, 144, 145, 153, 156, 158, 163, 168, 178, 190, 201, 232, 233, 244, 274, 299, 306, 340, 346, 364, 415
Johnson-Sabine, E.C., 163
Jonas, J., 126, 127, 129, 130, 131, 147, 252, 402
Jourard, S., 215, 216
Jupp, J.J., 221

Kaler, M., 124
Kalin, N.H., 128
Kaslow, N., 128
Kasser, T., 231
Katch, F.I., 213, 214, 356
Katch, V.L., 213
Katz, J.L., 128, 129, 130, 392
Katzman, M.A., 97, 261, 364
Kauff, P.F., 390
Kaufman, M.R., 6
Kaye, W., 117, 119, 147, 244

Keesey, R.E., 26, 34, 36, 42, 48, 49, 115
Kelley, M.L., 165, 189, 190, 222, 299, 340, 364, 415
Kendall, P.C., 275, 276
Kennedy, S.H., 165, 166
Kenshole, A., 19
Keys, A., 40, 49, 52–53, 114, 124, 243
Khazam, C., 79
Killen, J.D., 101
Kinder, B.N., 162, 184
Kirkley, B.G., 29, 35, 131, 253, 261, 277, 340
Kirschenbaum, D.S., 165, 189, 270
Kiser, S., 126
Klanjner, F., 45, 125
Klein, R.H., 390
Knopes, K.D., 49
Kog, E., 147, 148
Kohut, H., 264
Koopman, R., 63, 223
Krall, E.A., 230
Kranz, J.S., 19
Krass, J., 222
Kreisberg, J., 20
Krener, P., 164
Kuldau, J.M., 19, 96, 97, 100
Kupfer, D.J., 39
Kurland, L.T., 19

Laakso, W., 5
Lacey, J.H., 80, 85, 86, 95, 100, 123, 151, 153, 159
Ladu, T.J., 246
Laessle, R.G., 321
Laine, D.C., 79, 95, 126
Larson, R., 145
Leblanc, C., 27, 30
Lechey, K., 106
Lee, N.F., 277
Lee-Benner, K., 395, 396, 397, 398
Leiberman, H.R., 47
Leiberman, M.A., 390
Leibman, R., 267, 404
Leibowitz, S.F., 115, 256
Leitenberg, J., 9, 15, 79, 107, 162, 222, 233, 297, 322
Leon, G.R., 81, 96, 106

502 ■ Name Index

Lerner, H.D., 264
Lerner, P., 166
Levendusky, P.G., 402
Levin, S., 164
Levine, A.S., 37, 118, 126, 176
Lewis, C., 56, 83, 97, 101, 150
Lewis, L.D., 56, 83, 97, 150, 153, 158
Liedermann, V.R., 59
Lindholm, L., 131
Lingswiler, V.M., 78, 80
Linton, P.H., 64, 220
Lipman, R.S., 188
Loriaux, D.L., 117, 246
Love, C., 56, 83, 85, 97, 101, 150
Luby, E.D., 118
Lucas, A.R., 19
Lund, R., 117
Lynch, B.S., 326

Machover, K., 215
Mack, D., 28, 201
Maddox, G.L., 59
Magnusson, D., 135
Malmberg, S.R., 16
Maloney, M.J., 241
Mann, L.M., 150
Marks, I., 306
Markus, H., 68, 69
Marlat, G.A., 158
Marlin, R.L., 106
Maron, D.J., 101
Marrazzi, M.A., 118
Martin, J.R., 94, 97
Mattingly, D., 22
Matusewich, E., 59
Mayo, L.L., 306, 340
McArdle, W.D., 213, 214, 356
McAvay, G., 164
McCabe, M.P., 221
McCance, C., 19
McCann, U., 133
McCrone, L., 19
McFall, R.M., 135, 146, 259, 278, 340, 363, 370
McGowen, C.R., 39
McKenzie, S.J., 73, 177
McMullin, R.E., 287, 293

McNeill, G., 43
Meichenbaum, D., 276
Merrill, C.A., 398
Messick, S., 197, 199
Mezey, A.G., 243
Mickalide, A.D., 21
Mickelsen, O., 40, 49, 52–53, 114, 124, 243
Miller, C.T., 59
Miller, J.G., 139
Mines, R.A., 398
Minuchin, S., 266, 267, 270
Mischel, W., 135, 362
Mitchell, D., 39
Mitchell, J.E., 27, 29, 30, 79, 80, 85, 86, 87, 95, 100, 101, 103, 104, 106, 108, 126, 144, 153, 158, 163, 164, 166, 203, 253, 261, 322, 340, 349, 364, 391, 397, 402
Mitchell, P.B., 133, 255
Moldofsky, H., 12, 22, 63, 147, 151, 153
Morawski, S.G., 100
Mori, D., 155
Morley, J.E., 37, 118, 126, 176
Morrell, W., 120, 130
Morrison, T.L., 164, 167
Morse, C., 322
Mullen, D., 242, 243
Murray, R., 120
Myburgh, K.H., 50

Nash, J., 50
Nassi, A., 167
Neuman, P.A., 29, 101, 103, 396, 397, 398
Nevo, S., 16, 20, 56
Nicholas, P., 55
Nielsen, S., 117
Niemen, L.K., 117
Nisbett, R.E., 41, 49, 143
Nishita, J.K., 49
Noakes, T.D., 50
Noles, S.W., 216
Norcross, J.C., 182
Norman, D.K., 83, 97, 261
Norring, C., 23

Norris, P.D., 129
Norton, K.R.W., 152, 153
Nudelman, S., 107
Nurnberger, J.I., 119, 147
Nylander, I., 51

O'Brien, R.M., 255
O'Connor, M., 322
O'Malley, B.P., 129
Ollendick, T.H., 19, 97
Olmstead, M.P., 16, 108, 152, 182
Oppenheimer, R., 22, 153
Orbach, S., 155
Ordman, A.M., 165, 189
Orsulak, P., 246
Owens, M., 165
Oyebode, F., 16

Palmer, R.L., 6, 21, 22, 86, 153
Parking-Feigenbaum, L., 270
Parloff, M.B., 390
Pasman, L., 107
Pepose, M., 83, 97
Perron, L., 39
Pertschuk, M.J., 20, 242, 243
Perusse, L., 27, 30
Petersen, R., 244
Phillips, T., 222
Pierce, W.D., 41, 244
Pierloot, R., 218, 245
Piran, N., 165, 166
Pirke, K.M., 49, 53, 114, 117, 124, 129, 321
Pliner, P., 155
Poehlman, E.T., 39
Pole, R., 271
Polivy, J., 28, 29, 45, 51, 124, 125, 182, 184
Pomeroy, C., 100, 103, 106
Pope, H.G., 10, 19, 20, 127, 129, 130, 131, 132, 147, 167, 252, 253, 255, 256, 402
Pope-Cordle, J., 124, 230, 231
Post, G., 101
Powers, P., 162, 184, 203, 205
Powley, T.L., 34, 42, 49
Prange, M., 162, 184
Prather, R.C., 73, 177

Price, J.M., 143
Pruitt, J.A., 150
Pyle, R.L., 27, 30, 80, 85, 86, 87, 101, 103, 104, 105, 108, 144, 153, 158, 163, 164, 166, 203, 322, 340, 349, 364, 391, 397

Raciti, M.C., 182
Ralph, A., 43
Rand, C.S.W., 19, 96, 97, 100
Ratlmann, L., 59
Rau, J.H., 123
Register, A., 223
Reitman, E.E., 218
Richardson, S.A., 59
Richert, A.J., 106
Rigotti, N.A., 83, 97
Rippon, C., 50
Risely, T.R., 135
Ritholz, M., 128
Rittmaster, R., 17
Rivinus, T.N., 246
Robinson, P.H., 16, 255
Robinson, T.N., 101
Rockert, W., 108
Rockwell, W.J.K., 49, 245
Rodahl, K., 214
Rodin, G.M., 19
Rodin, J., 40, 46, 51, 143, 164
Roose, S.P., 254
Root, A.W., 28
Root, M.P.P., 147, 268, 273
Roper, M., 182
Rosen, J.C., 9, 15, 20, 57, 78, 107, 162, 222, 233, 235, 297, 322
Rosen, L.W., 16
Rosenbaum, J.F., 246
Rosman, B., 267, 270
Rosmark, B., 23
Rossiter, E.M., 30
Rothblum, E.D., 59
Rothwell, N.J., 35, 42
Roy-Byrne, P., 395, 396, 397, 398
Rozin, P., 59
Ruderman, A.J., 28, 158
Ruff, G., 66, 162, 163, 220, 221, 376, 378

Ruggiero, L., 73, 165, 189, 190, 197, 222, 234, 299, 340, 364, 415
Rush, A.J., 277
Russell, G.F.M., 8, 21, 77, 80, 85, 86, 95, 121, 165, 220, 243, 255, 261, 269, 270
Ryan, R.M., 265

Saba, G., 268, 270, 273
Sabine, E.J., 132, 254
Salkin, B., 120, 130
Sansone, R.B., 167
Santa Ana, C.A., 100
Santmyer, K., 322
Sargent, J., 267
Saylor, K.E., 101
Sbrocco, T., 124, 157, 231, 233
Schachter, S., 142, 143, 144
Schaefer, C.A., 20, 96, 97, 101, 182
Scheier, M.F., 135, 278
Schildkraut, J.J., 246
Schlundt, D.G., 14, 29, 34, 48, 73, 124, 135, 136, 143, 144, 145, 146, 153, 156, 157, 158, 163, 168, 190, 195, 197, 201, 228, 229, 230, 231, 233, 234, 244, 274, 278, 299, 339, 340, 346, 363, 364, 415
Schmidt, U., 306
Schneider, J.A., 261, 277, 340
Schneider, W., 286
Schotte, D.E., 20
Schreiber, J.L., 119, 147
Schull, W.J., 27
Schulman, R.G., 162, 184
Schulsinger, F., 27
Schutz, Y., 43
Schwartz, D.M., 153, 155, 158
Schwartz, E., 20, 98, 108, 184
Schwartz, G.E., 135, 139
Schwartz, R.C., 268, 270, 273
Schweiger, M., 321
Schweiger, U., 321
Scott, D.W., 120
Sebok, M., 106
Secourd, P., 215, 216
Senate Select Committee on Nutrition and Human Needs, 323
Sentis, K.P., 69

Seppala, M., 103
Shafer, C.L., 16
Shapira, K., 16
Sharp, T., 124
Shields, T.W., 124
Shiffrin, R.M., 286
Shisslak, C.M., 20, 96, 97, 101, 106, 182
Shrager, E.E., 125
Siegel, M., 395, 397
Siladi, M., 69
Silber, T.J., 16
Silberstein, L.R., 51
Silver, M., 267
Silverstone, T., 48
Simms, E.A.H., 40, 42
Sinclair, F., 261
Slade, P.D., 184, 220
Slochower, J., 143
Smart, D.E., 85, 103, 153
Smith, J., 70
Smith, M.C., 150, 185, 197
Solyom, L., 63, 158, 163, 223, 261
Sondik, E., 326
Sorensen, T.I.A., 27
Spana, R.E., 223
Sparling, P.B., 124
Spitzer, L., 46
Stalonas, P.M., 340
Starkey, R., 398
Stein, D.M., 5
Stellar, E., 125
Stephens, M.A., 78, 80
Stetson, B.A., 124
Stewart, J., 254
Stewart, S.M., 270
Stierlin, H., 267
Stock, M.J., 35, 42
Stolmaker, L., 161
Strauss, J., 265
Streigel-Moore, R.H., 51, 164
Strober, M., 120, 128, 129, 130, 147
Stuckey, M.K., 56, 83, 97, 101, 150, 153, 158, 340, 395
Stunkard, A.J., 20, 27, 123, 144, 197, 199, 255
Suitor, C.J.W., 231
Swift, W.J., 126, 128, 166
Szmukler, G.I., 19, 261, 269, 270

Taylor, C.B., 101
Taylor, H.L., 40, 49, 52–53, 114, 124, 243
Taylor, J.J., 216
Teasdale, T.W., 27
Telch, C.G., 30
Telch, M.J., 101
Temoshok, L., 143
Teriault, G., 27
Teusch, R., 265
Thelen, M.H., 150, 185, 197
Thomas, C., 63, 223
Thompson, J.K., 8, 64, 107, 220, 223
Thompson, M., 155
Thompson, M.G., 260
Thompson, P., 222
Todd, T.C., 270, 273
Tondorf, R., 246
Toner, B., 148
Touyz, S.W., 221, 322
Tremblay, A., 27, 30, 39
Turnbull, J., 261

Uauy, R., 126

Vaitukaitis, J.L., 12, 50
Van Buren, D.J., 148
Van Der Beer, E.J., 207
Van Itallie, T.B., 58
Vandereycken, W., 147, 148, 245, 269, 270, 273
Veitia, M.C., 234
Vigersky, R.A., 246
Von Bertalanffy, L., 139, 266

Wakeling, A., 110, 118, 132, 163, 254
Waller, D.A., 126, 270, 402
Waller, J.V., 6
Walsh, B.T., 202, 254
Walster, E., 59
Walster, W., 216
Wambolt, F.S., 128
Warren, M.P., 19, 20, 50, 107
Watson, D., 192, 193
Weber, G., 267
Wedel, M., 207
Weiner, H., 117

Weinsier, R.L., 64, 220
Weiss, L., 261, 364, 392
Weiss, S.M., 139
Weiss, S.R., 147, 165, 189, 399
Weits, T., 207
Wells, L.A., 132, 254
Welsh, G.S., 191
Weltner, J.S., 273
Wermuth, B.M., 123
White, W.C., 5, 6, 398
Whitehouse, A.M., 21
Wildman, H., 33, 45, 125
Willard, S.G., 100
Willenbring, M.L., 176
Williams, R.L., 20, 96, 97, 101, 182
Williamson, D.A., 73, 148, 165, 177, 189, 190, 197, 222, 234
Wilmuth, M.E., 9, 15, 162, 222, 233
Wilson, G.T., 131, 158
Wingate, B., 218
Winick, C., 106
Winstead, B.A., 64, 216
Winstead, D.K., 100
Wolchik, S.A., 97, 261, 364, 392
Wolf, M.M., 135
Wolfe, E.M., 164
Wollitzer, A.O., 94, 97
Wood, K.H., 163
Wooley, O.W., 155, 382, 385
Wooley, S.C., 155, 382, 385
Wurman, V., 265
Wurtman, J.J., 47, 48, 125, 176
Wurtman, R.J., 125

Yager, J., 395, 396, 397, 398
Yalom, I.D., 390
Yates, A., 106
Yellowlees, A.J., 165
Yonace, A., 132, 254
York, C., 66, 162, 163, 220, 221, 376, 378
Young, D.E., 300
Young, R.R., 300
Yurgelun-Todd, D., 19, 20, 130, 131, 147, 252

Zaynor, L., 101
Zimering, R.T., 145, 339

Subject Index

Absolutism, 282
Abstinence violation effect, 158, 174
  (see also Restraint)
Activity, effect on eating, 138
Addiction, 118–119, 125–126, 391
  (see also Opiates)
Adipocytes, 326
Adjustable calipers, body image assessment, 222
Affective disorders (see Depression)
Alcohol consumption, 349
All-or-none thinking, 281
Alternative activities, 316–317
Alternative interpretation, 288
Amenorrhea, 12, 31, 116
Amino acids, 326–327
Anamorphic lens, 222
Anorectic Attitudes Questionnaire, 182
Anorexia nervosa:
  bulimia subtype, 3, 12, 21, 22, 28
    (see also Bulimia nervosa)
  clinical syndrome, 1–3, 11–12, 25–31, 40, 114
  restrictor type, 2–3, 12, 21, 28
  treatment, 44
Anticatastrophic counters, 288
Antidepressants, 246, 251–255
Appetite (see Hunger)
Arbitrary inference, 282
Assertiveness, 348, 362, 393–394
Assessment:
  behavioral, 181, 340, 354, 365, 414
  bingeing cues, 307–308, 354
  body image, 214–228, 376–381

cognitive schemata, 286–287, 378–379
eating disorders, 182–187
family interaction patterns, 267, 272
functional analysis of behavior, 178–179, 343, 354, 363, 365, 414
interview protocols, 201–203
physiological, 128–130, 203–214
problem identification, 363, 365–366, 415–417
psychological, 181, 188–194, 413
treatment outcome, 260–262, 370, 414
Astrand ergometer test, 214
Automaticity, 284

BITE, 187
BSQR, 218
BULIT, 185, 226
Beck depression inventory, 165, 191–192
Behavioral training (see Skill acquisition)
Behavior setting, 145
Behavior substitution, 342–343, 352–353, 368–369
Behavioral antecedents, 156
Behavioral assessment, 228–235
Behavioral consequences, 172
Behavioral contracting, 303, 403
Behavioral medicine, 139
Binge eating questionnaire, 184
Binge scale, 184

507

Bingeing:
  definition and analysis, 24, 27, 44–48, 53, 77–82, 141–142, 173, 329
  epidemiology, 20, 82–86
  treatment, 343–345
Biological cues, 168
Biopsychosocial model, 139–140
Black-and-white thinking, 281
Body image:
  assessment, 214–228
  assessment of schema, 222–228
  definition and analysis, 63–66, 107, 174, 375–380
  influence on eating behavior, 162–163
  treatment, 375–387
Body Cathexis Scale, 216, 226
Body composition, 27, 38, 43, 48–49, 53, 205–212, 240, 244
Body distortion index, 220
Body Image Automatic Thoughts Questionnaire, 216
Body Image Testing System, 225–228
Body Parts Rating Scale, 216
Body Shape Questionnaire, 215
Booster sessions, 317
Borderline personality, 166
Brown adipose tissue, 42
Bulimarexia, 5
Bulimia, diagnosis, 7, 8
Bulimia Cognitive Distortions Scale, 184
Bulimia interview form, 202
Bulimia nervosa:
  clinical syndrome, 3–5, 13–15, 27–31, 122–123
  diagnosis, 8, 13–15 (*see also* Bulimia, Bulimarexia, Dietary chaos syndrome, Dysorexia)

Calorie intake, 79–82, 95, 240–243, 324, 346–348
Carbohydrate (*see* Food intake, dietary carbohydrate)
Career (*see* Vocation)
Case descriptions, 3, 5, 60–62, 74, 88–91, 108–110, 419–425
Catastrophe thinking, 282

Catecholamines, 35, 115 (*see also* Neurotransmitters)
Cluster analysis, 145
Coaching, 371
Cognitive antecedents, 159–162
Cognitive consequences, 173
Cognitive science, 66–73
Cognitive therapy, 275–295, 301, 378–379, 418
Communication, 267
Competence, 363, 415
Complications, 28, 29, 30, 31, 48–50, 59, 95–96, 100, 104, 105, 124–125
Computerized assessment, 224–228, 230–232, 233–234
Coping statements, 288, 302
Coping with emotions, 351–353
Counter-regulation, 158 (*see also* Restraint)
Counterattacking, 289
Countering, 287–288, 301
Countering irrational beliefs, 291, 301
Craving, 44–48
Cue misidentification, 280
Cultural systems, 154–156

Dating, 150, 153
Decision making, 283
Depression, 48, 127–133, 164, 175–176, 351
Dexamethasone suppression test, 129
Diagnosis:
  anorectic-bulimic conflict, 23, 27
  anorexia nervosa, 11–12, 18, 25–31
  atypical eating disorders, 17
  borderline personality, 167–168
  bulimarexia, 5–6
  bulimia, 7, 8, 13, 184 (*see also* Bulimia nervosa, Bulimarexia, Dietary chaos syndrome, Dysorexia)
  bulimia nervosa, 8, 13–15, 18, 25–31, 77
  comparison of categories, 8–10, 11–12, 13–15, 18, 25–31
  compulsive overeater, 15, 30

Subject Index ■ 509

DSM-III, 5, 7, 8, 10, 13
DSM-III-R, 10–15, 17, 18, 77
dietary chaos syndrome, 6
dysorexia, 6
history of, 5–8
implications for treatment, 413–414
night eating syndrome, 144
pica, 17
rumination disorder, 17
spectrum of eating disorders, 21–31 (see also Diagnosis, comparison of categories)
three-dimensional model, 25–31
Diagnostic Survey for Eating Disorders, 202
Diet composition, 43–44, 46–48, 125, 138, 159–160, 229–232, 247, 322–327
Diet pills, 105
Dietary chaos syndrome, 6
Dietary recall, 230
Dietary restraint (see Restraint)
Dieter's Inventory of Eating Temptations (DIET), 145, 194–195, 340
Dieting, 23, 27–31, 48–54, 55–58, 104–105, 124–125, 141–142, 158–159, 160, 173, 324
Dietitian, 335
Discounting, 282
Distorted body image test, 222
Diuretics, 103–104
Draw-a-person test, 215
Dysorexia, 6

Eating Attitudes Test, 106, 182
Eating behavior (see also Food intake):
regulation of, 33–34, 45–46
style, 34–35, 195, 232–234
Eating diaries, 230, 233–234, 342
Eating Disorder Inventory, 182
Electrolytes, 50, 331–332
Emotional consequences, 175–176
Emotional eating, 29, 47, 163–165, 175–176, 233, 349–355, 361
Emotional reasoning, 282
Endogenous opiates (see Opiates)

Endorphins (see Opiates)
Energy balance training, 276
Energy expenditure, 38–39, 41–42 (see also Resting metabolic rate, Thermic effect of food)
Energy intake, 322–327
Environmental consequences, 170–172
Environmental systems, 146
Epidemiology:
anorexia nervosa, 18–19 (see also Diagnosis, anorexia nervosa, Dieting)
bingeing, 20
bulimia nervosa, 19–21
dieting, 55–58, 104–105
diuretics, 101–104
laxative abuse, 99–102
males, 16
vomiting, 20, 96–99
Exercise, 24, 27, 39, 41, 106–108, 244, 325, 341, 355–358
Exposure with response prevention, 297–305, 417–418
Externality, 143

Family interaction patterns, 268–270
Family resemblance, 119–121
Family systems, 147
Family therapy (see Treatment, family therapy)
Fasting (see Dieting, Starvation)
Fat (see Food intake, dietary fat)
Fear of Negative Evaluations Test, 192
Fear of obesity, 22, 23, 27–31, 58–63, 73–75, 141–142, 164, 329, 339
Feedback, 285
Fenfluramine, 48 (see also Serotonin)
Fiber, 251, 323–324
Field Independence Test, 215
Financial resources, 151–152, 171
Fluid balance, 331
Food cues, 49, 142, 233, 341–343
Food diaries, 230, 233–234
Food Frequency Questionnaire, 230

Food groups, 231–232, 335, 337
Food intake:
  assessment of, 228–232
  dietary protein, 47, 322, 326–327, 329 (*see also* Diet composition)
  dietary carbohydrate, 43, 47–48, 322–325, 328–329 (*see also* Diet composition)
  dietary fat, 43, 159, 322, 325–326, 329–330 (*see also* Diet composition)
  regulation of, 33, 39 (*see also* Eating behavior)
Food obsession, 49, 52–53, 86–87
Food phobia, 73–75, 196–199, 323, 328–329, 348
Food Survey, 74, 195–199, 329
Friendship, 62, 149–151, 170
Functional analysis, 136, 169, 178, 232–234

General systems theory, 139, 178, 266
Genetics, 27, 30, 119–121
Gluconeogenesis, 324
Glucose, 33, 36, 46
Glycogen, 47
Glycogenesis, 324
Goal setting, 342, 363–364, 366–368, 372
Group therapy, 389–399

Harvard Step Test, 214
Health care, 154
Health Habit Survey, 203
Homework assignments, 294, 303, 308, 348, 354, 371–372
Hospitalization, 154, 399–410
Hunger, 34, 40, 138, 168
Hyperalimentation, 240
Hypoglycemia, 46, 176 (*see also* Insulin, Glucose)
Hypokalemia, 31, 50, 96, 103, 176 (*see also* Complications)
Hypothalamus, 36–37, 114–118, 123

Image marking method, body image, 218

Imagery, 293
Indirect calorimetry, 212–213 (*see also* Resting metabolic rate)
Individuation, 265
Information processing, 72–73, 159–162, 278–286 (*see also* Cognitive science)
Insulin, 33, 40, 45–46
Interpersonal skills, 154, 340, 361, 393
Interpretive information processing, 281 (*see also* Information processing, Cognitive science)
Intimacy, 60, 150, 152–154, 170
Irrational beliefs, 161–162, 276–277, 291, 301

Knowledge representation, 67–73 (*see also* Cognitive science, Schema)

Label shifting, 290
Laxative abuse, 24, 99–102, 248–251
Light beam, body image assessment, 221
Lipids, 325–326
Lipogenesis, 324
Low-fat diet, 43–44, 329–330, 353 (*see also* Weight, regulation of)

MMPI, 165, 190
Magnification, 282
Males, eating disorders in, 16
Meal skipping, 35, 144
Medical model, 10, 291
Microanalysis of eating, 232–234
Minimization, 282
Misattribution, 283
Mislabeling, 283
Modeling, 371
Monoamine oxidase inhibitors, 248, 251–255
Monosaturated fats, 325
Mood altering effect of food, 47–48, 49, 164, 175–176
Mood, effect on eating, 138, 163–165
Mortality, 28, 29, 332 (*see also* Complications)

Subject Index ■ 511

Naloxone, 37 (see also Opiates)
Nasogastric tube, 241
Neuroleptics, 245–247
Neuropeptides, 115
Neurotransmitters, 35–37, 47–48 (see also Opiates, Catecholamines, Serotonin)
Night eating syndrome, 144
Nitrogen balance, 327
Nutrient analysis, 231
Nutrient density, 334–335
Nutrition:
  clinical intervention, 327–330
  knowledge of, 321–322, 335
  recommendations and guidelines, 323, 326, 327, 332–338, 345–346 (see also Diet composition)
Nutrition counseling, 247
Nutritional supplements, 240

Obesity, 27, 30, 40, 59, 136–138, 195
Objective counters, 292
Obsessive-compulsive disorders, 298
Opiates, 35–37, 41, 118–119, 125–126, 176
Outcome expectancies, 160–162
Overeating, 44–47 (see also Bingeing)
Overgeneralization, 282
Oxygen uptake, 213–214, 356

Peer influence, 149–151
Perceptual information processing, 279 (see also Information processing, Cognitive science)
Personality disorder, 127, 166–168
Personalization, 283
Physical setting, 137, 141–143
Physiological consequences, 176
Polyunsaturated fats, 325
Portion sizes, 343
Potassium (see Electrolytes, Hypokalemia)
Premenstrual syndrome, 50
Problem solving (see Treatment, problem solving)

Projective tests of body image, 215
Psychoanalysis, 152, 262–266, 273, 390, 402
Psychopathology, 165–168, 266 (see also Depression, Personality disorder)
Psychophysical assessment of body image, 216
Purging, 24, 141–142, 173

Queens college step test, 214

Recommended dietary allowances, 332–333 (see also Nutrition)
Rehearsal (see Role playing)
Reinforcement of behavior, 169–177
Relapse, 274, 395
Reproductive hormones, 50 (see also Amenorrhea)
Response execution, 284
Resting metabolic rate, 29, 37–39, 42–43, 48–49, 53, 124, 207–213, 240, 324–325
Restraint, 28, 46, 51, 78, 199–201
Restraint scale, 184, 200–201
Role playing, 294, 354, 371–372
Rorschach Inkblot Test, 215

SCANS, 184
SCL-90, 165, 188–189
Satiety, 34–35, 325
Saturated fats, 325
Schema, 66–73, 162, 173, 223, 280–286 (see also Cognitive science)
Seizure, 123
Selective attention, 280
Selective interpretation, 282
Self-management skills, 340
Self-monitoring, 231, 273, 307, 340, 372
Self-psychology, 264–265
Sequential analysis of behavior, 156–157, 163, 233
Serotonin, 35, 47–48, 176, 255–256 (see also Neurotransmitters)
Set-point theory, 26, 30, 36–37, 41–42

Subject Index

Sexual abuse, 153
Sexuality, 60, 152, 170
Situational cues, 141–146, 341–343, 379–380
Skill acquisition, 340, 348, 361–363, 370–373
Skinfolds thickness, 206–207
Social avoidance, 60, 346
Social Avoidance and Distress Test, 193
Social consequences, 170
Social context, 137, 145
Social skills (*see* Interpersonal skills)
South Florida Eating Disorders Questionnaire, 203
Specific Dynamic Action (*see* Thermic effect of food)
Starvation, 28, 48, 53–54
Stimulus control, 342
Submaximal fitness testing, 214
Sugar, 46, 323–324
Systems theory (*see* General systems theory)

Tasting, 87–89
Temptation exposure with response prevention, 305–319, 417–418
Test meals, 233–235
Theory:
  biogenetic, 113–134, 169
  psychosocial, 135–136, 139, 141–177
Thermic effect of food, 41–44, 49 (*see also* Energy expenditure)
Three-Factor Eating Questionnaire, 199–200, 226
Time management and exercise, 358
Time of day, 137–138, 143–144
Time/distance run, 214
Total parenteral nutrition, 241
Tranquilizers, 246
Treadmill fitness test, 213–214
Treatment:
  behavior therapy, 273, 297–319, 341–355, 361–374, 391–392, 402–404, 417–418

body image, 375–387, 394, 418
cognitive therapy, 275–295, 301, 348, 368–369, 383, 393–394, 417–418
eating habits, 322, 340, 341–355, 393–394
emotional eating, 349–355, 361, 393
energy balance training, 339–359, 417–418
exercise, 355–358
exposure with response prevention, 297–305, 417–418
family therapy, 266–273, 404
food choice, 345–346
food phobia, 348–349
group therapy, 389–399, 403
inpatient, 399–410
laxative abuse, 248–251
medication, 123, 131–133, 245–247, 251–256
nutrition knowledge, 322–338, 347–349
nutritional support, 239–244, 247–248, 345–349, 392, 417–418
planning, 413–418
problem solving, 351, 361–374, 418
psychotherapy, 259–262
resisting temptation, 341–343
social eating, 346–347
temptation exposure with response prevention, 305–319, 417–418
Treatment outcome, 260–262, 276
Triglycerides, 325
Tryptophan, 47–48 (*see also* Food intake, dietary protein)
Tyramine, 248

Underwater weighing, 207–211
Utilitarian counters, 292

Vegetarian diet, 327
Video distortion, body image assessment, 221–222
Video feedback for body image treatment, 385–386

Visual size estimation, body image
    assessment, 220
Vitamins, 325, 332–333
Vocation, 60–61, 151, 170, 364
Vomiting:
  description and analysis, 24, 27,
    93–96
  epidemiology, 20, 96–99
  psychogenic, 18

Weight:
  reduction of, 43
  regulation of, 38–44, 339–340
  relationship to diagnosis, 24 (see
    also Anorexia nervosa, Diagnosis, anorexia nervosa)
  restoration, 240–244, 329
Weight cycling, 125
Word Association Test, 215